On the Art of Building

Leon Battista Alberti

On the Art of Building in Ten Books

translated by
Joseph Rykwert, Neil Leach, and Robert Tavernor

The MIT Press
Cambridge, Massachusetts
London, England

Fifth printing, 1994

This book was set in Bembo by Asco Trade Typesetting Ltd., Hong Kong, and printed and bound in the United States of America.

Library of Congress Cataloging-in-Publication Data

Alberti, Leon Battista, 1404–1472.

On the art of building in ten books.

Translation of: De re aedificatoria.

Bibliography: p.

Includes index.

1. Architecture—Early works to 1800.

I. Title.

NA2515. A3513   1988   720   87–26271

ISBN 0-262-01099-2 (hardcover) 0-262-51060-X (paperback)

On the Art of Building

Introduction

Joseph Rykwert

Vitruvius and Alberti

When Alberti wrote his treatise on the art of building, *De re aedificatoria*, about the middle of the fifteenth century, his was the first book on architecture since antiquity. Indeed, it was only the second to be entirely devoted to architecture: the very first, the *De architectura* of the Augustan architect Vitruvius, was, like Alberti's, divided into ten books, and Alberti's very title was a deliberate challenge to the ancient author across a millennium and a half.

Vitruvius had written to record a passing epoch rather than open a new one. He rehearsed and even codified the building theories and practices of preceding generations, of the Hellenistic architects of Asia Minor and the Greek mainland during the three or four centuries before his time. Their books were still available to him: they seem mostly to have been monographs which architects wrote to justify the design of a single building. Probably none contained a general statement about architecture such as Vitruvius proposed. For his part he was clear about the novelty of his ambition, but conditioned by his admiration for the older architects, so that he emulated their attitudes and adopted their vocabulary. Many of his technical terms are simple transliterations of Greek words; even his obsessive habit of setting categories and notions in triplets was much favored by Hellenistic thinkers. The brief bibliography he provided in the preface to his seventh book is the only reliable guide to the theoretical writings of Greek architects.

Vitruvius was well aware of the technical advances of his own time, such as concrete vaulting and improved siege engines, as well as the development of new building types, such as the steam bath (one of the earliest to have survived was built in Pompeii, probably after his death) and the permanent stone stage set. He was nevertheless most interested in recording the way Hellenistic (and probably earlier Greek) architects had gone about designing the temples he proposed as the only exemplars by which all other building had to be guided and judged. In particular the elements of the design of columns—elements later to be called the *orders*—were codified by Vitruvius. Whatever brilliant achievements the future may hold, it is the glory of the past that Vitruvius extols—and regrets. In his writing there is no sense of the vast achievement of Roman imperial architecture that was to come; and yet he was considered by later ages as its harbinger.

Alberti was, on the contrary, consciously setting out on a fresh enterprise. While the buildings that Vitruvius theorized were those which he and his readers could see in the city of Rome as well as in the colonies of the empire, those to which Alberti appealed were either described in ancient literary sources or accessible only to the most intrepid travelers, or yet visible only as ruins. The very few antique buildings to have survived entire and gained his admiration, such as the Pantheon or the tomb of Theodoric in Ravenna, had been achieved by a building industry whose techniques and organization were a mystery to him and his contemporaries. Specific buildings of his own time are never mentioned. It is from the ruins and the texts that a new architecture, as solemn and as impressive as that of the ancients, will have to be derived. And, as Alberti insists, the ultimate criterion is neither the written nor the ruined examples, but nature herself.

The essential difference between Alberti and Vitruvius is therefore that the ancient writer tells you how the buildings that you may admire as you read him *were* built, while Alberti is prescribing how the buildings of the future *are to be* built. In order for his lessons to have the proper authority, however, the tone and the audience to which he addresses himself must be established. And there, too, the difference with Vitruvius is at once clear: whereas Vitruvius, for all his encyclopedic and philosophical pretension, writes to confirm his position as the custodian of a tradition, and to claim imperial patronage in its name, Alberti writes to claim a high place in the social fabric for the re-formed discipline of the architect, which has to be established anew. He writes, moreover, not just for architects and craftsmen, but for princes and merchants, for the patrons—perhaps for them primarily. That is why he writes in Latin only, and that is why the book, in its original form, required only the fewest and tiniest illustrations. He wants to hold their attention by the elevated tone of his argument and by the elegance of his language. In this matter, as in several others, he sets himself against Vitruvius, who (as he rather insists) was no great stylist. There is no place in his book for Vitruvius' Hellenizing technical neologisms; not Vitruvius, but Cicero—the Cicero of the legal and rhetorical treatises—is the model to whom Alberti appeals. And religion appears only in ancient dress: the deity is always plural (*dei, superi*), churches are always "temples." The ancient Romans are referred to as they might have been by a late Republican writer, as *patres nostri*, "our fathers," "our ancestors."

And his contemporaries read him as if he were another Cicero. He wrote *divinissimamente*, Cristoforo Landino, Latin secretary to the Florentine republic, opined. And the enterprise proved a very difficult one: he swears (*me superi!* "by Heaven!") that he would never have done it, had he known, when he set out on the hard slog of compiling his treatise, how much trouble it was all going to cost him—this invention of a whole new range of discourse about building.

Alberti's Childhood and Youth

When Alberti set out to project how architecture was to be ordered in the future so as to have something of a beauty "so ancient yet so new," he was already a famous man of letters and an accomplished diplomat, a member (albeit illegitimate) of the great Alberti clan of Florence, in whose villa outside the city Giovanni da Prato (a latter-day Boccaccio) laid the scene of his collection of novels and anecdotes, the *Paradiso degli Alberti*. These powerful merchants and bankers, like the Medici, had fought the old Florentine nobility in all the disturbances that followed the rebellion of the Ciompi; they were in temporary disgrace, having been exiled from Florence at the instance of Maso degli Albizzi in 1393. Some were exiled specifically to Spain or Flanders, others just a distance outside the city. Benedetto, the first major statesman of the family, had already been exiled in other troubles and had gone on a pilgrimage to the Holy Land. He died on his way back, on Rhodes in 1387.

His grandson Battista was born in January 1404 (February in the old style) in Genoese exile: the second illegitimate son of Lorenzo de' Benedetto degli Alberti and Bianca Fieschi, a Genoese widow (Grimaldi was her married name) who had already borne Lorenzo another son, Carlo. She seems to have died soon after Battista's birth during an outbreak of the plague, after which Lorenzo moved with his children to Venice and later to Padua, though he did marry in Genoa in 1408. Battista seems to have been very precocious and was sent to the most brilliant educational establishment in north Italy, the school, already called *gymnasium*, of Gasparino Barzizza, where the scabrous Panormita, as well as Francesco Barbaro and Francesco Filelfo, were also pupils; as was Vittorino da Feltre, who succeeded his master as professor of rhetoric at Padua University and later founded his own school in Mantua. In his teens, probably in 1421, Battista went to Bologna to take the usual degree of doctor *utriusque juris*, of canon and civil law, which was a standard introduction to a high clerical career. While a student he became extremely interested in mathematics and seems already to have met the mathematician-engineer-geographer-physician Paolo Toscanelli. During that time his father died, followed a few months later by Battista and Carlo's uncle Ricciardo, who was also their guardian. Apparently some greedy relations then decided to use the boys' illegitimacy as an excuse to strip them of their inheritance, which caused Battista great grief and unsettled him thoroughly—he seems to have passed through a time of bad health, caused (as his anonymous biographer, or perhaps he himself as autobiographer, suggests) partly by worry and partly by overwork.

At this time he worked his first literary triumph, the comedy *Philodoxeos*: a pseudo-antique play, which passed for a long time as the work of a fictitious silver-Latin writer, Lepidus. It was an elaborate joke, a literary forgery rather than an independent composition, but it showed the author as a wit, already an accomplished Latinist, and a literary inventor of some power. The comedy circulated in a version that was rather sultried-up by the naughty "epicurean" Panormita; later Alberti would reclaim his authorship so that he could return his juvenile effort to its proper integrity, though a century and a half later it was again published as a genuine "antique" play. At the same time he was becoming an accomplished writer in the vulgar tongue: from this period date some love poems, of a conventional cast, which imply an ill-starred entanglement with a young lady of whom we know very little—that she was of a lower social class, that she was jealous, and that she seems to have left him with a bitter distaste for female company; indeed, their conventional nature has been taken by some to imply that she was as much a fiction as Lepidus. Whatever the truth, the poems show Alberti as a master of Italian verse forms.

He was no mere highbrow, however. He prided himself on his reputation as an athlete: he was supposed to be able both to jump over a man's head with his feet joined and to throw a silver coin up to the vault of Florence Cathedral so that you heard it ring. He was also very sociable, a man of strong loyalties and friendships. The most important of those he made at university was with Tommaso Parentucelli of Sarzana, who was to become Nicholas V, the humanist pope. It may well be that Tommaso, the secretary of the saintly Carthusian Niccolo Albergati, archbishop of Bologna, brought him to that cardinal's notice.

Meanwhile in Florence, circumstances had changed. Pope Martin V interceded for the exiled Albertis, and the ban was lifted. Some members of the clan had in fact already returned, and Battista probably had his first opportunity to see the home of his family in 1428. The occasion proved intoxicating: for the first time Alberti came into contact with the new Florentine art. The frescoes of Masaccio in the Carmine and in Santa Maria Novella, the sculptures of Donatello and of the della Robbias, and the overwhelming bulk of the cathedral dome all made an enormous impression on him. A direct result of the visit was the little book on painting, *De pictura*, in which Alberti set out the new method, first formulated by Brunelleschi, of *constructing* three-dimensional space on a two-dimensional plane by the use of the *costruzione legittima* of monocular perspective, which was to dominate discussion about art for the next century. Although he wrote in Latin first, by 1435 he had translated it into Italian at Brunelleschi's request: he dedicated the translation to *Pippo architetto*, whose great structure "rose into the sky, so ample that it can cover all the people of Tuscany with its shadow."

The Papal Functionary

Soon after that first visit of Alberti's Florence, Martin V sent Cardinal Albergati on an embassy to make peace between Charles VII of France, Henry VI of England (or rather his uncles, who ruled in his infancy), and Philip the

Good of Burgundy. English readers may recall that Joan of Arc was burnt in 1431. In Alberti's biography there is a hiatus about this time—but little positive evidence to support the idea favored by some of his biographers that he traveled in the cardinal's suite through northern Europe, though it would have been the only opportunity of observing people skating on ice (which he describes in book 6, chapter 8) and would account also for some very telling details of northern European use of building materials. At any rate, in the course of that journey the cardinal probably sat for Jan van Eyck in Bruges during a brief visit there—a drawing and a painting are traditionally described as being of Albergati—and it is tempting to conjecture that Alberti met not only the great Florentines of his day, but Jan van Eyck also.

By 1432 the cardinal had been legate at the Council of Constance (no sign of Alberti there) and returned to Bologna, where the council had been adjourned. Alberti reappears in the records: this time as secretary to Biagio Molin, patriarch of Grado (and later of Jerusalem) and head of the papal chancery. At Molin's instance Alberti became a member of the College of Pontifical Abbreviators: the diplomatic office, where all the papal documents were edited and written out in fair copies for publication. It was one of the main agencies through which the newly reformed Italic hand became the standard civilized manner of writing throughout Europe. It had been developed in Florence in the late fourteenth and the beginning of the fifteenth century by Coluccio Salutati, Niccolo Niccoli, Ciriaco of Ancona, and Poggio Bracciolini (Poggio became the official scribe to Pope Martin V) out of the book hand of Carolingian scribes. Most of the writings of ancient Latin writers were preserved in Carolingian manuscripts, and the new calligraphy was a kind of programmatic declaration of loyalty. Inevitably, Alberti also practiced it. To oblige Biagio Molin, he began writing a series of new-style, Ciceronian saints' lives, though he seems to have completed only one, the life of a little-known martyr, St. Potitus.

By this time Pope Martin was dead, and in October 1432 his Venetian successor, Eugenius IV, removed the canonic disabilities of illegitimacy that affected Battista. It is not certain that Battista was actually ordained priest (though the phrase *aureo anulo et flamine donatus*, by which he describes himself, would suggest it), but the pope's action allowed him to hold church livings: he became prior of San Martino in Gangalandi at Signa, outside Florence, and later also rector of the parish of San Lorenzo in Mugello; he was a canon of Florence Cathedral—and there may have been other benefices. All this meant that he had a steady income.

In Rome his main concern outside official duties seems to have been the drawing up of a complete and accurate survey of the monuments of the city. He may at this time also have begun, though not completed, the book that gives him a permanent position in the history of sociology as well as in

Italian letters: *Della famiglia,* a dialogue on the duties and pleasures of family life—even if his particular family seems for the purpose of the dialogue to be composed exclusively of men: father and sons, brothers, uncles and nephews. Women exist only in reported speech.

But the stay in Rome was not long. Eugenius was expelled by the rioting Romans at the end of May 1434 and a republic proclaimed; although the rule of the Church was quickly restored, the pope continued to hold court in Florence and other northern Italian cities. Alberti followed him, and moved with the pope to Bologna. He was present at the consecration of his kinsman, Alberto Alberti, as bishop of Camerino (he later became a cardinal) in the autumn of 1437 in Perugia. More important was the visit— with the papal court—to Ferrara in 1438, for the opening by the now aged Cardinal Albergati of the council between the Eastern and the Western churches, which later moved to Florence because of an outbreak of the plague, or perhaps because the papal coffers were empty and that was Cosimo de' Medici's condition for financing the proceedings; it is in fact known as the Council of Florence. Alberti was to stay in Florence almost constantly until 1443. It was in Ferrara, however, that he befriended the learned and gentle marquess, Lionello d'Este. To him he dedicated the "purged" *Philodoxeos* and his little book about breaking in horses, *De equo animante,* as well as one of his Italian books.

Architecture, Virtue, Fortune
It may well be that Alberti's knowledge of horses led, indirectly, to his first "professional" involvement with the visual arts: Lionello d'Este declared a competition for an equestrian statue of his father, Nicholas III. Alberti was invited to help judge it. The prize was divided quaintly between one sculptor for the horse and another for the rider. The statue was then set in the cathedral square on a strange, I am tempted to say unique, podium: it looked like the fragment of a triumphal gate. At the same time the bell tower of the cathedral, which had been funded by Duke Nicholas, was completely redesigned. Building went on for another century and more, and it is not at all clear what part, if any, Alberti had in the wholly revolutionary design of both monuments; if he had no hand in them, there must have been some unacknowledged architectural genius working in Ferrara at the time.

Meanwhile the council was sitting in Florence. Between the cathedral and Santa Croce a covered walkway was built. The hundreds of prelates, as well as the Byzantine emperor and his suite (seven hundred persons are said to have arrived in Venice on ships—Greeks, Russians, later Syrians, Armenians, Copts—but only thirty signed the decrees in the cathedral), would proceed frequently through the center of Florence. Bessarion of Nicea and Gemistus Pletho, both recognized as the great Greek scholars of their time, were part of the Greek delegation, and Bessarion was to live his life out as a cardinal in Rome. Ambrogio Traversari, the vicar general of the Camaldolite monks, was one of the council's main protagonists and coauthor of its decree, since he was a fluent Greek writer and speaker. He died soon afterwards, and Alberti, who had been a friend, was commissioned to write a biography, though the project fell through. However slight Alberti's acquaintance with the Greek language before the council, as a working official of the papal chancery he must have come into contact with many of the Greeks.

The Florentine stay also meant that Alberti became a fluent and accomplished writer in his mother tongue, the Tuscan or Florentine dialect. It may well be that he finished the third (and most impressive) of his four books, *Della famiglia*, at this time. He was also becoming something of a connoisseur of Italian verse. The *Certame Coronario*, a competition for Italian verse on a given subject, was devised (and the prize partly paid) by him. Although the first occasion, in October 1441, was a solemn one, the competition did not establish itself as a yearly event.

However, Pope Eugenius had returned to Rome in 1443. A number of moves were made to restore St. Peter's Basilica, including the casting of new bronze doors by Alberti's contemporary, the sculptor-architect Antonio Averlino, who called himself Filarete; there is an allusion to this in book 2, chapter 6. The negotiations started at Florence were being continued in Rome with the Copts and the Armenians by Tommaso Parentucelli. When Eugenius died in Rome in 1447, Parentucelli was elected pope and took the name Nicholas V in honor of his old patron, Cardinal Albergati.

Alberti also returned to Rome with the papal court. Florence he regretted. "I am like a foreigner there," he wrote toward the end of his life; "I went there too rarely, and lived there too little." About this time he began the lengthy composition of *Momus*, or *The Prince*, which he thought of as his Latin masterpiece: a satirical dialogue on the model of Lucian's *Dialogues of the Gods* and *Dialogues of the Dead*—emulating the Latin of Cicero much as Lucian, writing in the second century A.D., had emulated the Attic style of Plato and Xenophon. Lucian's works were well known in Italy, and several Latin versions (by Poggio and Guarino of Verona) were in circulation. In at least one dialogue, *Musca* (the fly), Alberti imitates Lucian explicitly, and another, *Virtus dea*, was considered to be a translation from Lucian by Carlo Marsuppini, a man of letters who certainly should have known better.

Alberti's anti-hero Momus had made occasional appearances in classical literature as the god of mockery and satirical wit. He was the son of Night and Sleep. At the beginning of Alberti's book the gods are invited to provide some ornament to the world that Jove has made: Momus produces the insects that so much troubled Alberti's contemporaries. After a number of other misdeeds and misadventures, Momus is emasculated and set on a rock in the sea, like a eunuch Prometheus. The father of the gods becomes convinced at some point that the world he has made should be destroyed and replaced by one or more new ones. Much of the book is concerned with the gods' search for a world design, which they first think will be supplied by philosophers or other "experts"—who turn out, however, to be malicious, quarrelsome. The work of the ancient architects turns out to be the one guarantee against Momus' malignities and the proof of man's devotion to the gods, and therefore the only proper pattern for their project. How the world escapes destruction and Momus his rock, both to be restored to Jove's favor, is shown in the fourth book. It was almost certainly a satire on Alberti's contemporaries, and many commentators have seen the features of Eugenius IV in Jove, while Momus has been equated with the writer-humanist Bartolommeo Facio or Fazio. Whatever the truth of all this, *Momus* is, in a sense, an introduction to Alberti's main preoccupation during the second half of his life, the theory and practice of architecture. The first sure and committed record of it is his *De re aedificatoria*, but *Momus* provides the essential clue about the extraordinary change in Battista's career, in his way of life: architecture was to him the ransom that any public man must pay to fortune if he would display the mask of virtue to his fellow citizens.

About this time simple Baptista becomes the more familiar Baptista Leo or Leon Battista and seems also to have adopted his "device," the flashing, winged eye with the motto *Quid tum*, "what then?" It is possible, even probable, that both name and device were taken on by Alberti at the same time, perhaps when he joined a small but powerful literary society in Rome, the "academy" gathered round Pomponio Leto—and that the name and the device were interdependent. *Quid tum* is a question about the human condition of mortality, to which the device is Alberti's personal answer. The lion's eye, it was generally believed, had the unique power of retaining the lion's majesty after his body died—that is the significance of the flashes. That power was likened by the philosopher Philo and the poet Statius to the way in which the name of a famous man, a man of virtue, survived the death of his body; though the device of the eye, the winged eye in particular, had appeared in Alberti's earlier writings, *Intercoenales*, his table-talk, as an emblem of divine omnipresence and omniscience.

De Re Aedificatoria

It was to Pope Nicholas that Alberti presented a version of his architectural treatise about 1450. By then he seems to have acquired considerable experience of building problems. Lionello d'Este's court may have provided small beginnings; but even before that he had been engaged on the great survey of Rome. His mathematical writings had made him even more famous among his contemporaries than his literary compositions. Some time about 1445/6 Cardinal Prospero Colonna, who as nephew of Martin V had been persecuted by Eugenius IV, employed Alberti, as a great mathematician and renowned engineer, to raise a Roman ship that was known to have lain on the bed of Lake Nemi, in his estates, since ancient times. Alberti brought some expert divers from Genoa and had them fasten air-filled skins to the wreck, but only managed to raise half of it. This was, however, considered a great triumph and became material for much speculation. In 1450, chronicling the event, his abbreviator colleague Flavio Biondo describes Alberti as a "brilliant geometer and the author of most elegant books on the *arte dell'edificare*." It is not absolutely certain that he had *De re aedificatoria* in mind, but it is most likely. At any rate, there is plenty of internal evidence that the ten books were not written in one continuous redaction. Some have even taken the preamble of book 6, chapter 1, to suggest that Alberti had interrupted work and/or that he had second thoughts about the project. And it is only in the latter part of the text that the reader will find the many blanks left not only by the printer but by practically all the scribes, since the author did not have the time to check or verify his references.

The new pope certainly used Alberti as a consultant. There were a number of problems on which his immediate opinion was sought. Old St. Peter's was in very bad condition, as Alberti is constantly reminding his reader, and measures had to be taken to remedy the most threatening defects. The pope decided definitely to settle in the Vatican and identify his office with the cult of his first martyred predecessor, so that the whole access to the basilica, as well as the extensive papal headquarters to the north of it, had to be integrated. A number of other churches in the city also needed immediate attention, such as Santo Stefano Rotondo. Alberti's part in all this building activity is uncertain. However, when the pope declared a holy year in 1450, the number of pilgrims was unprecedented. The balustrades of the bridge of Hadrian, which was the main one connecting the two sides of the Tiber, collapsed during a rush, and some two hundred people were killed in the panic. Alberti was almost certainly in charge of its rebuilding, and is probably describing his design here in book 8, chapter 6.

If Vasari is to be believed, many of the Roman works were carried out in collaboration with Bernardo Rossellino, a Florentine sculptor-mason. He and Alberti were certainly friends. However, while records of payments to Rossellino confirm his participation in them, no such records exist for Alberti. As an amply beneficed papal official he may well not have been entitled to professional fees. It does seem certain, at any rate, that for these and for other works such as the Fontana di Trevi, which was finished in 1453, he was in the inner councils of Nicholas V.

It was not the pope, however, but a warlord who provided Alberti with his first opportunity to apply his principles to a building which has survived, at least as a fragment. Sigismondo Malatesta, lord—more often called tyrant—of Rimini, consulted him on the rebuilding of the old church of San Francesco in his city, turning it into an antique-modern *tempio*. With the building of the Tempio Malatestiano, Alberti's career as an independent consultant and architect begins. His book is written, his principles are stated: however much he develops those principles, it is on the basis of the ideas set forth in his book that he orders his practice.

Reception of the *De Re Aedificatoria*

Alberti's contemporaries accepted *De re aedificatoria* as a model of learned Latin writing immediately. When it came to be printed, in 1486, some fourteen years after its author's death, the introduction was written by the great scholar-poet Angelo Poliziano and addressed to Lorenzo de' Medici, who was the virtual ruler of Florence. It is known that the sheets of the book were taken to Lorenzo at his villa in Careggi as they came off the press. Before it was printed, he was jealous of his own manuscript copy of the book; in a letter addressed to Duke Borso d'Este of Ferrara in 1484, he agrees to loan him a copy of the as-yet-unprinted book on condition that it be returned soon, "because he is very fond of it and reads it often."

Versions of the Latin Text

The manuscript that Lorenzo lent Borso d'Este was not the only one available at that time, though it may be the one the printer used. Another, rather splendid one belonged to Bernardo Bembo, ambassador of the Venetian republic in Florence and father of the great humanist Pietro, from whose library it was most probably bought by Sir Henry Wotton when he in turn was King James I's ambassador in Venice. Wotton left it to the library of Eton College (of which he was provost) when he died in 1639. It has bound in with it a portion of the second half of book 9 taken from an earlier and rougher manuscript—perhaps the one that the printer used—with notes added in Battista's own hand.

Another manuscript was finished in 1483 for the very recondite bibliophile Federico da Montefeltre, duke of Urbino, whose library (he would have been ashamed to have a printed book in it, one of his suppliers said) became part of the Vatican when his heritage was absorbed into the papal states. Two manuscripts were copied out and illuminated in Florence for another great bibliophile, Matthew Corvinus, king of Hungary. One is in the civic library in Modena, the other in the cathedral library at Olomuc, in Czechoslovakia. There are four further manuscripts that seem earlier than the first printed edition: a second one in the Vatican, one in the Laurenziana library in Florence, one in the Marciana in Venice, and one in the University of Chicago library.

The first edition was finished on the fourth of January 1485; though since the Florentines counted the year of the Incarnation from the feast of the Annunciation on March 25, it was really 1486 in our accounting. The printer was Niccolo di Lorenzo Alamani, one of the very first to work in

Florence. The next, a Parisian one, was edited and laid out by the great humanist-typographer Geoffroy Tory, who first divided the books into chapters; it was printed in 1512 by Berthold Rembolt. In 1541 a much more handy but also much more crabbed one was printed in Strasbourg by Jakob Cammerlander: it was the last one in which the Latin text appeared alone. Within a decade it was replaced as the "authorized version" by Bartoli's translation, of which more later.

Early Translations

Alberti's treatise was being translated into Italian perhaps before it had even been printed. The earliest translations remained in manuscript. A much-corrected late-fifteenth- or early-sixteenth-century version of the first three books in the Biblioteca Ricciardiana in Florence was mistaken by one of Alberti's nineteenth-century editors, Anicio Bonucci, for a holograph. Slightly later (dated 1538) is the charmingly but rather anachronistically illustrated version by one Damiano Pieti of Parma, which is now in the civic library in Reggio Emilia. The first printed translation "into the vulgar tongue" was done by Pietro Lauro of Siena, a practiced translator from Greek (Arrian, Plutarch's *Moralia*) and Latin (Columella); it was published by Vincenzo Valgrisi in Venice in 1546 and almost immediately replaced by a more faithful—and the first illustrated—version by Cosimo Bartoli, a Florentine cleric, who was to translate many of Alberti's other works, particularly the mathematical ones. It had a charming title-page woodcut after a drawing by Giorgio Vasari that is in the print room of the Uffizzi in Florence. The title page proclaims (presumably polemically against Lauro) that it is not just in any "vulgar tongue" but in the "Florentine language." This is the most familiar version, which was not really displaced until 1966, when a new critical Latin text with an Italian translation based on it was published by Giovanni Orlandi and Paolo Portoghesi. There have been several Italian editions since the sixteenth century; a complete Italian translation from Latin by Simone Stratico of Udine, whose eight-volume edition of Vitruvius (Udine, 1825) is certainly the bulkiest one, has remained in manuscript.

A French translation came next, in 1553. It was the work of Jean Martin, who had already produced a translation of Vitruvius in 1546 and of the *Hypnerotomachia Polyphili* in 1547. A posthumous publication, it carried a long lament for Martin by Pierre Ronsard; it was illustrated with woodcuts, mostly after Bartoli's, though with some others taken out of Italian Vitruviuses. A variant edition of Bartoli's including a version of the *Della pittura* by Lodovico Domenici, first appeared in 1565. In 1582 in Madrid Alonso Gomez published a Spanish translation, without a translator's name: it was probably the work of Francisco Lozano. A passage of chapter 13 in book 7, which reproves certain abuses by the higher clergy in the name of the primitive purity of the church, was condemned by an Inquisitorial Index of 1611 and may be found crossed out in ink in some surviving copies, though it appears intact in the second, "corrected" Spanish edition published by Joseph Franganillo in 1797.

Modern translations begin with a German one by Max Theuer, published in Vienna in 1912 and reprinted in 1969. A Russian one, by V. P. Zoubov, was published in Moscow in 1935–1937, and a Czech one in Prague in 1956. A Polish translation, by Kazimierz Dziewoński, appeared in Warsaw in 1960.

English Translations

The first English version was signed by James Leoni, an émigré Venetian architect, though it was in fact the work of a little team that he had organized; it was published in London in 1726, in three volumes, with the English and Italian (in Cosimo Bartoli's translation) texts in parallel columns. He also included the three books on painting and the book on sculpture. This version was in demand and was reprinted in 1739; in 1755, after Leoni's death, it was condensed into two volumes by omitting the Italian text. The illustration for Leoni's version were astonishing copper-engraved fantasies on the original simple line woodcuts of Bartoli's edition. They were done in Amsterdam by Bernard Picart (1673–1733), the head of a highly successful engraving and publishing studio, who had also produced the frontispiece and several of the plates for Leoni's earlier publication, his translation of Palladio. These plates must have represented a considerable investment on Leoni's part; the translation of Palladio launched his English career.

On that occasion his team included Nicolas Dubois, more often known as "Captain" Dubois, a military engineer turned architect, who was employed at the Office of Works by the time the Alberti was begun: this was a source of income closed to Leoni, who seems to have remained a Catholic, and therefore barred from holding office under the crown. He could certainly not have mastered English well enough to produce the book on his own.

These two major publishing enterprises did not establish Leoni as the master of the new English classicism, as he had hoped. In fact, he was under a cloud: he had chosen to "improve" many of Palladio's buildings in the engravings that he used to illustrate his translation, and this infuriated the English enthusiasts of Palladio's architecture, particularly Lord Burlington, who commissioned an alternative version from one of his retainers, Isaac Ware. When this appeared in 1738, it replaced Leoni's version of Palladio definitively.

Leoni's Alberti translation from Bartoli's Italian, however, remained the only English one until the present version, which has been prepared on the basis of the new critical Latin text edited by Giovanni Orlandi (1966)—even if we have occasionally differed from him in details of reading and interpretation. We also used the *editio princeps*, of 1486, to which an invaluable *Index Albertianum* was added by Hans-Karl Lücke in 1975. Lücke also very kindly allowed us to consult his book on the textual problems in Vitruvius' and Alberti's treatises, to be published in 1988. His many suggestions and comments have been invaluable. We should also acknowledge the help and support we have obtained from staff at the University Library, Department of Architecture Library, Emmanuel College Library, University of Cambridge, and Cambridge University Computing Service. The index has been retyped and checked by Elizabeth Irish and Mario Canato, but our debt to Anne Engel, who has coordinated the whole enterprise, is perhaps the greatest.

As far as English usage would allow, we have attempted to make this a literal translation, even where it proved difficult, as for instance in maintaining certain rhetorical devices, particularly the shifts back and forth between first person singular and first person plural. It was our conviction that this was a text meant not to be looked at, but to be read aloud.

De Re Aedificatoria: Editions

Leonis Baptistae Alberti de re aedificatoria incipit . . . Florentiae accuratissime impressum opera Magistri Nicolai Laurentii Alamani. Anno salutis millesimo octuagesimo quinto quarto calendis januarias (1486 by modern reckoning).

Libri de re aedificatoria decem. . . . Paris: Berthold Rembolt, 1512.

De re aedificatoria libri decem. . . , per Eberhardum Tappium Lunensem. Strasbourg: Giacomo Cammerlander, 1541.

I dieci libri dell'architettura di Leon Battista degli Alberti fiorentino novamente de la latina ne la volgar lingua con molta diligenza tradotti da Pietro Lauro. Venice: Vincenzo Valgrisi, 1546.

L'architettura (De re aedificatoria) di Leon Battista Alberti trodotta in lingua fiorentina da Cosimo Bartoli . . . con l'aggiunta de disegni. Florence: Lorenzo Torrentino, 1550.

L'Architecture et l'art de bien bâtir . . . divisée en dix livres, traduicts de latin en françois, par deffunct Jan Martin, parisien. Paris: by Robert Massellin for Jacques Kerver, 1553.

L'architettura tradotta in lingua fiorentina da Cosimo Bartoli. . . . Venice: Francesco Franceschi, 1565 (reprint of 1550 edition).

Los diez libros de architectura . . . traduzidos de latin en romance. Madrid: Alonso Gomez, 1582 (reprinted 1640).

The Architecture . . . in Ten Books. Of Painting in Three Books. And of Statuary in One Book. Translated into Italian by Cosimo Bartoli. And Now First into English . . . by James Leoni, Venetian architect. London: Thomas Edlin, 1726, 3 vols. (reprinted 1739 and 1955).

Della Architettura, della Pittura e della Statua . . . Traduzione di Cosimo Bartoli. Bologna: Instituto della Scienza, 1782.

I dieci libri di Architettura di Leon Battista Alberti tradotti in italiano da Cosimo Bartoli. Nuova edizione diligentemente corretta e confrontata coll'originale latino, ed arricchita di nuova ricavati dalle misure medesime assegnate dall'autore. Rome: Giovanni Zempel, 1784.

Los diez libros de architectura. Segunda edition en Castellano, corregida por D. R. B. Madrid: Joseph Franganillo, 1797.

I dieci libri d'Architettura, ossia dell'Arte di edificare . . . scritti in compendio ed illustrati con note . . . da B. Orsini. Perugia: Carlo Baduel, 1804, 2 vols.

Della architettura libri dieci. Traduzione di Cosimo Bartoli con note apologetiche di Stefano Ticozzi, e trenta tavole in rame disegnate ed incise da Costantino Gianni. Milan: 1833, 2 vols. (in *Raccolta dei Classici Italiani di Architettura Civile da Leon Battista Alberti fino al secolo XIX*).

Dell'arte edificatoria. In *Opere volgari di Leon Battista Alberti*, ed. Anicio Bonucci, vol. 4. Florence: Galileiana, 1847, pp. 187–371.

Zehn Bücher über die Baukunst. In Deutsche übertragen, eingeleitet und mit Anmerkungen und Zeichnungen versehn von Max Theuer. Vienna: H. Heller, 1912.

Desat Knig'o Zodčestve. Perevodie V. P. Zoubov. *Klassiki Teorii Architektury.* Moscow, 1935 (text), 1937 (apparatus and commentary).

Ten Books on Architecture by Leone Battista Alberti, ed. Joseph Rykwert. London: Alec Tiranti, 1955 (reprint of 1755 edition with notes).

Deset Knih o Stavitelstvi, tr. and ed. Dr. Alois Otoupalik; preface by Ing. Arch. Vladimir Matoušek. Prague, 1956. Státni Nakladetelství Krásné Literatury, Hudby a Uměni.

Ksiąg Dziesięć o Sztuce Budowania, tr. Kazimierz Dziewoński. Warsaw: Paustwowe Wydawnictwo Naukowe, 1960.

Leon Battista Alberti, L'architettura (De re aedificatoria), Latin text and tr. edited by Giovanni Orlandi, introduction and notes by Paolo Portoghesi. Milan: Edizioni il Polifilo, 1966.

On the Illustrations in This Edition

The illustrations that accompany the text are taken from Cosimo Bartoli's Italian translation, published in Florence in 1550. A copy of this version in the University Library of the University of Cambridge was the source for the photographic reproductions used here.

On the Art of Building

From Angelo Poliziano to his Patron, Lorenzo de' Medici, Greetings.

Leon Battista the Florentine, of the great Alberti clan, was a man of rare brilliance, acute judgment, and extensive learning. Among the many excellent works that he left to posterity were the ten books he had composed on architecture. These he had corrected and edited with the utmost care; he was on the point of publishing them and dedicating them to you[1] when fate struck him down. His kinsman Bernardo,[2] a wise man and very devoted to you, wanting both to honor the memory and wishes of that great man, and to acknowledge his gratitude for the favors you have shown him, has had the original manuscripts transcribed and gathered into one volume to present to you, Lorenzo de' Medici.

It was his particular desire that I should commend both his gift and its author, Battista, to you. This did not seem at all advisable to me, for fear that my own poor talents would only diminish so perfect a work and so great a man. The work will gather much more praise to itself when it is read than I could bestow on it by any of my words; and my tribute to the author is constrained by the brevity of a letter, as well as the poverty of my style.

Surely there was no field of knowledge however remote, no discipline however arcane, that escaped his attention; you might have asked yourself whether he was more an orator or a poet, whether his style was more majestic or graceful. So thorough had been his examination of the remains of antiquity that he was able to grasp every principle of ancient architecture, and renew it by example; his invention was not limited to machinery, lifts, and automata,[3] but also included the wonderful forms of buildings. He had moreover the highest reputation as both painter and sculptor, and since he achieved a greater mastery in all these different arts than only a few can manage in any single one, it would be more telling, as Sallust said about Carthage,[4] to be silent about him than to say little.

I would like you, Lorenzo, to give this book a place of honor in your library, read it carefully yourself, and make sure that it is widely published. For it is worthy to live on the lips of the learned,[5] and the patronage of the arts, abandoned by all others, rests with you alone. Farewell. ◆

Here Begins the Work of Leon Battista Alberti on the Art of Building.[1] Lege Feliciter.

Many and various arts, which help to make the course of our life more agreeable and cheerful, were handed down to us by our ancestors, who had acquired them by much effort and care.[2] All of them seem to compete toward the one end, to be of the greatest possible use to humanity, yet we realize that each has some integral property, which shows it has a different advantage to offer from the others. For we are forced to practice some of these arts by necessity, while others commend themselves to us for their utility, and still others we appreciate because they deal with matters that are pleasant to know. I need not specify these arts: it is obvious which they are. Yet, if you reflect on it, you would not find one among all the most important arts that did not seek and consider its own particular ends, excluding anything else. If, however, you were eventually to find any that proved wholly indispensable and yet were capable of uniting use with pleasure as

Portrait of Alberti: "Leon Batista Alberti gentil huomo Fiorentino."

well as honor, I think you could not omit architecture from that category: architecture, if you think the matter over carefully, gives comfort and the greatest pleasure to mankind, to individual and community alike; nor does she rank last among the most honorable of the arts.

Before I go any farther, however, I should explain exactly whom I mean by an architect; for it is no carpenter that I would have you compare to the greatest exponents of other disciplines: the carpenter is but an instrument in the hands of the architect.[3] Him I consider the architect, who by sure and wonderful reason and method, knows both how to devise through his own mind and energy, and to realize by construction, whatever can be most beautifully fitted out for the noble needs of man, by the movement of weights and the joining and massing of bodies. To do this he must have an understanding and knowledge of all the highest and most noble disciplines.[4] This then is the architect. But to return to the discussion.

Some have said that it was fire and water which were initially responsible for bringing men together into communities,[5] but we, considering how useful, even indispensable, a roof and walls are for men, are convinced that it was they that drew and kept men together. We are indebted to the architect not only for providing that safe and welcome refuge from the heat of the sun and the frosts of winter (that of itself is no small benefit), but also for his many other innovations, useful to both individuals and the public, which time and time again have so happily satisfied daily needs.

How many respected families both in our own city and in others throughout the world would have totally disappeared, brought down by some temporary adversity, had not their family hearth harbored them, welcoming them, as it were, into the very bosom of their ancestors?[6] Daedalus received much praise from his contemporaries for having constructed a vault in Selinunte where a cloud of vapor emanated so warm and gentle that it induced a most agreeable sweat, and cured the body in an extremely pleasant manner.[7] What of others? How could I list the devices—walks, swimming pools, baths, and so forth—that help to keep us healthy? Or even vehicles, mills, timepieces, and other smaller inventions, which nonetheless play so vital a role in our everyday lives? What of the methods of drawing up vast quantities of water from hidden depths for so many different and essential purposes? And of memorials, shrines, sanctuaries, temples, and the like, designed by the architect for divine worship and for the benefit of posterity? Finally, need I stress how, by cutting through rock, by tunneling through mountains or filling in valleys, by restraining the waters of the sea and lakes, and by draining marshes, through the building of ships, by altering the course and dredging the mouths of rivers, and through the construction of harbors and bridges, the architect has not only met the temporary needs of man, but also opened up new gateways to all the provinces of the world? As a result nations have been able to serve each other by exchanging fruit, spices, jewels, experience and knowledge, indeed anything that might improve our health and standard of living.

Nor should you forget ballistic engines and machines of war, fortresses and whatever else may have served to protect and strengthen the liberty of our country, and the good and honor of the state, to extend and confirm its dominion. It is my view[8] moreover that, should you question all the various cities which within human memory have fallen into enemy hands by siege, and inquire who defeated and conquered them, they would not deny that it was the architect; and that they could easily have scorned an enemy armed with weapons alone but could no longer have resisted the power of invention, the bulk of war machines and the force of ballistic engines, with which the architect had harassed, oppressed, and overwhelmed them. On the other hand, those besieged would consider no protection better than the ingenuity and skill of the architect. Should you examine the various military campaigns undertaken, you would perhaps discover that the skill and ability of the architect have been responsible for more victories than have the command and foresight[9] of any general; and that the enemy were more often overcome by the ingenuity of the first without the other's weapons, than by the latter's sword without the former's good counsel. And what is more important, the architect achieves his victory with but a handful of men and without loss of life. So much for the use of architecture.

But how congenial and instinctive the desire and thought for building may be to our minds is evident—if only because you will never find anyone who is not eager to build something, as soon as he has the means to do so; nor is there anyone who, on making some discovery in the art of building, would not gladly and willingly offer and broadcast his advice for general use,[10] as if compelled to do so by nature. It often happens that we ourselves, although busy with completely different things, cannot prevent our minds and imagination from projecting some building or other. Or again, when we see some other person's building, we immediately look over and compare the individual dimensions, and to the best of our ability consider what might be taken away, added, or altered, to make it more elegant,[11] and willingly we lend our advice. But if it has been well designed and properly executed, who would not look at it with great pleasure and joy? Need I mention here not only the satisfaction, the delight, but even the honor that architecture has brought to citizens at home or abroad? Who would not boast of having built something? We even pride ourselves if the houses we live in have been constructed with a little more care and attention than usual. When you erect a wall or portico of great elegance and adorn it with a door, columns, or roof, good citizens approve and express joy for their own sake, as well as for yours, because they realize that you have used your wealth to increase greatly not only your own honor and glory, but also that of your family, your descendants, and the whole city.[12]

The island of Crete was much celebrated for the tomb of Jupiter,[13] Delos was revered more for the beauty of its city and the majesty of its temple than for the fame of the oracle of Apollo. As to the imperial authority and fame that the Latins got by their building, I need only mention the various tombs and other ruins of past glory still visible all around, which have taught us to accept much of the historical tradition that may otherwise have seemed less convincing. Of course Thucydides did well to praise the ancients who had the vision to adorn their cities with such a rich variety of buildings as to give the impression of having far greater power than they really had.[14] Has there been one among the greatest and wisest of princes who did not consider building one of the principal means of preserving his name for posterity? But enough on this.

To conclude, then, let it be said that the security, dignity, and honor of the republic depend greatly on the architect: it is he who is responsible for our delight, entertainment, and health while at leisure, and our profit and advantage while at work, and in short, that we live in a dignified manner, free from any danger. In view then of the delight and wonderful grace of his works, and of how indispensable they have proved, and in view of the benefit and convenience of his inventions, and their service to posterity, he should no doubt be accorded praise and respect, and be counted among those most deserving of mankind's honor and recognition.[15]

Aware of this, we have undertaken, for our own pleasure, to inquire more fully into his art and his business, as to the principles from which they are derived, and the parts of which they are composed and defined. Finding them to be very diverse in kind, infinite (almost) in number, admirable in nature, and marvelously useful, I wondered what human condition, what part of the state, what class of citizen owed more to the architect, since he is responsible for every comfort: was it prince or private citizen, religious or secular institution, business or leisure, or individuals as opposed to mankind as a whole? We therefore decided for many reasons, too lengthy to enter into here, to collect and commit them to these ten books.

They will be dealt with in this order:[16] first we observed that the building is a form of body, which like any other consists of lineaments and matter, the one the product of thought, the other of Nature; the one requiring the mind and the power of reason, the other dependent on preparation and selection; but we realized that neither on its own would suffice without the hand of the skilled workman to fashion the material according to lineaments. Since buildings are set to different uses, it proved necessary to inquire whether the same type of lineaments could be used for several; we therefore distinguished the various types of buildings and noted the importance of the connection of their lines and their relationship to each other, as the principal sources of beauty; we began therefore to inquire further into the nature of beauty—of what kind it should be, and what is appropriate in each case. As in all these matters faults are occasionally found, we investigated how to amend and correct them.

Each book, then, has been given a title according to its varying contents as follows: book 1, Lineaments; book 2, Materials; book 3, Construction; book 4, Public Works; book 5, Works of Individuals; book 6, Ornament; book 7, Ornament to Sacred Buildings; book 8, Ornament to Public Secular Buildings; book 9, Ornament to Private Buildings; book 10, Restoration of Buildings. Appended are: The Ship, Economics, Arithmetic and Geometry, and The Service That the Architect Provides.[17] ◆

Here Begins the First Book on the Art of Building by Leon Battista Alberti. The Lineaments.[1]

I

4—4v*

Since we are to treat of the lineaments of buildings, we shall collect, compare, and extract into our own work all the soundest and most useful advice that our learned ancestors have handed down to us in writing, and whatever principles we ourselves have noted in the very execution of their works. We shall go on to report things contrived through our own invention, by careful, painstaking investigation, things we consider to be of some future use. But since it is our desire to be as limpid, clear, and expeditious as possible in dealing with a subject otherwise knotty, awkward, and for the most part thoroughly obscure, we shall explain, as is our custom, the precise nature of our undertaking. For the very springs of our argument should be laid open, so that the discussion that follows may flow more easily.[2]

Let us therefore begin thus: the whole matter of building is composed of lineaments and structure.[3] All the intent and purpose of lineaments lies in finding the correct, infallible way of joining and fitting together those lines and angles which define and enclose the surfaces of the building. It is the function and duty of lineaments, then, to prescribe an appropriate place,[4] exact numbers,[5] a proper scale,[6] and a graceful order for whole buildings and for each of their constituent parts, so that the whole form and appearance of the building may depend on the lineaments alone. Nor do lineaments have anything to do with material, but they are of such a nature that we may recognize the same lineaments in several different buildings that share one and the same form, that is, when the parts, as well as the siting and order, correspond with one another in their every line and angle. It is quite possible to project whole forms in the mind without any recourse to the material, by designating and determining a fixed orientation and conjunction for the various lines and angles. Since that is the case, let lineaments be the precise and correct outline, conceived in the mind, made up of lines and angles, and perfected in the learned intellect and imagination.

Now, as we wish to inquire into the inner nature of building and construction as a whole, it may be of some relevance to consider what were the origins and what the evolution of those dwelling places we call buildings. And, if I am not mistaken, what follows may be taken as the correct account of the whole matter. ◆

2

4v—5v

In the beginning, men sought a place of rest in some region safe from danger;[7] having found a place both suitable and agreeable, they settled

---

*The corresponding folios in the *editio princeps* appear at the beginning of each chapter.

down and took possession of the site. Not wishing to have all their household and private affairs conducted in the same place, they set aside one space for sleeping, another for the hearth, and allocated other spaces to different uses. After this men began to consider how to build a roof, as a shelter from the sun and the rain. For this purpose they built walls on which a roof could be laid—for they realized that in this way they would be the better protected from icy storms and frosty winds; finally they opened windows and doors in the walls, from floor to roof, so as to allow entry and social gathering within, and also to let in the sunlight and the breezes at the right time, as well as to let out any moisture and vapor that may have formed inside the house. Whoever it was who first started to do these things, the goddess Vesta, daughter of Saturn, or the brothers Heurialus and Hiperbius, or Gallio, or Thraso, or the Cyclops Typhincius,[8] I believe that such were the original occasion and the original ordinance of building. The business has grown, I believe, through experience and skill, so that it is now almost without bounds, what with the introduction of the various building types; of which some are public, others private, some sacred, others profane, some of practical necessity, others merely for the permanent adornment of the city, while yet others are for more temporary pleasures. But no one will question our account of their origins.

Since this is the case, the elements of which the whole matter of building is composed are clearly six: locality, *area*,[9] compartition,[10] wall, roof, and opening. If these elements are clearly recognized, what we have to say will be understood more easily. We shall therefore define them as follows: by locality we mean all that land which is seen to surround the prospective building; the *area* is a part of this locality. We shall define the *area* as that certain, particular plot of land which is to be enclosed by a wall for a designated practical use; included in this definition is any surface within the building on which our feet may tread. Compartition is the process of dividing up the site into yet smaller units, so that the building may be considered as being made up of close-fitting smaller buildings, joined together like members of the whole body.[11] The wall we shall term all that structure which rises from the ground upward in order to support the weight of the roof, or which acts as a screen to provide privacy for the interior volumes of the building. We shall refer to the roof, not only as that uppermost part of the building which fends off the rain, but also, in general, as whatever is extended in length and breadth above the head of anyone walking below, such as ceilings, vaults, arches, and so forth. We shall call an opening anything within the building affording entry or exit to man or thing.

We shall deal with these matters and their every aspect, but first we will make some observations, which are fundamental to, and so much part of, the whole subject that they are highly relevant to our argument. If we were to consider those attributes with which each of the parts we have enumerated should be endowed, we would come up with three that should never be overlooked, and which are most becoming to roofs, openings, and so on. That is, their individual parts should be well suited to the task for which they were designed and, above all, should be very commodious; as regards strength and endurance, they should be sound, firm, and quite permanent; yet in terms of grace and elegance,[12] they should be groomed, ordered, garlanded,[13] as it were, in their every part.[14] Now that we have set down the roots and foundations of our discussion, let us continue our argument. ◆

3

5v—7

As for the locality,[15] the ancients put much effort into ensuring that it should contain (as far as possible) nothing harmful and that it should be supplied with every convenience. Above all, they took the greatest care to avoid a climate that might be disagreeable or unwholesome; it was a very prudent precaution, even an indispensable one. For while there is no doubt that any defect of land or water could be remedied by skill and ingenuity, no device of the mind or exertion of the hand may ever improve climate appreciably; or so it is said. Certainly the air that we breathe and that plays such a vital role in maintaining and preserving life (as we can ourselves observe), when really pure may have an extraordinarily beneficial effect on health.

Who can have failed to notice the extensive influence that climate has on generation, growth, nourishment, and preservation? As you may have seen, those who enjoy a purer climate surpass in ability others subjected to a heavy and damp one; for that very reason, so it was said, the Athenians were much sharper than the Thebans.

Climate, we may therefore agree, depends on the location and formation of the landscape; some reasons for this variation will seem quite obvious, while others, because of their very obscure nature, lie well hidden and totally evade us. We shall examine the obvious ones first and then those which are obscure, so that we will know how to select the most advantageous and healthy locality in which to live.

The ancient theologians called the atmosphere Pallas;[16] Homer makes her a goddess and calls her Glaucopis,[17] a reference to air so pure that it is completely transparent by nature. It is quite apparent that the healthiest form of air is that which is the purest and least polluted, the most easily pierced by sight, the most transparent and light, and which is always serene and largely constant; whereas we term as pestilential any form of air whose consistency is so cloudy and vaporous as to render it dense and fetid, so that it hangs heavy on the brow and dulls that keenness of sight. I believe that the sun and the wind, more than any other factor, are responsible for determining these two conditions. We shall not, however, discuss questions of physics here—that is exactly how the force of the sun manages to draw up vapors from the innermost bowels of the earth and then raise them to high heaven, or how once gathered together into a huge cloud in the vastness of the sky, either through their immense weight or from being dried out by the action of the sun's rays to one side, they topple over in that direction, thereby producing a great rush of air and arousing the winds, and driven by thirst, plunge into the ocean; finally, replenished by the sea and pregnant with moisture, wandering once more in the atmosphere, they are propelled by the winds and squeezed like sponges, and discharge the droplets of moisture they are carrying to form rain, thus renewing the vapors on land. Whether this theory we report is correct, or whether wind is some dry exhalation of the earth, or hot vapor expelled by the force of cold, or just a breath of air, or yet air that has been disturbed by the movement of the earth or by the course and radiation of the stars, or whether it is that general animating spirit that moves of its own accord, or even something that is not a separate entity in itself but rather consists of air that has been burnt by the heat of the highest ether and reduced to liquid form, or whether there is any further theory or explanation, sounder or based on more ancient authority, I suggest we should pass it by, as it may detract from the main argument.

All this will, if I am not mistaken, help us to appreciate the reason why some parts of the world are seen to enjoy the most delightful of climates, while others, which may be their very close neighbors, are marred by gloomy weather and murky days. I must suppose that the reason for this is their unfavorable position as regards the sun and the winds. Cicero says that Syracuse was sited so that there was not a single day in the whole year on which the inhabitants could not see the sun;[18] such a situation is very rare, however, and if there are no strong reasons or grounds for avoiding it, it is the location to be sought in preference to any other.

The locality to be chosen, therefore, should be quite free of raging clouds and all the dense thickness of vapors. Those who investigate such matters have observed that the rays and heat of the sun act more fiercely on dense than on rarefied materials, as they do on oil compared to water, or on iron compared to wool. From this they deduce that the air is thick and heavy wherever the heat is more oppressive. The Egyptians, striving to prove their ascendancy over all other nations of the world, boasted that man was first created in their country, and that he could only have been created in a land where he would be able to live in the best of health; for they had be endowed, above all else, with certain favors by the gods—a wonderful mate and a perpetual spring. But even among the Egyptians, writes H dotus, those who live nearest Libya, where the wind never varie the healthiest.[19] Certainly various towns in Italy, and other n to have become unhealthy and pestilential places for no oth their sudden temperature changes from hot to cold.

It is no bad thing, then, to consider the quality and angle of the sun to which a locality is exposed, so that there is no excess of sunlight or shade; the Garamantes cursed the sun at its rising and setting, so scorched were they by the excessive persistence of its rays, while other nations appear pallid from living in almost perpetual night.[20] This variation is not so much dependent on the lesser or greater inclination of the earth's axis (although that is an important factor) as on the configuration of the ground itself and its degree of exposure to the sun and the winds. Personally, I prefer gentle breezes to winds, though I would consider winds, however fierce and blustery, less irksome than a stagnant and heavy atmosphere. Water that does not move, Ovid tells us, absorbs badness.[21] What of air? I might almost say that it takes pleasure in movement. For it is my view that movement dissipates the vapors that rise from the earth, and movement consumes them. I would prefer, however, that these winds reach me broken down by intervening woods and mountains or exhausted by the length of their journey, and I would ensure that they do not pass over land where they might pick up and bring us anything harmful. For this reason it is advisable to avoid any location in whose neighborhood anything noxious is given off, such as offensive smells or unclean vapor rising from marshes, and in particular from polluted waters and ditches.

Naturalists agree that any river fed by the melting snows brings with it a cold, dense air; but of waters, none can be so foul as those which spoil away by remaining stagnant; the less it is dispersed by favorable winds, the greater the effect of the contagion on the neighborhood. The winds, they say, cannot all be classed as healthy or unhealthy of their nature. Pliny, on the authority of Theophrastus and Hippocrates,[22] considers Aquilo[23] to be the most favorable for the restoring and maintaining of health;[24] the naturalists all declare Auster[25] the most damaging to mankind, and they do not even consider it safe to leave cattle grazing in the fields while it blows. And again the stork will never hazard flying into Auster; when Aquilo blows, dolphins hear voices calling with the wind, but with Auster they hear much less well, and only against the wind. They say too that when Aquilo prevails, eels may survive for six days out of water, although such is not the case with Auster, so dense is it and its power so unhealthy. As Auster brings illness, and especially catarrh, so Coro[26] makes us cough.

South-facing coastlines are not recommended, primarily because the reflected rays of the sun afflict them with two suns, in effect: one burns down from the sky, the other up out of the water. Such places are subjected to sharp changes in temperature, as the chilling shades of night draw in at sunset. Some are even of the opinion that at sunset the overall effect of the sun, both direct and reflected off the water, sea, or mountains, is at its most harmful, since a place that has already been heated by the sun all day is made sweltering by the additional heat produced by the reflection. If on top of all these effects you are also exposed to oppressive winds, what could be more harmful or intolerable? Morning breezes too have been rightly reproved, as they bring with them raw vapors as they rise.

We have discussed the sun and the winds, and the obvious influence we feel they exert on the climate, whether it is healthy or not; we have done so briefly, as seemed relevant to our argument, and we shall deal with them in greater detail in their appropriate place.[27] ◆

4

7—9 When selecting the locality, it is worth ensuring that everything is to the liking of those who are to live there, be it the nature of the place or the company they will have to keep.

In no way would I build a city on a steep and inaccessible ridge of the Alps, as Caligula had intended, unless compelled by the utmost necessity.[28] I would also avoid the uninhabitable wilderness that Varro describes in Rhineland Gaul,[29] and Caesar in contemporary Britain.[30] Nor would I like to live on birds' eggs alone, as they used to on the island of Oenoe in the Black Sea,[31] or on acorns, as in Pliny's time in some regions of Spain.[32] In short, I would not wish the locality to lack anything that might prove useful.

Quite rightly, Alexander did not want to found a city on Mount Athos: the project of the architect Polycrates, although splendid in other respects, could not supply the inhabitants with sufficient provisions.[33] Yet Aristotle might have found a site with difficult access particularly pleasing for the foundation of a city,[34] while I notice that it was the practice of some nations to leave vast expanses on their borders deserted and forsaken, so as to deny any advantage to an enemy. The question of whether such methods should be condoned or not shall be dealt with elsewhere; but provided they are of public benefit, I find no reason to condemn their adoption.

In general, however, I would prefer to site buildings in a locality that has many different points of access, to allow the easiest possible provision by ship, cart, or beast, both in summer and in winter. The locality should not be too damp with excess of waters nor too parched by drought, but it ought to enjoy a comfortable, temperate climate. If this ideal condition is not possible, rather let it be somewhat cold and arid than too hot and humid, for it is possible to counteract the cold with roofs and walls, through clothing and the heat of the fire, or by moving about; dryness, meanwhile, is not considered particularly harmful to body or soul; indeed, they say that dryness may harden a man and cold make him rugged, but moisture will always make the body languid, and heat cause it to wilt. One may see how men are physically strong and free of disease during the cold season or in cold climates, although it is generally conceded that while those in cold places have superior physiques, those in warm places have sharper wits.

From Appian, the historian, I have learned that the main reason why the Numidians were so long-lived was that they never had to endure any cold winters.[35] The best locality of all, however, is a moderately warm and moist one, for it will produce men tall and elegant in stature and cheerful in character. The next most convenient are the sunniest parts of snowy countries or the most moist, shady zones of arid, sunburnt regions.

But there is no site less suitable or seemly for any building whatsoever than one that is hidden away in some valley; for (to pass over such obvious reasons as that, being out of sight, it can enjoy no honor, while being denied the delights of a view, it can have no charm) it will inevitably suffer the ruinous torrents of rain and swirling floods; by absorbing too much damp, it will always rot; and it will constantly exhale earthy mists so damaging to man's health. In such a place no man could retain any strength, as the spirit wilts, nor any body show stamina, as its joints are weakened; mold will grow on books; tools will rust away, and everything in the stores will decay from excess of moisture, until it is all ruined. Furthermore, should the sun break through, reflected rays would cause the heat to grow more intense, but if kept out, the shade will make the air coarse and stagnant. What is more, should the wind penetrate as far as that, it would only rage with more violence and fury by being forced through fixed channels, but should it not reach there, the air would become as thick as mud. It would not be unfair then to consider such a valley as a puddle or a stagnant pool of air.

Let the site therefore have a dignified and agreeable appearance, and a location neither lowly nor sunk in a hollow, but elevated and commanding, where the air is pleasant and forever enlivened by some breath of wind. It should, moreover, be well endowed with all the useful and pleasurable things of life, such as water, fire, and food. Care should be taken, however, to ensure that it contains nothing that might prove harmful to the inhabitants or their possessions. Springs should be laid bare and sampled, and their water tested by fire to check that it contains nothing sticky, putrid, or difficult to digest that might make the inhabitants ill. I shall not dwell here on the goiters and stones for which water may be responsible. I shall pass over the more remarkable and miraculous effects it may have, since the architect Vitruvius has already listed them in a most learned and elegant manner.[36]

There is an aphorism of the physician Hippocrates, that those who drink untreated water that is heavy and unpleasant to taste will develop a hot and swollen belly, while the rest of their bodies, their elbows, shoulders, and faces, will become remarkably weak and emaciated.[37] They will also suffer adverse clotting of the blood from defective spleens, falling prey to many infectious diseases; in summer runny bowel movements caused by bile secretion and discharge of humors will weaken them; and then all year round they will be troubled by more aggravating and permanent illnesses, such as dropsy, asthma, and pleurisy. The young will go mad because of black bile,[38] while older people will be consumed by burning humors; women will have difficulty in conceiving and great trouble giving birth, while everyone, of whatever age or sex, will be plagued by disease and driven to an untimely death. Nor will they be able to enjoy a single day of their lives free of sadness and without the affliction of bad humors and the harassment of every kind of trouble, so that their minds will be forever anguished by sorrow and grief.

We could mention many other fascinating anecdotes recorded by the ancient historians on the properties of water and the good and bad effects it may have on man's health, but they are curious ones that would serve to show off our erudition rather than illustrate our argument; in any case we shall deal more extensively with water in the appropriate place. But this much at least is obvious, and should not be overlooked: water provides nourishment for all that grows, plants, seeds, and anything that shares vitality, and by which we are refreshed and sustained. We ought, therefore, to inspect with the greatest possible care the quality of the water available in any locality where we intend to live. Diodorus relates that in much of India men have tall, strong bodies and alert minds, because the air they breathe is pure and the water they drink wholesome.[39]

We say that water has the best flavor when it has none, and the most pleasing color, when it is quite devoid of any; in fact the water that is considered the best is that which is clear, transparent, and light—so that when strained through white cloth it leaves no mark, when boiled no sediment—and which, wherever it flows, leaves the riverbed free of moss and the rocks without stain. Good water should also produce tender vegetables when used for cooking, and good bread when used in baking.[40]

In the same way, great care should be taken to ensure that the locality is not responsible for anything infectious or poisonous, which might put the inhabitants at risk. There are well-known ancient instances, hardly worth mentioning, such as the tree leaves of Colchis, which oozed a honeylike substance;[41] anyone who tasted it would fall unconscious for a whole day, as if dead. Or the disaster that they say befell Anthony's army, because of a toxic plant that the soldiers ate for want of grain, which drove them insane and made them intent on digging up stones, until their frenzy reached such a pitch that they collapsed from disturbance of the bile, and perished, there being (according to Plutarch) no antidote, except drinking wine:[42] all well-known tales.

But good heavens, what about our own times in Apulia, here in Italy, where small land-spiders are common,[43] with an incredibly poisonous bite that can send men into various forms of delirium, as though driven mad? Most surprisingly, there is no swelling, no telltale mark appears anywhere on the body to show the bite or sting of a poisonous insect; but to begin with men lose consciousness, fainting from the shock, and then, if there is no one to help them, they soon die. They may be treated with a remedy of Theophrastus, who maintained that snake bites could be healed by the sound of the flute.[44] Musicians caress the ears of the afflicted with various forms of harmony, and when they hit the right one, the victim will leap up as though startled, and then, through joy, straining every nerve and muscle, will keep time to the music in whatever manner takes his fancy. Some of the victims will, as you may see, try to dance, others to sing, while others will exert themselves attempting whatever their passion and frenzy dictate, until they are exhausted; they continue to sweat for several days more, and only recover when the madness, which had taken root, has been totally satiated.

We read a similar event that befell the Albanians who fought against Pompey with a large cavalry force. For it is said that spiders were found there which would cause the death of anyone who touched them, either by laughing or by crying.[45] ◆

5

9—10

When selecting the locality, it is not enough to consider only those indications which are obvious and plain to see, but the less evident should also be noted, and every factor taken into account.

It is a sign of good air and pure water, if the locality produces a fine and abundant harvest, if it sustains a large number of men to a ripe old age, if it rears young men who are strong and handsome, and if the births there are frequent and successful, provided they are all natural and the children are not marred by any deformity. I myself have seen cities (which out of respect for the times shall remain nameless) in which there is not a single woman who when giving birth does not realize that she has become the mother of both man and monster. I know of another town in Italy where there are so many born either with tumors, squints, and limps, or who are crippled, that there is scarcely a family that does not contain someone deformed or handicapped in some way; and it is a sure indication, when many marked discrepancies are to be seen in bodies or their members, that the climate is at fault or that some other latent deficiency is responsible. Here the old saying is relevant: a heavy atmosphere will reduce the appetite, and a rarefied one increase thirst.

Nor would it be wrong to take the physical appearance of animals as a guide to the likely condition of men who are to live in the locality. For should the cattle appear sturdy, with long, well-developed limbs, it is not unreasonable to expect human offspring to be similarly endowed.

Nor is it inappropriate to take inanimate objects into consideration when looking for indications of the climate and winds: we may deduce from neighboring buildings, for example, that if they are rough and rotting, it is a

sign of some adverse outside influence. If trees should all lean in one particular direction, as though by common consent, or have broken branches,
clearly they have suffered the violence of the wind. Similarly, when the
upper surfaces of tough stones,[46] whether local or imported, are unusually
eroded, they betray sharp changes in temperature between hot and cold.
Above all, any region beset by these storms and temperature changes
should be avoided: exposure to extremes of hot and cold weakens and im-
pairs the structure and composition of the body and its parts, and may lead
to disease and premature old age; indeed the main reason why a city lying at
the foot of mountains that face west is considered especially unhealthy is
that it is particularly exposed to sudden nocturnal exhalations and the
chilling darkness.

It is also useful to take careful account of any unusual feature of the locality,
by consulting what wise men have recorded of the events of the past; nature
has imbued some places with hidden properties, which may benefit or disadvantage the citizens; it is said, for example, that Locri and Croton have
never suffered a plague,[47] that poisonous animals are never found on the
island of Crete, and that deformed children are seldom born in France. In
some places, according to the naturalists, lightning occurs neither in the
heat of the summer nor in winter, yet in Campania, Pliny tells us, flashes of
it are seen in all south-facing cities during both these seasons;[48] the Ceraunian mountains in Epirus, meanwhile, are said to be named after the
frequent thunder they suffer,[49] and the continual thunder on the island of
Lemnos has, according to Servius, prompted the poets to claim that Vulcan
fell to earth there.[50] It is said that thunder and lightning have never been seen
in the Bosphorus and amongst the Insodones;[51] if it rains in Egypt it is considered a miracle, but on the banks of the Hydaspes, at the beginning of
summer, it rains continuously.[52] The wind blows so rarely in Libya that the
thickness of the atmosphere causes different shapes formed of condensed
vapors to appear in the sky; on the other hand, in a large part of Galatia the
wind blows so hard during the summer that stones are thrown up into the
air like sand,[53] and in Spain, along the Ebro, they say that the northwester-
lies are capable of overturning well-laden carts. The south wind does not
blow over all of Ethiopia,[54] yet historians would claim that this is the wind
that dries up all the vegetation in Arabia and in the land of the Troglodytes.
Thucydides writes that Delos has never suffered any earth tremors but has
always stood firm on the same rock, although earthquakes have brought
ruin to all the surrounding islands. We ourselves have seen that stretch of
Italy, along the whole range of the Hernician mountains, from Algidus[55]
near Rome as far as Capua, repeatedly shaken and all but destroyed by
earthquakes. Some believe that Achaia takes its name from the frequent
floods it suffers.[56] I have discovered that Rome has always been troubled by
some sort of fever, which Galen diagnosed as a form of semitertian ague,

and which requires the application of various and almost contradictory methods of treatment according to the different hours of the day.[57] It is an ancient poetic legend that whenever the giant Typhon, who is buried on the island of Procida, turns in his grave, the whole island shakes from its very foundations.[58]

The poets have sung about this because of the violence of the earthquakes and eruptions that plagued the place, and that forced the Eretrians and the Chalcidians, who had once settled there, to flee; similarly other colonists, sent there some time later by Hieron of Syracuse to found a city, also fled through the continual fear of danger and disaster.

All these things should be examined repeatedly and over a long period; they should be compared with the characteristics of other places, to provide a full understanding of the locality. ◆

6

10—11

Inquiry should also be made into whether the locality suffers any other, less obvious, disadvantage; Plato believed that some places would occasionally be ruled by some divine power or demonic government, which might be either favorably or ill disposed toward the inhabitants.[59] There are indeed some places where men are more likely to go mad, others where, for a trifle, they will seek self-destruction, and others where they are more likely to take their own lives by hanging, or leaping from heights, or by the sword and poison. After a close scrutiny of all the most hidden, obscure evidence that nature has to offer, you must weigh up anything else that may seem relevant.

It is an ancient custom, traced back as far as Demetrius, to inspect the color and condition of the livers of cattle grazing on the site when founding a city or a town, or even when just setting out a temporary military camp:[60] should they show signs of infection, the place is manifestly unhealthy and should be avoided.

Varro informs us of tiny atomlike creatures that he has detected, which flit about in the atmosphere, enter our lungs as we breathe, and stick to our entrails;[61] they gnaw away at them, causing violent and wasting disease, which leads to plague and destruction.

Nor should you fail to consider that some places may not in themselves be particularly inconvenient or treacherous, but are so unprotected that when strangers arrive from some foreign land, they often bring with them plague and misfortune; and this may be caused not only by arms and violence, or the work of some barbarian or savage hand: friendship and hospitality may also prove harmful. Some whose neighbors desired political change have themselves been put at risk by the upheaval and turmoil. The Genoese colony of Pera, on the Black Sea, is always prone to disease, because slaves are daily brought there sick of soul and neglected of body, wasting away from idleness and filth.

It is said to be the mark of prudence and wisdom to examine the destiny of a locality by interpreting auspices and through observation of the heavens; I do not think these methods should be despised, provided they accord with religion.[62] Who would deny the importance of that which we call chance in human affairs, whatever it may be? Can we deny that the public fortune of the city of Rome greatly favored the expansion of the empire? The town of Iolaus in Sicily, which was founded by the nephew of Hercules, although frequently assaulted by Carthaginian and Roman forces, remained forever free; and can the ill-fortune attached to the place have had no connection with the temple at Delphi, burnt down first by Phlegyas, and a third time destroyed by fire at the time of Sulla? And what of the Capitol? How often did it burn? How often was it in flames?

The town of the Sybarites,[63] after being harassed again and again, and having been repeatedly destroyed and deserted, was totally abandoned in the end. Misfortune dogged the inhabitants, even when they had fled the place; for although they moved elsewhere, and changed the original name of the town, they could in no way escape disaster: they were attacked by the natives of their new land, and the members of all the chief and most ancient families were put to the sword and slaughtered; they were annihilated together with their temples and the entire town. But there is no need to go on: history books are full of such examples.

It is generally agreed that it is no mark of a foolish man to make sure of everything that would justify the care and expense of construction, and to ensure that the work itself is as lasting and salubrious as possible; it is surely the duty of that wise and sensible man not to overlook anything which might be of use to this end. Is an undertaking that leads to your own well-being, that favors a life of dignity and pleasure, and that entrusts the fame of your name to posterity not one of great benefit to yourself and your family? For here you may devote yourself to noble studies; here you may enjoy your children and your dear family; here you may pass your days in business or at leisure; here you may pass every period of your life. I am of the opinion, therefore, that there is nothing, aside from virtue,[64] to which a man should devote more care, more effort and attention, than to the acquisition of a good home to shelter himself and his family; and who would expect to achieve this if he ignores the advice that we have just given? But enough of this: we will now move on to discuss the *area*.[65] ◆

7

11—12

In choosing the *area*, whatever advice we gave on the locality should also be respected; for just as the locality is a particular part selected out of some larger territory, so too the *area* is a precisely limited and defined section of the overall locality taken for future building. For this reason the *area* will display almost the same advantages and disadvantages as the locality; but nonetheless in this account certain precepts will appear, some of which might seem to concern the *area* specifically, while others relate not only to determining the actual *area* but also to questions about the locality as a whole, such as the following.

It is necessary to bear in mind the work we are undertaking, whether it is public or private, whether sacred or profane, and other such categories with which we shall deal in detail at the appropriate place. Fora, theaters, gymnasia, and temples all require quite different sites and conditions; and so the shape and position of the *area* should depend on the purpose and use to which it is to be put.

So as to keep the discussion general, we shall only deal with topics that we consider to be relevant; but let us first say a few words about lines, which might help us to state our argument more clearly; as we are dealing with the setting out of *areae*, it will be useful to describe the elements involved.

Every outline is made up of lines and angles; lines make up the outer perimeter, which encloses the whole extent of the *area*. Any part of the surface within this perimeter that is contained between two intersecting lines is called an angle. When two lines intersect, four angles are formed; if any one of them equals the other three, they will be termed right angles. Those which are smaller than right angles are called acute, and those greater, obtuse. A line may be either straight or curved: there is no need here to deal with lines that spiral like a snail shell or a whirlpool. The straight line is the shortest possible line that may be drawn between two points.[66] The curved line is part of a circle. A circle is the line made by one of two points moving on one plane, so that throughout the operation its course remains no farther or closer than the initial distance set between it and the other, the fixed and central point, which it circumscribes.

It should be added, however, that the curved line, which we called a part of a circle, will be known as an arc or bow (because it resembles one) to us architects; the straight line drawn between two separate points on a curve will for the same reason be called a chord; the line that extends perpendicularly from the center of the chord as far as the arc is termed an arrow; the line drawn from the fixed point at the center of the circle to the curved boundary of that same circle is referred to as the ray; the fixed point, which always stays in the middle of the circle, is given the name center: the straight line that passes through the center and transects two points on the curved edge of the circle is called the diameter. Then there are different types of arcs: some are complete, others segmented, yet others pointed. A complete arc is one that takes up half of a whole circle, that is, one whose diameter is the same as its chord. A segment of an arc is one whose chord is less than the diameter; such an arc is always the section of a semicircle. A pointed arc consists of two segments of arc, so that at the top these two intersecting arcs meet at an angle, which never happens with a complete or segmented one.

Now that we have established this, let us proceed. ◆

<table>
<tr><td>8
12—13v</td><td>*Areae* may be either polygonal or curved; polygonal ones may be described entirely by straight lines or by a mixture of straight and curved, but I cannot recall having come across any building of the ancients that has a polygonal *area* or is composed of several curved lines without any intervening straight ones.</td></tr>
</table>

As we deal with these matters, there is something we must watch, since we would be strongly criticized for its absence in any part of the building, while its presence contributes much to charm and convenience. I mean that certain variety[67] possessed by both angles and lines, as well as by individual parts, which is neither too much nor too little, but so disposed in terms of use and grace, that whole may correspond to whole, and equal to equal.

Right angles are the most useful. Acute angles are never used, even in the smallest and most insignificant of *areae*, except reluctantly and when forced to either by the constraints of the site or by important demands of the *area*. Obtuse angles are considered respectable enough, provided they are always even in number.

The circular *area* is said to have the largest capacity and to be the cheapest to enclose with a mound or wall; those considered next have a number of jutting-out corners, provided all the angles throughout the *area* balance out and match one another; the most commendable are those conveniently raised to their full height from hexagonal or octagonal plans,[68] although I have also seen a decagonal one,[69] which looks most practical and graceful. It is quite feasible to have twelve or even sixteen corners, and I have seen one with twenty-four, but they are somewhat rare.[70]

The lines along the sides should be of equal length to those opposite them, and nowhere in the work should the longest lines be joined to the shortest by a single stroke, but there should be a fitting and dignified proportion[71] between them, according to the demands of each case. The angles ought to be positioned counter to the pressure of rocks or the likely direction of violent water and winds, so as to divide and dissipate the destructive blows as they strike, by facing the trouble with the strongest part of the wall[72] rather than the weakness of a side. But if the other lineaments of the building prevent you from using a corner there, as you might wish, a curved wall must be used instead, the curve being part of the circle, and the circle, according to the philosophers, being all angle.

The *area* may be either on a level surface, on a slope, or on top of a hill. If it is on a level surface, a mound should be formed, so as to place the building on some kind of podium, which will ensure it greater dignity and also prevent several inconveniences: floods caused by swollen rivers or heavy rains are likely to deposit mud in flat places, which gradually raises the level of the ground; the surrounding plain is also raised simply through the negligence of man, who fails to clear away the rubble and refuse that gather daily. The architect Frontinus[73] claimed that in his time frequent fires had been responsible for increasing the height of the hills of Rome;[74] and we can see today how the whole city has been buried by dirt and filth. I myself have seen an ancient shrine in Umbria,[75] built at ground level, but which nonetheless has now been for the greater part buried by a buildup of soil, because it stands on a plain at the foot of mountains. But why should I mention only what lies at the bottom of a slope? That noble relic outside the walls of Ravenna, which has a single hollowed stone for a roof, although it is near the sea and well away from mountains, has nonetheless been one-quarter-buried by the sheer force of time.[76] The precise height to which each of the *areae* should be raised will be dealt with more thoroughly (and not summarily, as we do here) when we come to the appropriate place.[77]

It is at any rate essential to make sure that each *area* is made quite firm by artifice, if it is not so by nature; I therefore insist that the advice of those who want us to test the soil so as to see whether it is compact enough, or too loose and soft to bear the weight of the building, by digging one or two trenches at some distance from each other, should first be followed. If the building is to be placed on an inclined site, provision must be made to ensure that the higher parts do not exert damaging pressure, nor that any chance movement in the lower section drag the rest to ruin. Indeed, I would wish that the base of the whole structure be the most solid and best reinforced part of the building.

If the *area* is to be on top of a hill, the site should be leveled out, either by building up the sides at some point or by cutting away what had been the peak of the hill. We must go about this in a way that best preserves dignity, while incurring the least expense in terms of cost and labor. It may in fact be best to pare some earth away from the top and to build some onto the slope. Whoever the unnamed architect was who set the town of Alatri on a rocky peak in the Hernician mountains, he was well versed in these matters. He took great care to reinforce the foundations (whether of citadel or temple) with fragments of rock cut from the top of the peak, which is the only evidence still remaining, since the superstructure has been demolished.[78] But what I approve of even more is that wherever the sides fell away sharply, he set the corners of the *area* forward, strengthening them with the powerful bulk of huge rocks packed together; yet he so arranged the stones that the very economy gave a certain dignity to the structure. In the same way, another architect introduced a measure of which I approve: where he had an insufficient quantity of stone to withstand the thrust of the mountain, he constructed a series of hemicycles, their backs turned into the mountain. This structure was not only pleasing to see and extremely strong, but also very economical, for he had constructed a wall that, although not itself solid, had as much strength as one that was, and whose thickness was equivalent to the sagittae of the arches.

I also greatly approve of the technique recommended by Vitruvius, which was practiced by the ancient architects and may be seen throughout Rome, but especially in the wall of Tarquinius;[79] this was to employ the support of buttresses. They do not, however, always follow the rule that the distance between the buttresses should be equal to the height of the structure, but make them distant or close, according to whether the ground is stable or liable to slip, as it were. I have noticed too that the ancient architects were not content with just a single substructure by each *area*, but that they preferred several, like steps,[80] securing the whole slope to the very heart of the mountain; a measure which I feel should not be overlooked.

The stream by Perugia, which flows between Mount Lucino[81] and the hill on which the town itself sits, continually erodes and undermines the foot of the hill, causing the land above it to slide down; this has been responsible for much of the city slipping and falling into ruin.

Consequently, I also very much approve of the numerous chapels that have been added on both sides of the site of the Vatican Basilica;[82] for those built against the wall of the basilica, where dug out of the hillside, are of considerable help and convenience: they support the constant pressure of the slope and intercept any moisture seeping down through the hill, stopping it from entering the building, so that the main wall of the basilica remains dry and therefore stronger. The chapels on either side, at the base of the slope, are quite capable of sustaining the weight of the ground, which had been leveled above them, because of their arched construction and because they buttress any earth movement.

I notice how the architect who built the temple of Latona in Rome showed great ingenuity in designing the building proper as well as its foundations: he set an angle of the site into the hillside on which it sits, so that the pressure of the weight was split between two straight walls, which (being set at an angle) offset the danger by dividing and dissipating the load.[83]

Since we set out to praise the prudence with which the ancients designed their buildings, I would not wish to ignore one particularly relevant example that springs to mind. The architect of St. Mark's in Venice incorporated a most useful measure into the design: for although he made the foundations of the whole church compact and strong, he left a number of shafts running through them, to allow an easy escape to any vapors that might have built up underground.

To conclude: any *area* that you intend to cover with a roof ought to be perfectly level, but those that are to be exposed to the heavens should have just enough of a fall to allow rainwater to run off. But enough of this topic; we have said more perhaps than the occasion demanded, since many of our comments apply equally to walls. We have thus dealt in the same place with two things that are by nature inseparable. We must now deal with compartition. ◆

9

All the power of invention, all the skill and experience in the art of building, are called upon in compartition;[84] compartition alone divides up the whole building into the parts by which it is articulated, and integrates its every part by composing all the lines and angles into a single, harmonious work that respects utility, dignity, and delight.[85] If (as the philosophers maintain) the city is like some large house, and the house is in turn like some small city,[86] cannot the various parts of the house—atria, *xysti*,[87] dining rooms, porticoes, and so on—be considered miniature buildings? Could anything be omitted from any of these, through inattention and neglect, without detracting from the dignity and worth of the work? The greatest care and attention, then, should be paid to studying these elements, which contribute to the whole work, so as to ensure that even the most insignificant parts appear to have been formed according to the rules of art.

To achieve this properly, all that has been said above about the locality and the *area* is highly relevant: just as with animals members relate to members, so too in buildings part ought to relate to part; from which arose the saying, "Large buildings should have large members." This was a principle followed by the ancients, who would give everything, including bricks, a larger scale in grand, public buildings than in private ones. Each member should therefore be in the correct zone and position; it should be no larger than utility requires, no smaller than dignity demands, nor should it be strange and unsuitable, but right and proper, so that none could be better;[88] the most noble part of the house, for example, should not be left in some forgotten corner, nor should the most public be hidden away, nor anything private exposed to view. Account should also be taken of the seasons, so that rooms intended for summer use should not be the same as those intended for use in winter, in that they should have different sizes and locations; summer rooms should be more open, nor is it amiss if winter ones are more closed in; summer ones require shade and draught, while winter ones need sunlight. Care must be taken to prevent the inhabitants' moving from a cold place to a hot one, without passing through some intermediate zone, or from a warm place to one exposed to the cold and the wind. This can be very detrimental to the body's health.[89]

The parts ought to be so composed that their overall harmony contributes to the honor and grace of the whole work, and that effort is not expended in adorning one part at the expense of all the rest, but that the harmony is such that the building appears a single, integral, and well-composed body, rather than a collection of extraneous and unrelated parts.

Moreover, in fashioning the members, the moderation shown by nature ought to be followed; and here, as elsewhere, we should not so much praise sobriety as condemn unruly passion for building: each part should be appropriate, and suit its purpose. For every aspect of building, if you think of it rightly, is born of necessity, nourished by convenience, dignified by use; and only in the end is pleasure provided for, while pleasure itself never fails to shun every excess. Let the building then be such that its members want no more than they already have, and what they have can in no way be faulted.

Then again, I would not wish all the members to have the same shape and size, so that there is no difference between them: it will be agreeable to make some parts large, and good to have some small, while some are valuable for their very mediocrity. It will be equally pleasing to have some members defined by straight lines, others by curved ones, and still others by a combination of the two, provided, of course, that the advice on which I insist is obeyed, and the mistake is avoided of making the building appear like some monster with uneven shoulders and sides. Variety[90] is always a most pleasing spice, where distant objects agree and conform with one another; but when it causes discord and difference between them, it is extremely disagreeable. Just as in music, where deep voices answer high ones, and intermediate ones are pitched between them, so they ring out in harmony, a wonderfully sonorous balance of proportions results, which increases the pleasure of the audience and captivates them; so it happens in everything else that serves to enchant and move the mind.[91]

This whole process should respect the demands of use and convenience, and follow the methods sanctioned by those who are experienced: to contravene established customs often detracts from the general elegance, while conforming to them is considered advantageous and leads to the best results. Although other famous architects seem to recommend by their work either the Doric, or the Ionic, or the Corinthian, or the Tuscan division as being the most convenient, there is no reason why we should follow their design in our work, as though legally obliged; but rather, inspired by their example, we should strive to produce our own inventions, to rival, or, if possible, to surpass the glory of theirs.[92] We will deal with these matters, however, more thoroughly in the appropriate place, when we consider how the city, the members of the city, and their respective services ought to be disposed.[93] ◆

10

15—16

We shall now deal briefly with the outlines of walls. First, however, I would like to mention a precaution I have observed the ancients always took: they never allowed any one side of an *area* to be drawn too far in a straight line without being broken by being bent into some curve or cut by an angle. Why such experienced men should take this step is obvious: they wanted to reinforce the wall by offering support.

When considering the methods of walling, it is best to begin with its most noble aspects. This is the place therefore where columns should be considered, and all that relates to the column; in that a row of columns is nothing other than a wall that has been pierced in several places by openings. Indeed, when defining the column itself, it may not be wrong to describe it as a certain, solid, and continuous section of wall, which has been raised perpendicularly from the ground, up high, for the purpose of bearing the roof.

There is nothing to be found in the art of building that deserves more care and expense, or ought to be more graceful, than the column. Columns may differ from one another, but we shall deal here with their similarities, with what constitutes their general characteristics; their differences, which determine individual variations, we shall deal with elsewhere, when appropriate.

So to begin from the very roots, as it were, let it first be said that every column has a foundation. Once they had reached floor level, it was customary to build a little wall on top of the foundations which some may call a cushion but which we shall call a pedestal. On this would sit the base, on the base the column was set up, and above that the capital. Columns would be designed so that the lower half would swell out, and the upper contract, the bottom being one part thicker than the top.

In my opinion the column was originally developed to support the roof. Yet it is remarkable that mortals, once they had developed a passion for nobler things, grew concerned to construct buildings that would be permanent, and as far as possible immortal. They therefore built columns, beams, even entire floors and roofs out of marble. In this, ancient architects closely followed nature's example in their desire not to appear to deviate too far from common ways of building; at the same time they took every possible care to ensure that their work would be not only appropriate to its use and structurally sound, but also delightful in appearance. Certainly Nature first supplied us with columns that were round and of wood, but, later, utility demanded that in some places they should be quadrangular. And, if I judge correctly, noticing the bands of iron or bronze incorporated at either end of the wooden columns to prevent them from splitting under the continual load, the architects also attached a wide straplike ring to the very foot of the marble columns to protect them from the splash of raindrops. Likewise at the top they placed another strap, and above that a collar, devices that they had seen used to strengthen wooden columns. As for the bases of the columns, they would ensure that the lowest part would be rectilinear and rectangular, while the upper surface would follow the outline of the column diameter. Further, both the width and the depth of the base would be greater than its height, and proportionally greater than its top, while the pedestal would be broader than the base, by the same amount that the foundations would exceed the pedestal; all of these would be positioned above one another, centered on a single plumb line. Meanwhile the capitals would be similar, in that their lower surface would follow the form of the column, and their upper one be rectangular; the top of capitals never fails to be broader than the bottom. So much for columns.

The wall follows the same rules as the column, in that if its height is to equal that of the column complete with capital, its width must equal that of the bottom of the column. They also avoided having any column, base, capital, or wall that did not correspond to the other elements of the same order, in height, width, or indeed any dimension and form. And yet, although it is wrong to make either the width or the height of a wall greater or less than reason and scale[94] demand, I would prefer to err in excess rather than to underprovide. Here it is worth mentioning a few building defects to heighten our own awareness of the matter. For to have no defect is the greatest honor.

I have noticed in the Basilica of St. Peter's in Rome a crass feature: an extremely long and high wall has been constructed over a continuous series of openings, with no curves to give it strength, and no buttresses to lend it support. It is worth noting that the whole stretch of wall has been pierced by too many openings and built too high, and positioned where it will bear the violence of Aquilo.[95] As a result, the continual force of the wind has already displaced the wall more than six feet from the vertical; I have no doubt that eventually some gentle pressure or slight movement will make it collapse. Indeed it is quite likely that, had it not been restrained by the roof trusses, it would have collapsed of its own accord already, once it had begun to lean. But perhaps the architect may be excused a little, since, being hemmed in by location and site, he may have considered the hill overlooking the temple sufficient protection from the winds. I would prefer, however, those whole sections of wall to be strengthened on both sides. ◆

I I

16—17   Roofs are the most important elements; for not only do they help to maintain the good health of the residents by defending them from rain, and keeping out the night, and above all keeping out the summer sun, but they provide excellent protection for the whole building as well. Take away the roof, and the woodwork rots, the walls totter and their sides crack; gradually the whole structure falls apart. Even the very foundations, though you may hardly believe it, rely on the protection of the roof for strength. Nor have as many buildings fallen into ruin by fire, sword, enemy hands, or by any other calamity, as have tumbled down for no other reason than human neglect, when left naked and deprived of the roof covering. Indeed, in buildings the covers are the weapon with which they defend themselves against the harmful onslaught of weather.

Our ancestors then seem to have distinguished themselves here, as elsewhere, in attaching so much importance to the covering that they exhausted almost all their decorative skill in adorning it. For we have seen roofs made of copper, glass, and gold, and elegantly decorated with ceilings gilded or coffered in gold, and picked out with sculpted crowns and flowers, and even statues.

Roofs may be either exposed to the sky, or not. Those exposed to the sky are not intended for walking on, but serve simply to keep out the rain. Those not exposed to the sky are intermediate floors of trussed and vaulted construction, which seem as if one building has been built on top of another, so that what constitutes the roof for the members of the building below is also therefore the *area* for those above, although we should rightly call the covering that part of the flooring which is above our heads; this should also be called ceiling, while anywhere that we tread on should be termed flooring or paving. We shall deal elsewhere with the question of whether the outermost covering, which is exposed to the sky and intended to keep out the rain, may also serve as the pavement.

Although they may have a flat surface, coverings exposed to the sky ought never to be parallel to the floor that they cover, but should always slope and incline in one direction to throw off the rain. Coverings not exposed to the sky, however, ought to have a flat surface parallel to the floor. All roofs must follow the lines and angles of the *area* and the form of the walls which they are to cover; and since these vary—some are composed entirely of curves, others of straight lines, yet others of a mixture, and so on—the form of the roofs must also be manifold and varied. And indeed, roofs are varied of themselves, some being hemispherical, some groin-vaulted, some barrel-vaulted, others composed of several arches, and still others called "carinated" and others "double-pitched." Whatever its form, however, every roof ought to be so designed as to offer shelter to the pavement below and to keep all rainwater out of any part of the building it covers. For rain is always prepared to wreak mischief, and never fails to exploit even the least opening to do some harm: by its subtlety it infiltrates, by softening it corrupts, and by its persistence it undermines the whole strength of the building, until it eventually brings ruin and destruction on the entire work. For this reason the experienced architects have taken great care to provide rainwater with an unimpeded runoff and to ensure that it is nowhere allowed to stand or to leak through and cause damage. Therefore they recommended that roofs should be double-pitched and very steep in snowy places, to prevent the snow from building up and to allow it to fall off more easily; but in summery places, as it were, the roofs should be less sheer, and inclined at an oblique angle.

Finally, care must be taken to ensure that the covering is a single, even, and unbroken unit, and, while respecting the rights regarding ancient lights and party walls, that it covers the whole building to an extent sufficient to prevent water dripping from the eaves and making any part damp; it should also be built so as not to drip onto another roof. The rainwater ought not to have too vast a surface to run down, as otherwise after a heavy shower it will overflow in the gutter beyond the tiles and drain back into the building, with devastating effect on the latter. So, when the *area* is to be very large, the roof ought to be divided up into several planes, so that the rain flows off in different places—a solution as elegant as it is practical. If any house is to have several roofs, they should be joined one to another, so that those who come into the shelter of one may wander through the whole house under cover. ◆

12

17—19

We now come to the opening. There are two types of opening, one for light and ventilation, and the other to allow man or object to enter or leave the building. Windows serve for light; for objects there are doors, stairs, and the spaces between columns. Also included among openings are the ways through which water and smoke may pass in or out, such as wells, drains, the mouths, as it were, of fireplaces, oven doors, and vents.

Every part of the house should have a window to allow the air within to breathe and be regularly renewed, otherwise it will decay and become stale. The historian Capitolinus relates the tale of the exceedingly old gold casket discovered in the temple of Apollo in Babylon; when it was broken open, the air within, which had become bad and extremely poisonous, escaped, and spreading abroad not only killed those immediately present, but infected the whole of Asia as far as Parthia with a most savage plague.[96] Similarly, we learn from the historian Ammianus Marcellinus that in Seleucia[97] in the time of Marc Anthony and Verus some soldiers, after plundering the temple and carrying off the statue of Apollo Conicus to Rome, discovered a narrow opening, previously blocked up by the Chaldean priests; when their desire for booty prompted them to open it up, an infectious vapor was emitted, so offensive and detestable that from Persia to Gaul everything was infested with loathsome and fatal disease.[98]

Each individual chamber, then, should have windows, to admit light and to allow a change of air; they should be appropriate to the requirements of the interior and should take into account the thickness of the wall, so that their frequency and the light they receive are no greater or less than utility demands.

Also to be considered are the winds to which the windows are exposed. Windows facing healthy breezes may be made quite large, and it is worth opening them sufficiently to allow the air to circulate around those within: the best way to achieve this is to have the sills of the windows so low that one can see and be seen by passersby on the street. Windows, however, exposed to the onslaught of those winds which are not always healthy should be built to admit no less light than is convenient and no more than is needed, and should be positioned high enough for the wall to act as an obstruction and to protect those within from the wind. In this way there will be sufficient wind for a change of air, but it will be broken down, thereby losing much of its unhealthiness.

Another consideration is how the sun should enter the house, and how the requirements of the apartment should govern the size of windows. Summer apartments should have windows with generous dimensions if they face north; if they face south, they should be low and narrow, so as to freely admit the breezes but avoid the glare of the sun's rays. Anywhere that men go to seek shade rather than light, there the sun constantly shining from every direction will provide sufficient illumination. Meanwhile, winter apartments should have windows that are large, to receive the direct sun, and placed high up, to avoid exposure to the wind by denying it direct access to those standing within. Clearly any opening intended to admit light should also allow a view out to the sky, and any windows constructed for this purpose ought never to be given a low position: light is seen by the face, not by the feet. Furthermore, should one person or another obstruct the light, the rest of the room would be thrown into darkness. This never happens when the light comes from above.

Doors should follow the same rules as windows, their size and number depending on frequency of use and functional requirements. In public buildings, however, I have noticed that it was customary to have a large number of both types of opening: this is demonstrated by theaters, which, if I am not mistaken, are totally composed of either stairways or, more especially, windows and doors.

The method of locating openings should be to follow the demands of use, but do not incorporate small openings within too vast an expanse of wall, nor employ within short spaces those which are too large. Opinions may have differed on the lineaments of these openings, although the best architects used nothing but quadrangular and rectangular forms, wherever possible.[99] All, however, are agreed that the design should suit the building, whatever its size or shape. They recommend that doorways should always be higher than they are wide, the taller variety containing two whole circles, the shorter one with a height the diameter of a square whose baseline is the width of the door.

Doors would be positioned where they might afford access as conveniently as possible to every part of the building. Care had to be taken to give openings a graceful appearance, and those on the right and the left would have equal dimensions so that they balanced each other out. Although it was customary to give doors and windows an uneven number, those on one side would be equal to and would match those on the other, while those in the middle would be somewhat larger.

Great precaution was taken to preserve the strength of the structure, and therefore openings would be placed well away from corners and the points where columns sprang, particularly in sections of wall that were weak, although not incapable of bearing their load. They also ensured that as much of the wall as possible rose perpendicularly and complete, unbroken from ground to roof.

There is one particular type of opening that adopts the same positioning and form as doors and windows; it does not cut right through the whole thickness of the wall, however, but is carved out like a shell, and provides a dignified and appropriate setting for statues and paintings. We shall talk in greater detail about their placing, size, and frequency, when we deal with ornaments to a building; they contribute as much to reducing the cost, however, as they do to improving the appearance of the work, in that fewer stones and less cement are used to complete the wall. All that is worth mentioning here is that niches should be arranged in a correct number, in moderate scale, and with pleasant appearance, in that their arrangement closely follows the rules for windows.

I notice that it was customary in the works of the ancients never to allow openings of any kind to occupy more than a seventh or less than a ninth of a wall's surface.

The spaces between the columns should certainly be considered among the most important of openings. Their composition varies according to the type of building, but we shall deal with this more thoroughly in the appropriate place, in particular when we consider the furnishing of sacred buildings. Let it suffice here to bear in mind that openings should be positioned with particular regard for the properties of columns, whose purpose it is to hold up the roof: columns should be neither narrower nor farther apart than is required for them to be easily capable of bearing the weight of the roof; nor should they be wider or closer together than what allows the interior spaces and entrances to remain unimpeded for every event and circumstance. Furthermore, the form of the openings will depend on the distance that the columns are apart: if close together they will be connected by beams, if far apart, by arches. But for any arched opening, care should be taken to avoid having an arch of less than a semicircle with one seventh of the radius added. The experienced agree that, as regards durability, this is the most suitable form of all; every other they consider inefficient at bearing loads and prone to collapse.[100] Moreover, the semicircular arch is the only one thought not to require ties or other means of support. All others, when on their own and without the restraint of ties and opposing weights, seem to crack and give way. I shall mention here a remarkable technique that I have noticed employed by the ancients, and that deserves particular praise: the best architects constructed the openings and vaulted arches of their temples so that even when all the interior columns had been removed, the arches of the openings and the vaults of the roof would still remain and not collapse. All the arches bearing the weight had been drawn down to the ground with such admirable and uncommon skill that the work remained standing supported by the arches alone. Is it any wonder that these arches, with the solid earth for their tie, should be so solid themselves, and stand on their own for ever? ◆

13
19—20

The task of constructing a stairway is so demanding that it may be done correctly only by someone with much experience and a thorough understanding. For within a single stairway are included three openings, the first being the door providing entry to the stairs, the second the window admitting light to make each tread visible, and the third the opening within the joists of the ceiling, giving access to the floor above. For this reason staircases are considered an awkward element within the whole design; but anyone not wishing to find the stairs an obstacle should not in his turn create any for them: they should be allotted their own section of the floor, running free and unimpeded right up as far as the outermost *area*, the roof that is exposed to the sky. That the stairs should occupy so much of the plan ought not to give cause for concern: their convenience is greatest when they least inconvenience other parts of the building; what is more, the vaults and spaces left over below the stairs can be used to great advantage.

We have two types of staircase (I do not intend to deal with those for military campaigns and defense here): one ascended not by stairs but by an inclined ramp, the other by steps. Our ancestors used to make their ramps as easy and gentle as possible. According to my own observations of their buildings, it was considered acceptable to have their ramps at an incline of one part in height along the vertical to six in length along the baseline. They preferred an odd number of steps for their temples, claiming that this would ensure that they would be entered on the right foot, as was considered religious. I notice here that the best architects almost always avoided having an unbroken flight of more than seven or nine steps (representing, I imagine, the number of planets, or the heavens); instead, after every seventh or ninth step they wisely provided a landing to give the weary or infirm a place to rest from the task of climbing the stairs, and, should anyone happen to stumble while ascending, to offer a place to check his fall, and to recover and gather himself.

Personally, I strongly approve of stairs broken up by well-lit landings, and given ample and spacious dimensions, appropriate to the importance of the building. The ancients considered that stairs should be constructed so that their risers are no higher than three fourths of a foot, no lower than one sixth, their treads no shallower than one and a half, no deeper than two.[101] The fewer the stairs in a building and the less room they take up, the less of an inconvenience they will be.

Outlets for smoke and water ought to be free of any obstruction, and their ducts designed to avoid stagnation and overflow, and to prevent them from becoming soiled and offensive or endangering the fabric of the building. For this reason fireplaces need to be far away from any woodwork, lest sparks or the heat of the fire set light to nearby beams and timbers. Drains for water should be designed to draw off any overflow without damage to the building through corrosion or damp; for if any harm is done, no matter how little, the march of time and continual wear and tear will produce further deterioration. As regards drainage, I have observed that the best architects ensured that rainwater was either drawn off by drainpipes, to prevent it from dripping on anyone entering, or collected in impluvia to be either stored for human use or forced to flow somewhere to wash away human filth, making it less offensive to the noses and eyes of mankind. It seems to me that one of their greatest concerns was keeping rainwater out of the building, and draining it off far away, in particular to avoid the ground about becoming damp.

They seem to me to have placed every opening in the most suitable position, where it would most advantage the whole building. Wells, in particular, should be built in a public or accessible part of the house, provided the site they occupy is not too important or inappropriate. The naturalists maintain that those open to the sky produce the purest and most natural water; but in whatever part of the building wells are dug or drains laid, or wherever water and liquid are chaneled, openings should be made to allow sufficient ventilation for the circulation of air and breeze to keep the pavement free of damp vapors.

We have said enough on the lineaments of buildings, drawing on observations that seem relevant to the work as a whole, and noting the individual topics to be discussed. We must now speak of the way the building is put together, but first we shall deal with materials and the necessary preparations for construction. ◆

Here Begins the Second Book on the Art of Building by Leon Battista Alberti. Materials.

In my opinion, the labor and expense of building should not be undertaken lightly: apart from everything else that may be at stake, one's esteem and good name may suffer. A well-constructed building will enhance the renown of anyone who has invested understanding, attention, and enthusiasm in the matter; yet equally, should the wisdom of the designer or the competence of the workman be found wanting anywhere, it will greatly detract from his reputation and good name. Merits and defects are particularly obvious and striking in public buildings, though (for some reason, I do not understand) criticism of impropriety is more readily given than approval for a work elegantly constructed and with no imperfections. It is remarkable how some natural instinct allows each of us, learned and ignorant alike, to sense immediately what is right or wrong in the execution and design of a work. It is precisely with regard to such matters that sight shows itself the keenest of all the senses; consequently, if presented with anything in any way inadequate, unstable, redundant, useless, or imperfect, we are immediately struck by the desire to make it more agreeable. How this happens, we do not all understand, though were we to inquire, no one would deny that you can make improvements and corrections. By what method this should be done is not given to everybody to resolve, only to those well versed in such matters.

It is the mark of considerable experience to have so thoroughly thought out everything and determined it in the mind beforehand, that in the course of construction, or on completion of the work, one is not forced to admit, "I wish I had not done this: I would have preferred it done otherwise." And the penalty to be paid for poorly constructed work is surprisingly heavy: with time we eventually realize the rashness and foolishness of any move not considered carefully enough at the outset; if the work is not taken down or amended, the mistake committed is the source of continual grievance, and if it is demolished, we are tormented at the thought of the loss and expense, and full of remorse for the lightness and fickleness of our opinion.

Suetonius tells us that Julius Caesar completely demolished a house on his estate at Nemi, because it did not totally meet with his approval, although he had begun it from the foundations and had it finished at vast expense.[1] In this he deserves censure even from us, his descendants, either for his failure to take sufficient prior account of the relevant considerations, or perhaps for his fickleness, which allowed him to dislike an executed building, although it had been correctly constructed.

For this reason I will always commend the time-honored custom, practiced by the best builders, of preparing not only drawings and sketches but also models of wood or any other material. These will enable us to weigh up repeatedly and examine, with the advice of experts, the work as a whole and the individual dimensions of all the parts, and, before continuing any farther, to estimate the likely trouble and expense. Having constructed these models, it will be possible to examine clearly and consider thoroughly the relationship between the site and the surrounding district, the shape of the *area*, the number[2] and order of the parts of a building, the appearance of the walls, the strength of the covering, and in short the design and construction of all the elements discussed in the previous book. It will also allow one to increase or decrease the size of those elements freely, to exchange them, and to make new proposals and alterations until everything fits together well and meets with approval. Furthermore, it will provide a surer indication of the likely costs—which is not unimportant—by allowing one to calculate the width and the height of individual elements, their thickness, number,[3] extent, form, appearance, and quality, according to their importance and the workmanship they require. In this way it is possible to form a clearer and more certain idea of the design and quantity of columns, capitals, bases, cornices, pediments, revetment, flooring, statues, and everything else relating to the construction of the building and its ornamentation. There is a particularly relevant consideration that I feel should be mentioned here: the presentation of models that have been colored and lewdly dressed with the allurement of painting is the mark of no architect intent on conveying the facts; rather it is that of a conceited one, striving to attract and seduce the eye of the beholder, and to divert his attention from a proper examination of the parts to be considered, toward admiration of himself. Better then that the models are not accurately finished, refined, and highly decorated, but plain and simple, so that they demonstrate the ingenuity of him who conceived the idea, and not the skill of the one who fabricated the model. The difference between the drawings of the painter and those of the architect is this: the former takes pains to emphasize the relief of objects in paintings with shading and diminishing lines and angles; the architect rejects shading, but takes his projections from the ground plan and, without altering the lines and by maintaining the true angles, reveals the extent and shape of each elevation and side—he is one who desires his work to be judged not by deceptive appearances but according to certain calculated standards. It is advisable then to construct models of this kind, and to inspect and reexamine them time and time again, both on your own and with others, so thoroughly that there is little or nothing within the work whose identity, nature, likely position and size, and prospective use you do not grasp.[4]

In particular, great attention should be paid to ensure that the design of the roof is the best possible. For unless I am mistaken, the roof of its very nature was the first of all building elements to provide mankind with a place of shelter: so much so that it was for the sake of the roof that the need arose not only for the wall and all that goes with it, but also for anything constructed below ground, such as water conduits, rainwater channels, sewers, and the like. From my own not inconsiderable experience in these matters, I am aware of the difficulties encountered in executing a work in such a manner that it marries practical convenience with dignity and grace, so that, among other commendable advantages, these parts are imbued with a refined variety, in accordance with the demands of proportion and harmony:[5] that really is difficult! yet to cover all of the parts with a suitable and stable roof, one seemly and appropriate to its task, can be achieved, I maintain, only if planned with sufficient thoroughness and executed with enough skill.

Finally, when every aspect of the proposed work has been fully approved, so that you and the other experts are satisfied that there is no longer any cause for hesitation or opportunity for improvement, even then would I advise you not to let your desire to build impel you headlong into commencing the work by demolishing any existing buildings or laying extensive foundations for the whole of it: this is what a foolish or rash man would do. Rather, if you heed my advice, allow the proposals to settle a while, and wait until your initial enthusiasm for the idea has mellowed and you have a clearer impression of everything; then, once your judgment is governed by soberer thoughts than your enthusiasm for inventions, you will be able to judge the matter more thoroughly. For in every undertaking time brings to light many observations and considerations that might otherwise have escaped the notice of even the most capable of men. ◆

2

21v—22v

When examining the model, these are some of the considerations to be taken into account. First, nothing should be attempted that lies beyond human capacity, nor anything undertaken that might immediately come into conflict with Nature. For so great is Nature's strength that, although on occasion some huge obstacle may obstruct her, or some barrier divert her, she will always overcome and destroy any opposition or impediment; and any stubbornness, as it were, displayed against her, will eventually be overthrown and destroyed by her continual and persistent onslaught.

How many examples are there to be seen or read about of the failure of mankind's work to survive, simply because it has come into conflict with Nature? Who would not mock someone who intends to ride over the sea on a bridge of ships, and despise him not so much for his arrogance as for his folly?[6] The port of Claudius, below Ostia, or that of Hadrian, near Terracina, are works that might otherwise have been expected to last forever; yet now we see them in ruins, their mouths long since choked with sand, their harbors silted up, while the sea with its incessant wrestling continues its onslaught and daily increases its advantage. And what would happen, do you imagine, to any attempt to hold back and restrain the force of cascading water, or the weight of tumbling boulders? We ought to be careful, then, to avoid any undertaking that is not in complete accordance with the laws of Nature.

Second, we should beware of taking anything on without the resources to bring it to completion. Had the gods not been in favor of the grandeur of the city, had the expanding empire not provided sufficient funds to complete an undertaking of such magnificence, Tarquin, king of Rome, would have deserved universal criticism for having lavished on the foundations of a temple enough money to cover the cost of the whole work.[7]

Another, not unimportant, consideration is that the work should be not only feasible but also appropriate. I cannot approve of the contemporary accounts of that famous harlot, Rhodope of Thrace, who had a tomb constructed for herself at vast expense: for although her immoral earnings had left her the wealth of a queen, in no way did she deserve a tomb fit for one.[8] But on the other hand, I would not criticize Artemis, queen of Caria, for building her beloved and noble husband a most magnificent tomb, although even in this matter moderation is to be commended.[9] Maecenas was rebuked by Horace for his passion for building;[10] but I quite approve of whoever was responsible for constructing that modest but enduring tomb to Otho, which Cornelius Tacitus mentions.[11] Although modesty is generally expected of private monuments, and magnificence of public ones, occasionally the latter may also be praised for exhibiting the modesty expected of the former. We lavish praise and admiration on the theater of Pompey for its exceptional scale and dignity;[12] it is a work worthy both of Pompey and of ever-victorious Rome. But not everyone would approve of Nero's mania to build, and his passion for completing works of immense size.[13] And, again, whoever was responsible for the many thousands of men who tunneled through a mountain near Pozzuoli, would it not have been preferable to have invested the care and expense in a more worthwhile project?[14] Who would not condemn the extraordinary arrogance of Heliogabalus, for proposing to construct a huge column, on top of which, reached by an internal staircase, was to be seated a statue of himself as deified Heliogabalus, to whose cult it was dedicated? However, although he searched as far as Thebes, he was unable to find a large enough stone and so abandoned the idea.[15]

It is also advisable to avoid any undertaking, no matter how expedient, worthy, and easy to execute it may appear and even though the means and opportunity are at hand, if its very nature makes it prone to suffer immediately, or through the neglect of subsequent generations, or from the wear and tear of everyday use. One of my main criticisms of Nero's proposals for a canal from Avernus[16] to Ostia, which would have been navigable by quinqueremes,[17] is that it would have required the continual prosperity of the empire and a succession of emperors prepared to maintain it.[18]

To conclude, it is your duty to consider all the above questions, the nature of your undertaking, and the relative positions of the elements, and to take into account your own social standing as the one who commissions the building: it is the sign of a well-informed and judicious mind to plan the whole undertaking in accordance with one's position in society and the requirements of use. ◆

3

22v—23

Having dealt with these points, it remains for you to consider whether each element has been well defined and allocated its proper place. To achieve this, you need to be convinced when you are making decisions about such matters, that it would be to your dishonor were you to allow another work constructed anywhere else for the same cost, and offering similar advantages, to present a more pleasing appearance or to draw richer praise. It will not be sufficient simply to avoid contempt in this matter; seek rather to gain the highest admiration and to become in turn the object of imitation. We need to be strict and meticulous in our planning, therefore, and to take care that nothing is included except what is choice and well proven, and that everything fits together so well, in terms of dignity and grace, that were you to add, change, or take away anything, it would be to the detriment of the whole.

In these matters—as I repeatedly advise—be guided by the knowledge of experts and the counsel of those whose advice is honest and impartial. For it is through their opinions and teaching, rather than your own personal whim and feeling, that you will more likely achieve perfection, or something approaching it. Finally, hearing experts voice their approval of your proposals is indeed very satisfying; and their approbation is all the stronger when they are unable to suggest any improvements. As a result you will also enjoy the approval of anyone else who has an understanding of the subject. Indeed, it is useful to listen to everyone, for even those with no experience in the matter sometimes make suggestions overlooked by the experts.

When you have considered and examined the design of the whole building through the various parts of your model, until there remains nothing that has escaped your attention and observation, and when you are entirely decided on building the work in this way and have determined a suitable source of financing, you should then start making the other preparations necessary for the execution of the work, so as to ensure that nothing occurs amiss during the course of construction to affect the speed with which the work is completed. For many components are required to finish the work, and as the absence of any of them can impede or result in the ruin of the entire structure, it is your duty not to miss anything that will add to the overall scheme if present, but detract from it if absent.

Eusebius Pamphilius[19] wrote that the Hebrew kings David and Solomon, who were intending to build the Temple of Jerusalem, waited until they had amassed a vast quantity of gold, silver, bronze, timber, stone, and other materials;[20] and to ensure speed and ease of construction, they took care that nothing was amiss before they summoned architects and several thousand workmen from nearby kingdoms—a precaution I approve of strongly. The fact that it was skilfully and properly constructed, and promptly finished, contributes greatly to the dignity of the work and the esteem of its authors. The ancient writers praised Alexander [the Great] of Macedonia for constructing in the space of seven days—according to Curtius[21]—a town of no small size by the river Tanais;[22] as is Nabuchodonosor celebrated for completing the Temple of Bel, according to the historian Josephus,[23] in fifteen days, and for having surrounded Babylon with a triple wall, it is said, in the same time;[24] and similarly Titus, for constructing a wall a little short of forty stades[25] in the space of three days;[26] and Semiramis for erecting a gigantic wall in Babylon, at the rate of one stade a day,[27] and for constructing another wall to contain a reservoir two hundred stades long and of considerable depth and height, in no more than seven days.[28] But of this elsewhere. ◆

4

23—24v

These are the materials to be prepared: lime, sand, stone, timber; and likewise iron, bronze, lead, glass, and so on. And I consider it of primary importance to select workmen who are neither inexperienced, nor unreliable, nor inconsistent, and to whom you may confidently entrust the task of executing the work diligently, according to your precise instructions, and of finishing it on time.

In making these decisions it will be helpful to derive ideas and draw comparisons by studying completed buildings nearby, and to base your own proposals on their example. For by observing their merits and defects you will be able to speculate about your own work. The emperor Nero decided to build a gigantic statue in Rome, one hundred and twenty feet high, dedicated to the veneration of the sun, and larger and more magnificent than any previous one; it was to be made by Zenodarus, a famous and unrivaled artist of the time, but, according to Pliny, he did not entrust him with the task until he had already constructed in the territory of the Arverni[29] in Gaul a huge statue of incredible weight, to satisfy himself of the merits of building on so vast a scale.[30] Having dealt with these considerations, let us move on.

We shall now deal with the materials suitable for constructing buildings, and we shall relate the advice handed down to us by the learned men of the past, in particular Theophrastus, Aristotle, Cato, Varro, Pliny, and Vitruvius: for such knowledge is better gained through long experience than through any artifice of invention; it should be sought therefore from those who have made the most diligent observations on the matter. We shall proceed, then, to gather this information from the many, varied passages in which the best authors have dealt with the question; and to these, as is our custom, we shall add whatever observations are in any way relevant to the discussion from those which we have made ourselves by studying the works of our ancestors or by listening to the advice of artists with experience.

It would be most convenient, I believe, to follow the natural order and begin with the material that man first used for building; this, unless I am mistaken, was timber from trees felled in the forest, although I notice that historians are divided on this issue. Some maintain that man first lived in caves, and that master and herd were sheltered under a common roof: they accept the account given by Pliny, that it was one Taxius, a Gelian, who was the first to imitate nature and build himself a house of mud.[31] Diodorus states that the goddess Vesta, daughter of Saturn, was the first to invent the house.[32] Eusebius Pamphilius, a respected scholar in matters of the antique, maintains, on the basis of ancient manuscripts, that the descendants of Protogenes devised the first dwelling place for man from screens platted of reed and papyrus.[33] But let us return to the matter.

The ancients, then, especially Theophrastus, recommended that trees, in particular the fir, the pitch tree, and the pine, should be felled as soon as they germinate and begin to send out young shoots, in that the high quantity of sap produced at that time will facilitate the removal of the bark.[34] Yet they recommended that other trees, such as the maple, elm, ash, and linden, should be cut down after the vintage. Likewise they maintained that the oak would be prone to worms if felled in spring, but would suffer no defect and would not split if felled in winter. Equally relevant is their observation that timber felled in winter, when Boreas[35] is blowing, will burn beautifully and almost without smoke, although still green, showing that the sap it contains is not raw but well absorbed.

Vitruvius prefers that timber be felled from the beginning of autumn until Favonius blows.[36] Yet in the words of Hesiod: Reap the crops when the sun hangs over your head with raging heat and gives men a dusky tan; but do not fell the trees until their leaves begin to drop.[37] But this is Cato's advice on the matter: "Fell timber, if it is oak, during the solstice; for in the winter it is always ready. Fell all other timber when it is mature, if it bears seeds, or if not, whenever you wish; fell any whose seed is both green and ripe, when the seed falls, and the elm, when its leaves fall."[38]

The lunar cycle is considered another important factor in determining when to use the axe. Many authors, especially Varro, believe that such is the influence of the moon on this and other uses of the iron blade, that even someone having his hair cut, when the moon is waning, would soon go bald.[39] It was for this reason, they said, that the emperor Tiberius reserved a particular day on which to have his hair cut.[40] Astronomers maintain that you will never suffer from a depression if you cut your hair and nails while the moon is obscured or ill disposed. Here it is relevant to mention the old saying that material intended for movable objects ought to be cut and handled when the moon is in Libra or Cancer, but anything to be stable or immobile ought to be worked on while the moon is in Leo or Taurus, or the like. But all the experts recommend that timber should be felled when the moon is waning: for it is then, they say, that the thick gum that exudes from trees, and that is likely to bring on rapid decay, is quite exhausted; certainly any wood cut at that time is never infested with rot. Hence the proverb: Grain for sale should be harvested at full moon; for then too are the ears at their fullest; grain for the store should be harvested when the moon is dry.[41] It is well known that while the moon is waning, even leaves gathered from trees will not rot. Columella[42] thinks that the correct time to fell trees is between the twentieth and the thirtieth day of the old moon.[43] Vegetius,[44] however, prefers the period from the fifteenth to the twenty-second day of the new moon; this has led him to suppose that the ritual celebrating eternity was performed on these days alone because anything cut down then would last for ever.[45] They also advise us to wait until the moon sets. In Pliny's view, the best time to fell trees is when the constellation of the Dog Star is at its highest and in conjunction with the moon, the day called interlunar, and he recommends waiting until nightfall of that day, after the moon has set.[46] The reason for this, according to astronomers, is that the moon has influence over the humors of every single thing, so that only when the humors have been either abandoned or drawn into the very ends of the roots toward the moon is the rest of the wood rendered more pure.

It is also their opinion that timber will be more reliable if the tree is not felled immediately, but the trunk is ringed and allowed to stand and dry out; and that the fir, a tree with little other defense against contagion from moisture, will, if stripped of its bark while the moon is waning, never rot in water. Some maintain that the turkey oak and the common oak, particularly heavy types of timber, which by nature normally sink in water, will, if cut back all over at the beginning of spring and felled only when they have lost their leaves, be able to float for up to ninety days in water. Others advise that the tree be allowed to stand, but ringed more deeply, right to the very marrow, to allow any poison or harmful sap to ooze out and be drawn off more freely. They also recommend that no tree that is to be planed or sawn up be felled until its seeds have ripened and it has produced fruit; and once cut, it should be stripped completely of its bark, especially if it is a fruit tree, as infection may easily spread under the rind if the bark remains.[47] ◆

5

24v—25v

Once the timber has been cut, it should be laid down away from the severities of the sun or the harshness of the wind; above all, wood with an inherent tendency to split ought to be particularly well shaded. This was the purpose behind the ancient architects' practice of smearing the wood with dung, usually of oxen. Theophrastus argues that the reason for this was to close up the pores to force any congealed gum and any moisture that had built up to seep along the marrow and evaporate, so that the process of drying imparted a more even density to the whole length.[48] It is also believed that timber will dry out better if stood upside down.

Various precautions were taken to prevent deterioration with age and to allay the threat of disease. Theophrastus considered that burying timber made it much tougher. Cato recommended smearing wood with less of oil to protect it from woodworm and rot.[49] It is well known that pitch protects wood from sweet and salt water. Wood steeped in oil lees will burn, it is said, without the nuisance of smoke.[50] Pliny relates that the Egyptian labyrinth was constructed with beams of Egyptian blackthorn steeped in oil.[51] Theophrastus claims that timber smeared with birdlime will not burn.[52] Nor should I forget the story, which Gellius extracted from the annals of Quintus Claudius, of a wooden tower near the Piraeus, which Archelaus, an officer under Mithridates, had liberally coated with alum, and which therefore did not catch fire during Sulla's attack.[53]

There are various methods of hardening some types of timber, and of strengthening them against the ravages of time. The wood of the citrus tree, for example, may be successively buried in earth, coated with wax, and covered with a mound of grain, each treatment lasting for seven days and with the same interval in between; as a result it is both stronger and easier to work, having lost a surprising amount of weight. This same wood, so it is said, will become hard and dense, and immune from decay, if cured in seawater.[54] The wood of the chestnut tree is certainly purified by seawater. Egyptian fig trees, according to Pliny, are immersed in marshes to cure them and to reduce their weight: unless treated in this way they will sink in water.[55] We have seen our own carpenters immersing timber in water and leaving it covered in mud for a period of thirty days, especially if it is to be used for turning; they say that it will accelerate the curing process and make the wood easier to manage, whatever its intended use.

Some would maintain that, whatever the type of wood, if buried in damp ground while still green, it will last for ever; but whether you bury it, smear it with something, or store it away, anyone with experience will agree that it should not be touched for the first three months. The timber must have time to harden, and to soak up, as it were, the strength of maturity, before being brought into use. Cato advises that wood treated in this manner be brought out and exposed to the sun, when the moon is on the wane, and only after midday (though not during the four days immediately after the full moon); and he advises against timber being brought out while Auster[56] is blowing. Furthermore, when it is brought out, it should not be dragged through dew, nor planed or sawn while covered with dew or frost or when not entirely dry.[57] ◆

6

Theophrastus was of the opinion that wood will not be properly cured in less than three years, especially if it is to be used for posts and panels of doors.[58]

These are the trees whose wood is reckoned most useful for the construction of buildings: the turkey oak,[59] common oak,[60] bay oak,[61] winter oak,[62] poplar, linden, willow, alder, ash, pine, cypress, oleaster, olive tree, chestnut tree, larch, box tree, likewise the cedar, ebon tree, and the vine. Each has a different character and so is best suited to a different use. Some fare better when exposed to the sky, others keep better in shadow; some flourish in the open air, others grow hard in water, and others last longer underground. Therefore, while some are more suitable for lamination, paneling, statues, and internal furnishing, others make better posts and beams, and others strong supports for terraces and roofs.

In particular, the alder makes the very best stakes for restraining rivers and marshes, and is very resistant to moisture, although it will not last long when exposed to air and sun.[63] The winter oak, on the other hand, has little resistance to water. The elm hardens if left in the open, but elsewhere splits and does not last long, whereas the pitch tree and the pine, if buried underground, last for ever. The bay oak, being a hard, sinewy, dense wood, with only the smallest of pores, does not absorb moisture and is therefore thoroughly suitable for any work underground;[64] it is most usefully employed for bearing weights and makes extremely strong columns. Yet, although it has such innate natural strength that it cannot be drilled unless it is soaked, above ground it is said to be less reliable, and apt to crack and warp, while even in seawater it may be easily ruined. This will not happen to the olive or the holm oak or the oleaster (which are very like the bay oak in other ways) when soaked in water. The common oak does not deteriorate with age, but retains its sap as if it were young. The beech and the walnut tree never rot in water and are counted among the most suitable for use underground. The cork tree, meanwhile, the wild pine, mulberry, maple, and elm are not unsuitable for columns.

Theophrastus recommends the wood of the Euboean nut tree for trusses and posts, in that it gives a tell tale crack as it is about to break; on one occasion this enabled everyone in the baths at Andros to escape safely before the roof caved in.[65] The best of all, however, is the fir, a tree of great height and circumference, and such natural strength that it scarcely bends under load, but resists, straight and unyielding; it is, in addition, easy to work, and light enough not to overburden the walls with its weight. This one wood has very many other advantages ascribed to it and is useful for many purposes; yet it has one undeniable defect: it is quick to ignite and so easily damaged by fire.[66]

For the construction of domestic flooring the cypress is not inferior to the fir; it is for this and other similar reasons that it has earned itself the highest reputation of all our trees. The ancients rated it among the most notable and not inferior to the cedar or ebony. In India it is valued almost as highly as spice plants; and with good reason. Praise, if you will, the amomon of Chios or Cyrene, which Theophrastus claimed lasts for ever; but taking into account fragrance, sheen, strength, size, straightness, and durability, is there any tree to compare with the cypress?[67] It is claimed that the cypress is affected neither by decay nor by old age, and that it will never crack of its own accord. Surely it was for this reason that Plato felt that public laws and decrees ought to be inscribed on sacred panels of cypress, in the belief that they might last longer than those of bronze.[68] This seems the right place to mention a number of other remarkable observations about the cypress, which I have either made myself or read about. The cypress doors of the temple of Diana at Ephesus lasted—so it is said—four hundred years, but so maintained their luster that you might always have thought them new.[69] We were able to see for ourselves, when the doors of the Petrine Basilica in Rome were restored by Pope Eugenius, that, where human hands had not damaged them in stripping off the silver with which they were once faced, they had remained solid and unaltered for more than five hundred and fifty years; for, if our interpretation of the annals of the Roman pontifs is correct, that was the span of time between the pontificate of Hadrian III, who had them constructed, and that of Eugenius IV.[70] The fir, therefore, is recommended for the construction of floors; the cypress must be preferred for its greater durability, but it is heavier.

The pine and the pitch tree are also recommended. The pine is considered very similar to the fir in its resistance to imposed weight, but one of the differences between them is that the fir is less susceptible to worms, since pine has a sweeter sap than the fir.

For myself, I believe that the larch is second to none. It provides stable and lasting support for the great weight of structures, as I have often observed, most notably in the Veneto in the ancient buildings of the Forum. Indeed, it is said that the larch embodies the properties of all other trees put together: it is sinewy, steadfast, unyielding in storms, and unaffected by rot. The ancients believed that it could resist damage by fire and come through almost unscathed; and they recommended that any surface exposed to the danger of fire should have a protective facing of larch boarding.[71] We have observed ourselves that if you put fire to the larch, it will indeed burn, but in such a way that it seems to despise the flames and want to rebuff them. Its one defect is that in seawater it is very susceptible to shipworm.

The bay oak and the olive are considered to be of little use in trusses because of their excessive weight, their inability to sustain loads, and their tendency to bend under their own weight. Besides, timber will be unsuitable for trusses if it tends to break completely rather than merely crack, as do the olive, fig, linden, willow, and so on. What is claimed of the palm tree is quite remarkable: that its timber not only resists any imposed load, but even bends in a contrary direction.[72] For trusses exposed to the sky, the juniper is best of all. According to Pliny it has similar properties to the cedar, but is more solid.[73] The olive, meanwhile, is said to have eternal life, while the box tree is also considered one of the most durable. The chestnut, although prone to expand and twist, is not unacceptable for open-air work.

The wild olive is also highly prized, mainly for the same reason as the cypress, in that it never suffers from rot; any tree imbued with an oily or gummy sap, especially if bitter, also falls into this category, as clearly the worm cannot enter and all external moisture is kept out. The opposite applies to any timber that has a sweet sap and is easily inflammable, except the domestic and wild olive.

According to Vitruvius, the turkey oak and the beech tree have little natural resistance to the weather and do not reach old age.[74] Pliny claims that the common oak also decays quickly.[75] For interior furnishings (doors, beds, tables, seats, and so on) the fir is excellent, particularly when it comes from the slopes of the Italian Alps;[76] it is by nature a very dry wood, which holds glue extremely well. For these same purposes the pitch tree and the cypress are also suitable. The beech, although acknowledged to be too brittle for other purposes, may be put to good use in chests and beds, and can be cut into the thinnest layers;[77] the holm oak is also good for cutting. Walnut, however, is not suitable for cutting into planks, because it splits too easily; as do the elm and ash, despite their inherent flexibility. Nonetheless, ash has the reputation of being the most easily wrought.[78] But I am surprised how little praise the nut tree receives in the precepts of the ancients: experience shows how easy to work this wood is and how thoroughly suitable for a variety of uses, most notably paneling.

The mulberry tree is praised both for its longevity and for the fact that it gradually darkens with age and improves in appearance.[79] Theophrastus recalls that the rich used to have their doors built of lotus tree, holm oak, or box wood.[80] The elm is considered suitable for the hinges of doors, because it keeps its rigidity, although it is recommended that it be used upside down.[81] Cato suggests that pegs be made of holly, laurel, or elm, while the wood of the cornel tree is recommended for wooden pins;[82] for the steps of stairs, the mountain ash or the maple; and for water conduits, hollowed-out sections of pine, pitch, or elm (although it is said that they soon deteriorate unless buried underground).[83]

As far as interior decoration is concerned, it is well known that the female larch, which is honey colored, makes very good panels for paintings which will last for ever and will not crack.[84] Further, they used the palm for making statues of the gods, because its grain runs across rather than lengthwise, as they used the lotus and the box tree, the cedar and the cypress, the larger roots of the olive, and the Egyptian peach tree, which is said to be similar to the lotus tree. If they needed to produce slender forms on the lathe, the ancients would use the beech, the mulberry, or the turpentine tree, but most especially the box tree, which is the densest of all and extremely suitable for turning; while for very fine pieces ebony was used.

They did not despise the poplar, white or black, for statues or paintings, nor indeed the willow, hornbeam, sorbelder, elder or fig; their timber is not only dry and even, and therefore suitable to accept and preserve the resins and paints of the artist, but also easily modeled and wrought by the tools of the sculptor. Yet clearly none of these can compete with the delicacy of the linden, although for statues some may prefer the jujube tree.

The bay oak displays entirely the opposite characteristics: it will never join with other timber, or even with its own kind, and is hostile to all glues. This rejection of every form of resin is said to be shared by all wood that is wrinkled or that oozes sap. Equally, smooth or dense wood does not adhere well with glue. Nor do woods of differing nature remain bonded together for long, such as hot trees, like the ivy, laurel, or linden, with those that grow in a humid climate, all of which are cold by nature. Nor do dry trees, such as the elm, ash, mulberry, or cherry, agree with the plane tree or the elder, which are moist by nature. In fact, our ancestors were so against bonding together woods of incompatible or conflicting natures that they would prevent even simple contact, let alone physical connection; hence Vitruvius' advice that planks of winter oak should not be placed next to those of common oak.[85] ◆

7

27v—28v

To sum up what has been said so far: all authors are agreed that trees that do not bear fruit are more robust than those that do, and that wild trees, uncultivated by hand or steel, are hardier than domestic ones. For, according to Theophrastus, wild trees never suffer any fatal disease, but domestic trees, it is said, and especially fruit-bearing ones, are afflicted by the gravest disorders;[86] and among the fertile those which ripen earliest have less protection than those which ripen late, and those producing sweet fruit less than those producing bitter fruit. And of those with a sharp and bitter taste, the sourer and more infrequent the fruit, the more solid the wood. Those which bear fruit every other year, or which are entirely sterile, are more knotty than those bearing fruit annually. The shorter a tree, the more difficult it is to work; those without fruit grow better than those with.

Moreover, trees that grow in exposed places, unprotected by mountains or forests, but troubled by frequent gales and storms, are generally more sturdy and thickset, although shorter and more knotty than those which grow in valleys and places protected from the wind. Trees that have sprung up in shaded, damp surroundings are also considered more tender than those from dry, sunny areas, and those which have grown facing north are more useful than those facing south.[87] Any tree found outside its natural habitat should be treated as a miscarriage and discarded. Trees growing to the south will prove extremely hard, although their heart[88] may be twisted and the texture of their wood not uniform enough for use in construction. Moreover, those dry by nature and slow-growing are tougher than any that are tender and fecund: in Varro's opinion, indeed, one has a feminine character, the other masculine.[89] All white wood is less dense and easier to work than any that is colored. Certainly heavy timber is always denser and harder than light timber, and the lighter it is, the more fragile; while the knottier, the more compact. Those whom nature has endowed with the longest life, she has also granted the capacity to resist rot the longest, once felled. In every type of wood the less heartwood there is, the stronger and more robust it is. Sections closest to the heart are harder and denser than the rest; but those nearer the bark have tougher sinews. For trees may be likened to animals, their outer bark being their skin, what lies beneath, their flesh, what surrounds the marrow, their bones, while Aristotle compared the knots in plants with sinews.[90]

The worst part of wood is thought to be the alburnum,[91] the chief reason being its susceptibility to worms. Moreover, the side of the tree that faced the midday sun while the tree was still standing will be drier, leaner, and less developed than the rest, although its density will be greater; and the heartwood will be closer to the bark on that side. The trunk nearest the earth and the roots will be the heaviest, as is shown by the fact that they will tend not to float; the middle of every tree is the most wrinkled part, while veins of whatever kind are more contorted the nearer they are to the roots. Yet the inner parts are thought more reliable and useful than the outer.

The best authors, I find, make some amazing claims about certain kinds of tree. The vine, they maintain, will survive for centuries. In the time of Caesar, in the city of Populonia, a statue of Jupiter, many centuries old and made of this wood, was found to be intact;[92] thus, they say, no other wood exists of a more durable nature. According to Strabo, vines are common in Ariana, a region in India, with trunks of so great a girth that two men can scarcely embrace them.[93] It is recorded that in Utica a roof of cedar stood for one thousand two hundred and seventy-eight years, and, in another instance, that the beams of the temple of Diana in Spain, which were made of juniper, lasted from two hundred years before the destruction of Troy until the time of Hannibal.[94] The cedar, too, has extraordinary properties, if, as it is said, it is the only tree not to grip nails.[95] In the mountains by Lake

Garda there grows a kind of fir whose timber needs to be smeared with oil before it will hold wine. But enough about trees. ◆

28v—29v

8

We have also to prepare the stone to be used in the walls. There are two kinds of stone, one to be used as aggregate in mortar, the other suitable for the structure of the building. I shall begin with the latter, although I shall leave out a considerable amount either for the sake of brevity or because it is already well-known.

Here I shall not go into the theories of naturalists about the origins and rudiments of stone: as to whether it was derived from a viscous mixture of water and earth, which hardened first into mud and then into stone; or whether it is composed of matter condensed by the cold or, as is said of gems, by the heat and by the rays of the sun; or whether in fact stone is formed like everything else, from a seed that Nature had implanted in the earth.[96] Nor shall we discuss whether the coloring in stone is caused by a certain blending of water with particles of earth, or by some inherent property within the seed itself, or by the effect of the sun's rays. Although such digressions may serve to embellish our argument, I shall pass over them all, and, as though conversing about building with craftsmen of acknowledged experience and skill, I shall proceed with greater freedom and fluency than is perhaps permitted by those who follow a stricter philosophy.

Cato advises, "Quarry the stone in summer, leave it in the open air, and do not use it for two years."[97] It should be quarried "in summer" to allow the stone to become gradually used to wind, frost, rain, and any other ravages of the weather to which it may not be accustomed. If stone fresh from the quarry and still full of its own native fluid and juices is immediately exposed to the severity of wind and sudden frost, it will tend to crack and crumble. It should be left "in the open air" so that each block may be given a form of preliminary trial, before its perpetual battle with time, to test its strength and ability to withstand the onslaught of adversity. It should not be used "for two years" so that any stone weak in itself, and likely to spoil the work, should not escape detection, and be separated from the stronger.

Certainly variations will be found within any type of stone: some will harden with exposure to air, others, when covered in frost, will grow rusty and begin to break up, and so on. Practice and experience, however, provide the best method of ascertaining the natural qualities of any particular stone, and the situations to which it is best suited: more can be learned from inspecting the buildings of the ancients than from any of the writings or memoirs of philosophers. But to keep my discussion on stone brief, I will make the following observations.

White stone is easier to handle than dark, and translucent more workable than opaque, but the closer a stone resembles salt, the harder it is to work.

If a stone is coated with shining sand, it will be coarse; if sparkling with gold particles, stubborn; if it is, as it were, flecked with black, unmanageable. Stones dappled with polygonal markings are more solid than those with circular ones; and the smaller the markings on a stone, the greater the weight it can bear; the purer and clearer the color, the longer it will last; and the fewer veins it has, the sounder it will be; and the closer the color of the veins to that of the surrounding stone, the more uniform its structure; while the thinner the veins, the more capricious the stone will be; the more tortuous and twisted they are, the more troublesome; the more knotted, the more refractory. The veins most likely to crack are those whose center is streaked with the color of red clay, or the ochre of rot, followed by those tinted in places with a pale, faded grass color; but the most awkward of all are veins that have taken on the blue color of ice. A large number of veins means that a stone will be unreliable and apt to split, while the straighter the veins, the less trustworthy it will be.

The sharper and cleaner the edge of the pieces into which the stone breaks, the more compact it is; while the smoother their surface, the easier the stone will be to work. But those with rough surfaces will prove more awkward the whiter their color, whereas with dark stone, the closer the grain, the greater its resistance to the iron blade. With stone of inferior quality, the greater its porosity, the harder it is; and the longer it takes to dry out, when soaked all over with water, the coarser it is. A heavy stone will be more solid and easy to polish than a light one, and a light one will be more friable. A stone that rings out when struck will be denser than one that does not. Any stone that produces a sulphurlike smell when rubbed will be stronger than one that does not; finally, the greater its stubbornness to the chisel, the more rigid and steadfast a stone will be against the assaults of the weather.

If stone remains intact in large blocks at the quarry entrance, in spite of the roughness of the weather, it is considered very strong. Almost all stone is softer when fresh from the quarry than when accustomed to the open air; and when sprinkled or soaked with water, more easily worked with iron than when dry. The damper the point within the quarry from which it was extracted, the denser the stone will be, once dry. It is thought that it is easier to shape stone while Auster rather than Boreas is blowing, but that it is more easily cut during the Boreas.[98]

If you wish to conduct a brief experiment to test how a stone will age, look for the following signs: any stone that substantially increases its weight when soaked in water will break up in high humidity; and any that becomes soft in contact with fire will be unable to endure the heat of the sun.

At this point I feel I ought not to pass over several noteworthy observations that the ancients made on the various types of stone. ◆

9

It is not at all irrelevant to our purpose to have an understanding of the varied and remarkable properties of the different types of stone, which will enable us to employ each in the most appropriate manner.

They say that round the Volsinian lake[99] and in the countryside about Stratonicea[100] a type of stone is found suitable for any building purpose: invulnerable to either fire or the violence of the weather, it lasts for ever and does not deteriorate with age, and when carved into statues keeps its lineaments for an extremely long time.[101]

Tacitus relates that when Nero reconstructed the city of Rome after the great fire, he used beams of Gabinian and Alban stone, because they would be untouched by fire.[102]

In Liguria and the Veneto, in Umbria, Picenum, and the territory of the Belgi, a white stone[103] is found that can easily be sawn and chiseled, and were it not for its inherent weakness and brittleness, it would be superior to any other for building; however, it will break up in frost, cold, or rain and has little defense against sea breezes.[104]

Istria produces a stone not unlike marble, which under intense heat or in contact with fire will instantly split and fly apart: this inability to endure fire is said to be common to all hard stone, especially flint, white or black.

In Campania a stone is found that is very similar (in color) to black ashes, and seems to contain pieces of coal. It is unbelievable how light this stone is, and easy to work with iron, how thoroughly steadfast and durable, and how great is its resistance to fire and storms; but it is so dry and thirsty that it absorbs and swallows up any moisture within lime straightaway, leaving the masonry dried up and powdery; its joints weaken and it soon begins to totter and eventually collapses of its own accord. Round stones, especially those found in rivers, act in quite the opposite way: they do not adhere to the mortar, because they are always moist.

But what of the discovery that marble actually grows in the quarry?[105] Recently at Rome small pieces of porous Tiburtine were found underground, which had grown together, as though nourished by time and the earth, to form a single, solid mass of stone.[106] On Lake Piediluco, at the point where the water spills over and crashes down through a broken precipice into the river Nera,[107] it is possible to see how the upper lip of the bank has gradually grown, causing some to argue that this continual growth of the rock has been responsible for the closing off of the river's mouth and the formation of the lake. In Lucania, not far from the river Sele, toward the east where a waterfall gushes out from the high rocks, enormous stalactites are to be seen, which daily increase in length, and whose size is so great that several waggons would be required to carry a single one. While it is fresh and still full of its natural juices, this stone is quite soft, but on drying out it becomes extremely hard and is most suitable for every kind of use. I have seen the same phenomenon in a number of ancient aqueducts: the sides of the channels have fused together, encrusted with a layer of stone deposits. In Gaul there are two remarkable sights that may be witnessed to this day.[108] There is a torrent running through the Cornelian countryside[109] with very high banks, along which, in several places, a great number of large round stones are gradually brought forth, conceived within the very bowels of the earth. In the countryside around Faenza on the banks of the river Lamone there are vast naturally formed stone overhangs; these daily throw up a not inconsiderable quantity of salt, which, it is thought, eventually turns to stone. In Tuscany, in the Florentine countryside, a stretch of land beside the river Clatis[110] is covered over with extremely hard stones, which every seven years turn back into clods of earth. On the other hand, around the towns of Cizicus[111] and Cassandrea,[112] according to Pliny, the clods turn into stone.[113] By Pozzuoli a powder is found that, when mixed with seawater, hardens into stone.[114] They say that all along the coast from Oropus to Aulis,[115] wherever the sand is washed by the sea, it hardens and petrifies.[116] Diodorus relates that in Arabia clods of earth with a sweet smell may be dug up out of the ground; in fire these will melt like metal and then turn into stone. The nature of this stone is such that if rained upon, the joints will dissolve and an entire wall will fuse together into a single block. There is a stone, so it is said, to be quarried near Troy in Asia, which is called the "sarcophagus": it is composed of veins that split easily, and it is said that within forty days any corpse buried in the stone will have been totally consumed apart from the teeth; yet more remarkable is the claim that anything that is buried along with the body, such as clothes, shoes, and so on, will turn into stone. The "chernites," a stone in which Darius is said to have been buried, behaves in the opposite manner: it preserves the corpse perfectly intact.[117] But enough about this. ◆

IO

30v—32

It is agreed that the ancients were quite willing to use bricks instead of stone. I do believe that men were first prompted by necessity, in the absence of other suitable material, to build in brick. Noticing both how easy this method of construction was and how practical, graceful, solid, and reliable, they proceeded to use brick for other buildings, and even royal palaces. Finally, whether by accident or by careful investigation, they discovered that fire strengthened and hardened bricks, and went on to construct everything of earthenware. Indeed, from what I have observed from studying very ancient structures, I would be so bold as to state that there is no building material more suitable than brick, however you wish to employ it, though it must be baked rather than raw, and the correct methods of molding and firing must be strictly followed. Of the advantages of brick there will be more elsewhere.

It is useful to note here the opinion that a whitish, chalky clay makes very good bricks; likewise reddish clay and the so-called masculine sand. It is advisable to avoid clay that is sandy or full of gravel; but above all, clay containing pebbles ought to be discarded utterly:[118] clay of this type tends to warp and crack during firing and to break up afterward by itself.

Freshly dug clay should not be used to make bricks, they say: rather the clay should be dug in the autumn, allowed to macerate throughout the winter, and not used for making bricks until the beginning of spring. If bricks are made during winter, obviously the frost will split them, or, if during summer, the intense heat will crack them as they dry.[119] But if it is absolutely necessary to make them during the cold of winter, they should be covered immediately with a layer of very dry sand, and if in the heat of the summer, with damp straw: stored in this way they will neither crack nor warp.

Some prefer bricks to be glazed. If so, sandy clay or clay that is too thin and dry ought to be strenuously avoided, as this will absorb the glaze; instead, glazed bricks should be made of a white, chalky, rich clay. The bricks must be thin: if they are too thick, they will not bake properly and will be liable to crack. But if thick ones are required, the problem may on the whole be avoided if a number of holes are spiked here and there through the middle: these will act as vents and will improve the drying out and firing of the bricks by allowing moisture and vapor to escape. Potters coat their wares with white chalk, so that when the glaze melts, it forms a more even skin on the vessels. The same method may also be employed in the manufacture of bricks.

I notice that bricks in ancient buildings contain a certain proportion of sand, especially red sand, and I have found that it was common practice to mix red clay with marble.

We know from experience that the same clay will produce a much stronger brick if it is allowed, as it were, to rise, as dough does in bread making, and then is kneaded several times, until it becomes as soft as wax, and even the smallest stones have been removed. Baking will so harden a brick that, if it is left long enough in the oven, it will become as tough as flint; furthermore, as happens with bread, the bricks get a solid crust, either while they are baked in the oven or when they are left to dry in the open air. This is why it is better to bake them thin, so that there is more crust and less crumb. And if they are baked and polished, they may well prove impervious to the assaults of the weather; the same happens with stone of whatever kind: if first polished, it will not be eaten away by decay.

Bricks, they say, should be polished either immediately after their removal from the kiln and before they have been wetted, or after they have been wetted and before they have dried out; for once they have been dampened and allowed to dry out again, they become so hard that they will blunt or wear down the edge of any tool; but, in our opinion, they are easier to rub smooth as soon as they have been made, and while they are still warm.

The ancients used three types of brick: the first, one and a half feet long by one foot wide, the second measuring five palms in each dimension, and the third no more than four palms. Bricks measuring two feet by two feet are found in some buildings, especially in arches and bonding brickwork.[120]

We are told that the ancients did not use the same brick for public and for private buildings, but used large bricks for the former and small ones for the latter.[121] On this point I have observed that in many ancient remains, especially along the Appian way, various types of brick may be found, large and small, used in different ways: and so I believe that they were careful to build in such a way as was graceful to the sight but also impressive. To mention but one example, I have seen bricks no more than six inches long, one inch high, and three inches wide, although these were generally laid down in paving, in herringbone fashion.[122]

Of the various types of brick, I prefer the triangular ones, which were made like this: first, shape a brick so that it is one foot square and one and a half inches thick; while still fresh, mark it with two grooves, running diagonally from the angles, as deep as half the thickness of the brick; this makes four equal triangles. They have these advantages: they use up less clay, they are easier to fit together in the kiln and to take out again, and they are more convenient to transport onto the site. Also, take into account that they may be carried four in one hand, and that a mason may split them with a light tap while continuing to work. He then lays them along the face of the wall, in rows, the side one foot long facing outward and the angle pointing inward. As a result, the expense is less, the work has a more pleasing appearance, and the structure is more solid: it seems as if the wall is constructed entirely of complete bricks, while the right angles are wedged together like teeth into the infill, making the wall much stronger.[123]

Once the bricks are molded, it is not recommended to place them directly in the kiln, unless they are completely dry; it is said that they take at least two years to dry out,[124] and that they dry better in the shade than when exposed to the sun. But enough on this topic, except to add that for works of this kind, referred to as the art of pottery, some of the best clay is reputed to come from Samos, Aretium, Mutina, Saguntum in Spain, and Pergamon in Asia.[125] In my concern for brevity I should not neglect to mention that whatever has been said about bricks applies equally to pantiles and plaintiles on the roof, and to earthenware piping, in short to any pottery or earthenware work.

So much for stone; we must now deal with lime. ◆

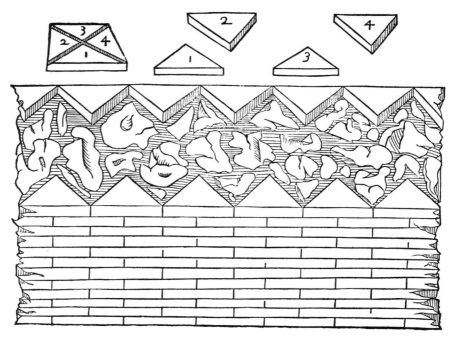

Brick wall construction: opus quadratum.

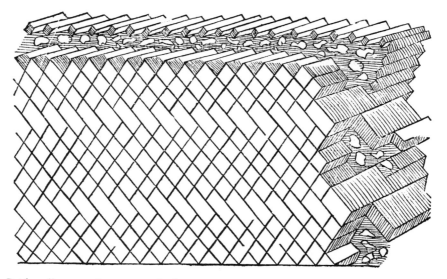

Brick wall construction: opus reticulatum.

Cato the Censor discourages the use of lime made up of different kinds of stone, and that made from flint he condemns as unsuitable for any work.[126] A stone will be utterly useless for producing lime if it is exhausted, dried up, or rotten, and if it does not contain anything for the fire to consume during the roasting process, as is the case with tufa and with the somewhat reddish and pale stone found in the countryside near Fidenae and Alba, around

Materials

Rome. Stone should lose a third of its weight in producing lime to meet with the approval of experts.[127]

On the other hand, any stone that is by nature too moist and damp, and that tends to vitrify in contact with fire, is equally unsuitable for making lime. Green stone, says Pliny, has a greater resistance to fire;[128] and we know well that porphyry will not only refuse to burn, but prevent any other stone that is in contact with it in the kiln from burning. Stone containing earth is also considered unacceptable, because of the impurities it leaves in the lime.

But the lime most highly praised by ancient architects is produced from extremely hard and compact stone, preferably white: it is thought suitable for many types of work and is particularly solid when used in vaulting. Their next preference is for lime made from stone which is porous, but neither light nor crumbly; this they consider the best for plastering, being easier to fashion and imparting a more splendid finish to the work.[129] In Gaul I have seen that architects use lime extracted solely from dark, round, hard stones found in riverbeds, which give the impression of being flint; nonetheless this lime has certainly shown itself strong and very lasting in both stone and brick buildings.

I read in Pliny that the stone used for millstones produces a lime that is naturally rich, and therefore most suitable for whatever use.[130] We know from experience, however, that if this particular stone is coated with salt crystals, it will be too rough and dry to serve its purpose; and the other variety, which contains no salt, will be more suitable, as it is denser, and can be ground more finely.

However, any quarried stone will make better lime than that gathered from the ground; a shady, damp quarry will contain better stone than a dry one; and lime from white stone, rather than dark, will be easier to plaster.

In France, in the coastal region of the Edui,[131] lime is made from the shells of oysters and mussels, for want of any stone.

There is another type of lime called gypsum; this is also made by roasting stone, although they say that in Cyprus and Thebes gypsum may be dug from the very surface of the ground, ready roasted by the sun.[132] However, stone that produces gypsum is quite different from that which produces lime, since it is very soft and friable, with the exception of that quarried in Syria, which is extremely hard. Further, stone for gypsum needs to be roasted for no more than twenty hours, whereas that for lime needs at least sixty. I have observed that there are four types of gypsum to be found in Italy: two translucent and two opaque. Of the two that are translucent, one resembles lumps of alum, or rather alabaster: this is called "squameola," as it consists of very slender scales attached and pressed together like thin layers; the other is also scaly, but more closely resembles dark salt than alum. Both of the opaque varieties resemble dense chalk, although one is whitish and very pale, and the other a pallid color tinged with red. The latter two are denser than the former, and of these the reddish one grips better. Of the first two, the purer one makes more lustrous stucco for cornices and figurines. A type of gypsum is to be found near Rimini that is so compacted that it gives the impression of being marble or alabaster: I have had this sawn into slabs that make excellent facing.[133] I should not forget to mention that all forms of gypsum must be pounded with wooden mallets and crushed into powder; this should be piled up and stored in a dry place, but once brought out, it ought to be mixed with water immediately and put to use without delay.

Lime is the opposite: it does not need to be crushed, but may be soaked while still in lumps; indeed, it should be allowed to soften in water for a good while before being mixed, especially if intended for plastering, so that any lumps not baked thoroughly enough by the fire will dissolve. If it is used too soon, before it has been properly steeped and softened, it may still contain some small half-roasted stones, which might with time begin to rot, soon developing blisters which disfigure the finish. It should be added here that lime ought not to be soaked by a single dousing, but ought to be dampened gradually with several sprinklings, until it is evenly saturated. It should then be left on its own, mixed with nothing else, in a damp, shady place with nothing but a layer of sand to protect it, until the process of time has fermented it into a more fluid paste. It is certain that this lengthy fermentation greatly improves the lime. We have ourselves seen lime that has been recently discovered in an old deserted cave, left for more than five hundred years, as numerous indications make abundantly clear, which stayed damp and viscous, and so mature that it was far softer than honey or the marrow in bones. Surely there is nothing else to be found more suitable for whatever purpose. Lime prepared in this way requires twice the sand as when mixed freshly slaked.

In this respect, then, lime and gypsum are different, though in other ways they are similar. Remove the lime from the kiln immediately, and store it in a shady, dry place, and then soak it. For if it is left in the kiln, or anywhere else where it might be exposed to the breezes, the moon, or the sun, especially in summer, it will very soon turn to ashes and become useless. But enough on this subject.

They advise us not to put stone into the kiln until it has been broken up into pieces no larger than clods of earth: apart from the fact that they burn more easily, it is well known that stones, especially round ones, often contain air-filled cavities, which cause a great deal of damage. Once the fire in the kiln has been ignited, the air inside the stone expands, as a result either of being constricted as the cold recedes, or of turning into vapor and increasing in size, as the stone eventually heats up; then, shattering the prison where it has been confined, it bursts out with a loud noise in its violent fury and totally demolishes the whole kiln. Many different animals have been seen flourishing in the center of these stones, including worms with hairy backs and many legs; these can cause great damage to kilns.[134]

I will not avoid mentioning here a number of memorable incidents about such things that happened in our own times: this book has been written not only for craftsmen but also for anyone interested in the noble arts. I shall therefore take pleasure in intermixing here and there some anecdotes intended to amuse, and anyway neither out of place nor foreign to our undertaking.

When Martin V was pope, a snake was brought to light discovered by workmen in a quarry in Latium;[135] it had been living inside a huge boulder without there being any passage into it for air. Several frogs and crabs have also been found, but these were all dead. Recently I myself have witnessed the discovery of tree leaves within a piece of marble of the purest white.

The summit of Mount Velinus, which divides the Abruzzo from Marsica and towers above the surrounding peaks, is quite bald, with white, tough stone;[136] on the slope facing toward Abruzzo broken pieces of stone may be seen full of imprints of seashells, no larger than the palm of a man's hand.

What is more surprising, in the Veronese countryside stones marked with a quinquefoil are found daily strewn across the open ground, where they have fallen out of the sky; so accurately have they been drawn, their lines exact and uniform, so beautifully have they been patterned by Nature with her extraordinary and consummate skill, that no human hand could ever quite match the subtlety of the work. And more amazing still, as if to protect the marking imprinted on it, not one of these stones is to be found facing upward; from this it is easy to understand that Nature has wrought these delights not for man to admire, but for herself alone. But to return to the discussion.

I will not dwell here on how best to line the opening and chamber of the kiln, nor how to set up the hearth inside, so that flames may breathe as they rage, yet be restrained to the right extent, and so that the whole force of the fire may be concentrated solely on the roasting process.[137] Nor will I go on to describe how the fire should be kindled gradually and with constant attention, until the flames come out through the top without smoke and even the highest stones glow red; nor will I explain that the stone will not have been roasted sufficiently until the kiln has settled back and again contracted, the flames having caused it to swell and open up. It is marvelous to watch how this substance behaves: if the fire below is removed after the lime has been roasted, the bottom of the kiln will gradually cool down, but the top will grow much hotter.

Since in order to build, not only lime is needed but also sand, we must now deal with the latter. ◆

There are three kinds of sand: that which comes from pits, that from rivers, and that from the sea. The best is from pits. This comes in several varieties: black, white, red, carbuncular, and gravelly. If anyone were to ask me of what sand is composed, I might reply that it is made up of tiny fragments broken off from some larger stone. Vitruvius, however, prefers to describe it—especially the Etruscan variety, known as carbuncular—as a form of earth, roasted by fire that Nature has entrapped within the mountains, which is no harder than unbaked clay and no softer than tufa.[138]

Of all these types of pit sand the carbuncular is the favorite, although I notice that red sand was not the last choice for public buildings in Rome. White sand is the worst type of pit sand. Gravelly sand makes a very suitable infill for foundations. Next, in order of preference, comes fine, gravelly sand, especially if the grains are sharp and quite free of soil, as is the variety found in great abundance in the territory of the Vilumbrians.[139] After that comes sand extracted from riverbeds, once the top layer has been removed. The most useful river sand comes from streams, and of these the best is provided by mountain streams with steep gradients. Sand extracted from the sea is considered the worst, although any that is black or vitreous is not entirely unacceptable.

In the territory of the Picenes, near Salerno, sand is extracted from the sea that is considered to be not inferior to pit sand—although this high-quality sand is not to be found on every beach in this region: in fact, it has been found that the worst sand comes from beaches exposed to Auster, while sand on beaches facing Libycus is not at all bad.[140] Among sea sands, that which lies under rocks and has a coarse grain is generally considered the most useful.

There are many differences among the various types of sand. Sea sand is difficult to dry: saltiness makes it soluble, so that it is always prone to take up moisture and dissolve; it is therefore unsuitable and unreliable for bearing weights. River sand is damper than pit sand and therefore easier to mold and more suitable for plastering. Pit sand, being fatter, holds together much better, although it tends to crack and therefore is more suitable for vaulting than for plastering.[141]

But the best sand of any kind will be one that crackles when rubbed or crushed in the hand, and when gathered in a clean garment leaves no stain, nor residue of soil.[142] On the other hand, a sand smooth in texture, without any harshness, and of a color and smell like those of a clayey soil will not be good, nor will any variety which when stirred in water leaves it turbid and muddy, nor will one that is covered by grass as soon as it is spread on the ground. It will be no good if, once procured, it is left in the open for a long time exposed to the sun, the moon, and the frost: this leaves it earthlike and rotten, and therefore quite capable of producing shrubs and wild fig trees, but with little strength for holding buildings together.[143]

We have dealt with the advice that our ancestors have given us on timber, stone, and lime. But it will not be possible to find materials everywhere at hand, ready to meet our requirements. Cicero relates that Asia always abounded in magnificent buildings and statues because of its plentiful supply of marble. But marble is not found everywhere: in some places there is no stone at all, or if there is any, not suitable for every use.[144] It is said that pit sand may be found throughout south-facing Italy, but none is to be found beyond the Apennines.[145] The Babylonians used bitumen, according to Pliny, and the Carthaginians mud.[146] In other places they built of wattle and daub for want of any stone. Herodotus relates that the Budini[147] constructed their buildings, be they private or public, solely of wood: everything was made of wood from their town walls to the very statues of their gods.[148] Whereas the Neuri,[149] according to Mela, were without any wood and were forced to use bones to kindle fires.[150] In Egypt they fuel their hearths with cattle dung. Thus people are forced to vary their dwellings according to necessity and the materials available. In Egypt even some of the royal palaces are built of reeds, while in India some are built with the ribs of whales.[151] Diodorus writes that at Dedalia in Sardinia they live in houses dug underground.[152] In the city of Carrae, in Arabia, they construct their homes and their walls with blocks of salt. But of this elsewhere.

To conclude, then, not every place will have the same supply of stone, sand, and so on, since the quality and quantity of natural resources vary from place to place. And so use should be made of whatever is available, and care must be taken to ensure, first, that only the most manageable and convenient materials are procured, and second, that in the process of construction all the right materials are used in the right places. ◆

13
34v—36

Having procured the materials mentioned above—that is, timber, stone, lime, and sand—it remains now to deal with the method and manner of construction. For as regards the provision of iron, copper, lead, glass, and so on, no more effort is required than to ensure that a sufficient quantity is purchased and stored to avoid any shortages during the building process; in any case, we shall deal with the selection and distribution of materials required for finishing and embellishing the work in an appropriate place. But we shall now proceed to set out the whole process, beginning from the very foundations, describing it as though we were ourselves about to construct the building with our own hands.

First, I must again warn you to take careful account of the current situation, both in terms of public affairs and in terms of your own personal circumstances and those of your family, to ensure that in unsettled times your undertaking does not incite envy if you continue construction nor cause needless expense if you abandon it. Another important consideration is the time of year: a close examination will show that buildings constructed in winter, especially in cold climates, will tend to freeze before they have fully set, and that those constructed in the summer, especially in hot climates, will tend to dry out prematurely. This was why the architect Frontinus advised that the best time to build was between the calends of April and the calends of November, with a break for the heat of the summer.[153]

But in my opinion consideration of local variations in terrain and climate should influence the decision whether to press on or to delay work. When you are finally satisfied with all the above factors, it will be time to plot out the *area* of your proposed building, by marking out the dimensions and angles of its composite spaces on the ground.

Some advise that construction not commence until an auspicious occasion, since great importance is attached to the moment in time when anything enters existence. It is said that Lucius Tarutius[154] was able to ascertain the precise date of the foundation of Rome by following the pattern of its fortunes.[155] In the eyes of the wise men of antiquity the moment of initiation had so great an influence on the future, that, according to Julius Firmicus Maternus,[156] some were able to plot the exact time at which the world came into existence, and to describe the event in great detail, by studying its history: Aesculapius and Anubis, supported later by Petosiris and Necepsus,[157] maintained that it happened as Cancer was beginning to rise, and the moon was in mid-course, the sun in Leo, Saturn in Capricorn, Jupiter in Sagittarius, Mars in Scorpio, Venus in Libra, and Mercury in Virgo.

Clearly, time, if our interpretation is correct, can have a great deal of influence on many things. For what about the things that they say happen on the winter solstice, when the dry pennywort comes into blossom, inflated bladders burst, and willow leaves and apple pips rotate? And the number of fibers in the livers of rats always corresponds to the day of the moon.

For my part, although I would not go so far as to believe that those who practice this art or who read the seasons can ascertain the destiny of everything, I would nonetheless concede that they ought not to be ignored when they argue that, on the basis of heavenly signs, a particular time is favorable or not. But whatever the case, either it will be extremely useful to heed their advice, if accurate, or, if inaccurate, it will do little harm.

I might mention here several ridiculous examples of measures that the ancients would recommend when embarking on anything;[158] I would not wish them to be misinterpreted. Certainly anyone who advises that nothing should be undertaken without good auspices, and includes the setting out of the *area*, deserves to be ridiculed. The ancients were so obsessed by superstition that they took care even when writing down the names of recruits, so as not to have the first one in any way inauspicious; and they would choose someone with a propitious name to lead out the victims when sacrificing to purify a colony or an army; when letting out contracts for taxes, the censors would put Lake Lucrinus at the top of the list, for its lucky name; then again, disturbed by the inauspicious-sounding name of Epidamnum (because it would sound as though anyone sailing there were traveling "to hell"), they changed it to Dyrrachium, and similarly the town previously called Maleventum was renamed Beneventum.

Ridiculous, too, is their practice of uttering various lucky words and prayers. Indeed, some would maintain that so great is the power of human speech, that even beasts and inanimate objects will obey it (although here I am not referring to Cato's remark that flagging oxen may be revived with words of encouragement). Apparently men would use words and prayers to implore their native soil to nourish any unusual or exotic trees, and entreat the trees themselves to allow their being transplanted to another place. Having entered this frivolous mood in recounting the follies of others, I ought to mention another tale for the sake of amusement: it is claimed that the human voice has such influence, that if a man requests turnips to look kindly on himself, his family, and his neighbors, as he sows them, they will grow all the larger. In which case I do not understand why it is thought that the herb basil will grow more luxuriantly the more it is cursed and insulted when sown. But let us move on.

I think it better to disregard all idle superstition, and to undertake our work in a holy and religious manner. "With Jove I begin, ye Muses; of Jove all things are full."[159] It will be proper to embark on such a work with a pure mind, and to make a holy and devout offering, and in particular to say prayers beseeching the gods above to lend their assistance and blessing to the undertaking, to ensure that it is carried through to completion favorably and prosperously, and that the builder, his family, and his guests continue to enjoy good health and prosperity, their positions secure, their minds free of anxiety, their fortune increasing, their work fruitful, their renown spreading abroad—in short, that they and their descendants continue to enjoy in the future benefits of every kind. But enough about this. ◆

Here Begins the Third Book of Leon Battista Alberti. On Construction.

The whole method of construction is summed up and accomplished in one principle: the ordered and skilful composition of various materials, be they squared stones, aggregate, timber, or whatever, to form a solid and, as far as possible, integral and unified structure. A structure may be said to be integral and unified when the parts it contains are not to be separated or displaced, but their every line joins and matches.

We need to consider, therefore, which are the primary parts of the structure, their order, and the lines of which they are composed. It is not difficult to discover the parts that make up the structure: clearly they are the top and bottom, the right and left, the front and back, and all that lies in between; but not everyone will comprehend their specific characteristics and why each is different.

The construction of a building does not entail just setting stone on stone, and aggregate on aggregate, as the ignorant may imagine; for, because the parts are different, so too the materials and methods of construction vary quite radically. The foundations need to be treated one way, the girdle[1] and cornices another, and the corners and lips of openings yet another, while the outer skins of a wall must be treated differently from the infill of the middle. We must now inquire what is appropriate in each case.

In this we shall follow, as we mentioned above, the same order as those who are to undertake the work with their own hands; we shall begin, therefore, with the foundations. The foundations, unless I am mistaken, are not part of the structure itself; rather they constitute a base on which the structure proper is to be raised and built. For if an *area*[2] could be found that was thoroughly solid and secure—of stone, for example, as may be found often around Veioi—there would be no need to lay down foundations before raising the structure itself.[3] There are colossal towers in Siena that have been built directly onto the bare ground, the hill below being a solid bed of tufa.

A foundation—that is to say, "a going to the bottom"[4]—and a trench will be necessary wherever a pit must be dug to reach solid ground, as is the case almost everywhere; more on this later. The following will serve to indicate whether the ground will be suitable: weeds that normally grow in damp places should not be present; the ground should bear either no trees at all or only those that grow in extremely hard, compact earth; all around, everything should be quite arid and dry, and if stony, the stone should not be small and round, but hard and sharp, preferably flint; there should be no springs or underground streams beneath, for it is the nature of the stream to plunder and deposit matter continually; for this reason solid ground will not be reached on a plain or by a river until you have dug below the level of the riverbed.

Therefore, before you start any excavation, it is advisable to mark out all the corners and sides of the *area*,[5] to the correct size and in the right place several times, with great care. In setting out these angles use an extremely large set-square, and not a small one, to make the direction of the lines more accurate. The ancients used a triangular set-square consisting of three straight rules, one three cubits in length, another four, and the other five.[6]

The inexperienced do not know how to set out these angles without first removing everything within the *area*, leaving the ground clear and absolutely level. Accordingly, they send in demolition men, wielding their mallets with less restraint than they would against their enemies, to ruin and destroy everything. Their mistake must be corrected. Misfortune, unforeseen developments, chance, and stringency may often hamper an undertaking and prevent the completion of what is begun. Moreover, it is not proper to show disrespect to the work of our ancestors or to fail to consider the comfort that citizens draw from their settled ancestral hearths; there will always be time enough to do away with, demolish, and level whatever is standing anywhere. Therefore, I would prefer you to leave all old buildings intact, until such time as it becomes impossible to construct anything without demolishing them. ◆

2

In setting out the foundations, it should be noted that the base of the wall and the plinth (which are also considered part of the foundations) must be somewhat wider than the proposed wall—for the very same reason for which people who walk through the snow in the Tuscan Alps strap to their feet rackets strung with cord, since the enlarged footprint will prevent them from sinking so much.

How to set out the angles would not be easy to explain using words alone: the method by which they are drawn is derived from mathematics and would require graphic illustration. What is more, it would be foreign to our undertaking, and in any case the subject has been dealt with elsewhere in our *Mathematical Commentaries*.[7] Nonetheless I shall attempt to describe the process as fully as I can here, so that any of you who have a ready intellect will understand enough to allow you to follow the matter on your own easily. Some things may still seem obscure, and if you wish to understand them exactly, find the answers in the work already mentioned.

Our usual method of defining the foundations is to trace out several lines, known as baselines, in the following manner. From a midpoint at the front, we extend a line right to the back of the work; halfway along it we fix a stake into the ground, and through this, following the rules of geometry, we extend the perpendicular. We then relate all the measurements to these two lines. This works wonderfully in every way: the parallel lines are easily drawn, the angles can be defined accurately, and the parts conform and correspond exactly to one another.

But if it so happens that existing walls of old buildings intrude and obstruct a view of where the corner is to be formed, you must trace out the parallel lines wherever there is some unobstructed space. Then mark out the point of intersection, and by setting the gnomon and projecting a transverse line, and tracing out further parallel lines at right angles, you will easily overcome the problem. Also it will be extremely useful to stake out the view, as seen from some high place, with a line from which the perpendicular may be dropped to check directions and distances.

Once the lines and angles of the trenches have been marked out, it would be good if we could have the same vision and intuition that a certain Spaniard was recently reported to have had: he was allegedly able to divine the veins of water snaking deep within the earth as clearly as if they were flowing on the surface. So much of what happens below ground is unknown, that to entrust it with the responsibility of bearing a structural and financial burden can never be done without risk. And so, especially in the foundations, where more than anywhere else in the building the thought and attention of a careful and circumspect builder are required, nothing must be overlooked. A mistake elsewhere will cause less damage, and be less difficult to rectify and more easily borne, but in the foundations a mistake is inexcusable.

The ancients used to say, "Dig until you reach solid ground, and God be with you." The ground has many layers, some sandy, some gravelly, others stony, and so on; and below these, its position ever changing and uncertain, lies a hard, compact layer of earth, extremely suitable for bearing the weight of buildings. The nature of this layer may itself vary, there being scarcely any similarities between the various types: some may be hard, almost impregnable to iron, others thick, some black, others white (the latter are commonly thought the weakest of all), some composed of clay, others of tufa, and others of a mixture of gravel and clay. Nothing can be said for certain as to which of these is best, except that any that resist iron, or scarcely dissolve when immersed in water, can be recommended. No substance is thought more sure and steadfast, then, than that found below a stream gushing through the bowels of the earth.

In our opinion, advice should be sought from those with any knowledge and experience in the matter, be they local residents or nearby architects: through their acquaintance with existing buildings or their daily experience in constructing new ones, they will have acquired a ready understanding of the nature and quality of the local soil. Methods do exist, however, of testing the consistency of the soil in advance. If a heavy object can be rolled along the ground, or dropped from some height, without shaking the ground, or disturbing the surface of a bowl of water positioned there, it will be a sure guarantee of the firmness of the soil. But solid ground may not always be found: in some places, such as along the Adriatic coast and in Venice, nothing but soft mire is to be found below the upper layers of silt. ◆

3

The design of the foundations must vary therefore according to the site. Some sites may be up high, others down low, and others in between these, such as slopes, for example; then again, some may be parched and arid, especially mountain ridges and summits, and others utterly saturated and damp, such as those which lie on the coast, by a lagoon, or in a valley. Others may remain neither totally dry nor utterly wet, because they are positioned on a slope, which is true for any place where water does not remain still and stagnant but always runs downhill.

No ground should be trusted simply because it resists iron; on a plain, for example, the ground might slide away, causing great damage to the whole work. We have ourselves seen it in the case of a tower in the Venetian town of Mnestor:[8] the ground there was clearly too thin and weak, and shortly after it was built the weight of the tower caused it to subside and sink right up to the battlements. All the more to be blamed are those who, without taking the trouble to seek out a naturally solid piece of ground suitable for bearing the weight of a building, find the leftovers of some ancient ruin and rashly use them as the base for a wall of considerable size, without inspecting the dimensions and their state of repair closely enough: greed to reduce costs will be responsible for destroying the whole building.

It is a wise expedient, therefore, to dig a few wells before digging anything else. There are several reasons for this, not least to make absolutely clear whether each stratum will support the work or undermine it; what is more, any excavated earth or water that is discovered can be put to a number of different uses; also, vents will be created, which will make the building more stable and less susceptible to damage from underground exhalations.[9] Having dug a well, cistern, drain, or indeed any other deep hole, and having ascertained the various layers hidden below the surface, you must next choose the most suitable layer to entrust with the task of bearing the work.

Whatever the location—whether it is elevated or otherwise—if a stream flows there, which is capable of causing erosion, the deeper you dig your trench, the better. The crags, which were originally cloaked in the fabric of the mountain but which daily appear more prominent, are evidence that mountains are reduced by being continually washed and worn away by the passage of rain. Mount Morello above Florence was thick with green fir in the time of our fathers; now erosion (by rain, if I am correct) has left it naked and rugged.

With a sloping site, Junius Columella recommends we start with the lower section of the foundations, at the deepest point;[10] and with good reason.

First, anything set down at the base will sit snugly upon the terrain and prove extremely durable; second, it will act as a form of buttress and provide firm support for anything added above, should you wish to extend the house. In addition, should fissures and earth slides occur, as they occasionally do with this type of trench, they will be more visible and less damaging.

On marshy ground it is best to dig a wide trench and to strengthen both of its sides with stakes, wickerwork, planks, seaweed, mud, and any similar materials to prevent the water from seeping in; next, any water remaining in the trench should be drawn off, sand dug out, and mud completely removed from the bottom, until the ground is quite firm beneath your feet. If the situation demands, the same procedure must be followed with sandy soil.

Finally, the whole base of the trench must be made absolutely level, without sloping in any direction, so that the imposed load will be distributed evenly; for it is in the very nature of weights to veer toward the lowest point.

A further measure is recommended when dealing with marshy ground, although it concerns the structure rather than the foundations. It is this: drive a number of inverted stakes and piles with charred ends into the ground; this work should cover twice the *area* of the proposed wall, and the length of the piles should be no less than an eighth of its planned height, while their thickness should be no less than a twelfth of their length; and they should be so closely packed together that there is room for no more. Whatever the machine used for driving the piles, it should not be equipped with extremely heavy hammers, but with such as deliver repeated blows: if they are too heavy, the timber will not be able to bear the impact and immense weight, and will split instantly; whereas the sheer persistence of repeated blows will break and wear down any soil, however great its resistance. You may see evidence of this when you try to fix a thin nail into hard timber: if you use a heavy hammer, it will not work, but with a suitably light one the nail will penetrate.

This may be enough on trenches, except perhaps to add that on some occasions, either to reduce costs or to avoid an insecure stretch of ground along the way, it may be better not to construct a solid work along a single, continuous trench, but to leave spaces between, as though only making foundations for pillars or columns; arches are then constructed from one pillar to the next, and the rest of the wall is raised on top. Here we must follow the same principle mentioned elsewhere, but the greater the intended load, the wider and firmer should be the foundations and footings. Enough on this subject. ◆

4

39—39v

It now remains for us to deal with the structure; but since the whole art of the mason and the method of construction depend in part on the nature, shape, and condition of the stone and in part on the adhesive capacity of the mortar bedding, we must first make a few brief, yet relevant comments on these.

Some stones are tough,[11] strong, and rich in moisture, such as flint, marble, and so on; these are naturally heavy and resonant. Others are lackluster, light, and dull, such as tufa and sandstone. And again, some have flat surfaces, straight edges, and equal angles; these are called squared stones; others have several different surfaces, edges, and angles; these we call irregular. Again, some may be so large that it is impossible for a man to move them as he wants, using his bare hands and without the help of sledges, levers, rollers, porters, and so on; others are so small that you may pick them up and arrange them at will even with one hand. There is a third category of stones, whose size and weight is in between; these are called "standard sized."

Every stone should be sound, free of mud, and well soaked. The noise it gives when struck will indicate whether the stone is sound or cracked. The best place to wash stones is in a stream. If the stone is of "standard" size, it is generally accepted that it will not be soaked properly before the ninth day; for a large stone it will take longer. Stone fresh from a quarry is better than that long-since quarried. Once stone has been separated from the lime to which it had been joined, it will not consent to a second match. So much for stone itself.

As for lime, if on removal from the kiln the lumps are cracked or broken, or extremely powdery, it is not to be recommended: such lime is thought to be too weak for use. The lime that is recommended either is purified by roasting, to become white, resonant, and light, or will give off a loud crack and throw up a great cloud of smoke when doused with water. The first kind, having less strength, clearly requires less sand, whereas the latter, being stronger, requires more. Cato decreed that for every foot of work one *modius*[12] of lime should be used to two of sand;[13] but opinions vary. Vitruvius and Pliny recommend that it be mixed with four measures of sand if the sand is from a quarry, or three if the sand is from a river or the sea.[14]

Finally, if the nature and quality of the stone (which we shall deal with below) require the mortar to be more fluid and supple, the sand must be sieved; but when a thicker mortar is required, half a measure of sharp gravel and tiny stone chippings should be mixed with one of sand. It is universally agreed that the addition of a one-third measure of crushed tiles will produce a far stronger mortar. Whatever the mix, you must constantly knead it until even the smallest particles are absorbed. And so some will stir and pound the mixture for some time in a mortar trough, in order to mix it thoroughly. So much for lime, except perhaps to add that lime adheres better to stone of its own kind (especially if it is from the same quarry) than to stone of a different kind. ◆

As regards the construction of the footings (that is to say, the section bringing the foundations up to the level of the *area*), I find that the ancients offer no advice on the matter, except, as we mentioned above, that any stone showing defects after two years in the open should be consigned to the foundations. As in the army, where lazy and cowardly soldiers, incapable of enduring the sun and the dust, are sent back home, not without a measure of disgrace, so too, soft or enervated stone is relegated to the depths to continue its idle ways in shameful darkness. In spite of this, I read in some historical works that the ancients would devote their every care and attention to constructing the underground footings, so that, as far as possible, they would be every bit as solid as the rest of the wall.

Asithis, son of Nicerinus and king of Egypt, under whom the law was passed allowing a debtor to borrow on the security of his father's dead body, when building a pyramid of brick, first drove wooden piles into the marsh to make the foundations and then laid bricks on top of this.[15] It is recorded that the excellent Cresiphus,[16] who was responsible for the very famous temple of Diana at Ephesus, was not so rash as to lay the foundations of so vast a building on land that was uncertain or insufficiently firm, and once a clear and level site had been chosen, which was likely to be free of earthquakes, he threw down a layer of crushed charcoal, and on top of this a layer of animal hides; coal was crammed into the spaces between the stakes, and on top of that a layer of squared stone, their joints as long as possible.[17] I hear that some stones used to build the foundations of public works in Jerusalem were twenty cubits long and at least ten high.[18]

I notice that in other large-scale works, however, the experienced architects of the past followed different methods and rules for laying the foundations. In the sepulcher of the Antonini,[19] for example, they filled the foundations with an aggregate bathed in mortar and consisting of fragments of hard stone no larger than the palm of a hand; in the Silversmiths' forum they filled them with an aggregate of assorted stone chippings, and in the Comitium with chips and lumps of common stone. But I am particularly impressed by those who built the work under the Tarpeian Rock; taking their example from Nature, they have produced a work particularly well suited to the hilly terrain. Like a hill that is composed of alternating bands of solid stone and soft matter, they have laid down as a base a layer of squared stone, two feet deep and as solid as possible, and on top of this two feet of a doughlike substance composed of aggregate; they have then filled in the rest of the foundations with alternating layers of stone and dough.

I have seen other examples of foundations of this type and buildings proper, which our ancestors constructed of pit gravel and even stone gathered from the ground, but which have been so strong that they have survived for centuries. When a particularly tall and solid tower was demolished in Bologna, the foundations were found to be an infill of round stones and clay, and to extend to a depth of almost six cubits; the remainder was then built with lime. Techniques in laying foundations vary therefore, and it would not be easy to say which I prefer: examples may be found of each that have proved extremely solid and strong. But in my opinion cost should be the overriding factor, so long as you do not fill the foundations with rubbish and material that might be perishable.

The types of footing also vary. There is one type for porticoes, or anywhere that is to support a row of colums, and another for coastal sites, where there is no guarantee that you will find solid ground to your liking. The latter will be dealt with when we come to the method for constructing deep-water harbors and moles: it is not a topic connected with constructional work in general, which we are discussing here, but with a specific part of the city; and it will be dealt with, along with other similar topics, when we discuss individual public works of this kind.

With rows of columns, then, there is no need to fill an extended trench with one continuous structure; it is better first to strengthen the seats or beds of the columns themselves and then to link each of these with an inverted arch, with its back facing downward, so that the level of the *area* becomes its chord. The ready support given by the arches will help to prevent the ground from giving way under the different loads that converge on a single point from all sides.

The northwest corner of the noble temple of Vespasian provides a good illustration of how prone columns are to sink into the ground, and of how great may be the pressure concentrated down on them. A corner of its *area* was obstructing a public thoroughfare, and in order to clear the way, they made a shortcut through the *area*, by tunneling into the fabric of the building; this left the corner resembling a wayside pillar, and although it was strengthened and supported by a buttress, the enormous weight of the building and soil subsidence eventually combined to bring about its destruction. Enough on this topic. ◆

6

40v—42

Once the foundations are laid, the walls may follow directly. But I must not neglect this advice on the completion of both the foundations and the whole wall. In buildings of immense size where the wall is to be very thick, the fabric of the wall should contain vents and flues, spaced not too far apart and extending from the foundations to the very top; these are to offer a free passage of escape to any vapors that might have built up and been trapped below ground, causing a disturbance—thus preventing them from damaging the structure in any way. The ancients would often include spiral staircases within their walls, both for this purpose and for the convenient access they would afford to the top, and perhaps also to reduce costs. But I now return to the subject.

The difference between the footings and the wall proper is this: the footings are supported by both sides of the trench and may be one mass of rubble alone, whereas the wall is composed of many parts, as I shall now explain. The main parts of the wall are these: the lower, that is to say the section immediately above the infill of the foundations[20] (this we may possibly call the podium, or platform); the middle, which encompasses and encases the wall (known as the apron); and the upper, the collar around the top of the wall (called the cornice). [21]

Among the other important, perhaps even more important, parts of the wall are the corners and inherent or additional elements such as piers, columns, and anything else that acts as a column and supports the trusses and roof arches. These all come under the description of bones. [22] So too the lips on either side of openings, which share the characteristics of both corner and column. Also included in the bones are the coverings to the openings, that is, the beams, whether straight or arched: for I call an arch nothing but a curved beam, and what is a beam but a column laid crossways? The zone stretching between these primary parts is referred to appropriately as "paneling." [23]

Throughout the wall there should be something common to all the above-mentioned parts; by this I mean the infill and the twin skins or shells on either side, one to keep the wind and the sun out, the other to protect the *area* within. The design of both infill and shell will vary according to the method of construction.

These are the kinds of construction: ordinary, reticulated, and irregular. It would be appropriate here to mention the passage in Varro where he refers to the walls around the villas in Tusculum being of stone construction, whereas in the Ager Gallicus they were of baked brick, in the country of the Sabines of unbaked brick, and in Spain of earth mixed with gravel. [24] More about this later.

Ordinary construction involves using stones (standard or, preferably, large-size) that have been cut square, and bonding these in a regular fashion along vertical and horizontal lines; there can be no method of construction stronger or more steadfast than this.

Reticulated construction involves using standard or, preferably, small-sized stones that have been cut square; these are laid not flat, but at an angle with their faces set flush and vertically aligned.

In irregular stonework, irregular stones are laid with each side, as far as its shape will allow, fitting closely into the sides of adjoining stones. This is the method of bonding used in the construction of flint roads.

However, the method of construction to be used will depend on the situation. For the facing of a plinth, for example, we will use nothing but extremely large, hard stone, cut square. Since the structure must be as solid

Construction

and firm as possible, as we said earlier, then surely this part of the wall requires greater strength and stability than any other. In fact, if at all possible, it should consist of a single stone, or at least of only so many as may give it the soundness and durability closest to that of a single one. The question of how to handle and transport these huge stones is related principally to ornament,[25] and will be dealt with in the appropriate place.

Build your wall, advises Cato, of solid stone and good mortar to at least one foot above the ground.[26] As for the rest of the wall, you may even use unbaked bricks, if you so wish. The reason for this is obvious: this part of the wall is liable to be eroded by rain dripping from the roof. But if we inspect the buildings of the ancients, we will notice that not only in this country but everywhere else, the bases of well-constructed buildings are made of hard stone; even in Egypt, where there is little fear of rain damage, the entire base of a pyramid was made of a black Theban stone. A more detailed explanation is required therefore. Just as iron, copper, and other metals, if bent repeatedly in opposite directions, will weaken and tire until they eventually break, so too any other material, if struck with alternating blows, will be badly damaged and will break. I have noticed this with bridges especially. Any side exposed to the vicissitudes of the weather, being first dried out by the rays of the sun and the breath of the wind, then moistened by the evening mist rising from the water, soon becomes rotten and riddled with decay. It is noticeable how this also happens to those parts of a wall that are low and closest to the ground: contact first with moisture and then with dust will soften and erode them. I am of the opinion therefore that the whole podium should be constructed of hard, extremely robust, and large blocks of stone, to give it the maximum protection from the frequent assaults of the elements. The question of which stones are hardest we have dealt with sufficiently in book 2. ◆

7

42—42v

It is particularly important to understand how stones are joined and bonded here, as elsewhere in the building. Like timber, stone may contain both veins and knots; and its strength may not be uniform; it is noticeable that marble, for example, will split and warp. Stone may contain abscesses and pockets of decayed matter, which eventually swell up, I imagine, by absorbing moisture from air that has been drawn in; this aggravates the pustules and leads to the scarring of columns and beams.

And so, aside from what has been stated about stone already, in the appropriate place, it must be understood that stone is formed naturally in layers, or so it is said, as we may see in liquid matter, which hardens as it gradually congeals, maintaining its original shape. As a result, the particles at the bottom are somewhat larger than those at the top, and veins are formed where one substance poured on top has adhered to another. Whether the veins consist of a mixture of scum from an earlier layer and sediment from a subsequent layer, or whether it is something quite different that has been inserted by Nature to prevent very different materials from being quite joined, it is certain that wherever they exist, the stone will be liable to crack. Moreover, it is self-evident, without looking for any less obvious reasons, that the assault of the weather will be responsible for loosening and breaking the bond of anything that has grown or been forced together. So too, the parts of stones that have been exposed to the weather will be softer and more likely to decompose.

It is advisable therefore, when laying stones, especially where the wall needs to be most robust, to ensure that only the strongest side, which will deteriorate the least, is exposed to the onslaught of the elements. It is best not to set the stones on their sides with the grain standing upright, as the weather will cause them to deteriorate in this position; rather, lay them flat, so that pressure from the load above will prevent them from splitting. Whichever side was hidden facing inward when the stone was in the quarry should now be exposed to the open; it will be richer in natural juices and stronger. But in any quarried stone the most resistant surface will be the one that has been cut not along the grain of the stone but transversely across it.

Moreover, the corners throughout the building need to be exceptionally strong, and so must be solidly constructed. In fact, unless I am mistaken, each corner represents half of the building, in that damage to one of the corners will inevitably entail the destruction of two of the sides. And a closer inspection will undoubtedly reveal that in almost every building where deterioration has set in, a structural weakness in one of the corners will have been responsible. Therefore it was sound practice that the ancients should have made their walls considerably thicker at the corner than elsewhere, and would add pilasters to reinforce the corners in colonnaded porticoes.

The reason why the corners need to be so strong is not only to enable them to support the roof—indeed, that is the task of the columns[27] rather than the corners—but mainly to help them keep the walls in position and prevent them from leaning away from the vertical in either direction. The cornerstones should be extremely hard and long, therefore, so that they extend into the adjoining wall like the elbow joint of an arm, and they should be wide enough relative to the depth of the wall to avoid the need for any infill. The bones within the wall[28] and around the openings should be treated in the same way as the corners, and strengthened according to the size of the load they may have to bear. It is most important that there be a system of claws—that is, stones projecting into each side in alternate courses—as a kind of armrest that supports the remaining paneling.[29] ◆

8

42v—43v

The paneling[30] consists of two components, which, as we mentioned above, are common to the whole wall: the skin and the infill. There are two types of skin, the inner and the outer. If the outer skin is made of hard stone, the durability of the building will be improved. I do not care how you prefer to construct the rest of the paneling—whether it be of reticulated or irregular stonework—so long as you protect it from the fierce hostility of the sun, the vexing winds, the fire and frost, by a layer of stone having great natural resistance to assault, pressure, and injury. And it is essential, as may be seen in all the buildings of antiquity, that a particularly robust material be used wherever rain, dripping from the gutters or the eaves, may be splashed; even marble can be damaged in this way, gnawed by the wind and eaten away by the damp; although most experienced architects would avoid this problem by using drainpipes to draw off the water collected on the roof.

Our ancestors observed, did they not, that in autumn leaves on the side of the tree facing south toward Auster[31] would be the first to fall. We have ourselves noticed how all buildings that collapse through old age begin to decay on the side facing Auster. Perhaps the reason for this is that the strength and heat of the sun dry the lime too soon, while the work is still fresh. In addition, the wall is constantly moistened by the southern breezes and then heated by the burning sun, causing it to weaken and decay. The wall must therefore be faced with a suitable material, capable of resisting this and other similar adversity.

In my opinion, one of the most important rules to be followed is that once it has been started, a wall should be built level and uniform round the whole structure, so that one side should not have large stones and the other small ones. For it is said that any imposed weight will put pressure on the structure, and the drying mortar have less grip, inevitably leading to cracks in the wall.

Yet I have no objections to your using soft stone for the inner skin and all of the wall facing. But whatever kind of stone is used, the skin inside and outside alike must be raised vertically and in line. It must follow the outline of the *area* exactly, without bulging out or caving in anywhere, or wavering at all: it should be straight and properly constructed throughout.

If during construction you apply the first layer of plaster to the wall while it is still fresh, whatever you add subsequently by way of rendering or stucco work will prove permanent.

There are two types of infill: one consisting of aggregate piled in to fill the gap between the two skins, the other simply consisting of common but rough stone, providing a structural center rather than just acting as infill. Both types seem to have been invented for the sake of economy, in that small, common stone of any kind is all that is required for this part of the wall. For if there were a ready supply of large, square-cut stone available, surely nobody would be willing to use small stone chips.[32]

And herein lies the difference between the paneling and the bones: with the former, the skins are filled with stone chippings and any rubble that is available—a quick task involving little more than shoveling; with the latter, irregular stones are never or only very seldom included, but ordinary-bond stonework is used to bind together the whole thickness of the wall.

I would prefer, for the sake of durability, to have each course of the whole wall composed entirely of squared stone; but however you decide to fill the gap between the two skins, as much care as possible should be taken to ensure that the courses on either side are bonded together and level. It is important also to include a number of ordinary stones, not too far apart, spanning across the wall, from the inside of one skin to the outside of the other;[33] connecting both skins to prevent the two outer surfaces that frame the work from bulging out when the infill is poured in.

When infilling the walls, the ancients made it a rule that no single section of infill rose higher than five feet without being bonded here and there with a course of long and broad squared stones; these acted as ligatures or muscles, girding and holding the structure together, and also ensured that should subsidence occur in any part of the infill, either by accident or as the result of poor workmanship, it would not bring down all the load resting on it, since the section above would have a form of fresh base on which to rest.

Finally, it is recommended—and I notice how strictly all the ancients followed this advice—that the infill not contain stone weighing more than one pound.[34] It is thought that small stones join together better and are more fit for bonding than large ones. It is appropriate to mention here what we read in Plutarch about King Numa: he divided up his people into their respective trades, in the belief that the smaller the parts into which a body is divided, the easier it is to govern and keep united.[35]

Another factor that I believe should not be overlooked is that every cavity must be filled and no pocket left empty; one of the reasons for this is to prevent any creature from gaining access and making nests there or accumulating filth and seeds, which might result in the wild-fig sprouting from within the wall. I have seen an incredible weight, a whole mass of stone, disturbed by a single root. Whatever you construct, therefore, must be carefully bound together and filled in. ◆

9

43v—44v

A number of courses of large stone should be included to act as bonds, and tie outer shell to inner, and bone to bone, just like those we mentioned that were to be inserted every five feet. There are other bonds—and these of great importance—which stretch the whole length of the wall and are intended to hold in the corners and support the work. The latter are less frequent, and I cannot recall having seen more than two or, occasionally, three in a single wall. Their main seat and place is to act as a cornice to clasp the top of the wall with a ledge of strong stones. The next rung runs immediately over the openings. Equally, they made sure that the podium at the bottom did not lack a decent cornice. Where the more common bonds, those every five feet, are more frequent, thinner stones are not amiss. But with the second type, known as cornices, because they are less frequent and the role they play more prominent, it is best to make the stones correspondingly stronger and thicker. But with either category, in general the longest, thickest, and strongest stone is required. The smaller bonds should be set square and flush with the rest of the wall; but the others should project from the facade like cornices. And their extremely long and wide stones should be set exactly level, and well connected between courses, so that those above cover the ones below like a pavement. This is how the stones should be laid: each fresh stone should be laid to fit tightly and neatly on those below, its center resting immediately above their joint and its surface spread evenly over the two. Although this pattern of laying stones should be practiced throughout the work, it is even more important that it is followed in bonds of this kind.

I notice that in reticulated work the ancients would include bonds usually of five, and certainly of no less than three, courses of masonry; of these at least one, if not all, would be of stone, the blocks no thicker than those adjoining, but longer and wider. In ordinary-bond brickwork, however, we find that they were content with a single course of double-height bricks every five feet to act as ligament. Some, we notice, have inserted long lead plates into the width of the wall to act as ligaments. But when they built with large stones, I notice that they were content with fewer bonds, and sometimes with cornices alone.

When constructing the cornice, none of the rules for bonds that we have so far mentioned should be overlooked, since it, too, binds the wall tightly together: only the firmest stone should be included, the blocks should be extremely long and wide, the joints continuous and well formed, and each course laid perfectly level and square as required. Its position demands that the cornice be treated with a great deal of care and attention, in that it binds the work together at a point where it is most likely to give way, and in addition acts as a roof to the wall below. Hence the saying: For walls of unbaked brick make a cornice of baked brick; this will cover and protect them from the damage of rain dripping from rooftops and eaves. For this reason ensure that every sort of wall is made with a firm cornice, serving as a covering, to prevent damage by rain.

We must now return to those methods of bonding and support required to unite a large number of stones into a single, solid, and compact wall. The most obvious consideration in this context is the importance of the lime, although I admit that not all stone can be bonded by lime. Marble, for example, when in contact with lime, not only loses its purity but is defiled by foul specks of blood; so prudish is marble that it will hardly tolerate contact with any but its own. Is this not so? It disdains smoke; anointed with oil it goes pale; bathed in red wine it grows murky; the sap of the chestnut tree turns it black, and stains it so deeply that no amount of scraping will remove the marks. This is why the ancients would leave marble naked in their work and avoid, as far as possible, laying any lime on it. But we shall deal with this later. ◆

The business of the experienced workman is not to demand the best possible materials, but rather to make sensible and appropriate use of those available; this then shall be the basis of our own discussion. One can tell that lime has been properly baked if, once it has been slaked and the heat has died away, a froth, like that from milk, rises from every lump. Equally, if you come across pebbly chips when you mix lime with sand, it shows that it has not been given long enough to macerate. If too much sand happens to have been added, it will be too coarse to adhere properly; if, on the other hand, less has been added than the quality and strength demand, it will become dull and clinging like mud, and difficult to manage.

Lime that has not been properly soaked, or that has some other fault, is more safely used in the foundations than elsewhere in the wall, and in the infill rather than in the outer skin. Lime with even the slightest defect should be kept away from the corners, the bones, and the ligaments, and for the arches especially only the most reliable should be used. The corners, bones, girdles, and cornices require a leaner, finer, and purer sand, particularly when they are made of polished stone. It is quite acceptable to use the lumpier sand for the infill.

Stone that is naturally dry and thirsty will go well with river sand, while any that is damp and moist will be well suited to quarry sand. I would not expose sea sand to Auster; it might do better when exposed to Septentrion.[36] Small stones need a rich mortar, dry and humorless ones a thick one, although the ancients considered a thick mix to have a better grip than a thin one in all types of construction.

Very large stones were laid, for preference, on a bed of fluid stuff. The main reason for this seems to have been not so much the need for adhesion as the need for a slippery bed that would allow the blocks to be more easily moved into position by hand during construction. On the whole it is best to make the mortar beds soft and slippery like this, as it will prevent the crushing of the stones when laboring under uneven loading. Those who have noticed that when very big stones are used in ancient buildings, the joints are pointed in red clay, have suggested that it was being used as a mortar. To me this seems unlikely, mainly because I have only seen this on one, and not both sides of the joint.

There is a further matter about walls that is not to be neglected. They must not be put up too quickly, or with hasty hands, or in one uninterrupted operation, nor should sloth be allowed to delay the work once in progress.

Construction

Rather, the work should proceed with method and purpose; speed should be combined with deliberation and proper care.

The experienced advise us not to raise the work any higher until that which has been completed already has set properly: soft and fresh work is too loose and weak to support any further addition. One can see how the swallows, who build their nests as nature taught them, having once daubed the twigs that act as base and root for the work with mud, lay the next course over this in the same way; they are never unduly hasty, but build patiently and gradually, interrupting their work until the preceding section has built up sufficient strength. It is said that lime has not hardened properly until it gives off a kind of down or florets, which anyone used to working with it will recognize.

A break in construction is necessary every now and then, the exact height being dependent on the thickness of the wall, and on location and climate. Whenever you decide to stop building, you should cover the top of the work with straw to prevent the juice from being drawn out by the wind and sun, and evaporating instead of drying in and making a timely bond. When you wish to resume work, pour clean water over it several times, until it is properly soaked, so that any dust that might encourage the growth of the wild fig is washed away. Nothing consolidates the strength and stability of the work more, than for the stone to be doused thoroughly in water. A stone, they say, is not saturated unless the inside appears completely darkened with moisture when it is broken open.

It is also recommended that during construction arches be set into the fabric of the wall wherever it may later prove expedient or desirable to introduce new openings, so that when the wall is eventually pierced, the arch will have a secure and prepared bed on which to rest. Words cannot describe how the removal of even one of the smallest stones can sometimes undermine the strength and cohesion of an entire structure. In fact we will never quite succeed in joining a new structure to an old one, without a break appearing between them; there is no need to explain that a wall weakened by such a scar is likely to collapse.

A thick wall needs no scaffolding if it is broad enough to offer the workmen footspace while building. ◆

II

45v—47

We have dealt with the standard method for construction that is raised in stone and bonded with mortar. But there are other kinds of masonry construction—some where mud, not lime, is used in the joints, and still others where the stones are fitted together without the support of any mortar, and other methods using rubble alone, or skin alone, and so on; we shall now deal with these very briefly.

Any stone[37] to be smeared with a mortar of clay should be cut square, but most importantly it must be dry; the bricks most suited to this are fired ones or, even better, unfired ones that have been well dried out. A wall of unfired brick is very healthy for those who live within, completely impervious to fire and little disturbed by earthquakes; on the other hand, unless it is reasonably thick, it will not be capable of bearing the weight of the flooring. For this reason Cato recommends that we incorporate masonry pillars in the structure to support the beams.[38] Some assert that mud, if it is to be used as mortar, should be like bitumen; and they consider the best mud to be that which dissolves slowly in water, is difficult to wash off the hands, and contracts markedly on drying. Others prefer it to be sandy, being easier to mold. This sort of work ought to be coated on the outside with lime, and on the inside, if you wish, with gypsum, or even silver clay. In order to make it adhere better, fragments of earthenware should be inserted occasionally into the cracks between the blocks during construction, so that they project like teeth and support the rendering more firmly.

Where the masonry is left uncovered, the blocks must be cut square, and they ought to be larger than usual, as well as being solid and extremely strong. There must be no infill, but the courses should be absolutely even and the joints continuous, and frequent use should be made of cramps and pins. Cramps are devices to link pairs of blocks on the same level to form a continuous row. Pins are devices to fix two blocks together one above the other so as to prevent any rows being pushed out of line. There is little objection to cramps and pins of iron, although if we inspect the works of the ancients, we will notice how iron rusts and does not last, in contrast to brass, which lasts almost for ever. I have noticed also how rust from iron can soften marble and make it crumble. Wooden cramps are also to be seen inserted into the masonry in some of the most ancient works; these I do not consider to be inferior to iron ones. Iron and bronze cramps should be fastened with lead, but wooden ones are held firmly enough in position by a shape, known, because of its appearance, as "swallow-tailed."[39]

Cramps should be inserted where they are safely out of reach of raindrops. Bronze cramps are considered to have greater resistance to old age if during casting they are mixed with a thirtieth part of tin, and they will have less to fear from rust if coated with bitumen, or even oil. It is said that iron, if tempered with white lead, gypsum, and liquid pitch, will not suffer rust. Wooden cramps, if anointed with pure wax and oil lees, will not rot. I have myself seen stones crack when a large quantity of exceedingly hot lead is poured over them to secure the cramps.

Throughout the buildings of antiquity extremely strong walls are to be found built of nothing but rubble. These are constructed in the same manner as the mud walls common in Africa and Spain: a temporary form, of paneling or wickerwork, is set up as shuttering to contain the material as it is poured in, until it has hardened. The only difference is this: with the former they pour in an almost liquid dough made of aggregate; with the latter they make the mud pliable by moistening and kneading it, and then pummel it down with beetles and their feet. The ancients would insert a rubble-like layer every three feet as bonding, consisting of reasonably large stones, mainly of the ordinary kind but including some sharp chips (round stones, however resistant to blows, are very unreliable in any structure unless it is fixed with much support). In Africa they mix the mud of their earth walls with Spanish broom or sea rushes; the resulting work has a remarkable resistance to wind and rain. Towers and lookouts built of mud on mountain ridges and dating from the time of Hannibal could still be seen in Pliny's day.[40]

Walls consisting solely of shell—as I prefer to call it, rather than skin—should be constructed using seasoned wickerwork and reed matting; this is not a work of any distinction but was often used by the plebeians of ancient Rome. The wickerwork is smeared with a mixture of mud and straw, which has been kneaded for three days. It is then dressed, as I have described already, with lime or even gypsum, and finally adorned with pictures or reliefs. If you mix your gypsum two to one with crushed tiles, it will have less to fear from being splashed. If mixed with lime, its strength will be enhanced. In the damp, frost, or cold gypsum will be utterly useless.

It remains for me to mention, as though in conclusion, an ancient rule among architects that I feel ought to be followed as advice from an oracle. It is this: Give your wall the firmest possible base; the top must be centered along the vertical and must correspond exactly to the bottom; the corners and the bones[41] must be reinforced from the ground right to the top with a stronger stone; soak your lime properly. Use no stone unless damp, and face the most exposed sides with harder stone. The structure must be built flush, level, and vertical. Make sure that each stone is laid centrally above the joint of the two below. Use complete stones for the courses on the outside and fragments for those on the infill. Lay several stones crossways to bind the rows together. Enough about the wall; I come now to the roof.

I can hardly omit a further consideration, which seems to me to have been taken more seriously by the ancients. Undoubtedly there are certain forces in nature that should not be underestimated. It is said, for example, that lightning never strikes the laurel tree, an eagle, or a seal.[42] Some may believe that if a work contains these objects it will never be struck by lightning. This I put on a par with other superstitions, such as that if you put a toad in a pot and bury it in the middle of your field, it will protect the seeds from the birds;[43] if you bring an oyster tree indoors, it will make childbearing difficult;[44] if you keep the leaves of the Lesbian euonymos under your roof, it will bring on dysentery, which will prove fatal.[45]

To return to the argument. We must now take up the discussion that we touched upon earlier, when dealing with the lineaments of buildings. ◆

Some roofs are exposed to the sky and others not; of these some may be composed of straight lines, others of curved ones, and others of a mixture of the two. A further distinction, which is appropriate here, is that a roof may be built either of timber or of stone. We shall begin our discussion by establishing exactly which features are common to the design of all roofs. They are the bones, muscles, infill paneling, skin, and crust,[46] and can be recognized in any roof just as in any wall; but let us consider whether this is really the case or not.

To begin with timber roofs composed of straight lines. In order to support the roof it is necessary to lay strong beams spanning from wall to wall. And, as we have just mentioned, there is no doubt that beams are columns laid crossways. Where bones should be, there is a beam. But, if finance permitted it, would not anyone prefer to make the work as strong as possible, of solid bone, so to speak, by making the columns continuous and linking all the beams together? We must take costs into account, however, and reckon anything that can be dispensed with without impairing the structural stability of the work superfluous. Therefore spaces are left between the beams, then cross-beams are added, and from these span the lathing and anything else similar. Each of these can quite acceptably be considered ligaments. To these are added planks, or wider boards, which surely take the place of infill paneling.[47] Equally, the pavement or the tiling undeniably serves as the outside skin, whereas the ceiling above our heads serves as the inside one.

If this is agreed, let us investigate whether they share any common feature, since in so doing we might more easily understand what is appropriate in the case of stone roofs. Let us then deal with them as briefly as the context will allow.

It is appropriate to mention here how unimpressed I am with modern-day architects, who, in order to accommodate the floor beams, leave gaps in the very bones of the wall and then, when the wall is complete, insert the heads of the beams into them; as a result the wall has less strength, and the house less protection from the ravages of fire, because it gives the flames easy access from room to room. I prefer therefore the custom of the ancients whereby sturdy corbels were fixed into the wall, and onto them were set the heads of the above-mentioned beams. But if you wish the walls to be connected to the beams, there is no shortage of cramps, bronze clips, and hooks that are eminently suitable for attaching to the corbels.

The beam must be perfectly intact and sound, quite free of any defect, especially midway along its length. If you position your ear at one end, and the other end is struck several ringing blows that sound dull and flat, this is a sure indication that the inside is diseased. Any beam containing knots should be rejected, especially if the knots are frequent or clustered together. The part closest to the marrow should be planed and laid upwards, whereas the lower surface of the beam should be stripped of bark or planed as little as possible. But any side with any defect running across it should be set on top. If any side has a crack running right down its length, it should not be left as one of the vertical surfaces, but be made the top or better the bottom. If you need to bore through a beam or perhaps to make notches in it, spare the central part of its length, and do not harm the lower surface.

If, however, you need to construct a twin beam, as are common in basilicas, leave a gap of several inches between the two beams, to allow them to breathe and to prevent any damage from friction. It is useful to lay the beams in opposite directions, so that their heads are not resting on the same pillow, but the foot of one rests next to the head of the other. In this way the stability and strength of the foot of one beam will compensate for the weakness in the lighter part of the other. The beams should be related, if at all possible; that is, they should be of the same type of timber, from the same forest, raised under the same climatic conditions, and felled on the same day, so that by having the same natural strength they will perform their function equally. The seat on which the beams rest ought to be totally level, and as solid and as strong as possible; take care when setting the beams in position that no lime touches the timber, and allow the beam to breathe freely on all sides, to prevent damage being caused by the least contact, or rot setting in because it is enclosed. As a pillow for the beams set down a layer of fern, which is a dry plant, or charcoal, or even better, the lees of oil mixed with olive stones.

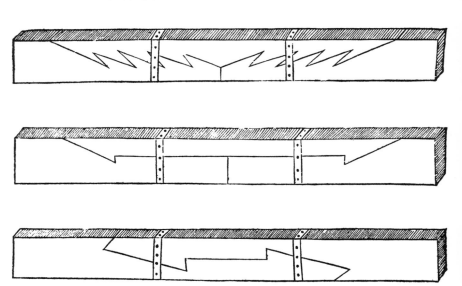

The binding of timber beams.

If, however, the trees are too small to make a complete beam out of a single trunk, join several together into a composite beam, in such a manner that they acquire the inherent strength of an arch, that is, so that the load will not compress the upper line of the composite beam nor stretch the lower line, which should act like a cord, to hold the trunks in tension, their opposing faces notched into one another.

Joists and other wooden members made from off-cuts of the beam are judged on the beam's condition and soundness. Panels that are too dense are considered unsuitable, in that as soon as they begin to warp, the nails are forced out. However thin the planks, it is recommended that the nails be used in pairs, especially for external boarding, where the corners, center, and sides must be held tight.

It is recommended that where nails need to bear transverse weight, thicker ones be used; elsewhere thinner ones will be quite acceptable, though they must be longer and have wider heads. I have found that brass nails last longer in the open air or in humid conditions, whereas iron ones are stronger indoors and in dry conditions. But when it comes to fixing flooring, wooden pins are preferred.

All that we have said about wooden roofs applies equally to masonry ones. Any stone with veins or blemishes running across it should be rejected and not used as a beam, but only as a column; or, if the marks are only moderate and light, it may be used in the construction, but the sides on which the marks appear should face upward. It is better that any veins in a beam run lengthways rather than crossways. Stone panels should not be made too thick, mainly because of their weight. Planks, posts, and beams used in either timber or masonry roofs should not be so thin or set so far apart, that they cannot bear their own weight and the load they carry; yet equally they should not be so stout and closely spaced as to leave the work inelegant and ungainly. But of the form and grace of buildings we shall speak elsewhere.

What has been said so far about rectilinear roofs will suffice; although I might perhaps add one piece of advice that I consider very important, whatever the work. The physicians[48] have noticed that Nature was so thorough in forming the bodies of animals, that she left no bone separate or disjointed from the rest. Likewise, we should link the bones and bind them fast with muscles and ligaments, so that their frame and structure is complete and rigid enough to ensure that its fabric will still stand on its own, even if all else is removed. ◆

I3

48v—49v

Now I come to roofs composed of curved lines. Let us consider the ways in which they correspond exactly to rectilinear ones. A curvilinear roof is made up of arches; and the arch, as we have demonstrated, is but a curved beam. Ligaments also recur here, and material for gaps. But I wish to clarify what exactly the arch is—what are the parts of which it is composed. The construction of the arch was learned, I suppose, when man noticed how two beams whose heads leaned against each other, while their feet were splayed apart, would be strong enough to stand up, provided they were joined and subjected to equal loading; he was pleased with this discovery and began to use this method to build double-pitched roofs for buildings. Then, perhaps as a result of the restrictions that the shortness of the beam imposed on his attempts to cover a larger *area*, he set an intermediate beam to span across the tops of the two trunks and form a shape similar to the Greek π; this additional piece was probably referred to as the wedge. The experiment proved successful, and so he added further wedges of this kind to form an arch, whose shape he found very pleasing. He then applied this method of fabricating the arch to masonry construction, and by adding further wedges he eventually formed an entire arch; therefore the arch must be recognized as a composition of several wedges, some of which provide the base for the arch with their lower ends, others lie on their backs and form the backbone, while others constitute the ribs and complete the curve.

It would not be out of place to repeat what we said in book 1. There are many different kinds of arches. There is the regular arch, which consists of a complete semicircle, and whose chord runs through the center of the circle. Then there is the one resembling a beam more than an arch. This we call an incomplete arch, because it is not a full semicircle but only a portion of it. Its chord passes not through the center but above it. There is also the composite arch, which some call the angular or pointed arch; this is composed of two incomplete arches, and its chord passes through the centers of two intersecting curves.

It is self-evident that the regular arch is the firmest; this can be proved further by reason and experiment. In fact, I do not see how the arch could possibly fall apart on its own, unless one of its wedges were to push another out of line; this would be most unlikely, as the wedges actually support and reinforce one another, and even if it should begin to happen, the natural thrust of either their support or their own weight will prevent the wedges from giving way. This is why Varro judges that in any vaulted structure the right is held up by the left, and the left is held up by the right.[49] Let us consider the matter: how can the uppermost wedge, which sits alone at the top of the spine, possibly be strong enough to thrust out the other wedges on either side? Or how could the outer wedges push the top one out, once it has been set in position? Those next in line along the ribs will be held in position quite easily by equilibrium. Finally, how could the other wedges, which provide support lower down, possibly move when they are held in position by the weight of those above? Thus, regular arches require no ties, because they are quite capable of supporting themselves, whereas incomplete arches must be reinforced either with an iron chain or by stretches of walling on each side that have the equivalent strength; the length of this walling should preferably be no less than that required to complete the semicircle from which the incomplete arch has been taken. The architects of antiquity never failed to take this precaution, and wherever possible would integrate any incomplete arches into the flank of a wall. Another remarkable precaution they took, wherever the opportunity presented itself, was to insert incomplete arches above any straight beams, then above these incomplete arches, regular ones; these were intended to assist the incomplete ones below, and to protect them from any damage that the imposed load might cause. Composite arches are never to be found in the works of the ancients. Some consider them necessary for openings in towers, to act as a prow to divide the thrust of any excessive loading, although composite arches are in fact strengthened and not overwhelmed by weight from above.

I would have the blocks of masonry for the wedges[50] that form the arches squared and as large as possible. For within any body the parts that have grown together and been joined naturally are more difficult to break asun-

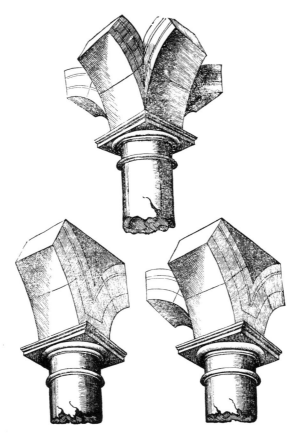

Convergence of four, two, and three arches over a capital.

Construction

der than those that man has used his strength and skill to force together and fuse. And the blocks on either side must be equal, so that the right balances the left in appearance, size, weight, and so on. With a series of arches springing from columns, as with the openings of a portico, the wedge from which two or more arches may spring together should not be divided into twin blocks, or whatever the number of the arches, but it should consist of one and the same block, quite undivided, so that it contains the base of the arches on all sides. If the second pair of wedges, set on top of the first wedge, are extremely large blocks of stone, make sure that they are linked, their backs meeting along a straight line. The third layer, set over the second pair, should be laid level, following the principles of good walling, with even joints on either side, so that it serves both arches to which it is joined and holds in their wedges. Make sure that throughout the arch the lines of contact and the joints point toward the center of the arch. Those with experience would always use a single, integral, large block of stone for the keystone; but if the wall is so thick that it is impossible to use a whole wedge of this kind, then it is no longer an arch; rather it is becoming a vault, which we shall call the barrel vault. ◆

<h2>14</h2>

49v—52

There are several different types of vaulting. We must inquire in what way they differ, and of what lines they are composed. To make myself as clear and straightforward as possible, which I have endeavored to be throughout this book, it will be necessary for me to invent new names. It has not escaped my notice that the poet Ennius refers to "the vast vault of the heavens,"[51] and that Servius calls every vault made in the manner of a ship's keel "a cavern."[52] But I ask this one favor, that in this book at any rate we consider acceptable Latin anything that is both accurate and easy to understand.

These are the various types of vaulting: the barrel, the camerated, and the perfectly spherical,[53] as well as any others consisting of a certain part of these three.[54] Of these the spherical by its very nature can be set only on walls that arise from a circular plan; the camerated requires a square plan, whereas the barrel covers any rectangular *area*, short or long, as may be seen in crypto-porticoes. Any vault constructed like a hole bored through a mountain shall be called a tunnel vault or barrel vault, because of the similarity of its name.[55] The barrel vault, then, is like a series of arches added one to the other, or like a curved beam stretched laterally, and hence it may be compared to a wall bent over our heads for protection. However, if a vault such as this, running from north to south, were completely transversed by another vault, running from east to west, it would create a vault resembling curved horns running out into the corners, which is therefore called "camerated."[56] But if the apexes of many identical arches were to meet at a point in the center, a vault would be created that is like the heavens; this then we prefer to call the perfectly spherical.

The vaults formed out of those parts mentioned are these: If nature had divided the hemisphere of the heavens into two parts by a straight vertical section running from east to west, she would produce two vaults fitting a semicircular niche. However, if nature had bounded the hemisphere of the heavens with lines running from the eastern corner to the southern one, from the southern to the western, from that to the northern, then from the northern to the original eastern corner by the same method, and then cropped them away, the vault left in the middle would resemble a billowing sail, and we would therefore call it a sail vault. Any vault that consists of several sections of barrel vaulting meeting together, such as may be seen spanning hexagonal or octagonal *areae*, we shall call an angular spherical vault.

The same method of construction should be followed for the vaults as is used for the walls. In fact, the bones[57] within the wall continue unbroken right up to the top of the vault; they are constructed in the same way and are set a correspondingly similar distance apart. The ligaments stretch from bone to bone, and the section between is filled in with paneling. But there is this one difference: in a wall the individual stones and courses are set and laid together in straight lines along the horizontal and vertical, but in a vault the courses are laid along a curved line, with the joints of all the stones pointing toward the centers of their respective arches. For the bones the ancients would almost always use baked bricks, generally two feet in length. It is advisable to complete the infill paneling with an extremely light stone, to prevent any eccentric loading putting a strain on the wall. I notice, however, that the bones were not made continuously solid by some architects; instead they would be interspersed here and there with bricks standing on edge, their ends fitting into one another like the teeth of a comb, as though someone were interlocking the fingertips of his right hand with those of his left. The middle they would fill in with aggregate, often of pumice, commonly regarded as the most suitable infill material for vaults.

For the construction of arches and vaults it is necessary to make use of centering. This is a form of temporary, rough wooden framework shaped like a curved line, with wickerwork, reeds, or any other cheap material laid down as a covering or skin; its function is to support the vaulting during construction, until it has hardened. The perfect sphere, however, is the one vault that does not require centering, being composed not only of arches but also of rings.[58] It is impossible to describe or even conceive in the mind the countless lines of mutual support, intersecting at equal and unequal angles, that these two provide. Consequently, wherever you insert a block within a vault of this kind, you realize that you are positioning a wedge for several arches and rings. And as you lay ring over ring, and arch beside arch, can you imagine the work ever being liable to give way, and if so, from which point, especially when all the wedges are inclined toward the center with equal force and pressure? Many of the architects of antiquity exploited the inherent strength of this structure, and would lay only a simple earthenware cornice every few feet, then fill in the remainder of the vault somewhat hastily, by just pouring in a cement mix. I would much rather that care be taken during the construction of the vault to ensure that the rings are not too infrequent and that they are connected one above the other, and so too the arches, side by side, with the same technique that is used to bond stones together in the wall, especially if quarry sand is in short supply and the work is exposed to sea breezes or Auster.[59]

The angular spherical vault may also be raised without centering, provided a perfectly spherical vault is inserted within its thickness, although it is particularly important that you use fixings to bind the weaker parts of the main vault to the stronger parts of the inner one tightly. It will be useful nonetheless, once one or two stone rings have been laid and have set firm, to fix below them some light thongs and eyes to which to attach sufficient centering to support a few feet of rings above, until they have dried. Then, once these also have hardened, the centering should be moved up a certain number of rows to construct the section above, until the work is complete.[60]

Cross vaults and likewise barrel vaults both require the support of centering. But I would prefer the first few courses and the feet of the arches to have a solid base. I do not approve of the practice whereby the entire wall is raised, leaving consoles as the only eventual support for the vault: it is far too weak and unreliable. If you want my advice, you should construct the arch and the wall to which it is fastened together, row by row, so that the work is tied by several connections of the strongest possible kind. The space left between the curving vault and the wall to which it is attached, which the workmen know as the hip, should be filled not with earth and dry stone fragments, but with ordinary solid stonework to keep it continually bonded with the wall. Also, I am impressed by the attempt to reduce weight by placing in the hips empty earthenware water vessels, which are cracked and turned upside down to prevent them from collecting water and gaining weight; over these is then poured a light but nonetheless strong stone aggregate.

In short, with every type of vault, we should imitate Nature throughout, that is, bind together the bones and interweave flesh with nerves running along every possible section: in length, breadth, and depth, and also obliquely across. When laying the stones to the vault, we should, in my opinion, copy the ingenuity of Nature.

Having completed the vault it remains to cover it, one of the most important elements in the whole building process, and one that is as vital as it is difficult; it is an operation that requires constant care and attention, and this is what we must now discuss. First, however, it seems relevant to include some advice that applies specifically to the construction of the vault. The manner in which vaults are constructed may vary: arches and vaults that are put together using the support of centering must be constructed speedily and without the least interruption; those put together without centering must be constructed with pauses after almost every course, to allow them time to set, and to avoid any new section working loose or slipping out of place because the one below has not gained sufficient strength. Also with vaults built over centering, it is useful to loosen slightly the supports for the centering as soon as the last wedges have closed up the vault. This prevents those wedges that have been recently set in position from floating around in their mortar bedding, but allows them to settle themselves and to reach equilibrium; otherwise the work will not set compactly enough, and cracks will be left as it settles. This, then, is how it should be done: the centering should not be removed straightaway, but should be gradually eased over the days, for if you take it away too soon, the result will be poor. After several days, depending on the size of the work, loosen it further. Continue like this until all the stone wedges in the vault have bonded, and the work has hardened. This is how the loosening should be done: when you set up your centering on posts, or wherever convenient, first position under the feet of the centering wooden wedges tapered like the head of an axe; then, when you want to loosen the work, you may knock these wedges gradually out of place with a mallet, as much as you wish, and without the least danger.

Finally, I recommend that the centering not be removed until winter has completely run its course. One of the reasons for this is to prevent damp from rain weakening and loosening the work, causing it to collapse; although it could be said that nothing is better for a vault than for it to absorb plenty of water and never go thirsty. Enough on this subject. ◆

I shall now turn to the covering of the roof. If I judge correctly, surely the most ancient function of the whole building was to provide a shelter from the burning sun and the storms raging down from heaven. And it is not the wall, nor the area, nor any other part that is responsible for maintaining this service for you, but primarily, as must be obvious, the outer membrane of the roof; yet, despite all the determination and skill that man has invested in his attempt to strengthen and reinforce it against the assaults of the weather, he has scarcely succeeded in protecting it as much as necessity demands. Nor do I imagine that this would be easy, faced as it is with the unremitting barrage not only of rain but also of ice and heat, and, most harmful of all, wind. Could anyone possibly hold out against enemies so relentless and so fierce for any great length of time? As a result, some decay straightaway,

15

52—52v

others crumble, others weigh down the wall, others split and fall apart, and others are washed away, so that no metal, however invincible it might otherwise prove against the ravages of the weather, could here possibly endure so continuous an onslaught.

Man met the inevitable as best he could, making use of whatever local material Nature had put at his disposal. As a result several different techniques in covering the roof have arisen. The Pyrgi, Vitruvius relates, used reeds as a covering, and, around Marseilles, clay kneaded with straw was used.[61] The Thelophagi, neighbors of the Garamantes, covered their vaults with a layer of shells, according to Pliny.[62] In much of Germany boarding is used. In Belgium a white stone is used for tiling, which is easier to cut into thin sheets than wood. In Liguria and Tuscany they cover their houses with slabs cut from a scaly stone. Others have tried paving slabs, which we shall deal with later.

Nevertheless, of all the techniques man has tried, his wit and energy have yet to discover anything more suitable than earthenware tiles. Frost will cause paviors' work to roughen, split, and settle; lead melts under the heat of the sun; copper, if laid in heavy plates, is costly, and if thin, may be damaged by the wind, and worn and eaten away by verdigris. It is said that the inventor of the tile was a Cypriot called Cinyras, the son of Agrippa.[63]

There are two kinds of tile: one is flat, measuring a foot in width by a cubit in length, with a rough ridge on either side a ninth of the width; the other is curved like the greaves that protect the legs; both are wider where they receive the flowing rain and narrower where they throw it off. But flat tiles are better, in that they can be joined in line and perfectly level without dipping on one side, and without any valleys, ridges, gaps, or anything to obstruct the rain as it runs off. If the surface of the roof covers a vast expanse, larger tiles will be required; otherwise the channels will be insufficient and the rivulets of rainwater will overflow. To prevent gales from dislodging the tiles, I would recommend that, particularly in public works, they be set firm in a bed of lime. In private ones, though, it will be sufficient simply to reinforce the guttering against the wind, in that it is easier to repair broken tiles, if they are not bedded.

There is another very suitable type of roof covering. With wooden roofs, instead of boarding, earthenware panels are fixed with gypsum to the transverse lathing; on top of these are laid plain-tiles held in position with lime. This produces a work with great resistance to fire, and one that is extremely convenient for the inhabitants; it will be even cheaper if, instead of panels, Greek reeds are laid and held down with lime.

Tiles that are to be fixed with lime, especially those for public works, should not be used until they have been exposed to the frost and sun for at least two years; if a weak one is laid in position, it cannot be removed without a great deal of effort.

It would be helpful here to mention a novel and useful technique; Diodorus, the historian, mentions that it was employed for the famous hanging gardens of Syria.[64] A layer of reeds daubed with asphalt was laid over the beams, and on top of this two courses of baked bricks held together with gypsum. The third layer consisted of lead plates welded together to prevent any moisture from reaching the first of the bricks. ◆

16

52v—54v

I now come to deal with the pavement, since it shares the same characteristics as the roof. Some are exposed to the sky, some are built of composite beams, and others not. But in each case the surface onto which they are laid must be solid and exact in its lines.

A surface exposed to the sky should have a fall of at least two inches in every ten feet. It should be so designed that the water running off is either collected in cisterns or drawn off into drains. If the water cannot be emptied into the sea or a river, find suitable places to dig wells deep enough to reach running water, then fill up the holes with pebbles. If even this is not possible, the final advice is to make a generous pit, throw in some coal, then fill it up with sand. This will absorb and remove any superfluous water.

If the *area* consists of piled-up earth, it must be leveled off accurately and covered with a layer of rubble rammed into place. But if the surface has a composite timber base, then further boarding should be laid crossways, rammed down, and covered with rubble to a depth of one foot. Some think that a layer of broom or fern should be laid as a base to prevent damage to the timber from its coming into contact with any lime. If the rubble is new, mix it three parts to one with lime; if old, five to two. Once it has been laid, it must be consolidated by being continually beaten with beetles. A pulp consisting of crushed tiles mixed three to one with sand is then laid over this to a depth of six inches. Finally, arrangements of marble or herringbone tiles or mosaic should be laid on top, in line and level. The work will be better protected if a layer of tiles bonded with lime, soaked in oil, is set between the hardcore and the dough.

For pavements not in the open Varro recommends the following for its exceptional ability to stay dry.[65] Dig to a depth of two feet, and pack down the soil, then lay a pavement of either rubble or brickwork. Leave a few openings for the water to drain away along channels; pile on some coal, then once this has been packed down and consolidated, cover it with a cake consisting of a mixture of gravel, lime, and ashes to a depth of a foot and a half.

All that we have mentioned so far is derived partly from Pliny,[66] but principally from Vitruvius.[67] I shall now refer to information that I have been able to gather myself about pavements, by careful and diligent inspection of the works of the ancients. And, I must confess, I have learned more on my own than I have from the author of any book.

I shall begin with the outermost surface. It is very difficult to make this strong enough and to prevent it from cracking. While it is still damp and full of moisture, the sun and the wind may dry out its outer surface, producing a result similar to the patches of mud we see deposited after a flood: their skins shrink, leaving cracks that cannot be repaired. There is no way to reset the parts that have dried out, while the damp parts yield and give way under the slightest tension.

I notice that the ancients used mainly baked clay or stone for their crusts. I have seen tiles, particularly where they would not be trodden on, measuring one cubit square, and bonded with lime mixed with oil. Small bricks are also to be seen, one inch thick and two inches wide, their length twice their width, placed edge-on in a herringbone pattern.[68] Stone surfaces are to be seen everywhere, in the form either of large marble slabs or of smaller sections and cubes. Old pavements may be seen with crusts consisting of a homogeneous mixture of lime, sand, and crushed tiles, mixed together in equal quantities, I imagine. I know that such crusts will be all the stronger and more steadfast if you add a fourth part of crushed Tiburtine.

Some prefer pozzolana powder (called "lapillum") for this. You may discover also that through beating the crust of a homogeneous pavement constantly for several days, it will acquire a density and hardness almost greater than that of stone. Certainly if the crust is sprinkled with limewater and spread with linseed oil, it attains a hardness comparable to that of glass and is unaffected by any weather. Pavements, it is said, containing oil worked into the lime are impervious to anything harmful.

I notice that a mortar of small tile chips in lime was laid under the crust to a depth of two or three inches. Below that was a type of infill composed partly of broken tiles and partly of stone chippings resulting from the workman's chisel. This layer was almost a foot deep. I have sometimes noticed a course of thin earthenware bricks between this and the layer above. Finally, at the bottom is a base of stones no larger than the size of a fist. Stones from a stream, referred to as "manly," such as pebbles, flint, and vitreous stones, dry as soon as they are out of water; but tiles, tufa, and so on retain their moisture for a long time. And some therefore maintain that if the base of the pavement is composed of this type of stone, no damp rising from the earth will ever quite reach the crusts. We may also find little pillars, a foot and a half high, laid out on the ground in rectilinear rows at two-foot spacings, and consisting of baked clay tiles; on these the pavement was constructed, as we have just described. But this type of paving is particularly appropriate to baths, and we shall deal with it in the appropriate place.

Pavements rejoice in being laid in damp and humid conditions, and remain stronger and more intact in the shade and the damp. They are most vulnerable to infirm soil, and also to being dried out too quickly. Just as the earth in the fields, which hardens with continual rain, likewise pavements, if they are kept saturated, will be welded together into a single, complete solid. Wherever rain drips from the drainpipes of the roof onto the pavement, the crust must be made of sound and very solid stone, to prevent the continual malice, so to speak, of the falling drops from wearing away and impairing it.

With pavements laid on top of framed wooden floors, care must be taken to ensure that the bones that provide the support are robust enough and that they all have the same strength. Otherwise, if any point in a wall or beam is stronger than the rest, there the pavement will split and be damaged. The strength and vitality of timber does not always remain constant, but varies with the conditions: timber will soften in the damp, but it will regain its rigidity and strength in the dry; and so, clearly, if any of the weaker parts strain and subside under the weight, the pavement will split. But enough on this subject.

There is, however, one pertinent consideration that I would not wish to pass over. The digging of the foundations and their infilling, the raising of the wall and the laying of the covering, should all be conducted at different times of the year and under different climatic conditions. The best moment to dig foundations is at the time of the Dog Star or during autumn itself, when the ground is dry and there is no water to flow into the trenches to impede the work. It is not at all unsuitable to fill in the foundations at the beginning of spring, especially if they are deep, as the earth will stand by and give them sufficient protection from the heat of the summer. The beginning of winter, however, is by far the best time to fill them in, except in polar regions and other cold places, where they will immediately freeze rather than set. The wall also dislikes excessive heat, biting cold, sudden frost, and, above all, northerly winds. The vault prefers an even and temperate climate, until the work has gained sufficient strength and has hardened. The most opportune time to set the outer shell is at the rising of the Pleiades, and, in general, any period when Auster[69] is blowing strong and full of moisture, because if the surface to which you apply the skin or rendering is not thoroughly damp, it will not adhere, but will peel, tear, and come away everywhere, leaving the work disfigured and full of blemishes. The surface and rendering, however, will be dealt with more thoroughly in the appropriate place.

Now that we have dealt with all the general characteristics of our subject matter, let us proceed to what remains to be considered in greater detail. First we shall deal with the various kinds of buildings, their differences and their individual requirements, then with the ornamentation of buildings, and then finally with how to repair and restore their defects, whether they result from faulty workmanship or from damages inflicted by the weather. ◆

Here Begins the Fourth Book of Leon Battista Alberti. On Public Works.

It is obvious that buildings were made to serve man. If our surmise is correct, man first made himself a shelter to protect himself and his own from the assault of the weather. Men's appetite then grew beyond what was essential for their well-being, to include all that would contribute to their unbridled demand for every comfort. They became so interested in and excited by the opportunities presented, that they conceived and eventually realized buildings intended to cater to pleasure alone. And so, if anyone were to comment that some buildings were designed for life's necessities, others offer themselves for practical requirements, while still others are for occasions of pleasure, he would not perhaps be all that wrong.

Yet, when we look around at the quantity and the variety of buildings, it is easy to understand that they were not all developed for this first purpose, nor indeed for the other reasons, but that the range of different works depends principally on the variation within human nature. If we wish to give an accurate account of the various types of buildings (as was our intention) and of their constituent elements, our whole method of investigation must open and begin here, by considering human variety in greater detail; since buildings arose on man's account, and for his needs they vary; so that they may be dealt with more clearly by distinguishing their individual characteristics.

We shall consult therefore the experienced men of antiquity, who founded republics and laid down their laws, to find out what they had to say about divisions within society, since they devoted zeal, diligence, and care to questions of this nature, and their conclusions have drawn much praise and admiration.

Theseus, reports Plutarch, divided the citizens into two groups, those who laid down and interpreted divine and human law, and those who worked at the trades.[1] Solon classified the citizens according to the size and extent of their property and wealth, and, in his eyes, anyone who receives less than 300 measures yearly from his land, he did not consider worthy of full citizenship.[2] The Athenians ranked men learned and skilled of intellect or experience highest, followed by ploughmen, and finally artisans.

Romulus distinguished the knights and the patricians from the plebeians, and Numa in turn divided the plebeians according to their various trades.[3] In Gaul, the lot of the plebeian was held to be almost that of the slave. Caesar relates that the rest were either soldiers or given over to wisdom and religion; the latter were known as Druids.[4] Among the Pantheans the priests were supreme, followed by the farmers, and then the soldiers together with herdsmen and shepherds.[5] The Britons were divided into four classes, the first being the royal families, the second the priests, the third the soldiers, and the last the common people. The Egyptians ranked their priests highest, then their royalty and governors, and in third place their warriors, while the remainder were divided up into farmers, herdsmen, artisans, and even, according to Herodotus, mercenaries and sailors.[6] They say that Hippodamus also divided his state into three: craftsmen, farmers, and combat troops.[7]

However, Aristotle seems to have been in favor of selecting the most worthy of the common people to serve as councillors, magistrates, and judges, and then of dividing the remaining people into farmers, craftsmen, merchants, mercenaries, cavalrymen, foot soldiers, and sailors.[8] According to the historian Diodorus, the state of India does not appear to have been very different: it was composed of priests, ploughmen, herdsmen, artisans, soldiers, ephors, and those who presided over public councils.[9]

Plato states that it will depend on the disposition of those in power, as to whether a nation is peaceful and eager for harmony and quiet, or passionate and warlike. So that divisions within society as a whole correspond to those between the different parts of the soul:[10] one group governs the whole state using reason and wisdom, the second pursues injustice with arms, the third affords and supplies sustenance for the previous two.[11]

These brief extracts I have digested from the many writings of the ancients. And from them I draw this lesson: that all the above are different parts of the state, and that each should be designated a different type of building. The following observations may be worth making, to keep the rest of the discussion as clear as we intended.

If anyone wishes to divide mankind into categories, surely the first thought to come to mind would be that it is not possible to treat the population taken as a whole in the same way as inhabitants of any one place divided into their constituent groups. Second, having observed Nature's own example, the groups should be distinguished one from another according to the features which separate individuals.

There is no respect in which man differs more from man, than that which differentiates him so markedly from the beasts: his power of reason and his knowledge of the noble arts, and also, if you wish, his prosperity and good fortune. Few mortals stand out and excel in all these gifts at once. Herein lies our first distinction: a few individuals stand out from the entire community, some of whom are renowned for their wisdom, good counsel, and ingenuity, others well known for their skill and practical experience, and others famous for their wealth and prosperity. Who would deny them the most important roles within the state? And so to these men of outstanding ability and great insight should be entrusted the care of government. They should administer divine matters according to the principles of religion, set up laws to regulate justice and equity, show us the way to a good and blessed life, and keep watch to protect and eventually increase the authority and dignity of their fellow citizens. When they have been worn out, as may happen, by the years, and are inclined more to a life of contemplation than to one of action, they might agree upon a suitable, useful, and necessary policy, and then should entrust its execution to those of practical experience who are free to put it into effect, so that they in turn can bring benefit to their country. Meanwhile, the latter, having undertaken their task, should dutifully carry it out with dexterity and diligence at home, and with application and patience abroad: they should give judgment, lead armies, exercise their own strength and diligence, and husband those of their men. Finally, they will acknowledge that were the means to carry out their functions not available, their efforts would be frustrated, and the next in line are therefore those who, either by working the land or by trading, supply those means. All other citizens should, within reason, owe allegiance to and respect the wishes of the leading group.

Perhaps this evidence is sufficient to demonstrate that some buildings are appropriate for society as a whole, others for the foremost citizens, and yet others for the common people. Then again, among the foremost citizens those presiding over domestic councils require different buildings to those involved in executing decisions or those engaged in accumulating wealth.

As we said before, each example owes a part to necessity and a part to commodity, but since it is buildings we speak of, let us give an equal part to the delight of the mind, given that in the introduction we set out to derive the origins of these divisions according to the first principles of philosophy. We must therefore now discuss what is appropriate for the people as a whole, what for the few important citizens, and what for the many less important ones.

But where shall we begin such an undertaking? Should we follow the gradual development of that which man first built for himself, the wretched poor man's hut, right up to those vast works that may be seen today: theaters, baths, and temples? Certainly it was a long time before the nations of the world needed to surround their towns with walls. The historians relate that when Dionysius wandered through India, there were no walled cities to be found among those people.[12] And Thucydides writes that once there were no defensive walls in Greece.[13] Likewise, in France, at the time of Caesar, the whole Burgundian nation was not gathered in towns, but in scattered villages.[14] Really, the first city that I find mentioned was Biblus, where the Phoenicians lived, and round whose houses Saturn drew a wall; although Pomponius recounts that Iope was founded even before the flood.[15] While the Ethiopians occupied Egypt, according to Herodotus, they would not kill any criminals, but forced them to dig mounds of earth around the villages where they lived;[16] this gave rise to the claim that it was in Egypt that cities were first founded. But we shall deal with this elsewhere. Now, although it is said that everything in Nature arose from lowly beginnings, I wish to start with grander matters. ◆

Everyone relies on the city and all the public services that it contains. If we have concluded rightly, from what the philosophers say, that cities owe their origin and their existence to their enabling their inhabitants to enjoy a peaceful life, as free from any inconvenience or harm as possible, then surely the most thorough consideration should be given to the city's layout, site, and outline. Yet opinions vary on these matters.

Caesar writes that the Germans counted it a great advantage to have their territory surrounded by a vast wilderness, because they thought it an effective measure in preventing any sudden incursions by the enemy.[17] The historians think that the Egyptian king Sesostris was only deterred from invading Europe by the scarcity of provisions and the difficulty of the terrain.[18] The Assyrians were never subjected by any foreign king, because they were defended by desert and arid land.[19] Likewise the Arabians have always remained free of any foreign invasion or assault, because their country has insufficient water or agricultural produce.[20]

According to Pliny, the only reason why Italy had been invaded by so many foreign armies was the popularity of her wine and figs. We might add that an overindulgence in anything concerned with pleasure is, according to Crates, harmful to old and young alike: it makes the old cruel, and the young effeminate.[21] The territory of the Emerici—according to Livy—is extremely fertile, but, as often happens with productive land, it rears a cowardly nation.[22] On the other hand, the Ligii are thoroughly industrious and robust, because they live in a stony land that forces them to spend their days continually at work, with very little nourishment.[23]

This is why some might not be adverse to founding their cities in a region such as theirs, with rough and difficult terrain. Others would have it different, and would prefer a region so well endowed with the benefits and gifts of Nature, that there would be nothing wanting either for their essential requirements or for their comfort and pleasure; their ancestral laws and customs, they maintain, could ensure that proper use be made of such resources. They also consider that the pleasures of life are sweeter when available at home than when they must be sought from elsewhere. For this reason they would no doubt prefer somewhere like the country around Memphis, which, according to Varro, enjoyed so healthy a climate that no tree or even vine lost its leaves during the year;[24] or that below Mount Taurus, exposed to the north wind, where Strabo claims that bunches of grapes are to be found two cubits long, and each vine will fill an amphora with wine, and a single fig tree will provide 70 modii of fruit;[25] or that found in India and the Hyperborean island of the ocean, whose fields, Herodotus claims, will yield two harvests a year;[26] or that in Lusitania, where the falling seeds yield crops time after time, or rather land like that at Talge on Mount Caspium, where the fields bear crops even if they have not been cultivated.[27] But such phenomena are uncommon, and easier to wish for than to find.

And so the foremost authors of antiquity, who recorded other people's views and their own ideas on the subject, considered the ideal location for a city to be one that provided for all its requirements from its own territory and would not need to import anything, as far as human needs could be calculated and circumstances would allow, and that would be so well fortified by its boundaries that no enemy could easily invade, or prevent you from dispatching your own soldiers abroad as you wish. A city such as this, they agree, could both preserve its liberty and also greatly increase its dominion. What should my example be? Egypt is praised above all for being so utterly inaccessible and so wonderfully fortified on all sides, protected on one by the sea, on the other by a vast desert, to the right by craggy mountains, and to the left by extensive marshes; so great is the fertility of the land, that Egypt was known in antiquity as the common granary of the world, and the gods would retreat there for peace and enjoyment. Yet, although its natural fortification and fertility were so great that it could boast of being capable of sustaining all other mortals, and hosting and protecting even the gods themselves, the region was unable, according to Josephus, to remain free for ever.[28] The old saying, then, is quite apt, that not even in the lap of Jove will human affairs be safe. It would be worthwhile therefore to follow the example of Plato, who when asked where that magnificent city which he had dreamed up could be found, replied, "That does not concern us; we are more interested in what type of city should be considered best. Above all others you should prefer that city which most closely resembles this ideal."[29] We too should project a city by way of example, which the learned may judge commodious in every respect, yet which will nonetheless conform to the requirements of time and necessity. In this we should follow Socrates' advice, that something that can only be altered for the worse can be held to be perfect.[30]

These therefore are the requirements we have laid down for our city: it should suffer from none of the disadvantages outlined in the first book; nothing required for economy should be lacking; its territory should be healthy, extensive, and varied in its terrain; it should be agreeable, fertile, naturally fortified, well stocked and furnished with plentiful fruit and abundant springs. There should be rivers, lakes, and convenient access to the sea to allow the importation of goods in short supply and the exportation of any surplus. Finally, to provide firm defence and encourage civil and military stability, there should be nothing wanting that might serve to protect the citizens and embellish the city, and to instill pleasure in their allies and fear in their enemies. And, in my opinion, it goes well with any state when it is able to cultivate a substantial part of its territory, despite its enemies.

Furthermore, a city ought to be located in the middle of its territory, where the view extends to its very boundaries, so that it can read the situation and be ready to intervene promptly if it should prove necessary; and in a position that allows farmer and ploughman to go out frequently and work in the fields, and return quickly laden with fruit and produce. It is particularly important to determine whether to locate your city in an open plain, on the coast, or in the mountains: each has advantages and disadvantages. When Dionysius was marching his army through India, and his men were overcome by heat, he took them up into the mountains. There, after breathing the healthy air, they regained their strength.[31] The reason why their founders sited cities on hilltops is that they felt them to be safe. But there, water is hard to come by. On the plains there are rivers and other convenient sources of water, but on the other hand, the atmosphere is denser; it is hot in summer and excessively cold in winter, and there is little protection from the enemy. The coast is convenient for importing merchandise, although it is said that no coastal city is ever calm: it will be continually troubled and churned by the attraction of political change and by the excessive power of the merchants. What is more, it will be exposed to many hazards and the dangers of foreign fleets.

This is my advice therefore: make every effort to ensure that, wherever the city is located, it enjoys the benefits of each type of terrain, yet none of its disadvantages. I would prefer to locate the city on a level surface when building in the mountains, and on a raised mound on a plain. But if there is insufficient variety to allow us an ideal choice, this is how to satisfy the essential requirements: a city on a plain should not be too close to the seashore, nor one in the mountains too far away. There are accounts of the coastline changing, and of many cities, notably Baia in Italy, being submerged by the sea. Faro, in Egypt, which was originally surrounded by sea, is now attached to the mainland like the Chersonese. The same, according to Strabo, happened to Tyre and Clazomenae.[32] And again, they say that the temple of Hamon was once on the coast, but that the sea has now receded, leaving it well inland.[33]

They advise us to build either on the shore itself or at a good distance inland. For the sea breeze is noticeably coarse and heavy with salt; so that when it is driven inland, especially onto a plain, and it meets moist air, the absorbed salt will dissolve and leave the air excessively thick and almost mucuslike. As a result threads like those of a spider's web are often found in such places twisting through the air. Air, it is said, reacts like water: mixing with salt clearly corrupts it and causes it to give off a foul stench.

The ancients, and Plato in particular, preferred a city to be ten miles from the sea.[34] But if so great a distance is impractical, it might be located where these sea breezes will only reach it when broken down, worn out, and purified. Set it back behind mountains to protect it from anything noxious picked up from the sea. On the coast the view of the sea itself can be quite delightful, nor is the climate there unhealthy. Indeed, Aristotle considered the healthiest region of all to be one continually disturbed by breezes.[35] But take care that the shore is not shallow and full of weeds, but deep, with cliffs of live rock standing sharp and rugged.

Siting the town on the "proud" ridge of a hill, as it were, contributes both to its dignity and charm and, above all, to its health and defense. For wherever there are mountains rising hard by, the sea is never shallow, and any dense vapors that might arise will be broken down by the ascent. And any sudden attack by a band of hostile men may be anticipated sooner, and fended off with less risk.

The ancients liked their hilltop towns to face east, although in hot regions they preferred them to be exposed to Boreas. Others might like them to face west, in the belief that crops grow better under that sun. Furthermore, the historians relate that below Mount Taurus the parts facing Aquilo are more fertile and therefore more healthy than the rest.[36]

Finally, whenever a city must be sited in the mountains, it is important to take account of the persistent and heavy buildup of mist, which leaves the day black and the sky always dark and harsh—a phenomenon common in such places, especially when encompassed by a range of somewhat higher mountains. And make' sure that when the winds, especially Boreas, are excessive and troublesome, they do not cause too much damage; since it is Boreas, according to Hesiod, that leaves everyone (the old in particular) torpid and hunchbacked.[37]

No site will be suitable for a city if there are crags above pouring down vapors raised up by the sun, or infernal valleys [below] overflowing with acrid air. Some recommend that one side of the city be on the edge of a deep ravine. But there are many examples, most notably Volterra in Tuscany, that illustrate how there is almost no ravine that can offer any inherent resistance to earthquakes or storms: eventually they collapse, bringing down with them anything built on top. Make sure, too, that there is no neighboring mountain overlooking the town, which the enemy might occupy as a base from which to bear down on it and do it harm; and that there is no plain below to offer the enemy shelter and sufficient room to set up a fortified camp for a siege or to draw up their line of battle for attack.

It is written that Daedalus founded the town of Agrigentum on a steep rock, which was so difficult to enter that it could be guarded by only three men[38]—an effective defense, provided that the exit could not be blocked by a small band of armed men with equal ease. Military experts strongly approve of Cingolum, a town in Picenum founded by Labienus;[39] they do so for a number of reasons, most notably because it does not share the disadvantage common to almost all hilltop towns, that once the summit is reached, it provides an open, level surface on which to fight: here any intruder would be repulsed by the steep and lofty rock; nor would the enemy be able to pillage and lay waste all the surrounding countryside at will in a foray; nor to besiege all the entrances at one time; nor can he safely retreat to a nearby camp, or send out men to forage, gather wood, or collect water without danger. On the other hand, these are the benefits to the townsfolk: the network of hills and valleys on all sides below would allow them to make sudden sorties to harass the enemy, and to break out and launch a surprise attack whenever a favorable opportunity arises. The town of Bisseium in Marsis[40] receives no less praise; sited at the confluence of three rivers and their corresponding valleys, and surrounded by rugged and impassable mountains, it has only a narrow entrance with difficult access, making it impossible for the enemy to besiege the town or to blockade the mouths of all the valleys; the townsfolk, meanwhile, are quite free to take in supplies and reinforcements, and to launch sorties against the enemy. So much for mountains.

But if you locate your city on a plain, and on a river, as is usual, and that river happens to pass through the middle of the walls, make sure that it does not flow either from or toward the south. In the first case it will be damper, in the second it will be colder, because of the passage of riverine mists. But if the river passes outside the town walls, take the surrounding region into account; stretches most exposed to the wind should be protected with a wall: keep the river behind you. Apart from that, it is relevant to note the opinion held by sailors, that winds by their very nature tend to turn their backs to the sun. The naturalists maintain that breezes from the east are purer in the morning and more humid in the evening, while those from the west are thicker at sunrise and lighter at sunset. This being the case, any river flowing either eastward or westward will not be all that unwelcome, because the breezes that arise with the sun will either disperse any harmful fumes passing through the city, or, with their arrival, do little to increase them. Finally, I would prefer any stretch of water, such as a lake, to lie to the north rather than the south, provided that [as a result] the town does not lie in the shadow of some mountain, the most wretched position of all.

I will not repeat other comments made above. It is well known that Auster is heavy and sluggish by nature, so that when the sails are burdened with its weight, a ship will lie lower in the water, as though it has taken on ballast; Boreas, on the other hand, seems to lighten both ship and sea. But whatever wind prevails, it is better kept at bay than allowed to penetrate the city or to blow directly against its walls.

Rivers with steep banks and deep, shady stone beds are roundly condemned for the foulness of their drinking water and the unhealthy air they give off. Then again, any man of wisdom and experience would keep well away from a swamp or muddy and stagnant marsh. I need not rehearse the diseases that infect the atmosphere in such places. Besides the pestilence inherent during the summer, the stench, mosquitoes, and other similarly foul vermin, even if they appear otherwise extremely clean and pure, they will not escape the disadvantages for which the plains have already been criticized: they grow extremely cold in winter and rage with excessive heat in summer.

Finally, every precaution must be taken to ensure that there is no mountain, rock, lake, marsh, river, spring, or whatever, that might protect and serve the enemy or in any way prejudice the town and its inhabitants. So much for the position of a town and its surrounding district. ◆

3

59v—61
It is understandable that the outline of a town and the distribution of its parts will need to vary according to location: in the mountains, for example, it is clearly impossible to lay out the walls in a circle, rectangle, or whatever shape you choose, as you might on a level and open plain.

The architects of antiquity were against having angles in their town walls, because they felt that they would be of more benefit to an enemy on the attack than to the inhabitants in defense, and that they had little resistance to damage from war machines.[41] Certainly angles may be of some benefit on the attack, when laying ambushes and launching missiles, in providing the opportunity to make a sortie and then retreat. Yet, on occasion, they may be of great assistance in the defense of hilltop towns, provided they dominate the entrance routes. The boroughs of the famous city of Perugia, for example, extend out over the hills on all sides like the fingers of a hand; should the enemy be intent on reaching the face of one of the angles, he will not find sufficient space to launch a large-scale attack, and as though trapped beneath some citadel, he will be unable to withstand the weapons hurled down and the sorties made against him. There is no one method, therefore, for laying out the town walls applicable in every situation.

And finally the ancients maintained that the city, like a ship, ought not to be too large, so that it rolls when empty, or too small, so that it is cramped when full. But while some prefer a crowded city, thinking it more secure, others prefer to plan for the future, and are delighted by more open spaces, while yet others may be more concerned with the city's renown and the name it will hand down to posterity. I have learned from the annals of antiquity that the city of the sun, founded by Busiris, and known as Thebes, was 140 stades in perimeter,[42] while Memphis was 150,[43] Babylon more than 350,[44] and Nineveh 480.[45] In some cases the area encompassed was so great that it was possible to gather sufficient produce all year round from within the city walls. But here I would follow the old proverb: To have everything is as much an excess as to have nothing. But if I should err on either side, I would prefer a place that may cater comfortably to an increase in numbers, rather than one that cannot decently accommodate the citizens already present. Furthermore, the city ought to be planned not only with a view to housing and other essentials; it should also provide pleasant areas and open spaces set aside as ornament and for recreation, away from the cares of civic business: race courses, gardens, ambulatories, swimming pools, and so on.

The ancients, Varro[46] and Plutarch[47] among others, mention that our ancestors used to set out the walls of their cities according to religious rite and custom. On an auspicious day[48] they would yoke together a bull and cow, to draw a bronze ploughshare and run the first furrow, which would establish the course of the town walls. The fathers of the settlement would follow the plough, the cow on the inside and the bull on the outside, turning any uprooted and scattered clods back onto the furrowed line, and piling them up to prevent their being dispersed. When they reached the point where the gates were to be, they carried the plough by hand, leaving the threshold of the gate untouched. By this means they deemed the whole course and fabric of the walls consecrated, with the exception of the gates, which could not rightly be called sacred.[49]

Dionysius of Halicarnassus says that in the time of Romulus it was customary, when founding a city, for the elders to make a sacrifice and light fires in front of the tents; they would then lead out the people to expiate themselves, by leaping through the flames.[50] Anyone unclean was thought unworthy to partake in the ceremony. This is what they did.

Elsewhere, I find that it was customary to mark out the line of the intended wall with a trail of powdered white earth, known as "pure." When Alexander founded Faro, for want of this type of earth he used flour instead.[51] This gave the soothsayers the opportunity to predict its future: the study of omens of this kind, during the first few days of existence, enabled them, so they thought, to foretell the destiny of a town.

The Etruscans were taught by their ritual books how to determine the future ages of the city, starting from the day of foundation; this was not through reading the sky, as mentioned above in the second book, but by examining the evidence and making deductions from it. This, as Censorinus recollects, is what they said: "The death of the longest-lived citizen born on the day of foundation marked the end of the first age of a city. Likewise the death of the last survivor who had been born by that time marked the end of the second age; and so too within the remaining ages. Portents sent by the Gods warned them when each age was finished."[52] This is what they did. And it is said that the Etruscans were able to work out their ages with great precision. This is how they entrusted it to memory:

the first four ages were each 100 years, "the fifth 123, the sixth 119, and likewise the seventh, the eighth was the period of the Caesars, while the ninth and tenth were yet to come."[53]

They also thought that indications such as these could give them insight into the nature of future ages. They were able to predict, for example, that Rome would hold dominion over the world, because one of those born on the day of foundation was given command of the city. This, I discovered, was Numa: Plutarch recalls that Numa was born on the very day that the city was founded, April 19.[54]

The Spartans prided themselves on not having walls around their city: trusting in their military prowess and the strength of their citizens, they thought their laws sufficient protection. The Egyptians and the Persians, on the other hand, felt that their cities ought to be defended with extensive walling. For example, Ninus and Semiramis, among others, planned the walls of their cities to be wide enough to accommodate two linked chariots being drawn on top, and to be more than one hundred cubits in height.[55] Arrian recalls that the walls of Tyre were 150 feet high.[56] Clearly some were not content with one set of walls: the Carthaginians surrounded their city with three. Herodotus mentions that Deioces surrounded the town of Cebatana with seven walls, despite its elevated position.[57]

For our part, when we think of the power that the walls offer for the safety and freedom of citizens against better-placed and more numerous enemies, we will side neither with those who want their city to be defencelessly naked nor with those who put all their hopes in the structure of the walls. With Plato[58] I say that it is of the nature of a city to expect that at some point in its history it should be threatened with conquest, since it is impossible, either in public or in private life, to curb that desire for possession and that ambition which are due to Nature or to human habits, within any reasonable limits: it has been the single most important reason for all armed aggression.[59] This being so, who would deny the need to add guard upon guard, and defense upon defense?

For the rest, the most capacious of all cities, as we mentioned elsewhere, is the circular one; the best defended, that protected by a wall of undulating bays,[60] as Jerusalem had been, according to Tacitus:[61] within the bays the enemy will not go unchallenged, and against the curtains he will not employ his war machines with any sure hope of success. We should look to ways of exploiting the nature of the site itself, as indeed we notice the ancients would do, depending on the advantages offered by the site, and their own requirements; for example, ancient ruins show that the old Latin city of Antium extended along the shore, in order to embrace the bay. Similarly, Cairo stretches along the banks of the Nile. According to Megasthenes, the Indian city of Polimbothra, belonging to the Grasii, was 80 stades in length and 15 in width, and extended downriver.[62] It is said that the walls of Babylon were quadrangular,[63] and those of Memphis set out in the shape of the letter Δ.[64] But in short, whatever shape it takes, all that is required of the wall (according to Vegetius) is that it should be wide enough for two armed guards to pass one another without hindrance, its height great enough to prevent anyone's bringing up a ladder and scaling it, and its mortar and construction strong enough to withstand the battering of war machines. For there are two types of war machine: one demolishes the wall by ramming and striking it, the other undermines it and digs away its foundations. Against either a ditch is generally a better defense than a wall. For with the second type of war machine, a wall cannot be recommended unless its foundations sit in deep water or on fim rock, but what is required is a ditch, both wide and quite deep. This prevents a "tortoise," mobile tower, or any such machine from being moved in close; also, if water or solid rock is met, it will thwart any attempt at mining. Military experts do not agree whether it is better to fill the ditch with water or to leave it dry. It is, however, conceded that the health of the inhabitants should not be the least consideration. Furthermore, they recommend that a ditch be easily cleared of debris caused by missiles, to prevent its piling up and so leaving the enemy a way in. ◆

4

61—62v

But I return to the subject of walls. This is how the ancients recommend they be constructed: Build two walls, one within the other and twenty feet apart. Then fill the center with earth excavated from the ditch and ram it down with beetles. The walls should be constructed so that it is possible to ascend from the level of the city right up to the battlements by a gentle incline similar to steps.[65] Others advise: Let earth excavated from the ditch be used to fabricate a rampart around the city, and a unified wall be raised from the very bottom of the ditch, thick enough to withstand the pressure of the earth weighing against it. Build a second wall farther in, toward the city, higher than the first, and far enough away to allow the line of battle to be drawn up and to give the detachments sufficient space in which to fight unhindered. Likewise, transverse walls should be constructed stretching from outer wall to inner: the connection and support provided by these links will restrain the main walls and reinforce them against the pressure of the earth in the center.

Besides these, we would commend any wall that is so laid out that it would leave sufficient space below for the debris to collect without filling the ditches with rubble, even if eventually demolished by the force of battery. Apart from that, I would agree with Vitruvius: "This is how I think a wall should be constructed: charred planks of olive should be set across the width of the wall as frequently as possible, to act as wooden ties and hold the two faces of the wall together and give them perpetual support."[66] Thucydides describes a similar wall being used by the Plataeans as a defense when besieged by the Peloponnesians; here timber was inserted to reinforce the brickwork greatly.[67]

Caesar records that almost all of the walls in Gaul were constructed in the following manner:[68] Unbroken straight lines of beams were laid parallel at equal intervals and bound across, but the space between them was filled with large stones, so that one beam did not touch another. Each course was laid in this manner until the wall reached the right height. The resultant work is agreeable to look at and provides an effective means of defense as well, since the stone protects it from the fire, and the timber from the battering ram.

Some, however, do not fully approve of this type of wall construction; they maintain that lime and timber do not last long together, because the timber is burnt by the heat of the lime and corroded by its salt. Furthermore, if the work were hit by missiles from the war machines, the entire wall, being interconnected, would be shaken and rocked as one, and be liable to collapse in ruins altogether.

But this, in our opinion, is the most effective method of reinforcing a wall against missiles: Buttresses with triangular bases should be built at ten-cubit intervals along the line of the wall, with one angle pointing toward the enemy. Arches should be constructed to spring from one buttress to another, and then be vaulted over. The niches in between should be filled with a mixture of clay and straw, and packed down. Thus the softness of the clay will deaden the force and impact of the engines. In addition, despite the continual onslaught of the engines, the wall can only be weakened here and there, where it can be repaired quickly. For this the plentiful supplies of pumice in Sicily work particularly well. Elsewhere, tufa provides a not unsuitable alternative to pumice or clay, and gypsum would also be quite acceptable.

Finally, whatever the material, if it is exposed to humidity, Auster, or nocturnal vapors, it must be dressed with a protective coating of stone. If the outer bank of the ditch is raised above the level of the surrounding land, and sloped, that will be very useful. This will cause all missiles aimed at city walls to miss them by overflying. There are others who contend that the best defense against a battery of missiles is for the line of the wall to follow the profile of the sawteeth.[69]

I find a stretch of wall, in the city of Rome, with a walkway halfway up its height, particularly impressive. Well-positioned gaps in the wall allow archers to ambush the enemy, should he make any hasty or incautious move.

The wall should be flanked by towers acting as buttresses every fifty cubits. These should be round, standing out from the wall, and somewhat taller, so that anyone venturing too close would expose his flank to missiles and be hit; thus the wall is protected by the towers and the towers by each other. Leave the side of the tower facing the town stripped of wall and open, to deny the enemy any protection should he happen to gain entry.

The cornices of the towers and walls act both as ornament and as a bond to strengthen them, while they prevent the use of scaling ladders. Some prefer to leave precipices along the wall, especially under the towers, and to provide wooden drawbridges, which can be speedily raised for safety or let down for use as the occasion demands.

On either side of the gates the ancients used to position a pair of larger towers, for the most part solid. These acted like arms to protect the entrance and its mouth.

The flooring within the towers should not be vaulted in stone, but of wooden boards, so that it can be taken up or set alight whenever the need arises. To make it easier to dismantle when the enemy gains advantage, it ought not to be fastened down with nails.[70]

These towers should not lack shelters and recesses to protect the guards from the winter frosts and other inclemencies of the weather. There should be holes beneath the battlements as they stand out from the wall, through which stones and firebrands may be cast down at the enemy, or water, if the gate is on fire. They say that if the gates are covered in leather and iron, they will be fireproof.[71] Enough on this subject. ◆

5

62v—63v

The positioning of the gates will depend on the number of military roads. Some roads of course are military ones, and others not. I do not intend here to enter into that legal distinction whereby *actus* is used for cattle and *iter* for men; I shall use the term "road" [*via*] for both.[72]

Military roads should be able to accommodate an army and its baggage setting out into the provinces. They must therefore be much wider than nonmilitary ones; I notice that the ancients usually built them to a width of no less than eight cubits. It is laid down in the Twelve Tables that roads, where straight, must be twelve feet wide, and where curved, sixteen feet.[73] Nonmilitary roads are those which lead off a military road, either to a villa or a town, or to another military road. There are cattle tracks in the countryside and alleyways in a town. There is a further sort of road, having the characteristics of a forum[74]—for example, those intended for a particular use, usually public, such as the avenues that lead to temples, racecourses, and basilicas.

Military roads in the country should not be constructed in the same way as in the city. Outside the city the following rules should apply: they must be spacious and open, and have views in all directions; they must be clear, and free of any water or rubble; they must leave brigands no place to hide or to lay an ambush; they should not have side roads entering from every direction, exposing them to robbers; finally, they should be direct and as short as possible. The shortest route is not, as some say, the straightest, but the safest; I prefer a slightly longer route over one that is inconvenient.

Some would think the countryside around Privernum[75] particularly safe, it being favored by deeply sunken roads, whose entrances are confusing and whose passage is uncertain, even dangerous; and whose high banks give no protection and make the enemy an easy target. Expert opinion considers safest such a one as runs through gentle hills along a level ridge. Next they would favor the old type of road that passes straight through the fields on a raised bank (this is why the ancients refer to it as an "embankment").[76] Certainly a road of this type has many advantages. Travelers walking along the raised causeway will find the view a pleasure and a great relief from the toil and trouble of the journey; second, and more important, it will enable them to see the enemy from afar, and will give them time to decide whether to attempt holding off the imminent danger with a modest band of men or, if outnumbered, to withdraw without loss of life. Here it is relevant to mention an observation I have made about the Portuensian Way: as a large number of men and a considerable quantity of goods come together there from Egypt, Africa, Libya, Spain, Germany, and the islands, they have laid out a double roadway, with a row of stones down the middle, one foot high and standing out like boundary markers, so that those approaching, travel on one side and those returning on the other, thus preventing any headlong accidents.

Such, then, should be a military road outside a city: clear, direct, and thoroughly safe.

When the road reaches a city, and that city is renowned and powerful, the streets are better straight and very wide, to add to its dignity and majesty. But with a settlement or a fortified town the entrances will be made safer if the road does not lead directly to the gate, but runs to the right or left along the wall, and preferably even directly under the battlements.[77] Within the town itself it is better if the roads are not straight, but meandering gently like a river flowing now here, now there, from one bank to the other. For apart from the fact that the longer the roads seem, the greater the apparent size of the town, no doubt it will be of great benefit in terms of appearance and practical convenience, while catering to the requirements of changing circumstances. And it is no trifle that visitors at every step meet yet another facade, or that the entrance to and view from every house should face directly onto the street; and while elsewhere too much openness will be disagreeable and unhealthy, here the large scale is welcome.

When Nero enlarged the streets, the city of Rome became hotter and therefore less healthy, according to Cornelius.[78] Although elsewhere the shade may grow harsh in the narrow streets, here this does not happen; the sun always shines down on the streets, even in winter. Although no house will be beyond the reach of the light of day, it will always remain shady during summer. Nor will the breezes ever be absent; from whichever direction they come, they will always find a straight and (for the most part) unobstructed path to flow along. For this same reason the wind will never be a nuisance; it will soon be checked by intervening walls. Furthermore, if the enemy gains access, he will risk injury, his front and flank being exposed as much as his back.

So much for military roads. Nonmilitary roads will be similar, except perhaps in this respect: if built in straight lines, they will make a better match with the corners of the walls and the parts of the buildings. But I notice that the ancients preferred to give some of their roads within the city awkward exits, and others blind alleys, so that any aggressor or criminal who entered would either hesitate, being in two minds and unsure of himself, or, summoning up the courage to continue, would soon find himself in danger.

It is also convenient to have even narrower roads of no great length, ending at the first cross road: these serve not so much to provide a public thoroughfare as to give access to the interlying houses, which will be of benefit both to the houses, by increasing the amount of light they receive, and also to the town, by impeding any hostile element seeking to escape. Curtius records that Babylon consisted of quite separate districts, in no way linked.[79] On the other hand, Plato preferred not only the quarters of the town to be joined, but even the walls of the houses, so as to act as a defensive wall to the whole town.[80] ◆

6
63v—67

A most important part of the street is the bridge. Not every site will be suitable for a bridge. It is best positioned centrally where everyone may use it, instead of being relegated to some distant and isolated corner for the benefit of only a few; and a bridge should moreover be located only where it can be easily built at no great cost, and where it might be expected to remain standing permanently. A stretch of river must be selected, therefore, where the water is not too deep, nor the banks steep, nor the riverbed uneven and unsure, but flat and reliable. Whirlpools, gulfs, and chasms must be avoided, along with other treacherous stretches of water, and most of all any section where the banks bend sharply to form elbows. Because, apart from the obvious fact that such banks would be liable to give way, tree trunks and other plants uprooted by floods will not pass freely through these elbows along a straight course, but will twist round and obstruct one another, accumulating and building up into a huge pile lodged against the piers of the bridge. The mouths of the arches will become blocked and begin to give way, until eventually the work will be torn down and demolished by the force and pressure of the water.

Caesar's bridge over the Rhine.

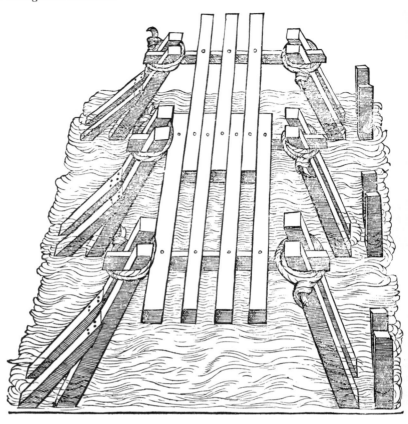

Bridges may be either of masonry or of wood. We shall deal with wooden ones first, since they are easier to build, and then go on to masonry ones. Both must be solidly constructed; a wooden bridge must therefore be reinforced with a good deal of strong timber. On the whole the best method of achieving this is to follow the well-known example of Caesar, who would build his bridges in this manner:[81] He took "a pair of posts, one and a half feet thick, sharpened a little way from the base, and their length varying according to the depth of the river; he fastened them together two feet apart. These were then lowered into the river with hoists, planted, and driven home with pile drivers, not vertically, like piles, but at an angle, sloping with the direction of the current. Opposite these two, others were planted, bound together in the same manner and positioned forty feet downstream, and turned against the force of the current. These two pairs, positioned as we have described, were linked by beams inserted from above, two feet in thickness and their length equivalent to the distance between the joints of the posts that had been set up.[82] Once the beams had been inserted in this way, they were each held in position by two brackets on the outside. This kept them the proper distance apart and braced them in the opposite direction; so rigid was this structure, and such the way in which Nature acted, that the greater the force of the current, the tighter the members were held together. On top of this, sections of timber were laid at right angles, then covered with a layer of poles and wickerwork. Beams, somewhat more slender but no less efficient, and called 'props'[83] because they were positioned below, were driven in aslant downstream to act as shoring, and linked to the rest of the work to resist the force of the current. In the same way further timbers were set into the river slightly upstream, as a form of protection to reduce the impact and prevent any damage to the bridge should the enemy launch any tree trunks or boats in an attempt to demolish the work." So much for Caesar's method.

It would not be irrelevant here to mention the device adopted in Verona of saddling wooden bridges with iron bars, especially where traversed by wagons and carriages.

This is how to deal with the stone bridge, which is composed of the following: the embanking abutments, the piers, arches, and paving. The embanking abutments differ from the piers since they must remain completely stable, in order not only to sustain the weight imposed by the arches (as the piles must do) but in addition to support the heads of the bridge and contain the thrust of the arches, so as to prevent them from opening. Therefore a stretch of bank composed of rock should preferably be chosen, since it is the most reliable support for the heads of the bridge.

The number of piers should relate to the width of the river. An odd number of arches will look pleasing, and also contribute to its strength. For in midstream the current, being farthest from contact with the bank, is least restricted, and the less restricted it is, the quicker and the more violently it rages. Therefore a through route must be left there, so that the struggle will not impair the strength of the piers. The piers must be positioned where the water slips by most calmly and, as it were, sluggishly. The silt will indicate where this is. Otherwise we should use the following method.

Imitating those who cast nuts into a river as food for those under siege to collect and eat, we should throw some similar buoyant material into the river along its whole breadth, at a distance of some 1,500 paces upstream, and preferably when the river is in full flow. The current is strongest wherever the cast objects group most closely; we should therefore avoid building the piers there, but choose instead a point where they are more spread out and their movement is less rapid.

When King Menes planned to build a bridge at Memphis, he diverted the Nile through the mountains, and when work was completed, he restored the river to its original course.[84] Nicocris, queen of Assyria, after preparing everything necessary for the construction of the bridge, had a vast lake dug out, into which the river was diverted. Then, while the lake was being filled, she had the piers of the bridge constructed on the dry riverbed.[85]

Such were their methods, but this is how we shall tackle the problem. During the autumn, while the river is low, foundations of the piers are laid inside an enclosure. This is how to construct the enclosure. Double rows of stakes are driven in close together, like a palisade, their heads above the water. Wickerwork is then wrapped around on the inside, to act as a wall that protects the piers. Then the spaces between these rows are filled with waterweed and mud, rammed down until they are sufficiently compacted to stop water filtering through. Next, anything left inside the enclosure is removed, be it water or, below that, mud, sand, or indeed anything else that would hamper the work. The rest of the operation is carried out as laid down in the previous book: a trench is dug down to a solid base, or, even better, stakes burnt at the end are packed tightly into the ground.

In this context, I record that architects of note used to make the base of the bridge continuous for all its length. Nor was this accomplished in a single operation, by closing off the river with one barrier, but by making gradual additions to what was already completed. For it would have been impossible to hold back and contain the force of the entire river. Therefore, while the work is in progress, channels must be left in the river to permit the buildup of water to escape. These may be on the riverbed itself, or, if more convenient, a wooden frame may be constructed supporting raised conduits along which any overflow may run off.

But if you find this too costly, build each pier its own base, drawn out like a Liburnian galley,[86] pointed at prow and stern, and aligned with the direction of the current, to divide and lessen the impact of the water. It must be borne in mind that the water will damage the stern more than the prow. The fact that the water rages more violently at the stern than at the prow provides proof of this; furthermore, at the stern, channels may be seen gouged into the riverbed, while the prow is the part that stands embedded in silt and sand. This being the case, the stern must have the most reinforcement of the whole work and must have the greatest resistance to the continual onslaught of the water. It is very valuable to ensure that the base of the foundations extends in every direction, especially toward the stern, for this purpose; so that even if some accident were to cause a large section of the foundations to fail or be carried away, enough would remain [in position] to bear the weight of the piers. It is particularly useful also to make the base slope from the bottom, so that the water passing over does not crash down, but easily slips over in a gentle motion; wherever water cascades headlong, it disturbs the bed, makes it turbid, carries away what it has disturbed, and causes erosion.

As far as possible we should build a bridge out of large blocks of considerable length and breadth, of a stone that is naturally resistant to frost, is not softened by water or easily dissolved by any other substance, and does not crack under load. Every care should be given to the bonding, so that the stones are flush, and vertically and horizontally aligned, their surfaces in continuous contact, and interlocking along their length and breadth, avoiding the need for any smaller stones to act as infill. Brass pins and cramps should be employed frequently, and the dimensions and position of their recesses should be such that the grooves do not impair the strength of the stones, but hold them firmly in their grip. The prow and the stern should be angled, and the work raised sufficiently high for the sides to remain above water level, even during a flood.

The thickness of the pier should be a quarter of the height of the bridge. Some prefer to terminate the prow and stern in a semicircle, rather than an angle, seduced by the greater elegance of the lines. Although I have previously stated that a semicircle has the same strength as an angle, here I would prefer an angle, provided it is not so pointed that it can be chipped or disfigured by the least injury. Yet I would have no objections to its being rounded off in a semicircle, provided it is not so blunt as to restrict the speed of the current. We consider the correct angle for the piers to be three quarters of a right angle, or, if you prefer it less, two thirds. So much for piers.

If the banks do not give as great a natural support as one would wish, it may be increased by pile driving in the same way as under the piers, and fresh piers linked by arches may be constructed out from the bank, onto dry land, so that if any of the bank were in time to be washed away by the continual passage of water, the extension of the bridge inland would ensure that there would be little disruption to the road.

The vaults of the arches need to be particularly strong, and wonderfully reinforced; this is for a number of reasons, not least because of the violent and constant shaking they receive from wagons. In addition, it may on occasion be necessary to draw extremely large weights over the bridge, such as colossi, obelisks, and so on; as happened when Scaurus dragged boundary stones across, causing the contractors for public works great concern over the damage likely to result.[87] For this reason allowances must be made both in the design and throughout its construction so the bridge may withstand the repeated and damaging jarring from the carts.

The example of the anvil demonstrates clearly why the stones of the bridge must be sound and extremely large: if the anvil is large and quite heavy, it will easily be able to bear the blows of the hammer. But if it is lighter, it will jump and move about under the blows. We have already mentioned that the vault consists of arches and infill,[88] and that the strongest arch is the regular one.[89] But if the curve of the whole arch is too high, in relation to the layout of the piers, we should use the incomplete arch, and reinforce the banking abutments by making them thicker.

Finally, whatever the arch used to face the vaults, it should be composed of large blocks of extremely hard stone, similar to that which would have been considered suitable for the piers. The blocks used in the arch should be no thinner than a tenth of the chord. The chords themselves should be no more than six and no less than four times the width of the piers. To hold the wedges[90] together, brass pins and cramps of no inconsiderable strength should be inserted. Then the uppermost wedge of the arch, known as the spine, should be shaped along the same lines as the others, but have a somewhat thicker head, so that it cannot be inserted without a pile driver nor driven into position without a light ramming machine. As a result the other wedges lower down in the arch will be held more tightly together and remain more firmly in position.

The infill panels should be made entirely of blocks of the soundest possible stone, and given the closest possible joints. But if there is no supply of strong stone to be found, I have no objections to the use of weaker stone for the infill paneling, out of necessity, provided that the entire spine of the vault itself and the adjacent rows on either side are made of hard stone.

Now to deal with surfacing. This operation has more to do with roads than it has with bridges, and relies totally on the methods of paving outlined in the previous book. The only difference is this: on a permanent road the ground must be consolidated, and covered with a layer of gravel one cubit thick, followed by stone embedded in pure river or sea sand. With a bridge, however, the substrata and base must be brought up with aggregate to a thickness equal to the arches. Then, whatever is laid on top must be bedded in lime.

This apart, the method used is the same. The sides are made as solid as possible, then stone is laid on top. The pieces of stone should be neither so small or smooth that they can be dislodged easily, nor again so large that they become slippery, causing the cattle to lose their footing and stumble before the hoof can gain a foothold.

Moreover, the type of stone used to surface the road is particularly important. What would be the effect, do you imagine, of the continual and protracted wear and tear by hooves and wheels, considering that ants can wear a path with their feet even into flint? In several places, and notably along the Tiburtine Way, I notice that the ancients would cover the middle of the road with flint, but on either side lay a covering of fine gravel. This prevented the surface along the sides from being broken up so much by the wheels, and the middle from shaking so much under the stamping of the hooves. Elsewhere, especially on bridges, the path would be contained by raised stone steps running the whole length, to provide pedestrians with a tidier pavement, while the center would be reserved for carriages and horses.

In general, the ancients much preferred to use flint for this, and of the various types the porous was their favorite, not because it was any harder, but because it was less slippery to walk on. However, any stone may be used, depending on its availability, and provided that only the hardest is selected to surface the path where the cattle tend to tread (they will prefer a level one, and always avoid any inclined plane). This should be surfaced with flint, or with any other stone, in blocks one cubit in width and no less than one foot in depth. The [upper] surface should be even and continuous, with no cracks between the stones, and it should be laid to a camber, to enable the rain to run off.

There are three types of camber. The slope may run into the middle (the most appropriate for wide streets), to the sides (the most convenient for narrow streets), or straight down its length. The choice will be determined by how the drains or ditches might best be emptied into the sea, lake, or river. The correct fall is half an inch in every two cubits.[91] I notice that the ancients used to construct mountain roads with an [uphill] gradient of one in thirty. In some places, as for example at the beginning of a bridge, there are gradients to be seen of one palm in every cubit;[92] but these are short stretches, which a well-laden beast could sail over at a single tug. ◆

7

67—68

We consider drains to be part of road construction for two reasons: they run under the center of the roads, and they affect their laying out, their leveling, and their drainage. They must therefore be included here. For what could be a better definition of a drain, than a bridge, or rather an arch extended in width? For which reason all the rules mentioned so far regarding the construction of a bridge should also be observed in the laying out of drains.

Such was the importance that the ancients seem to have attached to drainage, that in no other work do they appear to have invested so much expense and care. Indeed, the drains are considered the most astonishing of all the works in the city of Rome.

I need not stress here how important drains are in maintaining the sanitation of the city, the cleanliness of buildings, public and private alike, and toward preserving the wholesomeness and purity of the air. The city of Smyrna, where Trebonius was besieged until liberated by Dolabella, is said to have been otherwise very beautiful in the layout of its streets and the ornamentation of its buildings, but it had no drains to receive and carry away the sewage, and visitors found the filth repulsive.[93] The sanitation in Siena in Tuscany is poor, because there are no drains. As a result, not only does the whole town stink at the beginning and end of the night watch, when refuse receptacles are emptied out of the windows, but during the day as well, it is filthy and offensively vaporous.

There are two types of drains. One discharges the effluent into a river, lake, or the sea: this I call a "diffuser." The other is a "subsidence [cess] pit," where the sewage is collected and not discharged elsewhere, but disposed of by subsidence, as though being absorbed by the bowels of the earth. The bottom of the diffuser ought to be banked, sloping to falls, and solid, so that the effluent can flow freely; and of a material that will not deteriorate under the continual damp. It will also be best if it is high enough above river level that it will not be filled by raging floods or choked by silt. With a subsidence pit we need only the bare soil. For the poets call the earth "Cerberus," the philosophers, "the wolf of the Gods," because it devours everything, swallows everything. Thus the sewage, and any other refuse therein, will be consumed by the earth and disposed of, and fewer foul-smelling vapors will be given off.

I would recommend that drains for the disposal of urine be kept well away from the walls, as the heat of the sun may corrupt and infect them very much.

Meanwhile, rivers and canals, especially when they serve shipping, must, I feel, be treated in the same way as roads, since a ship may undoubtedly be considered a type of vehicle; and what is the sea, in essence, but a vast expanse of road? But here is not the place for such discussion: it requires extended treatment.

Should all the things above turn out to have been inadequate for the use of men, there are means and skills that will remedy them and restore their deficiencies: these will be discussed in the appropriate place. ◆

8

68—69

Now, if there is one part of the city specifically related to the topic under discussion, it is surely the harbor. The harbor may be compared to a confining pen, as on a racecourse; it is the starting point of your journey, and also the place to which you retire, once the course has been completed. Others might interpret the port as a stable for ships. But be it what you wish, pen, stable, or receptacle, clearly if its purpose is to receive and protect shipping from the force of the tempest, then surely the sides of every harbor must be strong and high. It must also have sufficient space for large and well-laden vessels to enter comfortably and be moored out of danger. If the coastline itself already offers such facility, you could ask for nothing more, unless perhaps there are several available options—as at Athens, where Thucydides claims there were three natural harbors—and there you will be unsure which to pick for preference so as to set up the buildings that any port needs.[94]

But it is clear from what we said in the first book that in some regions not all the winds blow, while in others certain winds are continually troublesome. We should therefore choose a harbor at whose mouth the breezes are soft and gentle, and where the wait for favorable winds before entering or leaving is not long. Boreas is thought to be the most placid of all winds;

when the sea has been disturbed by Aquilo it will grow calm again as soon as the wind dies, but after Auster it remains rough for some time.

Of the various alternatives, a site should be chosen that is the most convenient for the ships and that offers them the most room to maneuver. It is also desirable that the harbor be deep enough, not only at its mouth and within its embrace, but also along its banks, to accommodate ships even when laden with cargo and sitting heavy in the water. It is better for the bed to be clear and completely free of weeds, although thick, knotted weeds may sometimes be most convenient for securing anchors. Nonetheless, I would prefer the harbor to contain nothing that might pollute the air or harm the ships, such as algae or seaweed: these are responsible for woodworm and earth worm, which attack the hulls and cause a foul stench as they rot on the shore. Fresh water, if mixed with seawater, may also corrupt and infect the harbor, especially when it is rainwater running down from the mountains. Yet I would like to have springs and streams in the immediate vicinity, supplying pure water for storing aboard ship.[95]

I would also like the exits to be unobstructed, direct and reliable, free of sandbanks and other obstacles, and safe from ambush at the hands of the enemy or pirates. And I would have several lofty and conspicuous peaks towering above it to serve as well-known landmarks recognizable from afar, which the sailors might aim at as the target of their voyage.

Within the harbor a quay and a bridge should be constructed, making it possible to unload the ships close in. The ancients built them in various ways, but this is not the place to describe them. Their design comes under harbor maintenance and mole construction, and will be dealt with in the appropriate place.[96] The harbor must also have an ambulatory around it, with a portico and temple, where those disembarking might be received. Nor should columns,[97] hooks, and iron rings for mooring the ships be lacking. A number of warehouses should be set up to store the imported goods.

Tall and well-fortified towers should be erected at the harbor mouths, as lookouts from which to descry the approach of sails, and as nighttime beacons to show sailors the way in. Their battlements would protect allied shipping, and chains could be thrown across between them to deny the enemy entry. A military road should extend from the harbor into the center of town, with access to several neighborhoods, along which a counterattack may be launched from all sides against any intruding enemy fleet. Within the harbor there should be smaller outlets set aside for the repair of damaged vessels. One further relevant consideration must not be overlooked here: there have been, and there remain to this day, well-known examples of cities that are all the better defended for the inconsistency of the current at their harbor mouths and entrances; the current there is understood only by those who study its almost invisible, hourly changes in direction.

So much seemed worth saying about public works of general use. We might also mention the desirability of having large squares, as marketplaces and exercise areas for the youth during peace, and when at war as places to stockpile timber, grain, and other such commodities, essential for sustaining a siege.

As for temples, shrines, basilicas, show buildings,[98] and so on, these are not public domain so much as the province of certain groups, such as priests or magistrates. They will therefore be dealt with elsewhere, in the appropriate place. ◆

The Fifth Book of Leon Battista Alberti.
On the Works of Individuals.

How buildings, both in town and in the country, should vary to suit the different ways of citizens and other inhabitants we have already explained in the previous book; we established that certain buildings were appropriate for the public as a whole, others for the higher members of society, and others for the lower ones.[1] Those suitable for the general public have already been dealt with. Here, in the fifth book, we shall consider what is necessary or desirable in the case of individuals. This is a large and complicated matter, but we shall employ all our ability and energy in our attempt to expound it; and in so doing demonstrate our resolve to omit nothing that could be considered relevant to our argument, yet equally include nothing serving more to embellish our argument than to complete our undertaking.

Let us begin with the more exalted. The highest of all are those entrusted with supreme power and judgment: this may be entrusted to several individuals or to just one. The one who alone rules over the others is he who should have the greatest honor. Let us therefore consider what is appropriate in his particular case. Above all it is important to establish precisely what type of person he is: whether he is the sort who governs reverently and piously over willing subjects, motivated, that is, less by his own gain than by the safety and comfort of his citizens, or one who would wish to control the political situation so that he could remain in power even against the will of his subjects. For each building and even the city itself should differ when under the rule of those called tyrants, as opposed to others who take up their command and care for it like a magisterial office conferred on them by their fellows. For the city of a king it is sufficient defense to be capable of holding off an enemy attack. But for a tyrant, his own people may be just as hostile as outsiders, and he must therefore fortify his city against foreigner and fellow citizen alike, and the layout of the fortifications must allow him to receive outside reinforcements, even some of his own men against their fellow citizens.

In the previous book we dealt with ways of fortifying a city against the enemy; let us now consider appropriate methods of defense against one's fellow citizens. Euripides thought the common people to be a powerful adversary in themselves, but totally invincible when they combine deceit and guile.[2] Carrae[3] in Egypt was a city so heavily populated that when fewer than a thousand people died on a single day, it was considered healthy and thriving; prudently their princes had so divided it up with water conduits that it appeared not as one but as several small towns joined together. Their motive, I believe, was not so much to distribute the advantages of the

Nile more widely as to reduce the fear of any large-scale popular uprising, and to ensure that any such disturbance might be easily quelled; just as a colossus, if divided into two or more sections, is easier to manage and transport.

It was the practice of the Romans never to send a senator to Egypt as proconsul, but to delegate the individual regions to men of equestrian rank. The reason for this, according to Arrian, was to remove the risk of revolution under a single ruler.[4] They also observed that no city was ever free of civil discord when divided naturally either by a river or by being sited on several hills, or if it was partly on hills and partly on a plain.

The best means of dividing a city is to build a wall through it. This wall, I believe, should not run diametrically across the city but should form a kind of circle within a circle. For the wealthy citizens are happier in more spacious surroundings and would readily accept being excluded by an inner wall, and would not unwillingly leave the stalls and the town-center workshops to the marketplace traders; and that rabble, as Terence's Gnatho calls them, of poulterers, butchers, cooks, and so on,[5] will be less of a risk and less of a nuisance if they do not mix with the important citizens.

Nor is what we read in Festus beside the point: Servius Tullius ordered all the patricians to live in a district where any rebellion could be instantly put down from a hilltop.[6]

This internal wall should be planned so as to touch every district of the town. As in all other city walls, so especially in this case, the construction must be robust and bold in all its details, and so high as to dominate the roofs of any private houses. It is best to fortify it with battlements and turrets on both sides, and even perhaps a moat, so as to protect the guards stationed along it from either direction. The tops of the towers ought not to be open to the inside, but completely walled, and no more exposed to those on the inside than to the approaching enemy, especially where they overlook a road or the high roof of a temple. I would prefer there to be no route up into the towers except through the walls, and no access from the castle to the walls except where the prince allows it. No arches, no towers should stand along the roads through the town. There must be no projecting balconies, from which missiles could be thrown at soldiers as they patrol the neighborhood. In short, the whole town should be planned to give the one with supreme power sole possession of all the highest structures, and to make it impossible for anyone to restrict the movement of his men and prevent them from patrolling the town. Such are the differences between the town of a tyrant and that of a king.

There might perhaps be another difference in that a free people would find a plain more convenient, whereas a tyrant would be more secure on a hill. Apart from that, buildings inhabited by kings and tyrants have further characteristics in common, and even certain similarities with the ordinary private house, but so too differences. Their common features must first be dealt with, and then their individual requirements.

This type of building was established for necessity's sake, as is generally thought; yet it contains certain elements, such as porticoes, walkways, promenades,[7] and so on, that, although in essence items of convenience, have through use and habit come to be treated as indispensable. However, since our theory of building does not demand it, we will not distinguish convenient from necessary; we shall but state that in houses, as in towns, some parts are public, others restricted to the few, and others for single persons. ◆

2

70v—71v

The portico and the vestibule were not reserved for servants, as Diodorus thinks,[8] but are for citizens of all ranks, we would like to suggest. Within the house the corridors, yard, atrium, and salon (which I think is derived from the verb *saltare*, "to dance," because that was where the gaiety of weddings and banquets took place)[9] are intended for general use, rather than solely for those who live there. There are clearly two types of dining room, one for free men and one for slaves; then there are bedrooms for married women, young girls, and guests, almost all being single rooms. In the first book we dealt with the distribution of these parts in general terms. In their lineaments, number, size, and positioning they must be laid out in a manner appropriate to their respective uses. We shall now deal with them individually.

The portico and the vestibule are dignified by the entrance. The entrance in turn may be dignified by the road on which it lies, and also by the quality of its workmanship. Inside, the dining rooms, storerooms, and so on should be appropriately located where their contents will keep well, where the air is right and they will receive the correct amount of sun and ventilation, and where they can serve their intended uses. They should be kept separate, lest excessive contact between guests and attendants detract from the dignity, comfort, and pleasure of the former or increase the insolence of the latter.

The atrium, salon, and so on should relate in the same way to the house as do the forum and public square to the city: they should not be hidden away in some tight and out-of-the-way corner, but should be prominent, with easy access to the other members. It is here that stairways and passageways begin, and here that visitors are greeted and made welcome.[10]

Then again the house should not have several entrances, but only one, to prevent anyone's removing anything or entering without the knowledge of the doorkeeper. We should avoid having windows and doors open out, where thieves or (for that matter) neighbors may be of nuisance, watching

Works of Individuals

119

and finding out what is being said or done inside. The Egyptians built all their private houses with no windows looking out.

It might be desirable to have a back gate for bringing in provisions by cart or mule, without fouling the main entrance court; there should also be a more private side door, for the master of the house alone, to enable him to let in secret couriers and messengers, and to go out whenever the occasion and circumstances demand, without the knowledge of his household. To these I have no objections. I would also recommend the inclusion of secret hiding places, concealed recesses, and hidden escape routes, known only to the head of the family, where he might keep his silverware and clothing in difficult times, and even hide himself, should the situation become so grave. The tomb of David contained little niches where the hereditary treasures of the king were hidden so ingeniously that no one could ever find them. And from one of these the high priest Hyrcanus was able to draw, 1,300 years later, 3,000 gold talents to ransom the city when besieged by Antiochus, according to Josephus.[11] From another, some time later, Herod is said to have taken a considerable amount of gold.

These then are the similarities between the house of a prince and that of a private citizen. And yet between a prince's and a private citizen's house there is an intrinsic difference in character. Since the palace of a prince must accommodate a large number of people, it should have rooms notable for their number and size. Whereas a private house, being intended for smaller groups or for individuals, should have rooms that are elegant rather than large. Then again in the former, even private quarters must have a regal character, as though public, since there is no part of a royal household into which the crowd will not spill; whereas in a private house, even in public quarters it is best to avoid giving the impression that in having it built the head of the family has looked any further than to his own needs.

In a royal household the quarters of the wife, the husband, and the servants should be kept quite distinct, and each should contain its own services and whatever might contribute to its grandeur, to prevent the number of servants in any one quarter from causing confusion; surely a difficult objective, and practically impossible under a single roof. Each should therefore be allocated its own zone and *area*, and accommodated within its own pavilion, with its own separate roof. Yet they should be linked by a covered walkway, so that when teams of domestics or servants are rushing to perform some task, they appear not as if summoned from some neighboring house, but as though stationed there at the ready. The prattling and noisy hordes of children and housemaids should be kept well away from the men, as should the servants with their uncleanliness.

The rooms used by the prince for receiving guests and for dining should be given the noblest setting. This may be achieved with an elevated position and a view over sea, hills, or broad landscape. The apartments of his wife should be kept entirely separate from those of the prince, except for the most private rooms and the chamber containing the marriage bed, which should be common to both. Their quarters should be reached from the outside by the same door, guarded by a single keeper. Any further differences between the apartments of a prince and those of a private citizen belong more to the latter and will be dealt with in the appropriate place.[12]

Another characteristic common to the houses of princes is this: aside from their individual private requirements, they should all have an entrance off a military road, and especially access to a river or the sea; then there should be a generous reception area, serving as a vestibule, to receive ambassadors and distinguished company arriving by coach or on horse. ◆

71v—72v

3 There should be roofs and colonnades, in my opinion, not only for humans but also for beasts, to protect them from sun and rain. A portico, walkway, promenade, or whatever, is most welcome by the vestibule, where young men who are waiting for the elders to return from conversation with the prince may practice at jumping, playing ball,[13] throwing quoits, and wrestling. Then before the innermost rooms should be an atrium or hall, where clients can await the chance to discuss business with their patrons, and where the prince may sit on the tribunal and give judgment.[14] Then there should be a meeting room where the elders may gather to greet the prince and give their opinion when asked.

It might be convenient to have two such rooms, one for summer and one for winter. The advanced age of the elders must be taken into account, and consideration given to their comfort, so that there is nothing detrimental to their health and not the least impediment to prevent their debating and making decisions so long as reason and time demand.

I find in Seneca that Graccus, followed by Livius Drusus, was the first not to grant everyone an audience at once, but to divide up the people, and receive some in private, some in company with others, and some en masse, thus distinguishing close friends from secondary acquaintances.[15] If you are wealthy enough, you may prefer to have a number of different doors; these will enable you to dismiss your visitors in a different part from where you had earlier received them, and to exclude any whom you do not wish to receive, without causing offense.

Watchtowers should stand out above the building, to make any disturbances easier to trace.

These are the features that they have in common. But this is how they differ: A royal palace should be sited in the city center, should be of easy access, and should be gracefully decorated, elegant, and refined, rather than ostentatious. But that of a tyrant, being a fortress rather than a house, should be positioned where it is neither inside nor outside the city. Further, whereas a royal dwelling might be sited next to a showground, a temple, or the houses of noblemen, that of a tyrant should be set well back on all sides from any buildings. In either case an appropriate and useful guideline, which will lend the building dignity, will be to construct it in such a way that, if a royal palace, it should not be so large that it is impossible to throw out any troublemaker, or, if a fortress, not so constricted that it resembles a prison more than the apartment of a fine prince.

One matter must not be omitted: a tyrant will find it very useful to have secret listening tubes concealed within the fabric of the wall so as to eavesdrop on the conversation of guests or family.

Since it is expected of a royal household that it should differ from a fortress in almost every respect, and certainly in the most important ones, the palace must be linked to a fortress, so that in emergencies a king will not be without a fortress, nor a tyrant without a palace for his entertainment.

The ancients first gave each city a citadel as a retreat in times of adversity, where virgins and matrons could preserve their chastity and holy things be preserved from pollution. Indeed, Festus recalls that for the ancients the citadel was sacred ground and used to be called *augurialis*,[16] and that a certain arcane and secret sacrifice was performed there by virgins, away from the eyes of the crowd. This is why there is no ancient citadel to be found without a temple. But then tyrants took over the citadel and transformed a place of piety and religion into one of cruelty and excess, a sacred haven from adversity into a generator of distress.

But to continue. The citadel by the temple of the Hammonii is encompassed by three walls, the first to defend the tyrant, the next his wives and children, and the outermost to protect the quarters of his retinue;[17] a fine layout, apart from the fact that it caters more to defense than to attack. Indeed, it seems to me that just as a soldier cannot be commended for his bravery when all he can do is fend off an enemy attack resolutely, so a citadel should be expected to have the capacity not only to withstand an assault but also to drive back the attackers. It is necessary to cater to both defense and attack, yet in such a way as to make it appear that your sole concern is for the former. This may be achieved through the correct choice of site and design of walls.

I notice that there is disagreement among military experts over whether a citadel, intended to be as strong as possible, should be sited on a plain or on a hill. ◆

4

72v—73v

Not every hill to be found is impossible to besiege and destroy, nor every plain, if built up in the right way, possible to attack with impunity. This I accept. Certainly the whole question of location depends on what opportunities there are, so that all that was said about the city applies equally to the citadel.

In every case the citadel must have an unobstructed outlet, by road, river, lake, or sea, through which unimpeded it may seek or admit reinforcements or help from outside, against the enemy or, in the case of treachery or mutiny, against its own citizens and soldiers. The most suitable layout for the citadel is for all sections of town wall to be linked in a form of O, which is either in turn grasped, but not enclosed, by a huge C with bent horns, like so:

or from which several radial walls emanate to the circumference. Thus the citadel, as we have just recommended, is neither inside nor outside the town. But if one wanted to give a concise description, one might not go wrong in describing it as a well-guarded back door of the town.

Call it what you will—pinnacle of the whole work, or lock of the city—the citadel should be threatening, rugged and rocky, stubborn and invincible. A compact citadel is safer than a large one. The former can be entrusted to a few, the latter requires a large garrison; and as a character of Euripides' said, "never has there been a crowd without some mischievous element"—so here it is safer to put your trust in a few than to risk the perfidy of many. The base of the citadel must be solidly constructed out of huge stones, and must have an inclined surface, so that any ladder propped against it will bend and be weakened, and any enemy who tackles it will be unable to escape the stones hurled down by clinging to the wall, and the missiles of the war machines will not ram it so hard, but will bounce off at an angle.

The area inside should be paved throughout with slabs of stone of considerable width and thickness, to a depth of two and sometimes even three layers, to make it impossible for those laying siege to tunnel their way in secretly. The wall should be exceptionally high and solid, and extremely thick right up to the crowning cornice, if it is effectively to withstand the might of the war machines and their missiles, and at the same time to extend beyond the reach of ladders or even ramparts as far as possible. For the rest, what we have said about city walls should be followed.

It is essential with defensive walls to a town or citadel that every care be taken to prevent the enemy from approaching with impunity. This may be achieved with a deep, wide moat, as described above, together with loopholes positioned at the very base of the podium, where the enemy, although protected from above by his shield, will be struck where he is not covered. Indeed, this method of defense is superior to all others. It offers a more secure point from which to strike the enemy, leaving him at closer range and with a greater chance of being hit, because of the difficulties in protecting his whole body; and should your weapon miss one of the enemy, it will find another, and sometimes two or three at once. You cannot, on the other hand, fire from above without taking risks; your weapons will hit one man at a time—if that—since they can be seen coming, avoided by a slight movement, or warded off with a small shield.

If the citadel stands on the coast, stakes and rocks should be left along the shore as obstacles, to prevent any naval war machines from coming in close. If on a plain, the citadel should be surrounded by a moat; but to avoid corruption of the air, a ditch should be dug connecting it to a supply of fresh water. If on a mountain, the citadel should be protected by cliffs. Where possible, all three means should be used.

Any place where attack from catapults is possible should be protected with a curved wall or, better still, with one sharply pointed like the prow of a ship. The contention of certain military experts has not escaped my notice, that walls of great height are of little use against a barrage of missiles: when demolished, they fill the ditches with debris and present the oncoming enemy with an easy route in. This will not happen if the advice given above is observed.

To return to the subject. One main tower should be built within the citadel; it should be for the most part solid, of robust construction throughout, fortified on all sides, of greater height that anything else, difficult to reach, and entered only by a drawbridge. There are two types of drawbridge: one that can be raised to cut off the exit, another that can be extended or retracted according to use. The second type will be more suitable in any place plagued by high winds. Any surrounding towers from which missiles may be fired at the main one should be open on the side facing it, or protected only by a slender wall. ◆

5

73v—74

The sentry posts and the guards' quarters should be so distributed that each has a different area of responsibility: some should keep watch over the base of the citadel, others over the top, and so on. In short, entrances, exits, and every section of the citadel should be so planned and fortified that no harm may result either from the treachery of allies or from the violence and trickery of enemies.

To prevent the collapse of the roofs of the citadel under the weight of missiles hurled by war machines, they should be pointed, or reinforced with tough structure and thick beams; on this a covering should be laid, and over that hollow pipes to drain off the rainwater, their joints not laid in either lime or mud; finally this should be covered with broken tiles or, even better, pumice stone to a depth of two cubits. This method should reduce the fear of damage from heavy weights raining down, or from fire.

Book Five

124

In short: a citadel should be conceived and built like a small town. The same effort and skill should be invested in its fortification, and it should be fitted out with every other thing useful. There should be no shortage of water; and a garrison must be provided for the troops, along with storage space for arms, grain, pickled meat, vinegar, and, particularly important, firewood; and within the citadel itself the main tower, mentioned above, should be treated like a small-scale citadel and should be short of absolutely nothing expected of a citadel. It should have its own cistern and storeroom, well stocked with provisions and weapons for self-defense. It should have an outlet through which to launch an attack, even on one's own men, despite their opposition, and through which to receive any help requested.

Another point must not be overlooked: there are instances of citadels being saved by their own underground waterways, and of towns being lost because of their drains. Both may be of use for sending out messengers, but care must be taken to ensure that such devices do no more harm than good. They must therefore be suitably laid out: their path should be tortuous and sunk deep underground, so that no one armed might pass through them, nor anyone, even unarmed, enter the citadel, unless summoned and admitted. Ideally they should flow into some common drain or, better still, end in some deserted and abandoned sand pit or among the sepulchers and charnel houses of some remote temple.

But since in human life no chance may be left without provision, let there be some secret entrance into the center of the citadel, known only to you, through which entry may be forced with armed men, should you ever be shut out. To this end, it might be worth having a concealed section of wall, laid in clay instead of lime.

We have now dealt with the requirements of a person in sole charge of a community, be he king or tyrant. ◆

6

74—75

It now remains for us to deal with what is needed when control is not in the hands of one individual, but of several at the same time. Here government is either entrusted collectively to the magistrates or distributed among them. The republic consists of the sacred (involving divine worship, over which the clergy preside) and the temporal (involving the well-being of society, over which the senator and judge preside at home, and the generals and admirals abroad). Each of the above should have two separate types of abode, one for official business, the other a place to retreat with his household.

The family home should correspond to the character on whom he has modeled his life, whether king, tyrant, or private citizen. There are certain buildings most suitable to this class of person. Virgil puts it brilliantly: "The house of father Anchises lay withdrawn, screened by trees."[18] He understood that leading citizens would best have houses well away from the common crowd and working masses, for their own sake and for their families'. One reason for this was the delight and charm of living among open spaces, gardens, and country pleasures; in addition, it would prevent the lusty youth of a family so varied and large, of whom hardly any would live on his own, from being spoilt by the meat and drink of other men's tables, or from giving husbands cause for complaint; what is more, it will protect patrons from being unduly disturbed by the persistent flattery of well-wishers. I have noticed that the wisest princes have withdrawn not only beyond the range of the crowd but outside the city altogether, to avoid being continually plagued by common people with little motive behind their visits. And what is the use of all their wealth, if they are unable to take occasional time off to relax and laze?

But whatever the form, houses for people in such positions ought to contain a spacious reception area and a route out into the forum, wide enough not to be blocked by the retinue of domestic servants, clients, bodyguards, and others crowding around in their eagerness to accompany them, and swelling the number of hangers-on.

It is obvious where these men of high rank undertake their business: the senator in the senate house, the judge in the basilica or court of justice, the military leader in the camp or aboard the fleet, and so on. But what of the priest? For him there is not only the temple but also that which serves him as a military camp; since it is the priest, and those under him in charge of administering the sacraments, who must wage that fierce and arduous war (discussed in our book called *Pontifex*) of virtue against vice.

There are two types of temple: main temples, where a great prelate[19] solemnly conducts established ceremonies and sacraments, and those presided over by a lesser priest, such as chapels in built-up areas and oratories in the countryside. Perhaps the most suitable site for the main temple[20] would be the center of a town, but if removed from the pressing crowd, it would be more dignified; nobler set on a hill, though safer from earthquakes on a plain. In short, the ideal site for a temple would be the one to lend it the greatest reverence and majesty. Nothing unclean or indecent, which might offend the elders, matrons, and virgins who arrive to worship, should be seen near it, or distract them from carrying out their religious duties.

From the architect Nigrigeneus' writings about boundaries I have learned that the ancient architects thought the houses of their gods ought to have their fronts facing west, but that subsequent generations preferred to reverse this religious custom completely and have the temple and its boundaries face the direction where the earth was first lit up, to watch the sun as it rose above the horizon.[21] I notice, however, that with shrines and chapels, the ancients preferred them to face the direction from which people might arrive by river, sea, or military road. In short, it ought to be executed throughout with such wonderful and exquisite workmanship that those outside it are enticed to enter and those within are charmed into remaining longer.

A vaulted roof would be safer from fire, a trabeated one more resilient against earthquakes; the former will last longer, the latter would look much handsomer.

So much for temples. Much of what remains to be discussed concerns their ornament, more than their use, and will be dealt with elsewhere. Smaller temples and chapels follow the methods of the larger ones, scaled down according to the importance of the site and the requirements. ◆

<p style="margin-left:2em">

7

75—76

The monastery is a form of religious military camp,[22] where a number of men (such as those who dedicate their lives to religion, and who take the holy vow of chastity) may come together for a life of piety and virtue. There also exist priestly camps where scholars apply their minds to the pursuit of humane or religious studies. For if it is the duty of a priest to lead mankind to an existence as perfect as possible in every respect, the best way to reach that state is through philosophy. And surely the two human qualities that will allow us to succeed in this are virtue and truth (in that the former calms the mind and removes anxiety, and the latter unfolds and conveys to us the workings and laws of Nature, thus freeing the intellect from ignorance and the mind from contagion by the body); through this, then, we will reach a blessed existence, and an almost godlike state.

Further, it is to be expected of a man of good character—as a priest would consider himself, and indeed wish to be considered—that he should meditate upon, devote his energy toward, and carry out the duty that, in his opinion, one man owes to all mankind, of offering his services and generosity to assist the ill, the weak, and the destitute, and to ease their suffering. Herein lies the responsibility of the priest and those under him. This would appear to be a subject worthy of discussion, whether it concerns prelates or, more appropriately, those of lower rank.

To begin with the monastery. The monastery may be either closed—so that the occupants never appear in public, except perhaps to enter a temple or take part in some ceremonial procession—or more open, to the extent that it does not remain continually shut. Then again, it may be either for women or for men. I will not find fault with a nunnery that lies within a city, nor would I praise one sited completely outside. Although the isolation of this latter would ensure that there were fewer disturbances, anyone who wanted to enter for criminal purposes would have more time and freedom, since there would be no bystanders to watch, whereas in the former, the presence of many witnesses and onlookers would discourage any crime. In either case measures should be taken not just to dissuade the occupants from violating their chastity, but (more important) to make it impossible. For this reason all entrances must be barred, to prevent them from being entered, and those which are open must be watched, so that no one can loiter there without arousing suspicion. A military camp with its rampart and ditches need not be defended as strongly as this, fortified, as it should be, with a high, unbroken wall, not even pierced by a single aperture through which temptations of the eye or incitement of the tongue might enter to weaken resolve, let alone actual people with designs on their chastity. Light should be admitted through an open area on the inside. Around this area a portico, a walkway, the cells, dining hall, council chamber, and utility rooms should be arranged, as in a private house. Nor would I wish there to be any shortage of generous gardens and lawns, intended more for the recreation of the mind than for the pursuit of pleasure; for this reason it is not inadvisable to position them away from the main areas of circulation. Cloisters for men are best located outside the city: here they will be disturbed by fewer visits, totally committed as they are to a vow of continual sanctity and a religious peace of mind.

But I would have any cloister within the city, be it for women or for men, sited in the healthiest possible place, lest emaciation of the body and sleeplessness prevent the inmates from attending fully to their minds, and lest illness make their lives harsher than usual. Finally, I would consider it most important for any cloister outside the city to be located somewhere naturally well fortified, making it difficult for a raiding party of thieves or a small sortie from the enemy to plunder at will; for this reason it is as well to fortify the place with a wall, rampart, and tower, as far as its sanctity will allow.

For orders that combine religious duties with a study of the noble arts, the monastery should be sited, while not right amid the noise and bustle of industry, at least not too far from human concourse, so as to offer a closer involvement in human affairs, as their undertaking demands. Among the many reasons for this is that their own numbers are considerable, and many others will converge there to hear sermons, and for discussions on religious matters; for this a large building will undoubtedly be necessary. Such a building would be well sited alongside public places, such as theaters, circuses, and squares, so that the masses would gladly converge there of their own accord for amusement, and be more exposed to efforts to persuade, exhort, and advise them to denounce vice for virtue, and ignorance for an understanding of things noble. ◆

8

76—77

In the ancient world, in Greece especially, there would be a building called a palaestra in the center of a town, where one could engage in philosophical disputation.[23] This structure would consist of a well-fenestrated internal space, with outlooks and rows of agreeable seats; there would also be a portico running around a court green with grass and cloaked in flowers; such a setting is the best possible for these people, pious after their own kind. And in my view anyone interested in noble studies should be able to linger at length in the company of professors of the arts, in complete comfort and without irritation or annoyance.

I would therefore include a portico, court, and so on, that there be no diversion wanting. In winter they receive the gentle sun, and in summer they offer whatever grateful shade or breeze there may be. But attractions of this kind in buildings will be dealt with more thoroughly in the appropriate place.[24]

But should you wish to establish public auditoria and schools, places for the wise and learned to meet, position them where they are equally accessible to all. Any such institution must be sited away from the noise of workmen, and from any foul smells; let the distractions of the idle be kept out, let there be an air of solitude which befits serious men, those given to important and uncommon thoughts; it should also be given more to dignity than to charm.

To continue, the priest will need somewhere varied in form and carefully planned, to exercise his piety toward the weak and destitute; for the destitute and the ill must be received and looked after in different places. Then again, with the sick, care must be taken to avoid devoting too much attention to a few hopeless cases, at the expense of many more worthwhile. Some princes in Italy have banned from their cities anyone like that, ragged in clothes and limb, and known as tramps, and forbidden them to go begging from door to door: on arrival they were immediately warned that they would not be allowed to remain in the city out of work for more than three days. For there is no one so handicapped as to be incapable of making some form of contribution to society; even a blind man may be usefully employed in rope making. Anyone suffering a more serious illness would be assigned by the magistrate who is in charge of arrivals to one of the districts, to be cared for by lesser clergy. As a result they would not need to beg in vain from their pious neighbors, and the city would be spared their loathsome presence.

In Tuscany, in keeping with the long-standing local tradition for religious piety, wonderful hospitals are to be found, built at vast expense, where any citizen or stranger would feel there to be nothing amiss to ensure his well-being. However, since the ill comprise both those with contagious diseases, such as leprosy, the plague, and so on, which might be passed on to the healthy, and those who are, as it were, relatively healthy, I would recommend they be given separate quarters.

The ancients would dedicate these buildings to Aesculapius, Apollo, and Salus, through whose skills and divine intervention they thought man's health could be restored and preserved; they would only build them in healthy places, with wholesome breezes and the purest water, so that the rate of recovery would be enhanced by a combination of divine assistance and local benefits.[25] It is very desirable that the sick, whether cared for in public or in private, remain somewhere healthy. The ideal location for this, perhaps, would be dry, stony, and fanned by continual breezes, not scorched by the sun, but noted for its temperate climate, since damp encourages decay. But it is clear that in everything Nature thrives on moderation; and what is good health but a moderation composed of a fabric of different extremes? The mean is always pleasing.

As for the rest, those with contagious diseases should be kept well away not only from the city but also from any public road; all others may remain in the city. The buildings where they all live should be divided up and laid out as follows: the curable should be kept somewhere separate from those, such as the decrepit and the mentally insane, who are admitted not so much to be cured as to be nursed until struck down by fate. In addition, the women, whether patients or nurses, should be kept apart from the men. And, as in a family home, it is best to have some apartments more private than others, depending on the nature of the treatment and the inmates' way of life—a subject that we need not discuss further. Suffice it to say that every building of this type should be laid out according to the requirements of a private house. Enough on this subject; let us now move on to deal with what remains, in the order laid down. ◆

9

77—78

The republic consists of two parts, we said earlier, the sacred and the profane. The sacred has already been dealt with, and we touched upon the profane, to a certain extent, when we discussed the senate and the rooms in the prince's house for giving judgment. We shall now briefly list any further additions to be made, and then go on to discuss military and naval camps, and finally private buildings.

At first the senates of the ancients met in temples; the custom later developed of meeting outside the city; finally, in a move that increased both dignity and ease of business, they decided to construct a building specifically for the purpose, so that the elders, weary with old age, would not be deterred by length of journey nor prevented by inconvenience of location from meeting more frequently and staying together longer. They therefore positioned the senate house in the center of the city, thinking that it would be best sited close to the law courts and temple; this was not simply to allow those engaged in both electoral campaigns and legal cases to attend to both more easily, and without interrupting their zeal or their duty, but also to enable the elders themselves (since most older people are particularly religious) to say their prayers and return, when convenient, from temple to place of business without interruption to their work. Not only that, but should ambassadors or legates from some foreign country arrive to request an audience with the senate, it is as well to have somewhere worthy of both guest and city to receive them while they wait.

Moreover, in public halls of this type every measure must be taken to ensure that a group of citizens may be pleasantly received, decently treated while present, and conveniently dismissed; in particular make sure that there is no shortage of passages, lights, open spaces, and other such facilities. With the chamber of justice, because it may need to accommodate larger numbers for a debate, the apertures must be more frequent, large, and prominent than those in a temple or senate house. Then the entrance to the senate house must be as well fortified as it is dignified; this for a number of reasons, not least to prevent a reckless band of revelers within the crowd, incited by someone of mischievous intent, from having the freedom to break in at will and disturb the elders. This is the main reason why a portico, passageway, and so on must be added, where servants, clients, and their attendant domestics might provide protection in any unforeseeable circumstance.

Here is another consideration not to be overlooked: wherever people are to be heard reciting, singing, or debating, [stone] vaulting will not be suitable, because it reflects sound, whereas a composite timber ceiling will be, because it resonates. ◆

10

78—79

When laying out a camp, everything mentioned in previous books concerning the planning of cities must be reviewed and considered. For a camp is like a city in embryo; and you will find that many a city has been founded on sites chosen by experienced generals for camps.

With a camp it is important to understand what it must cater to. If there were no risk of sudden armed attack, or of being outnumbered by the enemy, there would be no need to pitch camp, and the work would be thought quite irrelevant; the nature of the enemy must therefore be considered. He may be equally well equipped and have equal numbers, or he may be more determined and strong, or he may be weaker. We have established, then, that there are three types of camp: the first is temporary and may be moved whenever necessary; it would be used for dealing with an enemy who is equally well equipped, its role being partly to keep the soldiers safe and partly to await the opportunity to bring the campaign to a successful close; the second type of camp is a permanent one, when the plan is to harass and lay siege to an enemy on the retreat, with little faith in his troops and confined to some fortified stronghold; then perhaps the third type of camp is one for holding off an enemy who is on the attack, until he is so worn down and exhausted from the siege that he has to abandon the enterprise and move on.[26]

Each of these camps should be carefully planned, and it is important to make sure that all which might contribute to your well-being and protection, and assist in withstanding and breaking down the enemy, is available; but, equally, make sure—to the greatest extent possible—that it offers the enemy nothing, either to be used against you or to improve his own comfort and safety. It is therefore most important to choose a site capable of providing abundant supplies and assistance, which are easy to gather and available when required. There should be no shortage of water, and provisions and timber to be found not far away; there should be a free route of retreat to your own, and easy access to the enemy, while every possible snare and difficulty should be left for the opposition.

I would have the camp overlook the entire enemy territory, so that no maneuver can be attempted or undertaken without being immediately seen and recognized. The site should be fortified on all sides with steep slopes and rugged cliffs, to make it impossible to surround by any large force, and to deny the enemy the chance to approach from any direction without grave danger; and again, should he eventually reach that far, to prevent him from sending in his war machines with impunity, and from holding his ground without grave loss of life. If there is any site to offer these advantages, seize upon it. If not, careful consideration must be given to the type of camp and the location that would best suit your expedition. For a permanent camp must be better fortified than a temporary one, and a site on a plain requires more extensive engineering and greater work than one on a hill.

We will begin with the temporary camp, which is the most common one. Indeed, frequent change of camp is thought to keep the troops healthy. One possible question to arise, in planning a camp, is whether to set it up in one's own territory or in that of the enemy. In Xenophon's opinion, a change of camp would harm the enemy but favor one's own side.[27] While, no doubt, to trample on foreign ground would give one a greater reputation for bravery, it would be safer and more advantageous to remain on one's own soil. But we should resolve to treat the relationship between camp and all occupied territory the same as that between citadel and city: it must have both an unbroken passage of retreat to its own territory and a ready and available route of advance into foreign lands.

There are various methods of fortifying a camp. The Britons would surround theirs with stakes, ten feet long, the ends burnt and sharpened; one end would be planted and rammed into the ground, the other would stand out and point toward the enemy.[28] The Gauls, according to Caesar, used to draw up their carts to form a sort of rampart to protect them from the enemy.[29] Curtius recalls that the Thracians used the same ploy against Alexander.[30] The Nervii used to splice saplings, then bend and tie together several branches, as an obstacle, primarily against cavalry.[31] Arrian recalls that Nearchus, one of Alexander's prefects, while sailing through the Indian

Ocean, would fortify his camps with a wall, as a defense against the barbarians.[32]

As for the Romans, it was their practice to be so well prepared for every eventuality of fortune and time as to have no cause for regrets, whatever happened. The training they gave their men in the fortification of camps was as thorough as in any other military drill; they were concerned more to protect their own men than to destroy the enemy. They felt that their ability to withstand and, in the process, frustrate and repulse an enemy played no small part in a victory. For this reason they would seize upon and use for their own convenience and safety any method of defense that could be either copied from anywhere or devised. If there was no high or craggy site to be found, they would form a precipice, with a ditch and rampart, held together with palisades and wickerwork. ◆

II
79—81

To continue with the method used by the Romans. The site on which we pitch our camp should be not only convenient but also such that none can be found more suitable for our current objectives. Besides the other considerations that we have already mentioned, it should be dry, in no way muddy, nor at all susceptible to flooding; it should be a site that neither inconveniences your men in any way nor offers the enemy the least protection. There should be no contaminated water in the proximity, but a supply of healthy water must not be far off; if possible, the camp should either contain springs of pure water or lie on the banks of some stream or river. But if not, make sure that there is a continuous supply of water nearby, within easy reach. Then, as for the camp, it should not be so large relative to the number of troops that passwords distributed among the sentries cannot be kept secret, and that shifts of guard cannot be covered without tiring the men; yet it should not be so cramped or confined that there is insufficient space for the soldiers to go about their duty.

Lycurgus thought corners of no use in a camp, and would make his camps circular, unless he had a mountain, river, or wall to give protection at the rear.[33] Others prefer quadrangular camps. But the siting and the outline of the camp should allow for considerations of time and place, and should depend on circumstances, and whether the enemy is in retreat or attack.

We should dig a ditch, large enough to require a considerable quantity of earth and wickerwork to fill; or, even better, two ditches, with a gap between. Again, the ancients considered it a religious observance to make the dimensions uneven, and the ditches would be constructed to a width of fifteen feet and a depth of nine. The sides of the ditch should be vertical, so that they are the same distance apart at the bottom and top. But where the soil is prone to slip, the bottom should be slightly narrower than the top. On a plain or in low-lying areas the ditches should be filled with water, from a river, a lake, or the sea. If that is not possible, make them bristle with stakes and trunks, hewn down and sharpened,[34] and likewise spikes and caltrops[35] buried all along the bottom.

Once the ditches have been dug and prepared, a rampart should be constructed, thick enough to withstand a manteler[36] and high enough to be beyond easy range not only of grappling hooks for pulling down the wall but also of darts thrown to terrify the soldiers. Obviously, the earth excavated with the ditches can be used for the rampart. For the latter the ancients preferred turf, cut from the meadows and held together by its roots. Others include green willow twigs in the construction: these germinate, and their roots entwine to strengthen the rampart. Thorns, stakes, spikes, hooks, and so on, should be implanted along the inside edge of the ditch and on the outside of the rampart, to impede the enemy as he climbs. The top edge of the rampart should be girt with a cornice of strong stakes, which are fixed into the ground, connected crossways, and supported by a layer of wicker-work and mud, the spaces between packed with clay. On the top of this, pointed merlons and fraises should be raised.[37] In short, every device should be incorporated in this work to make it harder to undermine, pull apart, or cross, and to increase the protection and safety it offers the soldiers.

Turrets should be raised every hundred feet[38] along the borders of the rampart, higher and more frequent anywhere prone to attack, so that the enemy can still be repulsed, even if he is already inside the camp. The *praetorium*,[39] the *porta quintana*, *porta decumana*,[40] and others, by whatever camp jargon they are known, should be located in a safe place, conveniently sited to repulse any intrusion, to receive provisions, and to readmit troops.

These measures apply, as I suggested, more to stationary than to temporary camps; but since allowance must be made for any accident that fate or circumstance might produce, they should also be applied to temporary camps, as far as they may be useful. As for stationary camps set up specifically to sustain a siege, their requirements will be very similar to those mentioned for the citadel of a tyrant, which is an object of constant hatred for the citizens; indeed, there can be no form of siege harder to bear, than to keep a citadel under constant watch, and to await continually the opportunity to release all the pent-up hate by its destruction. This is why, as we have already mentioned, care must be taken that it is powerful, strong, solid, capable of defending itself and of frustrating and forcing back the enemy; safe and impervious to any attack or to stubborn siege.

Finally, with camps for stifling and harassing an enemy already confined, all these measures are to be no less stringently observed. And rightly, since there is a saying that in war the besiegers become themselves very much the besieged. For this reason, you should not strive only for possession; you must look out that you are not yourself put on the defensive, either through the courage and ingenuity of the enemy or through the carelessness of your own troops. To gain possession, the best is to assault and surround; and for self-defense, to counterattack and be fortified. The whole aim of an attack is to break through the fortifications and into a town. Here I do not intend to deal with ladders for scaling defenses, despite enemy counterattack, nor shall I talk of mines, movable towers, war machines, or other methods of inflicting damage through fire, water, or any of Nature's resources. This is not the place to deal with them; we shall discuss war machines in greater detail elsewhere.[41] But here is some relevant advice: for protection against missiles, use beams, posts, boarding, wickerwork, ropes, fascines, sacks stuffed with wool, seaweed, or hay; it is important to pile them up steeply, so that they overhang the edge. To protect them from fire, wet them, preferably with vinegar and mud, and face them with unbaked brick; stretch skins over the brickwork to prevent its being washed away by water. Likewise, to prevent tearing and ripping of the skins by blows, cover them with soaking wet rags.

It is not inadvisable for the siegeworks around a city to be constructed close by the walls, for a number of reasons. The shorter their length, the easier they will be for the soldiers to construct, the smaller the quantities of materials, the less the expense, and the smaller the guard required, once they are complete. But they should not be so tight against the town boundaries that the inhabitants would be able to reach the soldiers, in their camp or on the siegeworks, by firing war machines from their walls. If the object of the siege is to deny the besieged outside reinforcements or supplies, however, then surely, provided it is applied from the onset at any entrance to be intercepted or blocked, the most effective method would be the following: barricade the bridges; elsewhere block all fords or roads with beams and rubble; link all ponds, lakes, marshes, and rivers with a watercourse; and attempt to raise the water level to inundate the low-lying areas.

To these must be added the effective measures of counterattack and self-defense. For it is essential to fortify the ditch, rampart, tower, and so on, both against those in the town breaking out, and against any band of reinforcements from the surrounding region rallying and launching an attack. Besides that, forts and lookouts should be built, where suitable, to give greater protection, freedom, and convenience to man and beast when foraging for water, wood, or provisions. But the troops ought not to be so dispersed that they find it impossible to come under one command, or to fight as a unified force, or, through their solidarity, to be of immediate mutual assistance. Here it is worth recalling that memorable account in Appian the historian:[42] when Octavius was besieging Lucius at Perugia, he dug a ditch up to the Tiber, 56 stades in length and 30 feet in both width and depth; along it he built a high wall, crowned with 1,050 wooden towers, 60 feet in height; and so great were the fortifications, that the besieged were not hemmed in so much as shut out, to prevent their doing the least harm to the army.

Works of Individuals

So much for terrestrial camps, except perhaps to add that the site chosen must be noble and conspicuous, where the banner of the republic may be displayed with majesty, and religious ceremonies may be conducted with much reverence, and where it is convenient to summon a military tribunal or council of war. ◆

Some, perhaps, would not accept that a fleet is a maritime camp, but would claim that the ship serves as a type of water elephant, controlled by its own form of bridle, and that the role of camp should belong to the port rather than the ship. Others, however, would contend that the ship is nothing but a mobile fortress. But we will skirt this problem, and simply state that there are two ways in which the theory and art of building may contribute to the safety and success of the captains and their crew, depending on whether you are in pursuit of the enemy or on the defensive: first, in the fitting out of the ships, and second, in the fortification of the port.

A ship serves, first, to transport you and your belongings; next, it may provide wartime service, if it is free from danger. Dangers may be either inherent—as though embodied in the ship itself—or external, such as the violence of the wind, the might of the waves, and rocks, obstacles, and sandbanks, all of which may be foreseen and avoided through practice in the art of sailing, and knowledge and experience of coast and winds. Intrinsic faults will be found in the lineaments or the materials. These faults must be forestalled.

All timber liable to split, break, sink, or rot should be rejected. Nails and straps of copper are better than of iron. Recently, during the preparation of this book, fragments of one of Trajan's ships were raised from the bottom of Lake Nemi, where they had lain submerged for more than 1,300 years: I noticed that the pine and cypress had lasted extremely well. The paneling had been covered on the outside with a double layer of fabric, consisting of linen soaked in black pitch, itself protected by sheets of lead fastened together with copper nails.[43]

In building a ship, the ancients would use the lineaments of a fish; so that its back became the hull, its head the prow; the rudder would serve as its tail, the oars as its gills and fins.

There are two types of ship: cargo ship and clipper. The greater its length, the better it will hold its course, especially in a straight line; the shorter, the easier to maneuver with a rudder. The length of a cargo ship should preferably be no less than three times the width, that of a clipper no more than nine. I have already dealt at length with the design of ships, in the little book called *The Ship*;[44] but I shall mention only what is relevant here. A ship consists of the following: keel, stern, prow, two sides, and, if you will, rudder, sails, and other rigging necessary for sailing. The capacity of the hold will be equal to the weight of the water required to fill it to the right level.[45] The keel ought to be straight, but all the rest should be modeled to a curve. The broader the keel, the greater the possible load, but the less the speed. An extended, tapered keel will increase the ship's speed, but unless you add ballast, it will also decrease stability. A wide keel is more suitable for the shallows, a narrow one safer on the high seas. A ship with high, elevated sides will prevail over oncoming waves but flounder under heavy winds. The sharper the prow, the more readily will it slip through the water; the thinner the stern, the steadier will it hold its course.

The bow and the breasts must be strong and sweep outward for the sails or the oars to drive the ship through the waves. Then the ship should taper in toward the stern, so that it glides smoothly through the water, as if of its own accord. To have additional rudders will improve stability but restrict speed. The height of the mast should equal the length of the ship. As for other nautical or military accessories, such as oars, anchors, ropes, rostra, towers, bridges, and so on, we shall pass them all over. It would be relevant to note that posts and beams suspended over the edge and along the sides, or left erect, may serve for ramming and as defenses against attack; while the raised masts may serve as towers; the sail yards, and the gangways[46] suspended from them, make excellent bridges.

The ancients would fix grapnels[47] to their prows; our own sailors have learned how to erect towers against the mast at the prow and stern, and to arrange a protective barricade of rags, ropes, sacks, and so on, and to drape rope netting over as an effective means of preventing anyone from boarding. And during a battle it is possible to make the ship's gangway so bristle with spikes in an instant, that the enemy will find it impossible to move a foot at all without injury; on the other hand, when convenient, they may be even more quickly removed, once the attack has been foiled: this is an invention of ours already noted elsewhere. I would not wish to describe it again here: anyone of ability need only be reminded. Another invention of mine was a method of collapsing an entire deck with one light tap of a mallet, throwing down anyone who has boarded, and then in no time at all, and with little effort, the whole work could be set back in place. Here I shall not mention my other inventions for sinking and burning enemy ships and throwing the crew into confusion, and putting them to a wretched death; perhaps there will be another occasion.

It should not be overlooked that the same length, height, and width of ship is not suitable everywhere. Between the islands in the Black Sea,[48] for example, a ship with a vast hull, and requiring a large crew, would be in difficulties as soon as the wind picked up; while in the waves of the open ocean by Cadiz, a small ship would flounder.

Included under naval matters are methods of defending or blockading a port. The most effective means is to employ a mole running out to sea, and a rampart, chains, or other such obstacles, dealt with in the previous book. Stakes should be driven into the ground, and boulders piled up to form an obstruction, and frameworks made up of planks and wickerwork should be filled with heavy objects and sunk. But if this is not feasible, because of the nature of the place or because of the excessive expense—when, for example, the sea bed is soft and muddy, or too deep—use the following alternative: Bind together a row of barrels, and on these fix a system of straight beams and timbers, connected transversely; onto this raft fasten several hard, sharp rostra and stakes, known as tonsils, pointing toward the enemy, and their ends clad in iron; these will deter any light enemy vessel from rushing the work, full-sail, or attempting to slip by. Cover the raft with earth to protect it from fire; surround it with a palisade of wickerwork and boarding; where suitable, erect wooden towers; reinforce it against the force of the waves with several anchors, where they can be securely fastened but not seen by the enemy. The work should preferably be curved, arched against the oncoming waves; this form will strengthen and reinforce it against them, and reduce the need for anchors and external support. Enough on this subject. ◆

13

Now, since an enterprise on this scale requires materials and financing, mention must be made of the magistrates responsible for them; the magistrates include the quaestor, collectors of taxes and public revenues,[49] and so on. These will require the following: a granary, a treasury, an arsenal, an emporium, dockyard, and stables. On this topic there is seemingly little to be said, but what there is, is important.

The granary, treasury, and arsenal must of course be located in the center, in the most crowded part of the city, where they will be better protected and more accessible. Because of the danger of fire, the dockyards should be quite separate from the residential quarters. It is particularly important to ensure that party walls continue uninterrupted from the ground to beyond the roof throughout the building, to contain the devastation of the flames and to prevent their spreading along the roof. Emporia should be sited on the coast, or at the mouth of a river, or at a junction of military roads. Dockyards should be linked to a bay and basin, where the fleet can dock, be refitted, and put out to sea again. Make sure that the water is in continual motion. Ships rot with Auster, crack under midday heat, but are preserved by the rays of the rising sun.

Clearly granaries—and any other structure used for storage—will be happiest in a dry location and climate. But these, with the exception of the salt store, will be discussed more thoroughly when we deal with private buildings, since that is the category with which they have most in common. I would make a salt store like this: Cover the ground with a layer of coal, one cubit thick, and pack it down; above this sprinkle sand worked in with pure clay, to a depth of three palms, and flatten it; finally, pave it with brick baked black. If this latter is in short supply, face the inside surfaces of the walls with squared blocks of stone, of an intermediate consistency, neither tufaceous nor tough;[50] otherwise use hard stone. This revetment should extend one cubit into the wall; construct the framework of the wall out of timber, held together with bronze nails or, better still, mortised joints. Fill the gap between the timber frame and the lining with reeds. It will be generally worthwhile to spread the timber with clay kneaded with oil lees and mixed with broom and broken rushes. Finally, it is obvious that any public building of this type ought to have walls and towers to protect it from thieving, raids by enemies or rebel citizens, and vandalism.

I appear now to have dealt at length with the subject of public works, though something should not be omitted of concern to the magistrates: that they should have somewhere to commit anyone judged worthy of punishment for disobedience, treachery, or villainy. This must not be overlooked. I find that the ancients had three types of prison: one where rough and untutored men might be rounded up to receive nighttime training from learned and experienced teachers of the noble arts in matters relating to their moral conduct and way of life; the second in which to confine insolvent debtors and those who require the tedium of prison life to set right their wayward lives; the third where to assign those who have committed abominable crimes, those who are unworthy of the light of day or of contact with society, and who are soon to suffer capital punishment or be given over to darkness and shame. However, anyone who determined that this last category be an underground chamber, like some fearful tomb, would be proposing a penalty for the criminal more severe than what the law itself or human reason should demand. Even if such men (who are beyond redemption) deserve the ultimate of all penalties for their crimes, it would be expected of republic and prince alike that they should not be wanting in compassion. Suffice it to make the walls, openings, and vaults of the work strong enough to make it difficult for any prisoner to escape; and, to achieve the necessary thickness, depth, and height, it is vital to use large blocks of hard stone, held together with iron and brass. You may also use a lining of boards, lofty barred openings, and so on, although not even these will prove large or strong enough to prevent anyone intent on freedom and safety from escaping, should you give him the opportunity here to demonstrate the extent of his natural strength and ingenuity. And to my mind they are quite right when they say that the only impregnable prison is the eye of a vigilant guard.

But in all other respects let us follow the customs and practices of the ancients. It would be relevant to mention that prisons must contain latrines and fireplaces, without the nuisance of smell or smoke. Then the prison as a whole should be as follows: select a space of ground in a secure and not deserted part of the city, and surround it with a strong, high wall, pierced by no opening, and supply it with towers and galleries; between this wall and the walls of the cells there should be a gap of three cubits for the guards to make nighttime patrols to intercept any conspiracy to escape. The central space must be divided up as follows: There should be a hall, none too depressing, to serve as a vestibule for assembling those sent to be taught a discipline; beyond this the first entrances should be to the quarters of the armed guards, protected behind bars and a palisade; next there should be an open court, flanked by porticoes on either side, containing a large number of openings into several of the cells. Here the bankrupts and insolvent debtors should be kept, not all together, but in separate cells. In front there should be a more restricted prison, where those convicted of minor crimes should be held. Anyone convicted of a capital offense should be kept in the innermost section. ◆

14

83v—84v

I come now to private buildings. We earlier described the house as a miniature city.[51] With the construction of a house, therefore, almost everything relevant to the establishment of a city must be taken into account: it should be extremely healthy, it should offer every facility and every convenience to contribute to a peaceful, tranquil, and refined life. These seem to have been already covered substantially in earlier books, in terms of their intrinsic nature, quality, and type. But here we shall deal with them from a different point of view.

The private house was obviously first constructed for the family, as a convenient place of repose. It will not be comfortable enough unless everything the family requires lies under the one roof. A large number of men and things cannot be accommodated as freely in the city as they can in the country. Why is this? In urban building there are restrictions such as party walls, dripping-gutters, public ground, rights of way, and so on, to prevent one's achieving a satisfactory result.[52] In the countryside this does not happen; here everything is more open, whereas the city is restrictive. This, then, is one of the many reasons why private buildings in the city should be distinguished from those in the country. And with either, the poor will have different requirements from those of the wealthy. For the poor it is necessity that governs the size of the dwelling, whereas the rich are seldom satisfied or able to limit their greed. But we shall pass on whatever sound advice and moderation would commend, in each case.

I think that I will begin with the easier. In the countryside there are fewer restrictions, and the rich are readier to invest money. But let us first rehearse briefly a few general comments on the design of villas: an adverse climate and porous soil[53] are to be avoided; building should be undertaken right in the countryside, at the foot of mountains, in a well-watered and sunny spot, in a healthy region, and in a healthy part of that region. It is thought that a severe and unhealthy climate may be caused not only by those disadvantages outlined in book 1, but also by thick woods—especially those containing trees with bitter leaves—in that the air will putrify if reached neither by sun nor by wind; another cause may be sterile or unhealthy soil, where all you will harvest will be timber.

In my opinion the site chosen by a proprietor for his country villa ought to be the most convenient to his town house. Xenophon would have us walk to the villa, for exercise, and then return by horse.[54] The villa, then, must be located at no great distance from the city, along an easy and unobstructed route, and in a convenient place accessible in summer and winter to visitors and for supplies of provisions, by foot, carriage, or perhaps even boat. Also, if the villa is not distant, but close by a gate of the city, it will make it easier and more convenient to flit, with wife and children, between town and villa, whenever desirable, without the need to dress up and without attracting anyone's attention.

It would be worthwhile siting the villa where the rays of the sun will trouble your eyes neither when you set out in the morning nor when you return in the evening. Then again the villa ought not to be consigned to some deserted, forsaken, and obscure location, but should be situated where others have been enticed to settle by the fertility and climate, and where provisions are plentiful, and life sweet and free of danger. On the other hand, anywhere too busy is to be avoided, as is anywhere next to a town, a military road, or a port that attracts many ships; the ideal location would be one that enjoys the benefits of the above, yet where your family life will not be plagued by visits from acquaintances who are passing by.

Windy places, according to the ancients, do not usually suffer from rust, whereas damp places, valleys, and locations undisturbed by the breezes are frequently troubled by injury of this kind. I do not always hold with the general rule that a villa must face the sunrise at equinox: comments about the sun and the breezes clearly vary from region to region, so that, for example, Aquilo is not always light, nor Auster everywhere unhealthy. Indeed, the physician Celsus made the wise observation that winds blowing in from the sea are denser, while those arriving from inland are always lighter.[55] In my opinion the wind is the reason why the very mouth of the valley is to be avoided; for if the wind blows from somewhere shady, it will be too cold, or, if from flat land exposed to much sun, it will be too hot. ◆

15

84v—85v

Country houses may be divided into those inhabited by gentlemen[56] and those by workers of the land, and further divided into those built mainly as a business and those intended more for pleasure. Let us now deal with the former, those concerned primarily with farming. These buildings ought not to be too far from those of the estate manager, so that he can be kept regularly informed of what each farmhand is doing and what remains to be done. The function of these particular buildings is to treat, collect, and preserve the produce reaped from the land, unless perhaps you think this latter [the storage of the harvest] should be entrusted to the master's town house rather than to his country estate. To carry out these operations, a large gang of men will be required, a supply of implements, and above all an industrious and diligent steward.

The ancients set the ideal number of farmhands at around fifteen. These must be provided with somewhere to warm themselves when cold and somewhere to retreat when driven from their work by the weather, somewhere to take their meals, to rest, and to make whatever preparations are necessary. A large, well-lit kitchen must therefore be provided, which is fireproof and furnished with an oven, fireplace, water supply, and drainage. Opening off the kitchen there should be an alcove[57] where the more respectable may pass the night, and where there might be a larder for daily supplies of bread, preserved meat, and lard. The others should be distributed each where he can take care of his charges, the steward by the main door, to prevent anyone's entering or removing anything at night without his notice, the herdsman by the stables, so as to be on call should the occasion demand.

So much for the manpower. The implements are either animate, such as the quadrupeds, or inanimate, such as vehicles, tools, and so on. For the latter erect a large shed by the kitchen, to store your cart, harrow, plough, yokes, hay baskets, and so on. The shed should face south, so that in winter the family may also enjoy the feast days there in the sun. You should also clear an open space for wine- and olive-presses, and provide a room for the storage and maintenance of buckets, baskets, pulleys, rope, hoes, pitchforks, and so on. Over the transoms and cross-beams of the shed lay a bed of wickerwork, on which to store props, poles, bars, rods, brushwood, leaves, bales of fodder for the cattle, hemp, raw flax, and so on.[58]

Quadrupeds are of two kinds: some are put to work, as oxen and beasts of burden, and some are bred for their produce, as are pigs, sheep, goats, and all other reared stock. Let us deal first with beasts of burden, since they serve primarily as instruments, and then go on to discuss reared stock, this being the province of the steward. Make sure that the stables for the cattle and horses are not cold in winter, and that the stalls are well fenced in, to keep the straw from being scattered. Hang up the baskets of hay sufficiently high that the horses, in order to reach it, must stand up, crane their necks, and expend some effort: this will ensure that their heads remain dry and their shoulders agile. On the other hand, with barley and seed, make sure that they have to eat it from the bottom of their trough: this will prevent them from gorging themselves or swallowing too much seed whole, and besides that, it will make their muscles and chests firmer and stronger.

Make quite sure that the wall of the pen facing the head of the animal is not damp: the horse has a thin skull, susceptible to moisture and cold. Take care that the windows do not let in the moon's rays: the moon can cause cataracts and heavy coughs, and its rays are harmful to any sick cattle. Set the food for the oxen at a lower level, so that they can chew it lying down. Horses are terrified if they see a fire, whereas oxen are more cheerful when they see light. If a mule is kept in a hot or dark place, he will go mad. Some think it sufficient protection for a mule to have his head covered but the rest of his body exposed to the air and cold. Give the oxen a stall with a stone floor, to keep their hooves from rotting in their filth. For a horse's stall, a trench must be dug and then covered with planks of holm or oak, to prevent the ground from becoming damp with the urine, and the pawing of hooves from wearing down floor and hoof alike. ◆

16

85v—87

The steward or manager is responsible not only for harvesting the fields but also, in particular, for farming the animals: quadrupeds, birds, and fishes: this we must mention briefly. Build the stalls for the cattle in a dry place, in no way marshy. Clear the ground and give it a slight incline, making it easier to sweep and clean. Leave it partly covered and partly open. Ensure that at night the cattle are not exposed to Auster or any damp breezes, and that the wind is not unduly troublesome from any direction. Build the walls for the rabbit hutch out of squared stone, the foundations deep enough to reach water level; and then fill the floor area with "male" sand, leaving raised mounds of Cimolean clay[59] here and there. Inside a court give the hens a south-facing shelter, sprinkled liberally with ashes, and above this a nesting place and perches, on which to roost overnight. Some would recommend the hens be confined in large, fenced-off coops, facing east. But for the laying and hatching of eggs, the more cheerful and open their surroundings, the more productive will the hens be; eggs laid in a shady, enclosed space will have less flavor.

Position your dovecote near water; make it conspicuous and moderately high, so that the pigeons, weary from flying and from performing their winged gymnastics and their clapping, will gladly glide in to land with outstretched wings. Some maintain that when a pigeon gathers food from a field, the greater the distance and effort to return to its young, the more it will feed them; this is because their food, stored by the pigeon in its throat, is half-digested by the delay; they therefore recommend the dovecote be given an awkward site. It might also be thought best to keep the dovecote well away from any water, to prevent the pigeons from cooling their eggs with damp feet. If you leave a kestrel in a cage at the corner of the tower, it will protect them from hawks. If, under the entrance, you bury the head of a wolf, sprinkled with cumin seed, inside a jar that is cracked so that the smell can escape, it will attract several pigeons away from their previous homes; and if you cover the ground with clay and repeatedly soak it in human urine, it will further increase their number. In front of the windows have a stone ledge or a shelf of olive wood, projecting out one cubit, on which the birds may land outside the shelter, and from which they may take off again.

Small cage-birds will waste away at the sight of trees and the sky. Bird-houses and bird tables should be put in a mild place; those for birds that walk rather than fly should be set lower down, if not on the ground itself; for all other birds they should be high up. Each should be bounded by a rack to contain eggs and young. In the construction of birdhouses, clay is better than lime, and lime better than gypsum. All tough stone is harmful; earthen-ware is better than tufa, provided it is not overbaked; the wood of the pop-lar or fir is best of all. Stalls for every kind of bird, but especially the pigeon, must be bright, clean, and spotless; as is also the case with quadrupeds, who develop scabies if the place where they lie is not kept thoroughly clean. Their stalls should therefore be vaulted, and the walls completely plastered, polished, and faced with marble; every gap should be diligently stopped, to keep eggs, young, and parents alike from being troubled by ferrets, mice, lizards, and other vermin. You must also have eating and watering places; for this you should dig a moat around the villa, where the geese, ducks, pigs, and oxen may wash and sleep; and make sure that the troughs where they take their food are well filled, even in rain and troubled weather. In the enclosures for smaller birds place the receptacles for water and meal in channels along the wall, to keep the birds from spilling or soiling the contents. These should be connected to the outside by pipes, through which the meal may be poured. In the middle should be a birdbath, with an abundant supply of clean water.

Dig the pond in chalky ground, and to a sufficient depth, to prevent its becoming too warm under the sun's rays or freezing over with the cold. Along the sides have hollows, where the fish can take refuge, when alarmed by a sudden disturbance, and not be consumed by panic. Fish feed off the earth's juices; fierce heat makes them torpid, and ice kills them, but they delight in the midday sun. The occasional influx of muddy rainwater is thought beneficial, although rain falling immediately after the Dog Star should be kept out, because it tastes of lime and kills fish; and thereafter it should rarely be admitted, as it infects water with foul-smelling moss and leaves the fish sluggish. It is important to make sure that there is a continual exchange of water, from a spring, river, or lake.

For ponds fed by seawater, the ancients go on to give the following sound advice: muddy ground produces flat fish, such as sole and oysters; other sea fish, such as bream and mackerel, fare better where it is sandy; where rocky, the wrasse and the whiting, and other fish that spawn among rocks.[60] Finally, in their opinion, the best type of pond is a lagoon, where one wave constantly follows another, and the old water inside is never allowed to stand and become stagnant. Water, they say, is slower to warm if it is gradually being renewed.[61] So much for the responsibilities of the steward.

Diligence is generally to be commended, but it is particularly appropriate in the harvesting and storage of produce and crops. These will require a threshing floor, open to the sun and wind, and positioned not far from the shed just mentioned, so that should there be any sudden cloudburst, the workmen may quickly remove the sheaves they have reaped and put them under cover. Where the threshing floor is to be, do not level the ground, but leave it slightly sloping, and dig it over; after that sprinkle it with oil lees, allowing them to be well absorbed; next thoroughly break up any clods; then level it with a roller or mallet, and tamp it down; after that sprinkle it once more with oil lees. When this has dried, neither mice nor ants will nest there, nor will it turn to mud, grass will not grow there, and no cracks will appear.[62] Clay makes the work particularly solid. So much for buildings for farm workers. ◆

17

87—90v

As for the master, some would maintain that he should have one villa for summer and another for winter. The following suggestions have been made: for winter the bedrooms should face the winter sunrise, and dining rooms the sunset at equinox; whereas for summer the bedrooms should face the midday sun, and dining rooms the winter sunrise; they would have the walkway exposed to the midday sun at equinox.[63] We, however, would prefer them to vary from place to place, according to climate and regional characteristics, so as to blend hot with cold, and damp with dry.

Moreover, I would prefer to locate the house of a gentleman somewhere dignified, rather than in a particularly fertile stretch of land, where it could enjoy all the benefit and delight of breeze, sun, and view. It should have easy access from the fields, and a generous reception area for the arrival of guests; it should be in view, and have itself a view of some city, town, stretch of coast, or plain, or it should have within sight the peaks of some notable hills or mountains, delightful gardens, and attractive haunts for fishing and hunting.

Each house, as we have already mentioned, is divided into public, semiprivate, and private zones. Of these, the public ones should imitate the house of a prince. There should be a large open area in front of the gates for chariot and horse races, its dimensions greater than the distance a young man could hurl a javelin or fire an arrow. Likewise within the gates there should be no shortage of semiprivate spaces, walkways, promenades, swimming pools, areas both grassed and paved over, porticoes, and semicircular loggias, where old men may meet for discussion in the welcome winter sun, and where on holidays the family might pass the day, and where in summer grateful shade may be found.

Clearly some of the house is occupied by members of the family, and the rest is given over to storing items for use. The family consists of the husband, wife, children, and grandparents, and their live-in domestics, including the clerks, attendants, and servants. Any guest is also to be included in the family. The items to be stored comprise essentials, such as food, and conveniences, such as clothing, weapons, books, and perhaps even a horse. The most important part is that which we shall call the "bosom" of the house, although you might refer to it as the "court" or "atrium";[64] next in importance comes the dining room, followed by private bedrooms, and finally living rooms. Then come the remainder, according to their use. The "bosom" is therefore the main part of the house, acting like a public forum, toward which all other lesser members converge; it should incorporate a comfortable entrance, and also openings for light, as appropriate. Clearly then everyone would prefer the bosom of his building to be a generous, open, noble, and prominent space. But whereas some are content with having one bosom to their building, others have added several, enclosed either completely by high walls or by a combination of high and low ones. They have covered some with roofs, others they have left open, and others partly covered and partly open; in some places they have added porticoes to one or more sides, and sometimes all four; some they have built on the ground, others on a vaulted base.

On this question I have nothing more to add, except that every consideration must be given to region, weather, use, and comfort—to keeping out biting Boreas and chill from air and ground in cold climates, or the troublesome sun in hot ones; and to letting in the refreshing breath of the heavens and a reasonable amount of pleasant light from all directions. Make sure that there is no marshy land to give off poisonous fumes, nor higher ground to produce a bank of mist to darken the atmosphere.

In the center of the bosom of the building should be the entrance with a vestibule; this should be dignified and in no way narrow, tortuous, or poorly lit. There should be a consecrated chapel, immediately visible, with an altar; here any guest on entry may make a pledge of friendship, and here the head of the family on his return home may pray to the gods above for peace and calm for his family; then in the vestibule he may embrace anyone who has come to greet him, and consult with friends over any decision to be made, and so on.

Here it would be convenient to have glass windows, balconies, and porticoes; apart from the attraction of the view, they may admit sun or breezes, depending on the season. According to Martial. "Glass casements facing the wintry Notus let in clear sun and daylight undefiled."[65] The ancients preferred their porticoes to face south, because in summer the arc of the sun would be too high for its rays to enter, whereas in winter it would be low enough. Mountains to the south, when viewed from afar, are not as pleasant, because the side that is visible is in shade, and they themselves will be obscured by a white haze common to that quarter of the sky; yet, when closer to, and seemingly right overhead, they make the night frosty and the shade freezing; but in all other respects they are more pleasant close at hand, and more useful, because they shut out Auster. A mountain to the north, when close by, will reflect the sun's rays and increase the temperature; but when some distance away, it will be most delightful: the clear atmosphere, ever present in that quarter of the sky, and the bright sun flooding down will leave it wonderfully distinct and resplendent. Mountains to the east, if close by, leave the dawn cold; conversely, those to the west throw a heavy dew at daybreak. Mountains to the east or west are most agreeable in the middle distance.

So too with rivers and lakes; these are a great inconvenience when too close, and are not as delightful when too far away. On the other hand, the sea from the middle distance leaves the breeze thick with salt; closer to, it is less of a nuisance, as the climate there is more constant; when viewed from afar, the sea has greater charm, because it inspires longing. The direction in which the sea lies is important, however: if to the south, it will scorch: to the east, increase the humidity; to the west, cause mist; and to the north, exacerbate the cold.

The dining rooms[66] should be entered off the bosom of the house. As use demands, there should be one for summer, one for winter, and one for the middling seasons, as you might say. The principal requirements of a summer dining room are water and greenery; of a winter one, the warmth of a hearth. Both should preferably be spacious, cheery, and splendid. It is easy to prove that the chimneys of the ancients were not the same as those to which we are accustomed. It is written, ". . . and the tops of the roofs smoked."[67] To this day nowhere in Italy (apart from Tuscany and Cisalpine Gaul) are there smoke flues to be seen projecting through the roof.

The vaults of winter dining rooms, according to Vitruvius, are not worth adorning with delicate cornice work, because it will be ruined by the smoke and constant soot from the hearth.[68] Indeed, they used to paint the vaulting above the fireplace black, to give the impression that it had been darkened by smoke. Elsewhere I read that they would use a wood called "cooked," which was purified to make it burn smokelessly;[69] this is why the lawyers felt that it could not come under the definition of "wood."[70] From this it may be deduced that they used mobile braziers of bronze or iron, to be moved wherever circumstances or the occasion demanded. It may even be that those barrack-room generations, hardened by military service to a man, had less use for the hearths. Nor do the physicians approve of our spending our whole time in front of a large fire. Aristotle maintains that it is cold that gives the flesh of animals its firmness.[71] Those who claim to understand these matters note that almost everyone who works in a foundry has an extremely rough, wrinkled complexion and skin; the reason they give for this is that fat and humors, the two substances of which flesh is composed, are congealed by the cold and then melted by the fire, so that they dissolve into vapor. The Germans, the Colchians, and other nations living where fire is needed to combat the rigors of the cold, use heated rooms; these will be dealt with in the appropriate place.[72] To return to the hearth.

These are the rules that apply to the hearth: it should be prominent, it should be capable of warming several people at one time, and it should have sufficient light but no draft (although there must be an outlet, to allow smoke to rise). The hearth, therefore, must not be confined to some corner or recessed deep within the wall; at the same time it should not occupy the most important position in the room, where the guests' table should be. It should not be troubled by gusts from any opening; the mouth at the bottom should not stand out much from the wall. The throat should be deep, with generous crossways, rising vertically until the entire chimney pot clears the apex of the roof; this was obviously intended to reduce the risk of fire and to avoid the roof's becoming an obstruction to the wind, causing the formation of air currents and eddies, which might check and force back the smoke. Smoke rises on its own, through its natural heat, but with the warmth of the flames and hearth its speed is increased. Once within the throat of the chimney, the smoke is constrained, as though in a tube, and with the force of the flames behind it, it is expelled in the same manner as sound is from a trumpet. And as with a trumpet, when it is too wide, air will enter and dull the sound, so it is with smoke.

The top of the chimney pot should be covered, to protect it from the rain; around the sides should be open vents, shielded by breaks from the assault of the wind. Between the breaks and the vents there should be sufficient space for the smoke to escape. Where this is not possible, I would have what I call a "vertula" mounted on a vertical pin. This is a copper cowl, wide enough to accommodate the upper mouth of the chimney; on the front of this stands a crest, which acts like a rudder and turns the back of the head against the direction of the wind.[73] Another convenient method is to fit a horn, of copper or terra cotta, over the chimney pot; this should be large, open, and hollow, and should be upturned, with its upper mouth sitting on the throat itself, so that smoke drawn in from the cheek below will be forced out at the top, despite the wind.

The dining rooms require a kitchen and a pantry for storing the leftovers of meals, along with vessels and tablecloths. The kitchen should be neither right in the lap of the guests, nor so far off that dishes intended to be served hot become cold in transit; those dining need only be out of earshot of the irksome din of scullery maids, plates, and pans. Take care that the dishes are carried along a route that is protected from the rain, has no tortuous corners, and does not pass through any dingy place, all of which may compromise the standard of the cuisine.

After the dining room comes the bedroom. As with dining rooms, a luxurious house would have different bedrooms for summer and winter. This brings to mind a comment made by Lucullus, that no man of free birth deserves a worse lot than that of a crane or swallow.[74] But we for our part shall only pass on what in each case good sense would recommend. I recall reading in the historian Aemilius Probo that it was the custom in Greece for women not to be admitted to table, except for meals with relatives, and the custom too for certain parts of the house, where the women resided, to be out of bounds to all but closest kin.[75] And certainly, to my mind, any place reserved for women ought to be treated as though dedicated to religion and chastity; also I would have the young girls and maidens allocated comfortable apartments, to relieve their delicate minds from the tedium of confinement. The matron should be accommodated most effectively where she could monitor what everyone in the house was doing. But in each case we should abide by whatever may be the ancestral custom.

The husband and wife must have separate bedrooms, not only to ensure that the husband be not disturbed by his wife, when she is about to give birth or is ill, but also to allow them, even in summer, an uninterrupted night's sleep, whenever they wish. Each room should have its own door, and in addition a common side door, to enable them to seek each other's company unnoticed. Off the wife's bedroom should be a dressing room, and off the husband's, a library. The grandmother, being weary with old age and in need of rest and quiet, should have a bedroom that is warm, sheltered, and well away from all the din coming from the family or outside; above all, her room should enjoy a little fireplace, and other comforts of the body and soul, essential to the infirm. Off this should be the strong room; here the boys and young men should pass the night, the girls and maidens in the dressing room, and next to them the nurse. Guests should be accommodated in a section of the house adjoining the vestibule, where they are more accessible to visitors and less of a disturbance for the rest of the family.[76] The young men of over seventeen[77] should be accommodated opposite the guests, or at least not far from them, to encourage them to form an acquaintance. Off the guest room should be a repository, where the guest might hide his more personal or precious belongings, and retrieve them as he wishes. Off the room for the young men should be the armory.

The butlers, domestics, and servants should be segregated from the gentry, and allocated accommodation decorated and furnished in keeping with their positions. The maids and valets should be stationed close enough to their areas of responsibility to enable them to hear commands immediately and be at hand to carry them out. The butler should be stationed at the entrances to the wine cellar and food stores. The stable boys should sleep in front of the stables. The stud horses should be kept apart from the pack horses, in a place where they will not offend anyone inside the house with their smell, or harm one another fighting, and where there is no risk of fire.

Wheat and all other seed is decayed by damp, faded by heat, impaired by rough treatment, and ruined by contact with lime. Therefore wherever you intend to store it, whether in a cave or a well, on wooden flooring, or heaped up on the ground, make sure that it is kept somewhere thoroughly dry and fresh. Josephus maintains that in Siboli grain was discovered intact where it had lain hidden for one hundred years.[78] Some are of the opinion that if barley is stored in a warm place, it will not perish, although after a year it will rapidly deteriorate. The physicians claim that while damp predisposes bodies to decay, it is heat that actually decays them. If the granary floor is composed of a paste of oil lees and clay over a base of broom and crushed straw, the grain will remain more solid and firm and will keep longer, nor will it be harmed by weevil or pilfered by ants.

Granaries for seed are best made of unbaked bricks. With seed- and even fruit-stores, Boreas is more favorable than Auster; but any breeze blowing in from somewhere damp will cause decay and leave the contents teeming with weevil and worm, while constant, excessive wind from any direction will cause them to shrivel. For vegetables, and especially beans, make the floor of ash and oil lees. Keep fruit on boarding in a cool, enclosed room. Aristotle was of the opinion that fruit, if stored in inflated bladders, would keep for an entire year.[79] The movement of air destroys everything; for this reason breezes from any direction are to be avoided; indeed, Aquilo is said to wrinkle and ruin fruit.

The approved wine cellar should be underground and enclosed, although some wines deteriorate in the shade. Even well-protected wine is ruined by exposure to any wind from the east, south, or west, especially during winter or spring; but under the Dog Star even Boreas disturbs it; the rays of the sun dry it up; the moon leaves it dull; movement throws a sediment and reduces the flavor. Wine is greedy for any odor, but a strong smell breaks it down and weakens it. In dry, cool, stable conditions wine will last for years. As Columella puts it, "Wine will keep properly as long as it is cool."[80] Therefore build the wine cellar somewhere solid, free from the vibration of carts. The walls and windows should face between the sunrise and Aquilo. Remove all filth, foul-smelling matter, any sources of damp, dense vapors or smoke, and any strong-smelling vegetables, such as onions, cabbage, and wild or domestic figs, and keep them well away. Pave the floor of your wine cellar as you might an outside surface, and leave a small dip in the center to collect any leakage from the vats. Some make their vats out of mortar or use techniques of wall construction; the larger the vat, the stronger and more full-bodied the wine.

Oil keeps better in warm shade; it dislikes cold drafts, and is ruined by smoke or soot. The storage of unclean matter, such as manure, can be passed over, of which they say there must be two heaps, one for fresh manure, another for old; manure thrives in the damp, but is drained by the sun or wind: let it only be said that anything at risk from fire, such as a hayloft, and anything unpleasant in appearance or smell should be removed and kept well away. Manure heaps constructed out of oak do not breed snakes.

I feel there is one comment not to be overlooked here: is it not wrong that although in the countryside manure heaps would be made in some secluded and remote spot, where the smell would not offend the farm household, nevertheless indoors, and almost below our beds in the main chambers, where we would take our otherwise unsullied rest, we choose to keep our private latrines, repositories, in effect, of the most infectious stink? If one is ill, it is indeed more convenient to use a bedpan and a chamber pot; but I see no reason why those in good health should not think it proper to keep anything so loathsome well away. And one may see the lengths to which birds, and swallows in particular, will go to ensure that their nests are completely clean for their young. It is remarkable what Nature teaches us: even the little fledglings during their first few days, as soon as their members are strong enough, empty their bowels only outside their nests; furthermore, to keep the filth well away, their parents are at hand to catch the droppings in midair in their beaks, and remove them. And so, in my opinion, the sound advice of Nature should be followed. ◆

18

90v—92

The villas and town houses of the wealthy differ in that the fortunate will own a villa as a summer retreat, but use the town house as somewhere to pass the winter in greater comfort. By this means they enjoy all the advantages to be found in the country, of light, breeze, open space, and views, and also the more shady and softer delights of the city. All that is required of a city dwelling is that it offer, within a dignified and salubrious setting, whatever is necessary for a civilized existence. Yet, as far as the limited space and light will allow, it should assume all the charm and delight of a villa.

Apart from a generous entrance, it should also contain a portico, walkways, promenades,[81] delightful gardens, and so on. But if the site is too cramped, sufficient space may be found for these members by building on level ground and increasing the number of stories. Where the nature of the site will allow, a cellar should be dug to provide storage for liquid and wood, and likewise the services; the noble floors of the house should be constructed on top. Then in turn further stories may be added, as needed, until all the requirements of the household are adequately met. The basic facilities should be at the base, the nobler rooms at a nobler level. Finally, make sure that there are discreet places to store grain, fruit, tools, and, in short, all household goods.

Also include a room for storing religious items, and one for the women's toilet;[82] have somewhere to keep what is used on feast days, and somewhere for the robes worn by men on holy days; have a cupboard for tools and weapons, and one for wool-making equipment, and somewhere else to store implements used at banquets or on the arrival of guests, and other objects reserved for certain special occasions. Things in monthly, yearly, and daily use should be kept in separate places. It is important to ensure that objects which cannot be locked away are kept within sight; the more so the less frequent their use. For anything in daily view is clearly in less danger of being stolen.[83]

For their own buildings, humbler folk should follow the example of the rich and emulate their magnificence, as far as their resources allow, though this imitation must be dampened, so that financial considerations are not sacrificed to pleasure. Their villas, then, should provide for the ox and herd almost as much as for the wife. They want a dovecote, fish pond, and so on, not for pleasure so much as for profit. Yet the villa should be pretty enough to ensure that the mother of the family will enjoy living there and will give careful devotion to its domestic upkeep. Nor should utility and profit only be taken into account, since health also should be a primary consideration. "Whenever you have occasion for a change of air, do so in the winter," advises Celsus;[84] in winter it is less dangerous than in summer to endure an unhealthy climate. But we would rather visit the villa in summer; ensure, then, that it is extremely healthy.

Within the city, the shop that lies beneath the house and provides the owner with his livelihood should be better fitted out than his dining room, as would appear more in keeping with his hopes and ambitions. If at a junction, it should occupy the corner position, if in a forum, it should lie on one of the sides, and if on a military road, at a conspicuous bend; almost the sole concern should be to entice customers by the goods on display. For the internal construction it would not be unseemly to use unbaked brick, wicker work, clay, a straw-bound mud, or timber; on the outside, though, it must be taken into account that neighbors may not always be honest and polite; accordingly the wall should be reinforced against the assault of both man and weather. Neighboring buildings should be either far enough apart to allow the breeze to dry them quickly, or close enough together for the rainwater to be received and carried off in the same gutter. Buildings with interconnecting roofs of this type and the gutters themselves should be quite steep, to make sure that the rain does not collect or wash back, but is quickly removed along the shortest possible route.

Finally, to summarize all that seems worth repeating, along with what was discussed in the first book. Any part of the building to be protected from fire, or exposed to the onslaught of the weather, or shut off or free from noise should be vaulted. It is preferable to vault the ground floor of every building, but it would be more hygienic to make subsequent floors of composite timber construction. Parts that require light until dusk, such as reception halls, passageways, and, in particular, libraries, should face the direction of the sunset at equinox.[85] Anything at risk from moths, mustiness, mold, or rust, such as clothes, books, tools, seed, and any form of food, should be kept in the east or south side of the house. Anywhere an even light is required by painter, writer, or sculptor should lie on the north side. Finally, face all the summer rooms to receive Boreas, all winter ones to the south; spring and autumn ones toward the sunrise; make the baths and spring dining rooms face the sunset.[86] But if it is impossible to arrange the parts as you might wish, reserve the most comfortable for the summer. To my mind, anyone who is constructing a building will construct it for summer use, if he has any sense; for it is easy enough to cater to winter: shut all openings, and light the fire; but to combat heat, much is to be done, and not always to great effect. Make your winter living area, therefore, modest in size, modest in height, and with modest openings; conversely, make your entire summer living area in every way spacious and open. Build it so that it will attract the cool breezes but exclude the sun and the winds coming from the sun. For a big room filled with air is like a lot of water in a large dish: it is very slow to warm. ◆

Here Begins the Sixth Book of Leon Battista Alberti. On Ornament.

The lineaments,[1] the materials for construction, and the employment of craftsmen; also anything else that might seem relevant to the construction of buildings, both public and private, sacred and profane; again, anything that would protect them from the assaults of bad weather and make them adaptable to the requirements of place, time, man, or thing—we have dealt with all this in the five preceding books. How thoroughly we have done so you may yourself discover as you examine them. I do not think you would want greater application in dealing with such matters. As heaven is my witness, it was a more demanding task than I could have imagined when I embarked on it. Frequent problems in explaining matters, inventing terms, and handling material discouraged me and often made me want to abandon the whole enterprise. On the other hand, the very reasons that first induced me to embark on it summoned me back to my undertaking and encouraged me to continue. For I grieved that so many works of such brilliant writers had been destroyed by the hostility of time and of man, and that almost the sole survivor from this vast shipwreck is Vitruvius, an author of unquestioned experience, though one whose writings have been so corrupted by time that there are many omissions and many shortcomings. What he handed down was in any case not refined, and his speech such that the Latins might think that he wanted to appear a Greek, while the Greeks would think that he babbled Latin. However, his very text is evidence that he wrote neither Latin nor Greek, so that as far as we are concerned he might just as well not have written at all, rather than write something that we cannot understand.

Examples of ancient temples and theaters have survived that may teach us as much as any professor,[2] but I see—not without sorrow—these very buildings being despoiled more each day.[3] And anyone who happens to build nowadays draws his inspiration from inept modern nonsense rather than proven and much commended methods. Nobody would deny that as a result of all this a whole section of our life and learning could disappear altogether.

Since that is how things stood, I could not help but consider long and often whether it was not my duty to write a commentary on this subject. As I was exploring this matter, many noble, useful things, vital to the existence of man, came to my notice, which I decided not to neglect in writing. Moreover, I felt it the duty of any gentleman or any person of learning to save from total extinction a discipline that our prudent ancestors had valued so highly.

As I vacillated, and hesitated whether to press ahead or give up, my love of work and enthusiasm for learning prevailed; and where intelligence failed me, enthusiastic study and hard application supplied. No building of the ancients that had attracted praise, wherever it might be, but I immediately examined it carefully, to see what I could learn from it. Therefore I never stopped exploring, considering, and measuring everything, and comparing the information through line drawings, until I had grasped and understood fully what each had to contribute in terms of ingenuity or skill; this is how my passion and delight in learning relieved the labor of writing. Yet to collate material from sources so varied, heterogeneous, and dispersed, material from outside the normal range and skill of any writer, to review it in a dignified manner, to arrange in a proper order, to articulate precisely and explain rationally, surely all this required an ability and learning greater than I would profess to have. Even this will not cause me to repine, if I have succeeded in the general aim I set myself of convincing the reader that I would rather my speech seemed lucid than appeared eloquent. Those with any experience in this field of writing will appreciate how difficult this is, better than those who have never taken such a risk. What we have written is (unless I am mistaken) in proper Latin, and in comprehensible form. We shall do our utmost to continue like this in the remainder of the work.

Of the three conditions that apply to every form of construction—that what we construct should be appropriate to its use, lasting in structure, and graceful and pleasing in appearance—the first two have been dealt with, and there remains the third, the noblest and most necessary of all. ◆

2

93—94

Now graceful and pleasant appearance, so it is thought, derives from beauty and ornament alone, since there can be no one, however surly or slow, rough or boorish, who would not be attracted to what is most beautiful, seek the finest ornament at the expense of all else, be offended by what is unsightly, shun all that is inelegant or shabby, and feel that any short-comings an object may have in its ornament will detract equally from its grace and from its dignity.

Most noble is beauty, therefore, and it must be sought most eagerly by anyone who does not wish what he owns to seem distasteful. What remark-able importance our ancestors, men of great prudence, attached to it is shown by the care they took that their legal, military, and religious institutions—indeed, the whole commonwealth—should be much embel-lished; and by their letting it be known that if all these institutions, without which man could scarce exist, were to be stripped of their pomp and finery, their business would appear insipid and shabby. When we gaze at the won-drous works of the heavenly gods, we admire the beauty we see, rather than the utility that we recognize. Need I go further? Nature herself, as is everywhere plain to see, does not desist from basking in a daily orgy of beauty—let the hues of her flowers serve as my one example.

But if this quality is desirable anywhere, surely it cannot be absent from buildings, without offending experienced and inexperienced alike. What would be our reaction to a deformed and ill-considered[4] pile of stones, other than the more to criticize it the greater the expense, and to condemn the wanton greed for piling up stones? To have satisfied necessity is trite and insignificant, to have catered to convenience unrewarding when the inelegance in a work causes offense.

In addition, there is one particular quality that may greatly increase the convenience and even the life of a building. Who would not claim to dwell more comfortably between walls that are ornate, rather than neglected? What other human art might sufficiently protect a building to save it from human attack? Beauty may even influence an enemy, by restraining his anger and so preventing the work from being violated. Thus I might be so bold as to state: No other means is as effective in protecting a work from damage and human injury as is dignity and grace of form.[5] All care, all diligence, all financial consideration must be directed to ensuring that what is built is useful, commodious, yes—but also embellished and wholly graceful, so that anyone seeing it would not feel that the expense might have been invested better elsewhere.

The precise nature of beauty and ornament, and the difference between them, the mind could perhaps visualize more clearly than my words could explain. For the sake of brevity, however, let us define them as follows: Beauty is that reasoned harmony of all the parts within a body, so that nothing may be added, taken away, or altered, but for the worse.[6] It is a great and holy matter; all our resources of skill and ingenuity will be taxed in achieving it; and rarely is it granted, even to Nature herself, to produce anything that is entirely complete and perfect in every respect. "How rare," remarks a character in Cicero, "is a beautiful youth in Athens!"[7] That connoisseur found their forms wanting because they either had too much or too little of something by which they failed to conform to the laws of beauty. In this case, unless I am mistaken, had ornament been applied by painting and masking anything ugly, or by grooming and polishing the attractive, it would have had the effect of making the displeasing less offensive and the pleasing more delightful. If this is conceded, ornament may be defined as a form of auxiliary light and complement to beauty. From this it follows, I believe, that beauty is some inherent property, to be found suffused all through the body of that which may be called beautiful; whereas ornament, rather than being inherent, has the character of something attached or additional.[8]

This granted, I continue: Anyone who builds so as to be praised for it—as anyone with good sense would—must adhere to a consistent theory; for to follow a consistent theory is the mark of true art. Who would deny that only through art can correct and worthy building be achieved? And after all this particular part concerning beauty and ornament, being the most important of all, must depend on some sure and consistent method and art, which it would be most foolish to ignore. Yet some would disagree who maintain that beauty, and indeed every aspect of building, is judged by relative and variable criteria, and that the forms of buildings should vary according to individual taste and must not be bound by any rules of art. A common fault, this, among the ignorant—to deny the existence of anything they do not understand. I have decided to correct this error; not that I shall attempt (since I would need detailed and extended argument for it) to explain the arts from their origins, by what reasoning they developed, and by what experience they were nourished; let me simply repeat what has been said, that the arts were born of Chance and Observation, fostered by Use and Experiment, and matured by Knowledge and Reason.

Thus medicine, they say, was developed by a million people over a thousand years; sailing too, as almost every other art, advanced by minute steps. ◆

<table>
<tr><td>**3**
94—95v</td><td>Building, so far as we can tell from ancient monuments, enjoyed her first gush of youth, as it were, in Asia, flowered in Greece, and later reached her glorious maturity in Italy. It would seem to me quite likely that the kings of Asia, being men of considerable wealth and leisure, when reflecting on their own standing, their wealth, and the majesty and greatness of their thrones,[9] saw the need for grander roofs and more dignified walls, and began to search out and collect anything that might be of use to this end; then, perhaps, to make their buildings as large and splendid as possible, they used the largest trees available for their roofs and built their walls of a finer stone. Their buildings became impressive as well as graceful.</td></tr>
</table>

Then, thinking that it was the huge scale of their works that was admired, and that one of the primary tasks of a king was to build what lay beyond the capacity of the private citizen, these kings became enamored of the immensity of their works, until their rivalry led to the folly of constructing pyramids.

I believe that experience in building gave them an opportunity to discern differences in number, order, arrangement, and exterior appearance in their buildings, and allowed them to compare one to another.[10] In this way they learned to appreciate the graceful and to spurn the ill-considered.

Next came Greece, a country where upright and noble minds flourished, and the desire for embellishing what was theirs was evident, and, above all, great attention was given to the construction of temples. Therefore they began by examining the works of the Assyrians and the Egyptians, from which they realized that in such matters the artist's skill attracted more praise than the wealth of the king: for vast works need only great wealth; praise belongs to those with whom the experts find no fault. The Greeks therefore decided that it was their part to surpass through ingenuity those whose wealth they could not rival, in whatever work they undertook. As with other arts, so with building, they sought it in, and drew it out from, the very bosom of Nature, and began to discuss and examine it thoroughly, studying and weighing it up with great incisiveness and subtlety.

They inquired into the differences between buildings that were admired and those that were not, overlooking nothing. They performed all manner of experiment, surveying and retracing the steps of Nature. Mixing equal with equal, straight with curved, light with shade, they considered whether a third combination might arise, as from the union of male and female, which would help them to achieve their original aim. They continued to consider each individual part in the minutest detail, how right agreed with left, vertical with horizontal, near with far. They added, took away, and adjusted greater to smaller, like to unlike, first to last, until they had established the different qualities desirable in those buildings intended to endure for ages, and those erected for no reason as much as their good looks.[11] This was their achievement.

As for Italy, their inborn thrift prompted them to be the first who made their buildings very like animals.[12] Take the case of a horse: they realized that where the shape of each member looked suitable for a particular use, so the whole animal itself would work well in that use. Thus they found that grace of form could never be separated or divorced from suitability for use. But once they had gained dominion over the world, they were so obviously eager to embellish their city and property as the Greeks had been, that within thirty years a house that might have been considered the finest in the entire city would not rank in the first hundred. There was such an incredible surfeit of talent in this field that at one time, I read, seven hundred architects were being employed in Rome alone, whose work could scarcely be praised enough. The empire had sufficient resources to supply anything needed to provoke astonishment: they say that a certain Tacius gave the people of Ostia a bath building with a hundred columns of Numidian marble for which he paid with private funds.[13] In spite of all this, they preferred to temper the splendor of their most powerful kings with a traditional frugality, so that parsimony did not detract from utility, nor was utility sacrificed to opulence, but could also incorporate anything that might be devised to enhance comfort or grace.

Their concern and enthusiasm for building continued unbroken, until eventually they probed so thoroughly into the art that there was nothing so recondite, concealed, or abstruse as not to have been explored, traced out, or brought to light; all this with the help of the gods, and little resistance from the art itself. Since the art of building had long been a guest among the Italians, more particularly among the Etruscans, who, besides the miraculous works of their kings, of which we read, such as labyrinths and sepulchers,[14] have inherited from ancient Etruria very old and excellent precepts about the building of temples;[15] because, I say, the art of building had long been a guest in Italy, and because the desire for her was so evident, she seems to have flourished there, so that Italy's dominion over the world, already famous for every other virtue, was by her ornament made still more impressive. She surrendered herself therefore to their understanding and possession, thinking it a disgrace that the leaders of the world, the glory of all nations, should be rivaled in the splendor of their works by peoples surpassed in every other virtue.[16]

Need I mention the porticoes, temples, ports, theaters, and vast baths, which caused such amazement that experienced architects from abroad denied that some of those works could ever be built, although they saw them before their very eyes. Should I go on? They did not fail even to have their drains beautifully built. And they had such taste for ornament that they delighted in lavishing imperial resources on grace alone, and their enterprise in building was perfectly matched by the ornament.[17]

Through the example of our ancestors, therefore, and through the advice of experts and constant practice on our part, thorough understanding may be gained on how to construct marvelous buildings, and from that understanding well-proven principles may be deduced; rules that should not be ignored by anyone eager—as we all should be—not to appear inept in what he builds. These we must set down, as was our undertaking, and explain to the best of our ability. These principles either direct every aspect of beauty and ornament throughout the building or relate individually to its various parts.[18] The former are derived from philosophy, and are concerned with establishing the direction and limits to this art; the latter come from the experience of which we spoke, but are honed, so to speak, to the rule of philosophy and plot the course of this art. These latter ones have a more technical character, and I shall deal with them first, saving the former more general rules for an epilogue. ◆

4

95v—98

The pleasure to be found in objects of great beauty and ornament is produced either by invention and the working of the intellect, or by the hand of the craftsman, or it is imbued naturally in the objects themselves. The intellect is responsible for choice, distribution, arrangement, and so on, which give the work dignity; the hand is responsible for laying, joining, cutting, trimming, polishing, and such like, which give the work grace; the properties derived from Nature are weight, lightness, density, purity, durability, and the like, which bring the work admiration. These three must be applied to each part of the building, according to its respective use and role.

The parts of a building may be classified in several different ways, but here we would prefer to draw the distinction between characteristics common to all buildings, rather than according to individual differences. In the first book we established that every building must have a locality, *area*, compartition, wall, roof, and opening.[19] In this they all agree. Their individual differences lie in that some are planned as sacred, some profane, some public, others private, some for need, others for pleasure, and so on. We shall begin with their common characteristics.

It is difficult to establish how the hand and intellect of man may increase the grace or dignity of the locality, unless, perhaps, it is worth imitating those responsible for devising the fantastic schemes that have been documented—schemes that men of prudence would not criticize, provided they offered some advantage, but would not praise unless they were necessary. And rightly so. Who would praise[20] whoever it was—whether Stasicrates, as Plutarch claims,[21] or Dinocrates, as Vitruvius maintains[22]—who proposed to carve Mount Athos into an effigy of Alexander and in its hand to place a city capable of holding ten thousand people?

But equally, Queen Nitocris is not to be criticized for constructing vast ditches to divert a bend in the Euphrates into a huge loop, so that it passed three times in front of the same Assyrian village, if the depth of the ditch helped to fortify the locality, and the abundant irrigation to improve the fertility of the soil.[23] But let such projects be for the amusement of powerful kings. Let them join sea to sea by cutting through intervening land; let them level mountains and valleys; let them create new islands, and again join existing ones to the mainland; let them leave behind feats that could never be imitated, and in so doing preserve their name for posterity. In any case, the more useful their works will prove, the more they will be praised.

The ancients would use religion to add dignity to places and groves, and even entire regions. We read that the whole of Sicily was consecrated to Ceres.[24] But let us skirt this matter. What would be most agreeable would be some admirable and unusual property of the place, of great benefit and quite outstanding; as, for example, when the climate happens to be milder than anywhere else, and unbelievably consistent, as it is in Meroe, where men live as long as they wish;[25] or when the locality offers something to be found nowhere else, desirable and salutary to mankind, such as amber, cinnamon, or balsam; or when there is some supernatural influence, as on the island of Sonus Eubusius, which is said to be quite free of anything harmful.[26]

The *area*, being a certain portion of the locality, will be enhanced by all that may adorn the locality.[27] But natural advantages will be more abundant and readily available in the *area* than they are in the locality. There may be many different attractions all around, such as promontories, rocks, heights, chasms, grottoes, springs, and other reasons making it attractive to build there rather than anywhere else. Also there may be landmarks of some bygone era, records of the times and events to fill the eyes and mind with admiration. These I shall pass over; nor shall I mention the site where Troy once stood, the blood-soaked fields at Leuctra or Trasimene,[28] and the countless other examples.

It is not easy to describe what the hand or intellect of man may contribute to this end. I shall pass over the more obvious instances, such as the oriental plane trees transported by sea as far as the island of Diomede, to adorn an *area*,[29] or the erection of columns and obelisks by great men, or the planting of trees for posterity to venerate, such as the olive planted by Neptune and Mercury, which long stood on the acropolis of Athens.[30] Nor shall I mention objects preserved for long ages and handed down by our ancestors for posterity, such as the terebinth tree at Hebron, which is said to have lasted from the beginning of the world to the time of Josephus the historian.[31]

A most appropriate way to make a place more dignified is through good taste and ingenious measures, such as the laws that prohibit any male from entering the temple of Bona Dea,[32] or that of Diana by the patrician portico;[33] likewise at Tanagra no female may enter the grove of Eunostus,[34] nor the inner parts of the temple in Jerusalem;[35] and there is a spring in Panthia where no one but priests may wash, and they only for the purpose of making a sacrifice; nor may anyone spit in Doliola by the Roman Cloaca Maxima, where the bones of King Pompilius lie.[36] Inscriptions may be found in a number of chapels forbidding the entry of prostitutes.[37] No one is allowed to enter the temple of Diana in Crete, except in bare feet,[38] and no slave girl is permitted entry to the temple of Matuta.[39] No herald may enter the temple of Oridio at Rhodes,[40] nor flute player the temple of Tennes at Tenedos.[41] No one may leave the temple of Laphystian Jove without first offering a sacrifice.[42] No ivy may be carried into the temple of Pallas at Athens, or of Venus at Thebes. In the temple of Faunus the word "wine" could not be mentioned.[43] There was also a rule that in Rome the Porta Janualis could not be closed during war, nor the gate of the temple of Janus opened during peace;[44] and they preferred the temple of Hora to remain continually open.[45]

Should we decide to follow this example, then it might be appropriate to make it unlawful for any woman to enter temples of the martyrs, or men those temples of the virgin saints. There are other conditions that human ingenuity can fix, and that add great dignity; some of these, although we read of them, we would scarcely credit, if similar ones were not to be found in our own times. Some maintain that human art was responsible for the fact that in Byzantium snakes will not harm anyone, nor jackdaws fly indoors; and that around Naples crickets are never heard,[46] that there are no owls in Crete,[47] that no bird ever disturbs the temple of Achilles in the island of Boristene,[48] and that in the Forum Boarium at Rome no fly or dog has ever entered the temple of Hercules.[49] And in our own times it has been claimed that no kind of fly ever enters the public palace of the Censors in

Venice; in Toledo only one type of fly will enter the public slaughterhouse, and it may be distinguished by its whiteness.

Many such examples are recorded, but to review them would take too long. Nor do I know enough to say whether they are the result of artifice or of Nature. Is art or Nature, for instance, responsible for the following? A laurel tree is said to grow from the tomb of Bibrias, king of Pontus; if a sprig from it is taken aboard ship, it will lead to continual disagreement on board, until it is removed.[50] It never rains on the altar of the sanctuary of Venus in Paphos; in Troy, if any sacrificial remains are left about the statue of Minerva, they will not rot; if a hole is dug in the tomb of Anteus, the heavens will not stop raining until it has been refilled. Some maintain that these effects may be achieved using a technique now long out of use, based on the operation of figurines that the astronomers claim to understand.

I recall reading in the life of Apollonius that magicians fixed on the roof of the royal basilica of Babylon four gold birds, which they called the tongues of the gods; these, they claimed, had the power to reconcile the mind of the crowd to the heart of the king.[51] Even as serious an author as Josephus claims to have witnessed a certain Eleazar, who in the presence of Vespasian and his sons instantly cured a maniac, by putting a ring to his nose.[52] He also claims that Solomon had composed an incantation to reduce illnesses.[53] And Serapis of Egypt, whom we call Pluto, according to Eusebius Pamphylius, gave out symbols for expelling demons and taught how they took on the form of animals to taunt humans.[54] Servius, too, claims that men used to recite certain magical incantations to protect themselves from misfortune, so that they could not die unless the incantation were to be canceled.[55] If such stories are true, I could easily be led to believe an incident I find in Plutarch: there was in Pellene a statue that, if taken out of the temple by a priest, would fill everything, wherever it faced, with terror and great anxiety, because no eye could look at it without fear.[56] But these anecdotes are included for entertainment.

To continue. As for the general methods of dignifying the *area*, such as setting out, dyking, leveling, consolidation, and so on, I have no more to say, beyond what is to be found above in the first and third books. To have the greatest dignity, the *area*, as we mentioned above, must be extremely dry, level, and solid, and very appropriate and convenient for the purpose that it is to serve; it may well help to surface it with some material: this we shall deal with later, when discussing walls. Plato also gives some useful advice: a grand name will lend a place great dignity and authority.[57] That the emperor Hadrian approved of this is demonstrated by the famous names, such as Licus, Canopeius, Achademia, and Tempe, that he gave the rooms of his Tiburtine villa.[58] ◆

Compartition has, for the most part, already been dealt with in the first book, but we shall summarize it again here.[59] The chief ornament in every object is that it should be free of all that is unseemly. Compartition, therefore, will be seemly when it is neither jumpy, nor confused, nor disorganized, nor disconnected, nor composed of incongruous elements; it should be made up of members neither too numerous, nor too small, nor too large, nor too dissonant or ungraceful, nor too disjointed or distant from the rest of the body, as it were. But in terms of its nature, utility, and methods of operation, everything should be so defined, so exact in its order, number, size, arrangement, and form, that every single part of the work will be considered necessary, of great comfort, and in pleasing harmony[60] with the rest. For if the compartition satisfies these conditions completely, the cheerfulness and elegance of the ornament will find the appropriate place and will shine out; but if not, the work will undoubtedly fail to retain any dignity. The entire composition of the members, therefore, must be so well considered, conform so perfectly with the requirements of necessity and convenience, that this or that part should not give as much pleasure separately as their appropriate placing, here or there, in a particular order, situation, conjunction, arrangement, and configuration.

In adorning the wall and roof, you will have ample room to display uncommon gifts of Nature, techniques of art, diligence of the workman, and power of the intellect. But should you have the means to imitate the ancient Osyris, who is said to have built two temples out of gold, one dedicated to the celestial Jove, the other to the royal Jove;[61] or should you be able to incorporate in the construction a block of stone large beyond human belief, such as that quarried by Semiramis from the mountains of Arabia, measuring 20 cubits in height and breadth, and 150 in length;[62] or if there were available a block of stone so large that you could use it to complete one entire section of the whole work, such as the reported shrine of Latona in Egypt, 40 cubits in width across the front, carved out of one complete stone, and roofed by another similar one;[63] surely all such things would make the work more impressive; especially if the stone comes from abroad, and has been conveyed along a difficult route, like the block described by Herodotus, which measured more than 20 cubits along the front and 15 in height, and was dragged from the city of Elephanta as far as Sais, a journey lasting twenty days.[64] It will also greatly enhance the effect of ornament if a stone that is itself worthy of admiration is set in a noble, important place. There is a shrine on the island of Chemmis in Egypt, remarkable not so much for the fact that the roof consists of a single stone as for the fact that such a huge stone could have been set on walls so high.[65] A rare and exquisite stone will also add to the ornament, as, for example, the marble of which the emperor Nero reportedly built the temple of Fortune in the Golden House,[66] pure, white, and translucent, so that even when all the doors were closed, light seemed to be trapped inside.

In short, all such things will contribute. But whatever they are, they will look worthless unless their composition is precisely governed by order and measure. Each individual element must be arranged according to number,[67] in such a way that even is balanced by even, right by left, upper by lower; nothing must be introduced that might disturb the arrangement or order; everything must be set to exact angles and proportionate lines.

It may be observed that a common material skilfully treated will be more graceful than a noble one piled up in a disorderly manner. There is a wall in Athens, described by Thucydides, hastily built, even using statues seized from tombs;[68] but who would think it beautiful, simply because it was built of broken statues? On the other hand, in ancient rustic buildings, pleasant walls may be seen, built of random construction, using small, irregular stones, set in even rows, alternating between black and white; this, given the modest scale of the work, could hardly be faulted. But perhaps this is related more to the part of the wall called the revetment than to the construction of the wall as a whole. To conclude, all materials should be so distributed that nothing is begun without establishing a procedure to an end in view, nothing raised except according to the principles on which it was begun, and nothing considered finished that has not been brought to perfection with the greatest care and attention.

But, always excluding columns, the main ornament to a wall or roof (especially where vaulted) will be the revetment. This may take many forms: white stucco, plain or in relief, painted surfaces, paneling, mosaic work, glass work, or a mixture of all of these. ◆

6

We will now discuss these forms of revetment and describe how they are applied. But first, since we have mentioned the movement of huge blocks of stone, it would seem advisable to describe here how masses of such bulk may be transported, and set in difficult positions. Plutarch relates that Archimedes once drew a fully laden merchant vessel through the middle of the forum in Syracuse, as though leading an animal by its bridle:[69] a great mathematical invention! But we shall consider only what is appropriate to our needs; finally we shall make a few points, to enable anyone of intelligence to understand the whole matter clearly for himself.

I read in Pliny that an obelisk was conveyed from Foci to Thebes along a canal dug from the Nile, on ships laden with bricks, which could later be off-loaded in order to accommodate the weight of the stone to be transported.[70] I read in the historian Ammianus Marcellinus that an obelisk was transported from the Nile in a three-hundred-oar ship and then drawn on rollers from the third milestone outside the city, through the Ostian gate, and into the Circus Maximus; to erect it required several thousand men, and the whole circus was filled with machines of extremely tall beams and immense ropes.[71] We may read in Vitruvius that Chresiphones and Methagenes, father and son, transported columns and beams to Ephesus using an invention based on the rollers used by the ancients for leveling surfaces. At either end of the stones long iron pins were fixed in lead and projected to form axles; on either side wheels were mounted onto these axles, large enough for the stones to be freely suspended from them; they were then transported by being wheeled along.[72] It is said that when the Egyptian Cherrenis was building a pyramid, a work more than six stades in height, he constructed earth ramps on which to haul up the huge stones.[73] Herodotus writes that when Cleopa, the son of Rasmita, constructed a pyramid, on which hundreds of thousands of men labored for several years, he left steps on the outside, so that the huge stones could be moved using short props and suitable machinery.[74] It is recorded that elsewhere the following method was used to set vast stone beams on top of high columns: Under the beam two sleepers were laid side by side at right angles, halfway along its length. Baskets of sand were then hung from one end of the beam, their weight causing the other end, which was unencumbered, to rise, and leaving the sleeper nearer it free of weight. They then transferred the baskets to the other end, once this sleeper had been propped up, and by alternately weighing down and further propping up the side with the larger gap beneath it, they succeeded in making the stone rise, as though of its own accord.[75] We have only briefly described these examples, and we shall leave them to the authors themselves to explain more fully.

Finally, as we have undertaken, so we shall briefly make a few relevant observations. For my part, I shall not pause here to explain why weights have the natural tendency to press downward continually, obstinately tend to lower themselves, and resist all attempts to raise them, never yielding their position except to a superior weight or contrary force. Nor shall I describe the various types of movement—carrying, pulling, pushing, and so on. These questions will be dealt with more fully elsewhere.

We believe it to be true that there is no direction in which a weight will move more easily than downward, which it does of its own accord, and none with greater difficulty than upward, which it naturally resists; there is a third form of motion, halfway between the two, which probably embodies the characteristics of both, a movement that a body neither resists nor makes of its own accord, such as when it is dragged along a smooth, unobstructed surface. All other movements are correspondingly easier or more difficult, depending on whether they are closer to the first kind or second.

As for the way in which immense weights might be moved, that Nature herself seems to have shown in many ways. Anyone may see how any weight that is set upon an upright column may be upset with a little push, and as it begins to fall, no force may quite arrest it. It is also obvious that even circular columns, but also rounded wheels, and anything that rotates, can be moved easily, and are difficult to stop once they are set in motion; nor is it easy, should you attempt it, to drag these objects without causing them to rotate. Very heavy ships may be drawn through still waters with a light pull if it is constant; but ramming, however sudden or violent, will not budge them; while some objects that might require great force to shift them may be moved by sudden repeated blows; heavy objects may be dragged on ice without the least resistance; we also observe that anything may be moved easily for a certain distance when hanging from a very long rope. Such methods are worth bearing in mind and imitating; let us therefore discuss them briefly.

The base of a weight must be completely solid and even. The broader it is, the less it will damage the surface of the ground; the narrower, the easier to maneuver, but it will furrow and ruin the ground. If the base of the weight has any projections, they will dig into the ground like claws and create resistance. If the ground is slippery, solid, level, and constant, and does not give way, if it has no rises and is free of obstacles, the weight will undoubtedly find nothing to oppose its movement, other than its own natural fondness for rest, and its sluggish and morose character. It was probably on the basis of similar considerations, and a deeper examination of the phenomena mentioned above, that Archimedes was prompted to say that he could certainly turn the world, given a large enough mass as anchor.[76]

To prepare the bottom of the weight and the ground, this is the best method of achieving the desired result: Beams should be laid down, of sufficient number, thickness, and strength for the size of the weight; they should be close together, firm, and level, their surface smooth and without gaps. Between the bottom of the weight and the ground there should be some lubricant to make the path slippery. The lubricant may be soap, tallow, oil lees, or perhaps even a paste of wet clay. Another method of lubrication is to lay rollers beneath at right angles to the direction of movement. If there are too many of them, however, they will be difficult to keep parallel and in line with your intended direction: it is absolutely essential, in order to prevent the weight being damaged or scratched, or carried to one side, that the rollers perform their task in unison. With a small number, they might become overburdened and crack, and, once split, prove a hindrance; or else their single line of contact, either with the surface of the ground below or with the base of the weight above, will cause the latter to become fixed and to jam, digging in like a sharp edge. The body of a roller clearly consists of several equal circles joined one to another; and since the mathematicians would claim that a straight line cannot touch a circle in more than one place, we may call the point of contact of the roller a line, on which the entire weight of the cylinder rests. These difficulties may be avoided by choosing a material of sufficient density and by using a set-square to ensure that the lines of contact are at right angles to the intended direction. ◆

7
100v—102

In addition to the above, there are other instruments to be commended for their utility, such as wheels, pulley blocks, screws, and levers: we must deal with them in detail.

Wheels are on the whole similar to rollers: their weight will always fall perpendicularly on a single point. But there is one difference: rollers are not restricted in their movement, whereas a wheel is impeded by the friction of its axle. There are three parts to a wheel: the circumference, or outermost band of the circle, the axle at the center, and the circle into which the axle fits, as into a bracelet. This some may call the pole, but we, if permissible, shall call it the *axecla*, because in some machines it remains still, while in others it moves. If the wheel has a thick axle, it will turn with difficulty; if a thin one, it will not be able to bear much load. If the outer circumference of the wheel is too small, the same problem will occur as we mentioned would happen to rollers, and it will become stuck in the ground; if it is too large, it will shake in both directions, and should you need to turn to the right or left, it will be difficult to control. If the *axecla* is too loose, the [resultant] grinding will cause it to jam; if too tight, it will be difficult to rotate. Between the axle and the *axecla* there must be some lubrication, because their reaction is the same as between the base of the weight and the ground. Rollers and wheels should be of elm or ilex, the axle of holly, cornel, or, better still, iron; the best material for the *axecla* is bronze mixed with a third part tin.

Pulleys are little wheels. Levers act like spokes to a wheel. But anything of this kind—whether huge treadwheels, which men turn from inside with their feet, capstans, screws, pulleys, or any such instrument—all are based on the principles of equilibrium. It is said that the main reason why Mercury was considered divine was his ability to be clear and intelligible, using words alone, and without resorting to any gesture of the hand. I fear I could not match this, although I shall try to do so to the best of my ability. I set out to discuss these matters, not as a mathematician, but as a workman, intending to deal with no more than was absolutely necessary.

Imagine, to take an easy example, that you are holding a spear in your hand. On it I would like you to mark three positions, which I shall call points: one at either end, at the tip and the tail, and the third at the strap, halfway along. The distance between the points, that is from the strap to either end, I shall call the radius. I do not want to justify all this; it will become clear in the experiment. If the strap lies at the middle of the weapon, and the tail and iron tip have the same weight, then clearly the two ends of the javelin will resist one another and remain level. But should the iron end be heavier, the

Two arrows with alternative fulcrums: leverage.

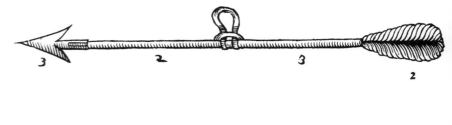

tail will be overcome; yet if the strap is then moved to a point along the javelin closer to the heavier end, the two weights will at once balance out. From that point the ratio between the lengths of the larger and smaller radii will equal the ratio between the weights of the heavier and lighter ends. Those who have researched into such matters have established that unequal radii and unequal weights may balance, provided that the numerical sum of the radius and weight on the right equals that on the left.[77] For example, if the iron tip weighs three units in weight, and the tail two, the radius from the strap to the iron tip would have to be two units in length, and the radius to the tail, three. Thus the five on one side corresponds to the five on the other, and as the sums of their radii and weights are equal, they remain in equilibrium and level; if the numbers do not correspond, the side with the larger sum will prevail.

I should also mention that if the radii extend equal distances on either side of the same strap, their ends, while in motion, will describe equal circles in the air; but if the radii are unequal, the circles they describe will also be unequal.

That the wheel is composed of circles, we have already mentioned. Thus, if two adjoining wheels are fixed to one axle and move with the same motion, so that while one is moving, the other cannot rest, and while one is resting, the other cannot move, the force within both may be calculated by considering the length of the radius of each.[78] It should be noted that the length of the radius is measured from the center of the axle. If this is understood well enough, our investigation into the whole theory behind machines of this kind, especially wheels and levers, will be self-evident.

About pulley blocks we must be a little more detailed. For the rope that is fed through the block, and the pulleys themselves inside, both act as the ground; the motion here is of the middle type, which we described as being

between the most difficult and the most easy: it travels neither up nor down, but continues about its center.

To make this easier to understand, take a statue weighing 1,000 pounds. Were this to hang from the trunk of a tree, attached by a rope, clearly that simple piece of rope would bear the full 1,000 pounds. Fasten a pulley block to the statue, and feed the rope on which the statue hangs through it, and tie it again to the trunk, so that it is hanging once more. Clearly the weight of the statue now hangs from two lengths of rope, and the pulley block in the middle holds it in equilibrium. To continue: Add another pulley block to the trunk, and again feed the rope through it. I ask you this: How much weight is borne by that portion of the rope which has been taken back up and through the pulley block? Five hundred pounds, you reply. Does it not then follow that the rope itself can impose no greater weight on this second

Supporting a weight by a double line and pulley.

pulley block than it holds itself? Thus it will hold 500 pounds. I need go no further. I think I have demonstrated satisfactorily that the weight is divided by the pulley blocks and that, therefore, a greater weight may be moved by a smaller one. And whenever the pulley blocks are redoubled in this way, the weight will be halved. From this it follows that as the number of pulleys is increased, the weight is, as it were, reduced and separated out, so that it becomes easier to move, though the rope takes longer to draw. ◆

8

102—103v

We have dealt with the wheel, the pulley block, and the lever. Now I would like you to understand that a screw consists of rings, whose function it is to sustain weight. If these rings were whole circles, so cut that the beginning of one joined the end of another, then clearly any weight moved

by it would go neither up nor down, but would travel in circles on a single plane. A lever is therefore used to force a weight to ride along the oblique rings. Again, if such rings have a short circumference and close to the axis, then surely the weight could be moved with a shorter lever and less strength.

Here I cannot avoid something that I did not think would require comment. If you could succeed in making the base of a weight—so far as the hand and skill of a workman may accomplish it—no larger than a point, and could propel it along a solid surface without marking the ground in any way by its movement, I dare say you would then be able to move Archimedes' ship, and perform any similar feat you should wish.[79] But of this elsewhere.

Each of the devices mentioned is very efficient in itself at moving weights. But were they to be combined together, they would work amazingly. All over Germany youths are to be found playing on ice wearing shoes with a thin, very straight, iron blade beneath: with but a light push they glide over the surface with a speed that could not be matched by even the swiftest of birds.[80] Since weights may therefore be either dragged, or pushed, or carried, it might be useful to stipulate that they are drawn by rope, pushed by levers, and carried on wheels and the like. How these devices may be used together is obvious. But with any such device there must always be some object, quite firm and solid, that acts as its immobile anchor, around which everything else moves. If the weight is to be dragged, there must always be some other heavier weight, to which the chains for the machines may be secured. If there is no such weight available, drive a strong, three-cubit-long iron stake deep into solid ground, reinforced with planks laid cross-wise around it. The chains of your tackle or capstans must be attached to the end of the stake that protrudes from the ground. If, however, the soil is sandy, lay down extremely long beams of one piece, to form the surface, and then fasten the chains to one end, as you might to the stakes.

I should mention something that the inexperienced would fail to believe, unless they had a full understanding. It is easier to drag two weights than one on a level plain. This is how. Move the first weight along to the very end of the surface laid down for it, then restrain it with wedges, so that it holds firm; once it is held down in this way, attach the machinery to it so as to pull the second weight along. Thus the movable weight may be drawn along the same surface as has been traveled by the weight that is equal to it but held fast.

If there is a weight to be lifted, the easiest method is to use a single beam, or a very strong mast. This we erect as follows: Fasten the foot of it against a stake, or some other stable object. Tie at least three ropes to its head, and extend them, one to the right, one to the left, and the third along the length of the beam. Then, at a certain distance from the foot of the mast, fix the pulleys or capstans firmly to the ground and draw the third rope through them. As the rope is being drawn through, the mast will follow and raise itself up. Then, using the two ropes attached to the head on either side as reins, we restrain the mast, so that it leans at whatever angle we choose and in whatever direction is required for positioning the weight. The two lateral ropes on either side must be fastened in the following manner, should there be no greater weight at hand by which to secure them. Dig a deep, square hole; set a trunk in the middle of the hole; to this attach chains, so that they lead back up out of the ground; across the top of the trunk lay boarding; then fill the hole with earth and pack it down; if you dampen the earth, it will be heavier still. As for the rest, follow the instructions that we gave for flat surfaces: fasten tackles to the head of the beam and the weight itself, and

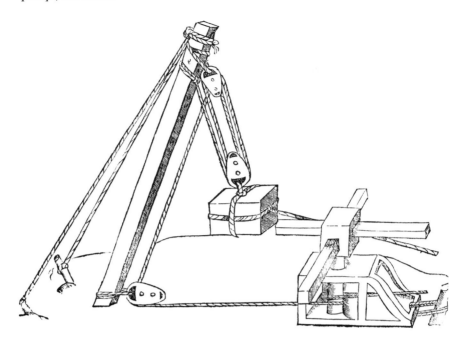

by the foot fix a capstan or some similar mechanism, which relies on the principle of the lever.

It is essential, when using any of these machines, to observe the following rules: When moving colossal weights, do not use machines that are too small or weak. With rope, spokes, and any other part used in moving weights, length implies weakness, for length is linked inherently to thinness, while thickness is derived from brevity. If the rope is too thin, its strength may be doubled by using pulleys. If it is too thick, use larger pulleys to prevent the rope's being cut by the edges of smaller ones. Axles should be of iron, in thickness no less than a sixth of the radius of the pulley and no more than an eighth of its diameter.

If the rope is damp, it will be protected from fire caused by friction or movement; it will also turn better within the pulley and be less liable to fray. For this purpose vinegar is better than water, and salt water better than sulphurous.[81] Rope soaked in fresh water and left in the heat of the sun will very soon rot. It is safer to twist the rope than to knot it. Always be careful not to let rope cut against rope. The ancients used to secure the first knots in their ropes and tackle to iron poles. For picking up weights, and especially stone, they would use iron pincers. These pincers were shaped like the letter **X**, the two lower arms forked inward to form a crablike claw for grasping the weight. Their top ends had rings attached, through which rope was threaded and bound, so that when the rope is pulled, the pincers grip tightly.

We have noticed that in large stone, especially columns that otherwise would have smooth and polished surfaces, projecting pinlike nodules have been left. Onto these ropes were fastened, to prevent them from slipping. Also incorporated, especially on cornices, were *impleola* (as I call them),[82] constructed in the following manner. A hole is made in the stone, the shape of an empty purse, as many palms large as the size of the stone requires, with its mouth narrower and its base wider on the inside (we have seen one such lewis a foot deep). This is then filled with wedges of iron, the two side wedges shaped like the letter **D**;[83] these are inserted first, so as to fill the sides of the lewis, while the middle wedge is inserted last to fill the space between these two. The ears of each of the wedges stand out from the cavity. An iron finger fastened to a strong handle is passed through a hole in these ears, and onto it, rope is attached for drawing the weight.

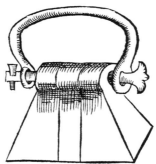

Top: *pincers for lifting weights.* Bottom: *lifting device for use with* impleola.

This is how to fasten rope to columns, door jambs, and other objects that are to be set vertical. Make a brace of iron or wood, strong and large enough for the size of the stone. Then in an appropriate place, girdle this around the column to be grasped; then strengthen it by driving in long, thin wedges, using a light mallet; finally, attach a rope sling to this brace. In this way neither the stone is scarred by the *impleola*, nor its edges damaged by a rope harness. Further, this type of binding is more straightforward, practical, and reliable than any other.

Elsewhere we shall deal more fully with questions relating to instruments of this kind. But here we need only consider the machine as a form of extremely strong animal with hands, an animal that can move weights in almost the same way as we do ourselves. These machines must therefore have the same extensions of member and muscle that we use when pressing, pushing, pulling, and carrying. One piece of advice: Whenever you intend to move vast weights, it is as well to approach the task gradually, with caution and in due time, on account of the various unforeseeable and irreparable accidents and dangers that are wont to beset such work, beyond even what the experienced might expect. Nor will you receive as much respect and praise for your ability if your undertaking follows your plan and succeeds, as the disrespect and contempt for your temerity if it fails. So much for this; I shall turn now to the subject of revetments. ◆

9

103v—105

For every revetment you must apply at least three coats of plaster.[84] The role of the first is to grip to the surface tightly, and to hold all other additional coats applied to the wall; the role of the outermost is to display the charm of the finish, color, and lineaments; the role of those in between is to remedy and prevent any defect in the other two. These are the defects that may occur. If the last, outermost coat, so to speak, binds the wall too strongly, as the first should have done, its sharpness will produce several cracks during drying. Yet, if the first coat is too delicate, as the last should be, it will fail to hold the wall in a sufficiently tight grip and will fall away.

The more coats of plaster there are, the smoother the surface and the longer they will last. I notice that some of the ancients added up to nine coats of plaster. Of these the first was always the roughest, made of quarry sand and brick, crushed not too finely but left in chips; its depth would vary from a finger to as much as a palm. For the middle coats, river sand is better, because it cracks less; they too must be rough, as otherwise the further coats will not adhere. The last coat should gleam like marble: for this a finely crushed white stone is used instead of sand. This last coat need only be half a finger thick; any thicker, and it will have difficulty drying. I notice that some, for reasons of economy, have made the outer skin no thicker than shoe leather. The thickness of the middle coats should vary according to whether they are closer to the inside or the outside.

In some mountain stone, veins may be found that are translucent, like alabaster; they are neither marble nor gypsum, but halfway between the two, and naturally very friable. If this stone is crushed and mixed instead of sand, it will gleam with an amazing sparkle, like white marble.

Nails may often be seen in the wall, to hold the revetment. Time has shown that brass ones are best. But it is preferable, instead of using nails, to make tiny holes in the wall, between the joints of the courses, and use a wooden mallet to insert chips of flint, so that they protrude slightly.

The fresher and rougher the wall, the more strongly the plaster will adhere. If, therefore, you apply your first coat of plaster, however thin, in the course of construction, while the work is still fresh, it will provide a fast and lasting grip for any additional coat. The best time for all revetment work is after Auster has been blowing; while Boreas is blowing,[85] and in periods of great cold or heat, the last coat in particular will soon blister.

Revetment may be either applied or attached. Gypsum and lime are applied. But gypsum may be used only in an extremely dry place: moisture found in old walls is hostile to all forms of revetment. Stone, glass, and so on are attached. These are the types of revetment that are applied: white plaster, relief work, and fresco. These are the types that are attached: paneling, intarsia, and mosaic. To deal with applied work first.

Lime is prepared like this. It should be soaked in pure water and allowed to macerate for a long time in a covered pool; it should then be chopped with a trowel, like wood. If, during this operation, the trowel meets no solid particle, it shows that the lime is fully macerated. Lime is thought to require three months before it is sufficiently mature. Preferably it should be thick and extremely glutinous; for if the trowel comes out dry, it shows that the lime is weak and not moist enough. When the sand or some other crushed substance is added, work it in over and over again with great vigor; then turn it over once more, until it appears to foam. For the outer coat the ancients used a mortar to pound the lime and temper the mixture, so that it would not stick to the trowel during application.

While this coat is drying and still fresh, apply a second coat; take care that all the coats dry uniformly. These coats should be consolidated by packing them down with a light tamper and baton.[86] If the final coat of pure plaster is rubbed carefully, it will shine like a mirror. And if, when quite dry, it is smeared with wax and mastic melted in a little oil, and warmed with burning embers from a fireplace, so that the mixture is absorbed, it will achieve a sheen superior to that of marble. In our experience cracks may be avoided in this type of revetment if, during application, as soon as a fissure appears, you brush it in with a hibiscus bundle or a broom of esparto grass.

Should you be applying the coat during the period of the Dog Star, or somewhere hot, beat some old rope and cut it into little pieces, then mix it into the paste. If, as you polish, you sprinkle it lightly with white soap dissolved in warm water, it will then take a fine polish; if it is soaked too much, it will turn pale.

Reliefs are easily added using molds. The mold is taken off a piece of sculpture, by pouring liquid gypsum over it. When the relief is dry, if treated with the mixture described above, it will take on a surface like marble. There are two types of relief: one stands out, the other is shallow and flat. The first, high relief, will not be unsuitable on a straight wall, but on a vaulted ceiling the second, low relief, will be more appropriate. For if the former is hung, its weight may easily cause it to become detached and fall, putting anyone inside at risk. Where there is likely to be a lot of dust, you would be well advised to have flat and shallow, not prominent, cornices to your ceiling, making them easier to wipe clean.

The revetment may be painted when wet or when dry. For frescoes, any natural color, extracted from stone, earth, minerals, and so on, will be appropriate. But all artificial colors, and especially those which are unstable in front of fire, will require a totally dry surface, and will abhor lime, the moon, and Auster.[87] It has recently been discovered that linseed oil will protect whatever color you wish to apply from any harmful climate or atmosphere, provided the wall to which it is applied is dry and in no way moist.[88] I notice, however, that in antiquity the prows of ships were adorned with a paste of liquid wax. We have noticed a gemlike substance, of wax or white bitumen, if I judge correctly, applied to the walls of ancient buildings; this has hardened with time, so that neither fire nor water can remove it; you might describe it as being like molten glass. We also see that milky flowers of lime have been used to adhere particularly glasslike colors, while the wall is still fresh. So much for this subject. ◆

IO Paneled revetment, whether plain or carved, is applied in the same way.
105—106 The degree of care with which the ancients cut and polished their marble is quite remarkable. Indeed, I have seen marble panels more than four cubits in length, two in width, and scarcely half a finger thick, and joined along an undulating line, to make the joint less obvious.

According to Pliny, for cutting marble the ancients preferred Ethiopian sand, with Indian sand a second best; Egyptian sand, although better than ours, was thought too soft. It is said that the ancients often used a particular sand found on a sandbank in the Adriatic.[89] The sand that we gather from the shore by Pozzuoli is one of the most suitable for this purpose. Also useful is the sharp sand found in any torrent. But the coarser the grain, the wider the cut and the deeper the bite; whereas the lighter it is to file, the smoother it will polish. Polishing begins with a coarse file but finishes with more of a lick than a bite. Thebaid sand is recommended for rubbing and polishing marble. Whetstone is also commended. There is a stone called emery, whose powder is second to none. Pumice is useful for the final polish.[90] Also most useful is the froth from burnt tin, burnt white lead, chalk especially from Tripoli, and any other such material, provided it has been reduced to minute particles, no bigger than atoms, while still remaining serviceable.

For holding thick sections of paneling, nails or projecting marble catches should be fixed into the wall, then the paneling applied directly; but with thinner sections, instead of lime after the second plastering, apply any molten mixture of wax, pitch, resin, mastic, or any form of gum, and then warm the paneling gradually, to prevent it from cracking under the sudden heat of the flame. If the joints and rows form a harmonious whole, when joining paneling, this will be commendable. Veining must join with veining, color with color, and so on, so that they each enhance one another. I am impressed by the cunning of the ancients, whereby the sections closest to the eye would be polished most brightly, while they invested less effort in those to be fitted farther away and higher up. And often, where the eye of even the most curious observer would scarcely notice, they did not polish them at all.

Intarsia and mosaic are similar, in that they both imitate a picture using stone, glass, or shells of various colors, arranged in an appropriate pattern. Nero is said to have been the first to have had mother of pearl cut and used in revetment.[91] Their difference lies in that in intarsia we inlay pieces of paneling as large as possible, whereas with mosaic, tiny cubes[92] are inserted no larger than a bean. The smaller these are, the more diffuse the splendor of their sparkle, as the light is reflected off the surface of the mosaic in different directions. They also differ in that it is easier to fix intarsia with a compound of gum, while lime is more suitable for mosaic, mixed with finely ground travertine.

Some recommend that with mosaic work the lime should be soaked repeatedly in warm water, to remove any saltiness and to make it softer and thicker. I have seen some extremely hard stone for use in intarsia polished on a wheel. With mosaic it is possible to gild the glass, using lead as a mortar, which is more fluid than any form of glass.

Almost all that we have said about revetment applies equally to paving, a topic we have promised to discuss; the only exception is that, to the latter, paintings and reliefs may not be applied, unless you count as painting, coloring the mortar in different shades, and pouring it into beds edged in marble, to make a picture. The coloring may be of burnt red ocher, brick, flint, iron filings, and so on. Pavements inlaid in this way, once dry, should be polished as follows. Take a lump of flint, or, better still, a five-pound weight with a flat base, and by means of a rope draw it back and forth across the pavement, having first sprinkled it with coarse sand and water; continue polishing until it is perfectly smooth, which is not achieved until the lines and edges of the blocks match. If the pavement is coated with oil, especially linseed oil, it will acquire a glazed finish. Oil lees make a good coating; water is also very useful, provided it contains no lime and is sprinkled on repeatedly.

In all the revetments described above, avoid using the same color or shape too frequently, or too close together, or in a disorderly composition; gaps between pieces should also be avoided; everything should be composed and fitted exactly,[93] so that all parts of the work appear equally perfect. ◆

The roof also has its attractions and charms, in its trusses, vaulting, and outer skin exposed to the sky. In the portico of Agrippa there remain to this day trusses composed of bronze beams 40 feet in length: you do not know what to admire more about it, the vast cost or the ingenuity of the builder.[94] We have mentioned already that in the temple of Diana at Ephesus there was a roof made of cedar, which stood for many years.[95] Pliny recalls that after conquering the Egyptian king Sesostris, Salauces, king of Colchis, had beams made of gold and silver.[96] There are also temples with roofs of marble plates, such as the vast, gleaming white one of the temple of Jerusalem, which from afar is said to have looked like a snow-covered mountain.[97] On the Capitol in Rome, Catulus was the first to gild bronze tiles;[98] I also find that later the Pantheon in Rome was covered with tiles of gilded bronze;[99] the basilica of St. Peter's was once totally covered with bronze plates by Pope Honorius, in whose time Mahomet established a new religion in Egypt and Libya. Germany glistens with glazed tiles.

Lead is used everywhere; it is a material that is durable, particularly pleasing in appearance, and not too expensive. But it has the following disadvantages: When it is applied to a cement surface, with no ventilation beneath, if under the sun's heat the pebbles on which it sits grow very hot, it will itself become too warm and melt. There is an experiment that may verify this phenomenon: a lead vase will not melt under flame, provided it is full of water; but throw in a pebble, and on contact with it the lead will immediately melt and form a hole. Another disadvantage is that it will easily be ripped off by the wind, unless it is fastened with frequent, very strong fixings. Also, it may be impaired and etched away by salts from lime, so that it would be safer to entrust the work to timber, provided there is no fear of fire; but here again nails, especially iron ones, have the disadvantage that they may grow warmer even than pebbles, or be corroded by rust. Therefore the cramps and pins to be inserted into the vault ought to be of lead, and soldered to the roofing sheets with red-hot iron. The work should be bedded in a thin layer of willow ashes, washed and mixed with white clay. Brass nails do not grow so hot, and suffer less from rust.

Lead is damaged by bird droppings; therefore make sure that there are no perches where the birds may conveniently land and roost; alternatively, make the surface thicker where the droppings are likely to accumulate. According to Eusebius, chains were stretched over the temple of Solomon, and four hundred bronze bells hung from them, the sound of which scared off the birds.[100]

Other parts of the roof that may be adorned include the gables, eaves, and corners. These may be fitted with spheres, garlands, statues, chariots, and so on, which will be dealt with individually in the appropriate place. No further comment comes to mind concerning this whole type of ornament, except that each should be applied wherever appropriate, so as to fit in with the rest of the work. ◆

12

107—108

Openings are an ornament that gives great delight and dignity to the work; but they present many grave difficulties too, which may be overcome only with the most careful workmanship and considerable expense. Openings require blocks of stone of huge size, sound structure, equal dimensions, elegant appearance, and uncommon material—characteristics rarely found together; nor may they be transported, laid, worked, or composed completely without forethought. If you listen to architects, says Cicero, you might think that no column could ever be set quite vertical.[101] In the case of openings, this is something utterly essential for the sake not only of strength but also of appearance. There are other inconveniences; yet all must be dealt with to the best of our ability.

The opening is, in essence, a form of access; yet sometimes one wall is backed by another, like a pelt on top of clothing, and a kind of opening is formed that does not continue through but is blocked off by the intervening wall: it would therefore not be inappropriate to call this a "false opening." This kind of ornament, like almost all others, was first invented by carpenters, as a means of strengthening the work and reducing costs; the masons then imitated it, thereby lending their works considerable grace.

Any of these openings would be more beautiful for having its bones[102] made entirely from one stone. Next best would be to compose all the parts so that there do not appear to be any joints.

The ancients raised the very large stones that were to be used for the columns and the other bones,[103] and even those for the false openings, and set them on their bases before the rest of the wall was built: a very wise move this; for the machines are less restricted, and it makes it easier to achieve the vertical. This is how to set a column plumb to perpendicular: Mark the center of the circle on the base, as well as at the bottom and top of the column; at the center of the base fix an iron pin with lead; at the bottom of the column make a hole in the center, deep enough to receive the pin protruding from the base; at the top of the machinery mark the point vertically above the center of the base pin. Once this is done, it will not be

Engaged columns protruding by half their diameter.

difficult to position the upper shaft of the column, with the center of its circle placed vertically beneath.

From inspecting the works of the ancients, I have learned that certain more delicate varieties of marble may be smoothed with the same tools that are used for planing wood. Also it has been observed that the ancients would lay stone in its rough state, and worked smooth only along the tops and edges where it was joined; then, once the work had been constructed, they would smooth and polish any surfaces that were still rough. The reason for this, I believe, was to risk as little expense as possible, considering the hazards that the machines cause. For if a polished and completely finished block of stone were damaged accidentally, the loss would be greater than in

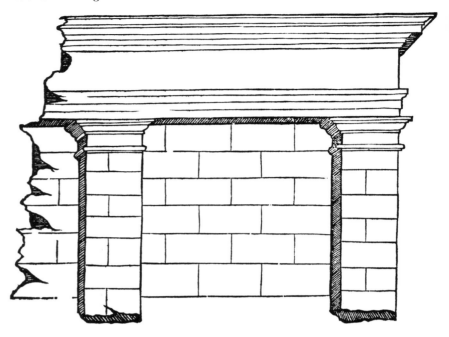

the case of an unfinished block. Added to this, they could take careful account of the seasons, in that there is one season for buildings, and another for dressing and polishing.

There are two kinds of false opening. One is part of the wall, so that a certain amount is concealed within and a certain amount stands out of the wall. The other has its columns standing completely free of the wall, like those of a portico. Thus the former is called "engaged,"[104] the latter "detached." With the engaged, the columns are either round or quadrangular. The round ones should project no more and no less than their radius; the quadrangular ones, no more than a quarter and no less than a sixth of their width. With the detached, the columns must never stand out by more than one and a quarter times their entire base, or by less than their column and base combined. With those, however, which stand out one and a quarter times, there must be a corresponding quadrangular one engaged to the wall. With the detached, the beam is not continuous across the whole face of the wall, but is interrupted at right angles, directly above the columns, so that at that point the ends of the lowest beam break out from the wall and extend to meet the capital of each individual column. Similarly, other members of the beam must run around these detached capitals. With the engaged, however, you may, if you so wish, either use a continuous beam and a cornice uninterrupted for the whole length of the building, or follow the layout for the detached columns, with the beam going out and returning.

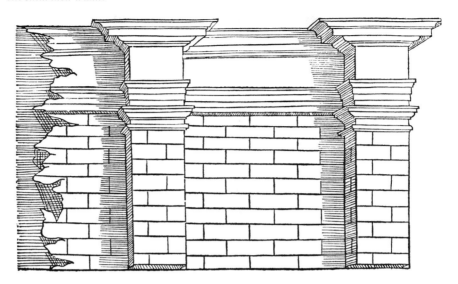

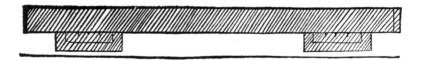

We have [now] dealt with ornament pertinent to parts common to all buildings. The respects under which they differ must be dealt with in the next book, the present one being long enough already. But since in this book we have taken it upon ourselves to investigate diligently into anything relevant to the ornament mentioned earlier, nothing useful may be overlooked. ◆

I3

108—109v

In the whole art of building the column is the principal ornament without any doubt; it may be set in combination, to adorn a portico, wall, or other form of opening, nor is it unbecoming when standing alone. It may embellish crossroads, theaters, squares; it may support a trophy; or it may act as a

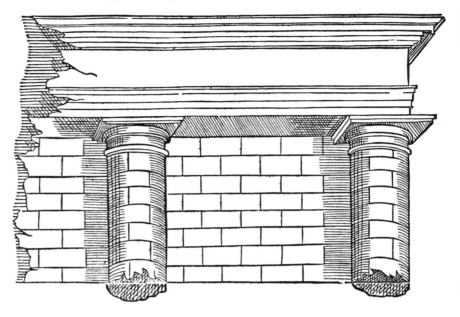

monument. It has grace, and it confers dignity. Just how much expense was invested by the ancients in making columns as elegant as possible is not easy to describe. Indeed some, not content with columns of Parian or Numidian marble, alabaster, and other forms of marble, would commission famous sculptors to carve figures and images on them; there are said to have been over 120 such columns in the temple of Diana at Ephesus. Others have added bases and capitals of gilded bronze, such as in the double portico at Rome constructed during the consulship of Octavius, the one who triumphed over Perseus.[105] Still others have made them completely of bronze, or plated in silver. But let us not dwell on such matters.

Columns must be rounded and turned. I read that two architects, a certain
Theodorus and Tholus, built in their workshop at Lemnos a series of wheels
whereby columns could hang and be so well balanced that they could be
turned by a child.[106] But this is a Greek story.

A matter relevant to our discussion is to establish which are the longest lines
in a column—to wit, the axis and the profile; the shortest are the diameters
of the various circles that surround the column in various places. The most
important of these circles are the plane surfaces, one at the top of the column
and one at the bottom, to be known as the end plates.[107] The axis is the
straight line extending through the core of the column from the center of

the top circle to the center of the bottom one; this may also be called the perpendicular through the center of the column. The centers of all the circles lie along this axis. The profile is the line drawn from the outermost band of the top circle to the corresponding point on the bottom band, joining the ends of all the diameters running through the center of the column; this line, then, is not a single straight line, like the axis, but is composed of many lines, some straight, some curved, as will be explained later.

The diameter is taken at five different points along the column, in order to determine the respective circles. These are the points: the projections, the recession[s], and the belly.[108] There are two projections, one at the top of the column and one at the bottom, so called because they protrude and stand out from the rest of the column. The recessions, also two in number, lie next to the projections, at both the top and the bottom, and are so called because there the projections pull back into the body of shaft. The belly has its diameter below the midpoint of the column, and is so called because there the column seems to swell out. Then again the two projections differ in that the one positioned at the bottom consists of a fillet[109] and a curve running from the fillet into the body of the column; but the projection at the top of the shaft has, in addition to the fillet and oblique curve, a collar.[110]

I have told you that I desire to make my language Latin, and as clear as possible, so as to be easily understood. Words must therefore be invented, when those in current use are inadequate; it will be best to draw them from familiar things. We Tuscans call a fillet the narrow band with which maidens bind and dress their hair; and so, if we may, let us call "fillet" the platband that encircles the ends of the column like a hoop. But the ring positioned at the top next to the fillet, which binds the top of the shaft like a twisted cord, let us call "collar."

Finally, this is how to determine the profile. On a stretch of pavement or level piece of wall, to be known as the "tracing," a straight line is drawn, equal in length to the proposed column, which the workmen have yet to quarry from the rock: this line is called the axis. We then divide the axis into fixed portions, as determined by the design of the proposed work and the type of column (which will be discussed in the appropriate place). The diameter of the cross-section at the bottom must be proportional to these sections, and this we mark on the drawing with a short line running across at right angles at the bottom end of the axis. We divide this diameter into twenty-four parts; we make the fillet one part high, and mark this on the drawing with a thin line. Then take three twenty-fourths of the diameter, and make the center of the next recess along the axis at that height, and through its center draw a line parallel to the base. This then will be the diameter of the bottom recess, in length one seventh shorter than that at the base. Having marked these two lines, the diameters, that is, of the recess

*Method for determining the entasis of a
column.*

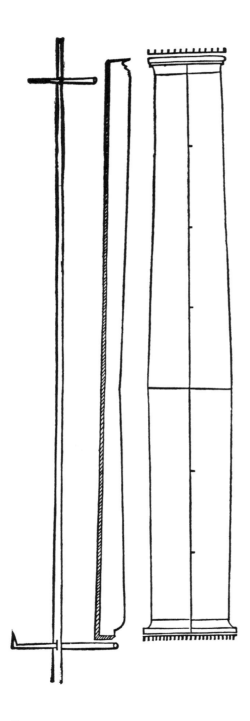

Ornament

187

and fillet, we make a curved line from the end of the recess to the end of the fillet, bending in toward the axis with as gentle and graceful a curve as possible. This curve should begin with a quarter circle, whose radius equals the height of the fillet. We then divide the whole length of the axis into seven equal parts, and mark the divisions with points. Then on the fourth point from the bottom I set the center of the belly, and through this the diameter is drawn, its length equal to that of the bottom recess.

The top recess and projection are then determined in the following way: according to the size of the column (a subject to be debated in the appropriate place), the length of the diameter of the top circle is derived from that of the bottom recess, and marked on the drawing at the top of the axis. Once drawn, we divide this diameter into twelfths, one of which is occupied by the collar and the fillet of the top projection together, with the collar taking up two thirds, and the fillet the rest. Below this projection lies the recess, its center one-and-a-half twelfths distant from the center of the projection to the top circle, and its diameter one ninth less than the maximum diameter of the projection. After this, draw a curved line, similar to the one below.

Finally, once the projections, recesses, oblique curves, and diameter of the belly have been added to the tracing, make two straight lines, one from the end of the top recess and, likewise, one from the end of the bottom one, both leading to the ends of the diameter that marks the belly. Using the above instructions, then, the line known as the profile may be constructed. Along this line a thin template may be fashioned, with which workmen may obtain and define the correct shape and definition for the column. The base of the shaft, if the column has been turned properly, should be at right angles to the line dropped vertically from the center of the circle that constitutes the top of the column.

The above is not a discovery by the ancients, handed down in some writing, but what we have noted ourselves, by careful and studious observation of the works of the best architects. What follows principally concerns the rules of lineaments; it is of the greatest importance, and may give great delight to painters. ◆

The Seventh Book of Leon Battista Alberti on the Art of Building. Ornament to Sacred Buildings.

I

110—112

We have noted that the art of building consists of different parts, some of which—such as the *area*,[1] roof, and so on—are common to all structures, whatever their type, while some vary from building to building. Ornaments to the first category we have considered as extensively as was relevant to our purpose. Now let us deal with the second. Our inquiry will prove so valuable that not even painters, who are most exacting seekers of delight, would be without it; it will also prove so delightful that—to put it simply—you will not regret having read it.

But I hope that you will not disapprove if this new argument is introduced with a new preface. We shall develop our argument as clearly as possible,[2] beginning with the articulation, description, and annotation of the parts of which the whole subject consists. With a statue made from a mixture of bronze, gold, and silver, the respective weights are the concern of the man who casts it, while the sculptor looks to the lineaments, and there may be others concerned with different aspects; in the same way, we shall divide up the different parts of building art, to establish a clear and appropriate order in which to deal with the relevant considerations. We shall now describe compartition, which contributes more to the delight and splendor of a building than to its utility and strength;[3] although these qualities are so closely related that if one is found wanting in anything, the rest will not meet with approval.

Buildings are either public or private; both public and private may be further subdivided into sacred and profane. To deal with public buildings first.

The ancients would set out the walls of their cities with great religious ceremony[4] and would dedicate them to some deity for protection. They thought that no method of government could be devised to resist changes that result from violence and treachery between man and man; and they compared the city to a ship on the high seas constantly exposed to accidents and danger, through the negligence of its citizens and the envy of its neighbors. This was, I imagine, why legend had it that Saturn, out of a concern for human affairs, once upon a time appointed heroes and demigods to protect every city with their wisdom;[5] because we depend not only on walls for our safety, but also on the gods' help. It is said that Saturn did this because he realized that just as we put a shepherd and not one of the cattle in charge of a herd, similarly another race of beings, far superior in wisdom and virtue,[6] should be left in command of human communities. This is why the walls were dedicated to the gods. Others credit the providence of the great and good God with the allocation of guardian spirits not only to individual souls but to nations.[7] The walls were therefore considered particularly sacred, because they served both to unite and to protect the citizens; when on the point of capturing a city under siege, the ancients would call upon the protecting deities of that city with a sacred incantation that they might not emigrate unwillingly, so as not to appear to have acted in disrespect of the religion of the place.[8]

Who could consider a temple as anything but sacred? And this for a number of reasons, not least because that is where mankind offers the gods thanksgiving and worship, which they have deserved. This piety is the single most important part of justice, and who would deny that justice is in itself a divine gift? There is a further part of justice, closely related to the above, and of particular importance; one that is also highly pleasing to the gods, and, consequently, most sacred: it is the means by which men achieve peace and tranquility, by dispensing to each his just deserts. For this reason the basilica, where justice is dispensed, we grant to religion also.[9]

As for the monuments of noble events, which are to commend their memory to posterity, unless I am mistaken, they depend entirely on justice and religion. We shall therefore discuss walls, temples, basilicas, and monuments together; but before touching on this, we cannot avoid making a few brief but important comments about the city itself.

The *area* of the city, and the surrounding region, will be greatly enhanced if the buildings are appropriately distributed and arranged. Plato preferred the urban center and the surrounding countryside to be divided into twelve districts,[10] each with its own temple or chapel.[11] For our part, we would also include crossroad altars, courts for lesser judgments, garrisons, racecourses and recreation grounds, and other similar facilities, provided sufficient homes flourish in the surrounding countryside to warrant them.

Some cities are large, and others, such as castles and little forts, are small. The authors of antiquity were of the opinion that since cities on a plain must have been founded after the flood, they were less ancient and consequently less important. At any rate, for grace and comfort, a flat and open site is more appropriate to a city, and a tortuous and inaccessible one to a castle. On the other hand, they need complimentary qualities: I would make any flat site slightly raised, for the sake of hygiene, and would take a level plateau in a mountainous site, for the sake of the roads and buildings. Cicero appears to have preferred the city of Capua to Rome, because it was not perched on hills, nor disrupted by valleys, but flat and level.[12] The reason why Alexander refrained from founding a city on the island of Faro[13]—an otherwise well-fortified and convenient site—was that he realized that there would not be enough space to expand.[14]

Another thing must not be forgotten here, that the wealth of its citizens is a great mark of distinction for a city. We read that when Tigranes[15] founded the city of Tigranocerta,[16] he forced a large number of the noblest and wealthiest men to settle there with all their possessions, by publishing an edict that threatened the confiscation of anything discovered not to have been taken with them.[17] But any neighbor, or even foreigner, would do this of his own free will, if he knew there was somewhere that he could lead a healthy and happy life, among honest citizens of good character.

The principal ornament to any city lies in the siting, layout, composition, and arrangement of its roads, squares, and individual works: each must be properly planned and distributed according to use, importance, and convenience. For without order there can be nothing commodious, graceful, or noble.

In a state that is morally sound and well ordered, according to Plato, the law should forbid the importation of any foreign luxury and prevent anyone from going abroad before he is forty years of age;[18] any outsider to enter the city for instruction should be sent home again as soon as he has been instilled with the noble disciplines. This was because contact of any kind with foreigners would cause the inhabitants gradually to forget their ancestral frugality and to grow resentful of their traditional customs, which in itself would be a great detriment to the city. The elders of Epidamnium, according to Plutarch, realized that trading contact with the Illyrians would corrupt their citizens; and mindful that moral decadence could bring about revolution, they selected each year, as a precaution, one of their most serious and circumspect citizens to go to Illyria and negotiate trade and contracts on behalf of the others, according to their individual requests.[19] In short, anyone of experience would agree that it is best to take every precaution to prevent the state from being corrupted through contact with foreigners. Yet I do not think that we ought to follow those who exclude strangers of every kind.

In Greece there was an ancient custom among nations that were not in league, but nonetheless not unfriendly to one another, that should one pass through another's territory bearing arms, he would not be received within the city, nor, equally, would he be inhospitably driven away; instead, a market for provisions would be set up not far from the city limits,[20] ensuring that the new arrivals found all the refreshments they required, while the citizens would not fear for their safety. Personally I prefer the Carthaginian system: while they were not unreceptive to foreigners, they would not allow them the same privileges as their own citizens; they permitted them access to certain roads leading to the forum, but denied them any view of the more private parts of the city, such as the dockyards and so on.

Mindful of this precedent, we should divide the city into zones, so that not only are foreigners segregated into some place suitable for them and not inconvenient for the citizens, but the citizens themselves are also separated into zones suitable and convenient, according to the occupation and rank of each one.

The charm of a city will be very much enhanced if the various work-shops are allocated distinct and well-chosen zones. The silversmiths, painters, and jewelers should be on the forum, then next to them, spice shops, clothes shops, and, in short, all those that might be thought more respectable. Anything foul or offensive (especially the stinking tanners) should be kept well away in the outskirts to the north, as the wind rarely blows from that direction, and when it does, it gusts so strongly as to clear smells away, rather than carry them along. Some might prefer the residential quarters of the gentry to be quite free of any contamination from the common people. Others would have every district in the city so well equipped that each would contain all its essential requirements; thus it would be quite acceptable to have common retailers and other shops mixed in with the houses of the most important citizens. So much for this subject. Clearly utility demands one thing, and dignity another. To return to the argument. ◆

2

112—113

The ancients, especially the Etruscans, preferred to use vast, squared stone for their walls, just as the Athenians had for the Piraeus, on the advice of Themistocles.[21] In Tuscany and Vilumbria, and also in the territory of the Hernicians, ancient towns may be seen, constructed of huge, irregular blocks of stone;[22] I approve of this form of construction very much: it has a certain rugged air of antique severity, which is an ornament to a city. This is how I would build the city walls, that the enemy might be terrified by their appearance and retreat, his confidence destroyed.

If along the wall there is a wide, deep moat with sheer sides—such as that of Babylon, said to have been 50 royal cubits wide and more than 100 deep[23]— it will add considerable grandeur. The height and thickness of a wall may also add grandeur, as in the works attributed to Ninus, Semiramis, Tigranes, and many others who had a mind to magnificence.

Along the walls of Rome we have seen turrets and walkways, their pavements patterned with mosaic and their walls faced with the prettiest revetment. But not every treatment is suitable for every city. The refinement of a cornice and revetment are not appropriate to a town wall: instead of a cornice, there should be a projecting row of large stones, slightly smoother than the rest and set flat and level; instead of revetment, while still preserving a rough, austere, and almost menacing appearance, I would have the stones fit so tightly together along their edges and corners that there are no gaps to blemish the work. This is best achieved with a Doric rule, cited by Aristotle to describe his interpretation of how the law should be;[24] the Doric rule is one made of flexible lead. When employing extremely hard blocks of stones, which are awkward to shape, labor and expense may be spared by leaving them unsquared and laying them randomly, wherever they will fit. It is an exceedingly laborious task to arrange blocks of stone until they fit in a suitable position; this flexible rule is therefore employed, and wrapped around the edge and sides of the block onto which another is to be joined; it is then used as a bent rule, to gauge the spaces between the blocks already in place, and, before inserting a new block, to select where it might add the most strength.

Then, to inspire greater reverence, I would have an open road describing the city limits[25] and running in front of the walls, and I would dedicate it to the freedom of the commonwealth; here no one may dig a ditch, build a wall, or plant a hedge or a tree.

I come now to temples. The first who founded a temple in Italy was, I find, father Janus; this is why the ancients would always say a prayer to the god Janus before they sacrificed.[26] Others maintain that the first temple was dedicated by Jupiter in Crete;[27] and so of all the gods to be worshiped, he is thought the most important. Then again, in Phoenicia, a certain Uso is said to have been the first to set up statues to Fire and Wind, and to construct a temple.[28] Others record that before any cities existed, Dionysius gave a temple to every town he founded, and instituted certain religious rites during his expedition through India;[29] and others maintain that, in Achaia, Cecropus was the first to build a temple to Ops,[30] and that the Arcadians were the first to build one to Jove.[31] It is said that Isis (also called the goddess lawgiver, as the first immortal to institute a code of laws) was the first to construct a temple in honor of her parents, Jupiter and Juno, and to appoint priests.[32]

In each case what form the temple was to take in the generations that followed is not clear at all. Personally, I could easily believe that it would have been similar to that on the Acropolis at Athens,[33] or the Capitol at Rome.[34] Even when the city was flourishing, these were roofed in straw and reeds,[35] on the basis that it was important to uphold ancestral traditions of frugality. But as kings and other citizens grew wealthier, and were tempted to dignify their city and their own names with buildings of great size, it seemed disgraceful that the houses of mortals should receive higher praise for their beauty than the temples of the gods; soon the stage was reached when even in the humblest of towns King Numa laid out four thousand pounds of silver for the foundations of a single temple.[36] I strongly applaud him for this, because he catered both to the dignity of the city and to the worship of the gods, to whom we owe everything.

Yet some with a reputation for wisdom are of the opinion that the gods require no temple. This is what persuaded Xerxes, so it is said, to burn down the temples in Greece, on the basis that the gods ought not to be enclosed by walls, but everything should be open, and the world should serve as their temple.[37] But to return to our argument. ◆

No aspect of building requires more ingenuity, care, industry, and diligence than the establishment and ornament of the temple. I need not mention that a well-maintained and well-adorned temple is obviously the greatest and most important ornament of a city; for the gods surely take up their abode in the temple. And if we decorate and splendidly furnish the houses of kings and visiting notables, what should we not do for the immortal gods, if we wish them to attend our sacrifices, and hear our prayers and supplications? But although men value them so highly, the gods have little concern for such perishables—they are moved solely by purity of mind and divine worship. There is no doubt that a temple that delights the mind wonderfully, captivates it with grace and admiration, will greatly encourage piety. To the ancients a people seemed to be truly pious when the temples of the gods were crowded.

This is why I would wish the temple so beautiful that nothing more decorous could ever be devised; I would deck it out in every part so that anyone who entered it would start with awe for his admiration at all the noble things, and could scarcely restrain himself from exclaiming that what he saw was a place undoubtedly worthy of God.[38]

The Milesians, according to Strabo, once built a temple that was so large that it was never roofed—this I do not commend.[39] The Samians boasted that they had the largest temple of all.[40] I am not against a temple being such that it can scarcely be enlarged, but it must be possible to adorn. Ornament is never completed: even in a small temple there is always something left over, it seems, that could and should be added. For my part, I like the temple that is no bigger than the size of the city requires; a large expanse of roof I consider offensive.

But I find it most desirable in a temple that, on the evidence of what is seen there, it should be truly difficult to decide whether the brilliance and dexterity of the artist or the enthusiasm of the citizens deserves the greater praise in gathering such rare treasures; and whether it is to be valued more for its grace and seemliness or for its endurance. This last is a quality that in other buildings, both public and private, must be given repeated and thorough consideration; but especially in a temple, since the investment which it involves must be protected as well as possible against accidental destruction. And, in our opinion, age will give a temple as much authority, as ornament will give it dignity.

Following the Etruscan Discipline,[41] the ancients were advised that every place was not suitable for every god. Those who patronize peace, chastity, and the noble arts should have their temples located within the custody of the walls; but those who incite pleasure, strife, and fire—Venus, Mars, and Vulcan—should be excluded.[42] Vesta, Jupiter, and Minerva, whom Plato called the guardians of the city, they would place in the town center or on the citadel;[43] and Pallas, goddess of craftsmen, Mercury, to whom the merchants sacrificed in the month of May, and Isis, in the forum; Neptune on the coast, and Janus on some high mountain. They sited the temple to Aesculapius on the Tiberine island, thinking water to be one of the primary needs of the sick;[44] elsewhere, according to Plutarch, this temple was generally sited outside the city, because there the air was healthier.[45]

Moreover, they thought that the temples to the different gods should take different forms:[46] those to the sun or to Father Liber[47] should preferably be round; and, according to Varro, the temple of Jupiter ought to have a perforated roof, because it is he who opens the seeds of everything.[48] The temple of Vesta, whom they associated with the earth, they made round like a ball.[49] Buildings to other heavenly gods they raised above the ground, and those to the infernal gods they built below ground, and those to the terrestrial gods, at a level in between.

They also developed, as I interpret it, different forms of temple for different types of sacrifice: some would pour blood over the altar, others would use wine and meal, and others would change the rite each day. In Rome the *Lex Postumia* decreed that no wine may be sprinkled on a funeral pyre; this is why, it is said, the ancients would use milk, and not wine, for their libation.[50] The capital on the ocean island of Hyperborea,[51] where Latona[52] is reputed to have been born, was consecrated to Apollo; everyone there could play the cithara, because they daily sang hymns of worship to their god.[53] I read in Theophrastus, the philosopher, that it was customary in the Isthmus [of Corinth] to sacrifice an ant to Neptune and to the Sun. In Egypt it was unlawful to appease the gods with anything but prayers within the city. This is why all temples to Saturn or Serapis, gods to whom cattle were sacrificed, would be built outside the city.

Our people, however, have used the basilican form for all our sacrifices, both because people originally used to meet and congregate in private basilicas, and because in them there is a dignified position for the altar in front of the tribunal, and around the altar a perfect space for the choir: the rest of the basilica, such as the nave and the porticoes, may be used by the congregation as spaces in which to walk around or to attend a sacrifice. Furthermore, in a timber-roofed basilica the voice of the priest as he preaches may be heard more distinctly than in a vaulted temple. But of this elsewhere.[54]

What has been said, that temples dedicated to Venus, Diana, the Muses, Nymphs, and other more delicate goddesses must take on the slenderness of a virgin and the flowery tenderness of youth, is very pertinent; buildings to Hercules, Mars, and other great gods must impose authority by their solemnity, rather than charm [the worshiper] by their grace.[55] Finally, you should situate the temple in a busy, well-known, and—as it were—proud place, free of any profane contamination; to this end it should address a large, noble square and be surrounded by spacious streets, or, better still, dignified squares, so that it is perfectly visible from every direction. ◆

All temples consist of a portico and, on the inside, a *cella*; but they differ in that some are round, some quadrangular, and some polygonal.[56] It is obvious from all that is fashioned, produced, or created under her influence, that Nature delights primarily in the circle. Need I mention the earth, the stars, the animals, their nests, and so on, all of which she has made circular? We notice that Nature also delights in the hexagon. For bees, hornets, and insects of every kind have learned to build the cells of their hives entirely out of hexagons.

The round plan is defined by the circle.[57] In almost all their quadrangular temples our ancestors would make the length [of the plan] one and a half times the width. Some had a length one and a third times their width, and others a length twice their width. It is a considerable defect in a four-sided plan if the angles are not exact right angles.

For many-sided plans, the ancients would use six, eight, or even ten angles. The corners of all such plans must be circumscribed by a circle.[58] Furthermore, they may be plotted exactly using the circle. For half the diameter of the circle will give the length of the sides of the hexagon [that it circumscribes]. And if you draw a straight line from the center to bisect each of the sides of the hexagon, it is obvious how to construct a dodecagon. From a dodecagon it is obvious how to derive an octagon, or even a quadrangle. But there is a better way to construct an octagon: mark out an equilateral, rectangular quadrangle,[59] and draw in the diagonals to each of the right angles; then from each point of intersection[60] draw an arc, its radius half the diagonal, to cut the sides of the quadrangle on either side; then the line joining these two cuts made by the arc will become the side of the octagon. We may also use a circle to define the decagon: we draw a circle with two diameters intersecting one another at right angles, and divide any one of the semidiameters into two equal parts. From this point of division we take a straight line slanting up to the top of the other diameter. If you then subtract from this line one quarter of the diameter, the distance remaining will equal the length of one side of the decagon.[61]

To the temple are added tribunals;[62] sometimes many, sometimes few. With quadrangular temples there is almost invariably one at the further end, opposite the door, where it is immediately obvious to anyone entering. With a quadrangular plan, tribunals along the side look best when they are twice as long as they are wide; on each side there should preferably be only one tribunal, but if more are required, they should be odd in number.[63] With round and, likewise, polygonal plans several tribunals may conveniently be added; depending on the number of sides, either each side should have a tribunal or they should alternate, one side having one, the next one being without. Round plans may conveniently accommodate six or even eight tribunals. With polygonal plans, make sure that the corners are equal in size and shape.

Then the tribunal itself may be rectangular or semicircular. But if there is to be only one tribunal, at the head of the temple, it should be semicircular for preference; a quadrangular one would be the second choice; but where there are to be a number of tribunals, close together, they will look more pleasing if, in plan, they alternate between the quadrangular and the semicircular, with elevations corresponding to each other.

The opening of the tribunal should be set out like this: In a quadrangular plan, where there is to be a single tribunal, divide the width of the temple into quarters, of which the mouth of the tribunal then takes up two; alternatively, if a more generous space is required, divide the width into sixths, and allow the opening to take up four. This will allow the ornament (such as the columns), the windows, and so on, to fit conveniently into their respective positions. When there are to be several tribunals around the plan, you may, if you so wish, make those along the side as deep as the main one. But, for the sake of dignity, I would prefer to make the main tribunal one twelfth part larger than the others. This also applies to quadrangular plans, in that it is quite permissible for the main tribunal to have equal sides, but if so, the rest must have a breadth, from right to left, twice their depth.[64]

Let the solid part of the wall—the bones, that is, of the building, which separate the various openings to the tribunals in the temple—be nowhere less than a fifth of the gap, nowhere more than a third, or, where you want it particularly enclosed, no more than a half. With a round plan, if the tribunals are six in number, make the intervening section—the bones, that is, and solid part of the wall—half the size of the opening; but if there are eight openings, then, in large temples especially, make it equal to the width of the tribunals; if there are more sides, however, make it a third of the tribunal.

Here and there are temples that, following ancient Etruscan custom, have small chapels along the walls on both sides, instead of a tribunal. These temples are laid out as follows: In plan, their length, divided into six, is one part longer than their width. A portico, serving as the vestibule to the temple, takes up two parts of that length; the remainder is divided up into three, to give the width of each of the three chapels. Then the width of the temple is divided into tenths, three of which were given to the chapels on the right, and likewise the left, and the four remaining were taken up by the nave in the center. A tribunal was added to the head of the temple, and to the middle chapel on either side. The width of the wall at the openings to the chapels was one fifth the intervening gap.[65] ◆

5
115v—117

So much for the interior. With a quadrangular temple, the portico may be attached either to the front or to both front and back, or it may be wrapped around the whole cella. Wherever a tribunal projects, there should be no portico.

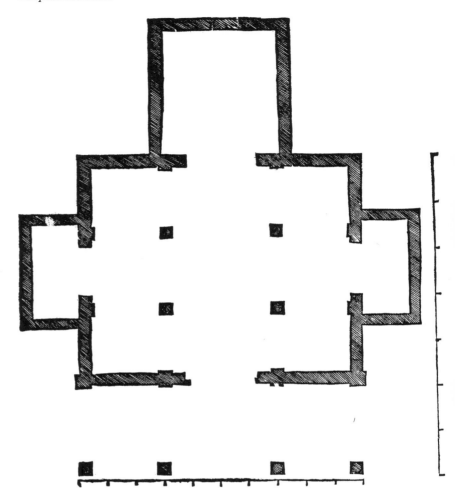

Porticoes on the front of quadrangular temples must never be shorter than the whole width of the temple, and never wider than a third of the length [of the temple]. Porticoes along the sides should have columns the same distance apart as they are from the wall of the interior. Those to the rear may take either form, according to preference.

Round temples should either be completely encompassed with a portico or have one only on the front. In either case the width should be calculated as with a quadrangular temple. But a portico on the front must always be quadrangular: its length should either equal the width of the whole interior or be between one eighth and as much as one quarter less.

The stairs to the temple of ——— at ———[66] have one hundred steps. The Hebrews have an ancestral law that states, "Have but one principal and sacred city, in a suitable, convenient location; in it construct one temple, with one altar, and built of stone not worked by hand, but as found, white and shining; the ascent to the temple should not be up steps; for you should be one people, of common feeling and common undertaking, given to religion, and preserved and defended by a single god."[67] To both of these I have objections: the first is impractical and inconvenient, especially to those who have frequent recourse to the temple, such as the old and the infirm; while the second greatly detracts from the majesty of the temple. I have also seen examples of sacred buildings, constructed not long before our time, where the entrance level is reached up several steps, and then the same number are descended to arrive at the temple pavement; I shall not say that this is a ridiculous device, but I fail to understand its purpose.

In my opinion, the space taken up by the portico and indeed the whole temple should be raised above the level of the city: this will give it a greater air of dignity. What is more, just as the head, foot, and indeed any member must correspond to each other and to all the rest of the body in an animal, so in a building, and especially a temple, the parts of the whole body must be so composed that they all correspond one to another, and any one, taken individually, may provide the dimensions of all the rest.[68] Thus I find that in antiquity almost all the best architects derived the height of the podium from the width of the temple, and would make the height of the podium a sixth of that width. With larger temples some preferred to make it a seventh, and with the very largest a ninth.[69]

The portico, by definition, consists of one continuous, complete wall only, the other sides being perforated with openings. Consideration must be given to what sort of opening you require. There are two types of colonnade, one where the columns are less frequent and spaced some distance apart, and one where they are more cramped and positioned closer together. Both have their disadvantages: With the distant spacing, the gaps between the columns will be so great that they cannot be spanned with a beam, without it breaking; yet an arch will not sit happily on a column. And with the closer spacing, the narrowness of the gap will restrict movement, obstruct the view, and keep out light. This is why a third, in-between variety was developed, which had elegance, avoided these disadvantages, catered to convenience, and was, in short, preferable to the others.[70]

With these three we could have been content; but the ingenuity of the artist has added a further two. This, in my opinion, is how they evolved: When the number of columns proved to be insufficient relative to the size of the *area*, they were inclined to abandon that perfect compromise in favor of slightly more generous spacing; and when there were more columns available than required, they decided to set them somewhat closer together. There were therefore five degrees of spacing, which we might term as follows: the wide, the close, the elegant, the not-so-wide, and the not-so-close. I would conjecture further that a shortage of blocks of stone of sufficient length might have forced the architect to reduce the height of the columns; these he adopted, but realizing that the result was lacking in grace, he set them on top of pedestals to give the work the right height. For measurement and inspection of various works had established that the columns of a portico would not appear graceful unless their height and thickness were based on fixed rules.

On these rules they gave the following advice. The number of gaps between columns should be odd, the number of columns always even; make the central opening, opposite the door, more generous than the rest; where the spaces between the columns must be narrower, make the columns more slender; use thicker columns where the spaces are wider. Thus the thickness of the columns was restrained by the intercolumniation, and the intercolumniation by the columns, usually according to the following rules: in "close-set" colonnades, the intercolumniation should be no less than one and a half times the thickness of the columns; in "wide-set" colonnades, it should be no more than three and three-eights the thickness of the columns; in "elegant" colonnades, it should be two and a quarter; in the "not-so-close-set," two; and in the "not-so-wide-set," three. The central gap in the row should be a quarter part wider than the rest. This, then, was their advice.[71]

From measuring the ancient buildings ourselves, however, we notice that the central opening did not always follow these rules. With "wide-set" colonnading, no good architect would make it a quarter part wider; most made it a twelfth part wider—a wise move, this, as a beam of excessive length would have been incapable of supporting itself, and would crack. The central opening was often a sixth part wider than the rest, and not infrequently a seventh, especially with "elegant" colonnades. ◆

6

117—118

Once the intercolumniation has been established, the columns must be raised to support the roof. There is a considerable difference between erecting a column and erecting a pier, and between spanning the opening with an arch and spanning it with a beam. The arch and the pier are appropriate for a theater, and even in a basilica the arch would not be amiss; but in a temple, the noblest work, nothing is found but the trabeated portico. Of this we shall now speak.

The columnar pattern comprises the following: the pedestal and, on top of that, the base; on the base, the column, followed by the capital, then the beam, and on top of the beam, the rafters, their cut-off ends either terminated or concealed by the frieze; finally, at the very top comes the cornice.

I feel that we should begin with the capital, being the element that varies the most. Here I ask those who copy out this work of ours not to use numerals to record numbers, but to write their names in full; for example, twelve, twenty, forty, and so on, rather than XII, XX, and XL.[72] It was Necessity who instructed that a capital should sit on top of the column, to serve as a base for the joints of the beam timbers; originally it was a shapeless piece of roughly squared wood. The inhabitants of Doron[73] (if the Greeks are to be believed in everything) were the first to put it to the lathe, and to make it look like a round dish set under a quadrangular lid; because this seemed too cramped, they raised it on a slightly higher neck. The Ionians, on viewing the Doric work, found the dish on the capital to their liking, but not the bareness of the dish, nor the junction of the collar; they therefore added the bark of a tree, draping it on either side and spiraling in to hide the edge of the dish. The Corinthians followed at Callimachus' instigation; he preferred a high vase covered with leaves to the squat dish, one he had seen overgrown with acanthus by the grave of a young girl. Thus three types of capital had now been established and incorporated into the vocabulary of the experienced architect: the Doric—although I have discovered that this was already in use in ancient Etruria—the Doric, then, the Ionic, and the Corinthian.[74]

What do you think might be the reason for this? Everywhere one is accosted by a host of different capitals, works of great effort and careful study, produced by men intent on some new discovery. Yet none of them deserves comparison with these former, except that capital which—to distinguish it from all foreign imports—we shall call the "Italian." It combines the gaiety of the Corinthian with the delight of the Ionic, and, instead of handles, has hanging volutes; the result is graceful and thoroughly commendable.[75]

If the columns are to confer elegance on the building, they should be governed by the following: the Doric capital requires a column with a base one seventh of the height from top to bottom thick; the Ionic a column, its base one ninth of the overall height thick; the Corinthian a column one eighth its height thick.

With each type of column the base, they felt, should have the same height, but different lineaments. Not only that: they should differ in the lineaments of almost all their parts, although on the whole the column should be similar. As we mentioned in the last book, the Ionians, Dorians, and Corinthians all favored the same lineaments for their columns. Their columns have a further similarity, in that, as in Nature, the top of the trunk is always more slender than the bottom. Some maintained that the bottom should be one and a quarter times as thick as the top. Others, realizing that objects appear smaller, the farther they are from the eye, sensibly decided that with a tall column the top should not be reduced as much as with a short column, and applied the following rules.

When a column is to be fifteen feet tall, the diameter at the base must be divided into sixths, five of which give the diameter at the top; but for columns of between fifteen and twenty feet, they felt that the diameter at the top of the shaft should be eleven thirteenths that at the base; for columns of between twenty and thirty feet, the top is to be six sevenths of the base; then for those of up to forty feet, thirteen fifteenths; finally, for columns of up to fifty feet in height, the diameter at the top should be seven eighths that at the bottom. Thereafter, this same progression must be used to calculate how the width at the top increases, as the height of the column increases.

In these respects, then, all orders agree; although we have discovered, by measuring the works ourselves, that the Latins did not always follow these rules exactly.[76] ◆

7

118—120

In the previous book we discussed the lineaments of the column; here I shall go over them once more, looking at them from a different, but no less useful, point of view. Out of the stock of columns generally used by our ancestors in their public works, I shall choose one whose size is neither too large nor too small, but in between: its length I shall set at thirty feet. The maximum overall diameter is divided into nine equal parts, of which the diameter of the projection at the top takes up eight, giving it the ratio nine to eight, called the *sexquioctave*. The ratio of the maximum overall diameter to that at the base of the bottom recess I make the same, nine to eight; and the ratio of the maximum diameter of the upper projection to that of the upper recess I make eight to seven, the *sexquiseptima*.

I come now to the lineaments of the parts that differ with each order. The base is composed of die,[77] tori, and scotia. The die is that quadrangular element at the bottom, so called because it has a face to every side. The tori are thick collars forming part of the base, one below the column itself, the other on top of the die. The scotia is a circular recess, like that in the wheel of a pulley, sandwiched between the tori.[78]

The measurements of all the parts are taken from the diameter at the base of the column, according to the rule first established by the Dorians. They

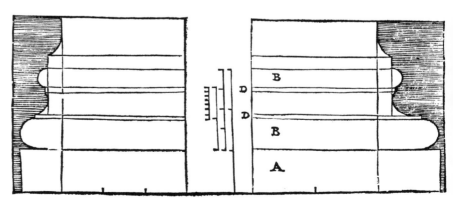

Doric base: A *plinth,* B *torus,* D *astragal,*
with scotia between.

made the height of the base half the diameter. The width of the die in either dimension would be no more than one and a half and no less than one and a third times that diameter. The height of the base was then divided into three parts, one of which was taken up by the thickness of the die. Thus the thickness of the base was three times the thickness of the die, and the width of the die three times the thickness of the base. The thickness of the remainder of the base, excluding the die, was then divided into quarters, the top one being taken up by the upper torus. Then the distance remaining in the middle, between the torus at the top and the die at the bottom, was divided in half, the bottom being given over to the lower torus, the top hollowed out for the scotia sandwiched between the two tori. The scotia consists of a hollow channel and two thin fillets running around the edges of the channel. Each fillet takes up a seventh of the thickness; the remainder is hollowed out.

It is essential in all building, as we said, to take care that everything rests on a solid base. Nor will it be solid, if a plumb line dropped from any masonry above meets air or void. When carving out the channel of the scotia, they were always careful not to cut beyond the vertical of whatever was built on top. The tori projected five eighths of their thickness; and the thicker torus at its widest point was vertically aligned with the profile of the die within the base. So much for the Doric.

The Ionians found the thickness of the Doric base to their liking, but doubled the number of scotias, and added two thin rings in the middle, between the scotias. Thus the height of the base was made equal to half the diameter at the bottom of the column; this height was divided into quarters, one of which constituted the thickness of the die, and eleven its width. The ratio, then, between the thickness and the width of the base was four to eleven. Once the die had been marked off, the rest of the height was divided into sevenths, two of which gave the thickness of the lower torus; then the space left over by the torus and the die was further divided into thirds, the top one being given over to the upper torus, the two remaining to two scotias and two rings, sandwiched between the two tori.

The method for the scotias and rings was as follows: the space between the tori was divided into sevenths, one of which was taken up by each of the rings, and the five remaining divided equally between the two scotias. The tori had the same projections as in the Doric, and, when channeling out the scotias, they did not cut beyond the vertical of whatever was built on top. They made the thin fillets an eighth of the scotia.

Some did it another way: apart from the die, the thickness of the base was divided into sixteen parts, called modules; four of these were taken up by the lower torus, three by the upper torus, three and a half by the lower scotia and, similarly, by the upper one, and two by the intermediate rings. So much, then, for the Ionic.

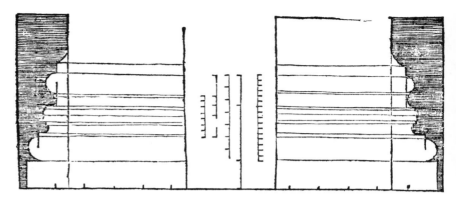

The Corinthians found both the Ionic and the Doric base to their liking, and used both throughout; in fact, they added nothing to the columnar system except their capital. The Etruscans, it is claimed, made the die in the base round instead of quadrangular; we have yet to find any such base in an ancient work, although we have noticed that in circular temples, where the portico runs around the temple, the ancients used to give the base a continuous die, as an uninterrupted socle to all the columns, with a height equal to that of a die. The reason for this, I imagine, was their realization that the quadrangle and the circle do not go well together. We notice also that some have pointed the abaci in temples toward the center of the temple; had they done the same at the base, the result, while not perhaps to be rejected, would, nonetheless, not be totally satisfactory.[79]

Here I might make a brief digression, for the sake of clarity.[80] The following are the minor moldings of ornamental work: platband, corona, ovolo, astragal, channel, wave, and gullet. All of them project, but each has a different outline: The platband has a lineament like the letter **L**; it is similar to the fillet, only wider. The corona is a particularly prominent platband. The ovolo I was almost tempted to call ivy, because it extends and clings; its lineament is like the letter **C** surmounted by the letter **L**, like so:

The astragal is a little ovolo. The letter **C**, if reversed and surmounted by the letter **L**, like so,

produces a channel. But if the letter **S** is surmounted by the letter **L**, like so, it is called a gullet,[81] because of its resemblance to a man's throat. If, however, below the letter **L** an inverted **S** is attached, like so,

it is called a wave,[82] because of its similar curve.

Again the moldings are either plain or in relief. The platband may be carved with seashells, volutes, or even with a lettered text; in the corona there may be dentils, their width half their height, and the space between two thirds their width. The ovolo is carved with eggs, or sometimes adorned with leaves; the eggs are sometimes whole and sometimes cropped along the top. Beads are cut into the astragal, as though threaded along a string. The gullet and wave are not covered except with leaves. The fillet, in any position, is alway left plain.

When two moldings adjoin, the upper one always projects farther. Fillets are used to separate one molding from another; they also provide a border to the moldings (the border being the top of the lineament to each molding). In addition, their polished surface provides a contrast to the texture of the relief. The width of these fillets is one sixth that of their adjoining molding, whether dentils or egg carvings, except in the case of the wave, where it is a third. ◆

8

120—121v

To return now to the subject of the capital. The Dorians gave their capital the same height as the base, and divided it into thirds, the first being occupied by the abacus, the second by the echinus, and the third and last by the collar of the capital, which lay below the echinus.

The abacus has a width and depth one and one twelfth times the diameter at the base of the column. The abacus contains a border and a die. The border is formed by a gullet, and takes up two fifths of the abacus. The upper edge of the echinus meets the end of the abacus. Running around the bottom of the echinus there are either three tiny rings or a gullet, serving as ornament and taking up no more than a third of the height. The collar (the bottom part of the capital), as in the case of all capitals, is no wider than the column itself.

In other cases—as we have observed in the lineaments of ancient buildings—the height of the Doric capital has been made three quarters the diameter of the base of the column, and the overall height of the capital has been divided into elevenths, four being allotted to the abacus, and also to the echinus, but three to the collar. The abacus has then been divided in two, the top being a gullet and the bottom a fascia; the echinus is then also divided in two, the bottom being given over either to rings or to a gullet, running around the base of the echinus. To the collar are attached either roses or leaves in relief. So much for the Doric.[83]

We shall form the Ionic capital like this: The overall height of the capital should be half the diameter through the bottom of the column. Divide the height into nineteen modules. Give three modules to the abacus, four to the scrolls of the volute, six to the echinus, and leave the remaining six at the bottom to the volute, where it hangs down on either side and folds into a scroll. The width and depth of the abacus should be the diameter at the top of the shaft of the column. The depth of the scroll, from front to back of the capital, should equal that of the abacus. Crosswise the scroll spills over the sides and hangs in a shell-like spiral. The navel[84] of the spiral on the right should be twenty-two modules from the equivalent navel on the left, and twelve from the top of the abacus.

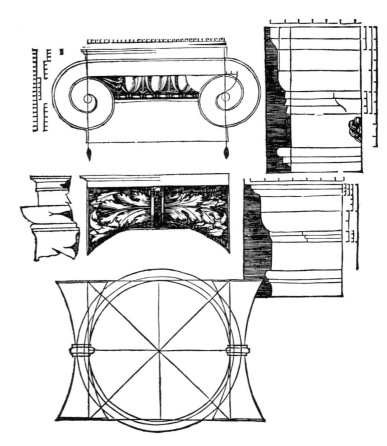

Left: *Ionic capital—front, side, and plan.*
Right: *Doric capital—two variants.*

This is how to form the spiral. Around the center of the navel trace a small circle with a radius of one module. At the top of this circle make a mark, and at the bottom another. Then set the fixed end of your compasses on the upper mark, and with the free end construct a line from the point where the abacus meets the scroll, turning down in a complete semicircle as far as the end of the capital, to exactly below the center of the small circle. Retract the compasses at that point, drawing in the fixed end to the mark at the bottom of the original small circle; then turn the free end to continue the incomplete curve from the point so far reached up to the upper edge of the echinus, to form a single, continuous curve out of two unequal semicircles. Then continue the line in the same manner, until the spiral, which is the curve so far described, reaches the eye,[85] which is the small circle.[86]

The edge of the echinus[87] extends two modules beyond the scroll; but at its base it is equal in thickness to the top of the column. The sides of the capital, where the volutes at the front meet those at the back, contract to within half a module of the thickness of the echinus. The ornament to the abacus is bordered by a gullet of one module. A channel is cut into the scroll half a

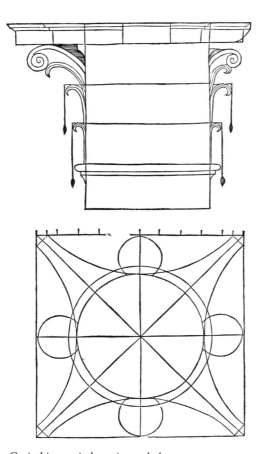

Corinthian capital: section and plan.

module deep, bordered by a fillet one-quarter module wide; into the middle of the front surface are carved leaves and seeds. The portion of the echinus on the front of the capital is carved with eggs and, below them, a string of beads. The contractions at the sides, between the volutes, are adorned with scales or leaves. Such, then, is the Ionic capital.

The height of the Corinthian capital is equal to the diameter at the base of the column and is divided into seven modules. The abacus takes up one module and the remainder is occupied by the vase, whose base has the same width as the top of the column, without its projections, and whose upper rim has the same width as the bottom of the column.

The abacus is ten modules wide, but half a module is clipped off at each corner. The abaci of all other capitals consist of straight lines; those of the Corinthian curve inward until the distance between them is the same as the width at the bottom of the vase. The border of the abacus takes up a third of its height, and its lineaments are identical to those at the top of the shaft of the column.

The vase is girt with a fillet and an astragal, which cover it with two interlapping rows of leaves standing out in relief; each row contains eight leaves. The first row is two modules high, as is the second. The remaining space is taken up by the stalks sprouting out from the leaves to the full height of the vase. These stalks are sixteen in number; four of them unfold on each face of the capital, two from the same knot on the right, and two from the same

Corinthian capital.

Italic (Composite) capital.

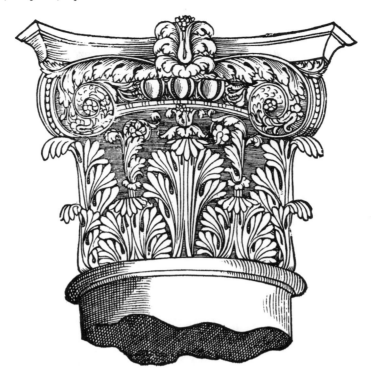

knot on the left; the two end ones hang below the corners of the abacus in a form of spiral, while the middle ones also curl, so that their ends meet in the center. Between these middle two a flower sprouts prominently from a vase, as far as the top of the abacus. The rim of the vase, where it is visible and not covered by stalks, is one module thick. Each leaf should be articulated into five or, possibly, seven lobes. The tips of the leaves hang forward half a module. As with all carving, deeply incised lineaments will add great charm to the leaves of the capital. Such, then, is the Corinthian capital.

The Italians combined in their own capitals all the ornament to be found in the other three; they used the same design as the Corinthians for the vase, abacus, leaves, and flowers; but instead of the stalks, they had handles, two complete modules in height, protruding beneath each of the four corners of the abacus. The otherwise plain front of the capital took its ornament from the Ionic, with stalks sprouting into the volutes of the handles, and the rim of the vase, like the echinus, carved with eggs and lined below with a string of beads.

There are many other variations on the above, capitals composed of different lineaments, their elements enlarged or reduced; not, however, approved by the learned.

Composite capital: section and plan.

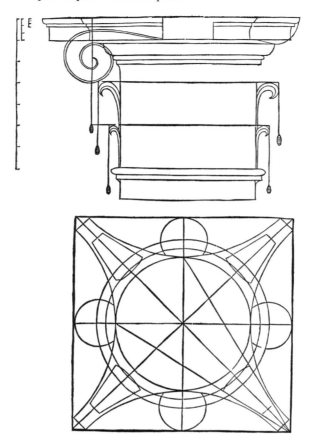

So much for the capital, except perhaps to mention the practice of including, above the abacus of the capital, a second small quadrangular abacus, hidden behind the construction. This gives the capital below more room to breathe, and makes the main beam appear less oppressive; during construction, it helps protect the more delicate and slender parts of the work. ◆

9
121v—124v

The beam[88] is set on top of the capitals, once they have been placed in position, and on top of the beam are set the cross-beams, boards, and other parts that make up the roof. In all this the Ionic, in particular, differs considerably from the Doric, although in certain respects they all agree. For example, the beam is generally fashioned with a soffit no wider than the diameter at the top of the column, and a top surface equal in width to the diameter at the bottom of the column.

"Cornice" we call the top section, protruding above the rafters. The general rule given for all projections also applies here, in that the distances that any section projects from the wall must also equal its height. The cornice would also be made to lean forward, by a twelfth of its height, as it was realized that if it were vertical, it would appear to lean backward.[89]

Here I repeat my request—and I do so most strongly—that in order to reduce errors, those who transcribe this work should record all numbers mentioned with their full names, and not with numerals.[90]

The Dorians made their beam at least as wide as half the diameter at the base of the column. They gave their beam three fascias; below the top one, several short battens were attached; on the underside of each of these were fixed

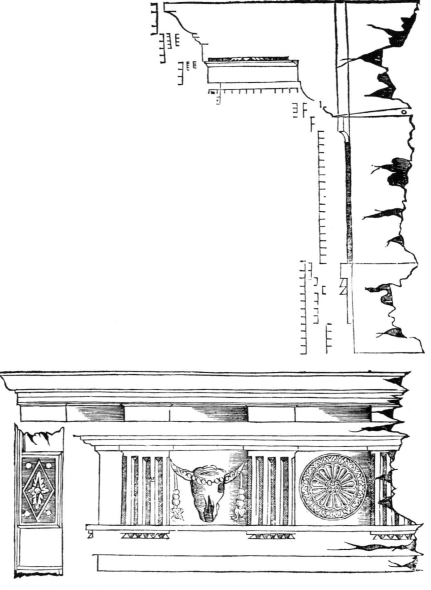

Doric entablature: section and elevation.

six nails, intended to hold in place the cross-beams, which projected from the wall to the level of the battens: clearly this device was to prevent them from slipping inward. The overall height of the beam was divided into twelve units, from which were derived all the measurements of the elements described below. The lowest fascia was four units high, the middle one, next to it, six, and the top one took up the remaining two units. Of the six units of the middle fascia, one was taken up by the battens, and another by the nails fixed beneath. The battens were twice six units in length. The blank spaces between the ends of the battens were twenty minus two units wide. Over the beam are set the cross-beams, whose ends are cut at right angles, and which stand out half a unit. The width of these cross-beams should equal the thickness of the beam, and their height should be half as much again, or twice nine.[91] Up the face of the cross-beams are incised three straight grooves, cut at right angles, equidistant, set at intervals of one unit. The edges on either side were chamfered to a depth of half a unit. The gaps between the cross-beams in more elegant work are filled with tablets,[92] as broad as they are high. The cross-beams are set vertically above the solid of each column. The faces of the cross-beams stand out half a unit from the tablets; the tablets, meanwhile, are flush with the lowest fascia of the beam below. In these tablets are sculpted calves' skulls,[93] roundels,[94] rosettes, and so on. Each of the cross-beams and tablets has, as a border, a platband two units high.

Above this there is a plank, two units thick, its lineaments those of a channel. In its thickness there extends a pavement[95]—as I might describe it— three units wide, its ornament of small eggs based, unless I am mistaken, on the stones that stand out from the mortar in paving. On this are set mutules, of equal width to the cross-beams and equal thickness to the "pavement," one positioned above each of the cross-beams, projecting out twelve units and cut perpendicularly to the level. The mutules are bordered by a gullet three quarters of a unit thick. On the underside, between the mutules, were carved rosettes and acanthus.

Above the mutules sits the cornice, four units in height. This consists of a platband with a gullet border. The latter takes up one and a half units. If the work is to have a pediment, every layer of the cornice is to be repeated in it, and within each layer each particular element should be set at the correct angle and be aligned exactly with the others along the plumb. The difference between the pediment and the top of the cornice, however, is that at the top of a pediment there is always a border of a wave, four units high in the case of the Doric order, to act as a rainwater drip; but in a cornice it is only included when there is to be no pediment above. But more about pediments later. So much for the Dorians.[96]

The Ionians not unwisely decided to make the depth of the beam increase with the height of the column, a principle that might equally well apply to the Doric. They therefore laid down the following rules: for columns of up to twenty feet, the height of the beam should be one thirteenth that of the column; for those up to twenty-five feet, a twelfth: then for columns of up to thirty feet, the beam should be one eleventh of that height; this same progression was then used to calculate the remainder.[97]

Besides a border, the Ionic beam should also contain three fascias. Its height should be divided into ninths, of which the border should take up two. The lineament of the border should be that of a gullet. What lies below this border should then be further divided into twelve units, three of which go to the lowest fascia, four to the middle, and the remaining five to the top one, immediately below the border. The fascias sometimes have a border, and sometimes not. If they do, it is either a wave, one fifth the height of the fascia, or an astragal, one seventh its height. Examples may be found of ancient works where the lineaments have been borrowed from elsewhere or are a mixture of other styles; the result can be quite commendable. But the most popular version would seem to be a beam with no more than two fascias: in other words, the Doric, as I interpret it, without battens and nails. This is how it was composed: the overall thickness was divided up into nine units, of which one and two-thirds was given over to the border. The middle fascia took up three and a third units, and the bottom one the remaining two.[98] The top half of the border of the beam consisted of a channel and a fillet, and the bottom half consisted of an ovolo. Below the ovolo, the middle fascia had an astragal as its border, taking up an eighth of its depth, and the lowest fascia had a border of a gullet taking up a third of its depth.

Above the beam are set cross-beams; but their ends are not visible, as they are in the Doric: they are cut vertically, flush with the beam, to produce a continuous panel, which I call a "royal fascia."[99] The depth of this fascia equals the thickness of the beam below. On the fascia there would be carved at regular intervals either vases and sacrificial items, or calves' skulls; from their horns would hang garlands of apples and other fruit. Above the royal fascia would be a border consisting of a gullet, no more than four and no less than three units in height.

Above this would be set boards serving as a soffit;[100] these would project to form a step no less than three units in depth. They would sometimes be carved with dentils, to look like cut planks, and sometimes be left continuous, unbroken by any carving. On the planking there would be either the above-mentioned soffit or a cross-bracket, off which the mutules spring; it would project three units and be carved with little eggs; on this they set the mutules, sheltered and backed by the fascias of the tablets. The fascia on the front would be four units high, and the underside would be six and a half units deep. Directly above the mutules would come the drip mold, two units thick and adorned with a gullet and an ovolo. At the very top would be a wave, three or, if you prefer, four units thick. Along this molding, in

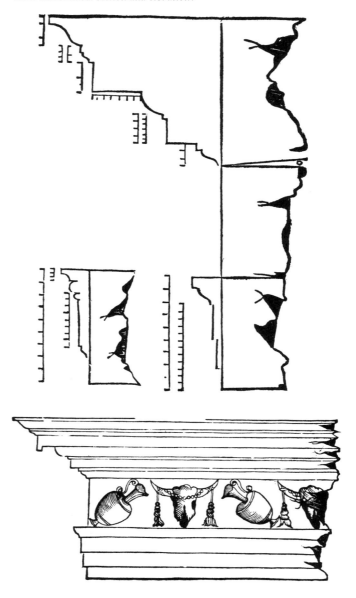

both the Ionic and Doric systems, lions' heads would be carved,[101] to throw off any water that might have collected. They took great care not to shower water either on the interior or where people would enter the temple, and accordingly would block the mouth of any head positioned above an opening.

The Corinthians made no new contribution to the beam or to any of the framework of the roof, except, if I judge correctly, not to make the mutules covered or square, as in the Doric, but to leave them bare and cut into like a wave; the gaps between the mutules equaled the distance they projected

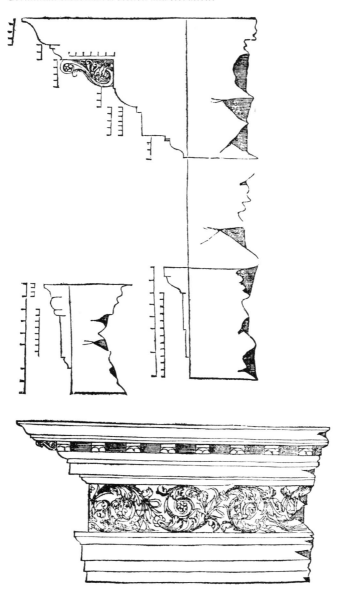

from the wall. But apart from that, the Corinthians followed the Ionians. So much for trabeated systems of columns; we shall deal with arched systems later, when we discuss the basilica.

There are certain matters relevant to these systems of columns that must not be overlooked. It is obvious, for example, that columns seem narrower in the open air than in an enclosed space; secondly, the number of flutes may increase the apparent thickness of a column. For this reason the following advice is given for columns on a corner: make the columns thicker or increase the number of their flutes, because they stand in the open air and appear somewhat narrower than the rest.[102]

Channels run down the column in either a straight line or a spiral. In the Dorian one, the channels run straight down the column and are referred to as "flutes"[103] by the architects; the Dorians have twenty such flutes. In the other orders there are twenty-four; these are separated one from another by fillets, no more than a third and no less than a quarter the width of the groove. The groove itself has a semicircular lineament. The Dorians, on the other hand, have no fillets: the flutes are simple, sometimes straight, more often with grooves no greater than a quarter circle, and meeting con-

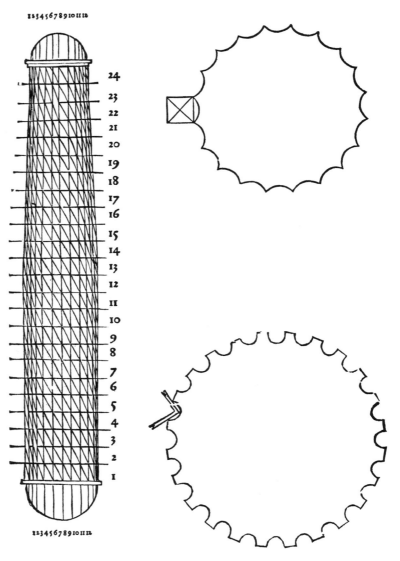

Method used to outline column flutings.

tinuously along an edge. The fluting along the bottom third of the column was almost always filled in with an ovolo, to protect the column from injury or damage. When the flutes run straight down the length of the column from top to bottom, they give the column a greater apparent thickness.

Of spiral fluting there are different kinds, but the less the line deviates from the vertical, the thicker the column appears. The fluting would run no more than three and no less than one complete spiral. Whatever form the fluting takes, it should run from base to top in continuous, parallel lines, so that all the grooves agree. The best way to regulate the groove is to use a set square. According to the mathematicians, if two lines are drawn from any point on the circumference to either end of the diameter, they will form a right angle. And so, once the ridges have been marked, the groove must be hollowed out until the angle of the set square can sit comfortably within it.[104] With all fluting a proper gap must be left at either end, to separate the hollow of the fluting from the next molding, the fillets running around the column. Enough on this subject.

Around the temple in Memphis—so it is said—colossi, twelve cubits in height, were used instead of columns.[105] Elsewhere there are reports of columns completely bedecked with spiraling vine leaves and sprinkled with

Various Doric intercolumniations.

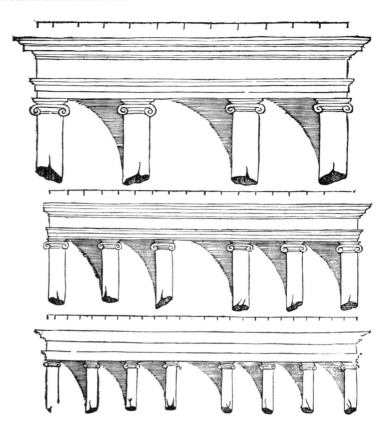

little birds in relief. A smooth, plain column, however, is more in keeping with the solemnity of a temple.

Here below is a list of dimensions of particular use to the workman in setting out the columns. The method is based on the number of columns to be contained in the work. To begin with the Doric: If there are to be four columns, the front of the elevation is divided into twenty-seven parts; if there are to be six, it is divided into forty-one; but if there are eight, it is divided into fifty-six. Each column takes up two of these parts. With the Ionic, however, if there are to be four columns, the front of the elevation is divided into eleven parts; if there are to be six, it is divided into eighteen; and if eight, into twenty-four and a half; each column takes up one of these parts.[106] ◆

10

124v—126

There are some who recommend that the floor and the interior of the temple should be reached up several steps, and that the altar for the sacrifice should be established higher than anything else. As for the chapels flanking the sides, some left their entrance and openings quite free and open, without any intervening section of wall; others put a pair of columns in them, their beams and ornament taken from the portico as recently described, and the remaining space above the cornices filled with statues and candelabra; others still closed them off by a wall, stretching from one side to the other.

Anyone who thinks that extremely thick walls lend a temple dignity is mistaken. For who would not criticize a body for having excessively swollen limbs? Besides, thick walls restrict the light. With the temple of the Pantheon, since the walls needed to be thick, the architect very commendably employed nothing but ribs, rejecting any form of infill. He used spaces that someone of less experience might have filled in, for niches and openings, thereby reducing the cost, while resolving structural problems and contributing to the elegance of the work. [107]

The thickness of the wall is determined in the same way as that of the column, so that the ratio of height to thickness must be the same for both wall and column. I notice that the ancients used to make the walls of their temples a twelfth—or, where they wanted the work to be particularly strong, a ninth—of the width of the front.

With a circular temple, the height of the wall on the interior, up as far as the vault, was never less than half the diameter: it would generally be as much as two thirds, and sometimes three quarters. But the more experienced would divide the circumference of the *area* into four parts, and extend one of these lengths vertically upward to give the height of the wall on the interior, to a ratio, say, of eleven to four. [108] This method is often also used for quadrangular buildings, whether temples or some other form of vaulted work.

But when the walls on either side were to be flanked with chapels, they would sometimes raise the height of the wall to equal the width of the *area*, so that the interior might appear more open. With a circular building, however, the wall would not have the same height on the inside as on the outside; on the interior the wall stops where it meets the vaulting, whereas on the exterior it should continue right up to eaves level. This section on the outside should rise a third of the height of the vaulting measured from the springing on the wall, if the roof has a stepped profile, or one half, if the roof is straight and sloping. The walls of a temple are best built of brick, but they should be decorated with some form of ornament. [109]

Opinions vary on how to adorn the walls of a sacred building. The wall of a chapel in Cizicus was adorned with polished marble and joints of solid gold. [110] The brother of Phidias used a paste of saffron and milk as stucco for the temple of Minerva in Elis. [111] The kings of Egypt surrounded the temple of Osimandia, where Jupiter's concubines were buried, with a circle of gold, one complete cubit in thickness and three hundred and sixty-five in circumference, one for each day of the year. [112]

This is one view; others take a different line. Cicero follows Plato's teaching, and holds that citizens should be compelled by law to reject any variety[113] and frivolity in the ornament of their temples, and to value purity above all else. "Let us have," he added, "some dignity for all that."[114]

I could easily believe that in their choice of color, as in their way of life, purity and simplicity would be most pleasing to the gods above; nor should a temple contain anything to divert the mind away from religious meditation toward sensual attraction and pleasure. Yet, to my mind, with temples as with other public buildings, provided it in no way diminishes their solemnity, it is thoroughly commendable to attempt to execute wall, roof, and flooring skilfully and elegantly, and to make them as durable as possible.

For this reason, the most convenient method of facing all unexposed sections of the interior would be to use marble or glass, in the form of either paneling or mosaic; the exterior, in keeping with ancient custom, should preferably be faced with stucco in relief; in either case great care should be taken to set paneling and reliefs in appropriate and seemly positions. The portico, for example, makes a fine setting for pictures commemorating great events. Within the temple I favor detached painted panels rather than pictures applied directly to the walls, although I would prefer reliefs to paintings, unless they are like those two which the dictator Caesar acquired for the temple of Venus Genetrix, at the cost of eighty talents.[115] I look at a good painting (to paint a bad picture is to disgrace a wall) with as much pleasure as I take in reading a good story. Both are the work of painters: one paints with words, the other tells the story with his brush. They have other things in common: both require great ability and amazing diligence.

I would have nothing on the walls or the floor of the temple that did not have some quality of philosophy. I find that bronze tablets were kept on the Capitol, and on them were inscribed the laws for governing the empire; three thousand of these were restored by the emperor Vespasian, when the temple burned down.[116] It is recorded that the threshold of the temple of Delian Apollo was inscribed with verses instructing men how to prepare herbal remedies against poison of every kind. But in our opinion any advice to be posted should instruct us on how to make ourselves more just, modest, and frugal, and to equip ourselves with every virtue and make ourselves more acceptable to the gods above; there should be maxims such as, "Behave as you would wish to appear," and, "Love if you would be loved," and so on. I strongly approve of patterning the pavement with musical and geometric lines and shapes, so that the mind may receive stimuli from every side.

The ancients would use precious objects to adorn their temples and porticoes; such as the ants' horns brought from India to the temple of Hercules,[117] or the chaplets of cinnamon deposited in the Capitol by Vespasian, or the great root of cinnamon that Augusta placed in a gold dish in the main temple on the Palatine.[118] In Aetolia, the country laid waste by Philip, the portico of the temple at Thermus was said to have been decorated with more than fifteen thousand suits of armor and over two thousand statues; according to Polybius,[119] all were destroyed by Philip, except those bearing the name or image of a god. In such matters diversity may be just as valuable as quantity. In Sicily, some make their statues of salt: Solinus is our authority on this.[120] Pliny mentions that glass was also used. Certainly, whether for their natural materials or for their ingenuity, objects of such rarity deserve great admiration. But of statues elsewhere.

Columns may either be added to the wall or inserted into an opening, but the method used is not the same as for a portico. I notice that in large temples, perhaps because the columns cannot relate to a work of vast scale, the arches of the vault are extended to have a total height[121] one and a third times the radius; this turns out to be more graceful, because the vaulting, rising higher, is more agile and relaxed, as it were.

Here is another point, I feel, not to be overlooked: in vaulting, the springing of the arches must be lower than the semidiameter by at least as much as the projection of the cornices, so as to be hidden from the view of someone standing in the middle of the temple. ◆

I I

126—127

I would expect the roof of a temple to be vaulted, for the sake of dignity and also durability. I do not know why, but there is scarcely a famous temple to be found that has not suffered from some disastrous fire. We read that Cambyses burned every temple in Egypt, and removed the gold and ornament to Persepolis.[122] Eusebius relates that the oracle at Delphi was burned down three times by the Thracians;[123] it is also recorded in Herodotus that Amasis[124] restored it, when on a further occasion it caught fire of its own accord.[125] Elsewhere it is written that the oracle was burned down by Phlegyas,[126] around the time that Phoenix invented an alphabet for his citizens, and was once more ablaze during the reign of Cyrus, a few years before the death of Servius Tullius, the Roman king; finally, it is also known to have gone up in flames around the time of the birth of those luminaries of invention and learning, Catullus, Sallust, and Varro. The Amazons burned down the temple at Ephesus during the reign of Silvius Postumius; it was burned down again about the time Socrates drank his poison in Athens. We read that a temple in Argos[127] was destroyed by fire the year that Plato was born in Athens, and while Tarquin was king of Rome.[128] What need I say about the sacred portico in Jerusalem? What of the temple of Minerva at Miletus? What of the temple of Serapis in Alexandria? And what of the Pantheon in Rome, the temple of Vesta, or the temple of Apollo, where, it is recorded, the Sibylline verses[129] were burned? Almost every temple may claim to have suffered some such calamity. Diodorus writes that in his time the only temple to have remained undamaged was that dedicated to Venus in the city of Eryx.[130]

Caesar maintained that the vaulting of roofs saved Alexandria from catching fire when he attacked the city.[131] There are ornaments particularly suitable to vaults. For their spherical vaults, the architects of antiquity borrowed the ornament used by silversmiths for their sacrificial bowls. For barrel- and cross-vaulting, they copied the patterning commonly found on bedspreads. Thus vaults may be seen patterned with quadrangles, octagons, and other figures of equal angles and sides, picked out with radiating lines and circles, to produce a result that could not be more graceful.

Here I should mention the coffering found in many buildings, including the Pantheon, undoubtedly a splendid way of adorning the vault, but one whose method of construction has not been handed down in writing. We have developed our own method, which requires little labor or cost: The outlines of the intended pattern of coffering, whether quadrangular, hexagonal, or octagonal, are drawn directly onto the supporting framework; the hollow sections in the vault are then filled to a set level, using unbaked brick, and clay instead of lime. Once these mounds, as it were, have been raised along the back of the centering, the vault is built on top, using brick and lime, and taking great care to link and reinforce the more slender sections with the thicker and more secure ones thoroughly. Once the vault has been closed, and while the centering is being dismantled, the clay mounds originally set in position are extracted from the solid structure of the vault. This method, then, may be used to achieve whatever type of vaulting is required.[132]

To return to the discussion. I am highly pleased by the description given by Varro of the vault at ————,[133] which was painted to represent the sky; it also contained a mobile star with a ray to indicate the hour of the day and the direction of the wind outside.[134] I am delighted by such devices.

A pediment is said to lend a work so much dignity that for the sake of appearance not even the heavenly house of Jove was thought to be without one, although it never rained there. This is how the pediment to the roof is composed. The section up to the vertex (that is, the ridge at the top) takes up no more than a fourth and no less than a fifth of the width of the facade, measured at cornice level. Bases, to accommodate statues, are set at the top of this ridge and at both ends of the eaves. Those at the corners of the eaves should have a height equal to that of the entire cornice excluding the royal fascia. The one at the center of the ridge of the pediment should be one-eighth higher than the two at the corners.

Buccides, it is said, was the first to introduce ornamental masks of red clay to the outer tiles of the roof;[135] later, like all the tiles, they were made of marble. ◆

The window openings of a temple should have modest dimensions and should be placed high up, where they have a view of nothing but the sky, which will not divert the minds of celebrant or supplicant from divine matters. The awe that is naturally generated by darkness encourages a sense of veneration in the mind; and there is always some austerity about majesty. What is more, the flame, which should burn in a temple, and which is the most divine ornament of religious worship, looks faint in too much light.

For this reason, surely, the ancients were usually content with a doorway as the only opening. But, for my part, I would prefer to make the entrance to a temple thoroughly well lit, and the interior and nave not too gloomy. I would place the altar, however, in a place of majesty rather than of elegance. To return to the subject of openings for light.

Let us recall what we said earlier, that the opening consists of void, jambs, and lintel. The ancients would never make their windows and doors other than quadrangular. To deal with doors first. All the best architects, whether Ionian, Dorian, or Corinthian, would make the jambs one fourteenth narrower at the top than at the bottom. The lintel and the top of the jambs would be the same thickness, and their ornament would share the same profile; their joints would fit exactly; the cornice at the top of the door, above the lintel, would have the same height as the capitals on top of the column in the portico. Everyone observed the rules we have set out.

But otherwise they differed greatly. The Dorians divided the overall height into thirteenths, of which the height of the void took up ten, which the ancients called "a light," the width five, and the jambs one. So the Dorians. The Ionians divided that same overall height, which equals that of the top of the capitals of the columns, into fifteenths, of which the height of the void took up twelve, the width six, and the jambs one. The Corinthians divided theirs into seventeenths, seven of which were given over to the width of the void, the height of the light was twice the width, and the jambs of the door were a seventh the width of the void. In each case on all sides the door frame would take its shape from the beam.[136]

Here, unless I am mistaken, the Ionians preferred to use their own standard beam, adorned with three fascias, and the Dorians theirs, minus the battens and nails.[137] For the ornament to the lintel each relied generally on the grace of the cornices. But the Dorian beams did not represent the exposed ends of the cross-beams, with their three grooves;[138] instead they used a royal fascia, equal in thickness to one of the jambs of the door. To this they added a border of a gullet, and above that a simple corona, to serve as a parapet, and on that a row of little eggs, followed by covered mutules with their own border and at the top a wave; the dimensions for each element are taken from the rules listed above for the Doric entablature.

Doric portal.

The Ionians, on the other hand, had no royal fascia, but included instead a band laden with garlands of leafy sprigs, tied together with ribbons; its thickness took up two thirds of the beam. Above this came a border, dentils, a row of little eggs, a thick band of mutules covered by a fascia, with its own border on the front, and, at the top, a wave. They also included, at the top of both jambs and below the thick band of covered mutules, little projecting ears, as I would call them, because of their resemblance to that breed of dog with a keen scent and a fine sense of hearing. The shape of

Ornament to Sacred Buildings

these ears was that of a large, extended **S**, its ends curving inward as in a volute, like so:

At the top their thickness was equal to the width of the band [of leaves], and at the bottom it was one quarter less.[139] The ears hung down lengthwise to the level of the top of the void.

For their doors the Corinthians borrowed the arrangement of their porticoes. Their doors, especially if exposed (we need not repeat this matter), were adorned with a little portico as follows: once the jambs and the beam had been constructed, a column, sometimes freestanding, sometimes engaged, would be added to either side. The bases of the columns would be far enough apart to completely contain the door frame. The length of the columns, complete with capitals, should equal that of the diagonal [of the void] from bottom right to top left. Above these columns are set the beam, fascia, cornices, and tympanum, using the same method as for the portico, described above in the appropriate place.

Instead of using the molding from the beam, some have adorned the jambs of the door with cornices, thereby increasing the size of the opening—a detail more in keeping with the nicety of a private house, especially for its windows, than with the solemnity of a temple. With larger temple doorways, especially if such a doorway is the only opening, the height of the void is divided into thirds. The upper third alone is left as a window, and adorned with a bronze lattice; the remainder is taken up by the leaves of the door.

There are also rules governing the details of the leaves. The main component is the hinge. This hinge may take two forms: the door may either be hung from iron pins and hooks along one side, or rest and rotate on a pivot at its corner. It would be safer to entrust the doors of a temple to a pivot than to a system of pins, since, for the sake of durability, they must be of bronze, and consequently extremely heavy.

Here I do not mean doors like those about which we read in historians and poets, so heavily weighed down with gold, ivory, and reliefs that they could be opened only by a team of men, and would give off a terrifying creak. I much prefer temple doors that are easy to open and close.

The bottom end of the pivot should therefore sit in a socket made of copper mixed with tin. Both the socket and the end of the pivot attached to the door should be hollowed out, so that they are concave, like a fishbowl, and may contain between them an iron ball, perfectly round and smooth. There

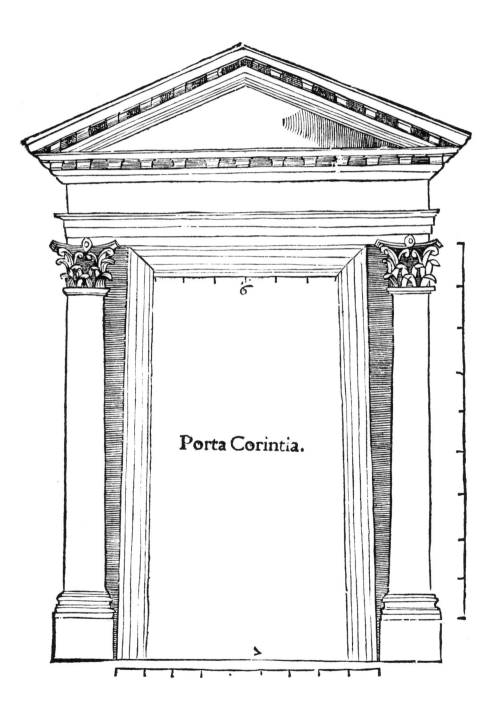

Porta Corintia.

should be a brass female joint set into the lintel at the upper end of the pivot, at the top of the door, and around the axle there should also be a free-moving iron washer, polished smooth on all sides. These will ensure that the door is never stiff, but will swing open with a light push whenever required.

Each door should have twin leaves opening in opposite directions to one another; they should be one twelfth as thick as they are wide. Their ornament should consist of stiles—as many as you like, two, three, or even one—applied to the surface and running around the edge; when there are two stiles, one should overlap the other like a step, and together they should take up no more than a quarter and no less than a sixth of the width of the door. The one on top should be a fifth wider than the one underneath. When there are three stiles, they should take their lineaments from the Ionic beam. But when there is a single stile, it should have a width of between one fifth and one seventh that of the door. The inside edge of the fascia should be a gullet.

The door should be divided lengthwise by crosspieces, the upper section taking up two fifths of the overall height.[140]

The windows of a temple have the same ornament as the doors; but because they occupy the upper part of the wall, immediately below the vault, their voids curve in at their corners to follow the line of the vault above, and, as a result, the section below the vault is also the inverse of the door: their width is twice their height. The overall width of the window is subdivided by two columns, to the same design as in the portico, although here the columns are almost always quadrangular.[141]

The niches, to contain paintings and statues, derive their lineaments from doors. They should take up a third of the height of the wall.

The windows that provide the temple with light would have, instead of leaves, either fixed, thin slabs of translucent alabaster or a lattice of bronze or marble, to keep out the frost and wind. In the latter case the spaces were filled, not with fragile glass, but with transparent stone, imported mainly from the Spanish town of Segovia, or from Bologna in [Cisalpine] Gaul. These are sheets of translucent and extremely pure gypsum, rarely larger than a foot in size, and with the natural capacity not to deteriorate with age.[142] ◆

13

129—130v

The next point to be considered, when dealing with the temple, is where the sacrificial altar is to be set up so as to give it the greatest dignity: the ideal position, surely, is before the tribunal. The ancients would make their altars six feet high, and twelve wide; on top they would set a statue. I shall leave it to others to decide whether it is proper to have further sacrificial altars arranged around the temple.

In ancient times, in the primitive days of our religion, it was the custom for good men to come together and share a common meal. They did not do this to fill their bodies at a feast, but to become humbler through their communication, and to fill their minds with sound instruction, so that they would return home all the more intent on virtue. Once the most sparing of portions had been tasted rather than consumed, there would be a lecture and a sermon on divine matters. Everyone would burn with concern for the common salvation and with a love of virtue. Finally they would leave an offering in the center, each according to his means, as a form of tax due to piety and a donation toward those who deserved it. This the bishop[143] would distribute among the needy. Everything would be shared in this way, as between loving brothers.

Later, when princes allowed these meetings to become public, there was little deviation from the original custom, except that as the congregation grew, so the size of the libation decreased. Throughout the commentaries of the Fathers, records of the eloquent sermons preached by the bishops of those days have been preserved for us. There would be a single altar, where they would meet to celebrate no more than one sacrifice each day.

There followed the practice of our own times, which I only wish some man of gravity would think it fit to reform. I say this with all due respect to our bishops, who, to preserve their dignity, allow the people to see them scarcely once in the year of festivals, yet so stuff everything with altars, and even. . . . I shall say no more. Let me simply state that within the mortal world there is nothing to be found, or even imagined, that is more noble or holy than the sacrifice. I would not consider anyone who wanted to devalue such great things, by making them too readily available, a person of good sense.[144]

There are other kinds of ornament for a sacrifice that are not fixed, and further means of adorning the temple for which the architect is responsible. What, you may question, is more beautiful: a playground, alive with gamesome youth; a stretch of sea, packed with a fleet; a plain, thick with troops and their triumphal banners; a forum, crowded with elders wearing civic dress; and so on; or a temple, illuminated with bright lights? But I would wish there to be a certain majesty to the lighting of a temple, a majesty that is singularly lacking in the tiny, blinking candles in use today. They have, I do not deny, a certain charm, when arranged in some form of pattern, such as along the lines of the cornices; but I much prefer the ancient practice of using candelabra with quite large lamps, which burn with a scented flame.

The candelabrum should be divided lengthwise into sevenths. Two of these would be taken up by the base, which was triangular, and ——— longer than it was wide, and ——— [145] wider at the bottom than at the top. The stem of the candelabrum rose up with a series of dishes, one above the other, to catch the drips. On top was set a lamp, brimming with gums and aromatic woods. It is recorded that the amount of balsam requested by the princes to be burned at public expense in the great basilicas of Rome every feast day was five hundred and eighty pounds.

So much for candelabra. I come now to other objects that make excellent ornaments for a temple. We read that Gyges[146] made a gift to Pythian Apollo of six solid gold craters, weighing 30,000 pounds;[147] and that at Delphi there were vases of solid gold and silver, each with a capacity of six amphorae. Some value the skill and invention of the craftsman higher than gold itself. It is said that in the temple of Juno at Samos there was an iron crater encrusted all over with relief; this had once been sent by Sparta as a gift to Croesus,[148] and was large enough to contain three hundred amphorae.[149] I find also that the Samians once sent to Delphi a gift of an iron caldron on which there were sculpted with remarkable skill the heads of animals; it was supported by kneeling colossi, seven cubits high. Another remarkable tale is that of the temple to the god Apis built by Sanniticus of Egypt: it was adorned with columns and various reliefs, and contained a statue of the god Apis that continually revolved to face the sun.[150] Still more amazing is the claim that the weapon of Cupid in the temple of Diana in Ephesus was suspended in air, without any support whatsoever.

I have nothing to say about objects of this kind, except that each should be allocated its own appropriate place, where it can be displayed with dignity, for all to admire. ◆

14

130v—131v

It is quite clear that the original role of the basilica was to provide a covered assembly room where princes met to pronounce justice. A tribunal was added to give it greater dignity. When the main enclosure proved too small, porticoes, opening inward, were added on either side, in order to increase the space; first simple porticoes, then double. Others added a further aisle transversely to the tribunal: this we shall call the "causidiciary," being the place where the orators and advocates would operate. These two naves joined together to form a shape similar to the letter T.[151] It would appear that later, for the sake of the servants, further porticoes were added to the outside. The basilica, then, is composed of nave and porticoes.

Since the basilica has the character of a temple, it should adopt much of the ornament that is appropriate to it; but in so doing, it should give the impression of seeking to imitate rather than rival the temple. Like the temple, the basilica should be set on a podium, but the height of the podium should be one eighth less,[152] in keeping with its lower religious standing. All its other ornament should lack the gravity of that of a temple. A further difference between a basilica and a temple is that the former, because of its almost rampaging crowd of litigants, and because of the need to read and record documents, should have clear passages and well-lit openings. It would be

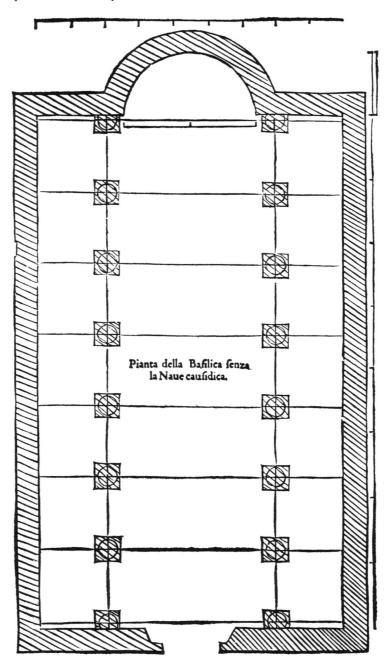

Basilica plan without a transept.

Pianta della Bafilica fenza
la Naue caufidica.

commendable if the plan of the basilica were to allow anyone arriving in search of a patron or a client to find where they are at first glance. For this reason columns should be wider apart; they should ideally be arched, although the trabeated form is also acceptable.[153]

The basilica, then, may be described as a form of wide, quite open walkway, roofed and surrounded by inward-facing porticoes. For any without porticoes might be considered not so much a basilica as a curia or senate house, a building type that will be dealt with in the appropriate place.[154]

The basilica ought to have a plan[155] with a length twice its width. It should also have a central nave, and a free and unimpeded causidiciary. If it is to have no causidiciary, but only the simple porticoes on either side, it should be laid out as follows: The width of the plan is divided into ninths, five of which are allocated to the central nave and two to each of the porticoes. The length also is divided into ninths, one of which is taken up by the depth of the alcove of the tribunal, and two by the width of the alcove at its mouth.

If, in addition to a portico, there is also to be a causidiciary, then the width of the plan is divided into quarters, two of which are taken up by the central nave and one by each of the porticoes. Then the length is divided up as follows: the depth of the alcove of the tribunal takes up a twelfth of the

Basilica plan with transept.

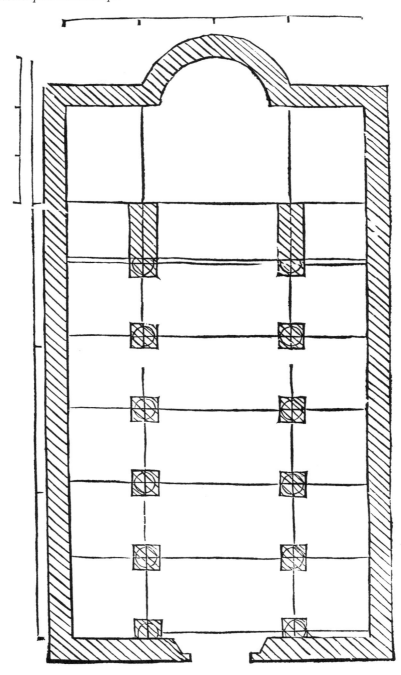

overall length, and the width of its opening two and a half twelfths; the width of the causidiciary should take up one sixth of the length of the plan.

If, however, there are to be both a causidiciary and a double portico, the width should be divided into tenths, four of which are taken up by the central nave, three by the porticoes on the right, and three by those on the left, each individual portico taking up half the space. The length is divided into twentieths, one and a half of which are taken up by the alcove of the tribunal, and three and a third by the width of the opening. The causidiciary takes up no more than three complete parts.

The walls of the basilica need not be as thick as those of a temple, for they do not have to support vaulting, but only the beams and gutters of the roof. Their thickness should therefore be a twentieth of their height. The height of the wall along the front should be one and a half times the width, and never more.[156]

Piers should be added to the wall at the corners of the nave, in line with the columns, and their thickness no less than twice and no more than three times that of the wall. Sometimes, for greater reinforcement, an extra pier is added, halfway between every two columns; its width should be triple or, at the most, quadruple that of a single column.

The colonnading need not have the same solemnity as that of a temple. It is therefore modified as follows, especially if trabeated: with the Corin-

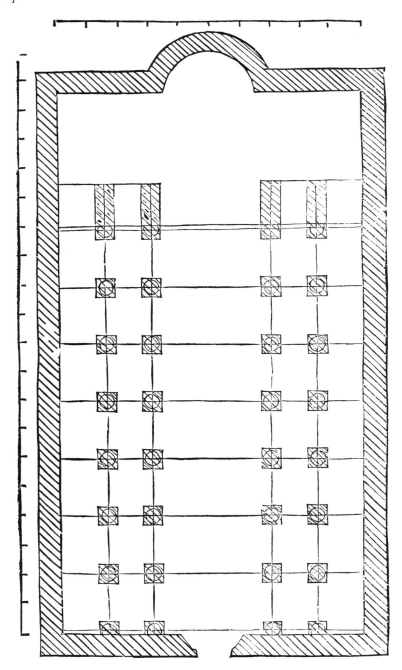

*Internal elevation of nave, having three
superimposed orders, Ionic, Corinthian,
and Composite.*

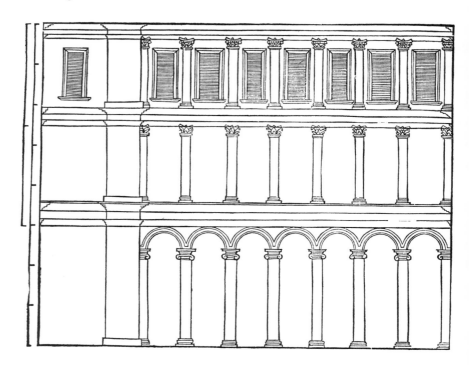

thian, the thickness is reduced by a twelfth; the Ionic by a tenth; the Doric
by a ninth. In the composition of every other member—the capitals,
beam, fascia, cornices, and so on—the same rules are adopted as for a
temple.[157] ◆

I5

131v—133

For arched colonnades quadrangular columns are required. The work
would be defective with round columns, since the springings of the arches
could not be fully supported by the solid of the column, and whatever lay in
plan beyond the circle contained by the square would rest on nothing but
thin air. To remedy this, on top of the capitals to the columns the experienced architects of antiquity would add a quadrilateral plinth, with a height
either a quarter or a fifth the diameter of the column, and a lineament of a
gullet. At its base this additional quadrangular element is as wide as the
maximum cross-section of the capital, and at its upper projection its width
equals its own overall height: this gives the sides and corners of the arches a
more convenient and secure seat.

Arched colonnades have as many variations as trabeated ones. The spacing
may be "distant," "close," and so on. With close spacing the gap between
the columns has a height seven times half its width; with distant spacing the

height equals five thirds of the width; in the not-so-distant spacing the width is half the height; in the not-so-close spacing it equals a third.

We have described the arch elsewhere as a form of curved beam. The same ornaments which were appropriate to the beam[158] should also apply to the arch, therefore, according to the columns from which it springs. Whoever wants the building to be especially ornate will have straight lines added to run above the tops of the arches along the whole length of the wall, representing a beam, fascias, and cornices, as may be thought appropriate to a colonnade of that height.[159] But since a basilica has either a single or a double portico around it, the position of the cornice above the columns and arches must also vary. With a single portico the cornices run five ninths, or as high as four sevenths, the way up the wall; but with a double portico the cornices lie at no less than a third and no more than three eighths the overall height.

Then, for the sake of both ornament and utility, a second set of columns, preferably quadrangular,[160] may be added to the wall, on top of the original cornices and centered vertically above the first set of columns. In addition to maintaining the solidity of the ribs and increasing the dignity of the work, these will also help to reduce considerably the weight and cost of the wall; projecting cornices may also be added above this second colonnade, as the type of work requires.

Basilicas with double porticoes may have three colonnades, one above the other, between floor and ceiling, whereas a single portico may only have two. When there are to be three colonnades, the stretch of wall between the lowest set of columns and the joists of the ceiling is divided in two, and along this division runs the second set of cornices. Between the first and second cornices the wall continues unbroken, and is adorned with inlaid revetment, but the section between the second and third is pierced by windows and other openings for light.

The windows in the blank spaces of the upper colonnading of a basilica should be uniform and matching, their width no less than three quarters of the gap between those columns, and their height preferably twice their width. If the windows are quadrangular, their lintels should be level with the top of the columns, without their capitals, and if arched, they may almost touch the beam; a reduced arch is also permissible, if so desired, but it must not exceed the height of the adjacent column.

Below the windows should run a parapet with a border consisting of a gullet and a band of little eggs. The openings of the windows should be latticed, but not glazed with gypsum, like those of a temple. Obviously they must contain something to ward off the bitter wind and keep out the irksome cold, to prevent any damage. On the other hand they must also provide continuous and unobstructed ventilation, to prevent the dust disturbed by the numerous feet from irritating eyes or lungs. I would therefore strongly advise the use of thin sheets of bronze or lead, patterned with numerous, tiny perforations, to admit light and breezes to purify the air.

The ceiling will look very fine if the soffits are perfectly level and the paneling fits together exactly. It should contain large circles in relief, of an appropriate size and mixed with polygonal patterns. Each shape should be separated by a molding, its lineaments taken from one of the elements of the cornice, in particular a gullet containing eggs, berries, and leaves. The moldings should be edged with bejeweled fascias, making a dignified and prominent projection, and containing between them resplendent leaves and acanthus forms; the spaces themselves should be gracefully and elegantly adorned through the ingenuity of the painter.

Pliny mentions a paste, called "leucophoron," used for laying gold onto wood. It was prepared as follows: six pounds of sinoper from Pontus are mixed with ten of clear yellow ocher; some Greek honey is then stirred in. This mixture is then left for a full twelve days before being applied.[161] There is a liquid mastic, made of linseed oil and well-roasted Elban sinoper, which proves altogether indelible.

The height of the doors to a basilica is governed by that of the portico. If there is a portico attached to the outside, to serve as a vestibule, it should have the same height and width as one on the inside. The opening, jambs, and so on, of the doors take their proportions from those of a temple; but the basilica is not important enough to have bronze doors: they should therefore be made of cypress, cedar, or the like, and adorned with bronze knobs. The whole structure should be put together with an eye to strength and durability, more than to delight. Or, if it is to have a greater appeal, instead of fiddly intarsiae, in imitation of pictures, bas-reliefs should be applied, so as to provide a method of decoration less easily damaged.

Round basilicas have also been undertaken. Here the height of the central space equals the overall width of the work. Then the same principles that apply to polygonal basilicas are used for the porticoes, colonnading, doors, windows, and so on. So much for this subject. ◆

16
133—135

I come now to the subject of commemorative monuments. Here it might be more entertaining to make our argument somewhat less dry than it has been up till now, during our discussion of numerical measurements. Yet I shall also attempt to be as succinct and concise as possible.

When our ancestors drove back their enemies and extended the boundaries of their empire with armed force, they would set up markers, to record their victorious progress and to brand territory gained in battle and distinguish it from that of their neighbors. And so the original purpose of posts, columns, and other such objects was to serve as boundary markers. After that, as a form of thanksgiving, they began to consecrate to the gods a portion of their booty, and to use religious ceremony as a public method of expressing their joy. This gave rise to altars, chapels, and other structures of a similar purpose. They also decided to take their future reputation into account, and strove to make their appearance and virtues known to all mankind. This gave rise to displays of spoil, statues, inscriptions, trophies, and other inventions to celebrate their glory. This form of display was eventually adopted not only by those who had served their country in some way, but also by the wealthy and the fortunate, so far as their means would allow.

But different methods were chosen to achieve this. Father Liber[162] used boundary markers consisting of stones, set up at frequent intervals, and tall trees, their trunks wreathed in ivy, to mark the extent of his expedition into India.[163] In Lysimachia[164] there was a huge altar, erected by the Argonauts during their expedition. By the banks of the river Hipparis near the Pontus, Pausanias set up a bronze crater, six inches thick, and with a capacity of six hundred amphorae.[165] Alexander built twelve altars of huge, squared stone on the river Alcestes,[166] across the ocean, and by the Tanais[167] built a wall to encompass all the land occupied by his camp, a work of sixty stades. When Darius had pitched camp in the land of the Odrisi on the river Artesroe, he ordered each soldier to cast one stone onto a pile, so that when future generations saw it, they would greatly marvel at the number of stones and the size of the pile.[168] While Sesostris was on campaign, he erected columns with magnificent inscriptions in honor of those who had resisted him like men; but to those who had surrendered without resistance, he left stone monuments and columns carved with the privy parts of women.[169] In each region through which he traveled, Jason erected a temple;[170] these were all destroyed by Parmenion,[171] so that the name of no one but Alexander would be celebrated there.

Such, then, was the tradition during a campaign; once victory had been achieved and peace established, other monuments would follow. The shackles used by the Spartans were hung up in the temple of Pallas the Worker.[172] Not only did the Eviani store in their temple the stone with which the king of the Inachians was struck and killed by King Phymius, but they even worshiped it like a god.[173] In their temple, the Eginitae[174] would consecrate the beaks of ships captured from the enemy. Augustus copied this, and after conquering the Egyptians, had four columns constructed out of the beaks of their ships; Domitian later transferred these to the Capitol. Julius Caesar added a further two, one in front of the rostrum, the other in front of the senate house, following a naval victory over the Carthaginians.[175] Need I discuss here the references made to towers, temples, obelisks, pyramids, and so on, in the works of the historians?

Enthusiasm grew for such works, as a means of self-glorification, until eventually individuals founded entire cities in order to preserve for posterity their names or those of their families. In addition to those which he had founded in his own name, Alexander, to give but one example, built the city of Bucephala in memory of his horse. Yet, to my mind, it was far more appropriate that after Mithridates had been put to flight, Pompey founded the city of Nicepolis, in Asia Minor, on the very site of victory. But Seleucus,[176] it would appear, has outdone them all, by naming three cities Apamia after his wife, five Laodicia after his mother, nine Seleuca after himself, and ten Antiochia after his father.

Others have ensured the immortality of their names not through the size of their wealth, but through something they have instituted. Caesar planted a wood from the berries of the laurel he had worn during his triumph, and he dedicated that wood to future triumphs. There was a famous temple in Ascalum in Syria that contained a statue of Dercetis,[177] given the face of a man and the body of a fish, because it was there that he had thrown himself into a pool; moreover, it was forbidden for Syrians to eat any fish from that pool.[178] At Lake Fucino the Mutinii made a statue of Medea Angistes in the shape of a snake, because she had helped save them from the danger of snakes.[179] This is like the Hydra killed by Hercules, or Io, or the beast of Lerna,[180] and the various creatures described in the verses of the early poets; I strongly approve of such devices, provided they convey some virtuous message—the carving, for example, on the tomb of Simandis,[181] in which there is a judge surrounded by magistrates in sacred robes; hanging from around their necks down to their chests is an image of Truth, its eyes closed and its head seemingly nodding; in the center is a pile of books, inscribed with the motto, "This is the true medicine of the mind."[182]

But, unless I am mistaken, the greatest ornament of all is the statue. It may serve as ornament in sacred and profane buildings, public and private, and makes a wonderful memorial to man or deed. Whatever the outstanding genius actually responsible for it, the statue is thought to have originated along with religion, and is said to have been invented by the Etruscans. Some believe that the Telchines of Rhodes were the first to make statues of gods; these would be consecrated to some magic cult, so as to induce clouds, rain, and so on, and could take on different animal forms as required.[183] Cadmus, son of Agenor, was the first Greek to consecrate a statue of a god in a temple. According to Aristotle, the first statues to be set up in the Athenian forum were of Hermodorus and Aristogiton, who had originally delivered that city from tyranny.[184] Arrian, the historian, recalls that Alexander returned these statues to Athens, after they had been removed to Susa by Xerxes.[185] Rome is reported to have had so many statues that it was said to contain a second population, made of stone. Rapsinates, the ancient king of Egypt, had stone statues of Vulcan carved, twenty-five cubits in height.[186] Another Egyptian, Sosostris, had statues thirty-two cubits high sculpted of himself and his wife.[187] In Memphis, Amasis had a statue, forty-seven feet long, made of himself prostrate; its base contained two other statues, twenty feet tall.[188] On the tomb of Simandis there were three statues of Jove, marvelously carved by Memnon from a single block of stone; one of these was seated, and so large that its foot measured over seven cubits; and besides the skilful workmanship and the size of the stone, it is quite remarkable that so large a block of stone should contain no cracks or blemishes.[189] Subsequently, when no stone could meet the scale of their projects, they began to use bronze to cast statues of up to one hundred cubits in height. But Semiramis surpassed everyone: because of the inadequacies of stone, and because she was eager for something of a scale beyond the capacity of bronze, she had an effigy, seventeen stades high, of herself along with one hundred men bringing her gifts in veneration, carved into the rock of a mountain in Media, called Bagistanus.[190]

While on the subject of statues, I feel that I ought hardly to overlook the claim made by Diodorus that Egyptian sculptors, although working in different places and using different blocks of stone, were so skilful and ingenious that they could fashion a single statue, with its joints so perfect that it seemed to have been made in one place by one artist. The famous statue in Samos of Pythian Apollo was reportedly made using this astonishing technique, with one half being completed by Thellesius and the other by Theodorus in Ephesus.[191]

These anecdotes have been included purely for amusement: although they bear a particular relevance to the present discussion, I would prefer to consider them in the context of the next book, where we discuss the private monument, a subject to which they are more closely related. For private citizens, being reluctant to let even princes surpass them in the amount spent, and being themselves consumed with greed for glory, were eager for every opportunity to heap lustre on their names, and would therefore spare no expense, provided they had the means; and they would use all their resources to attempt whatever lay within the ability of the artist or the strength of the imagination. I therefore believe that in their struggle to rival the greatest kings in the elegance of their designs and the seemliness of their work, they managed to lag not far behind. But this subject will be reserved for the next book; and I promise that it will give the reader great pleasure. But let us first not overlook this one relevant comment. ◆

I7

135—136

There are those who maintain that a temple should contain no statues. King Numa, it is said, being a follower of Pythagoras, forbade there to be any effigy in a temple.[192] It was also for this reason that Seneca ridiculed both himself and his fellow citizens: "We play," he said, "with dolls like children." Yet instructed by our elders and appealing to reason, we would argue that no one could be so misguided as to fail to realize that the gods should be visualized in the mind, and not with the eyes. Clearly no form can ever succeed in imitating or representing, in even the slightest degree, such greatness. If no object made by hand could achieve this, they thought it better that each, according to his own powers of imagination, should fashion in his mind an impression of the principal sovereign of all, the divine intelligence. In this way the veneration of the majesty of his name would be all the more spontaneous.

Others think differently; they maintain that it would be sound and prudent to give the gods the image and likeness of man: if the presence of statues were to cause the ignorant to believe that as they approached, they were approaching the gods themselves, it would make it easier for them to turn their minds from the depravity of life. Still others felt that effigies of those worthy of mankind's praise, and deserving to be commemorated along with the gods, should be set up and displayed in sacred places, so that future generations, when paying their respects, might, in their zest for glory, be incited to follow such example.

But in a temple especially, the type, location, spacing, and material of the statue are all particularly important. For example, I feel that those absurd garden statues of scarecrow gods would hardly be appropriate, nor those of warriors, and the like, found in porticoes; nor should the statues be placed anywhere constricted or demeaning. To deal with material first, and later with the rest.[193]

According to Plutarch, statues were originally made of wood, such as that of Apollo in Delos, and, in the city of Populonia, that of Jove, made from vine and said to have survived intact for many years,[194] and that of Diana at Ephesus, said by some to be of ebony, although Mutianus[195] claims it to be of vine.[196] Peras, who founded the temple of Argolica and made his daughter the chief priestess, had a statue of Jove carved from the trunk of a pear tree.[197]

Some forbade the use of stone in statues of the gods, because it was a hard and insensitive material. Gold and silver were similarly rejected, because they are found in soil that is infertile and unlucky, and because they have a sickly hue. "There stood Jupiter," the verse runs, "scarcely covered in his cramped abode, / And in his right hand an earthenware thunderbolt."[198] In Egypt some believed that God was composed of fire, and lived within an etherial flame, and thus could not be perceived by the human senses; for this reason they preferred the statues of their gods to be of crystal. Others thought black stone to be the most appropriate, because its color could never be grasped; still others preferred gold, because it matched the stars.

I myself am undecided as to which material is best for statues of the gods. It might well be said that they ought to be made of the most dignified material, and that scarcity is the closest thing to dignity. Yet I am not for having them made of salt, as Solinus describes was customary in Sicily,[199] nor of glass, such as ———— mentioned by Pliny;[200] equally I would not have them made of solid gold or silver—not that I agree that they should be rejected because they are mined from sterile ground and because they have a sickly hue. I would be influenced by many factors, not least the conviction that in terms of religious veneration any object of worship intended to represent a god should resemble that god as far as possible. For this reason I feel that they should be as lasting and immortal as mortal hands can make them. And why, I ask myself, is the old belief still so popular, that a painting of a god in one place should be more receptive to the prayers and votive offerings of the righteous, than a statue of that same god positioned right next to it? What is more, you will find that if any statue, once the object of considerable veneration, is moved elsewhere, people will treat it as bankrupt, withdraw their credit, and no longer invest their votive offerings there. Each statue, then, should be allotted its own dignified position, and should remain there.

They say that within human memory no elegant work was ever made of gold: as though the prince of metals refuses to allow himself to be handled by craftsmen. If this is so, gold ought not to be used for any statue of a god that we want to be splendid. Besides, if it were of gold, there would be the temptation, not so much to steal his golden beard, as to melt down the entire god.

I would like bronze most, were it not that the candor of pure marble is very attractive. One of the main advantages in using bronze is its durability, provided, of course, that the statue be such as to make the sense of outrage at its destruction outweigh any financial incentive to melt it down for reuse. The statue should therefore be either beaten into shape with a mallet or cast in a thin skinlike layer.

It is written that ——— an ivory statue ——— was made so large that it would scarcely fit under the roof of the temple.[201] I cannot commend this; for the statue must be appropriate in its size, in the lineaments of its form, and in the disposition of its parts. And then, the severe countenance of the great gods, with their beards and eyebrows, might not go well together with the soft expressions of maidens. And again, the rarity of the statues increases the veneration for them, unless we are very much mistaken.

On an altar there should ideally be two statues, and certainly no more than three; others may find appropriate places in niches. Each statue of god or hero should, I suggest, have a gesture and garb that convey, as far as the artist can, his life and customs. Here I do not mean that they should strike some stance like a wrestler or an actor, as some think appropriate, but I would like the expression and the overall appearance of the body to convey the grace and majesty of a god, so that they seem to give a nod or gesture of the hand, to beckon on those who approach, and appear receptive to the prayers of the supplicants.

This, then, is the sort of statue appropriate to a temple; the rest should be consigned to theaters and other profane buildings. ◆

The Eighth Book of Leon Battista Alberti on the Art of Building. Ornament to Public Secular Buildings.

We have already noted the importance of the application of ornament in the art of building.[1] It is quite clear that each building does not require the same ornament. With sacred works, especially public ones, every art and industry must be employed to render them as ornate as possible: sacred works must be furnished for the gods, secular ones only for man. The latter, being the less dignified, should concede to the former, yet still be ennobled with their own details of ornament.

What is proper to sacred public buildings we dealt with in the previous book. It remains for us to treat of secular ones. We shall describe, then, the ornament appropriate in each instance.

The road, as I interpret it, is something essentially public, in that it is designed to convenience both residents and visitors. But since there are two ways to travel, by land and by sea, we must deal with both. Recall, if you will, our earlier distinction between military roads and nonmilitary roads.[2] These may be further subdivided into urban and rural roads.

The countryside along a route may be a considerable ornament to a military road, provided it is well maintained and cultivated, and full of villas and inns, and plenty of attractions; with views now of the sea, now of mountains, now of lakes, rivers, or springs, now of a parched rock or plain, and now of groves and valleys. If the road is neither steep, nor tortuous, nor obstructed, but rolling as it were, level,[3] and quite clear, it will also be an ornament.

Indeed, what measure did the ancients not take to achieve this? I need not mention their hard flint roads, running for up to one hundred miles and built of vast blocks of stone. The Appian Way was paved from Rome to Brindisi. All along these military roads there are examples to be seen of rocks pierced, mountains cropped, hills excavated, and valleys leveled—works of incredible expense and extraordinary labor; clearly each provides not only for utility but also for ornament.

Moreover, if the traveler often comes upon objects that stimulate conversation, especially if it is about high matters, that is an ornament of the greatest dignity. As Laberius put it, "A witty comrade at your side, to walk's as easy as to ride."[4] Certainly conversation does much to alleviate the tedium of a journey. I have always had a high regard for the various customs of the ancients, and here I find further cause to praise them (although I discover that their primary concern was not to entertain travelers, but something rather different, of which we shall now speak): there is a law in the Twelve Tables which orders that "No body may be buried or cremated within the city."[5] Furthermore, an ancient decree issued by the senate ordained that no corpse may be buried within the town walls, except those of Vestal Virgins and emperors (who were exempt from law).[6] According to Plutarch, the Valerii and the Fabritii were granted the privilege of being buried in the Forum; their descendants would lay down the body, but would remove it as soon as the torch had been applied, thereby indicating that the privilege was theirs, but that they did not wish to avail themselves of it.[7] The ancients, then, would choose a suitable, conspicuous roadside location in the country for their family tombs; they strove to adorn them with as much ornament as their resources and the hand of the artist would allow. As a result, their tombs would be built to the most exquisite design;[8] they would not be short of columns; their revetment would gleam; they would be resplendent with statues, reliefs, and panels, and show elegant busts of bronze or marble.

How much these prudent men and their practice benefited both the state itself and standards of moral behavior is a subject on which I need not dwell. I shall touch upon it only as far as is relevant to our argument. And what would be your opinion? Would a traveler along the Via Appia, or some other military road, not be greatly delighted gazing at its remarkable number of monuments, as he encounters first this sepulcher, then that, then another, and then one more, all splendidly ornate, and recognizes on them the names and titles of famous men? And would not all these monuments to the past provide numerous occasions to recall the deeds of great men, and so provoke conversation that itself serves both to make light of the journey and to enhance the reputation of the city?

But this was a minor consideration; more important was their concern for the prosperity and well-being of country and citizen. According to the historian Appian, one of the main reasons given by the wealthy for rejecting the Lex Agraria[9] was that they considered it a sacrilege to hand the tombs of their ancestors over to others.[10] How many inheritances that would have been squandered or gambled away, as we might well imagine, have passed instead to great-grandchildren through this single act of charity, devotion, and religious observance? Furthermore, it provided an ornament to the name and posterity of both town and family, constantly encouraging others to imitate the virtues[11] of the most famous. Finally, what would your reaction be, should you ever happen to witness an intruder ransacking the tomb of your ancestors? Who would be so idle or feckless as not to be instantly aflame with the desire to avenge both country and honor? And what power informs the mind, once indignity, devotion, and shame are aroused!

For this the ancients are to be praised. Yet I would not presume to criticize our own custom of having sacred burial grounds within the city, provided the corpses are not brought into the temple, where the elders and magistrates meet to pray in front of the altar, as occasionally this may cause pestilential vapors of decay to defile the purity of the sacrifice.[12] But how much more convenient is the practice of cremating bodies![13] ◆

2

137v—140

Here we might include a few comments that would seem necessary on the rules for sepulchers. These could almost be thought of as public works, because of their connection with religion. As the law reads, "Wherever a dead body is buried, let that place be considered sacred."[14] Likewise we maintain that laws about burial come under religion. Since religion must be considered before anything else, I think that in spite of the fact that these are matters of private rights, I should deal with them before moving on to public and secular works.

Scarcely any race has been so savage as not to feel the need of sepulchers; an exception was a nation called the Ictophagi from farthest India:[15] it is said that they used to throw their dead into the sea, maintaining that it was of little consequence whether they were consumed by earth, water, or fire.[16] The Albanians, too, thought it wrong to show concern for their dead.[17] The Sabaeans treated their dead like excrement, and even cast the bodies of their kings onto the dungheap.[18] The Troglodytes used to snatch up their dead, necks bound to their feet, and carry them away with mockery and jests; they would then bury them with no thought given to the location, and set a goat's horn at the head of the grave.[19] But no one with any concern for humanity would approve of these customs.

Elsewhere in Egypt and Greece monuments would be built not only to the body but also to the memory of friends, a display of devotion that no one could fault. One tribe in India deserves, I feel, particular attention: they maintained that the greatest monument of all was for the memory of a man to be preserved for posterity, and they would celebrate the funerals of their most distinguished citizens with nothing but hymns of praise. Yet I feel that it is also for the sake of those who remain that the body must be treated properly. What is more, the sepulcher will clearly be an effective means of preserving a name for posterity.[20]

Our ancestors used to erect statues and sepulchers at public expense to honor those who, by their life or their death, had proved notably deserving of the Commonwealth's gratitude, and to encourage others to such glory. Sepulchers were perhaps less popular than statues, because it was realized that they would deteriorate with the seasons and old age. Yet, according to Cicero, the sanctity of a sepulcher lies in the very ground, which cannot be destroyed or removed: while everything else becomes extinguished, the sanctity of the sepulcher increases with age.[21]

The sepulcher was consecrated, if I am not mistaken, to ensure that anyone whose memory had been entrusted to the surety of structure and soil would be protected by religion and fear of the gods even from the hand of man.

Hence the law in the Twelve Tables forbidding the use of the vestibule or entrance to a sepulcher for any other purpose.[22] There exists a further law imposing a heavy penalty on anyone who violates a tomb, or scratches or damages the columns of a sepulcher.[23]

In short, reverence for the sepulcher was customary among all civilized nations. The Athenians had such respect for the sepulcher that if any commander failed to honor his war dead with one, he would be sentenced to death. The Hebrews had a law forbidding them to leave any of the enemy unburied. If I were to digress, there would be much I might add on the types of funerals and sepulchers, such as the tale about the Scythians, who, as a mark of honor, would eat their dead at a banquet;[24] or that others would keep dogs to devour them when they died. But enough on this subject.

Almost anyone concerned for the sound and legal constitution of a state has taken particular care to ensure that lavish funerals and sepulchers are avoided. One of the laws of Pittacus restricted what could be built above a burial mound to a small, temporary column, no more than three cubits in height.[25] They thought it fair that in a condition in which Nature made everyone equal, riches should make no difference, but plebeian and wealthy alike should be treated in exactly the same way. In the ancient manner, therefore, they buried in the bare earth: they considered it right, since the body, which was of the earth, was laid, as it were, in its mother's womb. They decreed that no one could erect a sepulcher more elaborate than ten men might take three days to build. But no nation was more diligent than were the Egyptians with their sepulchers: they maintained that men were wrong to make the house unduly sumptuous—being their residence for so brief a time—at the expense of the sepulcher, which would be their place of rest for so long.

To me it would seem quite likely that in remote antiquity men first instituted the practice of marking any place where a corpse was buried with a stone, or possibly, as Plato recommended in the *Laws*, with a tree;[26] later it became customary to build something on or around the place, to prevent animals from digging up and rooting out the remains. When that same season returned, and the countryside was once more to be seen in blossom or laden with crops, as it had been when their familiars had left this life, their minds would no doubt have been filled with grief for those they loved; at once they would recall their words and deeds, and, visiting the place, would honor the memory of the deceased however they could. This was perhaps how the custom developed, common especially in Greece, of making a sacrifice at the tombs of the deserving. Here, as Thucydides relates, they would meet in their ceremonial robes, bearing the first fruits of harvest.[27] Such piety and religious significance was attached to this act, that it was also performed in public. As a result—to continue my speculation—

beyond merely erecting a mound or little column to mark or cover the grave, they began to construct shrines, to give the sacrifice a dignified setting, and made sure that they were thoroughly decent and handsome throughout.

But the ancients would choose varying sites for these sepulchers. According to the pontifical law it is not permitted to erect a sepulcher in a public place. It was Plato's opinion that no man, whether alive or dead, should be of any nuisance to the rest of mankind; he therefore decreed that burial sites should be consigned to land that is not only outside the city but also quite sterile.[28] Some have followed this, and have allotted a special place for sepulchers, out in the open and well away from human concourse; I strongly approve of this practice.

On the other hand, some have kept their dead at home, coated in gypsum or salt. Mycerinus, king of Egypt, encased the dead body of his daughter in a wooden bull, and kept it in the palace by his side; he commanded those who presided over the mysteries to offer her a solemn sacrifice[29] every day.[30] Servius relates that the ancients used to choose sites on top of lofty and very conspicuous mountains for the sepulchers of their most distinguished and noble citizens.[31] At the time of the historian Strabo the Alexandrians would reserve enclosed gardens for burying their dead.[32] More recently our own fathers would attach chapels to contain tombs onto their main temples. Throughout Latium there are family tombs to be seen, dug into the earth, their walls lined with small individual urns containing the remains of cremated bodies; there would also be short inscriptions to the baker, barber, cook, masseurs, and other members of the household. As a solace for mothers, the urns in which infant children were buried would also contain images of them, made of gypsum. Images of ancestors, especially when freemen, would be made of marble. That was their way.

But we should not criticize whatever custom is chosen for burying the body, provided the name is given a memorial in some place of great dignity.

Finally, delight in a monument of this kind lies in the form of the work and the inscription. It is not easy to say what form of building the ancients thought most appropriate for a sepulcher. The sepulcher of Augustus in Rome was built of squared blocks of marble and shaded by evergreens; at the top stood a statue of Augustus.[33] On the island of Tyrina, not far from Carmania, lies the sepulcher of Erythras,[34] a huge mound planted with palms.[35] The sepulcher of Zarina, queen of the Sacae, consisted of a triangular pyramid surmounted by a golden colossus.[36] The tomb of Artachaes, one of Xerxes' generals, was constructed with earth piled up by the whole army.[37]

It appears to me, however, that the main aim in each case was to offer a design different from anything else—not so as to criticize the works of others, but to attract attention through novelty of invention. With the increasing use and popularity of sepulchers, new designs were constantly being invented, until nothing further could be devised that had not already been employed and refined to perfection; and each is to be commended. Yet, if we examine this entire stock, we notice that sometimes they are intended to do no more than embellish whatever contains the body, while sometimes they go further, and attempt to construct a beautiful setting for an epitaph and memorial. And so some would be content with a simple marble casing, or would add a chapel on top, as the sanctity of the place demanded; others would add a column, pyramid, cairn, or similar large structure, whose primary function was not to preserve the body but to preserve the name for posterity.

We have already mentioned that at Assos in the Troad there is a stone called Sarcophagon, which quickly consumes corpses;[38] ground that is made up or composed of rubble quickly absorbs any moisture. But I shall not digress on such minor matters. ◆

3

140—142v

Now, although the sepulchers of the ancients may be approved generally, I do notice that some consisted of chapels, some of pyramids, some of columns, and others of different structures, such as cairns and so on. I feel that we must deal with each of them, individually; to begin with chapels.

I would make these chapels as if they were small temples. Nor will I object if lineaments are incorporated from any other building type, provided they contribute to both grace and permanence. It is not quite clear whether monuments intended to last for ever should be built of noble or cheap material, because of the danger of theft. But the ornate certainly delights, and, as we have mentioned already, there is no means more effective in protecting an object and preserving it for posterity.[39]

Of the once undoubtedly splendid tombs of the great emperors C. Caesar and Claudius,[40] nothing remains visible today save a few small squared stones, two cubits in size, on which their names are recorded. And, if I am not mistaken, had their names been committed to larger blocks of stone, these also would have long been missing, snatched or broken off, together with the rest of the ornament. Elsewhere, ancient sepulchers may be found that no one has violated, because they have been constructed of *opus reticulatum* [41] or of stone that cannot be put to any other use; consequently, they have had no difficulty in evading greedy hands. The lesson to be learned here, I feel, for anyone wishing to make his possessions really long-lasting, is that they should be constructed of stone that is neither weak nor yet so elegant that it will be promptly desired or may easily be removed.

In these matters I do feel, however, that even when the dignity of the individual is considered, a sense of measure must be maintained, and that even kings may be criticized for overexpenditure. Certainly I abhor those monstrous works that the Egyptians built for themselves—works also resented by the gods themselves, since none of them would be buried in tombs as sumptuous. Some might commend our own Etruscans, whose magnificence in such works almost rivaled that of the Egyptians; and in particular Porsenna, who, close to the town of Clusium,[42] built for himself a sepulcher of squared stone, whose pedestal, fifty feet in height, contained a totally impenetrable labyrinth; on top sat five pyramids, one at each corner and one in the center, each seventy-five feet broad at its base; a bronze globe rested on top of each of them, from which bells hung on chains; whenever they were agitated by the wind, their chimes were heard far away. Above this stood four further pyramids, one hundred feet high, and on top of these others still, remarkable not only for their size but also for their lineaments.[43] Such prodigious works, which serve no useful purpose, will never gain my full approval.

The tomb of Cyrus, king of Persia, has been commended, and its moderation thought preferable to all the extravagance of larger works. He built his vaulted home in Pasargadae[44] out of squared stone, and with a tiny entrance barely two feet wide. Inside, the body of Cyrus was contained within a golden urn, as befitted a king. This little chamber was surrounded by an orchard, planted with every variety of fruit tree; all around lay a green and well-watered meadow, with roses everywhere and an abundance of flowers; all was fragrant, delightful, and lovely. In keeping with the setting there was inscribed, "I am Cyrus, son of Cambyses, who, you will recall, established the Persian Empire. Grudge me not, then, this little home of mine."[45]

But I return now to the subject of pyramids. Some might have made their pyramids triangular, but in general they are quadrangular. Their height should preferably equal their width. Someone was praised once for designing a pyramid whose sides were never shaded from the sun. Almost all pyramids were built of squared stone, but some were made of brick.

Columns may either serve as structural elements—such as those commonly employed throughout building—or, when size makes them too big for civic buildings, be designed purely as markers or as memorials for posterity. To deal, then, with the second type.

This type of column is composed of the following parts: steps, serving as a podium and base, rise directly from the ground; a quadrangular dado[46] sits above these, and on top of this another, no smaller than the first; third comes the base to the column, then the column itself, and on top of that the capital, and finally a statue sitting on a plinth. Sometimes a sort of die is inserted between the first and second dadoes, in order to increase the height and make the work more graceful.

As with the columns in a temple, the lineaments of all the parts are taken from the diameter at the bottom. Here, however, if the work is particularly large, the base has only one torus, and not several, as in other types of column. The height of the base is divided into fifths, of which two are taken up by the torus and three by the die. The width and depth of the die should equal five quarters of the diameter of the column.

The dadoes on which the base sits should be composed of these parts: along the top, as with every other part of the structure, there projects a border; at the bottom there is a socle, as I call it, because of its resemblance to one; this strip of ornament consists of a corona, wave, or gullet, serving as a base to whichever part. But here I must make a few comments about the dado, a subject passed over in the last book and deliberately saved until now.

I mentioned that it was originally thought that columns needed to be supported by a low wall.[47] Then, once this had been built, it became desirable to make the passage through less restricted, and everything intermediate was removed to leave only as much walling beneath the base of the columns as was necessary to bear their weight. We call the section remaining the dado. The ornament along the top of this low wall would be a border in the form of a gullet, a wave, or something similar. The socle echoed them at the bottom. Both elements were retained therefore in the dado; the border would be either one fifth or one sixth the height of the dado, while the width of the dado would be no less than that of the base of the column, so that nothing built above rested on thin air. To strengthen the work, some would increase the thickness of the low wall by an eighth the width of the die. Finally, the height of the dado, excluding the border and socle, would either equal its width or be one fifth greater. These, then, are the proportions for the low wall and dado as found in the work of the best architects.

I now return to the subject of the column. Below the base of the column is a dado whose dimensions, as we have just stated, relate to those of the base. This dado should have a border consisting of a complete cornice, generally in the Ionic style. The Ionic cornice, you will recall, is composed of the following lineaments: at the bottom there is a gullet, followed by a corona, then an ovolo, and after that the overhang of the mutules, and finally, at the top, a wave. Running around the bottom, serving as a socle to this dado, is a gullet, and astragals and a fillet in reverse order. The second dado below this is composed of identical lineaments, so that nothing built above rests on thin air. Between this and the ground itself rise three or five steps of variable height and depth. The overall height of the steps should be no more than a quarter and no less than a sixth that of the dado immediately above. This lower dado should contain a doorway, embellished with either Doric or Ionic ornament, as described in the section on temples. The other dado

on top is carved with inscriptions and trophies piled high. If anything is to be inserted between these two dadoes, it should have a height one third its width, and the space should be filled with figures in relief, such as applauding gods, Victory, Glory, Fame, Wealth, and so on. Some would face the upper dado in gilt bronze.

Once the dadoes and base have been completed, the column should be set on top. It should have a height seven times its diameter. If the column is to be very large, the top of the shaft should be no more than a tenth narrower than the bottom; with smaller examples, the rules given in the previous book should be observed. Some build columns up to one hundred feet in height, completely encrusted with figures in relief and historical scenes. A spiral staircase would be cut through its center, climbing to the very top. Columns such as these would be given a capital in the Doric style, but

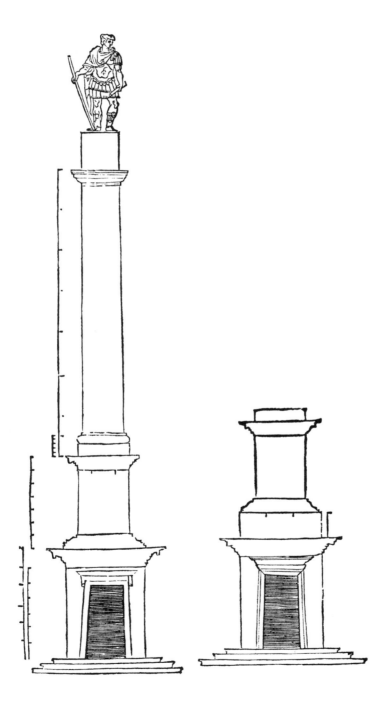

Ornament to Public Secular Buildings

without the addition of a collar to the top of the abacus. Smaller columns have a beam, fascias, and cornices, their ornament trimmed on each side; but with larger columns these are omitted, because of the shortage of stone of sufficient size, and difficulties in positioning it on top.

In either case something would be added on top to serve as the base for the statue. Should this happen to be a square dado, then its corners ought not to extend beyond the solid of the column, but if round, then it must be contained within the square outline of the above. The size of the statue would be one third that of the column. So much for columns.

As for moles,[48] the ancients used to draw their lineaments as follows: First of all, as with a temple, a quadrangular *area* would be raised.[49] Then a wall would be built, its height no less than one sixth and no more than one quarter the length of the *area*. Ornament would be added only at the top and

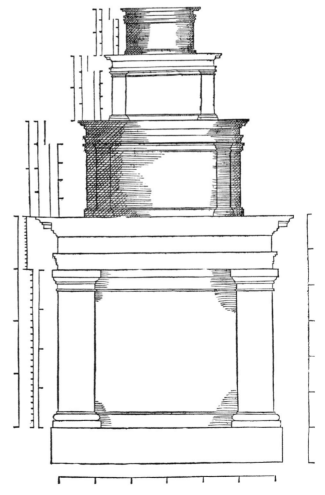

Elevation of a mausoleum.

bottom, and at the corners, or else it would consist of engaged orders projecting from the wall.

If columns were added only at the corners, the height of the wall, excluding the steps at the base, would be divided into quarters, three of which would be taken up by the columns, complete with base and capital, and the top one by the remaining ornament, that is, beam, fascia, and cornice. This top section would itself be divided into sixteenths, of which the beam, and likewise the fascia, would take up five, and the cornice, with its wave, six. The section, meanwhile, between the beam and the podium would be divided into twenty-fifths, three of which would be taken up by the capital and two by the base; the remainder in between would be filled by the length of the column. The columns at the corners would always be quadrangular. The base would be formed of a single torus, taking up half its height. Instead of a fillet, the profile at the bottom of the column would have the same lineaments as the top of the shaft. In structures of this kind, the width of the column would be a quarter of the height.

But when the wall was covered with colonnading, those at the corners had a width one sixth their length; the other columns along the wall were derived, together with their ornament, from the lineaments of the temple. The difference between this and the previous type of colonnading is that with the former, the base along the bottom, and the collar and fillet of the column at the top, below the beam, run the entire length of the wall from corner to corner; this does not happen where there are a number of engaged columns projecting from the wall, although sometimes, as in a temple, the base would run continuously around the whole work.

Within this quadrangular section of walling, an attractive, round structure would be built, rising to a height no less than one half and no more than two thirds the diameter of that already in position. The width of this round structure would take up no less than one half and no more than five sixths of the maximum dimension of the quadrangular *area*; generally it would take up three fifths. They would then alternate round with quadrangular, adding a second round structure on top of a second quadrangular one, according to the methods listed above, until the fourth story was reached. The ornament would consist of the lineaments described already.

Inside the mole itself there would be sure to be some easy steps and religious chapels, while rising from above the wall would be colonnading, with splendid statues and inscriptions carefully arranged between the columns. ◆

4

142v—143v

Now I come to the subject of inscriptions. Their uses were many and varied among the ancients. They were employed not only in sepulchers, but also in sacred buildings and even private houses. The names of the gods to whom a temple was dedicated would be inscribed, according to Symmachus, on the pediment.[50] It has been our own custom to inscribe on our chapels details of their dedication and year of consecration. I approve of this strongly.

It might be appropriate to mention that when Crates, the philosopher, reached Cizicus, and found inscribed on all the private houses verses such as, "Here lived Hercules, son of Jupiter, and a man of great strength; let nothing evil enter this house," he laughed, and suggested that they should have written instead, "Here lives Poverty," as this would have proved a more prompt and effective deterrent than Hercules to any manner of monster.[51]

Inscriptions should be either written—these are called epigraphs—or composed of reliefs and emblems. Plato decreed that no more than four verses might be written on a tomb.[52] And ———— said,[53] "Brief, half up the column, your verse to read, for him departing at full speed." Certainly, verbosity is thoroughly objectionable here—more than anywhere else. But should the inscription be somewhat longer, let it be so elegant and learned that its contents may be an inspiration to piety, compassion, and grace, a pleasure to read, a delight to memorize and recite. That of Omenea has drawn praise: "Were cruel fate to let us exchange our lives, my dear Omenea, I would gladly give up mine for yours; now nothing more remains for me but to flee the light and the sky, and with an untimely death to follow you across the Styx."[54] Another reads, "Let no one give me a funeral, for I shall live on by flitting from the mouths of learned men."[55] On the tomb of those who had fallen at Thermopylae the Spartans wrote the following inscription, "Stranger, tell the Spartans that here obedient to their commands we lie."[56] Nor should we despise an epitaph for its arresting wit, such as, "Hello, passerby, here lie a husband and wife who aren't quarreling. Who are we, you ask. —I'm not saying. —But I'll tell you! He is babbling Belbus, and I'm Brebia, whom he calls Peppa. —Oh wife, can't even death stop your prattling?" Such verses are delightful.

Our ancestors would gild their letters onto marble with bronze. The Egyptians employed the following sign language: a god was represented by an eye, Nature by a vulture, a king by a bee, time by a circle, peace by an ox, and so on. They maintained that each nation knew only its own alphabet, and that eventually all knowledge of it would be lost—as has happened with our own Etruscan: we have seen sepulchers uncovered in city ruins and cemeteries throughout Etruria inscribed with an alphabet universally acknowledged to be Etruscan; their letters look not unlike Greek, or even Latin, yet no one understands what they mean. The same, the Egyptians claimed, would happen to all other alphabets, whereas the method of writing they used could be understood easily by expert men all over the world, to whom alone noble matters should be communicated.

Many have followed this lead, and added various sculptures to their sepulchers. A column was erected at the sepulcher of Diogenes the Cynic,[57] and on it was set a dog of Parian marble.[58] Cicero of Arpinum boasted that at Syracuse he had rediscovered the long-neglected sepulcher of Archimedes, which was covered in brambles and unknown even to the locals. His assumption was based on a sculpture, consisting of a cylinder and little sphere, which he had noticed on some protruding column.[59] In his sepulcher, Simandis, king of Egypt, had a statue of his mother carved out of a block of stone twenty cubits high; she was represented wearing three royal diadems, to show that she was both daughter, wife, and mother of a king.[60] There was a statue on the tomb of Sardanapallus,[61] king of Assyria, seemingly clapping its hands in applause; below was inscribed, "I founded Tarsus and Archileus[62] on the same day; but you, my guest, eat, drink, and be merry; for hardly any other human business is worthy of what I am doing, this applause."[63] Such inscriptions and reliefs were popular elsewhere.

Our own Latin ancestors chose to express the deeds of their most famous men through sculpted histories. This gave rise to columns, triumphal arches, and porticoes, covered with histories in painting or sculpture. But I would only use monuments of this kind to record events of the greatest importance or gravity. So much for this.

We have dealt with routes by land. Any recommendation to be made for land routes will apply equally to watercourses. But since watchtowers are essential both to maritime routes and to some by land, they must be dealt with next. ◆

5

143v—145

Watchtowers provide an excellent ornament, if sited in a suitable position and built on appropriate lines; if grouped closely together, they make an imposing sight from afar. Yet I cannot commend the mania prevalent two hundred years ago for building towers even in the smallest of towns. It seemed that no head of a family could be without a tower; as a result, forests of towers sprouted up everywhere.[64] Some think that the movement of stars may influence men's minds. Thus between three and four hundred years ago there raged such religious fervor that man seemed to have been born for no other purpose than to construct religious buildings. To give but one example: we have calculated that there are currently over two and a half thousand religious buildings in Rome, although more than half are in ruins.[65] And what is this we now see, the whole of Italy competing for renewal? How many cities, which as children we saw all built of wood, have now been turned into marble?

I return to the subject of watchtowers. Here I shall not mention the description given by Herodotus of the watchtower in the center of the temple at Babylon, which measured an entire stade across its base and consisted of eight stories, one above the other.[66] I would approve of this type of construction for watchtowers: the vertical stacking of stories contributes both grace and strength; their intersecting vaults ensure that the wall is bound together perfectly.

A watchtower may be either quadrangular or circular in plan. In either case the height must be a set proportion of the width. The quadrangular, being the more slender of the two, should have a width one sixth its height; the circular should have a diameter one quarter its height. If they are to be very stout, the quadrangular should have a width no greater than one quarter its height, and the circular a height three times its diameter. A wall up to forty cubits in height must be at least four feet thick; one of up to fifty cubits must be five feet thick; one of sixty cubits, six feet thick; and so on, according to the same gradation.[67]

Now, these are the rules for a plain, simple watchtower. But some would add a gallery of freestanding columns to the outside of the watchtower halfway up; others would make the gallery spiral around the outside. Some would encircle it with galleries, like cornices, all the way up; yet others would clothe it completely with carved animals. In each case the method of colonnading does not differ from that of any other public work, although it may be made more slender to allow for the weight of the structure.[68]

But any tower that is to be utterly secure against the might of the weather, and wholly pleasing in appearance, must have a round story sitting on top of a quadrangular one, followed by a quadrangular on top of a round, with each story being reduced gradually, according to the rules of columns. I shall now describe what is the most handsome form of tower as far as we are concerned.

First, a quadrangular base is built up from the ground. This takes up a tenth of the overall height of the work from top to bottom. Its width should take up one quarter of that height. Engaged columns are then applied to the wall along each side of the base, two in the middle and one at each corner, each distinguished by its proper ornament, like that prescribed just now for sepulchers. On top of this base sits a sort of quadrangular chapel, its width twice the height of the base and equal to its own height; against which we may set columns in the same way as those prescribed for temples. Then, on the third, fourth, and fifth stories there should be round chapels; these we shall make three in number, and we shall call them "nodes," because they resemble the joints of cane. The height of each node should exceed the width by one twelfth, that extra section being intended as a socle. The width is clearly derived from the lowest quadrangular chapel, sitting immediately above the base, as follows: The width of this quadrangular chapel is divided into twelfths. Remove one, and give the remainder over to the first node. Likewise divide the diameter of this first node into twelfths, and give eleven over to the second node. By the same method make the third node one eleventh more slender than the second. As a result of this gradual

diminution, the stem of the work is one quarter thicker at the bottom of the base than at the top, as most learned ancients recommended. To these nodes no more than eight and no fewer than six columns are added, together with their ornament. Then, in suitable places in each node or chapel, windows and niches are added, together with their appropriate ornament. The window void takes up no more than half the gap between the columns. Above the third node (mentioned earlier) sits the sixth and uppermost story; this should be quadrangular. Both its height and its width should be no more than two thirds the diameter of the uppermost node.[69] Its ornament should consist entirely of polygonal columns attached to piers supporting the vault. It should also have beams, capitals, and other such ornaments. There should be an opening through the center of this structure, a kind of crossroad. Should there be a seventh and final story,[70] it should consist of a round

portico, open in every direction, its columns plain and freestanding. The height of the columns complete with ornament should equal the diameter of the *area* of that story, while the diameter itself must be three quarters the width of the chapel below. This circular portico has a spherical roof.[71]

To the outside corners of both rectilinear and quadrangular chapels, crests[72] are added; they should rise to the level of the entablature beneath, with its cornice, fascia, and beam. The central space of the initial quadrangular chapel above the base at the bottom takes up five eighths of its overall external dimension.[73]

A favorite among the ancients was that built on the island of Faro by King Ptolemy;[74] he ordered bright fires to be lit on top of this high watchtower to help nocturnal shipping; these would be mobile and in constant motion, so that from afar their flames could not be mistaken for stars. In addition, moving dials to indicate the direction of the wind, the angle of the sun, and the time of day would also be very useful.[75] So much for this subject. ◆

6

145—148

Next we must enter the city. Both inside and outside the city, however, there are certain roads, such as those leading to temples, basilicas, and show buildings,[76] that have greater importance than they would naturally warrant. We must therefore deal with these first.

We read that Heliogabalus paved all the wider and more important streets with Macedonian stone and porphyry.[77] Historians praise the road leading up to the temple in the Egyptian town of Bubastis: it passed straight through the forum, and was paved with fine stone; it was four plectra wide, and lined with huge trees on either side.[78] Aristeus relates that there were narrow but elegant passageways running through the city of Jerusalem, to provide a more dignified route for the elders and other important citizens; their main purpose, however, was to protect those carrying sacred objects from contact with the profane.[79] Another celebrated road is that described by Plato, leading from Knossos through a cypress grove[80] to the grotto and sanctuary of Jupiter.[81] In Rome there are two roads of this type that I find worthy of the greatest admiration: one runs from the gate as far as the basilica of St. Paul, a distance of roughly five stades, the other from the bridge to the basilica of St. Peter; the latter is 2,500 feet in length and protected by a portico of marble columns and lead roofing.[82] This is a remarkably appropriate form of ornament for a road of this kind. But I return to the subject of military ones.

The end or terminus, as it were, of a land route, be it inside or outside the city, is a gate, and, unless I am mistaken, that of a maritime route is a port. This is, of course, provided that the route is not underground, such as the one described in Egyptian Thebes, which allowed the kings to dispatch their army without the knowledge of the townsfolk; or the tunnels that I have discovered in great number at Penestrum in Latium, cut with astonishing workmanship from mountaintop to plain, in one of which Marius is said to have died, trapped by siege.[83] In the *Life of Apollonius* I have found a description of a road worthy of recollection: a Babylonian called Meda[84] built a wide road of stone and bitumen under a riverbed; this enabled her to walk with dry feet from her palace to her other house on the opposite side of the river.[85] But Greek historians may not always be believed.[86]

I return to the argument. A gate is adorned in the same way as a triumphal arch; a subject to be discussed shortly. The ornament to a harbor consists of a portico running around it, with a rusticated base and generous interior, and a temple, prominent, crowded, and splendid; the temple should address an extensive forum, and at the mouth of the harbor itself should be some colossi, of which there are several examples, notably that of Rhodes[87] and the three set up by Herod at ———,[88] said to have been larger still. There is

Ornament to Public Secular Buildings

261

a famous account in the works of the historians of a mole built in the harbor at Samos; it was said to have been 20 fathoms deep, and to have extended two stades into the sea.[89] Such should be the ornaments of a harbor; but they must be built with outstanding skill and no common materials.

Apart from being properly paved and thoroughly clean, the roads within a city should be elegantly lined with porticoes of equal lineaments, and houses that are matched by line and level. The parts of the road that need to be particularly distinguished by ornament are these: bridges, crossroads, fora, and show buildings.[90] For a forum is but an enlarged crossroad, and a show ground nothing but a forum surrounded with steps.

I shall therefore begin with the bridge, which is the most important part of the road. The bridge consists of piers, arches, and surfacing. Further parts of the bridge include the central section, where the cattle trudge, the pavements on either side, where the citizens may walk, and the edging along the sides. Some bridges even have a roof, like that of Hadrian in Rome, the most splendid of all bridges—a memorable work, by heaven: even the sight of what I might call its carcass would fill me with admiration. The beams of its roof were supported by forty-two marble columns; it was covered in bronze, and marvelously decorated.[91]

We should construct the bridge in the same way as a wide road. Let the piers be even in number and size, and have a width one third that of their span. The piers should be extended as a prow against the current, increasing the width of the bridge by half; this prow must stand out above the flood level.[92] The piers should also be given a stern; yet it would be wrong to make this less sharp, as though blunted. It would be advisable on both prow and stern to continue the supports upward, so as to reinforce the sides of the bridge; their base should take up no more than two thirds the width of the pier. The arches of the openings must have their springings completely clear of the water. They should take their lineaments from the Ionic or, better still, the Doric beam. In a large bridge they should take up no more than one fifteenth of the total opening. At the parapet, and as a reinforcement, an edging of quadrangular dadoes should be built, level and in line; these may also serve, if so desired, as the bases for columns to support the roof. The height of this parapet, complete with socle and border, should equal four feet. The gaps between the dadoes should be filled with a balustrade. Dado and balustrade should be bordered with a gullet, or preferably even a wave, for the whole length of the parapet. The base of the socle should correspond to this border. Between the central section of the road and the edging there should be pavements for women and pedestrians, standing one or two steps above the central roadway, which should be of flint for the sake of the animals. Let the height of the columns, complete with ornament, be equal to the width of the bridge.

The covered bridge.

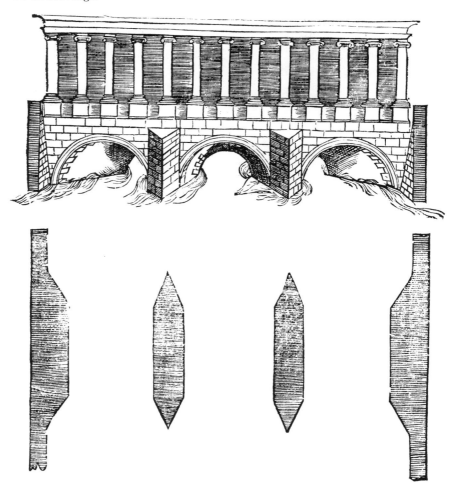

The crossroad and the forum differ only in size. In fact the crossroad is but a small forum. Plato recommended that at every crossroad there be a space where nurses with children could meet occasionally and be together. I believe that the purpose behind this was not only to strengthen the children in the fresh air, but also to encourage the nurses to be neat by exposing them to the eyes of so many curious observers, and to make them less sloppy, since they are eager for praise. The presence of an elegant portico, under which the elders may [stroll] or sit, take a nap or negotiate business, will be an undoubted ornament to both crossroad and forum. Furthermore, the presence of the elders will restrain the youth, as they play and sport in the open, and curb any misbehavior or buffoonery resulting from the immaturity of their years.

A forum may serve as a marketplace for currency or vegetables, for cattle or wood, and so on; each type of forum should be allocated its own site within

Plan of the forum.

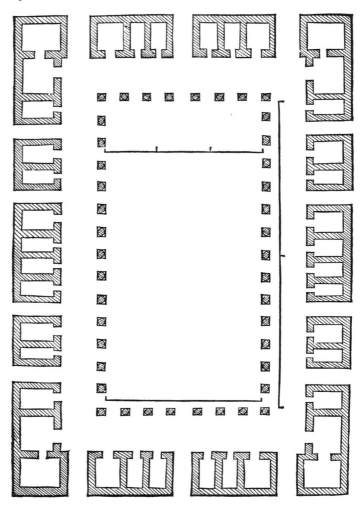

the city and have its own distinctive ornament. But the currency market ought to be the most splendid.

The Greeks would make their fora square; they would surround them with a generous double portico, adorned with columns and stone beams; on the upper floor they built a gallery.[93] Here in Italy our fora had a width two thirds their length; and because they had long been the traditional sites for gladiatorial displays, the columns to their portico would be spaced farther apart. Currency shops would line the portico, and above, on top of the entablature, would be balconies and storerooms for the public revenue. So much for the customs of the past.

Nowadays we prefer to make the *area*[94] of the forum a double square; the portico and other surrounding buildings must have dimensions that relate strictly to those of the open space, so that it appears neither too extensive

and the surrounding buildings too low, nor too confined if hemmed in by the buildings stacked up all around. The ideal roof height would be between one third and a minimum of two sevenths the width of the forum. I would give the portico a base one fifth its width high; the depth should equal the height of the columns.[95] The lineaments of the colonnading should follow those of the basilica, although here the combination of cornices, fasciae, and beam should take up one fifth the height of the column. But if you want a second row of columns above the first, their diameter and height should be reduced by a quarter, and below them should run a socle, like a base, its height half that of the base below.

But the greatest ornament to the forum or crossroad would be to have an arch at the mouth of each road. For the arch is a gate that is continually open. Its invention I ascribe to those who enlarged the empire; according to Tacitus, they were the ones traditionally responsible for extending the boundaries of the city;[96] so it was said of Claudius.[97] As the city increased in size, it was decided to retain the old gates for practical purposes, one of the reasons being perhaps to provide a further safeguard against the incursion of the enemy in times of adversity. Subsequently spoils and victory standards captured from the enemy would be deposited by the gates, standing as they did in a busy place. Hence the practice developed of decorating the arches with inscriptions, statues, and histories.

The most suitable place to build an arch is at the point where a road meets a square or a forum, especially if it is a *royal* road (the term I use for the most important road in a city). An arch, not unlike a bridge, contains three lanes, a central one for soldiers and one on either side for the mothers and families accompanying the victorious army as it returns to pay homage to the gods of the fatherland, while cheering and celebrating the heroes. When constructing an arch, its dimension in plan parallel to the road should be half that which intersects the road from right to left; the latter should be no longer than 50 cubits.

This work is very similar to the bridge, except that it consists of no more than four piers and three openings. Of the shorter dimension (that is, the one which is parallel to the road) an eighth part adjacent to the side facing the forum and an eighth part adjacent to the rear are reserved for dadoes to support the columns for the arches. The other, longer dimension (that is, the one which stands athwart the road) is divided into eight modules, two of which are allocated to the central opening and one to each of the piers and side openings. The innermost walls of the piers, which rise vertically up to the springing of the arch of the central opening itself, should be two and one-third modules high. The same method applies to the bearing walls of the two other side openings: they should relate to their internal spaces by a similar proportion.

The through passages should be barrel-vaulted. The ornament running along the top of the piers, below the arches and the vaulting, should be taken from the Doric capital; but instead of an echinus and an abacus, there should be a projecting Corinthian or Ionic cornice, and under the cornice, like a neck, a plain fascia, and under this, as at the top of a column, a collar and a fillet. The overall height of this ornament takes up a ninth the height of the pier. This ninth is itself further divided into nine smaller elements, of which the top five are taken up by the cornice, three by the frieze, and one by the collar and the fillet. The bent beam or arch, which faces the front, should take up no less than a twelfth and no more than a tenth the depth of the opening.

The columns applied to the center of the face of each pier should be standard and disengaged; they should be constructed so that the top of the shaft is level with the highest point of the opening, although their overall length should equal the width of the central opening. Below the column should sit base, dado, and socle; above it, the capital, be it [Ionic] or Corinthian, and above that, the beam, fascia, and cornice, Ionic or Corinthian. Each should be given the appropriate lineaments, which we have already discussed earlier.

Above the columns rises an additional section of wall, increasing the height of the work by half the distance between the bottom of the base and the uppermost line of its cornice.[98] The height of the further section of wall is divided into elevenths, of which the top one is given over to a simple cornice, without any fascia or beam beneath it, and the bottom one and a half are taken up by a socle, its ornament being a wave, which takes up a third of its height. Statues may best be set up on the ends of the beams where they project from the work to embrace the columns; these statues should be

Triumphal arch: plan and elevation.

COSMO MEDICEO
IO. FI. PA.
CONSERVATORI.

Ornament to Public Secular Buildings

freestanding and should sit upon a dado equal in thickness to the bottom of the column. The overall height of the statues, complete with dadoes, should take up eight elevenths of the wall. Along the upper edge of the work, especially on the side facing the forum, should be set four-horse chariots, statues of greater size, sculptures of animals, and so on. They are directly supported by a low wall serving as a socle; this should be three times as high as the continuous cornice immediately below. The height of the statues set at the very highest level should be no less than one sixth and no more than two ninths greater than that of the first set, positioned above the columns.

Along the face of the wall inscriptions and carved *historiae*[99] should be added in square or circular panels. Within passages they should be applied down as far as the halfway mark of the wall supporting the central vault; they would best be applied above that line, the lower section not being suitable because of splashback.

To avoid being struck by the wheel axles, the piers should be supported by a high step, serving as a socle, with a height no greater than one and a half cubits; it should be chamfered with an inverse gullet; this should take up one quarter of the height of the socle. Of these also enough. ◆

7

148—152v

I now come to show buildings.[100] They say that Epimenides[101] (who slept for fifty-seven years—in a tomb) rebuked the citizens when they constructed a sports ground in Athens, saying, "You have no notion what damage this place will cause: when you find out, you will tear it down, even with your teeth."[102] Nor dare I criticize pontiffs or any other moral teachers for their well-considered condemnation of the use of show buildings. Moses is praised for being the first to gather his entire nation into a single temple on feast days, and for bringing them together at set times to celebrate the harvest. His motive, I might suggest, was but the desire to cultivate the minds of the citizens through concourse and communion, and to make them more receptive to the benefits of friendship. Thus to my mind our ancestors established show buildings within their cities as much for functional reasons as for any festivity or pleasure. And surely, if we think the matter over carefully, we find frequent cause to regret that so splendid and useful an institution is now long obsolete. For some show buildings cater to leisure and peaceful recreation, and others to business and military training; the former clearly encourage intellectual energy and mental ability, the latter are remarkably effective in developing toughness and strength of body and soul. Yet within both there lies a sure and certain way to enhance the well-being and honor of the fatherland.

It is said that the Arcadians, whose lives were hard and severe, invented games, as a means of refining the minds of their citizens; when they abandoned games, they became so uncouth, according to Polybius, that they were despised by the whole of Greece.[103] Yet the tradition of games is very old, and their origin ascribed to many inventors. Dionysus is said to have been the first to have introduced dancing and games. Hercules, I find, was the inventor of contests.[104] The Olympic Games are said to have been conceived and invented by the Aetolians and the Epians, after their return from Troy.[105] In Greece Lenaean Dionysius,[106] who was the first to introduce the chorus in a tragedy, is also credited with establishing seats in a show ground.[107] In Italy L. Nummius[108] was the first to put on theatrical games during a triumph, two hundred years before Nero became emperor.[109] Actors migrated to the city from Etruria, horse races were introduced from Tyre, and almost every other type of game was imported to Italy from Asia.

I could easily believe that in the good old times, when the image of Janus appeared on coins, games would have been viewed from under the beech or elm. "You, Romulus," sang Ovid, "first disturbed the games, when the rape of the Sabines consoled your widowed men. No awnings then hung over the marble theater, nor was the platform ruddy with crocus spray; there, simply arranged, were leaves that the wooded Palatine had borne; the stage through no art was made. On steps of turf sat the audience, their unkempt hair carelessly wreathed with leaves."[110] But Iolaus, son of Ipsicles, is said to have been the first to introduce stepped seating, when on the isle of Sardinia he received the Thespiadae from Hercules.[111]

To begin with, theaters were made of wood, according to custom. This is why Pompey was criticized for providing show-ground seating with permanent steps, and not temporary ones, as before. Eventually the City contained three large theaters, several amphitheaters (one of which could accommodate more than two hundred thousand spectators), and, largest of all, the Circus Maximus; each built of squared stone and resplendent with marble columns. What is more, not content with this, they fitted out even temporary show buildings with marble, glass, and an incredible number of statues. Until it was burned down in the war waged by Octavian, the show ground with the greatest capacity was that at Placentia in Gaul.[112] But of this enough.

Show grounds cater to both leisure and sport. Connected with leisure are diversions such as poetry, music, and acting; martial contests consist of wrestling, boxing, cestus,[113] javelin throwing, chariot racing, and any preparatory contests in arms, such as Plato recommended should be held each year because of their extraordinary benefit to the well-being of the state and the honor of the city.[114]

These require different buildings, each with a different name. Buildings in which poetry, comedy, tragedy, and so on take place we call theaters, to distinguish them from the others; those in which noble youths exercise with chariots (with two- or four-horse teams) are called circuses; while those in which the hunting of caged beasts takes place are called amphitheaters.

Almost all show buildings are shaped like an army drawn up with wings extended in order of battle; they consist of a central *area*,[115] where actors, boxers, charioteers, and the like perform, and steps on which spectators sit. Yet each differs in the lineaments of its *area*. Any shaped like a moon on the wane are called theaters. But when the wings extend to form an oblong, the building will be called a circus, because of the circuits the two- and four-horse teams make as they race toward the finish. Here naval battles may be staged using water from either a canal or an aqueduct. Some maintain that the ancients called them circuses because they used to practice this sport between wars and rivers.[116] The inventor of these games is said to have been a certain Monagus, from Elis in Asia.[117] When two theaters were joined face to face, the resultant enclosed space was called a "pit,"[118] and the work itself an "amphitheater."

First of all, a thoroughly healthy location must be chosen for a show ground, avoiding harsh breezes, the sun, and other nuisances discussed in the first book. The theater, in particular, must be well protected from the sun, since it is where the populace comes in August to listen to poetry and to seek the shadowed and gentle delights of the mind. For the body, roasted by the rays of the sun concentrated within the building, may easily fall ill once its humors have been warmed. The site must also be sonorous and not dull in any way.[119] There should also be a portico, attached to the building or close by, where the audience might take refuge from any sudden shower or storm.[120] Plato preferred the theater to be inside the city, the hippodrome outside.

The theater is composed of a clear open *area*, surrounded by stepped seating, a raised stage at the mouth, where everything relating to the narrative takes place, and, at the top, a covered portico to concentrate the diffusion of the voice and make it more sonorous. Greek theaters differed from Latin ones in the size of their stage: they required a smaller one, because the chorus and theatrical dancers performed in their central *area*, whereas we preferred a larger stage, because there all our action took place.

One common feature is that all are based on a semicircular *area*, with its wings extended; but some are composed of straight lines, others of curves. Where straight lines are employed, they continue parallel until they have increased the wings of the semicircle by one quarter of its diameter. Where curved lines are employed, they describe a complete circle, with one quarter of the overall circumference removed, leaving the rest to the theater.[121]

Once the extent of the *area* had been established, the steps of the seating were laid out. First of all, they decided how high they wished the steps to be, and, on the basis of that, they defined the amount of space to be occupied at the bottom. Most theaters were given a height equal to the width of their central *area*. For it was well known that in a low theater voices fade and disappear, and that in a very high one they reecho and are difficult to catch. But some of the better architects have made the height of the theater four fifths the width of the central *area*. The steps never occupy less than one half or more than two thirds the overall height of the work. The steps themselves have a height of two fourths or two fifths their depth.[122]

We shall now describe what we believe to be a completely perfect and satisfactory form of theater. The distance between the base of the steps on the outside (that is, the wall bounding the uppermost tier of the seating) and the center of the semicircle should be one and a third times the radius of the central *area*. The steps do not begin at the level of the central *area*; instead there is a wall rising from here up to the first (that is, the lowest) step. In a large theater this wall has a height one ninth the radius of the central *area*, and in a small theater it has a height of at least seven feet.

These steps have a height of one and a half feet, and a depth of two and a half. Beneath them run vaulted passageways, all similar and modest in size, but some leading into the central *area* and some ascending to the uppermost steps; their number and size should depend on the dimensions of the theater. Seven of them should be main passageways, leading to the center and quite unobstructed; their entrances should be set at equal intervals. One passageway, aligning with the center of the circumference of the semicircle, should be more generous than the rest: this I call the "royal" entrance, because it leads to the "royal" road; similarly there is another entrance at the extreme right of the diameter, and another at the extreme left. Then on either side of the semicircle there are two intermediate passageways, and again further entrances between these, their size and number depending on the dimensions of the theater.

In large theaters the ancients divided the seating into three tiers and bordered each with a step twice as broad as the rest; this separated upper from lower as though an aisle had been inserted. Opening onto these breaks, as I would like to call them, were the vaulted access stairs rising up from under the seats. I notice that in some theaters distinguished architects and experienced workmen have ensured that internal staircases are added to either side of each of the main passageways; one has continuous steps giving a steeper and quicker ascent for the more eager and agile, the other rises more sedately, with landings and breaks, to let the matrons and the aged climb slowly and pause during their ascent. So much for the tiers.

Finally, at the theater mouth would be an elevated space where the actors perform the play. Wherever the local custom held that the elders and magistrates sat apart from the crowd, in some set place of honor such as on elegantly decorated seating in the central *area*, the stage would be quite large, enough to accommodate actors, musicians, and chorus. This stage would

Plan of the theater.

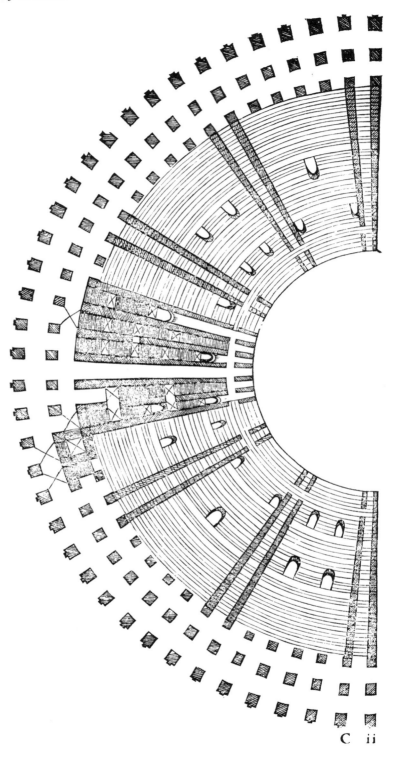

C   ii

extend to the center of the semicircle, and would be raised five feet, to give the senators at ground level a fine view of the artists' every gesture. But wherever it was the local custom not to accommodate the distinguished citizens in the central *area*, but to reserve it completely for dancers and players, the stage would be more restricted, but raised on occasion as high as six cubits.[123]

In either case, this section would be adorned with columns and entablature, one above the other, as in a house. In appropriate places portals and doors would be added, one in the center like a "royal" door, its ornament taken from a temple, and others nearby, giving the actors access on and off the stage, as the action demands.[124] Three types of drama are performed in a theater: tragedy, recounting the misfortunes of tyrants; comedy, unfolding the cares and anxieties of the head of a family; and satire, singing of countryside delights and pastoral romance. There would be rotating machinery, therefore, capable of presenting at an instant a painted backdrop, or of revealing an atrium, house, or even a wood, according to the type of drama and the action of the play. Such then were the *area*, tiers, and stage for theatrical artists.[125]

We have already mentioned that one of the most important parts of a theater is the portico, a device invented to amplify the voice and other sounds. The portico would be set over the top tier, with the openings of its colonnade facing the central *area* of the theater. This we must now discuss.

They had learned from the philosophers that air, once struck by the voice or shattered by sound, moves in waves like the circles formed when water is disturbed by an object emerging all of a sudden; and they realized that, as inside the lyre,[126] or in a valley, especially a wooded one, sounds and voices become more sonorous and clear if the expanding spheres of disturbance, so to speak, meet some obstacle that checks the outward movement of the rays of sound and throws them back, like a ball bouncing off a wall, thereby condensing and reinforcing the spheres.[127]

This is what first prompted men to make their theaters circular. Next, to allow the voice to flow freely to the top of the theater without obstruction, they set out the steps so that their outer edges all align. On the very top of the steps they added a portico, a particularly useful device, facing, as we mentioned, toward the central *area* of the theater; the front of the portico remained open, but the colonnade was completely walled along the back.

Then, as a form of base, they set the colonnading upon a perimeter wall; this served to contain the expanding spheres of the voice, which the denser air within the portico had cushioned and reinforced rather than reflected in full. Furthermore, to roof the theater, they would add a temporary awning, which not only provided shade but also improved the acoustics; this would be spangled with stars and, once fastened and extended, would shade the entire central *area*, together with the tiers and spectators.

The construction of this portico required considerable ingenuity. It was supported from below by further colonnades and porticoes opening onto the outside of the theater. In large theaters these would be double, to protect those walking beneath, should rain or foul weather driven in by a fierce wind enter the building. The openings and colonnading of the first of these supporting porticoes would not be like those we described for a temple or a basilica, but would be constructed solidly with robust walling, their lineaments taken from the triumphal arch. First, then, we must deal with these lower porticoes, which serve the upper ones.

The openings to these porticoes should be arranged so that there is one opposite each passageway leading into the central *area* of the theater. These must be joined by further openings according to fixed criteria. All the openings should match one another in height, in width, and in their every lineament and ornament. There should also be a passage running the length of the portico, its width equal to the gap between the columns. And the piers themselves should be of walling, their thickness half the width of the opening. Finally, the columns should not be freestanding, as in a triumphal arch, but engaged, attached to the center of the face of each pier, and supported by a dado one sixth the height of the colonnading. The rest of the ornament is taken from the temple. The height, including the ornament to the columns and the cornice, should be half the vertical dimension of the tiers on the inside.

There are two rows of external colonnading, therefore: the vaulting of the second row should reach the level of the top tier; and the floor of the portico on the inside of the theater—which, as we mentioned, faced the central *area*—should be level with this as well. The theater takes the lineament of its *area* from the hoofprint of a horse.

Once this is done, the uppermost portico is built on top. The facade and colonnade of this portico do not receive light from outside, as those we have described below it do, but face instead toward the central *area* of the theater, as we have mentioned already. This work prevents sound from escaping, and compresses and fortifies it; we shall therefore call the work the circumvallation.

This circumvallation has a height three halves that of the first row of external colonnading. It should consist of the following parts: A wall to support the columns, which we shall call the plinth; in a large theater it should take up no more than a third, and in a small theater no less than a quarter the overall height of the circumvallation. The columns should stand on this wall, their height, including their base and capital, equal to half the overall height of the circumvallation. Above these columns should come the orna-

ment, together with a further section of walling, as in a basilica, which takes up the remaining sixth of the overall height of the circumvallation.

The columns here should be freestanding, their lineaments taken from the basilica. In number they should match the engaged columns of the external portico, and they should be aligned to the same radii. "Radius" is the term I apply to the straight lines running from the center of the theater to each of the external columns. The wall that supports the columns of the circumvallation is referred to as the plinth; there are openings along it that align vertically with the passageways running below into the theater; in suitable places such as these, at equal intervals, niches may be fashioned, where you may, should you wish, hang bronze vases upside down, so that the resonance of the voice improves as it reaches and strikes them. Here I do not intend to go into Vitruvius' theory, based on the divisions in music, from which he derives his method of arranging vases around the theater to reflect principal, middle, and highest voices, as well as those in unison;[128] an effect that is easy enough to describe, but that only those who have experience know how to achieve. We should not ignore, however, the conviction also held by Aristotle, that any empty vessel or well improves the resonance of the voice.[129]

To turn to the portico of the circumvallation. The rear of this portico is unbroken; it encloses the whole wall work and prevents any voice that reaches it from escaping; as ornament to the external wall, the one that faces your approach, engaged columns are added, corresponding in number, size, vertical alignment, and so on, to the colonnade that lines the porticoes beneath.

From what has been said, the differences between a large and a small theater are obvious. The former has a double external portico at its base, whereas the latter is only single; and again the former always has two levels of external porticoes, whereas the latter may have a third.[130] Another difference is that in some smaller theaters no internal portico is added: the circumvallation consists solely of wall and cornice, so that the task of reinforcing the voice is left not to the circumvallation with its portico, as in a larger theater, but to the cornice. In large theaters the uppermost portico is sometimes doubled.

Finally, all exposed surfaces in the theater should be given a protective coating of plaster and laid to a fall, so that all rainwater runs off toward the steps. Any rainwater that has collected should be channeled into gulleys at the corners of the wall and discharged down hidden piping into secret drains. Around the top outer cornice of the theater should be fitted mutules and pad stones; on these, as an ornament to the public games, masts may be erected to receive and hold the ropes and fastenings of the awning stretched over the top.[131]

Ornament to Public Secular Buildings

In order to raise so massive a structure to its full height, it is necessary to ensure that the wall is thick enough to bear the load. The external wall to the first colonnade must therefore have a thickness one-fifteenth its overall height. With a double portico, the wall running between the two, separating one portico from the other, should have a thickness one quarter less than the external wall. Then any walling raised on top should have a thickness one twelfth less than that below. ◆

8

152v—154v

So much for this. We have dealt with the theater; next we shall discuss the circus and amphitheater. All buildings of this type are derived from the theater: a circus is nothing but a theater with its wings extended along parallel lines, although its nature does not require the addition of a portico; an amphitheater, meanwhile, consists of two theaters, their tiers linked into a continuous circle. They differ in that the theater is a form of semi-amphitheater; another difference is that the central *area* of the amphitheater is quite empty and free of any stage. In every other respect they are similar, especially in their tiers, porticoes, passages, and so on.

The amphitheater, we think, was built originally for the hunt; this was why they decided to make it round, so that the wild beast, trapped there and baited, with no corner into which to retreat, would be easier for the hunters to provoke. Here men were admitted to fight the most ferocious beasts with remarkable techniques: some would use poles to vault in the air to escape a charging bull; others would don an armor of sharp canes and allow themselves to be mauled by the claws of bears; others, hiding under a perforated cage, would taunt a lion with frequent turns; others would trick him, trusting in a cloak and an iron mallet; in short, if anyone devised any ingenious method of trickery, or possessed exceptional strength of mind and body, he would risk going down into the center, in search of fame or reward. I have also discovered that in theaters and amphitheaters emperors used to cast apples into the crowd, and release little birds, so as to incite childish squabbles among those who grabbed them.

Although encompassed by two theaters joined together, the central *area* of the amphitheater was not as elongated as it would be, were the extended arms of both theaters to be incorporated in the work; rather, the width would be derived from the length according to a set method. Some of our ancestors would make the width seven eighths of the length, and some three quarters. That aside, the same rules apply as for theaters: two porticoes are included, the one running around the outside, the other sitting on top of the uppermost tier and referred to as the circumvallation.

To move on to the circus. The circus was based, so it is said, on the heavens: there are twelve entrance gates, the number of heavenly mansions;[132] there are seven turning posts, the number of the planets; at the east and west ends there are finishing posts far enough apart for two- and four-horse teams to race around the central space of the circus, like the sun and the moon chasing through the zodiac; from the number of hours in the day there are twenty-four starting pens; likewise, the competitors are divided into four teams, each wearing its own sporting colors, green for spring, the grassy season of the year, pink for the fiery air of summer, white for fading autumn, and black for gloomy winter.[133]

Unlike that of the amphitheater, the central *area* of a circus was not empty, nor was it filled with a stage, like that of a theater; but turning posts were erected in appropriate positions along the length of the line that divides the width into two carriageways (that is, into two equal parts): around these the contestants, be they men or two-horse teams, would make their circuits. There were three principal turning posts. The central one was the most important; this would be quadrangular, tall, and slightly tapered, which was why it was called an obelisk. The two remaining turning posts consisted either of colossi or of stone prows, their beaks thrusting upward, and formed with grace and charm, according to the fancy of the artist. Between these, columns and smaller turning posts were inserted, two on either side.

I discover from the historians that the Circus Maximus in Rome was three stadia long and one wide.[134] At present it is so dilapidated as not to offer the least impression of its original appearance. But by measuring other similar works, I have discovered that the ancients used to give the central *area* a width of no less than sixty cubits and a length seven times that distance.[135] The width was divided into two equal halves by the line running lengthways on which were set the turning posts. The length itself was divided into sevenths, one of which was taken up by the curve, where the competitors rounded the final turning post and turned from the right-hand straight into the left-hand one. The remaining turning posts, arranged at equal distances down its length, would take up five sevenths of the overall length. A form of socle, at least six feet in height, would stretch from post to post, separating the two straights on either side, so that should any horse, competing on its own or as part of a team, stray from its lane, it would not be able to cross. The circuses would be lined on either side by tiers of seating, which occupied no more than a fifth and no less than a sixth the overall width of the central *area*; and, as in an amphitheater, these tiers would sit upon a base, to protect spectators from any danger from the beasts.

Also included among public work are parades,[136] where youths may play ball,[137] jump, and practice armed combat, and where the elders, on the other hand, take their recreation, by strolling or, if infirm, by being carried in a chair. "Better to exercise in the open," said Celsus, the naturalist, "than in the shade." But for the convenience of also being able to exercise in the shade, porticoes would be added to completely enclose the *area*. The *area* itself was sometimes laid with marble or mosaic, and sometimes would

Plan and section of the circus.

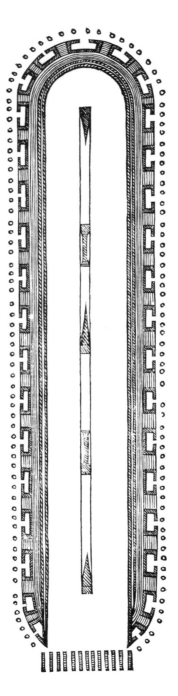

present a view of greenery,[138] planted with myrtle, juniper, citrus, and cypress.

This work was flanked on three sides by a very wide, simple portico, its width two ninths greater than those in a forum. On the fourth side, the one that faced south, there was a double portico, which would be considerably more spacious. There would be Doric columns along its facade, their height related to the width of the portico. It was recommended that the internal columns, separating the outer portico from the inner, should have a height one fifth greater than the main columns, their function being to support the ridge and to make the roof slope. These, then, had to be Ionic, being naturally taller than the Doric. But I see no reason why the ceilings could not be flat on both sides: it would certainly make them more graceful.

The thickness of the columns for either colonnade would be determined as follows: with the Doric, the bottom diameter of the column would be two fifteenths of the overall height, including its entire capital and base; but with the Ionic and the Corinthian, the bottom diameter of the column would take up three sixteenths of the entire shaft. Apart from that, their dimensions would be the same as in a temple. The external wall to this portico would be lined with thoroughly dignified sitting rooms, where distinguished citizens and philosophers might debate noble topics. Some would be for summer, and others for winter. The summer ones would face Boreas or Aquilo,[139] while the winter ones would receive cheery sun and be protected from the wind; the latter would therefore be enclosed with continuous walls, whereas the former would have a wall on either side to support the roof, and windows or, better still, colonnaded openings facing Boreas, with unrestricted views of the sea, mountains, lakes, or any other pleasant scene, so as to admit as much light as possible. Onto the porticoes on both the left and the right-hand side of the parade, other sitting rooms would be added, protected from the outside wind and receiving the morning or afternoon sun from the central *area*. The sitting rooms would vary in their lineaments. Some would be semicircular, and others rectilinear, but in either case their dimensions would relate to the *area* and the portico.

The width of the entire work would be half the length. The width would be divided into eighths, six of which would be taken up by the open *area* in the center, and one by each of the porticoes. But when the sitting rooms had a semicircular shape, their diameter would be two fifths the width of the central *area*. The rear wall of the portico would open out into the sitting rooms themselves. In a large work, the height of these semicircular sitting rooms would be the same as their width; but in a small work, it would take up at least five quarters of the width. Above the roof of the portico, along the face of the semicircular sitting rooms, windows would project to receive the sun within the semicircle and to fill the place with light. If, however, these sitting rooms were quadrangular, their width would be twice that of the portico, and their length twice their width. (By length I mean that dimension along the portico which, for anyone entering the sitting room, runs from right to left. . . .)[140]

Also to be included among public works is the portico for litigation before the lower judges; this should be constructed as follows. Its size should depend on the importance of the town or location, but should not be too small. The portico would be linked to a continuous row of chambers, where business relating to the decisions of the presiding judges would be attended to.

The buildings discussed so far are those which seemed to me to be particularly public: there patricians and plebeians meet frequently and freely. But some public buildings exist, such as the comitium, curia, and senate house, that are open only to prominent citizens and those involved in public business. These must be dealt with next. ◆

9

154v—156

According to Plato, the comitium should be held in the temple. In Rome there were special places reserved for the comitia. In Ceraumnia[141] there

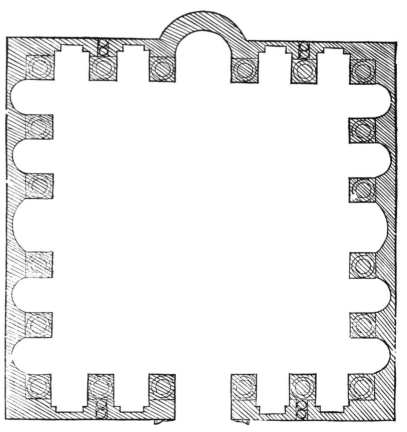

Plan of the sacerdotal curia.

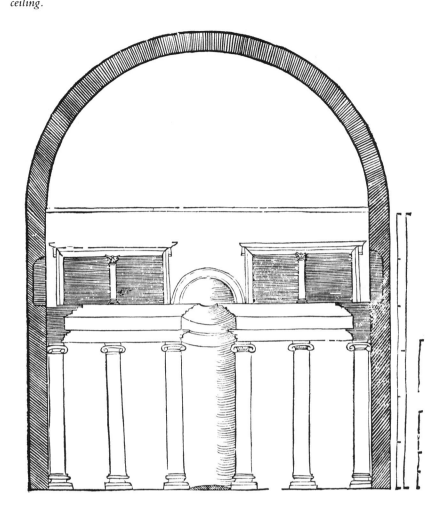

was a wooded grove dedicated to Jove, where the Achaians would meet to discuss affairs of state. Several other states would hold their meetings in their central forum. The Romans were allowed to convene their senate only in a place approved by augury; generally they would meet in a temple. Later they had their own curiae. According to Varro, there were two types of curia, one where priests took charge of religious affairs and one where the senate governed human ones.[142] I cannot describe with any certainty their individual characteristics, but we could well suppose that the former resembled a temple and the latter a basilica.

The priestly curia should therefore be vaulted, the senatorial trussed. In either case the consultants being questioned will use words, and the voice must therefore be taken into account. There ought, then, to be some device to prevent the voice from straying too high and, particularly with a vaulted roof, from echoing too harshly on the ears. While no doubt contributing to grace, cornices may be added to the wall primarily for practical reasons. I notice, from inspecting the works of the ancients, that the curia would be quadrangular in plan.[143]

When the roof is vaulted, the height to which the wall rises is one seventh less than the width of the facade. The type of vaulting used is the barrel vault. Opposite the entrance door lies the tribunal, its *sagitta* one third its chord. The door opening takes up one seventh of the facade. About five eighths of the way up the wall, cornices project along with a fascia, beam, and columns; the number of columns is sometimes large and sometimes small, depending on whether close or wide spacing is preferred; the method of colonnading is taken from the portico of the temple. Above the cornices on both the right- and left-hand walls, statues and other religious

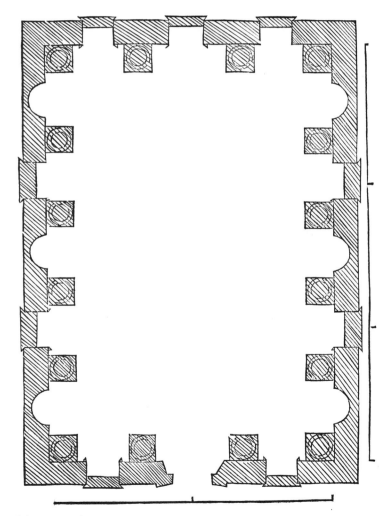

Plan of the senatorial curia.

items would be arranged in niches. Along the facade of the work, level with the niches, windows would open, their width twice their height, with two colonnettes inserted to support the lintel. Such would be the pontifical curia.

The senatorial curia should be as follows. The width of its *area* should be two thirds its length; its height, up to the level of the roof beams, should equal one and a quarter times the width of the *area*. Along the wall cornices are added as follows. The height as far as the trusses is divided into ninths, one of which is taken up by the solid section serving as a socle and podium, on which the columns sit. This section of solid wall should be taken up at the backs of benches. What remains above is then divided into sevenths, four of which are taken up by the first row of colonnading. On top of this row a second is added, together with a royal fascia and its associated ornament. The colonnading of both the first and second rows should be given the bases, capitals, cornices, and so on, that we prescribed for basilicas. Let the number of spaces be odd on both right- and left-hand walls, and no more than five. The spaces should all be equal. There should be no more than three spaces along the facade, the central one being one quarter wider than the rest. For each gap between the columns or mutules above the intermediate cornice there should be a window: curiae of this type must be well lit. Below the windows should run a parapet like that prescribed for the basilica. The windows that adorn the upper half of the facade should go no higher than the adjacent column, without its capital. The height of the window opening is divided into elevenths, of which the width takes up seven.

But if you prefer to dispense with columns and to employ mutules in place of their capitals, you should use the same lineaments as in the Ionic door. Here, as there, "little ears" should be suspended, to the following design. Let the width of the mutule have the same diameter as the top of the column shaft within a colonnade, excluding the collar and the fillet. The depth to which it hangs should equal the height of a Corinthian capital without its abacus. The projection of the mutule should not exceed that of the cimatium on the royal beam.

In many places there were such things as out of either necessity or pleasure turned out to be an ornament to the city and gave it great dignity. It is said that near the Academy[144] there was a most beautiful grove consecrated to the gods; Sulla cut it down to construct a rampart against the Athenians.[145] Alexander Severus planted a grove next to his baths, and added some excellent pools to the Antonian ones.[146] After the victory of Zelo over the Charchedonians, the Agrigentines built a pool seven stades long and twenty cubits deep, from which they even derived some revenue.[147] I remember having read in —————— that at Tivoli there was a famous public library. In Athens Pisistratus[148] was the first to make books available to the public; Xerxes removed the entire collection to Persia, but Seleucus returned it.[149] The Ptolemys, the kings of Egypt, had a library containing seven hundred thousand volumes.[150] But why marvel at public works? I discover that there were sixty-two thousand books in the library of the Gordians.[151] In the country around Laodicea there was a famous medical school founded by Zeuxis in the temple of Nemesis.[152] Appian writes that in Carthage there were stables for three hundred elephants and four thousand horses, a port for two hundred and twenty ships, an armory, a granary, and places to store and keep provisions for the troops.[153] The city of the sun, known as Thebes, had one hundred public stables, each large enough to shelter two hundred horses. On the island of Cyzicus in the Propontis[154] there were two ports, and between them lay a shipyard that could provide cover for two hundred ships. The harbor of the Piraeus contained the famous armory of Philo[155] and a splendid port for four hundred ships. Dionysius built a dockyard in the port of Syracuse containing one hundred and sixty buildings, each able to hold two ships, and an armory that in a few days could assemble more than one hundred and twenty thousand shields and an incredible number of swords. The Spartan naval base at Gythium was more than one hundred and forty stadia in length.[156] These are various works I have discovered in the different countries. As to how they ought to be, I have nothing special to say, except that anything which is to be practical should follow the rules for private buildings, and anything which you wish to be dignified or ornamental should be derived from those for public works.

One point not to be overlooked is this: the principal ornament to any library will be a large collection of rare books, drawn, preferably, from the learning of the ancients. It would also be an ornament to have mathematical instruments like the one Possidonius is said to have devised, where the seven planets followed their own orbits; or the map that Aristarchus is said to have made of the whole world and all its provinces engraved upon a metal plate.[157] Tiberius quite rightly recommended that a library should contain statues of the ancient poets.[158]

I seem to have dealt with almost everything connected with the ornament to public works. We have discussed the sacred, we have discussed the profane, we have discussed temples, porticoes, basilicas, monuments, roads, ports, crossroads, fora, bridges, arches, theaters, racecourses, curiae, sitting rooms, parades, and so on; there remains nothing to be considered, apart from baths. ◆

10

156—157v

Some have despised baths, claiming that they weaken the body; others have so approved of them that they bathed several times a day. Our own physicians back in antiquity erected numerous baths at incredible expense, so as to wash and care for the body. Heliogabalus, for example, built baths in several places; but he tore each one down as soon as he had washed there once, lest he become attached to baths.[159]

I am still not quite sure whether baths should rather be considered private or public. But clearly, as far as one can tell, they are a mixture of both. They contain many elements derived from private buildings, and many from public ones. Since the building of a bath requires a very large *area*, it should be sited in a part of the city that is neither too busy nor yet too out of the way: for the elders and matrons must come there to wash.

Bath buildings are surrounded by open space, and that open space is enclosed by a wall of no small height; entrance into this space is afforded only at certain, appropriate points. In the middle, as in the center of a house, there is an atrium, roofed, spacious, and majestic; off this are rooms, their lineaments taken from the Etruscan temple, as we have described it.[160] The entrance to this atrium is through the main vestibule, whose facade faces south. (Thus anyone entering from the vestibule would be going north.)

Plan of the xystus.

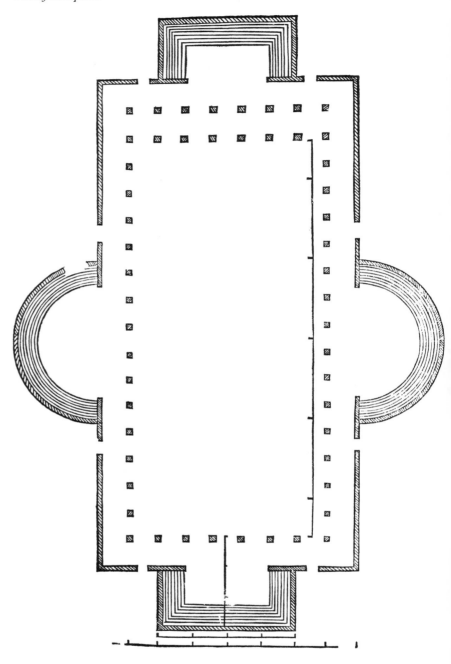

Off this main vestibule is a further, more constricted vestibule, perhaps better termed a passageway, leading into the aforementioned grand atrium. Off the atrium to the north there is a generous exit into the great open space. At the right end of this open space, on both the right- and left-hand sides, there is a large and very spacious portico, and, lying immediately behind it, a cold bath.

Let us return to the main atrium. At the extreme right of this atrium, toward the east, runs a vaulted passageway, reasonably open and quite wide; this is furnished with rooms, three on each side, matching each other. This passageway then leads on into an open *area* surrounded by porticoes: this I term a *xystus*.[161] Off this, the portico directly opposite the entrance to the passageway has a reasonably large sitting room to its rear. This portico, which faces the midday sun, contains that same cold bath mentioned above. In addition, the portico to the large open *area* is linked to the changing rooms. The portico directly opposite this has the warm baths behind it, whose windows receive the midday sun. Where appropriate at the corners of the porticoes there are *xysti*, smaller vestibules, for those going into and out of the outer space around the bath buildings. Such, then, should be the sequence of rooms on the right-hand side of the atrium; the left-hand side, toward the west, corresponds exactly to this: there is a passageway

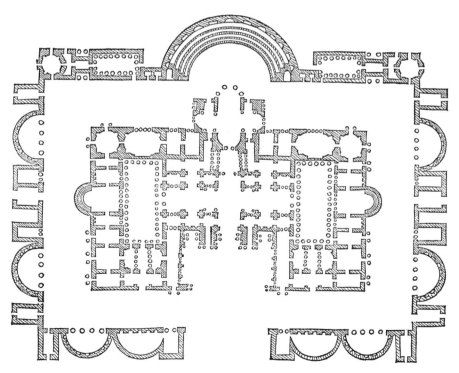

Plan of a bath building.

furnished with three matching rooms, then an identical open *area*, and *xysti*, together with their porticoes, sitting rooms, and corner vestibules.

To return to the main vestibule of the whole work, which, as we mentioned, faces south. To the right, along a line running east, are resting rooms, three in number, and a further three on the left, along a line running west; the former are for the use of women, and the latter for men. The first is where they deposit their clothes, the second where they are anointed, and the third where they wash. Sometimes a fourth is added for the sake of space: this might be a reception room for domestics and for companions who remain clothed. These bathing apartments receive the sun through large south-facing windows.

Between these apartments and the rooms described as flanking the main passageways that run from the atrium to the porticoed *area* of the *xystus*, there would lie an open space, which also provides light for the south side of internal rooms lining the passageway to the atrium.

This entire building complex was surrounded, as I said, by an extremely large open space, capable of accommodating even running contests. In appropriate places there would be turning posts around which the competitors would race. The space to the south, which extends in front of the vestibule, would open out to the south into a semicircle; this would be surrounded by steps, as in a theater, and there would also be a wall to ward off the southern breezes. A continuous wall ran around the outside, to enclose and fence in the entire open space, as though it were a town. This wall would be lined with splendid sitting rooms, both semicircular and rectangular, looking out onto the main bath building. In these sitting rooms the citizens could find sun or shade, as they preferred, on one side in the morning, on the other in the evening, depending on the time of the day. Beyond this main wall, particularly to the north, further open spaces were added, of moderate width, but elongated and bounded by a gentle curve. These spaces would be enclosed by a curved portico, walled in along its rear; they would have a view of nothing more than a small portion of sky (that is, what remained of the open space between the boundary wall and the curved portico itself). This would be a refuge in summer: the sun could scarcely penetrate the space, even at the summer solstice, because of its narrowness. There would be vestibules and chapels at the corner of the main wall, where, according to some, the women would appease the gods, once they had been purified.

This, then, summarizes the parts of which baths are composed. Their lineaments are taken from works that we have mentioned already, and from those we have yet to discuss, according to whichever is more suitable, that is, whether public or private. The *area* of the overall structure would almost always measure over one hundred thousand square feet.[162] ◆

The Ninth Book of Leon Battista Alberti on the Art of Building. Ornament to Private Buildings.

I

157v—159v

It should be recalled that private buildings may be either in the town or in the country; of these some are for the less well off and some for the wealthy. We shall discuss how each is to be adorned. But let us be sure that we do not pass over some things relevant to our argument.

I notice that the most prudent and modest of our ancestors much preferred frugality and parsimony in building as in any other matter, public or private, judging that all extravagance on the part of the citizen ought to be prevented and checked, and that both admonitions and laws were issued to this end with the utmost vigor and persistence. Plato in his writings therefore praises those responsible for the decree, mentioned elsewhere, that no one should produce a picture more splendid than was kept by his ancestors in their temples; it was forbidden for the temple to be adorned with more than one picture, which one painter might take one day to complete.[1] Likewise, statues of the gods were to be made of nothing but wood or stone, bronze and iron being reserved for instruments of war. Demosthenes esteemed the ways of the ancient Athenians far higher than those of his contemporaries. "The public buildings," he said, "that they have left us, especially their temples, are so numerous, ornate, and majestic that there is nowhere left for us to surpass them. Yet they displayed such modesty in their private buildings that there was scarcely any difference between the buildings of even the most eminent citizens and those of the commonest. They did this that glory might overcome envy among mortals."[2] Yet not even they who had glorified their city by the hand of the artist rather than by the fame of their deeds seemed deserving of praise to the Spartans; praise was due instead to those who had adorned their city not with buildings but with valor.[3] In Sparta, under a law issued by Lycurgus, it was forbidden to build a roof except with an axe, or to make a door with anything but a saw.[4] When Agesilaus noticed that at ——— in Asia they squared the beams of their houses, he laughed, and inquired whether they would make something round if it grew square.[5] He was right: their ancestral modesty dictated that a house should be built for convenience, not for charm or delight. In the time of Caesar the Germans took care, especially in the country, not to build anything too highly finished, for fear of provoking quarrels due to envy of the possessions of others.[6] Valerius had a house in Rome high up on the Esquiline, but, to avoid envy, he pulled it down and rebuilt it on the plain.[7]

The best of later generations were faithful to this frugality in works both public and private, as far as the maintenance of decent custom would allow. Later, as the empire expanded, so much did excess grip almost everyone (with the exception of Octavian, who was so upset by overextravagance in building, that he demolished a villa which was too lavish),[8] so much, I repeat, did excess grip the city, that the Gordian family, for example, built a house on the road to Praeneste with two hundred columns, all of the same size and style, of which, as ———— recalls, fifty were of Numidian marble, fifty of Claudian, fifty of Simidian, and fifty of Tistean.[9] What of Lucretius' story? "Golden are the statues of youths around the house; each holds up a flaming torch in his right hand to illuminate the nocturnal feast."[10]

Why enumerate these? To reiterate through examples what I said earlier, that everything is best when it is tempered to its own importance. And if you want my advice, I would rather the private houses of the wealthy were wanting in things that might contribute to their ornament, than have the more modest and thrifty accuse them of luxury in any way. Nevertheless, the need to hand down to posterity a reputation for both wisdom and power is universally accepted (for that reason, as Thucydides said, we build great works, so as to appear great in the eyes of our descendants);[11] equally, we decorate our property as much to distinguish family and country as for any personal display (and who would deny this to be the responsibility of a good citizen?). For both of these reasons, it is preferable to make the parts that are particularly public or are intended principally to welcome guests, such as the facade, vestibule, and so on, as handsome as possible. Although I may think that any excess must be censured, yet I feel that those who spend so much on the bulk of their buildings that they cannot afford to adorn them deserve even greater censure than those who overspend slightly on ornament.

I therefore conclude that anyone who wants to understand correctly the true and correct ornament of building must realize that its principal component and generator is not the outlay of wealth but the wealth of ingenuity. I firmly believe that any person of sense would not want to design his private house very differently from those of others, and would be careful not to incite envy through extravagance or ostentation. On the other hand, no sensible person would wish that anyone else should surpass him in the skill of his workmen, or in praise for his counsel and judgment; as a result the overall division and compartition of lineaments[12] will draw much praise, which is itself the primary and principal form of ornament. To return to the subject.

The royal palace and, in a free city, the house of anyone of senatorial rank, be he praetor or consul, should be the first one that you will want to make the most handsome. We have already discussed how to adorn their public sections appropriately. We shall now set out how to adorn those parts restricted to private use. I would give each house a dignified and splendid vestibule, according to its importance. Beyond this should be a well-lit portico; there should be no shortage of magnificent open spaces. As far as possible, in short, every element that contributes to dignity or splendor should follow the example of public works; yet they should be handled with such restraint as to appear to seek delight rather than any form of pomp. Just as in the previous book, on public buildings, [we said that] the temporal ought to concede to the sacred in dignity as far as is reasonable, so in refinement and quantity of ornament, private buildings should allow themselves to be surpassed easily by public ones.[13] They should not presume to have doors of bronze—such as were counted among Carvillo's crimes[14]—or of ivory; nor should the ceilings sparkle with large quantities of gold or glass; Hymettian or Parian marble should not glisten everywhere: such things are for temples. But in the private house modest materials should be used elegantly, and elegant materials modestly. Cypress, larch, or box will suffice. The revetment should be of plain white stucco, decorated with simple murals. The cornices should be of stone of Luna, or better still Travertine.[15]

Not that precious materials should be completely renounced and banished; but they should be used sparingly in the most dignified places, like jewels in a crown. If I were to sum up the whole question, I would say that sacred buildings ought to be so designed that nothing further may be added to enhance their majesty or cause greater admiration for their beauty;[16] the private building, on the other hand, must be so treated that it will not seem possible to remove anything, because everything has been put together with great dignity. To the others, that is, the profane public, must be left, I feel, a position midway between these two.

The severest restraint is called for, in the ornament to private buildings, therefore, although a certain license is often possible. For instance, the whole shaft of a column may be over slender, too swollen, or too retracted at its entasis perhaps, compared to what is strictly permissible in public buildings, yet it should not be faulted or condemned, provided the work is not malformed or distorted. Indeed, sometimes it may be more delightful to stray a little from the dignity and calculated rule of lineaments, which would not be permitted in public works. How charming was the practice of those more fanciful architects of stationing huge statues of slaves at the door jambs of a dining room, so that they support the lintel with their heads;[17] and of making columns, especially for garden porticoes, that resembled tree trunks, their knots removed and their branches tied into bundles, and the shaft scrolled and plaited with palms and carved with leaves, birds, and channels,[18] or, where the work is intended to be very robust, even quadrangular columns, flanked on either side by half-columns;[19] for capitals they would set up baskets laden with hanging bunches of grapes and fruits, or palms sending off new shoots from the tops of their stems, or a mass of snakes tangled in various knots, or eagles clapping their wings, or a gorgon's head full of wrestling snakes, and other such examples that would take too long to describe.

In doing this, the artist must, as far as he is able, guard each part in its noble form by skilfully maintaining the lines and angles, as if he would not wish to cheat the work of the appropriate *concinnitas*[20] of its members, yet seeming to entertain the viewer with a charming trick—or, better still, to please him by the wit of his invention. And since dining rooms, corridors, and chambers may be either public or enclosed and thoroughly private, the former should combine the splendor of the forum with civic pomp, provided it is not too offensive, but in more private examples a degree of license may be taken according to taste. ◆

2

159v—160v

Since some private houses are in the city and others are outside, let us consider what ornament is appropriate in either case. Aside from the differences mentioned in earlier books,[21] there is a further difference between a town house and a villa: the ornament to a town house ought to be far more sober in character, whereas in a villa the allures of license and delight are allowed. Another difference is that with a town house the boundary of the neighboring property imposes many constraints that may be treated with greater freedom in a villa.[22] Care must be taken that the basement is not prouder than harmony with the neighboring buildings requires;[23] while the width of a portico is constrained by the line of the adjoining wall. In Rome the thickness and height of a wall were not determined by opinion, since an ancient law restricted the thickness to ———. And because of the risk of collapse, Julius Caesar made sure that within the city no wall was raised higher than ———.[24] A villa is not bound by these laws. The inhabitants of Babylon were praised for having four-story houses to live in.[25] In his votive speech in praise of Rome, the orator Elius Aristides noted how astonishing it was that great buildings could be built on top of great buildings—praise indeed;[26] although he was in fact commending the size of the population rather than the method of construction. Tyre, it is said, surpassed Rome in the height of its houses; this was why it was once all but totally destroyed by an earthquake.[27]

A building will gain in comfort and even more in delight, if there is no need to go up and down a great deal. Those who say that stairs disrupt a building are quite right; I notice how strenuously the ancients avoided these obstacles. But with a villa there is no need to add story above story. The greater openness allows the villa to take up the most appropriate distribution of space, with one part leading off another, all on the same level; I would also be delighted to find this in a city, if only it were possible.

There is one type of private building that combines the dignity of a city house with the delight of a villa—a topic passed over in previous books, and saved until now. This is the suburban *hortus*,[28] something that, I feel, must not be overlooked on any account. The discussion will be all the briefer—and I am very concerned that it should be short—if I deal with the requirements of both kinds of building together. But first there are a few comments to be made on the *hortus* itself.

There was a saying among the ancients: "Anyone who buys a farm should sell his house in the town." And also, "If your heart is set on city life, you need no country business." By this they meant, perhaps, that a *hortus* was the best solution. The physicians advise us to breathe air as clear and pure as possible; this, I do not deny, may be found in an isolated hilltop villa. On the other hand, urban, civic business requires the head of the family to make frequent visits to the forum, curia, and temples. To do this easily you need a house in town; yet one may be inconvenient for business, the other damages health. Generals used to shift camp lest the stench prove too offensive. What then would you expect of a city, full of festering piles of filth which have accumulated over the centuries? This being the case, of all buildings for practical use, I consider the *hortus* to be the foremost and healthiest: it does not detain you from business in the city, nor is it troubled by impurity of air. [29]

Cicero charged Atticus to acquire a *hortus* in some busy place. [30] Yet I would not want it to be so busy that it is never possible to come to the door without being properly dressed. Let it have the advantage of which the character in Terence brags, "that I should never grow tired of country or town." [31] And as Martial so neatly put it,

> *How in the country do I pass the time?*
> *The answer to the question's brief:*
> *I lunch and drink, I sing and play,*
> *I wash and dine, I rest. Meanwhile*
> *I Phoebus quiz*
> *and Muses frisk.* [32]

It is useful both to have the city close by and to have places to which you withdraw easily and do what you will. A place close to a town, with clear roads and pleasant surroundings, will be popular. A building here will be most attractive, if it presents a cheerful overall appearance to anyone leaving the city, as if to attract and expect visitors. I would therefore make it slightly elevated; and I would make the road leading up to it rise so gently that visitors do not realize how high they have climbed until they have a view over the countryside. Meadows full of flowers, sunny lawns, cool and shady groves, limpid springs, streams, and pools, and whatever else we have described as being essential to a villa—none of these should be missing, for their delight as much as for their utility.

Moreover, I would certainly have the whole outer face and address of a building of whatever kind, bright and conspicuous on every side, since that increases its grace. It will receive much light from the joyous sky, much sun, and healthy breezes. I would not have it overlooked by anything whose gloomy shade would cause offense. Let everything smile at the visitor and greet him as he arrives. And once he has entered, let him be unsure whether it would be more pleasurable to stay where he is or to venture further, enticed by its gaiety and splendor. Let him then pass from quadrangular *areae*[33] to round ones, and from round ones back to quadrangular ones, and then on to those which are neither completely round nor rectilinear. You should not need to ascend steps to enter the inner "bosom" of the house;[34] it should be possible to penetrate to the innermost chamber of the house along even ground, or within a reasonable change of level. ◆

3

160v—162

Since the parts of a building differ greatly one from another, in their nature as well as in their appearance, I feel that we must next examine all these matters which we have mentioned earlier but left until now. With certain parts, it hardly matters whether you make them round or quadrangular, provided they serve their purpose properly; yet their size and position are of great importance. Some must be large, such as the "bosom" of the house, while others require a smaller *area*,[35] such as the closets and all internal rooms; yet others are of an intermediate size, such as the dining room and the vestibule. We have already discussed the proper arrangement of each member within the house. I need not discuss their individual differences in *area*, since such differences depend largely on personal choice and local variations in custom.

The ancients used to add either a portico or a hall onto their houses; not always composed of straight lines, but sometimes of curved ones, like a theater. Off the portico they would add a vestibule, almost always a round one.[36] Then there would be a passageway running into the bosom of the house, and other members already dealt with in their respective places, whose lineaments would take too long to describe. The following comments, however, may be of use.

If the *area* is round, it should be set out according to the lineaments of the temple, the only difference being that the walls ought to be higher than those of a temple; the reason for this you will see shortly.[37] If the *area* is quadrangular, it will differ somewhat from the description we gave for sacred buildings and for public profane ones, yet will have something in common with the senate house and the curia. In accordance with common practice of long standing, our ancestors used to give the atrium a width of two thirds its length, or a length either five thirds or seven fifths the width. In either case it seems that the ancients raised the wall to a height four thirds the length of the *area*.[38] From our own measurements of their work, we have established that with a quadrangular *area* the height required for walls would vary depending on whether the roof was vaulted or of timber construction. Similarly, the rules would vary between large buildings and much smaller ones, because the distance between the center of the visual

Book Nine

296

rays and the highest visible point differs from one to another.[39] But of this elsewhere.

The size of the *area* is determined by the roof, and the size of the roof by the length of the beams required to span it. A roof may be called medium-sized when supported by middling posts and timbers.

Apart from those we have mentioned, there are many other highly suitable[40] dimensions and relations between lines, which we shall attempt to describe here as succinctly and lucidly as possible. If the length of the *area* is twice the width, with a timber roof, the height should be one and a half times the width. With vaulted roofs, the height of the wall will be the same as the width to which a third is added. So much for medium-sized roofs.

In a large building, if the roof is vaulted, the height [of a room] from top to bottom will be five times a quarter of the width, and if the roof is of timber construction, seven times a fifth. But if the roof is of timber construction and the length of the *area* is three times the width, let the height be three quarters more than the width; if the roof is vaulted, let the height be one half more than the width. But if the length is four times the width, the height of the wall will take up half the length in the case of a roof of timber construction, and seven quarters of the width with vaulting. If the length is five times the width, the height of the wall will be one sixth more than it is for an *area* with a length four times the width. If the length is six times the width, the same applies, except that it is one fifth rather than one sixth more. With vaults, if the *area* is equal-sided, the ratio between height and width is the same as when the length is three times the width, but with trabeated roofing, the height remains the same as the width.[41]

With rooms of an even larger *area*, the height may be reduced, so that the width is one quarter more than the height. Where the length is one ninth greater than the width, the height is likewise one ninth greater than the width, but only when the roof is trabeated. When the roof is of timber construction and the length is four times a third of the width, raise the wall to a height one sixth more than the width; but if it is vaulted, increase the height further to equal the width plus a sixth of the length. With roofs of timber construction, when the length is one and a half times the width, the height is one seventh more than the width; with vaulting, however, add a seventh of the longer line of the larger dimension to the height. If, finally, the relationship of the lines is such that one equals 5 and the other 7, or one 3 and the other 5, and so on, as local constraints, variety of invention, or the method of ornament demand, make the height half the sum of their two dimensions.[42]

Something else I ought not to pass over here: the length of the atrium must never be more than twice the width; nor should the width of drawing rooms be less than two thirds their length. A ratio, length to width, of three, four, and so on, though no longer than six, is required for a portico.

Within the wall there should be openings for both windows and doors. Window openings along the width of a wall (which is naturally shorter than the length) should number no more than one. This should have either a height greater than its width or a width greater than its height, the latter version being known as a "reclining" window. When the width is narrower, as it is with a door, then make the opening, from right to left, no more than a third and no less than a quarter the overall internal width of the wall. Let the base of the opening itself be no more than four ninths and no less than two ninths of the overall height above floor level. The height should be one and a half times the width. These are the proportions for the opening whose width is less than its height. But if the opening is broader from right to left, and squatter from top to bottom, make the width of the opening no less than half and no more than two thirds the overall width of the wall. Equally, its height should be half its width, or two thirds that dimension. Two colonnettes may be added to support the lintel.[43]

If the longer wall is to contain windows, they should be more frequent, and their number odd. The ancients, I notice, preferred to make them three. Let them be as follows. Divide the overall length of the wall into no more than seven and no less than five parts; take three of these, and give each a window. Make the height of the opening seven quarters or nine fifths its width. But if more windows are needed, seeing as the work now assumes the character of a portico, their dimensions should be borrowed from the portico (especially that in a theater), as described above in the appropriate place.[44]

Let the door openings be the same as those prescribed for a senate house or curia.[45]

Make the ornament to the window openings Corinthian, to the main entrance Ionic, and to the doors of the dining rooms, chambers, and so on, Doric.

So much for lines, so far as they are relevant to our purpose. ◆

4

162—164

There are certain features of ornament which you might want to apply in private buildings and that must not be overlooked. The ancients used to pattern the floors of their porticoes with square and circular labyrinths on which the youths could play.[46] We have seen floors depicting climbing plants, their tendrils curling all around; and bedroom floors may be seen inlaid with an imitation carpet of marble mosaic; others are strewn with garlands and branches. Sosus has been praised for his device of having a floor in Pergamum paved to depict the remains of a meal[47]—a work, ye gods![48] not inappropriate for a dining room. Agrippa, in my opinion, was right to tile his floors in earthenware.[49]

Extravagance I detest. I am delighted by anything that combines ingenuity with grace and wit. For the revetment to a wall there can be no project more pleasant or attractive than the representation of stone colonnading. Titus Caesar had the portico where he used to walk inlaid with Phoenician stone, whose polish reflected everything like a mirror.[50] The emperor Antoninus Caracalla had a portico painted to represent the achievements and triumphs of his father;[51] as did Severus, too;[52] whereas Agathocles did not have his father's achievements shown, but his own.[53] In Persia an ancient law forbade anything to be painted or sculpted except wild beasts killed by the king. It is surely most appropriate for a portico or a dining hall to be painted or sculpted with scenes of bravery by the citizens, portraits and events worthy of recollection. When C. Caesar set up statues in his portico of those who had extended the commonwealth, his action was greeted with universal applause.[54] I approve of all this as well, but I would not have a wall overwhelmed with statues and reliefs, nor overcrowded with *historiae*.[55] It is remarkable with gems, and pearls in particular, how dull they become when clustered too close together. For this reason I would therefore have separate stone frames in appropriate and noble situations along the wall, in which to place pictures and also panels like those borne by Pompey in his triumph, depicting his glorious achievements by land and sea.[56] Or, better still, I would prefer illustration of the tales that poets make for moral instruction, like that which Daedalus painted on the gates to the temple at Cumae, showing Icarus in flight.[57]

Since painting, like poetry, can deal with various matters—some depict the memorable deeds of great princes, others the manners of private citizens, and still others the life of the simple farmer—those first, which are the most majestic, will be appropriate for public works and for the buildings of the most eminent individuals; the second should adorn the walls of private citizens; and the last will be particularly suitable for *horti*, being the most lighthearted of them all.[58] We are particularly delighted when we see paintings of pleasant landscapes or harbors, scenes of fishing, hunting, bathing, or country sports, and flowery and leafy views. It is worth mentioning the emperor Octavian, who collected rare and enormous bones of huge animals as an ornament to his house.[59]

To their grottoes and caves the ancients used to apply a deliberately roughened revetment of tiny pumice chips, or Travertine foam, which Ovid called "living pumice."[60] We have also seen green ocher used to imitate the bearded moss of a grotto. Something we once saw in a grotto gave great delight: where a spring gushed out, the surface had been made up of various seashells and oysters, some inverted, others open, charmingly arranged according to their different colors.

Wherever man and wife come together, it is advisable only to hang portraits of men of dignity and handsome appearance; for they say that this may have a great influence on the fertility of the mother and the appearance of future offspring. Paintings of springs and streams may be of considerable benefit to the feverish. It is possible to verify this: if some night as you lie awake in bed, unable to sleep, you visualize in your mind the clearest springs and streams you have ever seen, that dryness of insomnia will be quenched immediately, and sleep will steal you away into the sweetest slumber.

There should be gardens full of delightful plants, and a garden portico, where you can enjoy both sun and shade. There should also be truly festive space; and small streams breaking out in several unexpected places. Walks should be lined with evergreen plants. In a sheltered place plant a hedge of box; it will be damaged and waste if exposed to the open sky, to the wind, and particularly to sea spray. Some plant myrtle in a sunny place, claiming that it thrives in summer, although Theophrastus maintains that myrtle, laurel, and ivy prefer shade; accordingly he recommends that they be placed close together to shield each other from the heat of the sun.[61] Nor should cypresses cloaked in ivy be lacking. In addition, circles, semicircles, and other geometric shapes that are favored in the plans of buildings can be modeled out of laurel, citrus, and juniper when their branches are bent back and intertwined. Phiteon of Agrigentum[62] had in his own private house three hundred stone vases, each with a capacity of one hundred amphorae; such vases make a good garden ornament in front of fountains. As for vines, the ancients would train them over their garden walks, supported by marble columns, whose thickness was one tenth their height and whose ornaments were Corinthian. Rows of trees should be laid out in the form of the *quincunx*[63] as the expression is, at equal intervals and with matching angles. Let the garden be green with rare herbs and those which physicians value. How charming was that custom of our ancestors whereby the gardeners would flatter their master by writing his name on the ground with box or fragrant herbs! For hedges, use rose entwined with hazel and pomegranate. As the verse runs, "Bushes bearing cornels and plums, the oak and ilex yielding plenty of food to the cattle, shade to the master."[64] But these, perhaps, are more proper to the commercial farm than to the garden. In spite of what they give as Democritus' opinion, I shall not approve of anyone who thinks it unwise to surround his garden with stones or a masonry wall: since precautions must be taken against wanton recklessness.[65] Of comic statues in the garden I do not disapprove, provided they are not obscene. Such, then, should be the garden.

In a town house the internal parts, such as the drawing rooms and dining rooms, should be no less festive than those of a country one; but the external parts, such as the portico and vestibule, should not be so frivolous as to appear to have obscured some sense of dignity. The portico of the highest citizens ought to be trabeated, and that of the ordinary man arched; both should preferably be vaulted. The ornament to the beam and the cornices that rest on the column should take up one fourth the height of the colonnading. If there is to be a second row of columns above the first, its height should be one quarter less. If there is to be a third row, its height should be one fifth less than that below. In each case the height of the dadoes and the plinth should be one quarter that of the column they support. But when only one row of colonnading is required, it should follow the methods for public works of a temporal nature.

The pediment to a private house should not emulate the majesty of a temple in any way. Yet the vestibule itself may be ennobled by having its facade heightened slightly, or by being given a dignified pediment. The remainder of the wall may be crowned on either side with the slight projection of acroteria.[66] Acroteria standing just proud [of the roof] will add elegance, especially at each of the main corners. I do not approve of turrets and crenellations on the houses of private citizens; such elements are foreign to peaceful citizens and the well-ordered state: they belong rather to the tyrant, in that they imply the presence of fear or of malicious intent. Balconies along the front of a building may be a charming addition, provided they are not too large, lavish, or ungainly. ◆

5

164—167

Now I come to a matter with which we have promised to deal all along: every kind of beauty and ornament[67] consists of it; or, to put it more clearly, it springs from every rule of beauty. This is an extremely difficult inquiry; for whatever that one entity is, which is either extracted or drawn from the number and nature of all the parts, or imparted to each by sure and constant method, or handled in such a manner as to tie and bond several elements into a single bundle or body, according to a true and consistent agreement and sympathy—and something of this kind is exactly what we seek—then surely that entity must share some part of the force and juice, as it were, of all the elements of which it is composed or blended; for otherwise their discord and differences would cause conflict and disunity. This work of research and selection is neither obvious nor straightforward in any other matter, but it is at its most ambiguous and involved in the subject about to be discussed; for the art of building is composed of very many parts, each one, as you have seen, demanding to be ennobled by much varied ornament. Yet we shall tackle the problem to the best of our ability, as we have undertaken. We shall not inquire as to how a sound understanding of the whole might be gained from the numerous parts, but, restricting ourselves to what is relevant, we shall begin by observing what produces beauty by its very nature.

The great experts of antiquity, as we mentioned earlier, have instructed us that a building is very like an animal, and that Nature must be imitated when we delineate it. Let us investigate, then, why some bodies that Nature produces may be called beautiful, others less beautiful, and even ugly. Obviously, among those which we count as beautiful all are not such that there is no difference between them; in fact it is precisely where they most differ that we observe them to be infused or imprinted with a quality through which, however dissimilar they are, we consider them equally graceful. Let me give you an example: one man might prefer the tenderness of a slender girl; yet a character in a comedy preferred one girl over all others because she was plumper and more buxom;[68] you, perhaps, might prefer a wife neither so slender of figure as to appear sickly nor so stout of limb as to resemble a village bully, but such that you might add as much to the one as you could take away from the other without impairing dignity. Yet, whichever of the two you prefer, you will not then consider the rest unattractive and worthless. But what it is that causes us to prefer one above all the others, I shall not inquire.

When you make judgments on beauty, you do not follow mere fancy, but the workings of a reasoning faculty that is inborn in the mind. It is clearly so, since no one can look at anything shameful, deformed, or disgusting without immediate displeasure and aversion.[69] What arouses and provokes such a sensation in the mind we shall not inquire in detail, but shall limit our consideration to whatever evidence presents itself that is relevant to our argument. For within the form and figure[70] of a building there resides some natural excellence and perfection that excites the mind and is immediately recognized by it.[71] I myself believe that form, dignity, grace, and other such qualities depend on it, and as soon as anything is removed or altered, these qualities are themselves weakened and perish. Once we are convinced of this, it will not take long to discuss what may be removed, enlarged, or altered, in the form and figure. For every body consists entirely of parts that are fixed and individual; if these are removed, enlarged, reduced, or transferred somewhere inappropriate, the very composition will be spoiled that gives the body its seemly appearance.

From this we may conclude, without my pursuing such questions any longer, that the three principal components of that whole theory into which we inquire are number, what we might call outline, and position. But arising from the composition and connection of these three is a further quality in which beauty shines full face: our term for this is *concinnitas*;[72] which we say is nourished with every grace and splendor. It is the task and aim of *concinnitas* to compose parts that are quite separate from each other by their nature, according to some precise rule, so that they correspond to one another in appearance.

That is why when the mind is reached by way of sight or sound, or any other means, *concinnitas* is instantly recognized. It is our nature to desire the best, and to cling to it with pleasure.[73] Neither in the whole body nor in its parts does *concinnitas* flourish as much as it does in Nature herself; thus I might call it the spouse of the soul and of reason. It has a vast range in which to exercise itself and bloom—it runs through man's entire life and government, it molds the whole of Nature. Everything that Nature produces is regulated by the law of *concinnitas*, and her chief concern is that whatever she produces should be absolutely perfect. Without *concinnitas* this could hardly be achieved, for the critical sympathy of the parts would be lost. So much for this.

If this is accepted, let us conclude as follows. Beauty is a form of sympathy and consonance of the parts within a body, according to definite number, outline, and position, as dictated by *concinnitas*, the absolute and fundamental rule in Nature. This is the main object of the art of building, and the source of her dignity, charm, authority, and worth.

All that has been said our ancestors learned through observation of Nature herself; so they had no doubt that if they neglected these things, they would be unable to attain all that contributes to the praise and honor of the work; not without reason they declared that Nature, as the perfect generator of forms, should be their model. And so, with the utmost industry, they searched out the rules that she employed in producing things, and translated them into methods of building. By studying in Nature the patterns both for whole bodies and for their individual parts, they understood that at their very origins[74] bodies do not consist of equal portions, with the result that some are slender, some fat, and others in between; and observing the great difference in purpose and intention between one building and another, as we have already observed in earlier books, they concluded that, by the same token, each should be treated differently.

Following Nature's own example, they also invented three different ways[75] of ornamenting a house, their names taken from the nations who favored one above the others, or even invented each, as it is said. One kind was fuller, more practical and enduring: this they called Doric. Another was slender and full of charm: this they named Corinthian. The one that lay in between, as though composed of both, they called the Ionic; they devised these for the body as a whole. When they observed the particular contribution of each of the three factors mentioned above, number, outline, and position, in the production of beauty, they established how to employ them, having studied nature's works, basing their argument, it seems to me, on the following principles.

They realized that numbers were either odd or even; they employed both, but the even in some places, the odd in others. Taking their example from Nature, they never made the bones[76] of the building, meaning the columns, angles, and so on, odd in number—for you will not find a single animal that stands or moves upon an odd number of feet. Conversely, they never made openings even in number; this they evidently learned from Nature: to animals she has given ears, eyes, and nostrils matching on either side, but in the center, single and obvious, she has set the mouth.

Among the odd and even numbers, some are found more frequently in Nature and are particularly favored by the wise; these have been adopted by architects when composing parts of their buildings, mainly because they have some property that distinguishes them as the most noble. That Nature is composed of threes all philosophers agree. And as for the number five, when I consider the many varied and wonderful things that either themselves relate to that number or are produced by something that contains it—such as the human hand—I do not think it wrong that it should be called divine, and rightly be dedicated to the gods of the arts, and Mercury in particular. And as for the number seven, it is clear that the great maker of all things, God, is particularly delighted by it, in that he has made seven planets to wander the heavens, and has so regulated man, his favorite creature, that conception, formation, adolescence, maturity, and so on, all these stages he has made reducible to seven. According to Aristotle, when a child was born, the ancients would not give it a name for seven days, as, until then, it was not certain to survive. For both the seed in the womb and the new born baby are at grave risk for the first seven days. Another popular odd number was nine, that of the orbs which provident Nature has set in the sky. Then again the physicians are all agreed that many of the most important things in Nature are based on the fraction one ninth. For one ninth of the annual solar cycle is about forty days, the length of time, according to Hippocrates, that it takes the fetus to form in the uterus. And we notice that as a rule it takes forty days to recover from a grave illness. Menstruation ceases forty days after conception, if the child is to be a boy, and starts again a similar period after the birth, if a boy has been born. And during the first forty days you will not see the child laughing or crying while he is awake, although he will do both while asleep—so they say. So much for odd numbers.

As for even numbers, some philosophers maintain that the fourfold is consecrated to divinity, and that the most solemn oaths should be based on it.[77] The sixfold is one of the very few which is called "perfect," because it is the sum of all its integral divisors.[78] It is clear that the eightfold exerts a great influence on Nature. Those born in the eighth month will not survive, we have observed, except in Egypt.[79] They say also that a pregnant woman who gives birth to a stillborn baby in the eighth month will herself soon die. If the mother lies with a man during the eighth month, the child will be full of thick mucus and will have a foul skin full of thoroughly unpleasant scabs. Aristotle thought the tenth the most perfect number of all; perhaps, as some interpret, because its square equals the cube of four consecutive numbers.[80]

Architects have used these numbers extensively; yet, especially in the temple, they have employed no even number greater than ten, in the case of openings, nor odd number greater than nine. Next we must deal with outline.

For us, the outline is a certain correspondence between the lines that define the dimensions; one dimension being length, another breadth, and the third height. The method of defining the outline is best taken from those objects in which Nature offers herself to our inspection and admiration as we view and examine them. I affirm again with Pythagoras: it is absolutely certain that Nature is wholly consistent. That is how things stand.

The very same numbers that cause sounds to have that *concinnitas*, pleasing to the ears, can also fill the eyes and mind with wondrous delight. From musicians therefore who have already examined such numbers thoroughly, or from those objects in which Nature has displayed some evident and noble quality, the whole method of outlining is derived. But I shall dwell on this topic no longer than is relevant to the business of the architect. Let us therefore pass over what relates to the modulations of a single voice or the rules of the tetrachord; all that concerns our work is as follows.

We define harmony as that consonance of sounds which is pleasant to the ears. Sounds may be low- or high-pitched. The lower-pitched a sound, the longer the string that emits it; the higher-pitched, the shorter the string. From the different contrasts between these sounds arise the varying harmonies which the ancients have classified into set numbers corresponding to the relationships between the consonant strings. The names of the consonants are as follows: the *diapente*,[81] also called the *sesquialtera*;[82] the *diatesseron*,[83] also called the *sesquitertia*;[84] then the *diapason*,[85] which is a double; and the *diapason diapente*,[86] which is a triple; and the *disdiapason*,[87] which is called the quadruple. To these they added *tonus*,[88] which was also called the *sesquioctavus*.[89] The relationships between the above-mentioned consonants were as follows. *Sesquialtera* is so called because the length of the longer string is one and a half times that of the shorter. The prefix *sesqui* used by the ancients we might interpret as meaning "and another," as in *sesquialtera*. Thus the longer string should be given the number three, and the shorter the number two. The term *sesquitertia* is used when the longer string is one and a third times the length of the shorter: thus the longer string is given the number four, and the shorter the number three. In the consonance called *diapason* one number is double the other, such as two to one, or one to a half; in the triple, three to one, or one to a third; in the quadruple, likewise, four to one, or one to a quarter. To sum up, then, the musical numbers are one, two, three, and four; there is also *tonus*, as I mentioned, where the longer string is one eighth more than the lesser.

Architects employ all these numbers in the most convenient manner possible: they use them in pairs, as in laying out a forum, place, or open space, where only two dimensions are considered, width and length; and they use them also in threes, such as in a public sitting room, senate house, hall, and so on, when width relates to length, and they want the height to relate harmoniously to both. ◆

6

167—169v

We must now deal with such matters. To begin with the *area*,[90] since it is determined by two dimensions: an *area* may be either short, long, or intermediate.[91] The shortest of all is the quadrangle with all four sides of equal length, whose angles are all matching right angles.[92] After this come the *sesquialtera*, and another short *area* is the *sesquitertia*.[93] So these three relationships, which we call "simple," apply to the short *area* . There are three appropriate to the intermediate *area* as well, the best of which is the double, followed by that composed of a double *sesquialtera*. This latter is constructed as follows: having established the lesser dimension of the *area*— for example, four—construct the first *sesquialtera*, making the length six; to this add another, making the length nine. Thus the length is twice the width plus a further double *tonus*.[94] Another intermediate *area* is the double *sesquitertia*, constructed by precisely the same method; this produces a width of nine to a length of sixteen. Thus the greater line is twice the lesser, minus one *tonus*.[95] For a longer *area* use the following method: either the double square is enlarged by a *sesquialtera* to become a triple, or the double is enlarged by a *sesquitertia* so that the proportions are three to eight; alternatively, dimensions should be chosen to make the proportions one to four.

We have dealt with shorter *areae*, either with equal dimensions or with proportions of, say, two to three or three to four; and we have dealt with intermediate *areae*, where one dimension is twice the other or where the proportions are, say, four to nine or nine to sixteen. Finally we mentioned extended *areae*, with proportions of one to three, one to four, or, say, three to eight.

When working in three dimensions, we should combine the universal dimensions, as it were, of the body with numbers naturally harmonic in themselves, or ones selected from elsewhere by some sure and true method. Numbers naturally harmonic include those whose ratios form proportions such as the double, triple, quadruple, and so on. For a double may be constructed from the single by adding a *sesquialtera* and then a *sesquitertia*, as in the following example: let the lesser dimension of the double be two; to this add a *sesquialtera* to produce three; by adding a *sesquitertia* to the three, four is produced, which is itself twice the original two.

Alternatively, let the lesser dimension be three; enlarge it by a *sesquitertia* to produce four; add a *sesquialtera*; thus you have six, which is twice the original three. Likewise a triple may be formed of a double together with a *sesquialtera*. Let the lesser dimension here be two; doubled this becomes four; add to this the *sesquialtera* and it becomes six, which is three times the original two. Alternatively, it may be produced as follows. Make the lesser dimension two, and take its *sesquialtera*, to make it three; then double the three: you now have six, which is three times the lesser dimension. The quadruple may be formed by a similar enlargement, by adding the *sesquialtera* and then the *sesquitertia* to the double. This may also be produced by

Book Nine

306

doubling the double, known as the *disdiapason*, in the following manner. Let the lesser dimension be two; double it to produce the *diapason*, which has the proportions four to two; double it again, to produce the *disdiapason*, which has the proportions eight to two. The quadruple may also be constructed by adding the *sesquialtera* and the *sesquitertia* to the double. How to achieve this will soon become clear. For the sake of clarity, take the number two, for example; by the addition of the *sesquialtera* this becomes three, which in turn by the addition of the *sesquitertia* becomes four; the four is then doubled to produce eight. Alternatively, take the number three; by doubling this, you produce six; add a further half, and you have nine; to this add a third, to produce twelve, which is four times the lesser dimension of three.

These numbers which we have reviewed were not employed by architects randomly or indiscriminately, but according to a harmonic relationship. For example, anyone who wanted to build a wall around an *area*[96] with a length, say, double its width would not employ the triple proportion, but only ones made up of doubles. Likewise, in an *area* with a length three times the width, the same proportions are employed that make up the triple, and similarly with the quadruple, where no other proportions are used than its own. Thus in three dimensions, whatever numbers are judged most suitable for the work are drawn from the above list.

In establishing dimensions, there are certain natural relationships that cannot be defined as numbers, but that may be obtained through roots and powers.[97] A root is the side of a squared number, whose power equals the *area* of that square. The cube is a projection of the square. The primary cube, whose root is one, is consecrated to the Godhead, because the cube of one remains one; it is, moreover, said to be the one solid that is particularly stable and that rests equally sure and steadfast on any of its sides. However, if one is not an actual number, but the wellspring of number, which both contains and springs from itself, we might perhaps call two the first number. From it as root you produce an *area* of four, which, if extended upward to a height equal to a side, will form a cube of eight. From this cube is derived the rule for outlines. First of all it provides the side of the cube, called the cube root, which generates an *area* of four and the full cube of eight. From this we derive that line running from the one angle of the *area* to the opposite angle, the straight line dividing the square into two equal parts, for which reason it is called the diameter.[98] The numerical value of this is not known, but it is obviously the square root of eight. Next, there is the diameter of the cube, which we know for sure to be the square root of twelve.[99] Lastly, there is the line in the right-angled triangle[100] whose two shorter sides are joined by a right angle, one being the square root of four, the other the square root of twelve. The third and longest line, which is subtended by the right angle, is the square root of sixteen.[101] Such as we have reviewed, therefore, are the natural relationships between numbers and other quantities to be used in defining the diameter. Each should be employed with the shortest line serving as the width of the *area*, the longest as the length, and the intermediate one as the height. But sometimes these may be modified to suit the building.

Rules for the composition of outlines in three dimensions may be derived from other sources, apart from harmonies and bodies; these we must now discuss. There are several methods of three-dimensional composition that are particularly suitable; these are not only drawn from music and geometry but also arithmetic, and should now be examined. The philosophers have called these "means."[102] Rules for their composition are many and varied, but the wise use three principal methods, whose object is to find, given two other numbers, an intermediate one, which will correspond to the other two by a fixed rule, or, to put it another way, by a family relationship.

In this inquiry there are three dimensions for us to consider. One of these is termed the longest, and another the shortest; the third, the intermediate one, has a common relationship with both, that being the difference between it in the center and the other two. Of the three means principally favored by philosophers, the easiest to find is that which they call the arithmetical. Once two extreme numbers have been set, the longest being eight, for example, and the shortest, say, four, add them together, to produce twelve; divide this into two parts and take one of them: its value will be six. This number is called the arithmetical mean, being equidistant between both extremes, four and eight.

Another type of mean is the geometrical one, which is obtained as follows. Let the shortest dimension be four, for example, and the longest nine, say. Multiply these together to produce thirty-six, whose root, as it is called (that is, the dimension of the side that generates a square of equal size), fills an *area* of thirty-six. The root is therefore six; for six will give an *area* of thirty-six. This geometrical[103] mean is very difficult to ascertain numerically, although it may be found very easily using lines; a subject that I need not discuss here.

The third mean, called "musical," is a little more laborious than the arithmetical, yet numbers define it perfectly. Here the proportion between the shortest and longest dimensions is the same as that between the shortest and the middle, and again the same as that between the middle one and the longest, as in the following example. Let the shorter number be thirty, and the longer be sixty; one is double the other. Take the smallest possible numbers in the double: the first is one, and the other two; add them together to make three. Then take the difference between the longest number, sixty, and the shortest, thirty, and divide it into three equal parts; each of these parts will be ten; and so add one such part to the shorter limit; this equals forty. Such is the desired musical mean, its distance from the greatest number being double that from the shortest, the same proportion as that which we proposed between the greatest and smallest extremes.

By using means like these, whether in the whole building or within its parts, architects have achieved many notable results, too lengthy to mention. And they have employed them principally in establishing the vertical dimension. ◆

7

169v—170

The shapes and sizes for the setting out of columns, of which the ancients distinguished three kinds according to the variations of the human body, are well worth understanding. When they considered man's body, they decided to make columns after its image. Having taken the measurements of a man, they discovered that the width, from one side to the other, was a sixth of the height, while the depth, from navel to kidneys, was a tenth. The commentators of our sacred writings also noted this and judged that the ark built for the Flood was based on the human figure.[104]

The ancients may have built their columns to such dimensions, making some six times the base, others ten times. But that natural sense, innate in the spirit, which allows us, as we have mentioned, to detect *concinnitas*[105] suggested to them that neither the thickness of the one nor the slenderness of the other was suitable, so that they rejected both. They concluded that what they sought lay between the two extremes. They therefore resorted first to arithmetic, added the two together, and then divided the sum in half; by this they established that the number that lay midway between six and ten was eight.[106] This pleased them, and they made a column eight times the width of the base, and called it Ionic.

The Doric style of column,[107] which suited squatter buildings, they established in the same way as the Ionic. They took the lesser of the two previous terms, which was six, and added the intermediate term of the Ionic, which was eight; the sum of this addition was fourteen. This they divided in half, to produce seven. They used this number for Doric columns, to make the width of the base of the shaft one seventh of the length. And again they determined the still more slender variety, which was called the Corinthian, by adding the intermediate Ionic number to the uppermost extreme and dividing the sum in half: the Ionic number being eight, and the uppermost extreme ten, the two together came to eighteen, half of which was nine. Thus they made the length of the Corinthian column nine times the diameter at the base of the shaft, the Ionic eight times, and the Doric seven. So much for this.

Next we must deal with arrangement.[108] Arrangement concerns the site and position of the parts. It is easier to sense when it is badly done than to understand how to do it reasonably. For it relies to a large extent on the judgment Nature instilled in the minds of men, and also has much in common with rules for outlines.[109] Yet as far as this matter is concerned, these are the relevant categories.

When even the smallest parts of a building are set in their proper place, they add charm; but when positioned somewhere strange, ignoble, or inappropriate, they will be devalued if elegant, ruined if they are anything else. Look at Nature's own works: for if a puppy had an ass's ear on its forehead, or if someone had one huge foot, or one hand vast and the other tiny, he would look deformed. Even cattle are not liked, if they have one eye blue and the other black: so natural is it that right should match left exactly.

We must therefore take great care to ensure that even the minutest elements are so arranged in their level, alignment, number, shape, and appearance, that right matches left, top matches bottom, adjacent matches adjacent, and equal matches equal, and that they are an ornament to that body of which they are to be part. Even reliefs and panels, and any other decoration, must be so arranged that they appear to be in their natural and fitting place, as though twinned. The ancients attached such value to this balancing of the parts one against another, that they even tried to match their marble panels exactly in quantity, quality, shape, position, and color.

I have long been an admirer of a particular custom of the ancients in which they displayed outstanding skill: with statues, especially for the pediments of their temples, they took care to ensure that those on one side differed not a whit, either in their lineaments or in their materials, from those opposite. We see two- and four-horse chariots, sculptures of the horses, the commanders, and their lieutenants, so similar to one another that we might claim that here Nature herself has been surpassed; since never in her works do we see so much as one nose identical to another.

About the nature of beauty, therefore, and the parts of which it consists, and about the numbers employed by our ancestors, and the arrangement of outline, enough has been said. ◆

8

170v—172

I will next set out some brief but important suggestions, which must serve as rules not only in the ornamenting and beautifying of a work, but throughout the whole art of building. This also fulfills the promise we made to sum up the matter in a kind of epilogue. First of all, because we have already said that any fault of deformity must be strenuously avoided, let us consider the worst ones possible. Faults are due either to intellect and sense, such as judgment and selection, or to the hand, such as are committed by the craftsman. Errors and faults of intellect and judgment are prior both in their nature and in their timing, and once committed are far less easy to rectify than the rest. Let us therefore begin with them.

It will be a fault to choose a locality that is unhealthy, troubled, infertile, unlucky, gloomy, or plagued and afflicted by problems both obvious and latent. It will also be a fault to outline an *area* that is inappropriate or unsuitable; or to join together members mutually incongruous, which will not respond to the requirements and convenience of the inhabitants; or if you do not cater with sufficient dignity to individual needs, or to those of the entire range of the family, including sons, servants, matrons, girls, both in town and in the country—together with any guest or subject; or if you make anything more generous or mean than necessary, or too exposed or hidden, or too compact or disjointed, or too numerous or few; if there is no refuge from the heat and the cold; or if there are no apartments in which to take recreation and leisure when in good health, or others where those who are poorly and the infirm might be protected from the adversity of climate and season; or if there is insufficient protection or defense from human attack or sudden accident; or if a wall is too slender to bear its own weight and sustain the roof, or much thicker than the strength requires; or if the roofs have eaves that—if I might put it that way—do not agree with one another, and spill their contents within the walls in their course, or if they are set too high or too low; or if the windows are so open that they let in the violent wind, the irksome cold, and the harsh sun, or, on the other hand, so constricted that they produce a hateful murkiness; or if the openings encroach on the bones of the wall; or if the passageways are contorted, and if there is anything foul or obscene that causes offense; or if any other of the requirements that we described in previous books [are neglected].

To continue, the faults of ornament that must be avoided most of all are the same as those in the works of Nature, anything that is distorted, stunted, excessive, or deformed in any way. For if in Nature they are condemned and thought monstrous, what would be said of the architect who composes the parts in an unseemly manner? By "parts" here are meant the elements that define form, such as lines, angles, surfaces, and so on. Therefore they are right who maintain that there can be no defect of appearance more offensive or odious than for the angles, lines, or surfaces to be matched, balanced, and composed in their number, size, and position without due care and consideration. Who would not rebuke severely a person who, unconstrained by circumstance, built a wall that wandered like a worm, now here, now there, with no order, no method, with some sections long and some short, the angles unequal and the composition unshapely, especially if the *area* is obtuse on one side and acute on the other, its method confused, the order disturbed, without forethought or careful plan?

It will also be a fault if the work were built in such a way that even if raised from decent foundations, yet where ornament might be required, it will be impossible to refine it in any way by the additional elegance of such ornament; as do those who think the sole business of the wall is to support the roof, and there is no need to embellish it, in an appropriate and distinctive manner, with noble columns, magnificent statues, graceful paintings, and splendid revetment. Another and related fault occurs if you could at the same expense make everything more beautiful and graceful, and yet you will not invest your every effort in achieving it.

For about the appearance and configuration of a building there is a natural excellence and perfection that stimulates the mind; it is immediately recognized if present, but if absent is even more desired.[110] The eyes are by their nature greedy for beauty and *concinnitas*, and are particularly fastidious and critical in this matter. Nor do I know why they demand what is absent more keenly than they appreciate what is present. For they are continually seeking what would increase the elegance and splendor of objects, and are offended if whatever someone of the greatest application, insight, and diligence might be judged capable of foreseeing and executing is not evident in the skill, labor, and thoroughness of a work. Indeed, they sometimes find it impossible to explain what it is that offends us, apart from the one fact that we have no means of satiating our excessive desire to gaze at the beautiful.

In view of all this, surely it is our duty to strive with all enthusiasm, application, and diligence to make what we build as ornate as possible, especially those buildings which everyone would want to be dignified.[111] Within this group lie public works, and in particular sacred ones: since no man would allow them to be naked of ornament.

It would also be a fault to add to a private work ornament appropriate to a public one, or on the other hand to apply to a public work what is appropriate to a private one, especially if the ornament is too fulsome of its kind; and also if it is not lasting, as with pictures painted on public works in soluble materials, or perishable, rotting ones—public works ought to be indestructible.

One particularly bad fault we see committed by incompetent people, is that they have hardly begun a work when they cover it and cram it with paintings and sculpted statues; as a result these vulnerable items are destroyed before the work has even been completed. The work ought to be constructed naked, and clothed later; let the ornament come last; only then will you have the occasion and opportunity to do it conveniently without any form of hindrance.

But I would have the ornament that you apply be, for the most part, the work of many hands of moderate skill. If something more elegant or refined is wanted, such as statues and tablets like those of Phidias or Zeuxis, objects that are themselves somewhat unusual, set them up in an unusual and dignified place. I do not praise Deioces, the famous king of the Medes, who encircled the city of Ecbatana with seven walls distinguished by their colors; some were purple, some blue, some covered with silver, and some even with gold.[112] I also despise Caligula, who had a stable of marble and a manger of ivory.[113] All that Nero built was overlaid with gold and adorned with gems.[114] Still more outrageous, Eliogabalus strewed his pavements with gold, lamenting that he could not use amber.[115] Such ostentation of wealth, such insanity, is to be censured: human effort and sweat are invested in something of no particular use nor any role in the construction, which no admiration for its ingenuity can ennoble, nor the charm of invention endorse.

To avoid such pitfalls, therefore, I must urge you again and again, before embarking on the work, to weigh up the whole matter on your own and discuss it with experienced advisors. Using scale models, reexamine every part of your proposal two, three, four, seven—up to ten times, taking breaks in between, until from the very roots to the uppermost tile there is nothing, concealed or open, large or small, for which you have not thought out, resolved, and determined, thoroughly and at length, the most handsome and effective position, order, and number.[116] ◆

9

172—173

A prudent man would act like this: he would be forewarned and cautious in approaching the matter; he would study the strength and nature of the ground on which he was to build the house; he would learn from ancient buildings, as well as from indigenous practice and customs, what the climate is, and what materials—stone, sand, lime, and timber, local or imported—would be capable of resisting the weather. He would establish the width and depth of the foundations and footings, and the beginnings of the structure. Then, turning to the wall, he would investigate the necessary size and nature of the skin, infill, bonding, and bones. He would also review what materials were required for the openings, roof, revetment, outside pavement, and internal work. He would plan the position, path, and method for devices to draw away, prevent, and contain noxious and unpleasant waste, employing drains to remove rainwater, ditches to keep the *area* dry, and precautions against damp; he would also employ methods of restraining and overcoming the force, might, and violence of tumbling rocks, crashing waves, and driving wind. In short, he would set out everything, and leave nothing without some form of rule or measure. Although the prime concern of such precautions seems to be structure and use, they are almost all such that if ignored they will lead to considerable deformities.

The following reflections add most to the elegance of ornament. The method of decoration ought to be precise and, above all, unencumbered. The decoration should not be packed together too closely, piled up in a single heap; it should be arranged and positioned in so fitting, correct, and apposite a manner, that any alteration would be felt to disturb the delight of its *concinnitas*. Moreover, make sure that no part of the work is neglected or wanting in craftsmanship; but I would not make everything uniformly ornate and rich in ornament—variety is as useful as quantity. Set some of the outstanding features in the most dignified positions, others in between among the less elegant, and still others among those of little importance. Here you should avoid mixing worthless with precious, large with minute, or tight and narrow with diffuse and expansive; but items varying in importance and not quite similar in character may be skilfully contrasted, so that some display gravity and majesty, others gaiety and festivity.

All should be composed with such method and order that not only do they vie one with another to ennoble the work, but one could not exist on its own, nor maintain its dignity without the other. It would be helpful to include some sections treated with a little less care, so as to make the more refined ones shine by comparison. In each case make sure that the rules for the lineaments are not overturned, which would happen, as I mentioned, if Doric were mixed with Corinthian, Ionic with Doric, and so on.

Each story has appropriate parts, not scattered indiscriminately here and there, but arranged in their own appropriate places. Central elements should sit over central ones, and those equidistant from the center should be balanced. In short, everything should be measured, bonded, and composed by lines and angles, connected, linked, and combined—and that not casually, but according to exact and explicit method; so that one's gaze might flow freely and gently along the cornices, through the recessions, and over the entire interior and exterior face of the work, its every delight heightened by both similarity and contrast; and so that anyone who saw it would imagine that he could never be satiated by the view, but looking at it again and again in admiration, would glance back once more as he departed; and so that however much he searched, he would not find anything in the entire work inconsistent or incongruous or not contributing its every number and dimension to the splendor and grace.

Questions such as these should be projected and debated by the use of models; these models should be employed not only at the outset but also during construction, so that on their advice we may determine in advance what is necessary and make preparations in order to avoid any hesitation, change, or revision after the commencement of the work, and so that we may form a concise overall picture of the whole, in order that appropriate and useful materials might be procured, stored, and made readily available. Such are the considerations to which the architect must apply his wisdom and judgment.

I need not repeat the errors of craftsmanship; but make sure that the workmen make proper use of the plumb line, string, rule, and set square. Build when the season is right, interrupt and postpone the work when it is not; use materials that are pure, unspoiled, unadulterated, solid, sound, convenient, appropriate, and robust, distribute them in their proper place and setting, vertical, horizontal, or aslant, their face exposed or covered, as Nature and use require in each case. ◆

IO

173—175
If the architect is to succeed in planning, preparing, and executing the work properly and professionally, there are a number of considerations that he must not overlook. He must ponder the nature of his task, what skills he might offer, and what impression he would like to give; he must calculate the size of the project and the amount of praise, remuneration, thanks, and even fame he will achieve, or conversely, if he embarks on something without sufficient experience, prudence, or consideration, what contempt and hatred he will receive, and how eloquent, how obvious, patent, and lasting a testimony of his folly he will leave his fellow men.

A great matter is architecture, nor can everyone undertake it. He must be of the greatest ability, the keenest enthusiasm, the highest learning, the widest experience, and, above all, serious, of sound judgment and counsel, who would presume to call himself an architect. The greatest glory in the art of building is to have a good sense of what is appropriate. For to build is a matter of necessity; to build conveniently is the product of both necessity and utility; but to build something praised by the magnificent, yet not rejected by the frugal, is the province only of an artist of experience, wisdom, and thorough deliberation.

Moreover, to make something that appears to be convenient for use, and that can without doubt be afforded and built as projected, is the job not of the architect so much as the workman. But to preconceive and to determine in the mind and with judgment something that will be perfect and complete in its every part is the achievement of such a mind as we seek. Through his intellect he must invent, through experience recognize, through judgment select, through deliberation compose, and through skill effect whatever he undertakes. I maintain that each is based on prudence and mature reflection. But as for other virtues, in him I expect no more humanity, good nature, modesty, honesty, than in any other person given to any form of vocation; for anyone who lacks these qualities, in my opinion, does not deserve to be called a man. But above all he must avoid any frivolity, obstinacy, ostentation, or presumption, and anything that might lose him good will or provoke enmity among his fellow citizens.

Finally, I would have him take the same approach as one might toward the study of letters, where no one would be satisfied until he had read and examined every author, good and bad, who had written anything on the subject in which he was interested. Likewise, wherever there is a work that has received general approval, he should inspect it with great care, record it in drawing, note its numbers, and construct models and examples of it; he should examine and study the order, position, type, and number of the individual parts, especially those employed by the architects of the biggest and most important buildings, who, it might be conjectured, were exceptional men, in that they were given control of so great an expenditure.

Yet he should not mistake the mere bulk of the work for a true achievement (as someone said, it is a great enterprise, that of the farmer);[117] but above all he must inspect each building for the rare and precious artifice it might contain, the result of some considered and recondite artistry or of remarkable invention; and he should make it his practice not to approve of anything that is not wholly elegant or worthy of admiration for its ingenuity; and should he find anything anywhere of which he approves, he should adopt and copy it; yet anything that he considers can be greatly refined, he should use his artistry and imagination to correct and put right; and anything that is otherwise not too bad, he should strive, to the best of his ability, to improve.

The architect should strive constantly to exercise and improve his ability through keen and animated interest in the noble arts; in this way he should gather and store in his mind anything of note, either dispersed and scattered abroad, or hidden in the remotest recesses of Nature, that might lend his works remarkable praise and glory. And he should delight in displaying some product of his own invention that we might find admirable; such as the ingenuity of the person who constructed a sacred building without the use of any metal tool;[118] or the colossus that was transported to Rome, suspended in an upright position, an operation—another interesting fact—in which twenty-four elephants were employed; or he who can cut stone for a labyrinth or a temple from a quarry with astonishing skill, or anything else that might turn out to be unexpectedly useful.

They say that the architects employed by Nero were so prodigal that they would conceive of nothing that did not push to the very limits of human capacity. I cannot approve of them, and much prefer someone who gives the impression that he will always make utility and frugality his primary concern in anything. Even if everything has to be done for the sake of ornament, yet he should furnish the building in such a way that you would not deny that utility was the principal motive. And I would approve of any new invention that incorporates the established rules of ancient buildings, as well as the ingenuity of modern contrivance.

He should therefore develop his ability through practice and experience in any matter that might make some commendable contribution to his knowledge; and he should not think it his only duty to possess that skill without which he could not be what he professes to be, but he should apply himself to gain understanding and appreciation of all the noble arts so far as they are relevant, which understanding should be so ready and so serviceable that he will have no need of any further learning in this field; and he must not abandon his study, nor cool his application, until he feels that he is very close to those who are awarded the highest praise. He should not consider himself satisfied until he has employed every faculty with which art and talent have endowed him, and assimilated everything to the best of his ability so that he attains the highest degree of praise for it.

Of the arts the ones that are useful, even vital, to the architect are painting and mathematics. I am not concerned whether he is versed in any others. I will not hear those who say that an architect ought to be an expert in law, because he must deal with the rules for containing water, establishing boundaries, and proclaiming the intention to build, and with the many other legal constraints encountered during the course of building. Nor do I demand that he should have an exact understanding of the stars, simply because it is best to make libraries face Boreas, and baths the setting sun.[119] Nor do I say that he ought to be a musician, because he must place sounding vases in a theater; nor an orator, to instruct his client on what he proposes to do. Let him have insight, experience, wisdom, and diligence in the matters to be discussed, and he will give an articulate, accurate, and informed account of them, which is the most important thing in oratory.

Yet he should not be inarticulate, nor insensitive to the sound of harmony; and it is enough that he does not build on public land, or on another person's property; that he does not obstruct the light; that he does not transgress the servitudes on rain dripping from the eaves, on watercourses, and on rights of way, except where there is provision; and that he has a sound knowledge of the winds, their direction, and their names;[120] still, I would not criticize him for being better educated. But he should forsake painting and mathematics no more than the poet should ignore tone and meter. Nor do I imagine that a limited knowledge of them is enough.

But I can say this of myself: I have often conceived of projects in the mind that seemed quite commendable at the time; but when I translated them into drawings, I found several errors in the very parts that delighted me most, and quite serious ones; again, when I return to drawings, and measure the dimensions, I recognize and lament my carelessness; finally, when I pass from the drawings to the model, I sometimes notice further mistakes in the individual parts, even over the numbers. For all this I would not expect him to be a Zeuxis in his painting, or a Nichomachus in arithmetic,[121] or an Archimedes in geometry. Let it be enough that he has a grasp of those elements of painting of which we have written;[122] that he has sufficient knowledge of mathematics for the practical and considered application of angles, numbers, and lines, such as that discussed under the topic of weights and the measurements of surfaces and bodies, which some called *podismata* and *embata*.[123] If he combines enthusiasm and diligence with a knowledge of these arts, the architect will achieve favor, wealth, fame for posterity, and glory.

One piece of advice to the architect should not be neglected here. Do not offer your services to everyone who tells you that he is about to build, as do superficial people, those who are consumed with a greed for fame. I wonder if it might not be better to wait until you have been approached several times; people must show their confidence in you if they wish to make use of your advice. What can I gain if I explain my valuable and useful proposals to some completely untutored person, when I will not even receive any recompense for it? If you have gained some benefit from my experience, and this has saved you substantial expense or made a real contribution to your comfort and pleasure, do I not, for heaven's sake, deserve a substantial reward? A wise man will stand on his dignity; save your sound advice or fine drawings[124] for someone who really wants them.

Should you propose to supervise and execute the work, you will hardly be able to avoid having sole responsibility for all the errors and mistakes committed by others, whether through inexperience or neglect. Such projects require zealous, circumspect, and strict clerks of works,[125] to supervise the necessary work with diligence, application, and their constant presence.

I would also take care, wherever possible, to deal only with principal citizens who are generous patrons and enthusiasts of such matters: a work will be devalued by a client who does not have an honorable situation. How much, do you think, will the reputations of those outstanding men, to whom you would prefer to offer your services, contribute to your fame? For my part, I am one—aside from the fact that almost all of us are considered more sensible and better advised when we follow the opinion of the rich than is justified by reality—who would want the architect to have a ready and plentiful supply of all that is necessary for the construction of the work. Very often those of lesser means are not only less able but also less willing to do this. Moreover, it is obvious that of two buildings in which the workmanship, ingenuity, and application of the artists are equal, the one with the more precious and noble constituent materials will appear more graceful by far.

Finally, I advise you never to let greed for glory impel you to embark rashly on anything that is unusual or without precedent. Everything that is to be realized must be weighed and considered in the minutest detail. For to have others' hands execute what you have conceived in your mind is a toilsome business; and who is unaware of the complaints that always greet any proposal to spend someone else's money as you think fit?

I would urge you to avoid completely that common mistake which so often causes grave, much reproved errors in almost every major work; there will always be someone to criticize, instruct, and direct your life, your skill, your manners and practice. The brevity of human life and the scale of the work ensure that scarcely any large building is ever completed by the same man as begins it. While we, the innovative architects who follow, strive by all means to make some alteration, and take pride in it, as a result, something begun well by another is perverted and finished incorrectly. I feel that the original intentions of the author, the product of mature reflection, must be upheld. Those who began the work might have had some motive that escapes you, even though you examine it long and thoroughly, and consider it fairly.

Finally, I advise you not to embark on anything without the advice or, better still, the instruction of the greatest experts; this will help not only the process of construction but also yourself, by shielding you from the attacks of critics.

We have spoken of public and spoken of private buildings, of sacred and profane ones, and of those for use, dignity, or pleasure. It now remains for us to consider how defects that results from the inexperience or carelessness of the architect, from the damage caused by time or man, or from some unfortunate and unforeseen accident might be corrected and restored. Look kindly on these studies, men of learning! ◆

The Tenth and Final Book of Leon Battista Alberti on the Art of Building, in Which the Restoration of Buildings is Described.

If we are to discuss the faults of building and their correction, we ought first to consider the nature and type of the faults that may be corrected by the hand of man; as the physicians maintain that once a disease has been diagnosed it is largely cured.

Of the faults in both public and private buildings, some are integral and inherent, as it were, and the responsibility of the architect, while others result from some outside influence; they may be further divided into those which can be corrected by some form of art or ingenuity and those for which there is no remedy. Those that are the responsibility of the architect we have displayed in the previous book, almost pointing at them with a finger. Some are faults of the mind and others of the hand. Of the mind are displaced, dispersed, or confused selection, compartition, distribution, and outline;[1] of the hand are negligent or sloppy preparation, storage, stacking, bonding, and so on—errors that the unwise and careless may easily commit.

I think that those which result from some outside influence are almost too numerous and varied to list. The saying "Time conquers all things" refers to some of them; the batteries of old age are dangerous and very powerful; the body has no defense against the laws of Nature and must succumb to old age; some think even heavens mortal, because they are a body. We feel the sun burn or the shadows freeze; we feel the power of ice and wind. The working of this engine can crack and crumble even the hardest flint; vast storms will tear away and thrust out huge rocks from the highest cliff, so that they will crash down along with much of the mountain. Then there is damage caused by man. God help me, I sometimes cannot stomach it when I see with what negligence, or to put it more crudely, by what avarice they allow the ruin of things that because of their great nobility the barbarians, the raging enemy have spared; or those which all-conquering, all-ruining time might easily have allowed to stand for ever. Then there are frequent accidents by fire, lightning, earthquakes, battering of waves and floods, and so many irregular, improbable, and incredible things that the prodigious force of Nature can produce, which will mar and upset even the most carefully conceived plan of an architect.

According to Plato, the island of Atlantis has vanished, which was no smaller than Epirus.[2] We learn from the historians that Bura was swallowed up, and Helides swept away by waves;[3] the marsh Tritonis disappeared all at once;[4] while, on the other hand, the Stymphalian marsh near Argos flooded without warning;[5] at Theramene an island suddenly appeared, complete with hot springs; a flame burst out of the sea between Therasia and Thera, which heated the whole ocean for four complete days and made it hot; then an island of twelve stades suddenly appeared, on which the Rhodians built a temple to Neptune their patron;[6] elsewhere so many mice bred that a plague followed;[7] ambassadors were once sent from Spain to the senate to seek help to prevent damage from rabbits.[8] We have collected together many other similar stories in our short work called *Theogenius*.[9]

But not all faults produced by outside influence are irremediable; nor does every mistake made by the architect allow some remedy. Buildings that are utterly misconceived and thoroughly deformed from top to bottom cannot be put right. If a building cannot be improved without changing every line, the best remedy is demolition, to make way for something new. But I shall not pursue this question.

Let us now move on to those structures which the hand can improve, beginning with public ones. Of these the largest and most extensive is the city, or rather, if it can be put another way, the city region. A region in which a negligent architect would found a city might suffer the following faults that could be rectified. It might not be totally safe against an enemy incursion, it might have a harsh and unhealthy climate, or it might not have an abundant supply of basic necessities. Let us deal with these.

The road from Lydia to Cilicia is hemmed in so tightly by mountains that you might think it had been intended as a gate into the region. At the mouth of the pass, which the Greeks call Pylae, there is another road that can be guarded by three armed men, the path being constantly broken by meandering streams flowing out from the base of the mountain.[10] There is a similar pass in Picenum, commonly known as Fossombrone,[11] and many others elsewhere. But approaches that are naturally so well fortified are not to be found everywhere, as you might wish.

It seems possible to imitate Nature in this matter, however, as indeed the prudent ancients have done on frequent occasions. To fortify a region against incursions of the enemy, they would take the following precautions. Here I shall repeat briefly a few relevant extracts taken from the biographies of the most famous princes. Artaxerxes dug a ditch by the Euphrates 60 feet wide and 10 miles long to protect himself from the enemy. Of the Roman emperors, Hadrian constructed a wall in Britain 80 miles long to keep the barbarians off Roman land; on the same island Antonius Pius built a wall of turf; after him Severus cut a trench 122 miles long, which divided the island from one ocean to another.[12] In Margiana, a region of India, Antiochus Soter surrounded the site on which he founded Antioch with a wall 1,500 stades long.[13] Seososis built a wall from Pelusium, on the side of Egypt facing Arabia, to the city of the sun, which was called Thebes, running across deserts, and also having a length of 1,500 stades.[14] Mount Neritos was once linked to Leucadia, but when the isthmus was cut through by the sea, it became an island.[15] Moreover, the Chalcidians and the Boetians built the rampart of Euripus to link Euboea with Boetia, so that they could give each other support.[16] Along the river Oxus Alexander founded six towns not far from one another, so that should there be any threat of sudden enemy incursion, help would be at hand.[17] "Tyrses" is the name for those forts defended by a high rampart, much like castles, and commonly used to prevent enemy incursion.[18] The Persians built weirs on the river Tigris to obstruct it and prevent any ship from sailing upstream with hostile intent; Alexander destroyed them, saying that they were the work of a cowardly mind, and encouraged people instead to trust in their courage and their own strength.[19] Some regions have been flooded with water, to make them like Arabia, which is well defended, they say, from enemy incursion by the marshes and swamps of the Euphrates. Such were the defenses used to fortify a region against the enemy. These same methods were used to make enemy territory more vulnerable.

As for the factors that make a climate hard to bear, we have dealt with these at length in the appropriate place. If you compare them, you will find that they almost all fall into the following categories: either the sun is excessive, the shade harsh, or the wind strong, or harmful vapors emanate from the ground, or the very climate is responsible for some evil.

It is hardly possible—or so it is thought—to improve the climate by any human art; unless there is comfort to be derived from the report that when the gods have been placated or their warnings heeded—as when a nail was driven in by a consul—the most severe pestilence has been cured. There should be some means to protect those who dwell in a town or villa from the sun and wind; although we know of none satisfactory for an entire region, I will not deny that, on the whole, defects carried by the wind, such as harmful vapors arising from the ground, can be put right whenever they occur. I need not pursue the question, then, of whether it is by the force of the sun or through the building up of heat in its innermost bowels, that the earth breathes forth in two different ways: either from exhalations drawn up into the atmosphere and converted by the cold into rain or snow, or by a dry gust that is thought to generate the winds.[20] All we know for certain is that both are exhaled by the earth. Just as with breath from the bodies of animals, we can detect the conditions of the body that exhaled it—foul from a diseased body, sweet from a clear one, and so on (it is sometimes also obvious that although the sweat or breath is itself not the least bit bad, it may be infected by the odor of the garments, and smell foul)—so it is with the earth; for any field that is neither well drenched with water nor quite dry enough, but muddy and somewhere between the two, will give off infected and harmful exhalations and vapors for many reasons.

On this subject it is also relevant that waves feel cold where the sea is deep, and tepid elsewhere. They say the reason for this is that the heat of the sun cannot intrude or penetrate below a certain depth; just as when a fired, red-hot iron is plunged from the fire into a little oil, it will immediately send off clouds of acrid smoke, but will be extinguished and give off none if submerged in a larger quantity.[21]

But let us return to the subject with all the brevity with which we began. Servius writes that a plague developed in a certain town after a nearby marsh had begun to dry out, and that Apollo, when consulted, advised that the marsh be totally dried out.[22] At Tempe there was once a large stagnant lake, which Hercules drained by digging a channel, and, it is said, he burned the Hydra at the place from which the waters gushed, devastating the adjoining town; in this way, once the superfluous moisture had been drained and the ground had hardened, the openings through which the waters sprang were blocked.[23] The Nile once flooded more than usual and left many different creatures bogged down in the mud; as the ground dried, they rotted, causing widespread plague. According to Strabo, the city of Mazaca below Mount Argeo abounds in good water; but if in summer it has nowhere to flow, it leaves the atmosphere unhealthy and pestilential.[24] In the northern parts of Libya and likewise Ethiopia it never rains, and as a result, the lakes often dry out and become muddy; this gives rise to a whole host of locusts and other such animals, which breed on rotting bodies.[25]

Against such stench and decay the two remedies of Hercules may be conveniently employed: dig a channel to prevent the water from stagnating and sullying the ground, then expose it to the sun (for that is how we interpret the fire used by Hercules). It would also help to fill it with stone, earth, or sand. A simple method of using river sand to fill the hollow left by the stagnant water will be dealt with in the appropriate place.[26] Strabo writes that at his time Ravenna was often flooded by the sea, but that although this caused a foul smell, the air was not unhealthy;[27] this is extraordinary, unless—as they say happens in the cities of the Veneto—it is because the surrounding marshes are constantly agitated by the wind and by the action of the sea. They say that precisely the same happens at Alexandria, although the summer floods of the Nile remove the defect.[28]

Nature instructs us therefore about what we ought to do. We should either dry the ground out completely, or soak it with water from a river or the sea, or, finally, excavate down to the wellsprings of water. So much for this. ◆

2

Next we should make allowance for any practical needs that might not be catered for. What these needs are, I do not have to recount at length. They are obvious: food, clothing, shelter, and, above all, water. Thales of Miletus maintained that water was the basis of all things and the generator of human society.[29] Aristobolus says that in ——— he saw more than a thousand villages abandoned because the river Indus had changed its course.[30] I myself would not deny that for animals water is a source of energy and the food of life. And what about plants? And what of the other things that mortals use? I believe that without water all that grows and multiplies on the earth would come to nothing. Cattle are prevented from grazing along the Euphrates, because the luxuriant meadows make them too fat; this is attributed to excess of moisture. The main reason for the vast size of those animals which flourish in the sea is the abundant nourishment to be found in water. Xenophon recalls that as a mark of honor, the Laconian kings were allowed to have a pool of water fronting the gates to their house.[31] In the marriage rites, in purifications, and in almost every other sacred rite it is an ancient custom to use water.

All this shows what importance our ancestors attached to water. Who would deny that a plentiful supply of water is useful and profitable to mankind, when it is never thought sufficient unless there is a generous abundance of it for every manner of use? Let us begin, then, with water, since—as they say—it can be used for good health as for bad.

The Massagetae irrigated a region by cutting several canals from the river Araxes.[32] Because Babylon was built in a dry place, the waters of the Tigris and the Euphrates were channeled there. Semiramis brought water to the city of Ecbatana by cutting a canal 15 feet wide through a mountain 25 stades high. A king of Arabia brought water from the river Corys to an arid and deserted place where he was awaiting Cambyses, along an aqueduct made, if we are to believe everything in Herodotus, out of the hides of bulls.[33] Among the remarkable works in Samos that have drawn admiration was a canal 70 stades in length, running through a mountain 150 orgias high.[34] Also admired was the channel at Megara, a work 20 feet deep that brought springwater into the city. But to my mind the city of Rome easily outstrips all others, in the scale of its works, the ingenuity of its devices, and the quantity of water conveyed.

Rivers and springs are not always available to supply water. Alexander had wells dug along the Persian coast to provide water for his fleet. According to Appian, when Hannibal was being pressed by Scipio, near the city of Ucilla in the middle of the countryside, where there was no water, he provided for his troops by constructing wells.[35] Furthermore, not all water to be found is suitable for human use: apart from the fact that it may be either hot or cold, sweet, acidic, or bitter, perfectly clear or muddy, viscous, oily, or pitch-black, that it may petrify anything immersed in it, that its course may be partly clear and partly turbulent, and that in the same channel it may be sweet in one place, salty or bitter in another, there are other notable variations in the nature and quality of water, which may be either beneficial or harmful to man's health. Let us therefore say something entertaining about the wonderful properties of water.

The waters of Arsinoe, in Armenia, make holes in any garments washed in them.[36] The water of the fountain of Diana at Camarina will not mix with wine.[37] In the town of Debri in the country of the Garamantes there is a stream that is cold during the day and hot at night.[38] The Helbesus, a river in Segesta, suddenly becomes warm halfway along its course.[39] In Epirus there is a sacred spring in which anything alight is extinguished, and anything unlit ignited.[40] In Eleusis there is a spring that spurts out at the sound of a flute.[41] Wandering animals that drink from the Indus change color.[42] Similarly, there is a spring on the coast of the Red Sea whose water will immediately turn their fleece black if drunk by sheep.[43] Any quadruped conceived near certain springs in Laodicea will be born yellow.[44] If a beast drinks the water in the countryside around Gadara, it will lose its hair and hooves. By the Hyrcanian Sea there is a lake that causes anyone who washes there to develop a scab that can be cured only with oil. The water in Susa causes teeth to fall out.[45] By the Gelonian pond there is a spring that causes sterility, and another one that promotes fertility;[46] there is another in Chios that induces stupidity;[47] and there is a place ——— where it causes death by laughter, whether the water is drunk or merely tasted, and another one ——— in which anyone who washes will die.[48] In Nonacris in Arcadia there is another type of water that would be totally pure if it did not contain a corrosive property that makes any metal container impractical.[49] On the other hand, there are waters that promote good health, at Pozzuoli, Siena, Volterra, Bologna, and other famous places throughout Italy. But more surprising is what is said of the water in Corsica: there the water can reset broken bones and provide an antidote for the most virulent poison.[50] And there are waters ——— that inspire ingenuity and providence. Likewise in Corsica there is a spring that is good for the eyes; and should any thief who has denied his crime on oath wash his eyes there, he will go blind.[51] So much for this. Finally, the water found in many places is not completely pure or impure. This is why it is the custom throughout Apulia to collect and store rainwater in cisterns. ◆

3

There are four operations concerning water: finding, channeling, selecting, and storing. These we must deal with. But we must preface this with some recommendations on the use of water in general.

I believe that water can be stored only in a vessel; and I agree with those who for this very reason maintain that the sea is a huge vessel and who, by analogy, interpret the river as a greatly elongated one. They differ since in the latter the water flows and moves of its own accord without any external force, whereas in the first it would remain still quite easily, were it not disturbed by the force of the wind. Here I do not wish to pursue those philosophical questions of whether water seeks the sea as a place of rest, and whether the rays of the moon control the ebb and flow of the sea: such questions are irrelevant to our argument. Rather, let us not neglect what we may see with our own eyes: water tends downward of its nature; it never permits air below itself; it resents being mixed with any body lighter or heavier than itself; it seeps into every cavity of any container into which it is poured; the greater the force with which you constrain it, the more obstinately it struggles and resists; nor does it rest until it has achieved that repose for which it strives with all its might; only when it has found its level is it content; it despises association with anything else; its upper surface is always absolutely level with its rim and outer edges.

I recall something else on the subject of water in Plutarch. He raises the question whether, if a hole is dug into the earth, water gushes in like blood into a wound or seeps in gradually as when milk is produced in a nursing breast. Some maintain that perpetual springs are not poured out, as though contained in some vessel, but that wherever they appear, they are continually generated by air—and not any kind of air, but only that which is suitable for conversion into vapor; that the earth, and especially mountains, act as a porous sponge where any air absorbed is condensed by the cold and compressed; and that there is plenty of evidence for this, not least the fact that great rivers begin, or so it is thought, from great mountains. Others do not fully accept this. For, they claim, there are many rivers of no small size, including the Pyramus (which is even navigable), that spring not from a mountain but in the middle of a plain. For that reason the argument that the earth absorbs moisture from rain, and that the rain, because of its weight and fineness, penetrates and seeps into any gap, is the more plausible; since regions where it very seldom rains may be seen to have no water at all. It is said that the name Libya is derived from Lipygia,[52] because it rarely rains there, and as a result the country is short of water. And who would deny that rivers are fullest where it rains the most?

On this subject it should be noted that when digging a well, one will not find water until the level of the river has been reached. In the Etruscan hilltop town of Volsconium[53] they sank a very deep well—and had descended 220 feet before they reached any vein—until water was found at the same level as the springs gushing out elsewhere from the side of the mountain. You will find that this will almost invariably be the case with hilltop wells.

We know that a sponge will absorb humidity from the air; which provides a scale to measure the dryness or dampness of wind and air. Nor would I deny that it is possible for dew from the night air to be drawn to the dry earth, absorbed of its own accord, and so easily turned into liquid. Yet I am not sure where my true opinion lies: I find many different opinions on this subject among writers, and anyone examining this issue will encounter many different experiences.

It is agreed that springs often will erupt suddenly because of an earthquake, or of their own accord, then keep going for a long time; and that they may fail at different times, some disappearing in the summer, others in winter;

and after they have run dry, they may well up again with much water; and springs are not limited to land, but fresh water may even well up in the middle of the sea. It is said that water may also be drawn from plants: in an island of the archipelago called the Fortunate Isles,[54] there grow cane as tall as trees; from the black ones a bitter juice is extracted, and from the white there oozes pure water that is very good to drink. Strabo, a rather serious author, tells an extraordinary tale of the Armenian mountains: he claims to have seen wormlike animals that are hatched in the middle of the snow there and are full of a liquid that is very good to drink.[55] At Fiesole, and also Urbino, water is found as soon as you dig, despite the fact that they are hilltop cities: this is because the ground is rocky, the stone being compacted with clay. Also some clods of earth contain little pockets of the purest water within their lining.

From this it may be inferred that Nature is not at all easy to understand and very perplexing. ◆

4

180v—182

I return to the subject. There are signs for finding hidden water. They will be given by the shape and appearance of the countryside and the nature of the ground where you are looking for water; and there are others that a man can find if he uses his ingenuity. Such is Nature, that any place that is full of twisted valleys or caves seems to be intended as a vessel for water. Wherever there is much sun, little or no water will be found, because its rays burn up all moisture; and if some is found on a plain, it tends to be heavy, sluggish, and salty. On the north side of a mountain, wherever there is dense shade, water will always be available. Mountains that are covered with snow for a long time will be full of moisture. I have noticed that mountains which have flat meadows at their summits are never short of water. You will find that practically every river has its source in some such place. I also notice that springs are to be found only where they have sound and solid ground beneath and around them, or some flat land above, or where they are covered with thin or loose soil; if you consider the matter, you will realize that water appears where it spills out as though through a crack in the side of the vessel that contains it. Thus the densest soil has little water, and what there is lies only at the top, whereas looser earth is moister and has water only at the bottom.

According to Pliny, when woods are cut down, springs will sometimes arise. Flavius reports that when Moses was wandering through the desert and in danger of dying of thirst, he discovered veins of water by studying where the ground was grassy.[56] While Aemilius had his army near Mount Olympus in great difficulty because of a shortage of water, he found it where the trees were greenest.[57] A young maiden once showed soldiers who were looking for water a vein by the Collatian Way, which they then dug out to expose a plentiful spring; they built a chapel by the spring with a picture to commemorate the event.[58]

If the earth marks easily with footprints or adheres to the foot, it indicates that water is beneath. Another indication of water below ground is when plants grow or flourish there that like waters or are produced by them, such as willow, rushes, reeds, ivy, and other plants that could not reach any great size without a good deal of water for nourishment.[59] Where the ground supports leafy vines or, in particular, trees such as dwarf-elder, trefoil, and brambles, there will be good soil and veins of fresh water, according to Columella.[60] Likewise, an abundance of frogs or earthworms, mosquitoes, and clouds of gnats indicate the presence of water directly below where they are swarming.

Such are the ingenious devices for investigating these matters. Those who have researched them have observed that the whole crust of the earth, and mountains in particular, consists of pagelike strata, some denser, some more rarefied, some thicker, some thinner. And they have observed that in mountains these strata are heaped and piled up one above the other; so that on the outside their layers and joints run horizontally from right to left, but on the inside the strata slope toward the center of the mountain, and the entire outer surface is inclined equally, although the lines do not continue uninterrupted. About every hundred feet the strata are cut off abruptly by a diagonal line, to form steps; then by a similar gradation the layers run in continuous steps from either side of the mountain to the very center.

Once they had noted this, those of sharp wit realized quickly that water, whether rising or falling as rain, is collected in the spaces between the different strata or leaves of rock, making the inside of the mountain moist. They therefore deduced that by boring into the mountain they would find the hidden water, especially where the downward steps and the lines between the layers meet; the most obvious place is where the sinews of the mountain join, one to another, to form pockets.

What is more, they have established that the different strata vary in their capacity to hold and yield water.[61] There is almost no red rock to be found that does not contain water, although it is usually deceptive, because the water escapes along gaps between the veins common in this kind of stone; flint is thoroughly moist and tough, and at the base of a mountain, where it is cracked and very sharp, it yields water readily. Thin soil also gives out plenty of water, although it has a bad taste; male sand and the variety known as carbuncular are reliable sources of continuous, healthy water; the opposite is true of clay: because of its high density it will not hold water itself, although it traps any that comes from elsewhere; water found in sand is scarce, muddy, and low down; water given out by potter's clay is thin, but fresher than the rest; that of tufa is cooler; that of black stone more

limpid; with gravel, if it is loose, you cannot be certain of finding any water, but with compact gravel, once you begin to dig deep, it is not at all unlikely that you will find some; in either case, any water found tastes good.

Another method of locating underground veins of water has been handed down to us. It is done as follows. On a clear morning at daybreak lie down with your chin to the ground; then explore the immediate region that surrounds you. Wherever you see vapor forming wisps in the air, like a man's breath in the cold of winter, there you know you will find water.[62] But to be more certain, dig a trench there, four cubits deep and wide; around sunset, place in it a piece of pottery taken straight from the kiln, or a fleece of fresh wool, or a vase of unbaked earthenware or simple brass, upturned and anointed with oil; then lay planks over the trench and cover them with earth. The following day, if the pottery has become heavier, the wool damp, or the earthenware wet, or if water droplets cling to the vase, or again if a lamp left burning inside has consumed less oil, or if a fire lit there produces a lot of smoke, then certainly water is there.

What season is best for these tests has not been adequately explained, although in other authors I read the following: during the Dog Star the earth and the bodies of animals become very moist, so that at that time trees produce much humor under their bark; at the same period men suffer from loose bowels, and the excessive moisture in the body often causes fever; also at that time more water appears than is usual. Theophrastus attributes this to the fact that Auster blows then, a wind naturally humid and misty.[63] Aristotle maintained that the vapors emitted by the earth were caused by the pressure of the internal fire stirred up within its bowels.[64] If this is so, the best time for these tests would be when those fires are strongest, or under least pressure from excessive moisture, or when the earth itself is not too dry and burnt. I myself would prefer springtime if the place is dry, or in a shadier one, the autumn.

Encouraged by these signs, let us therefore begin to dig. ◆

5

182—182v

There are two kinds of excavation: the vertical well and the elongated channel. Digging a well is always hazardous: bad gases may rise, or the sides may fall in. In antiquity, slaves convicted of an offense were sent to the metal mines, where they soon died from the pestilential air. Against gas we are advised to take the following precautions. Keep the air ventilated and in continual motion, and use lamps, so that if there happens to be any light gas the flame will burn it, but if it is denser, the diggers will be able to protect themselves against the noxious danger and escape in time: for as the gas builds up, it will extinguish the flame. But if there are any heavy and persistent gases, they advise us to sink vents to the right- and left-hand sides, to give the noxious gases freedom to breathe.[65]

Against the danger of collapse construct your work as follows. At ground level, where you intend to build your well, lay a cornice of marble or some other very strong material, the same width as your desired well. This must serve as the base for your work.[66] On this raise the sides of the well to a height of three cubits and allow them to dry. Once they are dry, dig out the inside of the well, removing all the earth. As a result, the more you dig, the more this walled structure will sink, tending downward. Then, by gradually enlarging both hole and structure together, you will safely reach the depth you desire. Some prefer to build without plaster, so as not to obstruct the veins of water. Others recommend a triple wall, to purify the water as it seeps into the bottom.

The location of the well is particularly important. The earth is made up of different strata, one above the other, and sometimes rainwater is trapped at the first dense layer it reaches below the topsoil. This we should reject as being impure. On the other hand, sometimes when water has been found, it will disappear and vanish before your eyes, if you attempt to excavate any further. This is because you are digging through the base of the vessel in which it is contained. For this reason some prefer to make the base of the well as follows: as if they were constructing barrels, they line the inside of the excavated well with a double wall of wooden rings and panels, and allow a gap of one cubit to separate the two layers; into this gap they pour a paste of coarse gravel, or preferably chips of flint and marble, mixed with lime; they give the work between the two linings six months to dry out and harden. This acts as a complete vessel, through the base of which, and from nowhere else, the lightest and purest water wells up and flows in.

If you are making a conduit, take the same precautions against gases that we mentioned for excavations. To prevent its collapsing, the roof should be fortified with props and even vaulted. There should be frequent vents along the conduit, some vertical, others at an angle—partly to prevent the buildup of noxious gases, but mainly to open a clearer path for the removal of whatever is dug and cut away during construction.

When you are looking for water, if the ground does not grow ever damper and the tools easier to work with as you descend, your hopes of finding any will be dashed. ◆

Once water has been discovered, I would not let it be put to indiscriminate use; but since a city requires a large amount of water not only for drinking but also for washing, for gardens, tanners and fullers, and drains, and—this is very important—in case of a sudden outbreak of fire, the best should be reserved for drinking, and the remainder distributed according to need.

Theophrastus maintains that the colder the water, the better it is for plants.[67] And it is obvious that muddy and turbid water, especially if it runs off fertile soil, enriches the land. Horses do not like very clear water; yet on slimy and warm water they grow fat. Fullers prize extremely hard water. From physicians I hear that water is vital for the preservation of human life in two ways—it quenches thirst and also acts as a sort of vehicle to convey the nutrients extracted from food into the veins, where the juice is then purified and heated before being transfused into the members. Thirst they call a craving for liquid, and particularly for cold liquid. And cold water, especially when drunk after a meal, is supposed to fortify the stomach of the healthy. But if only slightly too cold, it will induce stupor even in the fit, make the bowels rumble and the nerves shake, and by its rawness extinguish the digestive process.

The river Oxus, according to ———, is very unhealthy to drink, because it is always turbulent.[68] The people of Rome are gripped by a heavy fever caused by the inconsistent climate, the nocturnal vapors arising from the river, and the afternoon winds; for throughout the summer, at the ninth hour of the day,[69] when the body is at its most heated, there blows a chilling breeze that numbs the veins. But to my mind the Tiber, with its constantly turbid water, which is drunk by almost everyone, is the chief cause of fever and other bad ailments. On this point I should mention that the ancient physicians prescribed squill vinegar and laxative as a cure for the Roman fever.[70] To return to the argument.

Let us inquire what is the best type of water. Celsus, the physician, said of water that the lightest was rainwater, the second springwater, the third river water, the fourth well water, and in the last place melted snow or ice.[71] Heavier still was lake water, but the worst of all was that of a marsh. The city of Mazaca, below Mount Argo, is rich with water that is otherwise good; but in summer, having nowhere to flow, it becomes unhealthy and pestilential.[72]

All experts are of the opinion that water, by its very nature, is not a compound body but a simple element, which is cold and wet. The best water, then, we might call that whose nature contains nothing foreign, nothing bad. For this reason, unless it is very pure, uncontaminated by any viscous element, and free of all defect in taste or smell, it will undoubtedly be very detrimental to health, by choking the internal respiratory tracts, so to speak, making the veins turbid, and stifling the spirit and the ministers of life. Hence the saying: rainwater, being composed of the finest vapors, is deservedly called the best, provided it does not suffer the ready defect of growing corrupt and rank when stored, and so becoming thicker and causing constipation. Some believe that this is because rainwater is drawn up into the clouds from a mixture of so many different places, such as the sea, into which every kind of spring flows; and that nothing is more ready or prone to corrupt than something confused and made up of different elements:[73] the juice [for example] of several varieties of grape all mixed into one is impatient of old age. There was an ancient law among the Hebrews that no one should sow any seed that had not been selected and was not of the same variety, showing that Nature quite abhorred an amalgam of different elements. Yet those who follow Aristotle take a different view, and believe that the vapors are drawn up from the earth into a cold region of the sky, and that first this cold compresses them into a form of fog, and that later they fall as drops of rain.[74]

According to Theophrastus, cultivated trees are more prone to disease than uncultivated ones: the latter, being tough and wild, have a stronger resistance to external influences, whereas the delicacy of the former gives them little defense, because they have been trained to be yielding and tame.[75] The same may be said of water: the more refined you make it (to use his words), the more susceptible it is. Hence they say that water that has been boiled or softened by fire is quicker to cool and quicker to heat up again. But enough about rain.

As a second choice, who would not prefer springwater? But those who prefer river water to springwater argue thus: how might we describe a river, other than as several springs flowing into a single channel, its water matured by sun, movement, and wind? They argue that a well is also a spring, only deeper. But if we do not deny that the rays of the sun improve water, it is obvious which is harsher; unless we accept that there is some fiery spirit in the bowels of the earth, which heats up the water underground. Well water, according to Aristotle, warms up after midday in summer.[76] Others maintain that in summer well water is not actually cold, although it appears to be so, relative to the hot air. And, contrary to established popular belief, it is noticeable that water recently drawn leaves no droplet on the glass, unless the glass is not fully polished or is smeared with grease.

Now, of the first principles of which everything exists, there are two, heat and cold, that the Pythagoreans call male. The nature and power of heat is to penetrate, dissolve, break up, to remove and absorb moisture; that of cold is to compress, tighten, harden, and solidify. To some extent, and especially with water, they both have the same effect, provided they are extreme and constant enough; that is, they both consume the delicate parts at almost the same rate, leading to dryness and scorching—hence we say that trees are burnt by both heat and cold, because when the more delicate parts are consumed and destroyed by frost or sun, we notice that the wood is left coarse and parched. Thus in the same way sun makes water viscous and frost leaves it ashlike.

Among the best waters there are further differences. With water from the sky, the season, hour of the day, type of rain, and wind direction at the time of collection are of particular importance, as are the location and duration of its storage. Rain falling after the winter solstice is considered the heaviest. That collected during winter is said to be sweeter than that collected during the summer. Rain immediately after the Dog Star is bitter and unhealthy, because it contains particles of burnt earth; earth is also said to taste bitter for the same reason, that it is burnt by the sun. Thus some prefer to collect rain from a roof rather than from the ground, and consider rain collected on the roof unhealthy if it is diluted with any previous rain.

The naturalists who wrote in Punic claimed that rain that falls during summer and especially during a thunderstorm is impure and unhealthy because of its saltiness. Theophrastus thought nighttime better than daytime rain.[77] Of this the healthiest is thought to be that which falls while Aquilo blows. Columella claims that rainwater will not go bad if it is drawn down earthenware pipes into a covered cistern, as it tends to grow infected when it is in the open and exposed to the sun.[78] Water also becomes defective if stored in a wooden vessel.

There are differences in springwater, too. Hippocrates considers that which comes from the roots of the foothills to be the best.[79] As for springs, the ancients reserved the first place among the best for those which faced north, or toward sunrise during the equinox; they consigned to the last place any spring facing south. Next best they thought those which faced the winter sunset; nor did they totally reject those facing west.

Any place usually moist from a heavy fine dew produces very pleasant water. Dew falls only in places with still, pure, and temperate climates. Theophrastus thought that water could be affected by the earth, just as the fruit of every vine or tree is flavored by the earth that nourishes it and by anything in contact with its roots.[80] The ancients maintained that there were as many kinds of wine as countries on the globe in which the vine was planted. The wine of Padua, according to Pliny, tastes of willow, because there they train the vine from willows.[81] Cato instructs us to treat the vine with the herb hellebore, by laying bundles of it at its roots during hoeing, to make a safe laxative.[82] This is why the ancients preferred water that burst out from tough rock to that which oozed through mud. But the best of all, they thought, was that which trickled out from the kind of ground that, if mixed with water in a basin until it becomes murky, settles as soon as you stop stirring, leaving the water not entirely impure in color, flavor, and smell. For this same reason Columella thought that the best water was that which tumbled down headlong through rocks, because it would not be contaminated by any foreign substance.[83]

But I do not recommend all the water that runs through rocks. It can grow corrupt by running along a hidden channel with very deep and shady banks; yet if it runs along an open riverbed, I agree with Aristotle: the heat of the sun will consume the lighter part of the water and leave it thicker.

Writers have preferred the river Nile to all others for the following reasons: it has a long course; it cuts through earth that is very clean, unaffected by decomposing matter and uncontaminated by harmful fluid; it flows north; and its channel is full and clear. Indeed it cannot be denied that waters that have a long and slow course are softened by movement, refined by exertion, and thereby purified, having jettisoned all their filth in the course of their journey.

Again, the ancients all agree that not only does water, as we have just mentioned, assume the characteristics of the earth in which it is contained, as though in the lap of a mother, but it may also be affected by the soil through which it flows, and even by the juice of the plants that it washes. The main reason for this is not that it makes direct contact as it flows past, but that its juices mingle with the earth in which the pestilential plant grows. Hence the saying that a bad plant makes water unhealthy. Sometimes you will find that the rain has a bad smell, and perhaps even a bitter taste. This, they say, is caused by some infection in the place where the moisture first evaporated. They also say that the juices of the land, when they have undergone a natural digestion and maturing, leave everything with which they mix sweet, while that which is undigested leaves it bitter.

Waters that run north are preferred because they are cooler, since they flee the rays of the sun and are illuminated without being burnt by them. The opposite happens with those which run south; it is as though they are throwing themselves at the flames. Aristotle said that Boreas,[84] being cold, blunts the fiery spirit with which bodies are naturally composed, and forces it inward, never to escape, leaving the water warm; and it is certain that this spirit is dissipated by the heat of the sun.

Wells and springs are unable to give off vapor if they are under cover, so Servius reports on the advice of experts.[85] The reason for this is that the fine wisp emitted is unable to pierce, penetrate, or clear the dense, heavy air contained by the wall and roof; whereas under the open sky it breathes more freely, and is exhaled and purified. This is why open wells are preferred to those housed in buildings. Otherwise, wells have almost exactly the same requirements as springs.

Wells and springs are related, and differ only in the way they flow, although you will not infrequently find a well whose veins move with an abundant flow; and they say that no continual source can ever be motionless (and stagnant water is unhealthy, wherever it is found). In fact, if you draw a large amount of water every hour from a well, it should work exactly like a deep spring. On the other hand, if the spring does not overflow but is quite still, it will be more like a shallow well than a spring. Some think that there can never be any water perpetual and continuous, as the expression goes, that is not influenced by the flow of some nearby river or torrent. I myself agree with this.

Lawyers distinguish between a lake and a pond in that the water of a lake is replenished continually, whereas that of a pond is seasonal and collected during the winter.[86] There are three kinds of lakes: the first I would call stationary, content with its own waters, and never overflowing; the second pours forth its water, to create a river; the third receives water from various sources and discharges into a river. The first has the character of a pond, the second is like a spring, and the third, unless I am mistaken, is like a river widening at one point. I do not need to repeat, therefore, what we said about the spring and the river.[87]

The following should be added: waters of every kind, if covered, will be colder and clearer, but harsher than those exposed to sunshine; on the other hand, any that are baked by excessive sun will become salty and sluggish. In either case depth is an advantage: in the latter it helps resist the raging heat, in the former the freezing cold.

Finally, the pond is not always thought a curse in every respect; for wherever eels are plentiful, the water is considered not altogether useless. The worst sort of stagnant water is said to be that which supports leeches; which has a layer of scum on top; which gives off a nauseating smell; which is black or livid in color; which remains thick even after it has been put into a vessel; which is slimy, heavy, or sluggish; or which, when used for washing your hands, takes a long time to dry.

To sum up all that has been said about water: it should be very light, limpid, fine, and clear. To this should be added those comments which we touched on in the first book.[88] Another useful test for water that otherwise conforms to our requirements is to examine whether cattle who have drunk or washed there for several months have strong limbs and are in good overall condition, and to inspect the condition of their livers to establish whether they are healthy. For they say that all that is harmful works through the passage of time, and that the worst is that which is felt last.[89] ◆

7

186—189

Once water has been discovered and its quality approved, provision must be made to convey it in the best manner and to use it most appropriately. There are two ways of conveying water: either by channeling it along a watercourse or forcing it down pipes. In either case the water will not move unless the place to which it is conveyed is lower than its starting point. But there is a difference in that channeled water must always flow downward, whereas piped water may rise for a portion of its journey. This we must discuss; but first there are some relevant considerations that ought to be mentioned.

Those who have studied the matter declare that the earth is spherical, although much of it is wrinkled by mountains and much of it clothed by sea; yet with a globe so large the roughness is scarcely noticed: it is like an egg that, although not smooth, has projections that seem minute and insignificant when compared to the size of its circumference. It is known that the earth is ——— stades in circumference;[90] whereas no mountain or sea is to be found with a height or depth of more than fifteen thousand cubits, except the Caucasus, whose summit is lit by the sun until the third hour of the night.[91] The mountain Cillene is the highest in Arcadia,[92] whose height is said not to exceed twenty stades. And the sea, in their opinion, should be thought of as a light sprinkling, like summer dew on an apple.

Some jest that the Maker of the world used the hollow of the sea as the original mold for casting the mountains. On this subject geometers add that if a straight line tangential to the globe is extended one mile from its point of contact, at its end the distance between the line and the circumference of the earth will not exceed ten inches; and that therefore water in a channel will not move, but stagnate, unless it descends a whole foot every eight stades from the point where the bank was first cut. (The lawyers call this point *incile*, "sluice,"[93] after the incision made in the rock or earth to allow the water to flow.) But a fall steeper than six feet every eight stades is thought to make the current too fast for ships.[94]

To find out whether the surface of the excavated channel descends from the sluice, and to what extent, an instrument and a useful method have been devised. The inexpert workman will place a ball in the ditch to ascertain this; if it rolls, he will consider it steep enough.[95] The expert will employ a level, set square, and any other such instrument for determining a right angle. The technique is somewhat less obvious, but I shall explain it only in so far as it is fully relevant. It involves taking certain sights, which we shall call "points."

If the place where the water is to flow is flat and clear, there are two methods of taking levels. Set up fixed staffs and markers either at shorter or at longer intervals. The nearer the extreme points of the intervals, the less the line of sight deviates from the curve of the earth; but the farther they are apart, the more the curve of the earth and the ground will appear to slope away from the level. By this method it may be observed that there is a fall of ten inches in every mile.

But if the place is not flat and clear, and broken by mounds, there are two ways of measuring it: one establishes the levels from the sluice, the other

from the outlet. By "outlet" I refer to the intended destination of the water, where it is to be discharged or to be put to a particular use. These heights are established by taking measurements in steps. I call them steps because they resemble those by which we ascend to the temple. One of these is the line of the ray extending from the eye of the observer to a point of equal height, which is fixed by means of a level and set square; the other line is that which falls vertically from the eye of the surveyor to his feet. Use these steps to mark out on the vertical the difference between one height and another, taking the vertical either from the sluice or from the outlet.

The other method is to draw a line from the sluice to the top of the mound that is causing the obstruction, and from there, further lines to the outlet; the sizes of their respective angles are determined by the rules of geometry. But this method is difficult to grasp, and not totally reliable in practice: over a large distance any error, however small, made by the eye of the surveyor in measuring the angle will be of great consequence.

Following the same principle there is a device, which we shall now describe, that provides a very efficient means of establishing direction, should it be necessary to channel water into a town by cutting through a mountain. It is done as follows.

At the top of the mountain, where there is a view of both the sluice and the outlet, mark out, on a level surface, a circle ten feet in diameter: this circle is called the horizon. In the center of the circle set a staff, so that it stands vertical. This done, the director of the works will walk round the outside of the circle until he finds the position where his line of sight, when looking toward one of the two ends of the channel, aligns itself with the base of the staff positioned in the middle. Having established and marked this spot on the circular horizon, the workman traces this line of direction onto the circle, so that it cuts the circumference on either side. This line will obviously be the diameter of that circle, because it runs straight through the center, cutting both sides of the circumference. If this is extended in a straight line away from the point of vision, and one end meets the sluice and the other

Method for measuring levels.

Method for measuring levels.

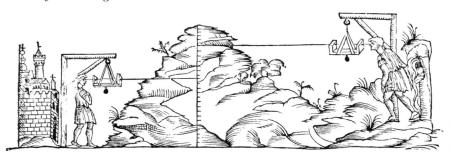

the outlet, its path will show that the course of the water will be straight; if it does not meet them, but the diameter aligned with the sluice has a different direction from the diameter aligned with the outlet, then the mutual intersection of their lines at the staff in the center will show the difference in their directions. This circle is very useful for marking and drawing maps of a city or province, and also for plotting underground conduits. But of this elsewhere.[96]

Whatever the size of the water channel, whether it is a small one for drinking water or a large one for the use of shipping, the same instructions apply. But the method of construction varies according to the greater or smaller volume of water. Let us therefore return to the subject of drinking water, something we have already begun, and then, in due course, deal with water for navigation.

A channel is either built up or constructed. There are two kinds of trench, one running flat over the countryside, the other through the center of a hill and called a tunnel. In each case, wherever you find stone, tufa, dense clay, or any other material that does not absorb water, there will be no need to build anything; but wherever the bottom or walls are not solid, then some masonry will be necessary. Conduits running through the bowels of the earth come under the rules listed above. With tunnels, air shafts should be sunk every hundred feet, and their sides should be reinforced, wherever the earth is not strong enough.[97]

In Marsian country, by the outlet to Lake Fucino, we have seen elegantly built wells of fired brick, of an incredible depth.[98] Four hundred and forty-one years after the foundation of the city, there was still not a single aqueduct in Rome; later hanging rivers came to be introduced.[99] And at one time it is said that there were ———— aqueducts in Rome, so that every house had an abundant supply of water.[100] At first, however, they began to build their conduits underground. These have some advantages: being hidden away, they were better protected from injury; and the tunnels, exposed to neither frost nor heat, provided water that was most acceptable and cool; nor could they be cut off easily by enemy action. Later, for delight, they began to build arched structures, in some places up to 120 feet high and stretching for up to 60 miles, in order to provide leaping waters for their garden fountains and baths. These also had their advantages: in Trastevere and elsewhere they milled their corn by means of an aqueduct (when this was destroyed by the enemy, they resorted to milling their corn on the Tiber aboard rafts);[101] also, the abundance of water meant that the city was cleaner and purer in its appearance and character. Architects also added mechanisms that served the citizens by revealing the time and the weather, with the most delightful movement: at the outlets to the aqueducts could be seen small figurines of brass that moved, or images to represent the games or the pomp of a triumph; and musical organs could be heard, and the sonorous and sweet accord[102] of voices, put in motion by the water.[103]

These artificial channels were covered with a slightly thicker vault, to prevent the water from being heated by the sun, and on the inside they were faced with a revetment such as we described for the pavement, to a depth of no less than six inches.

The parts of the artificial channel were as follows. At the *incile*, or sluice, was the barrier of the *septum*, or sluice gate; then along its length were inserted *castella*, or reservoirs; where a rise in ground was encountered, a *specus* or cistern was dug; at the very end by the outlet, a *calix*, or tap, was added. Such was their legal definition:[104] a channel is an elongated hollow; the *septa* are situated at the *incile* to control the flow of water; the *castella* are reservoirs for distributing public water; the *specus* is a place with deep banks, where the water is visible below; the *calix* is the very end of the watercourse, where the water is discharged.

All these must be built of solid masonry, with a thoroughly stable base, and a sound and reliable revetment. At the mouth of the sluice there should be a gate, which may be shut at will to restrict the turgid flow and to allow any collapsed section of the wall to be repaired without hindrance from water.

Beneath should be fixed a brass grate to clear the water, as it flows in, of all leaves, branches, and other debris.

One hundred cubits from the sluice gate there should be a reservoir, and 100 cubits farther either another reservoir or an underground cistern should be inserted, 20 feet wide, 30 feet long, and 15 feet deeper than the bed of the channel. This will allow any earth that has slipped into the water and been caught up by the flow to find a place of rest and immediately settle, purifying what flows on down the channel.

The *calix* controls the amount of water discharged, according to the rate of flow and the size of the piping that discharges it. The more plentiful and rapid is the supply of water, the less obstructed its course and the higher the pressure, the greater will be the discharge of water; whereas, if the flow is sluggish, the quantity discharged will be reduced. The amount will increase by having the piping level and straight. It is well known that the piping through which water flows is worn down by the passing of water, so to speak, and that no metal has a greater resistance than gold. So much for the channeling of water through excavated and artificial channels.

Water may also be conveyed in lead piping or, better still, earthenware tubes; for physicians maintain that lead causes scouring of the intestines; brass has the same defect. Experts tell us that whatever we eat or drink tastes better if stored in earthenware vessels, claiming that the natural place of rest for water and other products of the earth is surely the earth itself. Wooden piping eventually gives water an unpleasant color and taste. Piping should be very strong. Brass vessels cause elephantiasis,[105] cancer, and disorders of the liver and spleen.

The internal diameter of the pipe should be no less than four times the thickness of its wall. Tubes should slot one into the other with fitted joints. They should be smeared with quicklime mixed with oil and should be reinforced with a strong casing and further buttressed by a heavy weight of masonry, especially where the watercourse bends, or where it rises up again after a dip, or where the constriction of a bend causes a reversal in the flow. For the pipes could easily be ruined or crushed by the pressure of the water and by the weight and force of its current. To avoid this danger, the experts would use tough stone, and in particular a red variety, with a hole bored through for this purpose. We have seen pieces of marble, more than twelve feet in length, through which a hole one palm wide has been bored from top to bottom; we surmise, by conjecture and from studying the marking of the stone itself, that this was done using a rotating brass tube and sand.

To avoid the danger of any breakage, reduce the speed of the water not with sharp[106] bends, but with gentle curves, so that the water veers now to the right, now to the left, now up, now down. To this a form of sluice or reservoir may be added, to purify the water and to locate more easily any fault that may require repair. The reservoir should not be sited at the bottom of a valley, nor where pressure forces the water to ascend, but where the level remains constant.[107]

Should it be necessary to take the conduit across a pond or lake, this is how to do it at little expense. Take some oak timbers, and down the length of each cut a channel, of the same width and depth as the pipe; insert the pipe in that channel, set it with lime, and hold it firm with brass cramps; after that, lay a raft in a straight line across the lake, and link and bind together the ends of the posts as follows. Take some lead tubing, the same thickness as the pipes, and long enough for them to bend properly where necessary. Insert these tubes (as I might call them) into the pipe, smear them with lime mixed with oil, and bind them with bronze fastenings; join the posts together like this, and lay them out on top of the rafts until they stretch from one bank to the other, with the ends of the work resting on either bank on dry land. Then, starting where the lake is deepest, with the help of ropes, lower the timber posts containing the pipes into the lake, gradually and evenly, along with all their accompanying trappings. In this way the lead tubing will bend as required and the post construction will sit happily on the bottom of the lake.[108]

Once the conduit is ready, insert some ash before you let in water for the first time, so as to grout any joints that might not have been fully stopped.[109] And let in the water gradually, so that it does not gush in and trap air in the piping. It is remarkable how powerful Nature is, when air trapped like this is forced into a narrow passage. I am told by physicians that a man's shinbone was shattered by eruptions of trapped gas. Hydraulic engineers can force water to leap high out of a vessel, by trapping an air pocket between two columns of water. ◆

8

189—190v

I now come to cisterns. A cistern is a large container, not unlike a *castellum*. Its bed and all its walls must therefore be compact, solid, and firm. There are two kinds of cistern: one for drinking water, and the other for such other uses as extinguishing a fire. The former, in keeping with the ancient tradition by which silverware is known as *escarium* [eating ware], we shall call *potorium* [drinking cistern];[110] the latter, because it is intended solely for containing water for different purposes and is judged by its capacity, we shall call a *capaquia* [water holder]. With the drinking cistern it is particularly important that the water is pure. With both cisterns care must be taken that the water is correctly admitted, stored, and discharged for use.

Obviously, conduits can be used to convey river- or springwater to the cistern; also it is common practice to collect rainwater from a roof or courtyard.[111] But I am most impressed by the ingenuity of the architect who cut a reservoir, ten feet deep, into a huge, naked rock projecting from the top of a hill, which, like a circular crown, received all the rain falling on the naked mountain peak. Lower down, on the plain under the hill, he built a water-holder out of brick and lime, open on all sides, with a depth of 30 feet and a width and length of 40; into this he piped water from the upper reservoir along an underground conduit, the reservoir being much higher than the roof of the water-holder.

If you cover the bottom of your cistern with a layer of sharp gravel or well-washed male river sand, or, better still, do it to a certain level—say, three feet—it will provide pure, natural, fresh water; the deeper the layer, the more limpid the water.

Cisterns sometimes leak because the *capaquia* is poorly constructed or cracked. Sometimes the water itself becomes foul. And it is certainly very difficult to keep water captive behind walls, unless the structure is very strong, especially if it is built in "ordinary" bonding. Above all, the work ought to be completely dry before any water is let in; for the weight of the water exerts pressure, sweats through damp places, and once it has found a chink, will work its way through until it runs out freely, as though it were a conduit. The ancients would coat the wall with several layers of plaster as a protection, especially at the corners, and also line it with a carefully applied skin of marble. But there is no method more convenient for stemming a leak than to pack a layer of thoroughly pounded clay between the wall of the cistern and the side of the trench. We recommend that the clay used for this be absolutely dry and pulverized.

Some are of the opinion that if a glass vessel is filled with salt and sealed well with a paste of lime and oil, so that no water can enter, and then suspended in the middle of the cistern, the water there will never become corrupt with the passage of time. Others also add quicksilver. And others think that if you fill a new earthenware vessel with sharp vinegar, seal it well, as described above, and then insert it into the water, it will soon remove any slime. Cisterns and wells may be purified, they say, by releasing small fish into them: for fish are thought to feed off the slime and earthy moisture.

There is an old saying of Epigenes to the effect that water that has turned foul once will eventually be purified and restored, after which it will never turn foul again.[112] Water that has begun to turn foul, if stirred violently, and repeatedly moved and disturbed, will lose its stench. It is well known that the same happens to musty wine and likewise oil. According to Josephus, when Moses reached an arid place, where there was nothing but a well of bitter and foul water, he ordered the water to be drawn; that done, the soldiers shook and stirred it in this way, until it was drinkable.[113] Certainly boiling and distilling will purify water. They say that if barley meal is added to water that is nitrous and bitter, it will be sweet and ready to drink within two hours.

But to purify water in your drinking cistern, build a separate small well with its own wall, in a convenient position, and its base a little lower than that of the cistern. The side facing the cistern should have small openings packed with sponge or pumice, so that all water passing from the cistern into the well will be strained and its scum removed. In Tarragona in Spain is found a white pumice with particularly fine pores, and water strained through it will become very limpid. Another method of filtration would be to use a vessel perforated all over with many openings, and then fill it with river sand, so that the water is forced to filter through the fine sand. In Bologna a kind of yellow, sandy tufa is found, which leaves water very pure as it drips through.

Some make bread with seawater, which is more prone than anything else to cause disease; yet so effective are the methods of filtration which we have mentioned, that even this may be made healthy. Seawater, claims Solinus, when filtered through clay, becomes fresh.[114] And it is well known that salt can be removed by straining it repeatedly through fine sand from a stream. If you immerse a well-sealed earthenware pot in the sea, it will fill up with fresh water. While on this topic, we should mention that if you rub an almond above the rim of any turbid Nile water, it will immediately become clear. So much for this.

When pipes begin to block up with mud, insert a gallnut or a cork ball attached to a long, thin string. When the ball has been carried down to the bottom end, tie a stronger piece of string to the thin one, and then some rope of Spanish broom. Then, if you draw this rope up and down, you will remove any obstruction. ◆

9

190v—191

Let us now move on to other matters. We have mentioned that country people need food and clothes, which are supplied by farming, an art that does not concern our undertaking; but there are instances when the architect may be of service to the ploughman, as when a field is unsuitable for cultivation because it is too dry or spoilt by too much water. It would be useful to discuss these matters briefly.

This is how to plant a vine in a moist meadow. Dig some straight and parallel trenches, running from east to west; make them as deep as possible, 9 feet wide and 15 feet apart; pile up the excavated earth on the ground in between, and make it slope to face the midday sun. These artificial hillocks will protect the vine and make it more fruitful.

On the other hand, this is how to plant a vine on a dry hillside. On the upper part dig a long trench, not sloping but flat, its edges level and even. Into this channel water from nearby springs. The water will spill over the side, constantly and evenly, and irrigate the field below. In the country-side around Verona, where the land is full of round stones, and otherwise bare and completely infertile, they have managed to cover the ground with turf in some places and grow delightful meadows by using extensive irrigation.

To plant a wood in marshland, turn the ground over with a plough and root out all turf; then sow acorns at sunrise. These seeds will fill the place with trees, which will draw up much of the superfluous moisture. Then as the roots grow, and twigs and fallen leaves pile up on the ground, the level will rise gradually. And if you flood the place with turbid water, it will leave a layer of deposits as it subsides. But of this elsewhere.

But if the region is troubled by too much water, as we see in Gaul,[115] along the Po, in Venice, and so on, there are several factors to be considered: the problem may be the volume of water, its movement, or both. We shall deal with these briefly.

Claudius tunneled through a mountain by Lake Fucino and drained the excess water into the river Ripis.[116] M. Curius, probably for the same reason, tapped the Veline Lake so that it flowed into the Nar.[117] Likewise, Lake Nemi was drawn off into Lake Laurentum by cutting through a mountain, thereby draining the delightful gardens and fruitful grove below Nemi.[118] Caesar had planned to dig a number of trenches at Ilerda, so as to divert part of the river Sicoris.[119] The meandering Ethymantus is so depleted by the locals irrigating their land that what remains of it enters the sea without even a name.[120] Cyrus divided the Ganges into several channels; according to Eutropius, they numbered four hundred and sixty, and they so reduced its level that it was possible sometimes to cross it dry-shod.[121] At the tomb of Alyattes in Sardis, a work built mainly by female slaves, the artificial lake of Colous has been excavated to receive the floodwaters.[122] Moeris dug a lake above a city in Mesopotamia, which had a perimeter of 360 stades and a depth of 50 cubits, to hold the water of the Nile if it floods violently.[123] Apart from embankments to contain the Euphrates and prevent it from tearing down the houses in the city, several lakes were added, to absorb the violence of the river. They also excavated huge pits, whose still and calm water would act as a barrier against the impetus of the current.[124]

We have dealt with waters that are in excess, and partially also with those which cause damage by their movement. Anything that we have not covered will be dealt with shortly when we discuss the rivers and sea. ◆

IO

191—193

Next we shall take account of how best to import from abroad the provisions that people cannot obtain in their own land. For this highways and roads are used; they must be such as to allow easy and convenient transport of necessities whenever the occasion may arise.

There are two kinds of highway—as we have mentioned when dealing with the subject—by land and by water. To prevent the cluttering of a highway with filth and its being ruined by carts, apart from raising it on causeways, which we suggested elsewhere, make sure that the road is exposed to as much sun and wind and as little shade as possible. There is a road running through the woods near Ravenna, which was once in a state of decay but has recently been made very pleasant by widening it and cutting down trees to admit more sunlight. It is noticeable that where the ground is shaded by wayside trees, it is slower to dry, and as a result, the hooves of cattle leave potholes which fill up with rain to form ever increasing puddles.

There are two kinds of aquatic route: one that can be regulated—as rivers and canals—and the other—as the sea—that cannot. It seems to me that a river is liable to suffer the same faults as a vessel: its bed or sides might be unfit, unsound, or unsuitable. The quantity of water required for the transportation of ships is not small; therefore, unless it is contained by strong banks, it will burst them and flood the whole countryside, disrupting land routes as well. And if its bed is too steep, the current will certainly be too strong for any ship to sail upstream. What is more, if the bed is uneven or ridged, it will present obstructions. When an obelisk was transported to Rome from Egypt, the Tiber was found easier to navigate than the Nile, because, although the latter clearly had great breadth, the former was much deeper.[125] Although depth is more important than the volume of water for navigation, yet width must also be considered, since the banks slow down the current.

When the bed of the river is not solid, the banks will scarcely be strong. The bed will invariably be weak, unless (as we recommended for the foundations of a building) it is solid enough to defy even an iron tool. It will be quite unreliable if the banks are of clay, or if the river runs along a flat plain or through ground strewn with loose round stones. When the banks of the river are not firm, the channel will be obstructed with branches and rubble from buildings; tree trunks and stones will make dams across its width. The weakest of all and the least reliable are banks formed by a flood. From the weakness of their banks it followed in the case of the Meander and the Euphrates that the former, which runs through soft soil, daily made many new windings,[126] while the channels of the Euphrates were often blocked by the collapse of its banks.[127]

The main way in which the ancients would deal with these faults in riverbanks was to make embankments. They were built in ways analogous to other constructions. The line taken and how the work is built and reinforced are all of great consequence. If the embankment is in a straight line parallel to the stream, the current will not harm it; but when the river meets a bank across its path, it will demolish it if it is too weak, or flow over the top if it is too low. If the banks are not demolished, the riverbed will gradually rise as it collects sediment, and the channel will swell, as though building up for an assault, and having deposited what it has conveyed and can carry no farther, it will seek a different route. If its volume and strength destroy the bank, the river will act as we have already described: it will seep through any gap, drive out any air, and snatch up anything in its path; heavy objects and those not easily moved it will abandon as it gradually loses its force. Thus at the mouth of the breach itself, where the water floods out into the countryside, a thick deposit of coarse sand will be found, but thereafter the deposits of earth will be lighter and more muddy. But if the deposits rise up and over the bank, then the force of the rushing waters will crash down on the soil, and disturb it and carry some away, until a hollow is formed at the base, which will undermine the work and cause it to collapse.

If the current is neither parallel nor transverse to the bank, but meets it on a bend, depending on the bend and the width of the river, it will bear down on and consume either side equally, both the side receiving the impact and that which receives the washback. A bend is like a transverse obstacle and will therefore have to withstand the same attacks as those which are launched against the transverse bank, while it is also eroded by the harsh scouring it receives—all the more violent and damaging, the quicker and more turbulent the bubbling, as it were, of its whirlpools.

For the eddy, the whirling of water, is like a drill which nothing can resist, no matter how hard. It is noticeable how the beds downstream from stone bridges are hollowed out and deep; likewise, where a river with constricted banks opens out from a narrow mouth into a broader space, as the water spills and tumbles out, it devours and consumes any of the bank or the bed that lies in the way. I dare say that Hadrian's bridge in Rome[128] is the strongest work ever built by man; yet flooding has reduced it to such a state that I doubt whether it can last much longer. Over the years twigs and branches snatched from the land by the floods have burdened the piers and blocked most of the arches. This causes the water to rise and then crash down from a height, forming troublesome eddies, which undermine the prows of the piers and jeopardize the whole mass of the structure. So much for banks.

To deal now with riverbeds. Herodotus writes that in Mesopotamia Nitocris slowed the river Euphrates, which was too rapid, by making its route curved and tortuous.[129] It should be added that the slower the current, the longer-lasting the bed will be. It is as if someone were to come down a steep mountain, not straight down, but turning now to the right, now to the left. It is obvious enough that the speed of a river depends on the gradients of its channel.

Whether the current is too rapid or too slow, either will be inconvenient: the former will cause its banks to collapse, the latter will be prone to weeds and to icing over. To reduce the width of the river might raise its level, and to dredge its bed would make it deeper. Equipment for dredging, removing obstructions, and clearing shares almost the same rules and purpose, and will be dealt with later. But dredging will be in vain if the bed downstream toward the sea does not fall to an even gradient. ◆

I I

193—194v

I now come to canals. The canal should preferably neither be short of water nor have anything to obstruct its proper functioning. There are two ways of ensuring the former: the first is to have a plentiful supply channeled in from elsewhere, the second is to conserve water once it is held. (The channel should be dug following the principles listed above.) But to prevent any obstruction to its use, we should employ care and diligence to ensure that it is frequently cleaned and cleared of all deposits.

Canals have been described as sleeping rivers; and they have almost the same requirements as rivers. In particular they need a solid, firm bed and banks, so that none of the water they contain is absorbed or leaked. Their depth should be greater than their width, not only for the sake of shipping but also to reduce evaporation by the sun and to curb the growth of weeds.

Because the bed of the Euphrates is very high, a large number of canals have been dug from the Euphrates to the Tigris.[130] In Gaul, the whole of that part of Italy around the lower Po and the Adige is navigable by canal: this is possible because of the flatness of the land. According to Diodorus, when Ptolemy wanted to sail out of the Nile, he opened a canal, and then closed it up again once he had sailed through.[131]

These are the remedies for defects: constraining, cleaning, and closing. A river is constrained by artificial banks. The line of the banks should narrow the sides not abruptly but gradually. And where water passes from a narrow course back into a more open one, do not release it suddenly, but extend the channel, so that the river broadens and regains its original width gradually, and its sudden freedom does not lead to troublesome whirlpools and eddies.

The river Melas used to flow into the Euphrates. Perhaps King Artanatrix blocked its mouth in his greed for fame, and flooded the surrounding countryside. But soon afterward, the mass of dammed water broke through with so many whirlpools and such fury that it dragged with it many fields and laid waste much of Galatia and Phrygia. The Roman senate fined the man thirty talents for his insolence.[132] On this subject there is another tale that we read. When Iphicrates was besieging Stymphalus, he attempted to use vast quantities of sponge to block off the waters of the river Erasinus, which flows into a mountain and reemerges in Argos; but he was dissuaded by Jupiter and abandoned his attempt.[133]

The following advice might be deduced from all this: give the banks as much strength as possible. Strength is achieved by solidity of materials, method of construction, and size. Where the water falls over a bank, do not make the outside vertical, but allow it to slope gradually, so that the water flows over it smoothly, without the least eddy. But if in its fall it begins to excavate the ground, fill the hole immediately, not with tiny chips but with large, sound, durable, angular blocks of stone. It might be useful to lay bundles of brushwood to obstruct and break the fall of the water before it reaches the ground.

In Rome we see that much of the Tiber is restrained with solid masonry. Semiramis, not content with an embankment of brick, covered it with a four-cubit layer of asphalt; not only that, but she raised the structure by several stades to the level of the town walls.[134] But such are royal works. We should be content with a bank of earth, such as the mud one built by Nicotrix in Assyria;[135] or such as those which we see in Gaul, where great rivers seemingly hang in the air, so that in some places they stand above the roofs of cottages. There only the bridges need to be reinforced with stone.

When building the bank, some prefer to turf it over with grass cut from meadows; I too am in favor of this, because the intertwining roots bind the material, provided it is rammed together tightly. Indeed, the entire composition of the bank, and especially the part washed by the water, ought to be reinforced to an impenetrable and imperishable compactness. Some would plat the bank with sprigs of osier; this is certainly strong, but of a temporary nature. The sprigs rot easily, allowing the water to seep in where they have decayed, and to penetrate further, until it has increased the size of its passage and widened its bed. But there is less danger of this if green sprigs are used.

Some plant willow, elder, poplar, and other hydrophilic trees, in tight rows along the banks. This has its advantages, but it also suffers from the defect we ascribed to osier. The trunks may occasionally become diseased; tunnels and cavities will open up in the dead tree. Others—and this I prefer above all else—line the bank with bushes and a whole variety of hydrophilic plants whose roots are tougher than their branches; of these the most notable are the Celtic nard, rush, reed, and, above all, osier. This last has a large and widespread root, sending out long, tough fibers, while its branches are slight and flexible, and play with the waves without causing an obstruction; it has, moreover, another advantage, that in its greed for water it will continually advance below the waterline.

Wherever the embankment runs parallel to the stream, its shores ought to be quite naked and clear, so that there is nothing to obstruct the smooth flow of water. To reinforce the bank where it faces a curved section of river, strengthen it with planks. If it is necessary to check and hold off the whole might of the river with a dam, then during summer, when the water is lower and the channel exposed, construct a raft out of very long, tough logs, clasped and braced together; position this raft across the bed, against the flow of the current; drive sharp stakes into the bed, as deeply as the ground will allow, with special holes in them to fasten the raft; once the raft has been secured, lay alternate cross-beams; and over this caisson pile up a stone mole, cemented together with lime, or—where the expense will not allow that—fixed with twined juniper branches. Thus the waters will be held back by the sheer weight and the strength of the caisson. If any eddies threaten to undermine the work, they will actually be a help and advantage; for their effect will be to press and drag down the weight of the material, so that it settles more firmly. If, however, the river is always high and it is impossible to build this sort of raft, we should use the techniques that we described when dealing with the subject of constructing the piers of a bridge. ◆

12
194v—197

The seashore may also be reinforced with artificial banking, but not of the same kind as for rivers. For the water of a river makes mischief in a different way from ocean waves.

They say that the natural state of the sea is one of stillness and tranquillity, but that it is disturbed and whipped up by the pressure of the wind, producing the rows of waves that head for the shore. Where they meet any obstacle across their path, especially one that is hard and rugged, they hurl themselves against it with all their might, and when they are repulsed they leap up and collapse; thereby they disturb the ground as they fall from on high, and cause continual damage by excavating and demolishing whatever they encounter. Proof of this is in the depth of the sea found at the base of cliffs.

But if the waves are offered an easy and gentle slope by the beach, the violent sea, finding no opposition to its raging swell, renounces such assaults, and washes back on itself, its waves restrained; and whatever sand it has picked up and transported in the commotion, it abandons and leaves in a quiet place. As a result, it is noticeable how any such stretch of coast, although beginning as a humble plain, gradually extends into the sea. Where the sea meets some promontory, followed by a curved inlet or bay, the current runs rapidly along the shore and then washes back on itself; as a result, in many such stretches of coast, long channels have been gouged out.

Others claim that the sea breathes in and out naturally, and remark that no man ever breathes his last except when the tide is going out,[136] as though this is proof of some affinity and sympathy between our human life and the movement and spirit of the sea. So much for this.

Finally, it is obvious that the ebb and flow of the sea varies from place to place. In Chalcis there are six changes of tide each day.[137] In Byzantium it does not change except when it flows from the Black Sea into the Marmora. Such is the nature of the sea that it continually jettisons onto the shore whatever it has picked up from rivers. For anything that is disturbed by agitation is deposited wherever it finds a place of rest.

Restoration of Buildings

But since we notice piles of sand and stones thrown up on almost every shore, it would be useful to relate what we learn from the philosophers. We have already mentioned[138] that sand is formed out of mud, which is compacted by the sun, only to be fragmented later into tiny particles by heat. It is said that stones are produced by seawater. They argue that the water is heated up by sun and movement, dries up, is then thickened by the drying out of its lighter parts, and reaches sufficient thickness that, when the sea quiets down a little, it forms a slimy crust that is very bituminous. When this crust is later broken, the fragments are dispersed by further movement, until they collide and cluster together to form a spongelike substance; these balls are then carried to the shore, where they pick up any disturbed sand that sticks to them; they begin to clot and dry out with the action of the sun and salt, becoming denser, and they eventually harden to become stones. This is their theory.

We, however, have noticed that the shore always grows by the mouths of rivers, especially if the river is one that has flowed through soluble soil or one into which several streams run. Rivers build up vast piles of sand and pebbles on either side, and extend the shore where they enter the sea. The Hyster, the Phasis in Colchis,[139] amongst others, and the Nile in particular, provide proof of this. The ancients called Egypt the home of the Nile[140] and maintained that the sea once extended up to the marshes of Pelusium. They also say that much of the plain of Cilicia was added to by the river.[141] Aristotle argued that Nature was continually changing, and that some time in the future the sea and the mountains would change places. Hence the poet,

> Everything Time ever brings out of earth into light
> Time also buries, however splendid it is,
> And takes it back into the shade.[142]

I return to the argument. Waves have the characteristic that when they meet an obstacle in front of them, they strike it with all their fury and rise up, but as they recede, they dig up more sand the farther they have fallen. This is evident from the greater depth of the sea under rocks and cliffs, where waves have broken, compared with places where they have met nothing but a soft and sloping beach.

Such being the case, the greatest diligence and utmost care is demanded to restrain the fury and power of the sea. For the sea will often defeat all art and workmanship, nor will it be conquered easily by human effort. It would therefore be useful to have recourse to the kind of banking that we prescribed for the bridge.[143]

But if it is necessary to extend a mole into the sea to protect a harbor, we should begin our work on dry ground and then gradually extend the work into the sea. We should take care, above all, to build it on solid ground; and as you build it, make it of a vast pile of huge stones that confront the waves with a sloping wall, so that when they reach it, their fury is, as it were, extinguished, and finding nothing against which they may hurl all their might, they slip gently away, rather than crashing back. And as they retreat they meet the oncoming waves, and so hamper their assault.[144]

The mouths of rivers seem to share the same properties as the harbor, in that they are places where ships shelter from storms. I would make sure that they are fortified against the waves of the sea. As Propertius says,

> Conquer or be conquered,
> Such is the wheel of love.[145]

So it is here; for the mouths of rivers either are continually overwhelmed by the fury of the sea, and blockaded by its sand, or else by continual and obstinate onslaught themselves prove victorious. It is preferable therefore, as long as there is enough water, to provide the river with two different outlets into the sea. Not only does this give ships easier access as the wind varies, but also, if one of them is blocked by the violence of a storm or perhaps by blustering Auster,[146] the water will not rise and flood the land, but will have its own free outlet into the sea. So much for this.

Let us move on to the clearing of a stretch of water. Caesar took the greatest care in clearing the Tiber, when it was full of rubbish. Not far from the river, both inside and outside the city, there still remain vast mountains of pottery that have been removed from it.[147] I do not recall reading about the method by which he removed so much matter from so rapid a stream, but I imagine that he must have used enclosures to shut out the water, and removed the obstruction once the water had been pumped out.

Such enclosures are made as follows. Have some square posts ready, which have grooves running from top to bottom cut into each side, four inches deep and as wide as the thickness of the panels to be used in the work; and make all the panels of equal length and width. Once these have been prepared, drive in your posts so that they stand vertical, the distance between them equal to the width of the panels. When the posts are in position and firmly fixed, insert the panels at the top, and let them slide down along the grooves. These structures are commonly known as "cataracts." Then insert further panels on top, and wedge them in so that they hold together tightly. Then in suitable places position water screws, pumps, siphons, buckets, and any other instrument used for removing water,[148] employ a large number of workmen, and do not cease from your labor until all the water has been removed from the enclosure. If there is any leak, stop it up with rags. The work may then be continued as we desire.

There is a difference between this type of enclosure and the one we described earlier for the building of bridges: the latter must be stable and lasting, able to stand until the piers are built and the superstructure has set;

whereas the former is only temporary, and when the silt has been emptied, it must be moved and transferred elsewhere. But I advise you, whether you perform this operation with an enclosure or by diverting the course of the river, not to strive against the whole force of the stream in one place, but to proceed step by step with the work.

Any work intended to counter the might and force of water will have greater resistance if built with its back turned against the pressure of the current in the form of an arch. If you excavate a stream by laying a barrier across it, forcing the water to rise and swell up, this will ensure that as it spills over the top and falls, the water will carve out a ridge in the channel. Conversely, the lower you make the level downstream, the deeper will the bed be dug upstream toward the spring; because as the water falls it will continually disturb and carry away earth.

A river or canal may be cleaned by leading cattle into it, as follows. Dam the water, to make it rise; then drive the beasts to stir up the mud in the water with frequent and excited movement; release the dam suddenly, so that the water floods out and takes all the dirt away. If there is an obstruction buried or fixed in the river, a good idea—apart from the standard methods known to the workman—is to load up a barge and attach it to the object, whether stake or whatever that needs to be uprooted; then unload the barge. As the barge lightens it will rise, rooting up anything to which it is attached. It will be useful to keep swiveling the rudder like a key, as the vessel is rising. Around Praeneste we have noticed a moist clay that will not allow the force of a human hand to remove a stick or a sword inserted to a depth of just one cubit; but if, as you pull, you wriggle it backward and forward, as though you were drilling a hole, it will easily release it. At Genoa, a rock lying under the surface of the water blocked the mouth of the harbor. Recently a young man of exceptional skill and physique reduced it, thereby widening the entrance. It is rumored that he was able to stay under water for the best part of an hour without surfacing for air.

Dredge the mud from the bed with an oyster net clothed in tarpaulins; it will fill up as you draw it along. Where the sea is shallow, you may also dredge it using an instrument called the *palatia*, as follows.[149] Take two ketches. In the stern of one set up an axle, on which a very long pole pivots like the arm of a balance. Onto the end away from the ship attach a shovel three feet wide and six deep. Workmen lower this shovel into the water, scoop up the mud, and throw it into the other ketch, which lies alongside for that purpose. There are many other useful machines based on this principle, but they would take too long to describe. So much for this.

To move on to methods of closure. The flow of water may be shut off with sluices or doors. In either case the sides must be made as strong as the piers of a bridge. The weight of the sluice gate may be raised without risk to the workmen, by turning a cog with teeth, as in a clock, locked into those of a second cog that performs the task.

But the most convenient of all is the floodgate, with a fixed hinge in the center that rotates about a vertical axis. Onto this hinge is fastened a wide rectangular gate, like the square sail of a cargo ship, which can swivel to the prow or to the stern with either arm; but the two arms of the gate should not be equal: one should be up to three inches narrower than the other. This will allow it to be opened by one child, and to shut again of its own accord, because of its greater leverage on the larger side.

For a lock, two barriers must be made, to close the river in two separate places far enough apart to accommodate the length of a ship. Thus, if the ship is to ascend, once it has reached the lock, the lower gate is closed and the upper one opened; or, if it is to descend, the lower one is opened, and the upper one closed; in this way the ship is carried downstream as the water escapes, while the rest of the water is contained by the upper barrier.

I have one comment to make about roads (not to repeat what I have said elsewhere): in a town the bad habit of allowing the road surface to rise over the rubbish must be avoided; rather, cart away their rubbish and level them, and keep them swept and clear, so that the house blocks and open spaces in the city are not buried because of the accumulation of debris. ◆

13

197—198v

I shall now deal as briefly as possible with other less important remedies. Some places where water has been introduced have become warmer, others have become colder. Near Larisa in Thessaly the land was covered with stagnant water; this made the air thick and heavy. Once the water had been removed and the land had dried, the region became so cold that the olive, which used to flourish there, could no longer survive.[150] The opposite happened in Philippi: there, according to Theophrastus, when the water was drained and the land dried, the climate became less cold.[151]

They say that the purity or impurity of the air is responsible for these phenomena: for dense air, it is argued, is more difficult to move, but retains the heat and cold longer than thin air, which grows cold more readily and reacts more quickly to sunlight. Land that is uncultivated and neglected is said to have a dense and unhealthy air.

Also, where trees grow thickly, so that neither sun nor wind can penetrate, the air is very coarse. The caves around Lake Avernus were surrounded by a forest so dense that the sulphur they gave off killed any bird that entered their narrow spaces; but Caesar made the place healthy by cutting down the trees.[152]

The inhabitants of the Tuscan coastal city of Livorno used to be afflicted with heavy fever during the period of the Dog Star. After they built a wall to guard against the sea, their health improved; but when they later allowed water into their moats, to strengthen their defenses, they were stricken once more. Varro reports that when he was encamped on the island of Corfu, and his soldiers were dying of disease, he saved his men by keeping all the windows to the south shut.[153] The famous Venetian town of Murano is rarely affected by plague, although the neighboring city of Venice often suffers from it heavily. This has been attributed to the number of glassworks there; for it is certain that air will be largely purged by fire. That poison dislikes fire is demonstrated by the fact that the dead bodies of poisonous animals do not breed worms like any other. The nature of poison is to destroy and utterly extinguish the whole force of life; but if their bodies are struck by lightning, they will produce worms, because their poison is destroyed by fire. Worms are bred in a dead body by that certain fiery force in Nature producing that liquid which is here joined by fire; it is the property of poison to extinguish fire by overwhelming it, but if poison is itself overwhelmed it loses all its strength.

If you root out poisonous herbs, and especially squills, good plants will absorb the bad nourishment that they used to extract from the earth, and that corrupts our food. It may be useful to shelter your house from unwholesome winds with a grove, especially of apple trees; for the air you receive is greatly influenced by the leaves that shade it. Pitch trees are said to be very good for anyone suffering from consumption or for anyone convalescing after a long illness. Trees with a bitter leaf have the opposite effect, and make the air unwholesome.

And so, wherever the land is low, marshy, and humid, it would be well to make it bright and airy; this will ensure that the bad smells and poisonous animals that arise from such places will soon be destroyed by the aridity and the winds. In Alexandria there is a place reserved for the refuse and rubbish of the city. This has grown into such a mountain that it has become a landmark for sailors finding their way into port. But how much more convenient it would be to make it a legal constraint to fill up low-lying areas and dips. At Venice in my own time they have filled marshes with rubbish from the city—this I applaud. Herodotus informs us that those who live in the marshland of Egypt spend their nights up tall towers, in order to avoid the gnats and mosquitoes.[154] At Ferrara on the river Po very few gnats appear within the city; but outside the town, they are unbearable to those who are not used to them. It is thought that they are driven from the town by the great quantity of smoke and fire. Flies are not to be found in any place that is shady, cold, or very windy, especially if the windows are very high; some say that flies never enter where the tail of a wolf is buried, and also that if squill is hung anywhere it will ward off any venomous animal.

Our ancestors would employ many methods to counter the heat; among them I am delighted by their underground porticoes and vaults, which receive light only from the top. They also delighted in halls with large windows (provided they did not face south) which received shady air from covered places. Metellus, son of Octavia, the sister of Augustus, made an awning of sails over the forum, so that people might go about their business without prejudicing their health.[155]

But air is a more effective means of cooling than shade; as you will find by hanging a sail over a space to restrict the breeze. Pliny recalls that it was common to have shady places in a house, although he gives no description of what they were like;[156] whatever form they took, Nature would have provided the best model. We notice that when we gape open our mouths, the air we breathe out is warm; but when we blow with our lips tight, our breath comes out cool. So also in a building, when air reaches an open space, especially one exposed to the sun, it becomes warm; but if it passes through a more constrained and shady passage, it comes out quicker and cooler. If warm water passes down a tube through cold water, it will be cooled. The same holds true of air. The question is often asked, why it is that those who walk in the sun become less tanned than those who sit in it. The answer is simple: the air is disturbed by our movement, and the force of the sun's rays reduced.

Again, in order to make the shade cooler, it might be useful to protect a roof with a second roof, and the wall with a second wall; the greater the space between them, the cooler the shade will be. Anywhere sheltered and protected in this way will grow less warm. For the gap has almost the same effect as a solid wall of equal size; and it even has an advantage, in that whereas a wall would retain heat and be slower to absorb the cold, the air between the double walls that we have described will maintain an even temperature. Wherever the sun's heat is troublesome, a wall of pumice will not absorb so much heat nor retain it for so long.

If a doorway to a room has double leaves, so that one set opens inward, the other outward, with a gap of one cubit between them, whatever is said inside will not be overheard on the outside. ◆

14
198v—199

If we are to build somewhere very cold, we shall need fires. There are different kinds of fires, but the most convenient is the bright, open hearth: fire from smoky, vaulted ovens pollutes the air, makes our eyes water, and dims our vision.

What is more, the very sight of the light and flames of a live fire is a cheerful companion, they say, to old men chatting by the hearth. In the middle of the chimney breast above the fire there ought to be a transverse metal vent, which, when all the smoke has escaped and the coals have begun to warm up and glow, may be turned and shut, so that the opening does not allow any outside draft to enter the room.

Walls of flint and marble are both cold and damp; their very coldness compresses the air and turns it into moisture. Tufa and brick are more convenient, being thoroughly dry. Anyone who sleeps in a room whose walls are new and wet, especially if the ceiling is vaulted, will suffer painful and feverish illnesses or catarrhs. There have even been instances of people who have lost their sight because of this; others have had their muscles stiffen, and others still have lost their mind and reason, and gone mad. To let the rooms dry quicker, apertures should be left open to give the wind a through passage.

The most healthy type of wall is one of unfired brick that has been allowed to dry for two years. Plastering with gypsum thickens the air and makes it harmful to the lungs and brain. If you panel your walls with timber, and especially fir or even poplar, it will make the place healthier, warm enough in winter, and not too hot in summer; but it might cause you to be plagued with mice and bugs. To prevent this, line the gap with reeds, and stop all the hiding places and retreats for such vermin. For this a paste of clay and hair, mixed with the lees of oil, is very effective; for oil is utterly detested by every kind of animal that breeds in corruption. ◆

15
199—200

Since we have embarked on this argument, it might be useful to repeat a few comments of very serious authors whom we have read. One should make sure that any building is free of pests. The inhabitants of Oeta[157] sacrificed to Hercules, because he freed them of gnats; as did the Melians, because he rid their vines of caterpillars. The Aeolians sacrificed to Apollo for destroying their plague of mice. These were all acts of great benefit, although there is no record of how they were performed.

Elsewhere I read the following: The Assyrians would ward off all poisonous animals by hanging burnt lungs along with an onion and a squill over the door lintel.[158] According to Aristotle, snakes can be driven from the house by the smell of rue.[159] If you leave some meat in a pot, it will attract great numbers of insects, which you can then trap. If you lay sulphur and wild oregano in anthills, you will exterminate ants. Sabinus Tyro wrote in a letter to Maecenas that if their holes were stopped with sea mud or ash, it would kill them.[160] They may be cured very effectively, claimed Pliny, with the heliotrope herb;[161] others think that they also dislike water in which a soft brick has been soaked.

The ancients maintain that certain animals and certain things have such a natural aversion to one another, that one will ruin and destroy the other. Hence the weasel flees the smell of roasted cat, and snakes the smell of the leopard. They say that if a leech is sticking stubbornly to a human limb, it will relax its grip and drop off as soon as you hold a bug to its head. On the other hand, the smoke of the burning leech will dislodge and drive out any bug from its deepest hiding place. Solinus claims that sprinkling dust from the Isle of Thanet in Britain will soon drive away snakes;[162] and historians maintain that the earth of several other places, notably the island of Ibiza, will have the same effect.[163] The earth of Galeon, an island of the Garamantes, will kill both snakes and scorpions.[164] Strabo maintains that in Libya they rub the feet of their beds with garlic before going to sleep, for fear of scorpions.[165]

The Sasernae give us the following instructions on how to kill bugs: "Soak a wild cucumber in water; pour it wherever you want, and no bug will approach. Alternatively, daub your bed with ox gall mixed with vinegar."[166] Others instruct us to fill up cracks with lees of wine. "The root of the holm oak," says Pliny, "is lethal to scorpions";[167] ash is also excellent against such poisonous animals, and snakes especially;[168] snakes never hide under fern. Serpents are also driven away by burning women's hair or the horn of a goat or stag, or sawdust of cedar, or some drops of Galbanum,[169] or of willow, green ivy, or juniper; and anyone who rubs himself with juniper seed will be quite safe from snake bites. The smell of the herb called *haxum* intoxicates asps, makes them drowsy, and sends them to sleep.[170]

For dealing with colewort they advise us to set the skull of a mare on a post in the garden. Bats have an aversion to the palm tree. Wherever you sprinkle water in which elderflowers have been boiled, you will kill any flies, although hellebore is quicker; the black variety, when boiled, will also kill flies. Once you have buried a dog's tooth in a room, along with its tail and feet, they say you will be untroubled by flies. The tarantula cannot bear the smell of saffron. The smoke of burning lupine will kill gnats. Mice are killed by the smell of aconite, however far away. Both mice and bugs hate the smell of vitriol.

Fleas will vanish if you sprinkle a concoction of coloquintida or the sea thistle anywhere.[171] If you sprinkle goats' blood, they will swarm around it; but they are repelled by the smell of the cabbage, and even more effectively by that of the oleander. If you leave broad, flat vessels around the floor, they will be an easy trap for any flea that jumps too far. Moths are driven away by wormwood, aniseed, or the smell of savin; they say that clothes are safe from them, provided you hang them from ropes.

But we have said enough on this subject—indeed more, perhaps, than a serious reader would think appropriate. But you will pardon us if what we have said helps in any way to rid some place of pests; although there appears to be no means entirely satisfactory for combating the irritating and perennial problem of vermin. ◆

16

200—201v

I now return to the argument. It is remarkable that if you cover your wall with a woolen tapestry it will make the room warmer, yet if it is of linen it will make it colder. If the floor is damp, dig drains and trenches, and fill them with pumice or gravel, to prevent the moisture from causing rot. Then cover the ground with coal to a depth of one foot, and on top lay coarse sand or, preferably, terra-cotta piping, and over that the flooring.

It will be a great advantage if air can breathe beneath the flooring. Against the heat of the sun and the bitterness of winter, it will be very useful if the ground is not damp but dry. Excavate the *area*[172] of the dining room to a depth of twelve feet, and then cover it with boarding; if you lay a pavement with a revetment, this will make the air inside cooler than you could ever imagine, so that your feet will remain cold even when you are wearing shoes, there being nothing above the foundations except the boards. The ceiling of the dining room should be vaulted; and you will be surprised how warm it will be in winter, and cool in summer.

If you are troubled by the inconvenience about which the character in a satire complains,[173] whereby your sleep is disturbed by the passing of carts through the narrow, winding streets and the slanging of drovers when brought to a halt (so tiresome when he was ill in bed), take the advice of Pliny the younger in one of his letters on how to prevent this disturbance. "Have a bedroom annex for sleeping at night, where you will not sense the voices of the servants, the murmuring sea, raging storms, flashing lightning, or even the daylight, unless the windows are open, so deep and hidden is this den. The reason for this is that the walls of the room and the garden are separated by a corridor, an intervening space that absorbs all sound."[174]

I now come to walls. Walls are liable to the following faults: they may crack, they may fall apart, their bones may be broken, or they may lean away from the vertical. Each one of these faults may have a different cause, and also a different remedy. Some of the causes are obvious, but others are more obscure, and it is not always clear enough what needs to be done, until the damage appears. Other faults are not concealed at all, though men convince themselves in their idleness that they are not as damaging to the work as in fact they are.

Evident faults are, to take an example, when the wall is too slender, or when it is not properly bonded, or when it is full of dangerous openings, or, again, when the bones[175] are not strong enough to bear the assault of the weather. Faults that are concealed or unexpected are the following: earthquakes, lightning, and every natural inconsistency in the soil. But the primary cause of damage in all parts of the building is the carelessness and neglect of man.

The wild fig, one author said, is like a silent battering ram against a wall; it is hard to believe the huge stones I have seen moved and split under the force and leverage of a little root growing between their joints. If someone had torn it out while it was still young and tender, the work would have been spared the nuisance.

I thoroughly approve of the ancients' practice of employing gangs of workers at public expense to care for and maintain public works. Agrippa commissioned 250 men for this task, Caesar 460.[176] They would pave over the fifteen feet immediately around an aqueduct, so that no tree roots would grow and weaken the vaults or sides. This was a principle also followed by private individuals wherever they wanted to make a work particularly permanent: on their sepulchral monuments they would inscribe the extent of the ground which was to be hallowed; sometimes it would be fifteen feet, and sometimes twenty.

But not to repeat myself, a fully grown tree can be killed and destroyed, so they say, if it is cut down to one foot as the sun enters the Dog Star, and if the oil known as petroleum is mixed with powdered sulphur and poured into a hole in the heartwood; alternatively, it may be sprinkled liberally with cinders of burnt bean pods. According to Columella, to uproot a wood, sprinkle the roots with lupin flowers that have been soaked for a day in hemlock juice.[177] Solinus maintains that a tree will lose its leaves if in contact with menstrual blood;[178] others maintain that it will die. According to Pliny, a tree will die if it comes into contact with the root of the sea parsnip.[179] I now return to our previous discussion.

If the wall is too slender, either add a new section to the old to make a single wall, or, to save expense, build only the bones, that is, pilasters, columns, and beams. This is how to add one section to another: in several places in the old wall insert small catches of tough stone; these reinforcements project into the new wall as it is built, and act as cramps holding together two skins. The new wall should be constructed of nothing but ordinary brickwork.

This is how to add a pilaster to a wall. Mark out its intended width with red chalk on the old wall. Then, beginning from the foundations, cut a channel in the wall, whose width is slightly greater than that drawn on the wall with chalk. The channel need not go very deep. Then fill it very carefully with rows of level squared stone. In this way the remaining section of wall within the chalk outline is braced by the thickness of the column, and the wall is reinforced. Then above, using the same technique as with the base of the pilaster, add the remaining sections right up to the top of the work. So much for slender walls.

Where there are insufficient connections, use iron or, preferably, bronze ties, but make sure that the bones are not damaged and weakened.

If there happens to have been an earth slide, and it presses against a side of the wall, causing damp, dig a trench as broad as is required, parallel with the wall; within the trench construct semicircular arches to brace the weight of the earth that is falling in, leaving frequent outlets in them through which the water may seep and be drained away. Alternatively, lay posts along the ground whose ends will hold and restrain the wall that has been buckled by the weight of the earth. Fasten these posts to other transverse posts, and pile earth on top. This has the advantage that the mound of earth will consolidate before the timbers lose their strength. ◆

17
201v—203v

I come now to those faults which cannot be foreseen, but which it is possible to repair once they have occurred. Cracks in a wall and deviation from the vertical may sometimes be caused by the vaulting—the wall may either have been pushed out by the arches or be unable to bear an uneven loading; the foundations are almost always responsible. Checks can be made, however, to establish whether these faults are caused by the foundations or elsewhere.

I shall begin with cracks in a wall. The side on which the fault lies will be indicated by the direction in which the crack veers as it rises. If the crack does not veer at all, but continues straight up and spreads out at the top, we should inspect the courses of stonework on either side. If they depart from the horizontal on either side, it will indicate that there is a weakness in the foundations on that side. However, if the wall is quite sound at the top, but several cracks run up from the bottom, their ends meeting as they rise, it shows that the corners of the wall are strong, but that the fault lies with the foundations at the center. But if there is only one such crack, the wider it is at the top, the greater the movement at the corners.

When it is necessary to repair the foundations, a pit must be dug alongside the wall, its dimensions governed by the size of the work and the firmness of the soil, but of sufficient depth to reach solid ground. As soon as you have reached the bottom of the wall, pack "ordinary" stonework beneath it and allow it to harden. Once it has hardened, dig a similar pit in another place along the wall, prop up the wall in the same way, and allow it to set. By extending the trench in this way, you will be able to underpin the whole wall.

If, however, the ground is not as solid as you would wish, dig pits on both sides of the wall at its base, not far from the corners—that is, the part of the *area* that is under cover and the part opposite, on the outside; pack stakes into the ground, and on top of them lay particularly strong posts along the length of the wall. After that, set thicker and still stronger beams against the base of the wall, so that they rest on the layer of posts and hold up the wall with their back, like a bridge or yoke.

In all of the restoration we have described above, take care that no part of any old work to which something is added is incapable of properly sustaining its imposed load for a long time; for the whole mass of the wall will immediately lean on the weakest part.

If, however, the section between the foundations and the center of the wall has moved, but the upper section remains intact, mark on the surface of the wall in red chalk an arch as large as is required—that is, big enough to encompass the whole section that has moved. Then, starting at either end of the arch, dig a hole in the wall, no larger than one of the stones of the arch, which we referred to earlier as wedges; and insert one of these wedges in line with the radius extending from the center of the circle. After that, make another hole beside it and fill it with a similar wedge; continue the work in this way until the arch is complete. That is how the operation will be achieved without risk.

If a column or a bone has been damaged, this is how to repair it. Prop up the beam with a strong arch of tile and plaster supported by plaster piers designed for the purpose, so that the new relieving arch fills the old opening exactly; the operation must proceed at great speed, and without any interruption. Plaster naturally swells as it dries. Thus the new work lifts—as far as it is able—the load of the old wall or vault sitting on its shoulders. Having made these preparations, remove the damaged column and replace it with a sound one.

If you prefer to shore up the work with timber and raise it with struts, insert a form of balance arm beneath, and load its longer arm with bags of sand. The work is raised gradually and evenly, without shaking. If the wall deviates from the vertical, set up a system of posts fastened to the wall. To each of these attach a shore of very strong timber, with its bottom end set back from the wall. Then with levers or little wedges gradually increase the pressure on the wall. By distributing the load in this way, the wall will be restored to the vertical. If this is not possible, set timber props in firm ground and daub them well with pitch and oil, to prevent contact with the lime; next build a buttress of squared stone so that it encases the shoring that has been daubed with pitch.

Should the base of a colossus or a chapel happen to have sunk in one direction, you should either raise the part that has sunk, or sink the part that has risen. Either task is daunting. First, use posts and all manner of binding to wrap and secure thoroughly the base and anything that could be shattered by movement. A convenient method of binding is to use a cage tightened with wedges, and to lever it up by inserting a beam, which we earlier called a balance arm.[180] You may lower it by gradually enlarging a trench, as follows: Beginning at the middle of that side, below the base of the lowest footing, dig a hole that is not very wide, but deep enough to accommodate a layer of solid "ordinary" stonework as desired. Do not fill the opening completely with this substratum, but leave a gap of a few palms, where you might insert robust wedges spaced closely together. Use the same technique to dig out the whole side of the chapel that you wish to lower. When these are taking the whole weight, efficiently and carefully remove these wedges, thus restoring the leaning wall to the true vertical. Later you can reinforce the spaces between the wedges with further wedges of solid stone.

This is the method that I devised for the great basilica of St. Peter's in Rome, when sections of colonnading were leaning away from the vertical and threatening to bring the roof down.[181] Each leaning section of wall supported by a column I decided to cut out and remove; and to restore the sections that had been removed with vertical ordinary bond, having left stone teeth and strong clasps on both sides of the structure to tie the new sections to the old. Finally, where a section of sloping wall was to be removed, I proposed to support the roof beams with machines called *caprae* [goats], erected over the roof, with their feet secured on either side to more stable sections of roof and walling. I would have done the same, as the situation required, to each of the columns, one by one. The *capra* is a nautical instrument consisting of three posts that are bracketed and tied together at the top, but whose feet splay out to form a triangle. Used together with pulleys and capstans, this machine is very effective in lifting weights.

If you are about to lay a new coat of revetment on an old wall or pavement, wash it first with pure water, and with a brush whitewash it with a mixture of liquid flowers of lime and marble dust; this will allow the revetment to adhere.

If cracks appear in an open-air pavement, they may be grouted up by pouring and working in ash that has been sieved and mixed with oil (preferably linseed oil). Clay is very good for this, if well mixed with quicklime, roasted in a kiln, and immediately slaked with oil; but any dust must first be removed from the crack—this is done by brushing it with feathers or blowing it repeatedly with a pair of bellows.

Nor should we neglect the elegance of a work. If a wall happens to be unsightly because it is too high, insert a cornice or paint on lines where appropriate to articulate the height. If the wall is too long, break it up with columns running from top to bottom, and not too frequent but rather widely spaced. For the eye stops and dwells on them, as though offered a place of rest, and is less offended by the expanse.

On this topic I might also add that many things placed rather low or surrounded by unreasonably low walls will seem smaller and narrower than they in fact are; and, vice versa, many others, when the pavement or wall has been raised up, will seem far larger than they first appeared. It is also clear that dining rooms and drawing rooms will be made to look more dignified and elegant by a convenient arrangement of the openings and by locating the door well in view and the windows in the higher part of the wall.

Abbreviations Used in the Notes

Amm. Marc.   Ammianus Marcellinus, *The Histories*

Apollod.   Apollodorus, *Bibliotheca*

Apol. Rhod.   Apollonius Rhodius, *The Argonautica*

App.   Appian of Alexandria, *Roman History*

Arist. De Plantis   Aristotle, *On Plants*

Arist. *Pol.*   Aristotle, *Politics*

Arnob. *Adv. gent.*   Arnobius Afer, *Against the Gentiles*

Aul. Gell.   Aulus Gellius, *The Attic Nights*

Aurel. Aug. *De civ. Dei*   M. Aurelius Augustinus (St. Augustine), *The City of God*

Cato *De r.r.*   M. Porcius Cato, the Censor, *On Agriculture*

Cic. *Ad Attic.*   M. Tullius Cicero, *Letters to T. Pomponius Atticus*

Cic. *Brutus*   Cicero, *Brutus*

Cic. *De div.*   Cicero, *On Divination*

Cic. *Lael.*   Cicero, *Laelius*, or *On Friendship*

Cic. *De leg.*   Cicero, *On the Laws*

Cic. *De nat. deor.*   Cicero, *On the Nature of the Gods*

Cic. *De off.*   Cicero, *On Offices*

Cic. *De or.*   Cicero, *On Oratory*

Cic. *Philipp.*   Cicero, *Philippics against Mark Antony*

Cic. *De rep.*   Cicero, *On the Republic*

Cic. *In P. Vatin.*   Cicero, *Speech against Publius Vatinius*

Cic. *In Verr.*   Cicero, *The Verrine Oration*

Col. *De r.r.*   L. Junius Moderatus Columella, *On Agriculture*

Corp. agr. vet.   *Corpus agrimensorum Romanorum*, ed. C. Thulin, vol. 1, pt. 1, "Opuscula agrimensorum veterum," Leipzig, 1913

Dio Cass.   Dio Cassius, *The Roman History*

Diod. Sic. *Bibl. Hist.*   Diodorus Siculus, *The Historical Anthology*

Dion. Hal.   Dionysius of Halicarnassus, *The Early History of Rome*

Ennius   Quintus Ennius, *The Annals*

Eus. *Praep. Evang.*   Eusebius of Caesarea, *Gospel Demonstration*

Fest.   Sextus Pompeius Festus, *On the Meaning of Words*, with the Epitome of Paul the Deacon (*Sexti Pompeii Festi de verborum significatione . . . cum Pauli epitome*, ed. Wallace M. Lindsay, Leipzig, 1913)

F.G.H.   F. Jacoby, *Die Fragmente der Griechischen Historiker*, Berlin and Leyden, 1923–1958

Flav. Veg.   Flavius Vegetius Renatus, *On Strategy*

Front. *Aq. Rom.*   Sextus Julius Frontinus, *De aquis urbis Romae*

Front.   Julius Frontinus (in *Corp. agr. vet.*), *On Disputes about Land*

Front. *Strat.*   Frontinus, *On Strategy*

Herod.   Herodotus, *The Histories*

Hippocr. *Aphor.*   Hippocrates, *Aphorisms*

Hom. *Hymn.*   Homer, *The Homeric Hymns*

Hom. *Il.*   Homer, *Iliad*

Hom. *Od.*   Homer, *Odyssey*

Hor. *De ar. poet.*   Q. Horatius Flaccus (Horace), *On the Art of Poetry*

Hor. *Car.*   Horace, *Odes*

Hor. *Epod.*   Horace, *Epodes*

Hor. *Sat.*   Horace, *Satires*

Hyg. Grom.   Hyginus Gromaticus (in *Corp. agr. vet.*)

Hyg. Grom. *De castr.*   Hyginus Gromaticus, *On Military Camps*

Hyg. Grom. *De const. limit.*   Hyginus Gromaticus, *On the Drawing of Borders*

Hyg. Grom. *Fab.*   Hyginus Gromaticus, *The Fables*

Hyg. Grom. *De munit. castr.*   Hyginus Gromaticus, *On the Fortification of Camps*

Isid.   Isidore of Seville, *Origins*, or *On Etymology*

Joseph. *Antiq.*   Flavius Josephus, *Antiquitates Iudaicae*

Joseph. *Bell. Iud.*   Josephus, *Bellum Iudaicum*

Justin   M. Junius Justinus, *History* (abridging Trogus Pompeius)

Livy   T. Livius Patavinus, *History of the City since Its Foundation*

Lucil.   Gaius Ennius Lucilius, *The Satires*

Macrob. *Sat.*   Aurelius Theodosius Macrobius, *Saturnalia*

Mart. Cap.   Martianus Capella, *The Satyricon, On the Marriage of Philology and Mercury*

Nonnius   Nonnius Marcellus, *Knowledge in Brief*

Ovid *De a.a.*   Publius Ovidius Naso, *On the Art of Love*

Ovid *Pont.*   Ovid, *Ex Ponto*

Ovid *Metam.*   Ovid, *The Metamorphoses*

Paus.   Pausanias, *The Description of Greece*

Pind. *Nem.*   Pindar, *The Nemean Odes*

Pind. *Pyth.*   Pindar, *The Pythian Odes*

Pliny *N.H.*   Caius Plinius Secundus, *The Natural History*

Plutarch   Plutarch, *The Lives:* (Life of) *Aemilius Paulus; Alexander; Antony; Caesar; Camillus; Cimon; Lucullus; Lycurgus; Marcellus; Marius; Numa; Pericles; Pompey; Poplicola; Pyrrhus; Romulus; Solon; Theseus*

Plut. *G.Q.*   Plutarch, *Greek Questions*

Plut. *De Isid. et Os.*   Plutarch, *On Isis and Osiris*

Plut. *Par.*   Plutarch, *Parallels*

Plut. *R.Q.* Plutarch, *Roman Questions*

Plut. *De sort. Rom.* Plutarch, *On the Fortunes of the Romans*

Polyb. Polybius of Megalopolis, *The History*

P.W. A. Pauly, G. Wissowa, and W. Kroll, *Real-Encyclopädie der klassischen Altertumswissenschaft* (1893–1972)

Quint. Curt. Quintus Curtius Rufus, *On the Actions of Alexander the Great*

Sallust, *Bellum Iugurthinum* Gaius Sallustius Crispus, *Jugurtha*

Scr. Hist. Aug. Scriptores Historiae Augustae

Seneca *De brev. vitae* L. Annaeus Seneca, *On the Brevity of Life*

Seneca *De clem.* Seneca, *On Clemency to Nero*

Serv. *In Virg.* M. Servius Honoratus, *Commentary on Virgil*

Solinus Gaius Julius Solinus, *Collection of Things Memorable*

Soph. *Oed. Col.* Sophocles, *Oedipus at Colonnus*

Stat. *Theb.* P. Papinius Statius, *The Thebaïs*

Strabo Strabo, *On Geography*

Suetonius Gaius Suetonius Tranquillus, *Lives of the Caesars:* (Life of) *Augustus; Caligula; Claudius; Domitian; Julius; Nero; Tiberius; Vespasian*

Tac. *Ann.* Cornelius Tacitus, *The Annals*

Tac. *Hist.* Tacitus, *The Histories*

Tert. *Apol.* Tertullian, *The Apology*

Thuc. Thucydides, *The History of the Peloponnesian War*

Val. Max. Valerius Maximus, *The Memorabilia*

Varro *De L.L.* M. Terentius Varro, *On the Latin Language*

Varro *De r.r.* Varro, *On Agriculture*

Vell. Pat. Velleius Paterculus, *The Roman History*

Virg. *Aen.* L. Publius Vergilius Maro (Virgil), *The Aeneid*

Virg. *Culex* Virgil, *The Gnat* (attr.)

Virg. *Ecl.* Virgil, *The Eclogues*

Virg. *Geor.* Virgil, *The Georgics*

Vitr. M. Vitruvius Pollio, *On Architecture*

Xen. *Oecon.* Xenophon, *Economics*

Notes

Ancient works frequently cited are denoted by abbreviations here; see abbreviations list, above. Modern works listed in the bibliography are given shortened references here.

Foreword by Angelo Poliziano

1. Angelo Poliziano was one of the greatest literary figures of the fifteenth century, an intimate of Lorenzo de' Medici, and an enthusiastic student of architecture. For his Latin poems see F. Arnoldi, ed., 1964; the Italian poems were edited by G. R. Ceriello, 1952.

Alberti probably intended to dedicate the whole work to Federico da Montefeltro. After Federico's death in 1482, Angelo Poliziano seems to have persuaded Bernardo, Battista's executor, to alter the dedication to Lorenzo. So his seventeenth-century biographer, Bernardo Baldi; see Baldi, *Vita e fatti di Federigo di Montefeltro*, vol. 3, pp. 55f., and Dennistoun, *Memoirs of the Dukes of Urbino*, vol. 3, p. 258. Federico possessed a copy of the book (Vat. Urb. Lat. 264).

2. Although referred to as *frater* of the author, Bernardo was in fact his cousin—Bernardo's father, Santonio di Riccardo, being the brother of Lorenzo, Battista Leo's father. *Frater* is a much more generic term than the English "brother."

3. Alberti's work on the lifting of weights, *De motibus ponderis*, is lost, although the story of his efforts to raise the Roman galley from the Lake of Nemi is one of the best-known episodes of his life. See Mancini, *Vita di Leon Battista Alberti*, p. 9. The use of *pegma* and *automatum* reveals four years before the *Miscellanea* that Poliziano had reworked the text of Suetonius, *Claudius* 34. Cf. Grafton, *J. Scaliger*, p. 39.

4. Sallust, *Bellum Iugurthinum* 19.2.

5. A reference to his own epitaph by the Latin poet Q. Ennius, *Quur? Volito vivo per ora virum*, in which he forbids mourning, since he lives still in the mouths of men.

Prologue

1. Alberti's use of the term *res aedificatoria*, the art or matter of building, is in deliberate contrast to Vitruvius' use of the Greek neologism *architectura*; Alberti clearly intended his treatise at once to complement and to transcend Vitruvius' work. See Krautheimer, "Alberti and Vitruvius." For Alberti's criticism of Vitruvius' use of Greek terminology, see 6.1. *Lege Feliciter* translates literally as "Happy reading."

2. This is in deliberate contrast to the opening of Vitruvius' treatise, Vitr. 1.1.1. Art is used here in the wider sense, to refer to all branches of crafts and skills.

3. Alberti is here refuting the popular etymology of the word "architect": although it was in fact of Greek origin, and meant "chief builder," medieval tradition held that it was derived from the Latin words *archus* and *tectum*; the architect was thereby associated with the carpenter, the builder of roofs. Cf. Rykwert, "On the Oral Transmission of Architectural Theory." This definition can be found in Johannes Balbus, *Catholicon*. See also Cicero, *Brutus* 73.257.

4. See Vitr. 1.1.3–11; this theme is elaborated in Alberti 9.9–11.

5. Again Alberti is contrasting his view with that of Vitruvius (2.1.2) about fire as the origin of society.

6. Alberti is here alluding to the experience of his own family, who were exiled from Florence between 1401 and 1428, and not granted back their full rights as citizens until 1434.

7. Selinunte is a town on the southwest coast of Sicily. The legendary Daedalus, who is regarded as the builder of the Knossan labyrinth and as one of the founding fathers of architecture, is said to have escaped to Selinunte from Knossos. Alberti is presumably quoting from Diodorus Siculus 4.78.

8. Alberti is in part echoing Vitruvius. Cf. Vitr. 10.16.12.

9. The taking of auspices constituted an essential part of Roman life. The linking of *imperium* and *auspicium* (the right to take auspices from bird flight) was one of the essential elements of Roman military command. See P.W., s.vv.

10. Cf. Vitr. 2.1.3.

11. Alberti's definition of the beautiful as that harmonious and proportional composition from which nothing may be taken away and to which nothing may be added except for the worse, is contained in 6.2. The wording echoes Cicero's description of the perfection in the human body (*De or.* 3.45.179). Alberti compares the building to the human body throughout his book.

12. The notion that by patronizing a beautiful building a citizen is not only demonstrating private wealth but also exercising his civic duty had been generally accepted in the first half of the fifteenth century. See G. Befani Canfield in Zeri, *Scritti di storia dell'arte*.

13. Serv. *In Virg.: ad Aen.* 8.180; Solinus 11.7.

14. Thuc. 1.10.2.

15. Alberti's intention is to set architecture firmly among the liberal arts.

16. The structural clarity of Alberti's treatise is in marked contrast to the disorganization of Vitruvius' work, despite the latter's claim (2.1.8) to have followed a logical order.

17. These last four books have been lost, although references are made to the first and the third books (5.12 and 3.2). Orlandi questions the title of the fourth one and amends it to read, "What Might Help the Architect in His Work."

Book One

1. *Lineamenta* has provoked much discussion. The German *Risse* (as used by M. Theuer in his German translation, *Zehn Bücher über die Baukunst*, Vienna, 1912) provides an accurate literal translation, while the closest English translation might perhaps be "definitions" (as suggested by Krautheimer in "Alberti and Vitruvius"). The manner, however, in which Alberti uses the term throughout the work makes its meaning explicit. See glossary.

2. The desire to express everything with greater clarity runs throughout Alberti's work; cf. 3.14 and 6.1. He emphatically starts this passage in the first person singular, but continues in the plural, which cannot be done in English here (we have, however, followed him wherever it proved manageable.)

3. For the distinction between lineaments and structure, *lineamenta* and *structura*, see glossary, s.v. Construction.

4. Dealt with in 1.3–7.

5. Number is a more complex word in Alberti's Latin than in English: for the implication of *certum numerum*, see glossary, s.v. *Concinnitas*.

6. *Modum* in this instance means "manner," in the sense of "scale," and not "size," as Theuer interprets it (p. 19); see glossary, s.v. Scale.

7. This version of "origins" contrasts sharply with that given by Vitruvius in 2.1.

8. Alberti presumably used a corrupt manuscript of Pliny, since this version is given in all MSS; the correct version of this passage should read in translation, "Gellius accepts Toxius, son of Uranus, as the inventor of building with clay. . . . walls were introduced by Thrason, towers by the Cyclopes, according to Aristotle, but, according to Theophrastus, by the Tirynthians." Pliny *N.H.* 7.194–195.

9. See glossary, s.v. *Area*.

10. See glossary, s.v. Compartition.

11. Here the image of the building as a body (which is to recur throughout the book) makes its first appearance.

12. *Amoenitas* here translates as "elegance," but see also 7.1.

13. *Redimita*. This could also be translated as "decorated" or "embellished"; cf. Beauty and ornament, in glossary.

14. The Vitruvian triad of *firmitas, utilitas, venustas*: cf. Vitr. 1.3.2. On the use of the critical triad see Vitruvius, *Architettura*, trans. Silvio Ferri, pp. 48ff., and see glossary, s.v. Vitruvian triad.

15. Alberti's use of *regio* has a more parochial sense than the English "region"; "locality" may therefore provide a closer translation.

16. Cf. Diod. Sic. 1.12.7.

17. Glaucopis means "shining-eyed," an epithet Homer frequently uses in referring to Athene.

18. Cicero, *In Verr.* 5.26.

19. Herod. 2.77.3. Alberti uses a mistranslation of the Greek. Herodotus in fact wrote, ". . . the Egyptians are the healthiest of all men, next to the Libyans."

20. Cf. Herod. 4.184. According to Herodotus, it was the Atarantes, and not the neighboring tribe, the Garamantes, who cursed the sun. However, cf. Pliny *N.H.* 5.45.

21. Ovid, *Pont.* 1.5.6.

22. Hippocrates, *Air, Waters, Places* 8.

23. The northeast wind; see glossary, s.v. Winds.

24. Pliny *N.H.* 2.48.127. Pliny does not acknowledge or follow the advice of Theophrastus or Hippocrates on this matter.

25. The south wind; see glossary, s.v. Winds.

26. The northwest wind; see glossary, s.v. Winds.

27. See 10.1.

28. Cf. Suetonius, *Caligula* 21.

29. Varro *De r.r.* 1.7.8. Alberti appears to be following a corrupt text; Varro in fact writes, *intus ad Rhenum*, whereas Alberti has *inter Adienum*.

30. Alberti appears to be confusing Caesar's remarks on Britain with those he makes about Germany. Caesar, *De bello Gallico* 5.12; 6.23.

31. Cf. Pliny *N.H.* 4.95.

32. Pliny *N.H.* 16.15.

33. Cf. Vitr. 2.1.1. The architect's name was in fact Dinocrates; there has presumably been a scribal error at some stage, as Alberti records his name correctly elsewhere (6.4).

34. Arist. *Pol.* 7.10.2.

35. App. 8.71.

36. Vitr. 8.3; one of the few compliments Alberti pays Vitruvius.

37. Hippocrates, *Air, Waters, Places* 7.4.

38. Hypochondria, although Hippocrates refers to pneumonia. On black bile see also Cicero, *Tusculanae disputationes* 3.5.2.

39. Diod. Sic. 2.36.1. Diodorus, however, ascribes their physical size to their abundant supply of food.

40. Cf. Vitr. 7.4.

41. Cf. Xenophon, *Anabasis* 4.8.20–21. Xenophon does not mention the tree leaves. Pliny mentions *maenomenon mel*, a kind of honey in Pontus that was said to cause madness; Pliny *N.H.* 21.77.

42. Plutarch, *Antony* 45. Alberti omits to mention that unfortunately there was no wine to be had.

43. Tarantulas; although the word is now used for a wide variety of American, African, and Australian hunting spiders. Alberti's *Lycosa Tarantula* is usually about 5 cm. long, and not particularly poisonous, although it was generally believed that its bite caused a fatal melancholy only curable by the music of the tarantella. Tarantella dancers, however, already exhibited themselves for money, as Bishop Berdey saw on his trip to Apulia, but see Isaac Disraeli's *Curiosities of Literature*, Paris 1835, vol. 2, pp. 226ff.

44. Cf. Theophrastus, fragment 87, ed. Wimmer. Alberti clearly derives this information from Gellius (4.13), who attributes the cure to Democritus.

45. Cf. Strabo 2.4.56; Plutarch, *Pompey* 35. These Albanians lived on the Caspian shore of the Caucasus, not in Epirus.

46. See glossary, s.v. Tough stone.

47. Cf. Pliny *N.H.* 2.211.

48. Pliny *N.H.* 2.136.

49. *Keraunos* is the Greek for thunder.

50. Serv. *In Virg.: ad Aen.* 8.414; cf. *in Ecl.* 4.62.

51. Alberti presumably means the Essedones of Samatia.

52. Hydaspes is Jhelum in the Punjab.

53. Alberti is referring not to Galatia in Asia Minor, but to Gaul; cf. Strabo 4.182.

54. Cf. Pliny *N.H.* 46.121.

55. A high mountain, now Monte Compatri.

56. I.e. (Greek), the sea country; or an even more direct pun, Achaia/Aquaia.

57. Galen, *De febrium differentiis* (ed. Kuhn) 2.8.

58. Cf. Strabo, 5.247–248; Serv. *In Virg.: ad Aen.* 9.715.

59. There appear to be no references in Plato to local supernatural influences. Cf. *Leges* 5.744e.

60. Cf. Vitr. 1.4.9.

61. Varro *De r.r.* 1.12.2.

62. The conflict between classical precedent and contemporary religion was a constant concern of fifteenth-century humanists.

63. Cf. Diod. Sic. 12.10. The name of their town was Thurium.

64. Virtue: see glossary, s.v.

65. See glossary, s.v.

66. Within the "classical" vocabulary of "perfect" forms, to which Alberti is confining his argument, this is indeed the case.

67. This is Alberti's first introduction of *varietas*; see below, 1.9; and glossary, s.v. Variety.

68. Implicit in this is Alberti's belief that the height of a building section and elevations should relate to the dimensions, proportions, and form of the plan.

69. Alberti may be referring here to the Nymphaeum in the Licinian Gardens in Rome, known as the Temple of Minerva Medica.

70. There is a well-known twelve-sided monument, the tomb of the Calventii, on the Via Appia Antica, while the Mausoleum of Augustus could be said to be thirteen-sided.

71. Proportion: see glossary, s.v.

72. Cf. Vitr. 1.6.2; 1.6.8.

73. Sextus Julius Frontinus, superintendent of the Roman aqueducts under Nerva in the latter half of the first century A.D., whose works include *De aquis urbis Romae* and *Strategematica*.

74. Front. *Aq. Rom.* 18.

75. This may be, as Orlandi suggests, the temple at the source of the Clitumno, outside Spoleto.

76. Alberti is referring to the Mausoleum of Theodoric, at that time used as a church, Santa Maria Rotonda; the sea has now receded from Ravenna, and the ground about the building cleared.

77. See below, 3.5.

78. There are no such walls at Alatri. Alberti is presumably referring to the temple of Jupiter Auxur, or to the temple of Fortune at Palestrina.

79. More usually known as the *Agger Servii Tulii*, the inner wall of Rome, of which fragments still remain. Cf. Vitr. 6.8.6. P. Cluver (*Italia Antiqua*, Antwerp, 1624, vol. 1, p. 983) remarks on the absence of reference to walls in Latin literature. M. Todd, *The Walls of Rome* (London: Paul Elek, 1978), pp. 13ff.; Ian A. Richmond, 1917, p. 9.

80. Presumably Alberti means terraces.

81. Presumably Monte Moricino, not Lucino.

82. Alberti is referring, of course, to the chapels attached to the Constantinian Basilica of St. Peter, to which major changes were proposed by Pope Nicholas V in the 1450s, and which was destroyed completely by Pope Julius II, from the early sixteenth century onward, to make way for the building now standing. See also below, 1.10.

83. No record exists of any temple dedicated to Latona anywhere in Rome. The Basilica of Constantine in the Roman Forum was known as the *Templum Pacis* until

correctly identified by Antonio Nibby in 1819. It was described as *Templum Pacis et Latonae* in medieval documents. The northwest angle of the basement of the basilica is in fact fortified and impinges on the ruins of the Forum of Peace and of Nero's palace. Theuer (p. 611f., 6.2) suggested that the connection with Latona was due to the existence of an arched passageway called *Arcus Latronis*. See G. Lugli, *Roma Antica* (Rome: Bardi, 1968), pp. 227ff; and Krautheimer, "Alberti's *Templum Etruscum*," 1969.

84. "Compartmentalization" provides the closest translation of Alberti's *partitio*. However, Leoni's "compartition," though obscure, is perhaps more convenient, but see glossary, s.v. Compartition.

85. See glossary, s.v. Vitruvian triad; cf. above, n. 12 and n. 14.

86. See also below, 5.2. For the influence of this concept, see Wittkower, *Architectural Principles,* p. 67.

87. Although Vitruvius provides an accurate description of a *xystus* (5.11.4), its precise meaning in Alberti's time was probably somewhat vague; Flavio Biondo, for example, comments, "There were also curved *xysti* in the guise of a half circle, with other members of diverse Greek names, which the Greeks today, however, do not know how to interpret." F. Biondo, *Roma Trionfante*, trans. L. Fauno, Venice, 1544, pp. 332ff.

88. An opinion shared by Vitruvius (2.3.3), and mentioned elsewhere by Alberti (6.10).

89. Cf. Hippocrates, *Air, Waters, Places* 11.

90. Variety: see glossary, s.v.

91. For the relationship between music and visual harmony, see Wittkower, *Architectural Principles*; and below, 9.5–6; and glossary, s.v. Proportion.

92. This is a good example of Alberti's nondogmatic stance in relation to the classical canons of architecture.

93. See below, 4.1–5.

94. Scale, *modus*: see glossary, s.v. Scale.

95. See glossary, s.v. Winds.

96. Iulius Capitolinus (one of the Scriptores Historiae Augustae), *Verus* 8.2.

97. Seleucia: a celebrated city in Babylonia, near the river Tigris.

98. Amm. Marc. 23.6.24. Ammianus speaks of a hairy, *comaeus*, Apollo.

99. A point Alberti emphasized to the site architect of his Tempio Malatestiano in Rimini, in 1454: who, disregarding Alberti's model, had proposed using a circular window. See C. Grayson, *Alberti and the Tempio Malatestiano: An Autograph Letter from L. B. Alberti to Matteo de' Pasti, November 18, 1454* (New York: Pierpont Morgan Library, 1957). The circular windows seen at Sant'Andrea are most likely from the sixteenth century; see Rykwert and Tavernor, "Sant'Andrea."

100. This is a much-quoted argument against the Gothic pointed arch, which was still favored in northern Europe at this time for aesthetic and structural reasons.

101. Alberti refers to the antique system of measurement throughout his treatise; for Alberti's use of measure see glossary, s.v. Measures. Vitruvius (3.4.4.) recommends a rise of between nine and ten inches, and a tread of between one and a half feet and two.

Book Two

1. Suetonius, *Julius* 46.

2. See glossary, s.v. *Concinnitas*; and below, 9.7.

3. See glossary, s.v. *Concinnitas*; and below, 9.7.

4. Plato, *Sophist* 235e ff.; *Republic* 602c ff.

5. Variety: see glossary, s.v.; harmony: see glossary, s.v. *Concinnitas*; and below, 9.5–6.

6. In antiquity there were two instances of bridges of ships. Xerxes built one over the Hellespont. The bridge was destroyed by a storm, and the subsequent scourging of the sea, ordered by Xerxes, is reported in Herodotus (7.35). The bridge was rebuilt, but again destroyed by a storm. The other was built by Gaius Caligula between Baiae and the mole at Puteoli, the modern Pozzuoli (cf. Suet. *Cal.* 19).

7. See Livy 1.38.7. According to Dionysius of Halicarnassus (3.69), the temple was begun by Tarquin the Elder and completed by his son, Tarquin the Proud.

8. Cf. Pliny *N.H.* 36.82.

9. The tomb referred to is the Mausoleum of Halicarnassus, named after the husband of Artemis, Mausolus. Cf. Aul. Gell. 10.18.

10. Hor. *Car.* 2.18.

11. Tac. *Hist.* 2.49.

12. The theater of Pompey would in fact have been difficult to appreciate in Alberti's time, because it had been transformed into housing, and its exact location was uncertain.

13. Presumably Alberti is here referring to the *domus aurea* in particular. Cf. Suetonius, *Nero* 31; Tac. *Hist.* 2.42.

14. Alberti is perhaps referring to the Seianian Cave, a 900-meter-long tunnel through a hill near Naples, constructed by Cocceius Nerva in 37 B.C.

15. Cf. Scr. Hist. Aug. 24.7.

16. A lake near Cumae and Naples.

17. Quinquereme: the standard warship of the Roman republic, a large galley, probably with five rowers to each oar.

18. Cf. Suetonius, *Nero* 16.1; 31.3.

19. Eusebius (A.D. 265–340), bishop of Caesarea in Palestine and author (in Greek) of a *Chronicle*, an *Ecclesiastical History*, a *Gospel Demonstration*, a biography of Constantine, and a topography of Palestine.

20. Eus. *Praep. Evang.* 9.30.4–5.

21. Quintus Curtius Rufus. He wrote, probably under Claudius or Vespasian, a history of Alexander the Great in ten books, of which the first two are lost.

22. Quint. Curt. 7.26. According to Curtius, the city in fact took seventeen days to complete; Arrian (4.4.1) says twenty; Justin (12.5) agrees with Curtius.

23. Flavius Josephus (A.D. 37–c. 100), a Jewish statesman and soldier, the author of an *Early History of the Jews* (*Antiquitates Iudaicae*), to A.D. 66, and of a *History of the Jewish Wars* ((*Bellum Iudaicum*).

24. Joseph. *Antiq.* 10.224–225; *Contra Apionem* 1.138–140. It was a subsequent palace, not the wall or the temple, that took fifteen days to build.

25. Stade: a Greek furlong, 600 Greek feet, probably about 194 yards, or 185 meters; for Alberti's use of measures, see glossary, s.v. Measures.

26. Joseph. *Bell. Iud.* 5.508–509.

27. Diod. Sic. *Bibl. hist.* 2.7.3.

28. Diod. Sic. *Bibl. hist.* 2.9.1–3.

29. Arverni, a Gallic tribe, occupying modern Auvergne.

30. Pliny *N.H.* 34.45.

31. Pliny *N.H.* 7.194. The text used by Alberti was clearly corrupt: it should read, ". . . according to Gellius, Toxius was the first to. . . ." Gellius was a grammarian of the first half of the second century A.D. Strabo (11.503) mentions a people called the Gaelians.

32. Diod. Sic. 5.68.1.

33. Eus. *Praep. Evang.* 1.10.10.

34. Theophrastus, *Historia plantarum* 5.1.1–5.

35. See glossary, s.v. Winds.

36. Vitr. 2.9.1. Favonius marked the beginning of spring; see glossary, s.v. Winds.

37. Hesiod, *Opera et dies* 383–384, 415–421. In fact Hesiod recommends the harvest at the rising of the Pleiades, and is much more circumstantial about cutting wood.

38. Cato *De r.r.* 17.1–2.

39. Varro *De r.r.* 1.37.2.

40. Cf. Pliny *N.H.* 16.194.

41. *Luna sitiente*: literally, "when the moon is thirsty"; usually interpreted as meaning, "when the moon is cloudless, bright."

42. L. Junius Moderatus Columella, a well-known writer on husbandry in the first century A.D.

43. Col. *De r.r.* 11.2.11. There are, of course, only 28 days in the lunar cycle.

44. Flavius Vegetius Renatus, a writer on military affairs in the latter half of the fourth century.

45. Flavius Vegetius, *Epitoma rei militaris* 4.35.

46. Pliny *N.H.* 16.190–191.

47. Theophrastus, *Historia plantarum* 5.1.2.

48. Theophrastus, *Historia plantarum* 5.5.6.

49. Cato lists many uses for oil lees, but does not include this one. Cf. Cato *De r.r.* 130.111f. Cf. also Pliny *N.H.* 15.33–34. Alberti may be confusing Cato's comments with those of Pliny on cedar oil; cf. Pliny *N.H.* 16.197.

50. Cf. Pliny *N.H.* 15.34.

51. Pliny *N.H.* 36.89.

52. Theophrastus, *De causis plantarum* 5.15.4.

53. Aul. Gell. 15.1.4.

54. Cf. Pliny *N.H.* 13.99.

55. Pliny *N.H.* 13.57.

56. See glossary, s.v. Winds.

57. Cato *De r.r.* 31.2.

58. Theophrastus, *Historia plantarum* 5.3.5.

59. *Quercus cerrus*.

60. *Quercus*: and see below, n. 75, where Alberti's use of the generic term *quercus* causes some confusion.

61. *Quercus robur*.

62. *Quercus aesculus*.

63. Cf. Vitr. 2.9.10.

64. Cf. Vitr. 2.9.8.

65. Theophrastus, *Historia plantarum* 5.6.1. The baths were in fact at Antandros, a maritime town in Mysia, now Antandro.

66. Alberti borrows extensively from Vitruvius. Cf. Vitr. 2.9.6.

67. Theophrastus mentions the plant amomon, but makes no claims as to how long it lasts. Cf. *Historia plantarum* 9.7.2.

68. Plato, *Leges* 5.741c.

69. Cf. Pliny *N.H.* 16.213–215.

70. Hadrian III was pope A.D. 884–885, and Eugenius IV A.D. 1431–1447. Eugenius in fact commissioned the doors for St. Peter's from Filarete in 1439, giving the doors an age of at least 554 years and establishing a *terminus post quem* for Alberti's treatise, since the doors were completed in 1445.

71. Cf. Vitr. 2.15–16.

72. Cf. Pliny *N.H.* 16.223; Theophrastus, *Historia plantarum* 5.6; Aul. Gell. 3.6; Xenophon, *Cyropaedia* 7.5.11.

73. Pliny *N.H.* 16.198.

74. Vitr. 2.9.9.

75. Here Alberti appears confused. Pliny (*N.H.* 16.218) comments, "fagus et cerrus celeriter marcescunt." Vitruvius (2.9.9) comments, "cerrus quercus fagus . . . celeriter marcescunt." As Alberti elsewhere differentiates between *cerrus* and *quercus*, it would appear that here he is referring to Vitruvius.

76. Cf. Vitr. 2.9.7; Pliny *N.H.* 16.197.

77. Cf. Pliny *N.H.* 16.229.

78. Cf. Pliny *N.H.* 16.228.

79. Cf. Theophrastus, *Historia plantarum* 5.4.2.

80. Theophrastus, *Historia plantarum* 5.5.6.

81. Cf. Pliny *N.H.* 16.210.

82. Cato *De r.r.* 31.1.

83. Cf. Pliny *N.H.* 16.224.

84. Cf Pliny *N.H.* 16.187.

85. Vitr. 7.1.2.

86. Theophrastus, *Historia plantarum* 3.2.

87. Cf. Pliny *N.H.* 16.196.

88. *Medula*, literally "marrow."

89. Varro *De r.r.* 1.41.4.

90. Cf. Aristotle, *De plantis* 1.3; and also Pliny *N.H.* 16.185.

91. Alburnum: the new annual growth.

92. Cf. Pliny *N.H.* 14.9. Populonia was situated on the Tuscan coast, in the vicinity of Piombino.

93. Strabo 2.1.14.

94. Cf. Pliny *N.H.* 16.216.

95. Cf. Pliny *N.H.* 16.207.

96. Cf. Lucretius, *De rerum natura* 5.455–457; Theophrastus, *De lapidibus*, 1–3.

97. This advice is offered not by Cato, but by Vitruvius and Pliny. Cf. Vitr. 2.7.5; Pliny *N.H.* 36.170.

98. See glossary, s.v. Winds.

99. Lake Bolsena.

100. A town in Caria, now Eskişehir.

101. Hard white calcareous tufa. Cf. Pliny *N.H.* 36.168–169; Vitr. 2.7.3.

102. Two kinds of volcanic *peperino*. Tac. *Ann.* 15.43.

103. I.e., chalk.

104. Cf. Pliny *N.H.* 36.159, 167; Vitr. 2.7.1–2.

105. Cf. Pliny *N.H.* 36.125.

106. Presumably Alberti means a mass of stalactites and stalagmites.

107. Possibly the river Marmore, near Terni.

108. Alberti is here referring to Cisalpine Gaul.

109. Presumably that around Forum Cornelium, a town in the Lingones in Cisalpine Gaul, and not around Corneliana Castra on the African coast.

110. The river is now called the Chiana.

111. A town in Mysia, now Chizico, Atraki, or Balkiz.

112. A town in Macedonia.

113. Pliny *N.H.* 35.167.

114. Cf. Pliny *N.H.* 35.166. This *pozzolana* is the base of much of the cement used by the Romans. Cf. also Vitr. 2.6.1.

115. Oropus is a town, and Aulis a seaport in Boetia.

116. Cf. Pliny *N.H.* 35.167.

117. Cf. Pliny *N.H.* 36.131. Again the text used by Alberti appears to be corrupt. Pliny mentions "Assos in the Troad," not "Troy in Asia."

118. Here Alberti relies heavily on Pliny. Cf. Pliny *N.H.* 35.169; cf. also Vitr. 2.3.1.

119. Cf. Pliny *N.H.* 35.170; Vitr. 2.3.2.

120. See glossary, s.v. Measures.

121. Cf. Vitr. 2.3.3; Pliny *N.H.* 35.171.

122. For Alberti's use of antique measures, see glossary, s.v. Measures.

123. Alberti does not appear to have followed his own recommendations here, probably because of established and strictly followed traditions concerning the local manufacture of brick; see glossary, s.v. Measures.

124. Pliny *N.H.* 35.170; Vitr. 2.3.2.

125. Cf. Pliny *N.H.* 35.160.

126. Alberti is in fact quoting Pliny (*N.H.* 36.174). Cf. Cato *De r.r.* 38.2.

127. Cf. Vitr. 2.5.3.

128. Pliny *N.H.* 36.169.

129. Cf. Vitr. 2.5.1.

130. Pliny *N.H.* 36.174.

131. In fact, an inland area between the rivers Loire and Saône.

132. Alberti derives much of his information on gypsum from Pliny. Cf. *N.H.* 36.182–183.

133. This is presumably a reference to Alberti's work on the former church of San Francesco, Rimini, which he transformed for Sigismondo Malatesta into the Tempio Malatestiano. Alberti's involvement dates from 1450, providing a further *terminus post quem* for his treatise on architecture.

134. Presumably Alberti is referring to fossils. There seems to be some confusion between live and fossilized remains in stone. See two paragraphs below.

135. Martin V was pope from 1417 to 1431.

136. Tough stone: see glossary, s.v.

137. Cato provides a detailed account of the construction of the kiln and the method of producing lime. Cf *De r.r.* 38.1–4.

138. Vitr. 2.6.6.

139. A region situated between the Apennines and the rivers Tiber and Arno.

140. The southwest wind. See glossary, s.v. Winds.

141. Cf. Vitr. 2.4.2–3.

142. Cf. Vitr. 2.4.1.

143. Cf. Vitr. 2.4.3.

144. A problem that Alberti encountered when building in Mantua, where there is no local stone. Consequently his buildings there are of brick.

145. Cf. Pliny *N.H.* 36.175.

146. Pliny *N.H.* 35.182, 169.

147. Budini: a people of Sarmatia.

148. Herod. 4.108.

149. Neuri: a people of European Scythia.

150. Pomponius Mela, *De chorographia* 2.1.15.

151. Cf. Diod. Sic. 3.19.

152. Diod. Sic. 4.30.5.

153. Front. *Aq. Rom.* 2.123. Apart from the skilled masons, wallers, and so on, general labor was more abundant during the winter months, a time of year when farming required less manual labor. There is evidence that this affected seasonal work on building during Alberti's time more than the influence of the weather on building materials.

154. L. Tarutius Firmanus, a celebrated astrologer.

155. Cf. Cic. *De. div.* 2.98.

156. Julius F. Maternus, a Roman mathematician in the time of Constantine the Great, author of a work entitled *Matheseos libri octo*.

157. Petosiris: a celebrated Egyptian mathematician and astrologer. Necepsus: a mythic astrologer in Egypt.

158. The final passages of this book distance Alberti from certain revered antique beliefs and traditions, and serve to emphasize the objectivity of his approach to architecture.

159. Virg. *Ecl.* 3.60.

Book Three

1. Girdle: see glossary, s.v. Bones and paneling.

2. *Area*: see glossary, s.v.

3. Alberti is probably referring to the level of tufa rock near the ancient Etruscan city of Veio, in the locality now known as the Isola Farnese.

4. Alberti considers *fundatio* to be derived from *fundus*, "the bottom," and *itio*, "a passage"; it is more likely derived from the verb *fundere*, "to found," with the suffix *-atio*, thereby meaning "the process of founding."

5. See glossary, s.v.

6. This way of verifying the right angle was known to the ancient Egyptians. Vitruvius comments that it follows the theory of Pythagoras on the square of the hypotenuse (9. intro. 6).

7. These *Commentarii rerum mathematicarum* have not so far been securely identified and may be a lost work of Alberti's. See Grayson, "The Composition of L.B. Alberti's *Decem Libri*."

8. The mainland town of Mestre.

9. See 1.8; 3.6.

10. Col. *De r.r.* 1.5.9.

11. See glossary, s.v. Tough stone.

12. *Modius*: the Roman grain measure, containing 16 *sextarii*, or the equivalent of 8.73 liters. See glossary, s.v. Measures, for Alberti's use of measure.

13. Cato *De r.r.* 15.

14. Vitruvius in fact recommends the proportions three to one for pit sand and two to one for river or sea sand: Vitr. 2.5.1. Pliny *N.H.* 36.175.

15. According to Herodotus, the poles were driven into the marsh and then retracted to collect clay to be used for making the bricks. "Asithis" should read "Asuchis," and "Nicerinus," "Mycerinus." Cf. Herod. 2.136.

16. "Cresiphus" should read "Chersiphron"; Alberti describes in 6.6 his novel technique for the transportation of quarried stone.

17. The Chicago MS completes the lacuna between "hides" and "coal." The hides are in fact sheepskins. Further beams were laid on top, and above the beams, vast stones. We would omit sheepskins and only cram charcoal into the space. . . . This conflates Pliny (*N.H.* 36.95) and Vitruvius (3.4.2; 5.12.6).

18. See glossary, s.v. Measures. Cf. Eus. *Praep. Evang.* 9.4.

19. I.e., Hadrian's mausoleum in Rome, known more familiarly as Castel Sant'Angelo.

20. Alberti includes the footings within his definition of the term "foundations."

21. See glossary, s.v. Cornice.

22. See glossary, s.v. Bones and paneling.

23. In Latin, *complementum*. See glossary, s.v. Bones and paneling.

24. Varro *De r.r.* 1.14.4.

25. Cf. 6.2; see glossary, s.v. Beauty and ornament.

26. Cato *De r.r.* 14.4–5.

27. For the meaning of "columns" in this context, see ch. 6, above.

28. See ch. 6, above; and glossary, s.v. Bones and paneling.

29. See glossary, s.v. Bones and paneling.

30. See glossary, s.v. Bones and paneling.

31. See glossary, s.v. Winds.

32. In Mantua, where Alberti designed the churches of San Sebastiano and Sant'-Andrea, there was no local stone available, and the walls of his buildings are constructed with an inner and an outer skin of brick filled with rubble.

33. Vitruvius calls these *diatonos* (2.8).

34. I.e., Roman *libbra*, which equals 327.45 grams.

35. The codices have Mino and Nino; Orlandi is clearly correct, however, in amending the name to Numa; Plutarch, *Numa* 17.

36. See glossary, s.v. Winds.

37. *Lapis*, used by Alberti to mean brick as well as stone.

38. Cato *De r.r.* 14.1.

39. I.e., dovetailed.

40. Pliny *N.H.* 35.169.

41. See glossary, s.v. Bones and paneling.

42. Cf. Pliny *N.H.* 2.146.

43. Pliny notes the custom of hanging up a toad by one of its hind legs at the threshold of a barn before carrying the grain into it; *N.H.* 18.303.

44. Cf. Pliny *N.H.* 13.117.

45. Both Pliny and Theophrastus comment that the tree, if eaten, may prove fatal, and that diarrhea is the only way to purge it; Pliny *N.H.* 13.118; Theophrastus, *Historia plantarum* 3.18.13.

46. See glossary, s.v. Bones and paneling.

47. See glossary, s.v. Bones and paneling.

48. Physicians/*physici*: Those who deal with *physis*, Nature. The nearest modern equivalent would be "natural scientists."

49. The reference is not in Varro.

50. *Cuneos*; these wedges are of course voussoirs in modern terminology.

51. Ennius, *Tragedies* 5.423 (ed. Vahlen). This is reported by Varro (*De L.L.* 5.19).

52. Servius *In Virg.: ad Aen.* 2.19.

53. The "spherical" vault, by which Alberti presumably means "hemispherical," is, of course, more usually known as a dome.

54. Of the various types of vaults described here, Alberti proposed a barrel vault for the Tempio Malatestiano at Rimini with a spherical vault at the east end, probably on a circular plan; a spherical vault for the first project of San Sebastiano at Mantua,

on a cruciform plan; a spherical vault for the already existing circular plan of the choir of Santissima Annunziata, Florence; a long barrel vault flanked on either side by lower barrel-vaulted chapels at Sant'Andrea in Mantua. The only vault to have been constructed in his lifetime for which he was undoubtedly responsible was that to the chapel of the Rucellai sepulcher in San Pancrazio, Florence.

55. *Fornix*, which Alberti derives from *perforare*, "to drill, to pierce through."

56. Camerated or cross-vault: Alberti constructs another etymology here—*camura* is derived, following Servius (*In Virg.: ad Georg.* 3.55), from *camur*, meaning "folded over."

57. Bones: for this and the rest of the paragraph, see glossary, s.v. Bones and paneling.

58. Rings, *coronae*: see glossary, s.v. Cornices.

59. See glossary, s.v. Winds.

60. The herringbone construction and the movable centering were both used by Brunelleschi in Florence Cathedral. Alberti's preference for the structure of the Pantheon is quite explicit.

61. Vitruvius in fact mentions the Phrygians, whose primitive civilization was proverbial; Vitr. 2.1.5.

62. Pliny *N.H.* 6.109. Pliny in fact attributes this to "the Turtle-eaters in the angle of Carmania." Cf. also *N.H.* 6.19 and 9.35, where Pliny again mentions the practice of using turtle shells for roofing.

63. Cf. Pliny *N.H.* 7.195.

64. Diod. Sic. 2.10.

65. Vitruvius, and not Varro, gives this advice: 7.4.5.

66. *N.H.* 36.184–189.

67. 7.2.1ff.

68. *Opus spicatum*; cf. Vitr. 7.1.4.

69. See glossary, s.v. Winds.

Book Four

1. Plutarch, *Theseus* 25.1–2.

2. Plutarch mentions 300 measures (*metra* in Greek). Cf. Plutarch, *Solon* 18.1ff.

3. Plutarch, *Numa* 17.

4. Caesar, *De bello Gallico* 6.13.

5. Not a known place name. Orlandi suggests that this is a reference to Panchaia, "a fabulous island in the Red Sea," on which see Servius *In Virg.: Georg.* 2.115–117 and 4.379; and Pliny *N.H.* 7.197 and 10.2, where it is the home of the phoenix. It is more probably a reference to the utopian society of that name described by Euhemeros of Messene, which could have been known through the epitome given by Diodorus Siculus (5.41ff.) or Eusebius of Caesarea (*Praep. Evang.*).

6. Herod. 2.164–168. Strabo and Diodorus give the Egyptians as being divided into three classes, whereas Plato makes them five or more (cf. Diod. Sic. 1.29 and 1.74; Plato, *Timaeus* 24 A ff.). But cf. also Isocrates, *Busiris* 21.

7. Cf. Arist. *Pol.* 2.5.2.

8. Aristotle discusses the constitution of the ideal state in *Politics* 7 and 8. Cf. also 4.3.11ff.

9. Ephors were Dorian elective magistrates, who became particularly powerful in Sparta. Diod. Sic. 2.40–41.

10. See glossary, s.v. Soul.

11. Plato, *Republic* 9.580f.

12. Cf. Arrian, *Indike* 7.3; Diod. Sic. 2.38.

13. Thuc. 1.2.2.

14. The Burgundii were one of the barbarian tribes who invaded French lands in the fourth century A.D., and Alberti may have had the Helvetii in mind, who burned *all* their *oppida* and four hundred villages; see Caesar, *De bello Gallico* 1.5.

15. Pomponius Mela, *De chorographia* 1.64. Cf. Eus. *Praep. Evang.* 1, 10.

16. Herod. 2.137.3.

17. Caesar, *De bello Gallico* 4.3; 6.23. Caesar further comments that the Germans felt that if the land beyond their boundaries was uninhabited, it was a sign that no one dared be their neighbor.

18. Cf. Diod. Sic. 1.55.6; an approximate reading.

19. Orlandi has pointed out that Alberti (or his source) has conflated the two comments about Assyria and Arabia in Diodorus. See note 20.

20. Cf. Diod. Sic. 2.48.4–5.

21. As Diogenes Laertius points out (4.23), there were many who bore the name of Crates; it is likely that Alberti is here referring to Crates the Theban Cynic (fl. 326 B.C.), whose ascetic life is described by Diogenes (6.85–93).

22. Livy 29.25.12. Orlandi notes that Alberti appears to have used a corrupt text: instead of "the territory of the Emerici," Livy has "Emporia," which lies between Gabes and Sfax in Tunisia.

23. Cf. Diod. Sic. 4.20.1. The Ligii are in fact the Ligurians.

24. Varro *De r.r.* 1.7.6. Varro refers to a vine near "Elephantine," not "Memphis."

25. Strabo mentions the Taurus, but gives no details. The *modius* was the Roman grain measure, containing 16 *sextarii*.

26. Herodotus makes no such comment. Cf., however, Diod. Sic. 2.47, who quotes Hecateus, among others, as the authority on this myth.

27. This tale appears to have come from Pomponius Mela (*De chorographia* 3.58), who refers to "Talge in Caspio mari sine cultu fertilis"; i.e., Talge on the Caspian Sea.

28. Joseph. *Bell. Iud.* 2.386–387.

29. Plato, *Republic* 5.473a. Cf. also 9.592a–b.

30. This echoes the definition of beauty given in 6.2; where in the Platonic dialogues or Xenophon he found it is not evident. See, however, Plato, *Leges* 5.746c, and Cicero's description of the perfection of the human body (*De oratore* 3.45.1792).

31. Cf. Diod. Sic. 2.38.

32. Strabo 1.3.17.

33. Cf. Strabo 1.3.4. There seems to be no definite evidence that the temple was

once on the coast, although Strabo supports the theory of Strato, that at some stage this must have been the case for it to have achieved so much fame.

34. Plato, *Leges* 704b.

35. Arist. *Pol.* 7.10; *Problemata* 1.52; 5.34; 37.3.

36. Mount Taurus is the Taurian Mountains, a range in northeastern Asia Minor.

37. Hesiod, *Opera et dies* 518.

38. Diod. Sic. 4.78.

39. Cingolo, mentioned by Caesar, *De bello civili* 1.15.

40. Possibly Brixino in Rhaetia; Breixen.

41. Cf. Vitr. 1.5.2., on the angles that defend the enemy rather than the townsmen. How the corners of towers are susceptible to damage from the war machines is described in a later passage; Vitr. 1.5.5.

42. Cf. Diod. Sic. 1.45.4; it was the city of Zeus (Diospolis), not the city of the sun (Heliospolis).

43. Cf. Diod. Sic. 1.50.4.

44. Diodorus notes the tradition of Ctesias of Cnidus, who makes the circumference of the walls 360 stades, and that of Cleitarchus, who makes it 365, adding that it had been the intention of Semiramis to make it equal the number of days in the year. Quintus Curtius (5.1) also gives 365. Strabo (16.1.5) gives 385, although this has generally been taken as an error of the MSS for 365. Herodotus (1.178) gives 480.

45. Cf. Diod. Sic. 2.3.3.

46. Varro *De L.L.* 5.143.

47. Plutarch, *Romulus* 11.

48. Here Alberti is following Varro.

49. *Ne fas*, "wrong," in the religious sense. Cf. Servius *In Virg.: ad Aen.* 2.730. But it was also a juridical distinction; cf. Plut. *R.Q.* 27.

50. Cf. Dion. Hal. 1.88.

51. Cf. Amm. Marc. 22.16.7; Arrian, *Anabasis* 3.2.1; Strabo 17.1.6; Plutarch, *Alexander* 26.5–6; Quintus Curtius reports, however, that it was a Macedonian custom to use barley to mark out a city, 4.8.6. The omens were taken from the way the birds ate the grain or flour.

52. Transcribed virtually verbatim from Censorinus; cf. Censorinus, *De die natali* 17.5ff.

53. Censorinus, *De die natali* 17.6.

54. Plutarch, *Numa* 3.6; but Plutarch gives the date as April 21. And the birthday of Rome is still celebrated on April 21.

55. Ninus founded Nineveh, and Semiramis Babylon. Cf. Diod. Sic. 2.3.3; 2.7.4.

56. Arrian *Anabasis* 2.21.4.

57. Herod. 1.98. Herodotus gives the name as Agbatana.

58. Plato, however, appears disdainful of walls. Cf. *Leges* 6.778d.

59. Cf. Plato, *Leges* 9.870, for Plato's views on ambition.

60. Cf. Flav. Veg. 4.2.

61. Tac. *Hist.* 5.11.

62. Megasthenes' description of Palimbothra is recorded by Arrian (*Indika* 10.5–6).

63. Cf. Herod. 1.178.

64. Diodorus records that Memphis was sited on a "delta" of the Nile. Diod. Sic. 1.50.3.

65. Taken almost verbatim from Flavius Vegetius, 4.3.

66. Vitr. 1.5.3.

67. Thuc. 2.75.2.

68. Caesar, *De bello Gallico* 7.23.2.

69. Cf. Vitr. 1.5.7.

70. Cf. Vitr. 1.5.4.

71. Cf. Flav. Veg. 4.4.

72. A direct reference to the rustic praedial servitudes of Roman Law. Cf. *Institutiones* 2.3; *Digesta* 8.3.8.

73. Cf. *Digesta* 8.3.8; here, however, it is mentioned that a straight road should be eight feet wide.

74. Unfortunately, the only available English word, "square," has unsuitable geometrical associations in this context.

75. An ancient town of Latium, now ruins near Pipero.

76. By another homely piece of etymology Alberti draws the derivation of *agger,* "embankment," from *ager,* "field."

77. Cf. Vitr. 1.5.

78. Tac. *Ann.* 15.43.

79. Quint. Curt. 5.1.26–27.

80. Plato, *Leges* 6.779.

81. Caesar, *De bello Gallico* 4.17.3ff. The quotation is partially interpreted.

82. Alberti has added the word *longis,* presumably with the intention of clarifying the sense. In fact he alters the sense; Caesar (4.17.6) has ". . . two feet in thickness, equal to the gap where the posts were joined."

83. *Sublicae;* Alberti adds a philological gloss to Caesar's term.

84. King Min, the legendary first king of united Egypt. Herodotus describes how that king diverted the Nile into the hills, but no bridge is mentioned, only a dam. Herod. 2.99.

85. Cf. Herod. 1.186. In later references, her name is correctly spelled Nitocris.

86. A light, slim, quick ship; the Liburnei of Dalmatia supplied timber for such ships.

87. Cf. Pliny *N.H.* 36.6. A sewer contractor forced Scaurus to give him security against possible damage to the drains, when he had heavy columns hauled to the Capitol.

88. N.B. Vaulting, says Alberti, consists of arches, as a wall consists of columns; the arch here is a rib, expressed or not.

89. I.e., a semicircle plus a further tenth.

90. I.e., the voussoirs.

91. This represents a fall of one in ninety-six; in England modern standards require a fall of one in ninety.

92. This represents a gradient of one in six.

93. The two were in fact adversaries in the Civil War. Dolabella stormed Smyrna and killed Trebonius. Cf. Appian, *De bellis civilibus* 3.26.

94. Thuc. 1.93.

95. A verb seems to be missing in this sentence. Theuer supplies *malim*; the sense is clear enough in any case.

96. See below, 10.12.

97. *Columnae*; clearly bollards are meant.

98. *Spectaculum*; see glossary, s.v. Show buildings and show grounds.

Book Five

1. See above, 4.1.

2. Euripides, *Hecuba* 884.

3. Bartoli already read it as Cairo.

4. Arrian, *Anabasis* 3.5.7.

5. Terence, *Eunuchus* 2.2.26.

6. Fest. p. 247.

7. *Gestatio*; strictly, a place where one is carried in a litter.

8. Diod. Sic. 5.40.1.

9. Alberti derives the Italian *sala* from the Latin *saltatio*, *triclinium saltatorium* (see Macrob. *Sat.* 2.10), though in fact the Italian is an adaptation of a Lombard word, related to the German *Saal*.

10. A further analogy between the house and the city, suggested in 1.9.

11. Joseph. *Antiq.* 13.249.

12. See below, 5.18.

13. It cannot be said with any certainty what form this "game of ball" would have taken. Orlandi translates it as *palla*. It is tempting, since Alberti mentions that it should be played in *ambulationes*, to associate it with various ball games played in cloisters, of which games such as *palla*, *jeu de paume*, and real tennis are a direct derivative. Cf. Heiner Gillmeister, "The Origins of European Ball Games," *Stadion* 7 (1981), pp. 19–51; also Antonio Scaino, *Trattato del giuco della palla* (Venice, 1555), where the layouts of various early courts are illustrated.

14. Cf. Vitr. 6.8. Alberti has drawn on that passage for the terminology if not the plan of his house.

15. Seneca, *De beneficiis* 6.34.2.

16. Fest. p. 17. Festus in fact refers to *auguraculum*, by which name the citadel was called because the augurs observed the flight of birds there.

17. That is, the temple of Jupiter Ammon or Hamon in Cyrenaica. Cf. Diod. Sic. 17.50.3.

18. Virg. *Aen.* 2.300.

19. *Summus antistites*, "high prelate." *Antistites* is a term often used for bishops.

Alberti uses the term *pontifex* for all clergy, much as he uses *templum* for a church. Of course *Pontifex Maximus* was the title proper to the pope alone.

20. I.e., cathedral.

21. Nigrigeneus: corrupted form of Hyginus Gromaticus. Cf. Hyg. Grom. *De const. limit.*, p. 134, II. 17–21, in *Corpus Agrimensorum Romanorum* (ed. C. Thulin, Stuttgart: Teubner, 1971).

22. In the previous chapter Alberti has already described religion in military terms, as a war waged on the devil.

23. Cf. Vitr. 5.11.

24. See the remaining sections of this book as well as 8.8.

25. Cf. Vitr. 1.2.7.

26. Polybius (6.27ff.) suggests that the camp plan is derived from that of the Roman city.

27. Xenophon, *Polity of the Lacedaemonians* 12.5.

28. Cf. Caesar, *De bello Gallico* 7.73. Here Caesar attributes the technique to the Gauls, not the Britons. Cf. *De bello Gallico* 5.18.3.

29. Cf. Caesar, *De bello Gallico* 1.26.3.

30. Quint. Curt. 1.11.

31. Cf. Caesar, *De bello Gallico* 2.17.4.

32. Arrian, *Indika* 20ff.

33. Xenophon, *Polity of the Lacedaemonians* 12.1.

34. Cf. Caesar, *De bello Gallico* 7.73.

35. A caltrop is an iron ball with at least four spikes projecting, used to obstruct military movement.

36. A mantelet is a war machine used as a cover for advancing infantry.

37. Cf. Caesar, *De bello Gallico* 7.72.

38. Caesar (*De bello Gallico* 7.72) gives the distance between them as eighty feet.

39. The general's tent.

40. The *porta quintana* corresponded to the *via quintana*, one of the crossways of the camp, parallel to the *via decumana*, which ran from the *porta decumana* to the *porta praetoria*.

41. More of this matter is given in book 10. But it may well be that another book on war machines was contemplated.

42. Appian, *De bellis civilibus* 5.33. Appian gives 1,500 towers, at intervals of 60 feet.

43. Alberti had in fact supervised the raising of this ship from the bottom of Lake Nemi in 1447; Flavio Biondo in "Italia illustrata" in *Opera* (Basel, 1559), vol. 1, pp. 326f.; Mancini, *Vita di Leon Battista Alberti*, pp. 314f.

44. *Navis*. Although known in the sixteenth century to Leonardo da Vinci, it was not printed, and no manuscript has come to light.

45. Alberti observes that it is not volume, but the weight relative to that of the water displaced, that determines the capacity of the hold.

46. *Scaphae* or *scafae*, suspended planks used for boarding enemy ships.

47. *Corvus*, literally, "a raven." Here it refers to a grapnel, or grappling iron, shaped like a raven's beak and used to gain a hold on, or to damage, an enemy ship.

48. *Pontus*, a sea, usually the Black Sea if not qualified; but since it has no islands, Orlandi suggests either an emendation or taking the Hellespont as part of the Black Sea.

49. Alberti uses the ancient terms *quaestor*, *publicanus*, *decumanus* for the public financial officers, much as he uses *pontifex* for Christian clergy.

50. Tough: see glossary.

51. Book 1, ch. 9.

52. This is another reference to the urban praedial servitudes of ancient Rome. Cf. book 4, n. 72; *Digesta* 8.6.8.

53. Porous: *cariosus*, an expression used by Cato (*De r.r.* 5.6; 34.1; 37.1), and explained by Pliny (*N.H.* 17.3.34) as "dry, porous, rough, white, full of holes, and like pumice stone."

54. Xen. *Oecon.* 11.15–18.

55. Celsus, *De medicina* 2.1.4.

56. *Ingenui*: literally, "native, free man."

57. Cf. Vitr. 6.3.5.

58. Cf. Cato *De r.r.* 14.

59. Or cimolite, after the Cycladic island Kimolos: fuller's earth, or common mineral.

60. Cf. Col. *De r.r.* 8.16.7–8.

61. Cf. Col. *De r.r.* 8.17.1.

62. Cf Cato *De r.r.* 91 and 129.

63. Cf. Vitr. 6.4.

64. Vitruvius (6.3.3) calls it "atrium"; Varro (*De L.L.* 5.161) calls it *cavum aedium*, "inner court."

65. Martial 8.14.3.

66. Varro (*De L.L.* 5.162) observes that the term *coenacula*—as Alberti calls the dining rooms—should properly refer to rooms on the upper story. Cf. also Vitr. 2.8.17.

67. Perhaps, as Grayson suggests, a quotation of Virg. *Ecl.* 1.83, transcribed from memory. See Grayson, "The Composition of L. B. Alberti's *Decem Libri*," p. 155.

68. Vitr. 7.4.4.

69. Presumably charcoal.

70. Cf. *Digesta* 32.1.55.s7.

71. Aristotle, *De generatione animalium* 2.6.743a. Cf. *Problemata* 8.15.

72. See below, 10.14.

73. This kind of swiveling cowl was not generally adopted until the nineteenth century.

74. I.e., that he should be able to change his abode according to the seasons. Lucullus (Plutarch, *Lucullus* 39.5) in fact states, "Do you suppose, then, that I have less sense than cranes or storks, and do not change residences according to the seasons?"

75. Cornelius Nepos, *Praefecti* (*De excellentibus ducibus*) 6.7.

76. Alberti includes guests and servants as part of the family. See this chapter, above.

77. That is, those wearing the *toga praetexta*.

78. The grain was found in Masada. Siboli does not exist. Cf. Joseph. *Bell. Iud.* 7.296–297.

79. Aristotle, *Problemata* 22.4.

80. Col. *De r.r.* 12.30.1.

81. See glossary, s.v. Beauty and ornament.

82. *Mundus muliebris*: in fact, this was a cosmetic box in antiquity; cf. Livy 34.7.9; *Digesta* 34.2.25.

83. Cf. Varro *De r.r.* 1.22.6.

84. Celsus (*De medicina* 1.3.1) writes, "It is better to make the move from a salubrious into an oppressive place at the beginning of winter, from an oppressive into a salubrious one at the beginning of summer."

85. Here, and below, cf. Vitr. 6.4.1.

86. This westerly orientation of the baths is reiterated in 9.10 below (n. 119); cf. 8.10 below, where public baths are described as arranged on a north/south axis.

Book Six

1. See glossary, s.v. Lineaments.

2. The Latin word *professor*, which Alberti uses here, implies as much a practitioner of one of the arts as a university teacher.

3. Presumably Alberti is referring here to the common practice of pilfering marble from the ancient ruins for the production of lime, on which see the poem of Aeneas Silvius Piccolomini (Pius II), "De Roma," in *Pii Secundi, Opera inedita*, ed. J. Cugnoni (Rome: R. Accademia dei Lincei, 1883).

4. Ill-considered (*inconcinnus*, literally without *concinnitas*): see glossary, s.v. *Concinnitas*.

5. See glossary, s.v. Beauty and ornament.

6. Alberti has already given this definition of beauty in the prologue. See his definition of perfection in 4.2, and compare Cicero's description of the perfection of the human body (*De oratore* 3.45.179). But see also 9.7.

7. Cic. *De nat. deor.* 1.28.79.

8. See glossary, s.v. Beauty and ornament.

9. *Sceptrum*, figure for power; this cannot be rendered literally in English here.

10. See glossary, s.v. *Concinnitas*.

11. Unfortunately the inner rhyme *vetustas* (long ages) and *venustas* (good looks) is not translatable.

12. See glossary, s.v. Compartition.

13. It was the emperor Tacitus who supplied the funds. Cf. Scr. Hist. Aug., *Tacitus* 10.5.

14. Pliny (*N.H.* 36.91) mentions the labyrinth made by King Porsena of Etruria to serve as his tomb.

15. Cf. Vitr. 6.6 and 7.

16. See glossary, s.v. Virtue.

17. See glossary, s.v. Beauty and ornament.

18. See glossary, s.v. Beauty and ornament.

19. See glossary, s.vv. *Area*, Compartition.

20. To follow Orlandi's conjectural alteration to the text, *laudet* for *audiat*.

21. Plutarch, *Alexander* 72.4; the architect appears as Polycrates in 1.4.

22. Vitr. 2. pref.2.

23. Cf. Herod. 1.185.

24. Ceres, the daughter of Saturn and Ops, sister of Jupiter and Pluto, mother of Proserpine; the goddess of agriculture.

25. Cf Pomponius Mela, *De chorographia* 3.85. Meroe is an island in the Nile, in Ethiopia.

26. Cf. Pomponius Mela, *De chorographia* 2.125. Corrupt reading: Ebusus, Ibiza.

27. See glossary, s.v. *Area*.

28. Leuctra, a small town in Boetia, where Epaminondas defeated the Spartans; Trasimene, a lake in Etruria, where Hannibal defeated the Romans.

29. Cf. Pliny *N.H.* 12.6.

30. Cf. Pliny *N.H.* 16.240.

31. Joseph. *Bell. Iud.* 4.533.

32. Cf. Macrob. *Sat.* 1.12.27.

33. Cf. Plut. *R.Q.* 264c.

34. Cf. Plut. *G.Q.* 300d.

35. Cf. Joseph. *Bell. Iud.* 5.227.

36. Cf. Varro *De L.L.* 5.157; i.e., Numa Pompilius.

37. Alternatively, ". . . forbidding the wearing of skins." Cf. Varro *De L.L.* 7.84.

38. Cf. Solinus 2.8.

39. Cf. Ovid, *Fasti* 6.481.

40. Presumably the Odeon, although there is no clear reference.

41. Cf. Diod. Sic. 5.8.3.4.

42. Cf. Herod. 7.197.

43. Cf. Macrob. *Sat.* 1.12.25.

44. Cf. Varro *De L.L.* 5.165.

45. Cf. Plut. *R.Q.* 275f.

46. Cf. Solinus 2.40.

47. Cf. Solinus 11.14; Pliny *N.H.* 10.76.

48. Cf. Pliny *N.H.* 10.78; Solinus 19.1.

49. Cf. Pliny *N.H.* 10.79; Solinus 1.10–11.

50. Cf. Pliny *N.H.* 16.239.

51. The birds were wrynecks; these the ancient wizards used to bind to a wheel, which they turned round, believing that they drew men's hearts along with it and charmed them to obedience. Cf. Flavius Philostratus, *Vita Apollonii* 1.25.

52. Joseph. *Antiq.* 8.46.

53. Joseph. *Antiq.* 8.47.

54. Eus. *Praep. Evang.* 4.23.

55. Serv. *In Virg.: ad Aen.* 4.694.

56. Plutarch, *Aratus* 32.

57. Plato, *Leges* 4.704a.

58. Cf. Scr. Hist. Aug., *Hadrian* 26.5: the true names were Lyceum (the garden in Athens where Aristotle taught), Canopus (an Egyptian temple-island), Academia (a garden in Athens where Plato taught), and Tempe (a valley in Thessaly associated with the cult of Apollo and Daphne). But no Alberti MS gives the correct spelling.

59. See glossary, s.v. Compartition.

60. Harmony: see glossary, s.v. *Concinnitas*.

61. Cf. Diod. Sic. 1.15.3.

62. Diodorus Siculus (2.11.4) gives the dimensions as 130 feet in length and 25 in width and thickness. See glossary, s.v. Measures.

63. Herod. 2.155.

64. Herodotus (2.175) gives the dimensions as 18⅔ cubits in length and 5 cubits in height. See glossary, s.v. Measures.

65. Cf. Herod. 2.91.

66. The Golden House is described by Suetonius (*Nero* 31) and Tacitus (*Annals* 15.42). However, there does not appear to be any reference to a temple of Fortune therein.

67. *Numerus*; Alberti describes beauty as *concinnitas*, a combination of *numerus, finitio,* and *collocatio.* The meaning of number is explained further in the ninth book, where certain "perfect" numbers are described. Number is both a quantity—relating to the number of building elements, and so on, as well as to specific lengths—and a quality, as defined by Pythagorean-Platonic number theory and later Christian biblical commentators. Alberti is here referring to number ordered by Natural laws of symmetry. See glossary, s.vv. *Concinnitas.*

68. Thuc. 1.93.

69. Plutarch, *Marcellus* 14.8.

70. Ptolemy Philadelphus erected the obelisk at Alexandria, hewn by King Necthebis and transported by Phoenix. Orlandi conjectures that Foci and Thebes are corruptions of Phoenix and Necthebis. Cf. Pliny *N.H.* 36.67–68; Orlandi suggests that they were already corrupt in the MS of Pliny used by Alberti.

71. Amm. Marc. 17.14–15.

72. Vitr. 10.2.11–12.

73. Cherrenis was in fact Chephren. Cf. Pliny *N.H.* 36.80–81.

74. Cheops, son of Rhampsinitus, was responsible for the pyramid. Herod. 2.124–125.

75. This mechanism relied on the principle of the lever. The relatively light baskets, by using half the length of the beam as their lever, were able to move the vast bulk of the stone through the smallest of increments.

76. Cf. Plutarch, *Marcellus* 14.8.

77. Alberti is attempting an early formulation of bending moment, which was to occupy both Leonardo and Galileo, though its laws were not formulated until the eighteenth century. It is of course the *product*, not the *sum*, of distance and weight that must be equal on either side for the object to remain in equilibrium.

78. Alberti is here referring to the mechanics of the simple couple.

79. For Archimedes' ship, see above, 6.6.

80. This passage is often quoted as evidence of Alberti's journeys in northern Europe with Niccolo Albergati in 1430–31. It does read as if based on personal experience rather than hearsay. See also 2.11; 3.15; 5.17; 6.11.

81. Sulphurous, *aqua Albula*, so called after one of the many villages near Rome that have sulphur springs (cf. Pliny *N.H.* 31.10), although Alberti may have been thinking of sweet water generally.

82. *Impleola*, lewises.

83. Presumably the Greek letter delta.

84. Throughout this chapter, compare to Vitruvius (7.3–4).

85. See glossary, s.v. Winds.

86. A method of consolidation recommended for the threshing-floor. Cf. 5.16.

87. See glossary, s.v. Winds.

88. Linseed oil as a vehicle for color was a recent northern European invention; and the best oil came from Poland, Germany, and Holland.

89. Cf. Pliny *N.H.* 36.51.

90. Cf. Pliny *N.H.* 36.53–54.

91. Suetonius, *Nero* 31.

92. *Tesserae*, as they are still called.

93. Exactly: *ad unguem*, literally, "to the fingernail"; so that the nail drawn over it will not feel any unevenness or joint.

94. These were the trusses on the portico of the Pantheon, which were replaced with wooden ones at the time of Urban VIII Barberini. The bronze was used mostly for the baldacchino of St. Peter's, and the operation epitomized by the Romans in the distich, "Quod non fecerunt barbari, fecerunt Barberini."

95. See 2.7—where, however, Alberti mentions a temple to Diana in Spain. Cf. Vitr. 2.9.13.

96. Pliny *N.H.* 33.52.

97. Cf. Joseph. *Bell. Iud.* 5.223.

98. Pliny *N.H.* 33.57.

99. Cf. Pliny *N.H.* 34.13.

100. Reference not found in Eusebius; however, Josephus (*Bell. Iud.* 5.224) mentions "sharp golden spikes protruding, to prevent birds from settling upon and polluting the roof."

101. Cicero, *In Verrem* 2.1.133.

102. See glossary, s.v. Bones and paneling.

103. See glossary, s.v. Bones and paneling.

104. Engaged: *prominens*, literally, "projecting."

105. Cf. Pliny *N.H.* 34.13.

106. Cf. Pliny *N.H.* 36.90. The names of the architects were Zmilis, Rhoecus, and Theodorus.

107. End plate: *planta*.

108. The belly: i.e., the entasis; Alberti again shows his contempt for Greek terms, and resorts to human analogy.

109. Cincture.

110. Astragal.

Book Seven

1. *Area*: see glossary.

2. Cf. 1.1–2.

3. The Vitruvian triad of *firmitas, utilitas,* and *venustas* reappears here. See glossary, s.v. Vitruvian triad; see also Compartition.

4. Cf. Plutarch, *Romulus* 11; Livy 1.7–8.

5. Extrapolated from Virg. *Aen.* 8.319ff. and Servius ad loc. Diod. Sic. 5.66.

6. Virtue: see glossary.

7. Great and Good God, *Deus Optimus Maximus*: the epithet "best and greatest" was a common appellation of Jupiter, under which the Capitoline temple was dedicated to him.

8. On the rite of *evocatio*, see Pliny *N.H.* 28.18; Servius *In Virg.: ad Aen.* 2.351.

9. On the difference between temple and basilica see below, 7.14.

10. District: "parish" would be the modern Christian equivalent.

11. Plato, *Leges* 5.745c; cf. also 8:848d.

12. Cicero, *De lege agraria* 2.96.

13. Pharos, an island in the harbor of Alexandria, famous in antiquity for its lighthouse. See next note.

14. Quint. Curt. 4.8.

15. Tigranes: a king of Armenia, and son-in-law of Mithridates.

16. Tigranocerta: capital city of Greater Armenia, founded during the Mithridatic War.

17. Cf. Plutarch, *Lucullus* 26.

18. Plato, *Leges* 12.950.

19. Plutarch, *G.Q.* 29.

20. City limits, *pomerium*: an open space left free from buildings on each side of a town's walls. See note 25, below.

21. Cf. Thuc. 1.93.5.

22. The Hernician fortress of Alatri has already been praised for its walls: 1.8.

23. Herodotus describes the moat as being deep and wide, but gives measurements only of the city wall: 50 royal cubits in width and 200 cubits in height. The royal cubit measures 20.5 inches, 52.5 cm. Cf. Herod. 1.178.3; and see glossary, s.v. Measures.

24. In fact, Aristotle (*Nicomachean Ethics* 1137b) speaks of a *Lesbian* lead rule in such a context.

25. City limits, *pomerium*: on the *pomerium* and its freedom from building, see Tac. *Ann.* 12.24; Aul. Gell. 13.14.2; Varro *De L.L.* 6.34.

26. Janus was the god of doors and beginnings; the first month of the year, Januarius, is still dedicated to him. Cicero comments (*De nat. deor.* 2.67) that Janus was the first to be invoked during the sacrifice, because his name was derived from *ire,* "to go." On the Roman sacrificial prayer, which began with Janus and ended

with Vesta, see G. Dumézil, *La Religion de Rome archaïque* (Paris: Payot, 1967), pp. 323ff.

27. Diodorus Siculus (5.72 and 73) mentions that there still stood a temple where Athena was begotten by Zeus in Crete.

28. Cf. Eus. *Praep. Evang.* 1.10.

29. Cf. Diod. Sic. 2.38; Arrian, *Indika* 7.3.

30. On the cult of Ops (associated with Saturn and Kronos) see Varro *De L.L.* 5.74; 6.21, 22.

31. Cf. Serv. *In Virg.: ad Aen.* 6.21; 8.352.

32. According to Diodorus, Osiris, the brother of Isis, was responsible for the building of the temple. Cf. Diod. Sic. 1.14–15.

33. I.e., the Parthenon. The Parthenon could only have been known to Alberti from hearsay. Although in his lifetime it was under the control of Florentine dukes who resided on the Acropolis (1385–1458), the only antiquarian who recorded the Parthenon was Alberti's friend Ciriaco d'Ancona.

34. For the temple of Capitoline Jupiter see Vitr. 3.3.5; Tac. *Hist.* 4.53; Pliny *N.H.* 35.157.

35. For the tradition of thatched roofs in antiquity see J. Rykwert, *On Adam's House in Paradise* (Cambridge, Mass.: MIT Press, 1981), pp. 141ff.

36. The founding of cults and temples is an essential part of the Numa legend, on which see Plutarch's life of Numa; cf. Dion. Hal. 2.13ff.

37. This is taken by P.-H. Michel as a possible allusion to Alberti's "pantheistic" views (*Pensée*, pp. 536ff.): cf., however, Wittkower, *Architectural Principles*, pp. 14ff.

38. This remark may be a deliberate echo of the cry of Justinian on entering St. Sophia, as reported by Procopius: "Solomon, I have outdone you!"

39. Strabo 14.1.5. Presumably the Didymeon.

40. The great Heraion on the island of Samos was one of the oldest as well as largest classic temples; cf. Herod. 3.60; Strabo 1.14–16; Pliny *N.H.* 5.135.

41. On the *Disciplina Etrusca* (distinguished in Roman religious practice from the *Disciplina Graeca*), which was concerned primarily with divination and surveying, see C.O. Thulin, *Die Etruskische Disziplin* (Göteborg: Wald Zachrisson, 1906).

42. Cf. Vitr. 1.7.1.

43. *Leges* 745b: Plato has Hestia, Zeus, and Athene.

44. On the temple to Aesculapius on the Tiber Island, see Livy, *Epitomae* 11; Ovid, *Fasti* 1.289ff.

45. Plut. *R.Q.* 94.

46. This seems to echo Vitruvius (1.2.5), who only considers that the order of the columns must vary according to the god; but see n. 55, below.

47. Bacchus.

48. This is the Vitruvian *hypaethros* (1.2.5); the reason in fact given by Varro is that the name Jupiter is connected with *divum*, the sky, and hence the sky ought to be visible. Varro *De L.L.* 5.66.

49. Cf. Plutarch, *Numa* 11.

50. Cf. Pliny *N.H.* 14.88.

51. Hyperborea, literally, "beyond whence Boreas [the north wind] blows": a legendary country to the far north, which might possibly have been Britain.

52. Latona: Leto, the mother by Zeus of Apollo and Artemis.

53. Cf. Diod. Sic. 2.47.2–3.

54. See 5.9, last paragraph.

55. Compare Vitruvius (1.2.5), who states that this should be expressed in the order of the temple.

56. This is a variation on Vitruvius 3.2.

57. Throughout this passage we translate *area* with "plan." See glossary, s.v. *Area*.

58. In fact there were very few circular temples remaining from antiquity; many of the buildings called temples in the fifteenth century were in fact tombs. On the symbolism of the centralized church, see A. Grabar, *Ecclesia et martyrium*, 2 vols. (Paris, 1943–1946). Much information on the centralized plan is provided by medieval encyclopedic writers: Rhabanus Maurus, Isidore of Seville, Vincent of Beauvais.

59. In fact a square.

60. I.e., at each corner.

61. A compass must then be set to this distance, and used to mark off, along the circumference of the circle, the ten points where the decagon touches that circle. On the whole of this passage see Wittkower, *Architectural Principles*, pp. 3ff.

62. Apses or side chapels.

63. See the restoration of Alberti's church of Sant'Andrea at Mantua by Rykwert and Tavernor, *Architects' Journal* 183, no. 21 (21 May 1986), pp. 36–57.

64. These rules are a criticism of current practice. At his own church of San Sebastiano Alberti has semicircular sub-apses opening from the rectangular ones; the single apse that he added to the Santissima Annunziata is square, while the other, preexisting ones are semicircular; at Sant'Andrea the apses are square; the apse added to San Martino at Gangalandi is a semicircle on the short side divided into four, one unit being used as the radius of the apse.

65. Since Theuer's commentary on this passage, it has been reinterpreted by Wittkower (*Architectural Principles*, pp. 47ff.) and by Krautheimer, who makes a comparison between the Basilica of Maxentius-Constantine and Alberti's Sant'Andrea at Mantua, as a variation on the *Templum Etruscum* theme (Krautheimer, "Alberti's *Templum Etruscum*"; cf. also Tavernor, "*Concinnitas*," pp. 66–76, 153–168).

66. This is left blank in MSS and in the *editio princeps*, and may indeed have been left blank by Alberti himself, who intended to complete the work but failed to do so.

67. This is a radical precis of 1 Kings 6 and 7, presumably drawn from a medieval commentator.

68. Cf. Vitr. 3.1.1; see glossary, s.v. Compartition.

69. This is a paraphrase of Vitruvius 3.4.

70. *Elegans*," elegant," is presumably Alberti's latinization of *eustyle*; cf. Vitr. 8.3.6.

71. This is a paraphrase of Vitruvius 3.3: from *pycnostyle*, one-and-a-half-column-diameter intercolumniation, to *aerostyle*, over three diameters.

72. This instruction to the scribe was copied in all MSS, though the scribe did not always follow his wish. See also below, n. 90.

73. Cf. Vitr. 4.1.5; *in Doreion civitatibus*, "in the cities of the Dorians."

74. On the origins of the capitals, see Vitruvius 3.5.5 for the Ionic; 4.1.1f. for the Corinthian; 4.3.4 and 4.7.2f. for the Doric. Alberti provides very different explanations from Vitruvius, and prefers the Tuscan to the Doric, a preference that will be echoed by many later theorists.

75. This order appears on the arches of Titus and Septimius Severus. Alberti used it for the Tempio Malatestiano. Serlio was to make it the fifth canonic order, composite.

76. This follows Vitruvius 3.3.11 and 4.4.2.

77. *Latastrum*, "die": a term apparently coined by Alberti from *latus*, "wide," and *struere*, "to construct."

78. Vitruvius' Doric order has no base at all; the base described by Alberti is the one known as "Attic" and often used with the Ionic. Cf. Vitr. 3.5.2.

79. Some of these procedures may have been noted by Alberti on the temple of Vesta at Tivoli.

80. To follow Theuer's conjectural reading, *declarandorum gratia*; though not allowed by any of the MSS.

81. In Latin, *iugulum*; the technical term is *cyma reversa*.

82. In Latin, *undula*; the technical term is *cyma recta*.

83. This Doric capital was abused as "thoroughly Gothic" in R. Fréart de Chambray's handbook of orders, *Parallèle des ordres antiques et modernes*, of 1650.

84. The navel, *umbilicus*: the central point; this circle is now usually called the eye.

85. Eye, *oculus*: the center.

86. This construction was much debated by later theorists. The rule evolved by Giuseppe Porta (known as Salviati) and published in 1552 was adopted by Barbaro in his Vitruvius commentary, and became much more general than the one advocated by Alberti. It is based on a spiral constructed of quadrants, instead of semicircles, and the center moving more subtly through the eye. See Gianantonio Selva, *Delle differenti maniere di descrivere la voluta ionica* (Padua, 1814).

87. Echinus: Alberti calls it *labulum*, "lip."

88. The beam, "architrave": Alberti uses the term *trabs*, "beam," for Vitruvius' Greek term *epistyle*, "over the column." The term "architrave"—"main beam"—was not coined until the end of the sixteenth century, probably by Francesco Maria Grapaldi.

89. This again quotes Vitruvius' advice on optical corrections (3.5.9).

90. Cf. 7.6.

91. These of course were *triglyphs*. In spite of Alberti's distaste for the term, we shall now be obliged to adopt it for convenience.

92. This tablet was of course the *metope*.

93. Calves' skulls: *bucrania*.

94. Roundels: *patinae*, literally, "dishes."

95. In the accounts of both Doric and Ionic the word is used to signify "soffit."

96. The descriptions that Vitruvius and Alberti give of cornices differ more considerably than their descriptions of capitals. The most obvious difference in the case of the Doric entablature is the prescription of three instead of the usual two furrows in the triglyph. Theuer (*Zehn Bücher*, p. 625) points out certain resemblances between the Doric entablature of Alberti and the entablature of the Basilica Aemilia, which was still standing in the fifteenth century: see the drawing by G. B. da Sangallo (cf. C. Hülsen, *Il libro di G. da San Gallo*, Biblioteca Apostolica Vaticana, 1925, plate Q).

97. Cf. Vitr. 3.5.8. Alberti has simplified Vitruvius' rule considerably by not specifying for columns between 15 and 20 feet, which Vitruvius puts outside the series—½ diameter, i.e., ¹⁄₁₉ the height—and by reducing the other proportions of Vitruvius, ¹⁄₁₃, ²⁄₂₅, ¹⁄₁₂ to ¹⁄₁₃, ¹⁄₁₂, ¹⁄₁₁.

98. The components add up only to seven; perhaps a fascia of two units is omitted below the edging of one and two-thirds and the second fascia of three and a third.

99. In Latin, *fascia regia*. The term "frieze," a corruption of *Phrygium opus*, "Phrygian work," meaning an embroidered fringe, was also introduced very late.

100. Soffit: in the account of the Doric cornice, *pavimentum* seems to be used for "soffit."

101. Gargoyles.

102. Another reference to optical refinements; cf. Vitr. 3.3.11.

103. Channels: *canaliculi*; flutes: *striae*.

104. I.e., touching both sides and the bottom of the flute. Such a spirally fluted column is not mentioned by Vitruvius. On its use in antiquity see V. Chapot, *La Colonne torse* (Paris, 1907).

105. Herod. 2.153. This is a temple of Apis, or Epaphus in Greek. There were several such temples in Memphis, notably the Ramesseum. Cf. Herod. 2.38.1.

106. Vitruvius (4.3.3) recommends 27 parts for four columns, 42 for six. The octastyle as 56 is extrapolated by Alberti. See also Vitr. 3.3.7.

107. This principle, as Theuer has already pointed out, was followed by Alberti in his design for the remodeling of the tribune of Santissima Annunziata.

108. The proportion 4:11 seems to be completely foreign to Alberti's theory; cf. Wittkower, *Architectural Principles*, p. 7. Theuer (p. 628) gives an ingenious explanation of this ratio, based on the then accepted value of pi = 1¾. His explanation, which involves a rather rough approximation, is more ingenious than convincing. The cross-reference to the proportions of the *curia* in 8.9 does not really reinforce Theuer's case.

109. Although Alberti is recommending a wall that acts structurally like a pinnacle on a buttress, he gives no structural justification for it.

110. Cf. Pliny *N.H.* 36.98.

111. Pliny *N.H.* 36.177.

112. Cf. Diod. Sic. 1.49.5.

113. Variety: see glossary.

114. Cic. *De leg.* 2.18, quoting Plato, *Leges* 12.

115. Cf. Pliny *N.H.* 7.126; 9.26 and 9.136.

116. Cf. Suetonius, *Vespasian* 8.5.

117. Cf. Pliny *N.H.* 11.111. Pliny describes these "ants" as being gold diggers; they were reputedly the color of cats and the size of Egyptian wolves. He comments that the horns of an Indian ant installed in the temple of Hercules were one of the sights of Erythrae, a city in Boetia near Mount Cithaeron.

118. Cf. Pliny *N.H.* 12.94.

119. Polyb. 5.8-9.

120. Solinus 5.19.

121. Total height: Alberti uses the mathematical term *sagitta*, "arrow," by which he appears to mean, through its relationship to the arc, or bow, the line that runs perpendicularly from the middle of a chord to the circumference.

122. Cambyses, the son and successor of the elder Cyrus, king of Persia.

123. Eus. *Praep. Evang.* 4.2.8.

124. Amasis: pharaoh from c. 569 B.C.

125. Herod. 2.80.1.

126. Cf. Serv. *In Virg.: ad Aen.* 6.618.

127. Argos: a city in the Peloponnese.

128. Plato was born around 429 B.C., but the second of the Tarquins, Tarquin the Proud, reigned in the sixth century B.C.

129. The Sibylline verses: a collection of prophetic utterances, bought by Tarquin the Proud (on which see Servius,. *In Virg.: ad Aen.* 6.72) and put into the charge of a special priestly college, to be consulted only at the command of the senate. When they were destroyed in 83 B.C., a new collection was made from various sources to replace them.

130. Diod. Sic. 4.83.3. Eryx: a city in Sicily, founded by Eryx, son of Aphrodite and Butes.

131. Caesar, *De bello Alexandrino* 1. Although previously ascribed to Caesar, this work is now generally regarded as being of uncertain authorship.

132. It is not clear whether Luca Fancelli adopted this method when building Alberti's design for Sant'Andrea, with its coffered vaults in the entry porch. Here the coffers are square, with rosettes at their centers, each of an individual design in terra-cotta. The later north extension, with its vault of around 1550, is incomplete, and has plain brick coffers without the terra-cotta adornment of the entry porch, thus suggesting a reversal of the procedure recommended here by Alberti.

133. Omitted in all MSS.

134. Varro *De r.r.* 3.5.17. Varro here refers to his aviary at Casinum, whereon see A. W. Van Buren and R. M. Kennedy, "Varro's Aviary at Casinum," *Journal of Roman Studies* 9 (1919), pp. 59–66.

135. Cf. Pliny *N.H.* 35.152. His name was in fact Butades.

136. *Antipagmentum* is a term discussed both by Festus (s.v.) and Vitruvius (4.6.1f.); from the latter passage Alberti's measurements are extrapolated. However, Vitruvius' basic door proportion is 1:2 for all the orders.

137. I.e., the *regulae* and *guttae*.

138. I.e., the triglyphs.

139. The volutes that appeared in antiquity on the keystones of triumphal arches

(Titus, Septimius Severus) became a very common architectural feature after Alberti's time. Leoni thought that Alberti meant a spaniel.

140. The treatment of the doors is based on Vitruvius 4.6.4 and 5. Alberti made the thickness of the door identical with Vitruvius' specification for the stile.

141. This is a specification for the antique "thermal" window, much used by Palladio, though no example survives in any building of Alberti's. However, the filled-in windows of the side chapels at Sant'Andrea at Mantua were clearly of this kind.

142. This gypsum is "modern" (as against "ancient" or "oriental") alabaster.

143. *Antistes*: in the fifteenth century this meant a bishop or prelate, rather than a simple priest, though here it should perhaps be read as "the president of the community."

144. Theuer takes this rebuke, which looks somewhat less startling in the Latin text, to be a reference to the nepotism practiced by Calixtus III (1455–1458), the first Borgia pope and the successor of Nicholas V; he suggests 1455 as a *terminus a quo* for the passage.

The appeal to patristic literature, the stated desire for ecclesiastical reform, which appear here in conjunction with an all but express disapproval of more than one altar in a church, point to a close relation, at the most obvious level, between Alberti's professed religious views, expressed in books such as his life of Saint Potitus, and his theory of architecture. This connection, although questioned by some earlier authorities, is reaffirmed by Wittkower in *Architectural Principles*, pp. 3–9 and 24–28. In some copies of the Spanish translation of the book this passage is canceled in ink.

145. Left blank in MSS.

146. Gyges, king of Lydia (c. 685–657 B.C).

147. Cf. Herod. 1.14. According to Herodotus, the craters weighed 30 talents (the "Attic" talent weighed about 58 pounds, the "Aeginetan" about 82 pounds).

148. Croesus, a king of Lydia (560–547 B.C.), celebrated for his riches.

149. Cf. Herod. 1.70. Three hundred amphorae were roughly equivalent to 2,700 gallons, or more than 7,800 liters.

150. Cf. Herod. 2.153. Sanniticus should read Psammetichus, a king of Egypt said to have been the designer of the labyrinth (on which see Pliny *N.H.* 36.84). The statue that Herodotus describes does not revolve.

151. The "causidiciary" aisle is of course a transept. *Causidicum* existed in antiquity only as an abstract noun, "advocacy."

152. Cf. above, 7.5.

153. See above, 1.8; 1.10.

154. See 8.11.

155. In the passage that follows, *area* is translated "plan" throughout. See glossary.

156. Theuer reads *latitudo spatii* as referring to the internal measurement of the nave, rather than the width of the whole facade. Leoni reads Bartoli, whose Italian is as ambiguous as the original Latin, to mean the whole width of the facade, and Orlandi accepts this. One of the problems about the reading of this passage is that no ancient basilica facade survives, and the passage must therefore be read in reference to Alberti's church facades; it of course produces an arithmetic proportion between length and width of building.

157. Cf. 7.2. Alberti makes little reference here to Vitruvius 5.1, which deals with basilicas, and no mention of his building at Fano.

158. Beam: *trabs*; here, technically, architrave.

159. Alberti may have had the facade of Brunelleschi's Foundling Hospital in Florence in mind here. This became a standard motif after the fifteenth century.

160. I.e., pilasters.

161. Cf. Pliny *N.H.* 35.36. Again, Alberti appears to have used a corrupt text. The correct text reads in translation, "One half pound of sinopis from Pontus, ten pounds of bright yellow ocher, and two pounds of Greek earth of Melos, when mixed together and pounded for twelve days, produces 'leucophorum.'"

162. Father Liber: an old Italian deity who presided over planting and fructification; afterward identified with the Greek Dionysos.

163. Cf. Quint. Curt. 7.9.15.

164. This is likely to be the Lysimachia on the northeastern extremity of the Thracian Chersonese, not far from the Sinus Melas.

165. According to Herodotus (4.81), in the region of the Hypanis there stood a bronze vessel, as much as six times greater than the cauldron dedicated by Pausanias at the entrance to the Pontus.

166. Cf. Justin 12.9.1. The river was the Acesine, which runs into the Indus and is now known as the Chenaub.

167. Tanais: now the river Don.

168. Cf. Herod. 2.92. The river was called the Artescus.

169. Cf. Herod. 2.102.

170. For example, see Pomponius Mela, *De chorographia* 1.101; Solinus 2.7.

171. Parmenion: general and adviser of Philip of Macedon and Alexander the Great.

172. Pallas the Worker: Athene Ergane was what Pausanias called her (1.24.3).

173. Cf. Plut. *G.Q.* 13c. The Eviani were in fact the Ainianes, a people of central Thessaly.

174. Presumably the inhabitants of Aegina, an island in the Saronic Gulf. Cf. Cic. *De off.* 3.11.

175. Cf. Serv. *In Virg.: ad Georg.* 3.29. Orlandi notes that the text used by Alberti contained the corrupt *duas Julius*, for *Duilius*. Duilius was the famous conqueror of the Carthaginians in honor of whom the first *columna rostrata* was erected in 260 B.C.

176. Seleucus Nicator, a general of Alexander the Great, and subsequently king of Syria.

177. A Syrian goddess, linked with the Greek Aphrodite.

178. Cf. Diod. Sic. 2.4.2–3.

179. Cf. Serv. *In Virg.: ad Aen.* 7.750.

180. "The beast of Lerna," was another name for the Hydra. There seems to be some confusion here: Io, who was changed into a cow, is not relevant, but Herakles' nephew and companion Iolaus did help him to kill the beast of Lerna. The story of Io is alluded to in Alberti's *De pictura* 44, though she is not named.

181. Osymandyas, identified with Rameses II of Egypt.

182. Cf. Diod. Sic. 1.49. Alberti appears to have misinterpreted his source, though this expression is indeed said by Diodorus to appear on the wall of the library in Thebes.

183. Cf. Diod. Sic. 5.55.2. According to Diodorus, it was the Telchines, and not their statues, who could influence the weather and change their shapes.

184. This comes not from Aristotle but from Pliny, who gives the names correctly as Harmodius and Aristogeiton. Cf. Pliny *N.H.* 34.17; cf., however, Arist. *Pol.* 5.10, which does not mention the statues.

185. Arrian, *Anabasis* 3.16.7–8.

186. Cf. Herod. 2.121. "Rapsinates" should read "Rhampsinitus."

187. Cf. Herod. 2.110; Diod. Sic. 1.57.5. There were two statues, each thirty cubits high.

188. Cf. Herod. 2.176. According to Herodotus, the statue was seventy-five feet in length.

189. Cf. Diod. Sic. 1.47.

190. Cf. Diod. Sic. 2.13.2.

191. Diod. Sic. 1.98.5–6. "Thellesius" should read "Telecles." Alberti also refers to this legend in *De statua* 11.

192. Cf. Plutarch, *Numa* 8. According to Plutarch, Numa thought it impious to liken higher things to lower, and to give the gods human or animal form.

193. Alberti disposes of the iconoclastic arguments very rapidly.

194. Cf. Pliny *N.H.* 14.9.

195. Licinius Mucianus, an author much quoted by Pliny, was consul in A.D. 52, 70, and 75.

196. Cf. Pliny *N.H.* 16.213.

197. Cf. Eus. *Praep. Evang.* 3.8.

198. Cf. Ovid, *Fasti* 1.201–202. The manuscripts have both *rectus*, "upright," and *tectus*, "covered." Ovid has *totus*.

199. Solinus 10.

200. See 7.10, above. Many glass and obsidian statues are mentioned by Pliny: *N.H.* 36.66f.

201. Among others this was said of both the statue of Zeus at Olympia and the Athena Parthenos of Phidias.

Book Eight

1. See 6.2.

2. See 4.5.

3. *Vagans*, literally, "wandering."

4. Cf. Aul. Gell. 17.14. Gellius compares Publilius Syrus to Laberius, but this saying comes from the former.

5. Cf. Cic. *De leg.* 23.58.

6. Cf. Serv. *In Virg.: ad Aen.* 11.206.

7. Plutarch, *Poplicola* 23.3.

8. Although somewhat free, "design" is the only acceptable translation of *lineamenta* in this context; see glossary, s.v.

9. Lex Agraria: agrarian law of 133 B.C. relating to the division of public land among the poor, championed by Tiberius Gracchus.

10. Appian, *De bellis civilibus* 1.10.

11. See glossary, s.v. Virtue.

12. A sentiment echoed by Pius II in his decree forbidding the admittance of any corpse into the cathedral of Pienza.

13. This is an unusual plea for the ancient practice of cremation, which was not revived until the nineteenth century, but not explicitly condemned until 1894 by Leo XIII.

14. Cf. Cic. *De leg.* 2.22.

15. Ictophagi: in fact, the Ichthyophagi, "Fish Eaters," one of the numerous tribes dwelling on each shore of the Red Sea.

16. Cf. Diod. Sic. 3.19.6.

17. Cf. Strabo 11.4.8.

18. The Sabaeans: a large tribe in Arabia Felix.

19. Cf. Diod. Sic. 3.33.2.

20. This was certainly a motive behind Sigismondo Malatesta's transformation of the church of San Francesco at Rimini into the Tempio Malatestiano, according to a model by Alberti. The Tempio was to glorify the name of Sigismondo and his wife, Isotta, and to house their sarcophagi in arched panels by the entrance, and those of notable men within arched openings along the sides.

21. Cic. *Philipp.* 9.14.

22. Cf. Cic. *De leg.* 2.24.61.

23. Cf. Cic. *De leg.* 2.26.64.

24. Cf. Pliny *N.H.* 6.53; 7.9.

25. Cf. Cic. *De leg.* 2.26.66. Although Cicero also mentions Pittacus, a lawgiver of Lesbos, he attributes this law in fact to Demetrius Phalereus, the famous orator and pupil of Theophrastus.

26. Plato, *Leges* 12.947e.

27. For his description of the funeral rites of those who died in the Peloponnesian War, see Thucydides 2.34.

28. Plato, *Leges* 12.958d–e.

29. *Parentare*, to offer a sacrifice for deceased parents or relatives. The Parentalia, the Roman feast of All Souls, took place on the *dies parentales* (February 13–21).

30. Cf. Herod. 2.129–130.

31. Serv. *In Virg.: ad Aen.* 11.849.

32. Strabo 17.1.10.

33. Cf. Strabo 5.3.8.

34. Erythras: a fabulous king of southern Asia.

35. Cf. Strabo 16.3.5. Tyrina is a variant of the MSS. The island was in fact Ogyris, in the Red Sea.

36. Cf. Diod. Sic. 2.34.3–5.

37. Cf. Herod. 7.117. Artachaes was reputed to have had the loudest voice in the world, and, at 8 feet 2 inches tall, to have been the tallest man in Persia. He was one of two officers in charge of cutting the canal through the isthmus of Mt. Athos in 480 B.C. (cf. Herod. 7.22).

38. See 2.9; cf. Pliny *N.H.* 36.131.

39. See 6.2.

40. For the tombs of Caligula and Claudius, see Suetonius, *Augustus* 100, *Claudius* 45, *Nero* 9; Tac. *Hist.* 12.69.3.

41. *Opus reticulatum*: square-faced blocks of small size laid diagonally; Alberti used the pattern thus created, but not the technique itself, in the Palazzo Rucellai in Florence. Cf. Vitr. 2.7.1–2 and illustration to 2.10 above.

42. Clusium: the modern Chiusi.

43. Cf. Pliny *N.H.* 36.91–92. Pliny's text allows no clear reconstruction of the monument. A number of sixteenth- and seventeenth-century engravers, however, attempted it, with varying success. The Loeb translation takes *in earum summo aderat orbis aeneus* to refer to a single bronze disk resting on all of the pyramids.

44. Pasargades: a citadel in Persia, now the ruins of Darabgerd.

45. Cf. Arrian, *Anabasis* 6.29.4–8.

46. Dado: *ara*, literally, "fire altar," which was often a cube.

47. See 3.5.

48. The Latin word *moles* means "heap," "large mass," "bulk," and therefore any large building. Alberti uses it for "mausoleum."

49. Throughout the following passage, *area* is used in the sense of "plan." See glossary, s.v.

50. Quintus Aurelius Symmachus, *Relationes* 3.7.

51. A rather free version of Diogenes Laertius, 6.50, who tells the story about Diogenes, not about his disciple Crates. For Alberti's *Epistola ad Cratem*, see *Opera inedita*, ed. G. Mancini (Florence, 1890), p. 271.

52. Plato, *Leges* 950e; cf. also Cic. *De leg.* 2.26.

53. The name is omitted from all manuscripts; the verse is in fact taken from Propertius (4.7.83ff.)

54. Cf. F. Bücheler, *Carmina Latina epigraphica* (Leipzig: Teubner, 1895–1926), 995b, lines 1; 4–6.

55. The end of the epitaph of the poet Ennius; cf. the final paragraph of Angelo Poliziano's letter of dedication to this book.

56. A very popular inscription; first reported in Herod. 7.228.

57. Diogenes, son of Hicesias of Sinope, founder of the Cynic sect. From his nickname, "the Dog," came the term "cynic."

58. Cf. Diogenes Laertius 6.78.

59. Cicero, *Tusculanae disputationes* 5.64–65.

60. Cf. Diod. Sic. 1.47.5.

61. Sardanapallus: a celebrated effeminate king of Assyria, who eventually burned himself to death, together with his treasures.

62. Tarsus: the capital of Cilicia; Archileus: should read "Anchiale," a town in Cilicia.

63. Cf. Strabo 14.5.9.

64. The little town of San Gimignano in Tuscany provides a good example, although the Roman Forum was also crowded with towers during the Middle Ages.

65. The much-discussed phenomenon of religious building in the eleventh century has been summed up in the phrase of the chronicler Raul Gluber, "The whole world was covered with a white mantle of churches."

66. Herod. 1.181; this was of course a ziggurat, not a watchtower.

67. A consistent ratio of one to fifteen. See glossary, s.v. Measures, for the various unit lengths.

68. Alberti is referring to the apparent, not the physical weight.

69. With a notional tower height of 100 units, the base is 25 units wide by 10 high; the second story 20 by 20; the third 18⅓ wide; the fourth 16⅔ wide; the fifth 14.99 wide (i.e., ¼ of the second story width of 20); the sixth story 10 by 10. Each socle is 1⅔ units and the dome at the top is 5 units, making the total height of the tower 100 units. Bartoli's illustration does not convey this.

70. Alberti has already stated that in his ideal watchtower the sixth would be the final story; and see note 69 above.

71. Spherical: i.e., hemispherical, or domed.

72. Crests are in fact acroteria.

73. Alberti's theoretical tower was never built, although its description had a considerable influence on later architects. The tower follows his principle of emulating antiquity: the main proportions are derived by analogy with the general proportions of the column.

74. Pharos, an island that was part of the harbor of Alexandria in Egypt; the lighthouse was one of the seven wonders of the world. Cf. Pliny *N.H.* 36.83.

75. On Alberti's obvious delight at such devices, see his comments on Varro's aviary at Casinum in 7.11.

76. See glossary, s.v.

77. Cf. Scr. Hist. Aug., *Heliogabalus* 24.6. The genuine text has "Lacedaemonian" for "Macedonian." Lacedaemonian stone, a green porphyry, now called serpentine.

78. Bubastis: the modern Tel-Basta, situated on the eastern side of the Pelusian arm of the Nile; cf. Herod. 2.138. Plectra: the correct transliteration from the Greek would be "plethra"; one plethron is about 100 feet.

79. The passageways were merely pavements, raised slightly above the rest; for Pseudo-Aristeas and his letter on the Septuagint, see H. St. J. Thackeray in *Jewish Quarterly Review* 15.

80. Knossos, ancient capital of Crete, the residence of King Minos.

81. Plato, *Leges* 1.625b.

82. The first route is presumably from Porta San Paolo to San Paolo fuori le Mura, the biggest church in Rome after St. Peter's. Orlandi suggests that the second route ran from the Arco di Graziano, on the left bank of the Tiber, across the Ponte Elio, arriving at the Cortina San Petri—constructed after A.D. 379 to protect pilgrims, but in ruins by Alberti's time; but see the *Liber pontificalis*, ed. J. Duchesne, p. 507.

83. Penestrum in Latium: now Preneste in Lazio. Cf. Plutarch, *Marius* 46.6.

84. Meda: a queen of Babylon.

85. Philostratus, *Vita Apollonii* 1.25. The river was the Euphrates.

86. A criticism already aired in 6.13.

87. Cf. Pliny *N.H.* 34.41.

88. Diod. Sic. 13.75.1 mentions that there were three harbors at the city of Rhodes, but it is not clear to what Alberti is referring.

89. Cf. Herod. 3.60. But see Vitr. 5.12 on the construction of harbors.

90. Show buildings: see glossary, s.v.

91. On December 19, 1450, a crowd returning from St. Peter's panicked, and broke through the balustrades of the Bridge of Hadrian (Ponte Sant'Angelo). Nicholas V had the bridge repaired and had two chapels erected at its head. Vasari claimed to have had in his possession a drawing made by Alberti of the Ponte Sant'Angelo covered by a loggia. The passage that follows may be a description of that design.

92. See 4.6.

93. Cf. Vitr. 5.1.1.ff.

94. See glossary, s.v.

95. Cf. Brunelleschi's Foundling Hospital in Florence.

96. Boundaries of the city: *pomerium*, the open space left free of buildings within and without the walls of a town, bounded by stones, and limiting the city auspices.

97. Tac. *Ann.* 12.23. In this case the expansion was the conquest of Britain. There had been an old custom by which the expansion of the empire conferred the right to extend the boundaries of the city.

98. This description is clearly based on the arches of Constantine and Septimius Severus in Rome. It would perhaps be more consonant with the measurements of these arches if, as Theuer suggests (*Zehn Bücher*, p. 635), *a basi infima*, here translated as "the bottom of the base," were taken to mean the base of the column excluding the pedestals. Wittkower (*Architectural Principles*, pp. 33ff.) discusses Alberti's use of the triumphal column.

99. Alberti describes *historia* in his treatise on painting, *De pictura*, as a scene from literature or legend. It involves human figures in contrasting attitudes, and was considered the highest category of painting from Alberti's time onward into the nineteenth century. He thought the choice of subject, its organization, and its execution the most important consideration of the artist; see *On Painting*, trans. C. Grayson, pp. 71ff.

100. See glossary, s.v.

101. Epimenides: a famous Greek poet and wonderworker of Crete.

102. Cf. Diogenes Laertius 1.109, 1.114; Plato, *Leges* 642d.

103. Cf. Polybius 4.21.1–4.

104. Cf. Hieronymus (St. Jerome), *Chronica* 757.

105. Epians: possibly the descendants of Epeus, the son of Panopeus, the contriver of the Trojan horse. Cf. Pindar, *Odes* 54ff.

106. Lenaean: an epithet of Dionysus, derived from the Greek for a wine tub.

107. Cf. Diod. Sic. 4.5.

108. In fact Lucius Mummius.

109. Cf. Tac. *Ann.* 14.21.

110. Ovid *De a.a.* 1.101–108.

111. Cf. Diod. Sic. 4.29; Solinus 1.61. The father of Iolaus was in fact Iphikles.

112. In fact the war was waged by Otho against Vitellius; cf. Tac. *Hist.* 2.21. Placentia in Cisalpine Gaul is the modern Piacenza.

113. *Cestus*: literally, a strap of bull's hide loaded with balls of lead or iron, wound round the hands and arms, and used by pugilists.

114. Plato, *Leges* 7.796d.

115. See glossary, s.v.

116. Circus: *Circenses*. Theuer and Orlandi after him suggest that this is a quotation of Isidor of Seville, *Etymologia* 18.27.3. Isidor suggests that the word is derived from *circumeundo*, because *circumibant* (they walk around), in it; alternatively from *circum* and *enses*, the latter word meaning swords, or warlike exercises.

117. Flavio Biondo (*Roma Restaurata* 3.21) gives this same information on the authority of Cassiodorus.

118. Pit: *cavea*.

119. Cf. Vitr. 5.3.5.

120. Cf. Vitr. 5.9.1.

121. See M. Bieber, *The History of the Greek and Roman Theater* (Princeton: Princeton University Press, 1961), pp. 54ff., 108ff., 167ff.

122. Cf. Vitr. 5.6.3, for the dimensions of the steps in feet.

123. See glossary, s.v. Measures.

124. Alberti is referring to the *scaenae frons*, a fine example of which survived in Rome on the southeastern corner of the Palatine—the Septizonium. This was a three-story structure that was fortified and inhabited. It may have stimulated Alberti's design for the Rucellai Palace façade.

125. *Area*: see glossary, s.v. On Renaissance theater building see R. Klein and H. Zerner, "Vitruve et le théâtre de la Renaissance," in R. Klein, *La Forme de l'intelligible* (Paris: Gallimard, 1970); E. Battisti, *Rinascimento e barocco* (Turin: Finandi, 1960), pp. 96ff.; A. Pinelli, *I teatri* (Florence: Sansoni, 1973).

126. *Cithara* really means any plucked instrument; "lyre" is the closest approximation—"zither" is much more specific in English.

127. See Vitr. 5.3.6 and 7 for a similar account.

128. For his discussion of sounding vases, see Vitr. 5.5.1. In 5.4 Vitruvius expounds his theory of musical harmony, taken from Aristoxenus, a pupil of Aristotle. Although the stoneware analogy is a common one in ancient discussions of sound, Alberti seems to be following Boethius' discussion of reflection in *De musica* 1.14.

129. Aristotle, *Problemata* 11.8.

130. The number of porticoes for the larger and for the smaller theater seems to have been reversed.

131. Alberti would have been aware of this device from the Colosseum in Rome, particularly, where corbeled mutules are still to be seen on the upper story: this amphitheater is discussed in the next chapter. The only building of which enough remained to allow for restoration—that of Marcellus—was not even partially free

from post-Classical accretions until the 1520s; Alberti therefore had to rely on Vitruvius here more than in other parts of the book, and he had to supplement data with details taken from amphitheaters.

132. I.e., houses of the zodiac.

133. Cf. Dio Cass. 49.43.2.

134. See glossary, s.v. measures.

135. The best-preserved of the ancient circuses was the Circus of Maxentius on the Via Appia near the tomb of Cecilia Metella. Alberti's dimensions equal approximately 555 by 185 meters, whereas they should be nearer 600 by 150 meters.

136. These structures seem to combine the characteristics of the parade (cf. Vitr. 5.5) with the function of the palaestrum (cf. Vitr. 5.11).

137. See book 5, note 13, on ball games.

138. Vitruvius (5.9.5) mentions how air that comes from greenery benefits the eyes.

139. See glossary, s.v. Winds. For the above passage, cf. Vitr. 5.9.2–5; 5.11.1–2.

140. Here the text is corrupt. Alberti has identified the *palaestra* of Vitruvius (5.11) with its porticoes and walks connected with the theater (5.9), while omitting most of the ancillary rooms that Vitruvius recommends for the *palaestra* following Greek usage. Interestingly, he interprets Vitruvius' recommendation to make the central row of columns of the south portico Ionic as being done *displuviandi tecti gratia*, "to make the roof slope." Vitruvius was probably thinking of a flat ceiling, which Alberti says he would have preferred.

141. This Epiriot location has already appeared in 1.5.

142. Varro *De L.L.* 5.155.

143. The curia is now identified as the old church of Sant' Adriano, though the identification is not constant. Nardini in 1700 thought that Sant'Adriano was the Temple of Concord.

144. A gymnasium six stades from Athens, celebrated as the place where Plato taught.

145. Cf. Appian, *Mithridates* 30.

146. Cf. Scr. Hist. Aug., *Severus* 19.5.

147. Presumably the victory of Gelon, tyrant of Syracuse, over the Carthaginians at Imena in 400 B.C. Agrigento, Akragas, was allied with him. Cf. Diod. Sic. 13.82.

148. Pisistratus: tyrant of Athens in the sixth century B.C.

149. Seleucus: general of Alexander the Great, who on the latter's death became governor of Babylonia, founding the Seleucid dynasty.

150. Cf. Strabo 13.1.54.

151. See Julius Capitolinus, "Gordiani Tres," in *Historia Augusta*.

152. Zeuxis, an "empirical" commentator of Hippocrates, was well known to Galen. Nemesis: the goddess of requital, who punishes human pride and arrogance.

153. Appian, *Punic Wars* 95–96.

154. The Propontis, or the Sea of Marmara, lies between the Hellespont and the Thracian Bosphorus.

155. Philo: a renowned Athenian architect; cf. Vitr. 7.pref.12.

156. Alberti, or his source, may have misunderstood Strabo on this point. Cf. Strabo 8.5.2.

157. Possidonius: a Stoic philosopher and Cicero's master. Aristarchus: a distinguished mathematician and astronomer from Samos. Cf. Vitr. 9.8.1.

158. Cf. Suetonius, *Tiberius* 70.2.

159. Scr. Hist. Aug. *Elagabalus* 30.7.

160. See 7.4.

161. Vitruvius (6.7.5) comments that for the Greeks, *xystus* meant a wide colonnade where athletes trained in winter, but that for the Romans it was a promenade in the open, which the Greeks called *paradromides*. Alberti's description corresponds to the illustrated plan of a bath building here, whereas the plan of the *xystus* is the illustrator's own fantasy.

162. Alberti was familiar with the ruins of the imperial thermae, especially those of Caracalla and Diocletian, and therefore does not rely on the description given by Vitruvius of comparatively small baths in 5.10. For Alberti's own design for a semi-public bath see H. Burns, "A Drawing by L. B. Alberti," *Architectural Design* 49, no. 5–6 (1979), pp. 45–56. See also glossary, s.v. Measures.

Book Nine

1. Plato, *Leges* 656d–e, 956a.

2. Demosthenes, *Third Olynthiac* 25–26.

3. Valor: see glossary s.v. Virtue.

4. Cf. Plutarch, *Lycurgus* 13.5; *De esu. carnium* 997c. Lycurgus was a mythical lawgiver of the Spartans.

5. The story is told about Agesilaos II in Plutarch, *Apothegmata Lacedaemonia* 210d. On Agesilaos' Asian campaign (396–395 B.C.) see Xenophon, *Hellenica* 4.1. Plutarch does not specify the place: "in Asia."

6. Cf. Caesar, *De bello Gallico* 6.20, as part of a general description of German rudeness, though it is not quite as causal as Alberti makes it.

7. Valerius: P. Valerius Poplicola. The house in question is on the Velia of the Palatine, not the Esquiline, in Livy 2.7; Plutarch, *Poplicola* 10.3–6; and Val. Max. 4.1.1.

8. Suetonius, *Augustus* 72.3. The house belonged to his granddaughter, Julia.

9. Iulius Capitolinus in his life of Gordian III (M. Antonius Gordianus Augustus), *Historia Augusta* 20.32. The ruins of this villa, now called Villa dei Tre Imperatori, are on the Via Praenestiana, about three miles out of the Porta Maggiore, just beyond Tor dei Schiavi.

10. Lucretius, *De rerum natura* 2.24–26.

11. Thuc. 1.10.2.

12. See glossary, s.vv. Compartition, Lineaments.

13. See above, 8.1.

14. Cf. Pliny *N.H.* 34.7; Spurius Carvillius the Quaestor objected to the criminal display on the part of the dictator Camillus (though only of bronze-covered, *ostia aureata*, doors) as one motivation for his exile in 380 B.C.

15. Luna stone is the white stone of Carrara, which, with Travertine, was regarded as a relatively cheap stone.

16. See glossary, s.v. Beauty and ornament.

17. Caryatids and *atlantes*, though known from literary sources, do not appear until the sixteenth century. On the tree trunk with lopped-off branches as a column, which became relatively common around 1500, see E. Kris, "Der Stil rustique," in *Jahrbuch der Kunsthistorischen Sammlungen* (Vienna, 1926); and J. Rykwert, *On Adam's House in Paradise* (Cambridge, Mass.: MIT Press, 1981), pp. 97ff., 211ff.

18. Channels: *rivulis* in the *editio princeps*; in most MSS the text seems corrupt: *duulisque*.

19. Columns such as these would have been much more common in Byzantine and proto-Renaissance than in Classical buildings. Theuer has pointed out that Piranesi records a square column with two half-columns attached "ante Xenodochium Sanctae Mariae Consolationis" and two more "in Aedibus maximorum." Palladio has also noted such columns in the temple near Trevi. Cf. Andrea Palladio, *I Quattro Libri dell' Architettura* (Venice, 1570), pp. 98–102. There were of course many late-antique precedents for the sort of fanciful capital of which Alberti speaks here.

20. *Concinnitas*: see glossary s.v.

21. Cf. 5.14, above.

22. A problem experienced directly by Alberti with his facade for the Palazzo Rucellai, which was unfinished or amended because of delays in the acquisition of adjoining property by Giovanni Rucellai. See B. Preyer, "The Rucellai Palace," in *Giovanni Rucellai ed il suo Zibaldone*, part 2: *A Florentine Patrician and His Palace*, Studies of the Warburg Institute, ed. J. B. Trapp, vol. 24, pp. 155–228.

23. On the urban praedial servitudes see *The Institutes of Justinian*, ed. Thomas, vol. 2, p. 3.

24. For the blank spaces, see Vitr. 2.8.18; though Vitruvius makes no mention of Julius Caesar in this connection; but cf. Pliny *N.H.* 35.23. According to Strabo and Aurelius Victor it was Augustus who limited wall heights to 70 feet, while Trajan reduced it to 60 feet. In Florence, urban building heights were limited to 50 Florentine braccia maximum, according to a law dating back to 1325 or about 100 feet; see R. Davidsohn, *Storia di Firenze* (1956–1968), vol. 5, p. 401.

25. Herod. 1.180 speaks of many such houses, but says nothing about it being an honor to live in one.

26. P. Aelius Aristides, Encomium of Rome, 8.

27. Cf. Strabo 16.2.23.

28. *Hortus*: literally, "garden," and hence a form of suburban villa. Pliny comments (*N.H.* 19.4.50) that in the Twelve Tables the term was used to refer to a villa; cf. Cic., *De. off.* 3.14.

29. See also what Alberti has to say about the villa in the third book of *Della famiglia* (Opere volgari, vol. 1, pp. 198ff.) and in *Villa* (Opere volgari, vol. 1, pp. 359ff.)

30. It would appear, however, that Cicero meant by *celeber* "easily frequented." Cf. Cicero, *Ad Attic* 12.19.

31. The comment comes from the old man in Terence's play *The Eunuch*; cf. line 972.

32. The epigram is falsely ascribed to Martial; cf. *Anthologia Latina*, ed. Bücheler-Reise (Leipzig: Teubner, 1884), vol. 1, part 1, p. 98, no. 26, ll. 1, 7, and 4.

33. *Areae*: see glossary, s.v.

34. On *sinus*, the "bosom" of the house, see 5.17.

35. *Area*: see glossary, s.v.

36. In Alberti's time the circular vestibule was not a common feature of domestic architecture; nor did it ever become one, although such a suggestion would have seemed agreeable to him.

37. See above, 7.4 and 7.10.

38. The proportions 2:3 and 3:5 were already present in Vitruvius; 5:7, Orlandi suggests, is a close approximation to $1:\sqrt{2}$ (1.4 for 1.414). Cf. Vitr. 6.3.3. Alberti's hesitation in specifying the height was probably due to its seeming disproportionate to him. In fact, Vitruvius specifies 3:4, not 4:3, as the proportion of height to length.

39. This point about proportions that are modified by scale follows Vitruvius (3.5) and has already been made above.

40. Highly suitable: *concinnissimae*; see glossary, s.v. *Concinnitas*.

41. This series may be summarized as follows:

	width	length	height	
A	1	1	1	flat ceiling
	1	1	3/2	vaulted
B	1	2	3/2	flat ceiling
	1	2	4/3	vaulted
For a large building:	1	2	5/4	flat ceiling
	1	2	7/5	vaulted
C	1	3	7/4	flat ceiling
	1	3	3/2	vaulted
D	1	4	2	flat ceiling
	1	4	7/4	vaulted
E	1	5	13/6	
F	1	6	11/6	

42. The arabic numerals here are roman numerals in the text. These formulae may be summarized as follow:

	width	length	height	
A	10	9	8	
B	48	36	42	flat ceiling
	48	36	44	vaulted
C	21	14	16	flat ceiling
	21	14	17	vaulted
D	7	5	6	
E	5	3	4	

43. The medal of the Tempio Malatestiano, by Matteo de' Pasti, dated 1450, shows such a window. See C. Ricci, *Il Tempio Malatestiano*, repr. with an appendix by P. G. Pasini (Rimini: Bruno Ghigi Editore, 1974), ch. 10, pp. 253ff. Indeed, this is the only window to the width of the *area* as prescribed by Alberti here.

44. Above, 8.7.

45. Above, 8.9.

46. Cf. Pliny *N.H.* 36.84.

47. Cf. Pliny *N.H.* 36.184.

48. We translate literally, although it is a conventional formula, meaning something like "really," "truly."

49. Cf. Pliny *N.H.* 36.189. Agrippa was Augustus' son-in-law.

50. Cf. Suetonius, *Domitian* 14.4. According to Suetonius, the work was commissioned by Domitian, and the material used was phengite, a hard, white, and translucent stone (Pliny *N.H.* 36.163).

51. Antoninus Caracalla: emperor A.D. 211 to 217. Cf. *Historia Augusta* 13.9.6.

52. Severus Alexander: emperor A.D. 222 to 235. Cf. *Historia Augusta* 18.25.6.

53. Agathocles: tyrant of Sicily for a generation after the death of Alexander. Cf. Cicero, *In Verr.* 2.4.122.

54. The Caesar responsible for this work was Augustus. Cf. Suetonius, *Augustus* 31.5.

55. See 8.6.

56. Cf. Appian, *Mithridatic War* 117; Plutarch, *Pompey* 45.

57. Virg. *Aen.* 6.14ff. The fall of Icarus is in fact the part of his story that Daedalus did *not* paint or carve in relief.

58. This Aristotelian division of *genre* is also adopted by Vitruvius. The three style sets for the three *genres* were made famous by Serlio.

59. Cf. Suetonius, *Augustus* 72.3. The collection was housed in the emperor's villa at Capri.

60. Ovid, *Fasti* 2.315; *Metamorphoses* 3.159.

61. Theophrastus, *Historia plantarum* 1.10.8.

62. Presumably Phintias, tyrant of Agrigentum in the third century B.C.

63. I.e., in oblique lines; *quincunx*: the five spots on the dice.

64. Cf. Horace, *Epistles* 1.16.9–10.

65. Democritus of Abdera's *Georgica*, quoted by Columella, *De r.r.* 11.3.2.

66. Acroteria: see 8.5; pedestals originally used for statues (but often seen without) at either extremity of a pediment or at its apex.

67. See glossary, s.v. Beauty and ornament.

68. *Habitior*, not *habilior*, as Alberti has it; the personage is Pamphila in Terence, *The Eunuch* 310–318; in fact her lover Cherenus describes her as having "color verus, corpus solidum et succi plenum."

69. H. K. Lücke, *Vitruvius-Alberti-Vitruvius* (Munich: Prestel 1988 [in press]), MS p. 64.

70. See glossary, s.vv. *Concinnitas*, Lineaments.

71. Cf. 9.8. See also H. K. Lücke, *Vitruvius-Alberti-Vitruvius* (see n. 69, above).

72. See glossary, s.v.

73. This reads like Neoplatonic teaching, but it had been absorbed into standard scholastic doctrine. See, for example, St. Thomas Aquinas, *Compendium theologicum* 151.

74. The first beginnings of things, *primordia rerum*: an expression used by Lucretius (*De rerum natura*, 1.265ff.) to refer to the particles or atoms of which everything is composed.

75. Ways: *formas*, literally, "shapes."

76. See glossary, s.v. Bones and paneling.

77. On the Pythagorean oath by the "holy fourfold" see Iamblichus.

78. That is, $3 + 2 + 1 = 6$. And see Vitruvius on the number 6: 3.1.6 and chapter 1 for the number in general.

79. That is, the eighth month of pregnancy.

80. That is, $10^2 = 1^3 + 2^3 + 3^3 + 4^3$. Aristotle, *Metaphysics* pref. 1.5.5; cf. also Vitruvius (3.1.5), who gives Plato as the nominator of its perfection.

81. Literally, a "fifth," $3:2$.

82. Literally, "one and a half," i.e., $1:3$.

83. Literally, a "fourth," $1:4$.

84. Literally, "one and a third," $3:4$.

85. A whole octave, $1:2$.

86. One and a half octaves.

87. The double octave.

88. *Tonus*: the single note.

89. One and an eighth.

90. *Area*: see glossary, s.v.

91. "Short" and "long" refer to the shape of the rectangle, not its size.

92. I.e., the square.

93. The proportions of the *sesquitertia*, one and a third to one, make it shorter in fact than the *sesquialtera*, which has a proportion of one and a half to one.

94. I.e., the length is two and one quarter times, or nine quarters of the width. On the whole matter of the generation of ratios, see Wittkower, *Architectural Principles*, pp. 113ff.; G. Hersey, *Pythagorean Palaces: Magic and Architecture in the Italian Renaissance* (Ithaca: Cornell University Press, 1976). It is worth noting that the individual numbers are very important to Alberti in this generation, and cannot be reduced to simple ratios.

95. I.e., $9:16$; $16 = (2 \times 9) - 2$.

96. *Area* is used here in the sense of floor plan; see glossary, s.v.

97. I.e., square roots and squares.

98. Here, clearly, the diagonal.

99. This line is the diagonal of the cube, the third side of the triangle formed by the above-mentioned diameter of the square and one of the sides.

100. I.e., other than equilateral.

101. This is the cube of the "first" square, or the first "true" cube.

102. Means: *Mediocritates*; i.e., three numbers in a series, of which the middle one is the "mean" of those on either side. The practical use of "means" (known also as the Rule of Three or the Merchant's Key) by Alberti's contemporaries, in the arts and commerce, is described by Baxandall in *Painting and Experience in Fifteenth-Century Italy*, pp. 94ff. Also see glossary, s.v. Proportion.

103. All MSS have "arithmetical" here, but this is clearly wrong.

104. This is one of the very few direct references to scripture or to patristic writings; cf. *Genesis* 6.15, where the relationship to the human body is not mentioned. However, St. Augustine (*De civitate Dei* 15.26) sets this argument out very clearly. *Genesis* describes the ark as 300 cubits long, 50 wide, and 30 high.

105. *Concinnitas*: see glossary, s.v.

106. *Numerus*, "number," is the first part of the triad of which *concinnitas* is composed; see glossary, s.v. *Concinnitas*.

107. "Style of column": the modern term is of course "order," but this word was not applied to the "styles" or "kinds" of columns until the sixteenth century.

108. Arrangement: *collocatio*, the third part of the triad of which *concinnitas* is composed.

109. Outline: *finitio*, the second part of the *concinnitas* triad.

110. Cf. 9.5. See also H. K. Lücke, *Vitruvius-Alberti-Vitruvius* (see n. 69, above).

111. Dignified: *ornatissima*; see glossary, s.v. Beauty and ornament.

112. Cf. Herod. 1.98; each wall was of a different color, the remaining colors being black, white, and orange.

113. Cf. Suetonius, *Caligula* 55.3; Caligula was a passionate supporter of one of the four teams of charioteers who competed in the Circus. The stable and manger were for a horse called Incitatus, meaning "swift."

114. Cf. Suetonius, *Nero* 31.2.

115. Scr. Hist. Aug., *Elagabalus* 31.8.

116. See 2.1.

117. This passage, Orlandi suggests, is interpolated.

118. This obviously refers to the fact that metal tools were not heard during the building of the temple at Jerusalem; see 1 Kings 6.7.

119. Boreas: see glossary, s.v. Winds; "the sunset": a reiteration of a statement in 5.18 above (n. 86). Cf. the orientation of bath buildings in 8.10, where the main vestibule faces south, and the main spaces lie on a north-south axis.

120. See glossary, s.v. Winds.

121. Nichomachus: a second-century A.D. writer on arithmetic.

122. Alberti wrote his treatise on painting, entitled *De pictura*, in Latin at the end of 1435, and later translated it into the vernacular; see L. B. Alberti, *On Painting and Sculpture*, tr. C. Grayson.

123. These are Greek words, used by Alberti in spite of his prohibition. *Podismata* appears in technical literature to mean "pacing out," while *embates* is known only in Vitruvius and seems to mean "a module or unit of measurement."

124. Drawings: *lineamenta*; see glossary, s.v.

125. Clerks of works: *adstitores*, a word that seems to have been coined by Alberti, although the function of these personages is quite clear.

Book Ten

1. See glossary, s.vv. Compartition, *Concinnitas*, Lineaments.

2. Plato, *Timaeus* 25d, *Critias* 108e. Cf. Strabo 2.3.6.

3. Achaian cities, on the Gulf of Corinth. Cf. Strabo 1.3.18. Strabo has Helice.

4. The marsh Tritonis in Libya disappeared in the course of an earthquake. Cf. Diod. Sic. 3.55.3.

5. In northern Arcadia; cf. Paus. 8.22.8.

6. These islands are in the Cyclades. Cf. Strabo 1.3.16; Seneca, *Quaestiones naturales* 6.21.1; Pliny *N.H.* 2.102.

7. Cf. Strabo 3.4.18.

8. Cf. Strabo 3.2.6.

9. Also *De republica*. The exact date of its composition is uncertain.

10. Leoni takes this to be a reference to Thermopylae. However, it is more probably a pass called in antiquity Amynicae Pylae, which was on the Cilician road to Syria, not Lydia. Cf. Cicero, *Epistulae ad familiares* 15.4.9. *Pylae* is the Greek for "gates."

11. Near Urbino, on the river Metauro.

12. The fortifications against the Scots or Picts are still known as Hadrian's Wall. On these walls see Scr. Hist. Aug. 1.2.2; 3.5.4; 10.18.2.

13. This is Antioch in Margiana, now Soviet Turkestan. Cf. Strabo 11.10.2.

14. The City of the Sun is of course Heliopolis. Cf. Diod. Sic. 1.57.4.

15. In the Ionian Sea, to the west of the Gulf of Corinth; cf. Strabo 10.2.9.

16. Cf. Diod. Sic. 13.47.3f.

17. Cf. Quint. Curt. 7.10.15.

18. This is a simple transliteration of the Greek.

19. Cf. Arrian. *Anabasis* 7.7.7.

20. See glossary, s.v. Winds.

21. Some editors have inserted here, "so it is with the rays of the sun on water." This is a conjectural interpolation, where there seems to be a lacuna in the original text.

22. Serv. *In Virg.: ad Aen.* 3.701.

23. Cf. Diod. Sic. 4.18.6; 4.11.6–7.

24. In Cappadocia; Strabo 12.2.7. Strabo makes no comment about the quality of the water.

25. Cf. Strabo 17.3.10.

26. Below, 10.13.

27. Strabo 5.1.7.

28. Cf. Strabo 17.1.7.

29. Thales here probably quoted from Vitruvius—8.pref.*i*, perhaps. Much of the information that follows may also be found in Vitruvius' book 8.

30. Quoted in Strabo 15.1.19; here no precise location is given.

31. Xenophon, *Polity of the Lacedaemonians* 15.6.

32. Cf. Herod. 1.201ff.; Araxes: the modern Arax.

33. Cf. Herod. 3.9.

34. See glossary, s.v. Measures.

35. Appian, *Punic Wars* 40. Ucilla is near Zama, in the north of modern Tunisia.

36. Arsinoe: the name of several cities that derived their name from Arsinoe, the favorite sister of Ptolemy Philadelphus.

37. Cf. Solinus 5.16.

38. Cf. Solinus 29.1.

39. Cf. Solinus 5.17.

40. Cf. Solinus 7.2.

41. Cf. Solinus 5.20.

42. Cf. Solinus 52.14.

43. Cf. Solinus 33.1.

44. Cf. Vitr. 8.3.14.

45. Cf. Vitr. 8.3.23.

46. Cf. Solinus 5.21.

47. Cf. Vitr. 8.3.22.

48. The spaces were probably left by Alberti himself. Pliny (*N.H.* 31.2.16) mentions a fountain called Gelon (from the Greek verb for "to laugh") in Phrygia, whose water causes laughter. Vitruvius (8.3.15) mentions a lake at Chrobs in Thrace that would kill anyone who drank of it, or even bathed in it.

49. Cf. Vitr. 8.3.16; Vitruvius adds that the water could only be transported in the hoof of a mule.

50. Cf. Solinus 4.6. Solinus refers not to Corsica but to Sardinia.

51. Cf. Solinus 4.6–7.

52. The etymology comes from Serv. *In Virg.: ad Ecl.* 1.65, which follows Varro. Lipygia is derived from the Greek and means "lacking in rain."

53. Now Orvieto.

54. The Fortunate Isles: the fabulous islands in the Western Ocean, the abodes of the blessed, commonly associated with the Canary Isles; cf. Solinus 56.15; Mela 3.102; Pliny *N.H.* 6.203–204.

55. Strabo 11.14.4.

56. On Moses and his search for water, see Joseph. *Antiq.* 3.3.

57. Cf. Plutarch, *Aemilius Paulus* 14.

58. This spring supplied the Virgo aqueduct; cf. Front *Aq. Rom.* 1.10.

59. Cf. Vitr. 8.1.3.

60. Col. *De r.r.* 2.2.

61. For this whole section see Vitr. 8.1.2.

62. Cf. Vitr. 8.1.1.

63. Theophrastus, *De ventis* 2.16–37; see glossary, s.v. Winds.

64. Aristotle, *Meteorologica* 1.3.

65. Cf. Vitr. 8.6.13; Pliny *N.H.* 31.49.

66. Cf. Vitr. 8.6.14–15.

67. Theophrastus, *Historia plantarum* 4.50.55.

68. Polybius (*History* 10.48) describes the river as turbulent but does not comment on the quality of the water.

69. I.e., three o'clock in the afternoon.

70. Squill is a seashore plant whose bulbs are dried and used as diuretic, purgative, etc. Cf. Pliny *N.H.* 20.97.

71. Celsus, *De medicina* 2.18.12.

72. Cf. Strabo 12.2.8; Solinus 45.4.

73. Cf. Leviticus 19.19, and repeatedly in reference to vineyards in Deuteronomy 22.9.

74. Aristotle, *Meteorologica* 2.4.360a.

75. Theophrastus, *Historia plantarum* 3.2.1.

76. Aristotle, *Problemata* 24.2.

77. Source not found.

78. Col. *De r.r.* 1.5.2.

79. Hippocrates, *Air, Waters, Places* 7.

80. On the effects of situation and climate, see Theophrastus, *Historia plantarum* 2.2.

81. Pliny *N.H.* 14.110.

82. Cato *De r.r.* 114.1.2; "hellebore" is the ancient name given to various plants supposed to cure madness.

83. Col. *De r.r.* 1.5.2, although Columella in fact thinks rainwater the healthiest.

84. See glossary, s.v. Winds.

85. Serv. *In Virg.: ad Aen.* 7.84.

86. Cf. Varro *De L.L.* 5.25.

87. See above, 10.2.

88. See above 1.4.

89. Alberti is taking the side of Democritus, whom Cicero mocked for holding this view in *De div.* 2.12ff.

90. In one manuscript (*V*, Orlandi) a figure of 252,000 stades (41,832 km) is given. Vitruvius (1.6.9) gives a figure of 31,500,000 paces, after Eratosthenes; see Tavernor, "Concinnitas," appendix X, pp. 181ff., for further speculation on this.

91. Cf. Aristotle, *Meteorologica* 1.13.

92. Now Killini. See Paus. 8.17.i; Strabo 8.5.ii.

93. *Incile*: "a cut"; cf. *Digesta* 43.21.5.

94. Vitruvius (8.6.1) recommended a fall of 1/2 inch every 100 feet; Pliny (*N.H.* 31.31), of 1/4 inch every 100 feet.

95. A method still used by building inspectors to test drains in Britain.

96. See Alberti's *Descriptio urbis Romae*, written after 1432, in Accademia Naz. dei Lincei, Roma, 1974, Quad. 209, trans. G. Orlandi, pp. 112–137. A similar tool is described by Alberti in *De statua*: Grayson, *Painting and Sculpture*, pp. 129ff.

97. Cf. Vitr. 8.6.2; Vitruvius states that the shafts should be one *actus* (120 feet) apart.

98. This is the *Emissario* of Lake Albano, well known from Piranesi's engravings, and the subject of a war between Rome and the Etruscan city Veio, described by Livy, 5.15ff.

99. Cf. Front. *Aq. Rom.* 1.4.

100. The number is omitted; Frontinus (*Aq. Rom.* 64.2) lists nine aqueducts.

101. Such water mills existed on the Tiber in Alberti's time and were still working in the seventeenth century.

102. Cf. Vitr. 10.3 on water-driven instruments. "Accord" here translates *concinnitas*, on which see glossary, s.v.

103. On water organs, see Vitr. 10.8.

104. Cf. *Digesta* 43.20–21.

105. This is used not in the modern sense but rather for scurvy and other allied skin diseases.

106. Sharp: *geniculatus*, literally, "knee-jointed."

107. Cf. Vitr. 8.6.7.

108. According to Flavio Biondo, fragments of a similar conduit were found at the bottom of Lake Nemi; he goes on to quote Alberti's opinion that the conduits supplied springwater to pavilions on board the ships, turning them into luxury galleys. It was these galleys that Alberti was engaged in raising.

109. Cf. Vitr. 8.6.9.

110. *Argentum escarium*: literally, "an eating vessel of silver." Hence, *potorium*, "a drinking vessel." Cf. *Digesta* 34.2.19.12.

111. "Courtyard" here translates *area*, meaning any exposed horizontal plane.

112. Cf. Pliny *N.H.* 31.34. Pliny has *septies*, "seven times," instead of *semel*, "once."

113. Joseph. *Antiq.* 3.8.

114. The author is in fact Pliny, *N.H.* 31.70.

115. I.e., Cisalpine Gaul.

116. Cf. Tac. *Ann.* 12.56; the river was in fact the Liri.

117. Cf. Cic. *Ad Attic.* 4.15.5. M. Curius: Manius Curius Dentatus, consul and censor in the third century A.D. The Nar, a tributary of the Tiber, is now called the Nera.

118. Alberti's attempt to salvage a Roman galley from the bottom of Lake Nemi is well documented. W. Abeken (*Mittelitalien*, Stuttgart, 1843, p. 167) notes that although the lake has no visible outlet, the water is drawn off by an artificial emissary, probably of very ancient construction.

119. Ilerda: a city in Hispania Tarraconensis, now Lerida; Sicoris: now the river Segre. Cf. Caesar, *De bello civili* 1.61.

120. Cf. Quint. Curt. 8.9.

121. Eutropius: historian from the middle of the fourth century A.D.

122. Cf. Herod. 1.93. The lake is in fact called the Gygaean lake. Alyattes: king of Lydia and father of Croesus.

123. Cf. Herod. 2.149.

124. Cf. Herod. 1.185–186.

125. Cf. Amm. Marc. 17.4.

126. Cf. Pliny *N.H.* 5.113; Solinus 40.8.

127. Cf. Pliny *N.H.* 5.84; Solinus 37.1.

128. Hadrian's bridge: the Ponte Elio, in front of the Castel Sant'Angelo. See above, 8.6.

129. Herod. 1.185.

130. Cf. Arrian, *Anabasis* 7.7.3.

131. Cf. Diod. Sic. 1.33.11. Ptolemy was Tolomeus II Philadelphus, king of Egypt (285–246 B.C.).

132. Cf. Strabo 12.2.8. King Ariarathes of Cappadocia was the one responsible. Euphrates is obviously an error in Strabo for Halys.

133. Cf. Strabo 8.8.4.

134. Cf. Diod. Sic. 2.7.3f. See glossary, s.v. Measures.

135. Cf. Herod. 1.185. Thus in all manuscripts. This is another reference to Nitocris.

136. Cf. Pliny, quoting Aristotle, *N.H.* 2.220.

137. Cf. Strabo, 9.2.8, who gives seven changes.

138. See 2.12.

139. Hyster: the lower part of the Danube; the Phasis empties into the Euxine Sea and is now known as the Rion.

140. Cf. Herod. 2.5; Strabo 1.2.29; the epithet is in fact "the gift (*donum*) of the Nile," rather than "the home (*domum*) of the Nile."

141. Cf. Strabo 1.3.7.

142. Hor. *Epod.* 1.6.24–25.

143. Cf. 4.6; Theuer conjectures that *pontibus*, "bridges," should read *portibus*, "harbors."

144. Cf. Vitr. 5.12.

145. Propertius 2.8.8.

146. See glossary, s.v. Winds.

147. Alberti is referring to the so-called Monte Testaccio in Rome, a hill composed entirely of fragments of pottery. Caesar was Octavius Augustus; cf. Suetonius, *Augustus* 30.1.

148. On devices for pumping water, see Vitr. 10.6.1.

149. *Palatia*: a shoveling device.

150. Cf. Pliny *N.H.* 17.30.

151. Cf. Theophrastus, *De causis plantarum* 5.14.5; Philippi: a city in eastern Macedonia.

152. Cf. Serv. *In Virg.: ad Aen.* 3.442; Caesar was Octavius Augustus.

153. Varro *De r.r.* 1.4.5.

154. Cf. Herod. 2.95.1.

155. Cf. Pliny *N.H.* 19.24. Metellus: in fact Marcus Claudius Marcellus, the son of Octavia *minor*, who was adopted by Augustus and had a portico and theater named after him.

156. Alberti or his source appears to have misinterpreted Pliny here; cf. Pliny *N.H.* 2.115.

157. Oeta: a mountain range between Thessaly and Aetolia.

158. Here there appears to be a lacuna in the text.

159. Aristotle, *Historia animalium* 9.6.4.

160. Cf. Pliny *N.H.* 19.177–178.

161. Pliny *N.H.* 19.178.

162. Solinus 22.8; Thanet is in southeast Kent.

163. Cf. Solinus 23.11. Ibiza is one of the Balearic Islands.

164. Cf. Solinus 29.8.

165. Strabo 17.3.11.

166. Cf. Varro *De r.r.* 1.2.25. The Sasernae, father and son, were writers on agriculture.

167. Pliny *N.H.* 24.13.

168. Cf. Pliny *N.H.* 16.64.

169. Galbanum: the resinous sap of an umbelliferous plant in Syria.

170. Cf. Pliny *N.H.* 24.148. The herb mentioned by Pliny is *aron*, wake- robin.

171. Cf. Pliny *N.H.* 22.27.

172. See glossary, s.v.

173. Cf. Juvenal 3.236–238.

174. Pliny the Younger 2.17. The text has been slightly altered.

175. See glossary, s.v. Bones and paneling.

176. Cf. Front. *Aq. Rom.* 2.116ff. The gangs were for maintenance of the aqueducts. According to Frontinus, there were two gangs of men, one belonging to the state, the other to Caesar. The former was the first to be instituted and was left by Agrippa to Augustus, and by him made over to the state; it numbered around 240 men. Caesar's gang numbered 460 and was organized by Claudius when he brought his aqueduct into the city.

177. Columella (*De r.r.* 7.5.7–8) makes a similar suggestion as a cure for scabies.

178. Solinus 1.54–55.

179. Pliny *N.H.* 9.155; 32.25. Pliny refers not to the sea parsnip but to the sting projecting above the tail of the stingray (known as the parsnip fish), which, when driven into the root of a tree, will kill it.

180. Balance arm: *statera*.

181. See above, 1.10.

Bibliography

Alberti, Leon Battista. *L'architettura*, ed. Giovanni Orlandi and Paolo Portoghesi. 2 vols. Milan: Il Polifilo, 1966.

Alberti, Leon Battista. *The Family in Renaissance Florence* (translation of *Della famiglia* by R. N. Watkins). Columbia: South Carolina University Press, 1969.

Alberti, Leon Battista. *Opera inedita et pauca separatim impressa*, ed. G. Mancini. Florence: J. C. Sansoni, 1890.

Alberti, Leon Battista. *Opere volgari*, ed. C. Grayson. Bari: Laterza (Scrittori d'Italia), 1960–1966.

Alberti, Leon Battista. *Opuscoli inediti: "Musca," "Vita S. Potiti,"* ed. C. Grayson. Florence: Leo S. Olschki, 1954.

Alberti, Leon Battista. *On Painting and Sculpture*, ed. and tr. by Cecil Grayson. London: Phaidon Press, 1972.

Alberti Index: Leon Battista Alberti, De re aedificatoria (Florence, 1485), ed. Hans-Karl Lücke. 4 vols. Munich: Prestel Verlag, 1975–1979.

Andrews Aiken, J. "L. B. Alberti's System of Human Proportions." *Journal of the Warburg and Courtauld Institutes* 43 (December 1980), pp. 68–96.

Architectural Design 49, nos. 5–6 (1979) (also published as *A.D. Profiles 21*): *Leon Battista Alberti*, ed. Joseph Rykwert, with contributions by Cecil Grayson, Hubert Damisch, Françoise Choay, Manfredo Tafuri, Howard Burns, and Robert Tavernor.

Balbus, Johannes. *Catholicon*. Mainz: J. Gutenberg, 1460 (reprinted Farnborough: Gregg Press, 1971).

Baldi, Bernardino. *Vita e fatti di Federigo di Montefeltro Duca d'Urbino e memorie concernenti la città d'Urbino*. Rome: Francesco Zuccardi, 1824.

Baron, Hans. *The Crisis of the Early Italian Renaissance*. Princeton: Princeton University Press, 1966.

Baxandall, M. *Painting and Experience in Fifteenth-Century Italy*. Oxford: Oxford University Press, 1974.

Bialostocki, J. "The Power of Beauty: A Utopian Idea of Leon Battista Alberti." In *Studien zur toskanischen Kunst, Festschrift Ludwig Heydenreich*, ed. W. Lotz and W. W. Möller. Munich, 1964, pp. 13–19.

Bolgar, R. R. *The Classical Heritage and Its Beneficiaries*. Cambridge: Cambridge University Press, 1963.

Buck, August. *Die Rezeption der Antike in den romanischen Literaturen der Renaissance*. Berlin: Erich Schmidt Verlag, 1976.

Burckhardt, J. *The Architecture of the Renaissance in Italy*. London: Secker and Warburg, 1984.

Chastel, A. *Marsile Ficin et l'art*. Geneva: Librairie Droz, 1975.

Choay, Françoise. *La Règle et le Modèle*. Paris: Editions du Seuil, 1980.

Dennistoun, James, of Dennistoun. *Memoirs of the Dukes of Urbino*. 3 vols. London: Longman, Brown, Green, and Longman, 1851.

Doursther, H. *Dictionnaire universel des poids et mesures, anciens et modernes*. Brussels: M. Hayez, 1840. Reprinted Amsterdam: Meridian Publishing, 1965.

Gadol, Joan. *Leon Battista Alberti, Universal Man of the Early Renaissance*. Chicago: University of Chicago Press, 1969.

Garin, Eugenio. *L'Umanesimo Italiano: Filosofia e vita civile nel Rinascimento*. Bari: Laterza, 1952.

Gosebruch, M. "*Varietas* bei L. B. Alberti und der wissenschaftliche Renaissancebegriff." In *Zeitschrift für Kunstgeschichte*, 20, no. 3 (1957), pp. 229–238.

Grafton, A. *J. Scaliger: A Study in the History of Classical Scholarship*. Oxford: Oxford University Press, 1983.

Grayson, C. "The Composition of L. B. Alberti's *Decem libri de re aedificatoria*." *Münchener Jahrbuch der bildenden Kunst*, III, 11 (1960), pp. 161ff.

Krautheimer, R. "Alberti's *Templum Etruscum*" and "Alberti and Vitruvius." In *Studies in Early Christian, Mediaeval and Renaissance Art*. New York: New York University Press, 1969, pp. 65–72 and 323–332.

Krautheimer, R., and Krautheimer-Hess, T. *Lorenzo Ghiberti*. Princeton: Princeton University Press, 1982.

Lang, S. "*De lineamentis*: L. B. Alberti's Use of a Technical Term." *Journal of the Warburg and Courtauld Institutes* 28 (1965), pp. 331–335.

Mancini, Girolamo. *Vita di Leon Battista Alberti*. Florence: Sansoni, 1882. 2d ed. Florence: Carnesecchi, 1911.

Martini, A. *Manuale di Metrologia ossia misure, pesi e monete in uso attualmente e anticamente*. Turin, 1883 (reprinted Rome: Editrice E.R.A., 1976).

Matthias Corvinus und die Renaissance in Ungarn. Vienna: Niederösterreichische Landesregierung, 1982.

Michel, Paul-Henri. *La Pensée de L. B. Alberti*. Paris: Les Belles Lettres, 1930.

Morrison, Stanley. *Politics and Script*. Oxford: Oxford University Press, 1972.

Mühlmann, Heiner. *Aesthetische Theorie der Renaissance: Leon Battista Alberti*. Bonn: Rudolf Habelt Verlag, 1981.

Naredi-Rainer, P. von. *Architektur und Harmonie*. Cologne: Du Mont, 1984.

Onians, J. "Alberti and ΦΙΛΑΡΕΤΗ: A Study in Their Sources." *Journal of the Warburg and Courtauld Institutes* 34 (1971), pp. 96–114.

Panofsky, E. *Idea: A Concept in Art Theory*. New York: Harper and Row, 1968.

Parsons, W. B. *Engineers and Engineering in the Renaissance*. Cambridge, Mass.: MIT Press, 1968.

Pastor, Ludwig. *The History of the Popes*, ed. and tr. F. I. Antrobus. London: Kegan Paul, Trench, Trubner, 1923.

Poliziano, Angelo Ambrogini, called Il. Latin poems, ed. F. Arnoldi, 1964. Italian poems, ed. G. R. Ceriello, 1952.

Rykwert, Joseph. "On the Oral Transmission of Architectural Theory." *AA Files* 6 (May 1984), pp. 14ff.

Rykwert, J., and Tavernor, R. "Sant'Andrea in Mantua." *Architects' Journal* 183, no. 21 (21 May 1986), pp. 36–57.

Santinello, G. *L. B. Alberti: Una visione estetica del mondo e della vita*. Florence, 1962.

Splendours of the Gonzagas, ed. D. Chambers and J. Martineau. London: Victoria and Albert Museum, 1982.

Tavernor, R. "*Concinnitas* in the Architectural Theory and Practice of L. B. Alberti. Ph.D. Thesis, University of Cambridge, 1985.

Tommaso, A. di. "Nature and the Aesthetic Social Theory of Leon Battista Alberti." *Mediaevalia et Humanistica*, Case Western Reserve University, Cleveland, n.s. 3 (1972), pp. 31–49.

Ullman, B. L. *The Origin and Development of Humanistic Script*. Rome: Edizioni di Storia e Letteratura, 1960.

Vagnetti, L. "*Concinnitas*: Riflessioni sul significato di un termine Albertiano." *Studi e documenti di architettura* 2 (1973), pp. 139–161.

Vitruvius, M. P. *Architettura*, ed. and tr. Silvio Ferri. Rome: Fratelli Palombi, 1960.

Vitruvius, M. P. *De architectura*, ed. and tr. Frank Granger. London and Cambridge, Mass.: William Heinemann and Harvard University Press, 1945.

Westfall, Carroll William. "Society, Beauty and the Humanist Architect in Alberti's *De Re Aedificatoria*," *Studies in the Renaissance*, 16, 1969, pp. 61–79.

Westfall, Carroll William. *In This Most Perfect Paradise*. University Park, Pa.: Pennsylvania State University Press, 1974.

Wittkower, Rudolf. *Architectural Principles in the Age of Humanism*. London: A. Tiranti, 1952.

Wittkower, Rudolf. *Palladio and English Palladianism*. London: Thames and Hudson, 1974.

Zeri, Federico. *Scritti di storia dell'arte in onore di. . . .* Milan: Electa Editrice, 1984.

Glossary

Text citations include book, chapter, and page numbers, followed in parentheses by the corresponding page numbers in the *editio princeps*. For example, 7.4.196–197 (114v–115v) denotes book 7, chapter 4, pages 196–197 (pages 114v–115v in the *editio princeps*). References to works listed in the bibliography (pp. 417–419) and to the various translations of *De re aedificatoria* listed on pages xxii–xxiii are shortened here.

Area   There is no precise English equivalent for *area*. Alberti uses it to mean: all that is covered by the building; aspects of the locality; the arrangement of the plan; foundations, and even parts of the walls above ground.

For Alberti's discussion of *area* see book 1, chapters 7 and 8. Perhaps "area for the site" or even "site plan" is a more precise English equivalent. See, for example, 1.2.8 (5); 3.1.61, 62 (36, 36v); 7.4.196–197 (114v–115v); 7.14.232–234 (131); 8.3.254–255 (142); 9.6.306–309 (167–169v). In 7.14.232–234 (131), *area* is alternatively translated as building "plan," meaning "site" or "ground plan."

Beauty and ornament/*pulchritudo et ornamentum*   Alberti is quite precise about the nature of beauty and ornament in book 6, chapter 2 (6.2.156 [93v]): "Beauty is that reasoned harmony of all the parts within a body, so that nothing may be added, taken away, or altered, but for the worse." A theme initiated in the prologue and in 4.2.96 (57v), where he writes, "We should follow Socrates' advice, that something that can only be altered for the worse can be held to be perfect." On the other hand (6.2.156 [93v]): "Ornament may be defined as a form of auxiliary light and complement to beauty. From this it follows, I believe, that beauty is some inherent property, to be found suffused all through the body of that which may be called beautiful; whereas ornament, rather than being inherent, has the character of something attached or additional."

The distinction between beauty and ornament is clear here: beauty is the overall intellectual and primary framework—the essential idea—while ornament is the phenomenon—the individual expression and embellishment of this frame (and see beauty in relation to *concinnitas*, below). Thus, Alberti writes more specifically (4.7.113 [67v]): "The city of Smyrna . . . is said to have been . . . very beautiful in the layout of its streets and the ornamentation of its buildings," and (4.3.101 [60]): "The city . . . should also provide pleasant areas and open spaces set aside as ornament and for recreation . . . : racecourses, gardens, ambulatories, swimming pools, and so on."

In Book 5 (5.6.127 [75]), having described the orientation of temples, Alberti states that "what remains to be discussed concerns their ornament, more than their use. . . ." For further comparison see 5.3.121 (72): *ornatus*/decorated; and 1.2.9 (5v): *redimita*/garlanded or embellished.

For beauty in relation to Cicero's *honestas*, or "moral rectitude," see Onians, "Alberti and ΦΙΛΑΡΕΤΗ," especially p. 102; Bialostocki, "The Power of Beauty"; and the bibliography to *concinnitas*, below.

Bones and paneling/*os et complementum*   Alberti describes the "bones" of the building and "paneling" between them in 3.6.69 (41), and further in 3.8.71–73 (42v–43v). From the latter: "And herein lies the difference between the paneling and the bones: with the former, the skins are filled with stone chippings and any rubble that is available—a quick task involving little more than shoveling; with the latter, irregular stones are never or only very seldom included, but ordinary-bond stonework is used to bind together the whole thickness of the wall."

The body analogy that recurs throughout the treatise aids his explanation in 3.12.79 (47–47v). Features that are common to roofs, Alberti writes, "are the bones, muscles, infill paneling, skin, and crust. . . spaces are left between the beams, then cross-beams are added, and from these span the lathing and anything else similar. Each of these can quite acceptably be considered ligaments. To these are added planks, or wider boards, which surely take the place of infill paneling." And, more specifically, in 3.12.81 (48v), concerning walls: "The physicians have noticed that Nature was so thorough in forming the bodies of animals, that she left no bone separate or disjointed from the rest. Likewise, we should link the bones and bind them fast with muscles and ligaments, so that their frame and structure is complete and rigid enough to ensure that its fabric will still stand on its own, even if all else is removed." Also, in 3.14.86 (50v–51v): "In short, with every type of vault, we should imitate Nature throughout, that is, bind together the bones and interweave flesh with nerves running along every possible section. . . ." And, in 9.5.303 (165v): "Taking their example from Nature, they never made the bones of the building, meaning the columns, angles, and so on, odd in number—for you will not find a single animal that stands or moves upon an odd number of feet."

See also 3.1.61 (36–36v): *procinctus*/girdle (translated in Orlandi as *legamento*/ ligament or tie); and see Compartition.

Compartition/*partitio*   Alberti defines this term quite clearly in 1.2.8 (5): "Compartition is the process of dividing up the site into yet smaller units, so that the building may be considered as being made up of close-fitting smaller buildings, joined together like members of the whole body." A morphological analogy appears again in 7.5.199 (116–116v), after Vitruvius 3.1.1 and 9: "What is more, just as the head, foot, and indeed any member must correspond to each other and to all the rest of the body in an animal, so in a building, and especially a temple, the parts of the whole body must be so composed that they all correspond one to another, and any one, taken individually, may provide the dimensions of all the rest."

Alberti devotes book 1, chapter 9 (1.9.23–24 [13v–15]), to compartition: "All the power of invention, all the skill and experience in the art of building, are called upon in compartition; compartition alone divides up the whole building into the parts by which it is articulated, and integrates its every part by composing all the lines and angles into a single, harmonious work that respects utility, dignity, and delight" (see also *Concinnitas* and Vitruvian triad). Alberti continues with the well-known city-house/house-city analogy. See 6.5.163 (98) for a further summary of compartition.

Concinnitas   Jacob Burckhardt described *concinnitas* as Alberti's "most expressive term" (Burckhardt, *Architecture of the Renaissance*, pp. 30ff.), and other scholars have drawn attention to it when accounting for Alberti's particular approach to architecture (see bibliography here). Alberti introduces it in book 2 (2.1.35 [21v]): "I am aware of the difficulties encountered in executing a work in such a manner that it marries practical convenience with dignity and grace, so that . . . these parts are imbued with a refined variety, in accordance with the demands of proportion and *concinnitas*." Later, when defining beauty, he writes (9.5.302–303 [164v–165]): ". . . that the three principal components of that whole theory [of beauty] into which we inquire are number [*numerus*], what we might call outline [*finitio*], and position [*collocatio*]. But arising from the composition and connection of these three is a further quality in which beauty shines full face: our term for this is *concinnitas*; which we say is nourished with every grace and splendor. It is the task and aim of *concinnitas* to compose parts that are quite separate from each other by their nature, according to some precise rule, so that they correspond to one another in appearance. . . . Neither in the whole body nor in its parts does *concinnitas* flourish as much as it does in Nature herself; thus I might call it the spouse of the soul and of reason. . . . Everything that Nature produces is regulated by the law of *concinnitas*. . . . If this is accepted, let us conclude as follows. Beauty is a form of sympathy and consonance of the parts within a body, according to definite number, outline, and position, as dictated by *concinnitas*, the absolute and fundamental rule in Nature. This is the main object of the art of building, and the source of her dignity, charm, authority, and worth."

Of its three constituent components, *numerus*/number means quantity, and also quality—in the Pythagorean-Platonic sense and as interpreted through various Christian commentaries, such as Augustine's *City of God* (and see Alberti 9.5 and 9.6); *finitio* we have translated as "outline," though "measured outline" is possibly more precise (see Gadol, *L. B. Alberti*, pp. 108ff.; Tavernor, "*Concinnitas*," pp. 4ff.; and Lineaments, below); *collocatio*, or position, relates to decisions that determine the arrangement of a building (Westfall, "Society, Beauty," stresses the importance of *virtù* for these decisions; and see Virtue, below).

For further reading, see: Gadol, *L. B. Alberti*; Santinello, *L. B. Alberti*; Tavernor, "*Concinnitas*"; Westfall, "Society, Beauty"; Vagnetti, "*Concinnitas*"; Wittkower, *Architectural Principles*.

Construction/*structura*   The fundamental distinction that Alberti draws between *lineamenta* and *structura* in book 1 (1.1.7 [4])—of design and construction—may be compared to that which Vitruvius draws between *ratiocinatio* and *opus*, in 1.1.15. As Vitruvius writes: "The arts are each composed of two things, the actual work and the theory of it. One of these, the doing of the work, is proper to men trained in the individual subject, while the other, the theory, is common to all scholars. . . ." For Alberti and the art of building, design necessarily precedes construction, yet *lineamenta* and *structura* are interdependent.

Cornice/*coronix*   Alberti uses this term first of all to describe one of the three main parts of the wall: the collar to the top of the wall he calls the cornice ("hanc demum coronam nuncupant": 3.6.69 [41]). Later in book 3, however (3.14.85–86 [50v–51]), he uses *coronix* to describe what may best be called structural "rings" used with "arches" to form various configurations of vaults.

Lineaments/*lineamenta*   In his prologue, Alberti argues that architecture comprises two parts, the *lineamenta*—deriving from the mind—and the *materia*—

deriving from nature—mediated by the skilled craftsman: he makes *lineamenta* the subject of the first book. As Lang has pointed out (Lang, "*De lineamentis*"), the word *lineamenta* has been translated variously as *disegni* (Bartoli), meaning drawings and designs; *Risse* (Theuer); "form" (Panofsky, *Idea*; and by Krautheimer as "definitions," "plan," and "schematic outlines" (Krautheimer, "Alberti and Vitruvius" and "Alberti's *Templum Etruscum*"; Krautheimer and Krautheimer-Hess, *Lorenzo Ghiberti*, p. 230). Lang defines *lineamenta* as "measured ground-plan" (p. 333), but this reading is not consistently applicable and is too close to our preferred translation of *finitio* as "outline," meaning "measured outline" (see *Concinnitas*). We have translated it therefore as "lineaments" for the most part, which encompasses "lines," "linear characteristics," and so, by implication, design: indeed, "design" has been used in 8.1.245 (137), for reasons of clarity.

Measures: antique and modern   Alberti quotes measurements as reported by ancient authorities throughout his treatise. This seems reasonable: he uses the same "ancient" language, and sometimes the actual number of units is as important for his account as the overall absolute size (see *Concinnitas*). However, a further reason is surely that in his own time in Italy there existed no equivalent "universal" measure, and each Italian city-state employed a different system of mensuration. Consequently, in Florence a Florentine *braccio* equivalent to 0.5836 meters was used in commerce and for the making of artifacts, in Mantua one of 0.467 (see Proportion for ways of relating one system of measure to another). The local measure undoubtedly influenced the design of Alberti's buildings (for example, see Rykwert and Tavernor, "Sant'Andrea"), not least because the supply and manufacture of building materials were strictly regulated by locality: brick sizes were defined by statute. Alberti's specification for brick sizes in book 2 (2.10.52 [31v]) is a review of ancient preference and perhaps an appeal for standardization of measure—according to the "natural" principles followed by the ancients. The measurements he most often uses in this treatise, with their equivalent units and metric values, are

	digit★	inch★	palm	foot	cubit	pace	meters
digitus	1						0.0185
uncia/pollex		1					0.0246
palmus minor	4	3	1				0.0739
pes	16	12	4	1			0.2955★★
cubitus	24	18	6	1½	1		0.4432
passus	80	60	20	5	3	1	1.4775
centum pedes	1,600	1,200	400	100	66	20	29.5500
actus	1,920	1,440	480	120	80	24	35.4600
Greek *stadium*	9,600	7,200	2,400	600	400	120	177.3000
Roman *stadium*	10,000	7,500	2,500	625	416	125	184.6875
mile	80,000	60,000	20,000	5,000	3,333	1,000	1,477.5000

★Vitruvius describes the foot as composed of 16 digits after the Greeks (Vitruvius 3.1.8), though in his day the Roman foot was more commonly divided by 12 inches. It is not certain which subdivision of the foot Alberti assumed for his architectural treatise, and, to confuse matters further, in his treatise on sculpture, *De statua*, he adopts a "foot" subdivided by 10 "inches": see Alberti, *On Painting and Sculpture*; Andrews Aiken, "Human Proportions."

★★ There is no exact dimension for the foot, and this metric dimension is based on an average of 30 *pedes* that were well preserved (in collections at the Capitoline and Vatican museums). On this and metrology generally see Doursther, *Dictionnaire*; Martini, *Manuale*; Parsons, *Engineers*, appendix B.

Nature/*natura*   The word *natura* is notoriously difficult to translate; we have maintained "nature" wherever the sense of modern English has allowed it. The English use that is perhaps closest in meaning to the Latin is as in "natural philosophy."

Alberti advocated the imitation of nature: buildings should compare with the corporeality of natural creations (see Bones and paneling), and their builders should strive to understand and reflect the laws of nature (as *concinnitas*, q.v.)—particularly, "ideal" human proportions. Alberti probably learned much about the principles underlying nature from the researches of Florentine artists and architects, such as Ghiberti and Brunelleschi, ideas he developed and codified in his own treatises on painting and sculpture (see Alberti, *On Painting*, ed. Grayson, 1972). Following humanist precepts, Alberti overlays the natural philosophy of antiquity (the writings of Plato and Neoplatonists in particular) with Christian theology translated through early commentaries. In book 9, chapter 7 (9.7.309 and n. 104 [169v]), following Augustine closely, he compares the proportions of man with the biblical description of Noah's Ark. Biblical archetypes influenced the designs of Alberti's buildings and those of his contemporaries, as they had the great cathedral builders of the Middle Ages. (See Rykwert and Tavernor, "Sant'Andrea"; Tavernor, "Concinnitas"; Westfall, *Paradise*, chs. 6 and 7; Wittkower, *Architectural Principles*, appendix I.)

Proportion/*proportio*   Proportion comes from *concinnitas*: that is, the successful combination of number, measure, and form (*numerus, finitio*, and *collocatio*—and see Concinnitas). Correct aural and visual proportion should imitate nature (1.9.24 [14v]): "Just as in music, where deep voices answer high ones, and intermediate ones are pitched between them, and they ring out in harmony [*concentum*], a wonderfully sonorous balance of proportions results, which increases the pleasure of the audience and captivates them; so it happens in everything else that serves to enchant and move the mind." A detailed account of proportion is given in book 9, chapters 5 and 6, where certain rules are established for the numbers (ratios) of extremes and their mean, in relation to music, geometry, and arithmetic (see Wittkower, *Architectural Principles*, pp. 107ff. and appendix III; and Naredi-Rainer, *Architektur und Harmonie*). As each Italian city-state had its own system of metrology (see Measures), the rules underlying proportion in the visual arts and music also permeated everyday commercial life. A practical tool such as the Rule of Three was necessary to overcome exchange and trade difficulties between states. It involves an arithmetical combination of two extreme quantities that produces three terms in geometrical proportion, of which the middle term is the mean of two extremes: the mean is "in proportion" to the extremes. This is particularly well explained by Baxandall (*Painting and Experience*, pp. 94ff.). Perhaps the only major distinction to be drawn between this commercial tool and the process described by Alberti is that Alberti was concerned with the quality of the numbers used (see Concinnitas and Number). This is because proportion is a fundamental principle of natural philosophy, framing the activities of man and his well-being. As Alberti writes (5.8.130 [77]), "What is good health but a moderation composed of a fabric of different extremes? The mean is always pleasing."

Scale/*modus*   Theuer translates *modus* as "size" (*Zehn Bücher*, p. 19); Orlandi as "disposition" (*L'Architettura*, p. 18). We acknowledge the combined reasoning of Theuer and Orlandi in our translation of this word as "scale." Thus, for example, "It is the function and duty of lineaments, then, to prescribe [the] appropriate place [of lines and angles], [their] exact numbers, a proper *scale*" (1.1.7 [4v]); "It is wrong to make either the width or the height of a wall greater or less than reason and *scale* demand" (1.10.26 [16]).

Show buildings and show grounds/*spectacula*   In antiquity *spectaculum* (plural: *spectacula*) included the theater, circus, and gladiatorium. However, no permanent theaters or circuses existed in the fifteenth century in Europe, while performances of all kinds were watched from galleries or any open constructions. Therefore, since Alberti states in book 4 (4.8.116 [69]) that along with temples, shrines, and basilicas "show buildings. . . are not public domain so much as the province of certain groups, such as priests or magistrates," he presumably has a more intimate scale of building in mind than the huge arenas of antiquity. Perhaps the papal loggia, designated a theater building, in Pope Nicholas V's extensions to the Vatican palace was such a building (see Westfall, *Paradise*, pp. 152ff.).

In book 8 (8.6.262 [145ff.]) there are several references to what we have translated as show grounds, since they are clearly intended for large-scale public enjoyment: these are described specifically later in that book (8.7.268ff. [148ff.]). They include the theater (which Alberti relates was traditionally built of wood), amphitheater, and circus.

Soul/*animus/anima*   When in book 4 (4.1.93 [55v]) Alberti compares the constitution of society with that of the soul ("so that divisions within society as a whole correspond to those between the different parts of the soul"), he is, in part, rehearsing Plato's thesis set out in *The Republic*, 9.580f. Consequently, as Plato says that "the soul of each individual. . . is, like the city, divided into three forms," so Alberti concludes that "whenever a state establishes different parts, a different type of building should be designated for each of them." Though it is likely Alberti's reading went further than Plato's, the notion of *animus* having been overlayed and extended by later Christian commentators. For example, Augustine argued that the God-image is not in the corporeal man but in the *anima rationalis*, the possession of which distinguishes man from animals (Augustine, *Retractiones*, 1.26). Aquinas also stressed its importance to man: "The whole body and all its members receive substantial and specific being from the soul. . . . The human soul is the actuality of an organism that is its instrument. . . some activities of the soul surpass the range of body" (Aquinas, *Creation*, 175 and 176).

Tough stone/*redivivus*   In antiquity *redivivus* was used to mean "renewed," "renovated," and, in the context of buildings, the "reuse" of building material— stone in particular. Vitruvius uses it to mean "old stone" (Vitruvius 7.1.3), but

Alberti's usage is less specific. For the most part he applies *redivivus* to a category of stone that exhibits a certain life or vitality about it: flint, for example (e.g., 10.4.328 [181v]). Such stone may also be described as "manly" (3.16.90 [52v–54v]). Elsewhere he uses it to mean toughness (10.11.348 [194] and 10.16.359 [201]), which is the interpretation we have adopted for it generally.

Variety/*varietas*   Variety is an extension of ornament (see Beauty and ornament) and one of the visual highlights of a building. It is clear from the following extracts that, as much as any of the main principles that Alberti followed in his architectural theory, even variety needed careful consideration in a design (and see *Concinnitas*: as "refined variety," 2.1.35 [21v]).

"I mean that certain variety possessed by both angles and lines, as well as by individual parts, which is neither too much nor too little, but so disposed in terms of use and grace, that whole may correspond to whole, and equal to equal" (1.8.20 [12v]). "Variety is always a most pleasing spice, where distant objects agree and conform with one another; but when it causes discord and difference between them, it is extremely disagreeable" (1.9.24 [14v]). "Cicero follows Plato's teaching, and holds that citizens should be compelled by law to reject any variety and frivolity in the ornament of their temples, and to value purity above all else. 'Let us have,' he added, 'some dignity for all that'" (7.10.220 [125]). And see Gosebruch, "*Varietas*."

Virtue/*virtus*   The difficulty in translating this word is to clear it of its moralistic patina. In antiquity it meant "excellence" and "good action"—with the emphasis on the action. In fifteenth-century Italian it translates as *virtù*, which was used by Alberti to convey gifted activism in matters pertaining to civic life and society in general. It was considered that *virtù* shapes, conditions, and directs the actions of men, once acquired through a well-rounded education: *virtù* is "nature itself, complete and well formed" (see Tommaso, "Nature"; Alberti, *The Family*, p. 75). Westfall has argued that *virtù* is an extension of *collocatio* (see *Concinnitas*), because "it brings together the intentions and abilities of the architect and the intentions and achievements of God in creation and of man in society. Through his concern with *concinnitas* the architect enters society" (Westfall, "Society, Beauty," p. 66). Consequently, as Alberti states in 1.6.18 (11), apart from construction "there is nothing, aside from virtue, to which a man should devote more care, more effort and attention."

Vitruvian triad: *firmitas, utilitas, venustas*   This is familiar to many English readers in the form in which it is given by Sir Henry Wotton, after Vitruvius, in his *Elements of Architecture* of 1624: "Well building has three conditions, Commodity, Firmnesse and Delight." Without specific reference to Vitruvius (1.3.2), Alberti refers to (1.2.9 [5–5v]) "three [characteristics of building] that should never be overlooked. . . . Their individual parts should be well suited to the task for which they were designed and, above all, should be very commodious; as regards strength and endurance, they should be sound, firm, and quite permanent; yet in terms of grace and elegance, they should be groomed, ordered, garlanded, as it were, in their every part." Here he uses the terms *commoda . . . firmitatem . . . gratiam et amoenitatem*; elsewhere (1.9.23 [14]), *utilitatis, dignitatis, amoenitatisque*.

In book 7 this concept of building is allied to compartition (7.1.189 [110]): "We shall now describe compartition, which contributes more to the delight and splendor of a building than to its utility and strength; although these qualities are so closely related that if one is found wanting in anything, the rest will not meet with approval." (See also Compartition).

Winds   In book 9, chapter 10 (9.10.317 [174v]), when describing the necessary knowledge of an architect, Alberti writes that he should have "a sound knowledge of the winds, their direction, and their names. . . ." Eight winds were identified and given divine names by the Greeks. In Latin literature they are described by Virgil as imprisoned in a cave ruled by Aeolus (*Aeneid* 1.57). Vitruvius (1.6.4–5) describes the main winds as follows: Septentrio (north), Aquilo (northeast), Solanus (east), Eurus (southeast), Auster (south), Africus (southwest), Favonius (west), and Corus (northwest). Alberti adopts the same nomenclature (listed alphabetically below), except that he mainly uses *Boreas* for the north wind. Some of Alberti's descriptions of the winds are as follows:

Aquilo/northeast wind
"When *Aquilo* blows, dolphins hear voices calling with the wind, but with Auster they hear much less well, and only against the wind . . ." (1.3.11 [6v]). "Boreas is thought to be the most placid of all winds; when the sea has been disturbed by *Aquilo* it will grow calm again as soon as the wind dies, but after Auster it remains rough for some time" (4.8.114–115 [68]). Alberti comments that the sun and breezes clearly vary from region to region, so that, for example, "*Aquilo* is not always light, nor Auster everywhere unhealthy" (5.14.141 [84v]). "*Aquilo* is said to wrinkle and ruin fruit" (5.17.150 [90]).

Auster/south wind
"It is well known that *Auster* is heavy and sluggish by nature, so that when the sails are burdened with its weight, a ship will lie lower in the water, as though it has taken on ballast; Boreas, on the other hand, seems to lighten both ship and sea" (4.2.99 [59]). "In autumn leaves on the side of the tree facing south toward *Auster* would be the first to fall . . . [and] all buildings that collapse through old age begin to decay on the side facing *Auster*" (3.8.72 [43]). "Ships rot under *Auster*" (5.13.138 [82v]). "Ensure that at night the cattle are not exposed to *Auster* or any damp breezes" (5.16.143 [85v]). "Mountains to the south . . . are more pleasant close at hand, and more useful, because they shut out *Auster*" (5.17.146–147 [88]). See also 1.3.11 (6v) and 4.8.114–115 (68), under *Aquilo*; and 2.12.57 (34), under *Lybicus*.

Boreas/north wind and *Septentriones*/north winds generally
"Timber felled in winter, when *Boreas* is blowing, will burn beautifully and almost without smoke" (2.4.39 [24]). "I would not expose sea sand to Auster; it might do better when exposed to *Septentriones*" (3.10.75 [45]). "Keep out biting [cold] *Boreas*" (5.17.146 [87v]). "With seed- and even fruit-stores, *Boreas* is more favorable than Auster . . . Aquilo is said to wrinkle and ruin fruit" (5.17.150 [90]). "Face all the summer rooms [of the villa] to receive *Boreas*" (5.18.153 [91v]; and "It is best to make libraries face *Boreas* (9.10.317 [174v]). See also 4.2.99 (59), under *Auster*.

Corus/northwest wind
"As Auster brings illness, and especially catarrh, so *Coro* makes us cough" (1.3.11 [71]).

Favonius or *Zephyrus*/west wind

In 2.4.39 (24) Alberti mentions that Zephyr marks the beginning of spring.

Lybicus or *Africus*/southwest wind

"The worst sand comes from beaches exposed to Auster, while sand on beaches facing *Lybicus* is not at all bad" (2.12.57 [34]).

Index

Page numbers for illustrations are in italics.

in harbor, 115
location of, 107
ornament to, 262, *263*
stone, 109
Bridge of Hadrian (Ponte Sant'Angelo), 262, 346, 402n91
Brindisi, 244
Bronze, in statues, 243
Bubastis, 261
Bucranium, 212, 213, 393n93
Burgundian nation, 272
Burial customs, 245–249
Buttresses, 22, 104
Byzantium, 161, 349

Cadiz, 137
Caesar, Gaius Julius, 12, 33, 46, 92, 94–95, 104, 132, 220, 222, 239, 240, 249, 290, 294, 299, 344, 351, 353, 359
Caesar's bridge over the Rhine, *108*, 108–109
Cairo, 58, 102, 117, 118
Caligula, Gaius Caesar, 12, 249, 313
Calix, 339–340
Callimachus, 201
Cambyses, 221, 250, 324
Camerated vault, 84, 222, 379n56. *See also* Vaulting
Campania, 16, 49
Canaliculum, of column, 204–205, 394n103
Canals, 345, 347–349, 353
Candelabrum, 229–230
Capaquia, 341–342
Capital, of column, 182, 200–201, 205–210
composite, 201, *209*, 209–210, *210*
convergence of arches over, *83*
Corinthian, 201, *208*, 208–209
Doric, 201, 205–206, *206*, 393n83
Ionic, 201, *206*, 206–208
in monuments, 252, 254
origin of, 393n74
Tuscan, 393n74
types of, 200–201
Capitoline Jupiter, temple of, 391n34
Capitolinus, Julius, 28
Caprae, 362
Capua, 16, 190

Caracalla, Marcus Aurelius Antoninus, 299
Carmania, 248
Carthage, 1, 286
Carthaginians, 58, 102, 239, 286
Cato (Marcus Porcius Cato, the Censor), 38–39, 41–42, 44, 47, 53, 60, 66, 70, 77, 333
Caucasus, 336
Causidiciary. *See* Transept
Celsus, Aulus Aurelius Cornelius, 141, 152, 279, 331
Ceraumnia, 282
Ceraunian mountains, 16
Chalcidians, 17, 322
Chalcis, 349
Chapel
of Rucellai sepulchre, in Florence, 379n54
in watchtower, 258
Chios, 43, 325
Chiusi. *See* Clusium
Cicero, Marcus Tullius, 10, 58, 156, 180, 190, 220, 246, 257, 295, 386n6
Cilicia, 321, 350
Cillene, mountain, 336
Cincture, 390n109
Cingolum, 99
Circumvallation, 274
Circus, 270, 278–279, *280*
Cisalpine Gaul (Pianura Padana), 147, 228, 269, 344
Cistern, 341–343
Citadel, 122–125, *123*
City
drainage in, 113–114
location of, 95–100
ornament to, 190–191
planning of, 100–103
rectification of faults of, 321–343
zones in, 191–192
City of the Sun. *See* Heliopolis
Cizicus, 50, 219, 256
Clatis [Chiana], 50
Claudius (Tiberius Claudius Nero Germanicus), 249, 265, 299, 344
Clazomenae, 97
Climate. *See also* Weather
building site and, 9–12

senatorial, 283, *284*, 285, 285–286

Curtius, Rufus Quintus, 38, 107, 132

Cyma recta, 204–205, 393n81

Cyma reversa, 204–205, 393n81

Cyprus, 54

Cyrene, 43

Cyrus, 221, 250, 344

Dado, 250–252

Daedalus, 3, 98, 299

Darius, 50, 239

David (King), 38, 120

Decumanus, 385n49

Della Famiglia (Alberti), xiv–xv

Delphi, 18, 221

Democritus, 300

Demosthenes, 291

De re aedificatoria (Alberti), xvi–xxi
  early translations of, xix–xx
  English translations of, xx–xxi
  Latin versions of, xviii–xix
  reception of, xviii

Design. *See* Lineaments

Diana, temple of, at Ephesus, 43, 67,
  161, 179, 184, 230, 242

Diapason, 305, 307

Die, 393n77

Dining rooms, 148–149

Dinocrates, 160

Diodorus Siculus, 14, 39, 50, 58, 89,
  93, 119, 221–222, 240–241, 346–
  347

Diogenes, 257

Dionysius, 94, 97, 193, 269, 286

Dionysius of Halicarnassus, 101

Disdiapason, 305, 307

Domitian (Titus Flavius Domitianus),
  239

Door, 28–29, 298
  of basilica, 238
  ornament to, 223, 225–226, 228
  proportions of, 223, 225–226, 228,
  238, 395n136

Dorians, 201, 205, 211–212, 216, 223

Doric columns and beams, 192, 212,
  252, 262, 266, 281
  in basilica, 232
  doors and, 223, *224*
  in entablature, 212, 223, 394n96
  in structural column, 201–203, *202*,

205–206, *206*, 211, 211–212, *217*,
  218, 309

Dovecote, 143–144

Drainage
  of land, 344, 354
  of latrines, 151
  for rainwater, 32, 71–72, 113
  of roads, 113–114
  for sewage, 32, 113–114

Drawbridge, 124

Dredging, 352

Druids, 92

Durazzo. *See* Dyrrachium

Dyrrachium [Durazzo], 60

Ebro, 16

Ecbatana [Hamadan], 102, 312, 324

Echinus, 207, 393n87

Edui, 54

Egypt, 16, 58, 67, 70, 94, 96, 97, 106,
  117, 163, 195, 221, 240, 246, 248,
  257, 286, 304, 321, 345, 350

Egyptians, 10, 93, 102, 239, 247, 250,
  256

Elements of building, 8, 159–160

Elephanta [Elephantine], 163

Eleusis, 325

Embankment, 109, 345–349

Embata, 317

Ennius, Quintus, 84

Entablature, *182*, *183*, *185*
  Corinthian, 214–215, *215*
  Doric, 212, 394n96
  Ionic, 212–214, *214*

Entasis, 389n108

Entrance
  of house, 119–121, 151
  to theater, 271

Ephesus, temple of Diana at, 67, 179,
  184, 221, 230, 242

Epigenes, 342

Epirus, 16, 320, 325

Ethiopia, 16, 323

Etruria, 158, 269

Etruscans, 101, 158, 192, 204, 240,
  250. *See also* Tuscany

Etruscan temple, 287, 392n65

Euboean nut tree, 42

Eugenius IV, Pope (Gabriel Condul-
  mieri), 43

Euripides, 117, 123
Eusebius of Caesarea, Pamphylius, 162, 221
Eye, 393n84, 393n85

Facade
    of bath, 287
    of church, 396n156
    of curia, 284–285
    Palazzo Rucellai, 406n22
    of private house, 301
    of theater portico, 274
Faenza, 50
Farm buildings, 141–145
Faro, island of [Pharos], 97, 260–261, 401n74
Fascia, 212–213, 394n98, 394n99
Faults, 310–313, 320–321
Favonius (west wind), 39; and see glossary, s.v. Winds
Ferrara, 354
Festus, Sextus Pompeius, 118
Fiesole, 327
Financing, 36–38, 385n49
Fireplace. *See* Hearth
Floodgate, 353
Floor, 27, 298. *See also* Roof
Florence
    Alberti in, xiv–xv
    cathedral, construction techniques in, 379n60
    Palazzo Rucellai in, 400n41, 403n124, 406n22
    Rucellai Sepulchre in, 379n54
    SS Annunziata, 394n107
Flutes of columns, *216*, 216–217, 394n103, 394n104
Footings, 66–68
Fortification, 95–96, 98–99, 102–105
    within city, 117–119
    at harbor, 115
    of military camp, 132–136
    of monastery, 127–128
    of region, 321–322
    by tyrant, 121–125
Fortunate isles, 327
Forum, 263–265, *264*, *265*
Fossils, 56
Fossombrone, 321
Foundation, 21–23, 26, 61–69
    construction of, 91

of farm buildings, 143
    repair of, 360–361
Fresco, 177
Frontinus (Sextus Julius Frontinus), 21, 59
Fucino, Lake, 240, 344

Gabinian, 49
Gadara, 325
Galatia, 16, 347
Galen (Galenus Claudius), 16
Ganges, 344
Garamantes, 11, 88, 325, 357
Garden, 300
Gargoyles, 394n101
Gate
    of city, 105
    ornament to, 261
    for water, 352–353
Gaul, 12, 28, 38, 50, 54, 92, 104, 106, 347
Gauls, 95, 148
Gellius, Aulus, 41
Genoa, 352
Germans, 95, 148, 291
Germany, 88, 106, 172, 179
Gold, as material, 238, 242–243
Golden House (*Domus Aurea*), 164
Granary, 138–139, 150
Greece, 94, 128, 149, 157, 191, 193, 246, 247, 269
Greeks, 154, 157, 158, 201, 264, 321
Gullet (*cyma reversa*), 204–205, 393n81
Guttae, 395n137
Gypsum, 54–55, 176, 396n142

Hadrian (Publius Aelius Hadrianus), 162, 262, 321
Hadrian III (Pope), 43
Hamon, Temple of, 97
Hannibal, 46, 78, 324
Harbor, 114, 261–262, 350–352
Harmony. *See also Concinnitas*
    compartition and, 163
    defined, 305
    outline and, 307–308
Hearth, 32, 147–148, 355–356
Heating, of building, 355–358. *See also* Hearth
Hebron, 161
Height, calculation of, 336–337, *337*

Heliogabalus, 36, 261, 287, 313
Hernician mountains, 16, 21
Hernicians, 192
Herod, 120, 261
Herodotus, 10, 58, 93–96, 102, 163, 165, 221, 257, 324, 346, 354
Hesiod, 37, 39, 98
Hippocrates, 11, 13, 304, 333
Hippodamus (of Miletus), 93
Historia, 268, 402n99
Homer, 9
Honorius I (Pope), 179
Horace (Quintus Horatius Flaccus), 36
Hortus, 294–296, 299
Hospital, 129–130
Human body, analogy with building, 5, 302, 306, 309–310
Hydra, 240, 323
Hypaethros, 195, 391n48
Hyperboreans, 95, 195
Hyrcanian Sea, 325

Ibiza, 357
Icarus, 299
Impleola, *174*, 174–175, 389n82
India, 14, 43, 46, 58, 93, 94, 95, 97, 193, 220, 239
Indian Ocean, 132
Indus River, 323, 325
Infill paneling, 69, 71–73, 79, 111–112, 219; and see glossary, s.v. Bones and paneling
Insodones, 16
Intarsia, 178
Intercolumniation, 199–200 *217*, *218*, 392n71
Ionians, 201, 223, 225
Ionic columns and beams, 262, 266
    in basilica, *232*, *234*, *236*
    doors and, 223, *225*, 225–226
    in entablature, 212–214, *214*
    in structural column, 201, 203, *204*, *206*, 206–208, 212–214, *213*, *218*, 281, 309
Irrigation, 343–344. *See also* Water control
Istria, 49
Ivory, in statues, 243

Jerusalem, 38, 67, 102, 161, 221, 261
Josephus, Flavius, 38, 67, 96, 120, 150, 161–162, 342

Jupiter, god, 5, 46, 161, 219, 222, 241–242, 256, 261, 347
Jupiter, planet, 59

Knossos, 261

Laberius, Decimus, 244
Laodicea, 50, 240, 286, 325
Larisa, 353
Latium [Lazio], 56, 248, 261
Laurentum Lake, 344
Lead, 179–180
Lerna, 240
Leucophoron, 238
Leuctra, 161
Lever, 167–168, *168*, 171
Lex Agraria, 245
Lex Postumia, 195
Library, 286–287
Libya, 10, 16, 106, 323, 326, 357
Ligii [Liguri], 95
Liguri. *See* Ligii
Liguria, 49, 88
Lime, 53–56
    construction with, 66, 75
    in mosaic work, 178
    in revetment, 176
Lineaments, 7–32; see also glossary
    of column, 201–202, 251
    defined, 7
    of parade, 281
    rules for, 314
Lines, *areae* and, 19–22
Lipygia, 325
Livorno, 353
Livy (Titus Livius Patavinus), 95
Locality
    accessibility and, 12–13
    adornment of, 160
    for citadel, 122–125
    climate and, 9–13, 16
    conditions in, 14–16
    defined, 8
    faults in, 13–18, 311
    unusual features of, 16–17
    water and, 13–14
Lucania, 49
Lucino, Mount, 22
Lucretius Carus, Titus, 292
Lucrinus, 60
Luna (stone of Carrara), 293
Lusitania, 96

Lybicus (southwest wind), 57; and see
glossary, s.v. Winds
Lydia, 321
Lysimachia, 239

Machines, movement of weights and,
172–175, *173*, *174*
Magistrates, 138
Maleventum (Maloeton), 60
Mantua
church of San Sebastiano in, 392n56,
392n64
Sant'Andrea in, 392n64, 392n65,
395n132, 396n141
Marble, 74, 177–178, 181–182, 243,
356
Marc Anthony, 14, 28
Marcellinus, 28, 164
Margiana, 321
Marrubii. *See* Mutinii
Mars, god, 195
Mars, planet, 59
Marseilles, 87
Marsis [Marsical], 56, 99, 339
Martial (Marcus Valerius Martialis),
146, 295
Martin V, Pope (Otto Colonna), 56
Massagetae, 324
Materials. *See* Brick; Gold; Gypsum;
Lime; Marble; Sand; Silver; Stone;
Wood
Maternus Firmicus, 59
Mathematical commentaries (Alberti), 62
Matuta, Temple of, 161
Mausoleum, 254, *254*, 370n76, 372n9,
400n48
Mazaca, 323, 331
Meander, 345
Measurement
antique vs. modern, 371n101; see
also glossary, s.v. Measures
of column, 202
of height, 336–337, *337*
of levels, 336–338, *338*
Medici, Lorenzo de', 1
Megara, 324
Mela, Pomponius, 58
Memphis, 95, 100, 103, 109, 217, 240–
241
Meroe, 160
Mesopotamia, 344

Metope, 212, 393n92
Milesians, 194
Miletus, 221
Military camp, 131–136
Mithridates, 41, 240
Models, 33–37, 313
Molding
drip, 213–214
in ornamental work, 204–205
Moles. See Mausoleum
Momus (Alberti), xv–xvi
Monastery, 127–128
Monument, 36, 238–243, 245–257 *See
also* Arch, monumental; Column,
monumental; Sepulcher
Mosaic, 178, 298
Murano, 354
Music, 276, 305
Mutina [Modenal], 52
Mutules, 212–215, 403n131

Nature
beauty and, 155
imitation of, 25, 84, 86, 158, 196,
201, 301, 303–304; and see
glossary
relation to, 35–36 (*see also* Climate;
Weather; Winds)
Nave, 230, *232*, *234*, *236*
Nemi, 33, 136, 344
Nero (Nero Claudius Caesar), 36, 38,
49, 106, 163, 178, 269, 313, 316
Nervii, 132
Nicepolis, 240
Nicholas V (Tomaso Parentucelli,
Pope), xv–xvii
Nichomachus, 317
Nigrigeneus, 126
Nineveh, 100
Numa Pompilius (King), 73, 92, 102,
193, 241
Number, 164, 302–306, 388n67
Numidians, 13

Octavian, 29, 135, 269
Octavius. *See* Augustus
Olympus, Mount, 327
Omenea, 256
Openings. *See also* Door; Entrance;
Window
in basilica, 230–232
defined, 8

Tuscolum, 69
Twelve Tables, Law of the, 244, 247
Tyre, 97, 102, 269

Umbria, 21, 49
Urbino, 327
Utica, 46

Valerius Publius (Poplicola), 291
Variety, 24; and see glossary
Vaulting
  arches and, 382n88
  construction of, 85–87
  in curia, 283–285
  ornament and, 222
  room height and, 297
  in temple, 221–222
  types of, 84–85, 378n53, 378n54
Vegetius, Flavius, 40, 103
Veline, Lake [Piediluco], 49, 344
Venice, 43, 64, 162, 323, 344, 354
  St. Mark, Basilica of, 22
Verona, 109
Vespasian (Titus Flavius Vespasianus),
  162, 220
Vespasian, temple of. *See* Rome
Vestibule, 119
Villa, 140–141, 145–152, 294
Vilumbria, 192
Vilumbrians, 57
Virgil (Publius Vergilius Maro), 125–
  126
Virtue: see glossary
Vitruvian triad, 390n3; and see
  glossary
Vitruvius (Marcus Vitruvius Pollio),
  13, 38, 89, 154, 160
  Alberti and, ix–x
  capitals and, 393n74, 394n96
  on movement of stone, 165
  orders of architecture and, 391n46,
    392n55, 393n78
  ornament and, 147
  proportions and, 394n97, 395n136,
    396n140
  resonance and, 276
  on roof construction, 87–88
  on sand, 57–66
  on walls, 103
  on woods, 39, 44–45
Volsconium [Orvieto], 326

Volsinian Lake [Bolsena], 49
Volterra, 98, 325
Volutes, 225–226, 395n139
Voussoirs, 112, 361, 382n90

Wall
  of basilica, 234
  of city, 94, 102–105, 189–190, 192–
    193, 370n79
  within city, 118
  construction of, 69–78, 104
  defined, 8
  fortification and, 135 (*see also*
    Fortification)
  healthy types of, 356
  height of, 296–298
  lineaments of, 24–26
  ornament and, 163–164, 192–193,
    220–221, 298–299 (*see also*
    Revetment)
  parts of, 68–69
  restoration of, 358–360
  of temple, 219–221
  of theater, 278
  thickness of, 234, 278
  of water conduit, 338–341 (*see also*
    Embankment)
Watchtower, 257–261, *259, 260*
Water control. *See also* Drainage
  channeling of water and, 335–341
  clearing of stretch of water and,
    351–352
  embankments and, 345–349
  farming and, 144–145, 343–344
  improvement of climate and, 353–
    354
  storage of water and, 325, 341–343
  use of water and, 331
Water supply
  of citadel, 125
  for city, 97
  location of, 325, 327–330
  of military camp, 132–133
  properties of water and, 324–325,
    331–333
  quality of water and, 331–335, 342–
    343
  stagnation and, 323
Wave (*cyma recta*), 204–205, 393n82
Weather. *See also* Climate; Rainwater,